Saint Maria Faustina Kowalska

DIARY

Divine Mercy in My Soul

May God leads you into the
mystery of His merciful love
and may you find joy in
Him now and for ever.
                    Fr. Joseph, MIC

Marians of the Immaculate Conception
Stockbridge, Massachusetts 01263
2001

Original Polish Diary
Nihil Obstat: Krakow, April 17, 1979, Rev. Ignatius Rozycki
Imprimatur: Krakow, April 18, 1979, +Francis Macharski, Archbishop

English Translation
Imprimi Potest: Rev. Richard J. Drabik, M.I.C., Provincial Superior
February 22, 1987
Nihil Obstat: +George H. Pearce, S.M., Former Archbishop of Suva, Fiji
Imprimatur: +Joseph F. Maguire, Bishop of Springfield, Massachusetts
March 16, 1987

The NIHIL OBSTAT and IMPRIMATUR are a declaration that a book or pamphlet is considered to be free from doctrinal or moral error. It is not implied that those who have granted the NIHIL OBSTAT and IMPRIMATUR agree with the contents, opinions or statements expressed.

On the cover: the image of Saint Maria Faustina, painted in Poland by Helena Tchórzewska, which was placed in front of St. Peter's Basilica in Rome, on April 18th, 1993, during the ceremonies for Sister Faustina's beatification and then again on April 30th, 2000, during the ceremonies for Sister Faustina's Canonization.
copyright © 1993 Congregation of The Sisters of Our Lady of Mercy.

Notice to Reader: St. Faustina's full religious name was Sister Maria Faustina of the Most Blessed Sacrament. The name indicates her special devotion to Jesus in the Holy Eucharist. In the world, she was known as Helen Kowalska.

Library of Congress Catalog Card Number 87-090691
ISBN 0-944203-37-X

First published: 1987
Third edition with revisions (10th printing): 2001

copyright © 1987 Congregation of Marians

Available from the Association of Marian Helpers,
Stockbridge, MA 01263
Tel. 1-800-462-7426

Table of Contents

Preface

The diary of [Saint Maria] Faustina is the record of her life experience—the journey of her soul. She was graced by a special communion with God, and the diary expresses her conviction that this communion ought to be the center of our lives. Since the 1940's, the Marians of the Immaculate Conception, St. Stanislaus Kostka Province, have shared this conviction and have undertaken the promulgation of God's mercy throughout the world, particularly as it has been proclaimed by [Saint] Faustina.

In 1979, convinced of the importance of the diary, the Marians were instrumental in bringing it—in its rough typewritten form—out of Poland. We made the necessary corrections to the manuscript and published a critical Polish edition that has been promulgated throughout the world to Polish speaking people.

At the same time, we commissioned a couple in Poland, Adam and Danuta Pasicki, to translate the diary into English. Once they had completed this first, literal translation we asked Archbishop George Pearce, S.M., to re-translate portions of it in accordance with proper English terminology for the various theological concepts and spiritual experiences referred to throughout the diary. Archbishop Pearce was supported in this second translation by Fathers George Kosicki, C.S.B., Gerald Farrell, M.M., Leo McCauley, S.J., and an Oblate, Francis Bagan, O. M. I.

When this text was completed, it was given to Father Seraphim Michalenko, M.I.C., who was Director of the Divine Mercy Department from 1979-1986. Together with Sister Sophia Michalenko, C.M.G.T., he carefully reviewed the translation, often referring back to the original Polish to ensure exactness of expression. Father Joseph Sielski, M.I.C., and Father Kazimierz Chwalek, M.I.C., were then asked to review the text, re-reading it for authentic agreement with the Polish.

Finally, in the first part of 1987, the text was returned to the Divine Mercy Department, [then] headed by Father George Kosicki, C.S.B. Through his efforts, the tireless work of Sister Sophia Michalenko, C.M.G.T., and the assistance of Vincent Flynn, the diary was subjected to a complete editing, re-typing, and proofing process for clarity of expression and readability according to current English grammar and usage. The index, listing the main themes of the diary, was compiled by Father Eugene Ozimek and developed by Fr. George Kosicki and Sister Sophia. The design, composition, and mechanicals were then completed by Charles Parise and Pat Menatti, and the diary was printed by the Marian Press at the Marian Helpers Center. To all involved with this work, we wish to express our deepest gratitude and the assurance of our prayers.

Since the Polish diary is the official text, we have made every effort to be truly faithful to it, and to retain the various shades of meaning implied in the theological and spiritual terms used by [Saint] Faustina—a definite challenge, indeed! In translating the diary, we dealt with the same kind of challenge that faces the translators of Sacred Scripture. Some terms allow for a variety of expressions even though the meanings are the same, and the final translation thus becomes a personal choice of style and expression on the part of the translator.

For the most part, the texts that have already been published in the popular devotional booklets are the same as those used in the diary, though in some instances, there again may be slight differences of style and expression.

Special Features of this New English Edition

In the final editing process, inconsistencies of verb tense, capitalization, and punctuation were standardized as much as possible without losing [Saint] Faustina's unique style and powerful simplicity of expression. Our Lord's words to [Saint] Faustina were set in **bold type** for emphasis, while Our Lady's words were set in *italics*. The page numbers of [Saint] Faustina's original notebooks were also set in bold type, and paragraphs thought to be overly long or diversified in content were split into shorter paragraph units for readability.

The footnotes, too, have been reexamined, and additional clarifying notes have been added where necessary. Notes that were no longer pertinent, in light of changes incorporated into the English translation, were deleted; and, wherever possible, explanatory notes were placed in [square brackets] in the text itself to avoid unnecessary breaks in the reading.

Our deepest hope is that this diary may truly be a vehicle of grace for all who read it, for in reading it we can see that the mercy of God lives forever. Above all, we hope that all people will be struck by the truth that **mankind will not have peace until it turns with trust to God's mercy.**

May each one of you experience the power of the Blood and Water that poured out from the Heart of Jesus as a fount of mercy, and may each of you find confidence and trust in this ever-present mercy of God!

Gratefully in the Lord,

Very Rev. Richard J. Drabik, M. I. C.
Provincial Superior

Eden Hill, Stockbridge, Massachusetts
March 19, 1987

ORIGINAL PREFACE TO THE POLISH EDITION, 1981

In presenting this edition of the Diary of [Saint] Faustina Kowalska I am fully aware that I am introducing a document of Catholic mysticism of exceptional worth, not only for the Church in Poland, but also for the Universal Church. This publication is the critical edition, and thus reliable. It is the work of the Postulator of Sister Faustina, under the direction of the authority of the Archdiocese of Cracow.

The Diary, whose object is devotion to The Divine Mercy, has acquired tremendous interest lately for two reasons:

Firstly: The Sacred Congregation for the Doctrine of the Faith, in its revision more than two years ago [1978], withdrew the censures and reservations advanced earlier by the Holy See in relation to the writings of Sister Faustina. The withdrawal of the "Notification" caused the devotion to The Divine Mercy, as presented in the Diary, to grow in renewed vitality on all continents, as is evidenced by the numerous testimonies received by the Postulator and the Congregation of which Sister Faustina was a member.

Secondly: The recent encyclical of Pope John Paul II, *Dives in Misericordia*, happily fixed the attention of the Church, and even of the secular world, on this most wonderful attribute of God and extraordinary aspect of the economy of salvation, which is The Divine Mercy.

A comprehensive study in order to indicate the affinity of ideas found in the Diary of [Saint] Faustina and this encyclical (not to mention their probable interdependence) would be most welcome. These salient points certainly are numerous, for they draw their inspiration from the same source; namely, from the revelation of God and the teaching of Christ.

Furthermore, they come from the same spiritual environment, from Cracow, the city which, as far as I know, possesses the oldest church dedicated to the honor of The Divine Mercy. It is likewise necessary to stress that it was Karol Cardinal Wojtyla, the Archbishop of Cracow at that time, who made efforts to begin The Process of Beatification of Sister Faustina Kowalska and did inaugurate that process.

In this light, the Diary of [Saint] Faustina took on exceptional meaning for Catholic spirituality; and that is why it was fitting to prepare a credible edition, in order to prevent the distortion of the text by persons who perhaps are acting in good faith, but who are not adequately prepared for such work. Thus, publications containing differences and even contradictions, such as took place with the spiritual diary of St. Therese of the Child Jesus, *The Story of a Soul*, can be avoided.

The reader, after just a superficial skimming of the Diary, may be struck by the simplicity of the language and even by the spelling and stylistic errors, but he should not forget that the author of the Diary had but a limited elementary education. The theology alone which is found in the Diary awakens in the reader a conviction of its uniqueness; and if one considers the contrast between [Saint] Faustina's education and the loftiness of her theology, the contrast alone indicates the special influence of Divine Grace.

I would like to mention here my meeting with a well-known contemporary mystic, Sister Speranza, who in Collevalenza, not far from Todi [Italy], founded the sanctuary of "The Most Merciful Love," the site of numerous pilgrimages. I asked Sister Speranza whether she had heard of the writings of Sister Faustina and what she thought of them. She answered me with simplicity: "The writings contain a wonderful teaching, but reading them one must remember that God speaks to philosophers in the language of' philosophers and to simple souls in the language of the simple ones, and only to these last does He reveal truths hidden from the wise and prudent of this world."

To conclude this preface, permit me to mention yet one more personal recollection from the year 1952, when for the first time I took part in a solemn beatification ceremony in St. Peter's Basilica. After the festivity I was asked by some person who also participated, "Who exactly was this blessed one?" The question embarrassed me very much, because at the moment I could not recall who those blessed were, although I knew full well that the real purpose of a beatification is to present to the People of God a model to consider and imitate in their lives.

Among the candidates for beatification and canonization Poland has presently two persons familiar to the whole world which knows who they are, what they accomplished in their lifetime and what sort of message their lives proclaim. They are Blessed [now Saint] Maximilian Kolbe, the martyr of love, and Sister [now Saint] Faustina Kowalska, the Apostle of The Divine Mercy.

Rome, December 20, 1980

+ Andrew M. Deskur
Titular Archbishop of Tene

Introduction

1. **Saint Maria Faustina Kowalska**, known today the world over as the "Apostle of The Divine Mercy," is numbered by theologians among the outstanding mystics of the Church.

She was the third of ten children born into a poor and pious peasant family in Głogowiec, a village in the heart of Poland. At her baptism in the nearby Parish Church of Swinice Warckie she was given the name "Helena." From childhood she distinguished herself by her piety, love of prayer, industriousness and obedience as well as by her great sensitivity to human misery. She had hardly three years of schooling, and at the age of fourteen she left the family hearth to help her parents and to earn her own livelihood serving as a domestic in the nearby cities of Aleksandrów and Łódź.

When she was only seven (two years before her First Holy Communion), Helen already sensed in her soul the call to embrace the religious life. When later she made her desire known to her parents, they categorically did not acquiesce in her entering a convent. Because of this situation Helen strove to stifle this divine call within her. Pressed on, however, by a vision of the suffering Christ and by the words of His reproach: "How long shall I put up with you and how long will you keep putting Me off?" *(Diary, 9)*, she began to search for a convent to join. She knocked on many a convent door, but nowhere was she accepted. Finally on August 1, 1925, Helen crossed the threshold of the cloister in the convent of the Congregation of Sisters of Our Lady of Mercy on Żytnia Street in Warsaw. In her *Diary* she declared: "It seemed to me that I had stepped into the life of Paradise. A single prayer was bursting forth from my heart, one of thanksgiving" *(Diary, 17)*.

After a few weeks she experienced nonetheless a strong temptation to transfer to a different congregation in which there would be more time for prayer. It was then the Lord Jesus, manifesting to her His wounded and tortured face, said: "It is you who will cause Me this pain if you leave this convent. It is to this place that I called you and nowhere else, and [it is here] I have prepared many graces for you" *(Diary, 19)*.

Upon her entrance to the Congregation Helen received the name Sr. Mary Faustina. Her novitiate she spent in Cracow, and there, in the presence of Bishop Stanislaus Rospond, she pronounced her first religious vows, and five years later, she made her perpetual profession of the vows of chastity, poverty and obedience. She was assigned to work in a number of the Congregation's houses, but for a longer period in those of Cracow, Płock and Vilnius, fulfilling the duties of cook, gardener and doorkeeper.

To all external appearances nothing betrayed her extraordinarily rich mystical life. She zealously went about her duties, she faithfully observed all the religious rules, she was recollected and kept silent, all the while being natural, cheerful, full of kindness and of unselfish love of neighbor.

Her entire life was concentrated on constant striving for an even fuller union with God and on self-sacrificing cooperation with Jesus in the work of saving souls. "My Jesus" — she avowed in her *Diary* — "You know that from my earliest years I have wanted to become a great saint; that is to say, I have wanted to love You with a love so great that there would be no soul who has hitherto loved You so" *(Diary, 1372)*.

It is her *Diary* that reveals to us the depths of her spiritual life. An attentive reading of these records offers a picture of the high degree of her soul's union with God: the great extent of God's company keeping with her soul, as well as her efforts and struggles on the way to Christian perfection. The Lord endowed her with great graces: with the gift of contemplation, with a deep knowledge of the mystery of the mercy of God, with visions, revelations, the hidden stygmata, with the gift of prophecy and of reading into human souls, and also with the rare gift of mystical espousals. As lavishly gifted as she was, this is what she wrote: "Neither graces, nor revelations, nor raptures, nor gifts granted to a soul make it perfect, but rather the intimate union of the soul with God. ... My sanctity and perfection is based upon the close union of my will with the will of God" *(Diary, 1107)*.

The austere lifestyle and exhausting fasts that she imposed upon herself even before joining the Congregation, weakened her organism to such an extent that already during her postulantship it became necessary to send her to Skolimów near Warsaw to restore her to health. Towards the end of her first year of novitiate she was visited by unusually painful mystical experiences of the so-called dark night, and later by the spiritual and moral sufferings related to the accomplishment of the mission she was receiving from Christ the Lord. [St.] Faustina laid down her life in sacrifice for sinners and on this account she also sustained diverse sufferings, in order by means of them to come to the aid of their souls. During the last years of her life inner sufferings of the so-called passive night of the soul and bodily diseases grew in intensity. The spreading tuberculosis attacked her lungs and alimentary canal. For this reason twice she underwent several months' treatment in the hospital on Prądnik Street in Cracow.

Physically ravaged, but fully mature spiritually, she died in the opinion of sanctity, mystically united with God, on October 5, 1938, hardly 33 years old, having been a religious for 13 years. Her mortal remains were laid to rest in the common tomb in the convent's cemetery in Cracow-Łagiewniki. In 1966, during the informative process towards Sister Faustina's beatification, they were transferred to the convent chapel.

To this simple, uneducated, but courageous woman religious, who trusted Him without limit, Our Lord Jesus consigned the great mission to proclaim His message of mercy directed to the whole world: "Today," He told her, "I am sending you with My mercy to the people of the whole world. I do not want to punish aching mankind, but I desire to heal it, pressing it to My merciful Heart" *(Diary, 1588)*. "You are the secretary of My mercy; I have chosen you for that office in this and the next life" *(Diary, 1605)* ... "to make known to souls the great mercy that I have for them, and to exhort them to trust in the bottomless depth of My mercy" *(Diary, 1567)*.

2. [ST.] FAUSTINA'S MISSION. In short, her mission consists in reminding us of the immemorial, but seemingly forgotten, truths of our faith about God's merciful love for men, and in conveying to us new forms of devotion to The Divine Mercy, the practice of which is to lead to the revival of the spiritual life in the spirit of Christian trust and mercy.

[St.] Faustina's *Diary*, which Jesus Christ ordered her to keep during the last four years of her life, is a kind of journal in which the author recorded current or retrospective events related primarily to the "encounters" of her soul with God. A rigorous, scholarly analysis of her notebooks was necessary to extract from them everything which is considered essential to her mission.

This work was accomplished by an eminent and highly esteemed theologian, the Rev. Professor, Ignacy Różycki. A brief summary of his scholarly and theological work is published under the title *The Divine Mercy: Basic Characteristics of the Divine Mercy Devotion*.

Compared to this important theological work, all previous publications on the Divine Mercy devotion, related to us by [St.] Faustina, seem to be concerned only with some of its elements or with more secondary matters. For example, in some instances, emphasis is placed on the Litany or the Novena to The Divine Mercy, leaving aside the Hour of Mercy.

Fr. Różycki draws our attention to this fact by saying: "Before we acquaint ourselves with the specific elements of the Divine Mercy devotion, we need to notice that among them we won't find any of the well-known or beloved novenas or litanies."

The basis for selecting these, and not other, prayers or religious practices, as the new forms of the Divine Mercy devotion, are the specified promises attached to them, which the Lord Jesus promised to fulfill on the condition of one's trust in God's goodness and of mercy towards one's neighbors. Rev Różycki points out that there are five elements of the devotion to The Divine Mercy.

a. The Image of the Merciful Jesus. Its pattern was revealed in the vision [St.] Faustina had on February 22, 1931, in her convent cell at Płock. "In the evening, when I was in my cell," she recorded in the *Diary*, "I saw the Lord Jesus clothed in a white garment. One hand [was] raised in the gesture of blessing, the other was touching the garment at the breast. From beneath the garment, slightly drawn aside from at breast, there were emanating two large rays, one red, the other pale. ... After a while, Jesus said to me, 'Paint an image according to the pattern you see, with the signature: Jesus, I trust in You'" (*Diary*, 47). "I want this image ... to be solemnly blessed on the first Sunday after Easter; that Sunday is to be the Feast of Mercy" (*Diary*, 49).

For this reason, the content of this image is closely related to the liturgy of that Sunday. On this day, the

Church reads the Gospel according to St. John about the risen Christ appearing in the Upper Room and about the institution of the Sacrament of Penance (Jn 20:19-29). Consequently, this image represents the Savior risen from the dead who brings peace to people by means of the forgiveness of sins at the price of His passion and death on the cross.

The rays of blood and water that flow from the Heart that was pierced by a spear (not visible on the image) and the scars caused by the wounds of crucifixion call to mind the events of Good Friday (Jn 19:17-18; 33-37). The Image of the Merciful Savior, therefore, combines the two Gospel events that best bespeak the fullness of God's love for mankind.

The two rays are a distinctive feature of this image of Christ. The Lord Jesus, when asked about their meaning, explained: "The pale ray stands for the Water which makes souls righteous. The red ray stands for the Blood which is the life of souls. ... Happy is the one who will dwell in their shelter" (*Diary*, 299). The Sacraments of Baptism and Penance purify the soul, and the Eucharist most abundantly nourishes it. Thus, the two rays signify the Holy Sacraments and all the graces of the Holy Spirit, whose biblical symbol is water, as well as the New Covenant of God with men in the Blood of Christ.

The image of the Merciful Jesus is often called the "Image of The Divine Mercy," which is appropriate, since it is precisely in Christ's Paschal Mystery that God's love for humankind was most explicitly revealed.

The image not only represents The Divine Mercy, but also serves as a sign that is to recall the Christian obligation of trust in God and of active love toward neighbor. By Christ's will the image bears a signature comprised of these words: "Jesus, I trust in You." "This image," Jesus also declared, "is to be a reminder of the demands of My mercy, because even the strongest faith is of no avail without works" (*Diary*, 742).

To the veneration of the image understood in this way, as relying upon the Christian attitude of trust and mercy, Our Lord attached special promises, namely, of eternal salvation, of great progress on the way of Christian perfection, of the grace of a happy death, and of all other possible graces which people will ask of Him with trust: "By means of this Image I shall be granting many graces to souls; so let every soul have access to it" (*Diary*, 570).

b. The Feast of The Divine Mercy. It ranks highest among all the elements of The Divine Mercy devotion revealed to [St.] Faustina. Its institution was requested by the Lord Jesus for the first time in Płock, in 1931, while He was communicating His will regarding the painting of the Image: "I desire that there be a Feast of Mercy. I want this image, which you will paint with a brush, to be solemnly blessed on the first Sunday after Easter; that Sunday is to be the Feast of Mercy" (*Diary*, 49).

The choice of the first Sunday after Easter for the Feast of Mercy has a very deep theological significance, which points to the close relationship between the Paschal Mystery of the Redemption and the mystery of The Divine Mercy. This integral relationship is further emphasized by the Novena of Chaplets to The Divine Mercy which begins on Good Friday as a preparation for the Feast.

This feast is not only a day in particular for worshipping God in His mystery of mercy, but also a time of grace for all people. The Lord Jesus said: "I desire that the Feast of Mercy be a refuge and shelter for all souls, and especially for poor sinners" (*Diary*, 699). "Souls perish in spite of My bitter Passion. I am giving them the last hope of salvation, that is, recourse to My Mercy. If they will not adore My mercy, they will perish for all eternity" (cf. *Diary*, 965, 998).

The greatness of this feast is measured by the measure of extraordinary promises that the Lord attached to this feast: Jesus said "... whoever approaches the Fount of Life on this day will be granted complete remission of sins and punishment" (*Diary*, 300), and also, "On this day the very depths of My tender mercy are open. I pour out a whole ocean of graces upon those souls who approach the fount of My mercy. ... Let no soul fear to draw near to Me, even though its sins be as scarlet" (*Diary*, 699).

To profit from those great gifts we must fulfill the conditions of the Divine Mercy devotion (trust in God's goodness and active love toward neighbor), be in the state of sanctifying grace — having gone to Holy Confession, and worthily receive Holy Communion. Jesus explained: "No soul will be justified until it turns with confidence to My mercy; and this is why the first Sunday after Easter is to be the Feast of Mercy, and on that day, priests are to tell everyone about My great and unfathomable mercy" (*Diary*, 570).

c. The Chaplet of The Divine Mercy. This Chaplet was dictated to Sr. Faustina by the Lord Jesus Himself in Vilnius on September 13-14, 1935, as a prayer of atonement and for the appeasement of God's wrath (see *Diary*, 474-476).

Those who recite this Chaplet offer to God the Father "the Body and Blood, Soul and Divinity," of Jesus Christ in atonement for their sins, the sins of their loved ones, and those of the entire world. By uniting themselves with the sacrifice of Jesus, they appeal to the great love that our Heavenly Father has for His Son and, in Him, for all humanity.

By means of this prayer, the petitioners request "mercy on us and on the whole world," and by so doing, they perform a work of mercy. If the faithful add to this the foundation of trust and fulfill the conditions regarding every good prayer (humility, perseverance, matters in conformity with God's will), they can expect the fulfillment of Christ's promises which are particularly related to the hour of death: the grace of conversion and a peaceful death.

Not only will the people who say the Chaplet receive these graces, but also the dying at whose side others will recite this prayer. The Lord said: "When this chaplet is said by the bedside of a dying person, God's anger is placated, unfathomable mercy envelops the soul" (*Diary*, 811). The general promise says: "It pleases Me to grant everything they ask of Me by saying the chaplet" (*Diary*, 1541) "... if what you ask for is compatible with My will" (*Diary*, 1731). For, anything that is not compatible with God's will is not good for people, especially for their eternal happiness.

On a different occasion, Jesus said: "... by saying the Chaplet you are bringing humankind closer to Me" (*Diary*, 929). and again: "The souls that say this chaplet will be embraced by My mercy during their lifetime and especially at the hour of their death" (*Diary*, 754).

d. The Hour of Mercy. In October, 1937, in Cracow, under circumstances that are not fully described by [St.] Faustina, the Lord Jesus recommended that she honor the hour of His death: "... as often as you hear the clock strike the third hour, immerse yourself completely in My mercy, adoring and glorifying it; invoke its omnipotence for the whole world, and particularly for poor sinners; for at that moment mercy was opened wide for every soul" (*Diary*, 1572).

The Lord Jesus also determined the prayers that are appropriate for this form of the Divine Mercy devotion: "... try your best to make the Stations of the Cross in this hour, provided that your duties permit it; and if you are not able to make the Stations of the Cross, then at least step into the chapel for a moment and adore, in the Blessed Sacrament, My Heart, which is full of mercy; and should you be unable to step into the chapel, immerse yourself in prayer there where you happen to be, if only for a very brief instant" (*Diary*, 1572).

Prof. Różycki enumerates three conditions for prayers offered in this hour to be granted:

1. They are to be addressed to Jesus.

2. They are to be said at three o'clock in the afternoon.

3. They are to appeal to the value and merits of Christ's Passion.

The Lord Jesus promised: "In this hour you can obtain everything for yourself and for others for the asking; it was the hour of grace for the whole world — mercy triumphed over justice" (*Diary*, 1572).

e. Spreading the honor of The Divine Mercy. In discussing the essential elements of the Divine Mercy devotion, Rev. Różycki also mentions the spreading of the honor of The Divine Mercy as one of them since certain promises of Christ are related to this as well: "Souls who spread the honor of My mercy I shield through their entire life as a tender mother her infant, and at the hour of death I will not be a Judge for them, but the Merciful Savior" (*Diary*, 1075).

The essence of The Divine Mercy devotion is found in the Christian attitude of trust in God and of an active love toward neighbor. The Lord Jesus said: "I desire trust from My creatures" (Diary, 1059), and He expects them to exercise mercy through deeds, words, and prayers. And further: "You are to show mercy to your neighbors always and everywhere. You must not shrink from this or try to excuse or absolve yourself from it" (Diary, 742). Christ wants those who worship Him to perform at least one act of love of neighbor in the course of each day.

The spreading of the honor of The divine Mercy does not require many words, but always the Christian attitude of faith, of trust in God, and of becoming ever more merciful. In her lifetime [St.] Faustina gave the example of just such apostolic work.

f. The Divine Mercy devotion aims at the renewal of religious life in the Church in the spirit of Christian trust and mercy. It is in this context that the idea of the "new congregation" of which we read in the *Diary's* pages should be considered. This desire of Christ matured gradually in Sr. Faustina's own thinking, and underwnet a certain evolution — from a strictly contemplative order all the way to a movement which is made up also of active congregations (male and female) and of lay people.

This great, supranational community of people is one family, which is being united, first of all, by God in the mystery of His mercy, and secondly, by people's longing, both, to reflect that mercy in their own hearts and works, and for God's glory to be reflected in all souls. It is a community of people who is different ways, depending upon their state in life and vocation (priestly, religious, lay), live by the Gospel ideal of trust and mercy, proclaim the incomprehensible mystery of God's mercy by their life and words, and obtain Divine Mercy for the world with their entreaties.

[St.] Faustina's mission finds deep justification in Holy Scripture and documents of the Church; it superbly corresponds especially with the encyclical *Dives in misericordia (Rich in mercy) of the Holy Father, John Paul II.*

3. REMARKS REGARDING THE THIRD
ENGLISH EDITION OF [ST.] FAUSTINA'S DIARY.

The former scientific study by Fr. George Mrówczyński concerning the composition of [Saint] Faustina's *Diary*, that served as an introduction to its last two editions, has been replaced with the present text the aim of which is to bring the reader closer to the personality of the author herself and her mission, as an aid to understanding the *Diary*.

For the greater glory of The Divine Mercy!

Sr. M. Elizabeth Siepak, ZMBM

Cracow, December of 1991

Chronology of Events

in The Life of Saint Maria Faustina—Helen Kowalska
of The Congregation of
The Sisters of Our Lady of Mercy

August 25, 1905 — Helen Kowalska is born in the village of Glogowiec, Turek County, Lodz Province, Poland (Parish records of births).

August 27, 1905 — She is baptised in St. Casimir Church, Swinice Warckie, Turek County, by the pastor, Rev. Joseph Chodynski. She receives the name of Helen. (Acts of the Parish in Swinice).

1912 — At the age of seven, Helen hears for the first time a voice in her soul, calling her to a more perfect way of life (Diary 1:3).

1914 — She receives First Holy Communion from the hands of her pastor, Rev. Pawlowski (Acts of the Parish in Swinice).

November 1917 — She begins her primary education in Swinice (Minutes from Zbiorczej Szkoly Gminnej w Swinicach Warckich, April 6, 1976).

1919 — At the age of 14, Helen begins to work for the Goryszewski family in Aleksandrow near Lodz, in order to help her parents (Memoirs of her mother, Marianne Kowalska).

October 30, 1921 — She receives the Sacrament of Confirmation in Alexandrow near Lodz from Bishop Vincent Tymienecki.

1922 — After working for a year for the Goryszewski family, she returns home and announces that she wishes to enter a convent. Her parents decidedly oppose this move (Diary I:4; Memoirs of her mother).

Autumn 1922 — Helen leaves for Lodz to look for more work in order to help her parents. She works for three terciaries (Memoirs of her mother, p. 5; Memoirs of Stanislava Rapacka).

February 2, 1923 — Referred by an employment agency, she goes to work for Marcianne Sadowska, the owner of a store on 29 Abramowski St., Lodz, where she remains until July 1, 1924 (Memoirs of Mrs. Sadowska, p. 2).

July 1924 — Helen goes to Warsaw to enter a convent there (Memoirs of Mother General Michael Moraczewska, handwritten, p. 1; Diary I:4).

She applies at the Congregation of the Sisters of Our Lady of Mercy at 3/9 Zytnia Street in Warsaw. The superior, assesses her as "no one special" and puts her to the test, telling her to go to work so she can pay for her wardrobe (Memoirs of Mother Michael, p. 1; Memoirs of Sister Borgia, p. 1).

Summer 1924 — Helen goes to work as a domestic for Aldona Lipszyc, at Ostrowek, Klembow County, near Warsaw (Memoirs of A. Lipszyc, p. 1).

August 1, 1925 — She again applies to the Congregation of the Sisters of Our Lady of Mercy, and this time she is accepted (Memoirs of Mother Michael, p. 2; Memoirs of Sister Borgia, p. 1; Diary I:6).

**Circa
August 22, 1925 —** Helen wants to leave the Congregation to enter a stricter order. She feels

that there is too little time for prayer in the Congregation of Our Lady of Mercy (Memoirs of Mother Michael, p. 2; Diary I:6).

August 1925 — The superior sends her to Skolimow, a vacation house of the Congregation, near Warsaw, to regain her strength (Memoirs of Mother Michael, p. 2).

January 23, 1926 — She leaves for the Novitiate in Cracow to complete her postulancy period, make a retreat, and receive the veil (Memoirs of Sister Borgia, p. 1; Diary I: 7).

April 30, 1926 — After an eight-day retreat, she receives her habit and her name in religion. From now on Helen will bear the name Sister Mary Faustina (Cracow Chronicle III:177; Memoirs of Sister Clemens).

June 20, 1926 — An administrative change of the Directress of Novices influences Sister Faustina's spiritual formation (Cracow Chron. III:179).

April 3, 1927 — Sister Faustina experiences the spiritual dark night. The trial lasts almost to the end of the Novitiate. Mother Directress, Mary Joseph Brzoza, encourages her, excuses her from formal spiritual exercises, and urges her to great fidelity to God (Diary I:8).

April 16, 1928 — On Good Friday, the flame of Divine Love encompasses the suffering novice. She forgets past sufferings, and she more clearly recognizes how much Christ suffered for her (Diary I:10).

April 20, 1928 — In the evening Sister Faustina, together with other sisters, begins the retreat before taking temporary vows (Chronicle III:203; Memoirs of Mother Michael, p. 3; Diary I: 11).

April 30, 1928 — Sister Faustina makes her first profession of temporary vows, which she will renew each year for five years, until the moment when she will make her perpetual vows (Cracow Chron. III:203; Memoirs of Mother Michael, p. 3).

Dec. 6-10, 1928 — At the General Chapter of the Congregation of the Sisters of Our Lady of Mercy, Mother Michael Moraczewska is elected Mother General (Cracow Chron. III:210).

[Mother Michael will be superior throughout Sister Faustina's life, In difficult moments she will be her help and comfort. Into her hands Sister Faustina will place her perpetual vows. Before death she will ask pardon of the whole Congregation through Mother's hands for all the failings committed during her entire religious life (Memoirs of Mother Michael, pp. 5, 11, 12).]

October 31, 1928 — Sister Faustina leaves for 3/9 Zytnia Street, Warsaw, where she is assigned to work in the kitchen (Cracow Chron. III:212).

February 21, 1929 — She leaves for Vilnius to substitute for a sister going for her third probation (Vilnius Chron. I:9).

April 11, 1929 — By morning train, she leaves Vilnius to return to Warsaw (Vil. Chron. I:21).

June 1929 — She is assigned to work in a newly-formed house on Hetmanska Street, Warsaw (Memoirs of Sisters).

After a few months Sister Faustina returns to the house on 3/9 Zytnia Street. Meanwhile the students (wards) with whom she worked promise that they will follow her there (Memoirs of Sisters).

July 7, 1929 — For a short while, Sister Faustina is sent to a house of the Congregation in Kiekrz near Poznan, to substitute for an ailing sister in the kitchen (Memoirs of Sister Xavier; letter of July 6 with no year, placed in the memoirs; Diary I:74).

October 1929 — She is already back in Warsaw, as evidenced by a letter to Sister Justine, dated October 20, 1929. (Letters #25:66).

May-June 1930 — Assigned to the house of the Congregation in Plock, Sister Faustina works there by turns in the bakery, the kitchen, and the bakery store (Memoirs of Mother Michael, p. 3).

During her stay in Plock (from June 1930 to November 1932), she spends some time in Biala (a house of the Congregation situated in a village about 10 kilometers from Plock).

[Because the chronicles of Warsaw and Plock were ruined during World War II, it is difficult to fully ascertain the dates of her stay in these homes.]

A letter to Sister Justine Golofit, dated December 17, 1930, witnesses to the fact that Sister Faustina is, at that time, still in

Biala (Letters #26:68).

February 22, 1931 — Sister Faustina sees a vision of the Lord Jesus, who tells her to paint an image according to the pattern she sees (Diary I: 18; Memoirs of Mother p. 4).

November 1932 — She arrives in Warsaw for the Third Probation, which the Sisters of Our Lady of Mercy make before taking perpetual vows (Memoirs of Mother Michael, p. 5; Diary I:84).

Before beginning the Third Probation, she goes to Walendow to make a retreat (Memoirs of Sister Seraphina Kukulska; Diary I:84).

December 1, 1932 — Together with other sisters she begins the Third Probation under the direction of Sister Margaret Gimbutt (Memoirs of Mother Michael, p. 5; Diary I:89).

The Third Probation in this Congregation lasts for five months. During this time, Sister Faustina works in the vestry, helping Sister Suzanne Tokarski (Memoirs of Mother Michael, p. 5; Memoirs of Sister Suzanne; Diary I:89).

March 1933 — Sister Faustina's younger sister Wanda visits her (Diary I:97).

April 18, 1933 — With other sisters, Sister Faustina goes to Cracow to make an eight-day retreat and her profession of perpetual vows (Cracow Chron. IV:8).

April 21, 1933 — The eight-day retreat begins under the direction of Father Wojnar, S.J. (Cracow Chron. IV:8; Diary I: 102).

May 1, 1933 — Sister Faustina makes her perpetual vows. The celebrant for this ceremony is Bishop Stanislaus Rospond.

After the vows, Sister Faustina remains in Cracow for another month (Memoirs of Mother Michael, p. 5; Cracow Chron. IV:8; Diary I: 114).

May 25, 1933 — She leaves for Vilnius (Vil. Chron., p. 178). [The chronicle notes: "Sister Faustina, who made her profession of perpetual vows in Cracow, arrived Thursday evening, by train."]

January 2, 1934 — Sister Faustina goes for the first time to the artist Kazimirowski, who is to paint the image of The Divine Mercy (Memoirs of Rev. Sopocko, p. 1; Memoirs of Mother Michael, p. 6: Diary II:240).

March 29, 1934 — She offers herself for sinners, especially for those souls who have lost trust in The Divine Mercy (Diary I: 133).

June 1934 — The painting of the image of The Divine Mercy, executed by artist E. Kazimirowski under the guidance of Sister Faustina, is completed. Sister Faustina cries because the image of the Lord Jesus is not as beautiful as she had seen Him (Memoirs of Rev. Sopocko, p. 1; Diary I: 134).

July 26, 1934 — Sister Faustina lies sick—with a cold (Vil. Chron., p. 223).

July 28, 1934 — She begins to write the Diary again.

August 12, 1934 — She becomes gravely ill. Dr. Maciejewska is summoned along with Father Sopocko, who administers the Sacrament of Anointing of the Sick to her (Vil. Chron., p. 226).

August 13, 1934 — Her health improves (Vil. Chron., p. 226).

October 26, 1934 — Walking with the students from the garden to supper (10 minutes before 6:00 p.m.), Sister Faustina sees the Lord Jesus above the chapel in Vilnius in the same way as she saw Him in Plock; that is, with the pale and red rays. The rays envelop the chapel of the Congregation and the infirmary of the students, and then they spread out over the whole world (Archives — Sister Faustina documents).

February 15, 1935 — Sister Faustina receives news of her seriously ill mother and leaves immediately that evening for her home village of Glogowiec, near Lodz (Vil. Chron., p. 261; Diary I:165-169).

After leaving her home, Sister Faustina stops in Warsaw to see Mother General, Michael Moraczewska, and her former Directress, Sister Mary Joseph Brzoza. A few days later she returns to Vilnius (Diary I: 169).

[The Vilnius Chronicle does not note the date of her return.]

March 4, 1935 — Sister Petronilla and Sister Faustina go by wagon to the market held annually on St. Casimir's Feast Day, for tools and items needed by the house (Vil. Chron., p. 264).

September 29, 1935 — Sister Faustina accompanies some of the other sisters to the Church of St. Michael for the Forty-Hour

Devotions (Vil. Chron., p. 302).

October 19, 1935 — Sister Antonina and Sister Faustina leave for an eight-day retreat in Cracow (Vil. Chron., p. 307; Cracow Chron. IV:49).

November 4, 1935 — In the evening, Sister Faustina returns to Vilnius from the retreat (Vil. Chron., p. 311).

January 8, 1936 — She pays a visit to Bishop Jalbrzykowski and announces to him that the Lord Jesus is demanding the founding of a new congregation (Diary II:50).

March 17, 1936 — Sister Borgia Tichy, Superior of the house in Vilnius receives information from Mother General of the change of assignment for Sister Faustina from Vilnius to Walendow (Vil. Chron., p. 337).

March 19, 1936 — Sister Borgia confers with Archbishop Jalbrzykowski concerning Sister Faustina (Vil. Chron., p. 338).

March 21, 1936 — Sister Faustina takes the morning train from Vilnius to Warsaw (Vil. Chron., p. 338), and remains in Warsaw for a few days (Diary II:90).

March 25, 1936 — She arrives in Walendow—a country house of the Congregation, 20 km from Warsaw. The sisters welcome her joyfully and sincerely (Memoirs; Diary II:91).

April 1936 — After a few weeks, she is assigned to another country home, 1 km from Walendow, a place called Derdy (Memoirs of Mother Michael, p. 8).

This home is situated in a forested area, and Sister Faustina, enchanted with its natural beauty, writes of her joy to Fr. Sopocko in a letter dated May 10, 1936 (Letters #3:5).

May 11, 1936 — In company with Sister Edmund Sekul, she leaves Derdy for a permanent stay in Cracow (Cracow Chron. IV:60), where she works first in the garden and then as gatekeeper (Memoirs of Mother Michael, p. 8).

June 19, 1936 — With some of the sisters, she takes part in a procession in honor of the Sacred Heart of Jesus at the Jesuit house on 26 Kopernik Street (Cracow Chron. IV:62; Diary II: 111).

September 14, 1936 — Archbishop Jalbrzykowski, on his way to Tarnow, visits the convent at Cracow and spends a few minutes in conversation with Sister Faustina (Cracow Chron. IV:67; Diary II: 133; Memoirs of Sister Felicia and Sister Irene).

September 19, 1936 — Sister Faustina is given a physical examination at the hospital in Pradnik (Diary II: 133-134).

October 20, 1936 — In Cracow, she makes an eight-day retreat directed by Father Wojton, S.J. (Cracow Chron. IV:70; Diary II: 153).

December 9, 1936 — For health reasons, the superiors send Sister Faustina to the hospital in Pradnik, a sanatorium for tuberculosis patients in Cracow (Cracow Chron. IV:74; Diary II: 198).

December 13, 1936 — Sister Faustina confesses to the Lord Jesus (Diary II: 207).

December 24, 1936 — With the doctor's permission she returns to the convent for the

Christmas holidays (Cracow Chron. IV:74; Diary II:226).

December 27, 1936 — She returns to the hospital in Pradnik for further treatment (Diary II:230).

March 27, 1937 — She comes back from Pradnik, her health significantly improved (Cracow Chron. IV: 82; Diary III: 18).

April 13, 1937 — Her health becomes so much worse that she is forced to remain in bed (Diary III:22-23).

April 14, 1937 — Fatigued from sickness, she asks the Lord Jesus for health, and is heard (Diary III:23).

April 23, 1937 — During an eight-day retreat starting on April 20 in the Cracow convent, Sister Faustina takes this opportunity to make her three-day retreat (Cracow Chron. IV:82; Diary III:26).

April 29, 1937 — After the retreat, she converses with her former Directress of Novices, Sister Mary Joseph, who made her retreat in Cracow (Diary III:29-30).

May 4, 1937 — Sister Faustina receives permission from Mother General Michael Moraczewska to leave the Congregation (Memoirs of Mother Michael, p. 9; Diary III: 30-31).

July 20, 1937 — She learns that she is going to be sent to a house of the Congregation at Rabka (Diary III:54).

[The Chronicle makes no mention of this; however, it notes that the Superior went to Rabka for two days, which could have had some connection with Sister Faustina's departure (Cracow Chron. IV:88 — dated July 19; Memoirs of

Sister Irene).]

July 29, 1937 — Sister Faustina leaves for Rabka (Diary III:54-55; Memoirs).

August 10, 1937 — She finds that the climate at Rabka does not agree with her, but makes her feel more ill, so she returns to Cracow (Diary IV:4).

August 12, 1937 — Father Sopocko stops at the convent in Cracow and spends some time with Sister Faustina (Memoirs of Sister Felicia; Diary IV:4-5).

August 25, 1937 — Father Sopocko spends a few days in Cracow. Sister Faustina is happy because she is anxious to see him (Diary IV: 16).

August 29, 1937 — She receives permission to speak at length with Father Sopocko (Diary IV: 17).

[The Chronicles make no mention of this.]

September 6, 1937 — Due to increasing ill health, her assignment is changed from gardener to gatekeeper (Memoirs of Mother Michael, p. 10; Diary IV:25).

September 19, 1937 — Her brother Stanley visits her (Diary IV:40).

September 27, 1937 — Sister Faustina and Sister Irene Krzyzanowska, superior of the house, go to the printer to settle the matter of having some holy cards of the image of The Divine Mercy printed (Diary IV:45; Memoirs of Sister Irene, p. 2).

April 21, 1938 — Sister Faustina's health deteriorates, and her superiors decide to send her to the hospital in Pradnik again (Cracow Chron. IV:119; Memoirs of Mother Michael, p. 10).

June 2-5, 1938 — She makes a three-day retreat in the hospital (Memoirs of Sister Irene Krzyzanowska and Sister Felicia; Diary VI: 114).

June 1938 — She stops writing the Diary.

July 1938 — Mother General Michael Moraczewska pays a visit to her at the hospital (Memoirs of Mother Michael, p. 10; Memoirs of Sister Felicia).

August 1938 — Writing her last letter to Mother General, she begs pardon for all the faults of her whole life and ends with the words: "til we meet in heaven" (Letters #23:64; Memoirs of Mother Michael, p. 11).

August 24, 1938 — Sister Camille, who is also a patient at the hospital in Pradnik, telephones to the superior that Sister Faustina's health has significantly worsened. The superior rides to the hospital and spends the night at Sister Faustina's bedside (Cracow Chron. IV: 129).

August 25, 1938 — Rev. T. Czaputa, chaplain of the house of the Congregation in Cracow, goes to the hospital in Pradnik to administer the Sacrament of Anointing of the Sick (Cracow Chron. IV: 129).

August 28, 1938 — Father Sopocko, being in Cracow, pays a visit to the Congregation and visits Sister Faustina a few times in the hospital (Memoirs of Father Sopoctio, p. 3; Cracow Chron. IV: 129).

September 2, 1938 — Father Sopocko visits Sister Faustina in the sanatorium in Pradnik and sees her in ecstasy (Memoirs of Father Sopocko, p. 5;

Memoirs of Sister Felicia).

September 17, 1938 — Very weak and unable to keep much food, Sister Faustina is taken home from Pradnik. Calm and very uplifting, she waits for the moment of union with the Lord Jesus, not at all afraid to die (Cracow Chron. IV: 131).

September 22, 1938 — As she loses more and more strength, she asks pardon of the entire Congregation for her unintentional failings, and serenely awaits the coming of her Heavenly Bridegroom (Cracow Chron. IV: 132).

September 26, 1938 — Father Sopocko visits her for the last time in Cracow, and she tells him: "My one occupation is to live in the presence of my Heavenly Father."

[Father Sopocko notes that "She looked like an unearthly being," and he adds, "At that time I no longer had the slightest doubt that what she had written in her diary about receiving Holy Communion from an Angel was really true" (Memoirs of Father Sopocko, p. 5).]

October 2, 1938 — Sister Faustina, progressively weaker, but always uplifting, calmly awaits her departure (Cracow Chron. IV: 133).

October 5, 1938 — At 4:00 p.m., Father Andrasz, S.J., arrives, and Sister Faustina makes her confession for the last time (Cracow Chron. IV: 134).

At 9:00 p.m., the Chaplain Rev. T. Czaputa, together with the assembled sisters, prays at her bedside the prayers for the dying. Sister Faustina, conscious to the end, unites with those praying (Cracow Chron. IV: 134).

At 10:45 p.m., Sister Mary Faustina Kowalska, after long sufferings borne with great patience, goes to the Lord for her reward (Cracow Chron. IV: 134).

October 7, 1938 — The funeral of Sister Faustina Kowalska takes place on the First Friday of the month and the Feast of Our Lady of the Rosary.

The Jesuits, Father Wojton and Father Chabrowski from the Monastery of St. Barbara Square, and one cleric from 26 Kopernik Street, take part in the funeral services.

At 8:30 a.m., the Matins are sung, next Father Wojton celebrates the Liturgy at the main altar and Father Chabiowski at the altar of the Sacred Heart of Jesus (where the image of The Divine Mercy, renowned for countless graces, is presently found).

Fr. Chabrowski celebrates the Mass wearing white vestments. As the chronicle notes, everything is done very beautifully. No members of Sister Faustina's family are present at the funeral (Cracow Chron. IV: 134).

Sister Faustina is buried in the convent cemetery situated in the garden of the Congregation of the Sisters of Our Lady of Mercy, 3/9 Wronia Street, Lagiewniki, Cracow, in the common grave found on this cemetery.

October 21, 1965 — Twenty-seven years after the death of Sister Faustina, Bishop Julian Groblicki, specially delegated by Archbishop Karol Wojtyla, begins with a solemn session in the Archdiocese of Cracow, the Informative Process relating to the life and virtues of Sister Faustina. From this moment, Sister Faustina is worthy of the title, Servant of God.

November 25, 1966 — While the Informative Process relating to the virtues, writings and devotion of the Servant of God Sister Faustina is being conducted (October 21, 1965 to September 20, 1967), her remains are exhumed and translated to a tomb specially prepared for this purpose in the chapel of the Sisters of Our Lady of Mercy. Over the tomb is a black slab with a cross in the center. The slab usually has fresh flowers brought by the faithful, who plead for numerous graces through the intercession of Sister Faustina.

September 20, 1967 — His Eminence, Karol Cardinal Wojtyla, with a solemn session, closes the Informative Process of the Servant of God in the Cracow Archdiocese.

January 26, 1968 — The Acts of the Informative Process are received in Rome by the Sacred Congregation for the Causes of Saints.

January 31, 1968 — By a Decree of the Sacred Congregation for the Causes of Saints, the Process of Beatification of the Servant of God Sister

Faustina H. Kowalska is formally inaugurated.

April 18, 1993 — The Venerable Servant of God, Sister Maria Faustina Kowalska, is beatified by Pope John Paul II in Rome on the first Sunday after Easter, which is celebrated by many around the world as Divine Mercy Sunday.

April 30, 2000 — Blessed Maria Faustina Kowalska is canonized by Pope John Paul II in Rome on Divine Mercy Sunday during the Great Jubilee Year 2000. And the Pope states during his Canonization homily: "The Second Sunday of Easter from now on throughout the Church will be called 'Divine Mercy Sunday.'"

My daughter, be diligent in writing down every sentence I tell you concerning My mercy, because this is meant for a great number of souls who will profit from it.
(Diary 1142)

Divine Mercy
in my Soul

Diary

Sr. Faustina

Notebook I

(1)

1 O Eternal Love, You command Your Sacred Image[1] to
    be painted
And reveal to us the inconceivable fount of mercy,
You bless whoever approaches Your rays,
And a soul all black will turn into snow.

    O sweet Jesus, it is here[2] You established the throne of
        Your mercy
    To bring joy and hope to sinful man.
    From Your open Heart, as from a pure fount,
    Flows comfort to a repentant heart and soul.

May praise and glory for this Image
Never cease to stream from man's soul.
May praise of God's mercy pour from every heart,
Now, and at every hour, and forever and ever.

O My God

2 When I look into the future, I am frightened,
    But why plunge into the future?
    Only the present moment is precious to me,
    As the future may never enter my soul at all.

    It is no longer in my power,
    To change, correct or add to the past;
    For neither sages nor prophets could do that.
    And so, what the past has embraced I must entrust to
        God.

O present moment, you belong to me, whole and entire.
I desire to use you as best I can.
And although I am weak and small,
You grant me the grace of your omnipotence.

    And so, trusting in Your mercy,
    I walk through life like a little child,
    Offering You each day this heart
    Burning with love for Your greater glory.

(2)   +
                                 J.M.J.
                        [Jesus, Mary, and Joseph]

3   God and souls

                     King of Mercy, guide my soul.

Sister M. Faustina
of the Blessed Sacrament

                                        Vilnius, July 28, 1934

4 O my Jesus, because of my trust in You,
   I weave thousands of garlands, and I know
   That they will all blossom.
   And I know that they will all blossom
   When God's sun will shine on them.

      + O great and Divine Sacrament
      That veils my God!
      Jesus, be with me each moment,
      And no fear will enter my heart.

(3)₊   Vilnius, July 28, 1934
J.M.J.   +First notebook

God and Souls.

5 Be adored, O Most Holy Trinity, now and for all time.
   Be adored in all Your works and all Your creatures.
   May the greatness of Your mercy be admired and
   glorified, O God.

6 I am to write down³ the encounters of my soul with
   You, O God, at the moments of Your special visitations.
   I am to write about You, O Incomprehensible in mercy
   towards my poor soul. Your holy will is the life of my
   soul. I have received this order through him who is for
   me Your representative here on earth, who interprets
   Your holy Will to me. Jesus, You see how difficult it is
   for me to write, how unable I am to put down clearly
   what I experience in my soul. O God, can a pen write
   down that for which. many a time there are no words?
   But You give the order to write, O God; that is enough
   for me.

                                    Warsaw, August 1, 1925

                    Entrance into the Convent

7 From the age of seven, I experienced the definite call of
   God, the grace of a vocation to the religious life. It was
   in the seventh year of my life that, for the first time, I
   heard God's voice in my soul; that is, an invitation to a
   more perfect life. But I was not always obedient to the
   call of grace. I came across no one who would have
   explained these things to me.

8 The eighteenth year of my life. An earnest appeal to my
   parents for permission to enter the convent. My parents'
   flat refusal. After this refusal, I turned myself over to the
   vain things of life, paying no attention to the call of
   grace, although my soul found no satisfaction in any of
   these things. **(4)** The incessant call of grace caused me
   much anguish; I tried, however, to stifle it with

amusements. Interiorly, I shunned God, turning with all my heart to creatures. However, God's grace won out in my soul.

9 Once I was at a dance [probably in Lodz] with one of my sisters. While everybody was having a good time, my soul was experiencing deep torments. As I began to dance. I suddenly saw Jesus at my side, Jesus racked with pain, stripped of His clothing, all covered with wounds, who spoke these words to me: **How long shall I put up with you and how long will you keep putting Me off?** At that moment the charming music stopped, [and] the company I was with vanished from my sight; there remained Jesus and I. I took a seat by my dear sister, pretending to have a headache in order to cover up what took place in my soul. After a while I slipped out unnoticed, leaving my sister and all my companions behind and made my way to the Cathedral of Saint Stanislaus Kostka.

It was almost twilight; there were only a few people in the cathedral. Paying no attention to what was happening around me, I fell prostrate before the Blessed Sacrament and begged the Lord to be good enough to give me to understand what I should do next.

10 Then I head these words: **Go at once to Warsaw; you will enter a convent there.** I rose from prayer, came home, and took care of things that needed to be settled. As best I could, I confided to my sister what took place within my soul. I told her to say good-by to our parents, and thus, in my one dress, with no other belongings, I arrived in Warsaw.

11 When I got off the train and saw that all were going their seperate ways, I was overcome with fear. What am I to do? To whom should I turn, as I know no one? So I said to the Mother of God, "Mary, lead me, guide me." Immediately I heard these words within me telling me to

leave the town and to go to a certain nearby village where I would find a safe lodging for the night. I did so and found in fact that everything was just as the Mother of God told me.

12 Very early the next day, I rode back into the city and entered the first church I saw [St. James Church at Grojecka Street in Ochota, a suburb of Warsaw]. There I began to pray to know further the will of God. Holy Masses were being celebrated one after another. During one of them I heard the words: **Go to that priest** [Father James Dabrowski, pastor of St. James' Parish] **and tell him everything; he will tell you what to do next.** After the Mass I went to the sacristy. (5) I told the priest all that had taken place in my soul, and I asked him to advise me where to take the veil, in which religious order.

13 The priest was surprised at first, but told me to have strong confidence that God would provide for my future. "For the time being," he said, "I shall send you to a pious lady [Aldona Lipszycowa[4]] with whom you will stay until you enter a convent." When I called on this lady, she received me very kindly. During the time I stayed with her, I was looking for a convent, but at whatever convent door I knocked, I was turned away. Sorrow gripped my heart, and I said to the Lord Jesus, "Help me; don't leave me alone." At last I knocked on our door.[5]

14 When Mother Superior, the present Mother General Michael[6] came out to meet me, she told me, after a short conversation, to go to the Lord of the house and ask whether He would accept me. I understood at once that I was to ask this of the Lord Jesus. With great joy, I went to the chapel and asked Jesus: "Lord of this house, do You accept me? This is how one of these sisters told me to put the question to You."

Immediately I heard this voice: **I do accept; you are in**

My Heart. When I returned from the chapel, Mother Superior asked first of all, "Well, has the Lord accepted you?" I answered, "Yes." "If the Lord has accepted, [she said] then I also will accept."

15 This is how I was accepted. However, for many reasons I still had to remain in the world for more than a year with that pious woman [Aldona Lipszycowa], but I did not go back to my own home.

At that time I had to struggle with many difficulties, but God was lavish with His graces. An ever greater longing for God began to take hold of me. The lady, pious as she was, did not understand the happiness of religious life and, in her kindheartedness began to make other plans for my future life. And yet, I sensed that I had a heart so big that nothing would be capable of filling it. And so I turned with all the longing of my soul to God.

16 It was during the octave of Corpus Christi [June 25, 1925]. God filled my soul with the interior light of a deeper knowledge of Him as Supreme Goodness and Supreme Beauty. I came to know how very much God loves me. Eternal is His love for me. It was at vespers. In simple words, which flowed from the heart, I made to God **(6)** a vow of perpetual chastity. From that moment I felt a greater intimacy with God, my Spouse. From that moment I set up a little cell in my heart where I always kept company with Jesus.

17 At last the time came when the door of the convent was opened for me—it was the first of August [1925], in the evening, the vigil [of the feast] of Our Lady of the Angels. I felt immensely happy; it seemed to me that I had stepped into the life of Paradise. A single prayer was bursting forth from my heart, one of thanksgiving.

18 However, after three weeks I became aware that there is so very little time here for prayer, and of many other things which spoke to my soul in favor of entering a religious community of a stricter observance. This

thought took a firm hold of my soul, but the will of God was not in it. Still, the thought, or rather the temptation, was growing stronger and stronger to the point where I decided one day to announce my departure to Mother Superior and definitely to leave [the convent]. But God arranged the circumstances in such a way that I could not get to the Mother Superior [Michael]. I stepped into the little chapel[7] before going to bed, and I asked Jesus for light in this matter. But I received nothing in my soul except a strange unrest which I did not understand. But, in spite of everything, I made up my mind to approach Mother Superior the next morning right after Mass and tell her of my decision.

19   I came to my cell. The sisters were already in bed—the lights were out. I entered the cell full of anguish and discontent; I did not know what to do with myself. I threw myself headlong on the ground and began to pray fervently that I might come to know the will of God. There is silence everywhere as in the tabernacle. All the sisters are resting like white hosts enclosed in Jesus' chalice. It is only from my cell that God can hear the moaning of a soul. I did not know that one was not allowed to pray in the cell after nine without permission.[8]

After a while a brightness filled my cell, and on the curtain I saw the very sorrowful Face of Jesus. There were open wounds on His Face, and large tears were falling on my bedspread. Not knowing what all this meant, I asked Jesus, "Jesus, who has hurt You so?" And Jesus said to me, **It is you who will cause Me this pain if you leave this convent. It is to this place that I called you and nowhere else; and I have prepared many graces for you.** I begged pardon of Jesus and immediately changed my decision.

(7) The next day was confession day. I related all that had taken place in my soul, and the confessor answered that, from this, God's will is clear that I am to remain in this congregation and that I'm not even to think of another religious order. From that moment on, I have always felt happy and content.

20 Shortly after this, I fell ill [general exhaustion]. The dear Mother Superior sent me with two other sisters for a rest to Skolimow, not far from Warsaw. It was at that time that I asked the Lord who else I should pray for. Jesus said that on the following night He would let me know for whom I should pray.

[The next night] I saw my Guardian Angel, who ordered me to follow him. In a moment I was in a misty place full of fire in which there was a great crowd of suffering souls. They were praying fervently, but to no avail, for themselves; only we can come to their aid. The flames which were burning them did not touch me at all. My Guardian Angel did not leave me for an instant. I asked these souls what their greatest suffering was. They answered me in one voice that their greatest torment was longing for God. I saw Our Lady visiting the souls in Purgatory. The souls call her "The Star of the Sea." She brings them refreshment. I wanted to talk with them some more, but my Guardian Angel beckoned me to leave. We went out of that prison of suffering. [I heard an interior voice] which said, **My mercy does not want this, but justice demands it.** Since that time, I am in closer communion with the suffering souls.

21 End of postulancy [April 29, 1926]—My superiors [probably Mother Leonard and Mother Jane[9]] sent me to the novitiate in Cracow. An inconceivable joy reigned in my soul. When we arrived at the novitiate, Sister [Henry[10]] was dying. A few days later she came to me [in spirit, after her death] and bid me to go to the Mother Directress of Novices [Sister Margaret[11]] and tell her to ask her confessor, Father Rospond,[12] to offer one Mass for her and three ejaculatory prayers. At first I agreed, but the next day I decided I would not go to Mother

Directress, because I was not sure whether this had happened in a dream or**(8)**in reality. And so I did not go.

The following night the same thing was repeated more clearly; I had no more doubt. Still, in the morning I decided not to tell the Directress about it unless I saw her [Sister Henry] during the day. At once I ran into her in the corridor. She reproached me for not having gone immediately, and a great uneasiness filled my soul. So I went immediately to Mother Directress and told her everything that had happened to me. Mother responded that she would take care of the matter. At once peace reigned in my soul, and on the third day this sister came to me and said, "May God repay you."

22 The day I took the [religious] habit,[13] God let me understand how much I was to suffer. I clearly saw to what I was committing myself. I experienced a moment of that suffering. But then God filled my soul again with great consolations.

23 Toward the end of the first year of my novitiate, darkness began to cast its shadow over my soul. I felt no consolation in prayer; I had to make a great effort to meditate; fear began to sweep over me. Going deeper into myself, I could find nothing but great misery. I could also clearly see the great holiness of God. I did not dare to raise my eyes to Him, but reduced myself to dust under His feet and begged for mercy. My soul was in this state for almost six months. Our beloved Mother Directress [Mary Joseph[14]] encouraged me in these difficult moments. But this suffering became greater and greater.

The second year of the novitiate was approaching. Whenever I recalled that I was to make my vows, my soul shuddered. I did not understand what I was reading; I could not meditate; it seemed to me that my prayer was displeasing to God. It seemed to me that by approaching the Holy Sacraments I was offending God even more. But despite this, my confessor [Father Theodore[15]] did not let me omit one single Holy Communion. God was working very strangely in my soul. I did not understand anything at all of what my confessor was telling me. The simple truths of the faith became incomprehensible to me. My soul was in anguish, unable to find comfort anywhere.

(9)At a certain point, there came to me the very powerful impression that I am rejected by God. This terrible thought pierced my soul right through; in the midst of the suffering my soul began to experience the agony of death. I wanted to die but could not. The thought came to me: of what use is it to strive for virtues; why mortify oneself when all this is disagreeable to God? When I made this known to the Directress of Novices, I received this reply, "Know, dear Sister, that God has chosen you for great sanctity. This is a sign that God wants to have you very close to Himself in Heaven. Have great trust in the Lord Jesus."

That dreadful thought of being rejected by God is the actual torture suffered by the damned. I fled to Jesus' Wounds and repeated the words of trust, but these words became for me an even greater torture. I went before the Blessed Sacrament, and I began to speak to Jesus: "Jesus, You said that a mother would sooner forget her infant than God His creature, and that 'even if she would forget her infant, I, God, will never forget My creature.' O Jesus, do You hear how my soul is moaning? Deign to hear the painful whimpers of Your child. I trust in You, O God, because heaven and earth will pass, but Your word will last forever." Still I found not a moment of relief.

24 One day, just as I had awakened, when I was putting myself in the presence of God, I was suddenly overwhelmed by despair. Complete darkness in the soul. I fought as best I could till noon. In the afternoon, truly

deadly fears began to seize me; my physical strength began to leave me. I went quickly to my cell, fell on my knees before the Crucifix and began to cry out for mercy. But Jesus did not hear my cries. I felt my physical strength leave me completely. I fell to the ground, despair flooding my whole soul. I suffered terrible tortures in no way different from the torments of hell. I was in this state for three quarters of an hour. I wanted to go and see the Directress, but was too weak. I wanted to shout but I had no voice. Fortunately, one of the sisters [another novice, Sister Placida Putyra] came into my cell. Finding me in such a strange condition, she immediately told the Directress about it. Mother came at once. As soon as she entered the cell she said, "In the name of holy obedience[16] get up from the ground." Immediately some force raised me up from the ground and I stood up, close to the dear Mother Directress. **(10)**With kindly words she began to explain to me that this was a trial sent to me by God, saying, "Have great confidence; God is always our Father, even when He sends us trials."

I returned to my duties as if I had come out from the tomb, my senses saturated with what my soul had experienced. During the evening service, my soul began to agonize again in a terrible darkness. I felt that I was in the power of the Just God, and that I was the object of His indignation. During these terrible moments I said to God, "Jesus, who in the Gospel compare Yourself to a most tender mother,[17] I trust in Your words because You are Truth and Life. In spite of everything, Jesus, I trust in You in the face of every interior sentiment which sets itself against hope. Do what You want with me; I will never leave You, because You are the source of my life." Only one who has lived through similar moments can understand how terrible is this torment of the soul.

25 During the night, the Mother of God visited me, holding the Infant Jesus in Her arms. My soul was filled with

joy, and I said, "Mary, my Mother, do You know how terribly I suffer?" And the Mother of God answered me, *I know how much you suffer, but do not be afraid. I share with you your suffering, and I shall always do so.* She smiled warmly and disappeared. At once, strength and a great courage sprang up anew in my soul; but that lasted only one day. It seemed as though hell had conspired against me. A terrible hatred began to break out in my soul, a hatred for all that is holy and divine. It seemed to me that these spiritual torments would be my lot for the rest of my life. I turned to the Blessed Sacrament and said to Jesus, "Jesus, my Spouse, do You not see that my soul is dying because of its longing for You? How can You hide Yourself from a heart that loves You so sincerely? Forgive me, Jesus; may Your holy will be done in me. I will suffer silently like a dove, without complaining. I will not allow my heart even one single cry of sorrowful complaint."

26 End of the novitiate. The suffering does not diminish. Physical weakness dispenses me from all [community] spiritual exercises; that is to say, they are replaced by brief ejaculatory prayers. Good Friday [April 16, 1928] —Jesus catches up my heart into the very flame of His love. This was during the evening adoration. All of a sudden, the Divine Presence invaded me, and I forgot everything else. Jesus gave me to understand how much He had suffered **(11)** for me. This lasted a very short time. An intense yearning—a longing to love God.

27 First vows [First profession of temporary vows, April 30, 1928]. An ardent desire to empty myself for God by an active love, but a love that would be imperceptible, even to the sisters closest to me.

However, even after the vows, darkness continued to reign in my soul for almost a half year. Once, when I was praying, Jesus pervaded all my soul, darkness melted away, and I heard these words within me: **You are My**

joy; you are My heart's delight. From that moment I felt the Most Holy Trinity in my heart; that is to say, within myself. I felt that I was inundated with Divine light. Since then, my soul has been in intimate communion with God, like a child with its beloved Father.

28 Once Jesus told me, **Go to Mother Superior** [probably Mother Raphael[18]] **and ask her to let you wear a hair shirt for seven days, and once each night you are to get up and come to the chapel.** I said yes, but I found a certain difficulty in actually going to the Superior. In the evening Jesus asked me, **How long will you put it off?** I made up my mind to tell Mother Superior the very next time I would see her.

The next day before noon I saw Mother Superior going to the refectory and, since the kitchen, refectory and Sister Aloysia's little room are all close to each other, I asked Mother Superior to come into Sister Aloysia's room and told her of the wish of the Lord Jesus. At that, Mother answered, "I will not permit you to wear any hair shirt. Absolutely not! If the Lord Jesus were to give you the strength of a colossus, I would then permit those mortifications."

I apologized for taking up Mother's time and left the room. At that very moment I saw Jesus standing at the kitchen door, and I said to Him, "You commanded me to ask for these mortifications, but Mother Superior will not permit them." Jesus said, **I was here during your conversation with the Superior and know everything. I don't demand mortification from you, but obedience. By obedience you give great glory to Me and gain merit for yourself.**

29 One of the Mothers [probably Mother Jane], when she learned about my close relationship with the Lord Jesus, told me that I must be deluding myself. She told me that the Lord Jesus associates in this way only with the saints and not with sinful souls "like you, Sister!" **(12)**After

that, it was as if I mistrusted Jesus. In one of my morning talks with Him I said, "Jesus, are You not an illusion?" Jesus answered me, **My love deceives no one.**

30 +On one occasion I was reflecting on the Holy Trinity, on the essence of God. I absolutely wanted to know and fathom who God is. ...In an instant my spirit was caught up into what seemed to be the next world. I saw an inaccessible light, and in this light what appeared like three sources of light which I could not understand. And out of that light came words in the form of lightning which encircled heaven and earth. Not understanding anything, I was very sad. Suddenly, from this sea of inaccessible light came our dearly beloved Savior, unutterably beautiful with His shining Wounds. And from this light came a voice which said, **Who God is in His Essence, no one will fathom, neither the mind of Angels nor of man.** Jesus said to me, **Get to know God by contemplating His attributes.** A moment later, He traced the sign of the cross with His hand and vanished.

31 +Once I saw a big crowd of people in our chapel, in front of the chapel and in the street, because there was no room for them inside.[19] The chapel was decorated for a feast. There were a lot of clergy near the altar, and then our sisters and those of many other congregations. They were all waiting for the person who was to take a place on the altar. Suddenly I heard a voice saying that I was to take the place on the altar. But as soon as I left the corridor to go across the yard and enter the chapel, following the voice that was calling me, all the people began to throw at me whatever they had to hand: mud, stones, sand, brooms, to such an extent that I at first hesitated to go forward. But the voice kept on calling me even more earnestly, so I walked on bravely.

When I entered the chapel, the superiors, the sisters, the students,[20] and even my parents started to hit me with whatever they could, and so whether I wanted to or not, I quickly took my place on the altar. As soon as I was there, **(13)** the very same people, the students, the sisters, the superiors and my parents all began to hold their arms out to me asking for graces; and as for me, I did not bear any grudge against them for having thrown all sorts of things at me, and I was surprised that I felt a very special love precisely for those persons who had forced me to go more quickly to my appointed place. At the same time my soul was filled with ineffable happiness, and I heard these words, **Do whatever you wish, distribute graces as you will, to whom you will and when you will.** Then, instantly, the vision disappeared.

32 Another time I heard these words, **Go to the Superior and ask her to allow you to make a daily hour of adoration for nine days. During this adoration try to unite yourself in prayer with My Mother. Pray with all your heart in union with Mary, and try also during this time to make the Way of the Cross.** I received the permission, though not for a full hour, but only for whatever time was left me after I had carried out my duties.

33 I was to make this novena for the intention of my Motherland. On the seventh day of the novena I saw, between heaven and earth, the Mother of God, clothed in a bright robe. She was praying with Her hands folded on Her bosom, Her eyes fixed on Heaven. From Her Heart issued forth fiery rays, some of which were turned toward Heaven while the others were covering our country.

34 When I told this and certain other things to my confessor,[21] he replied that these might really be coming from God, but that they might also be an illusion. Because of my frequent changes [of assignments], I did not have a permanent confessor and besides, I had great difficulty in speaking of these things. I prayed ardently

that the Lord would give me that great grace—that is, a spiritual director. But my prayer was answered only after my perpetual vows, when I went to Vilnius. The priest was Father Sopocko.[22] God had allowed me to see him in an interior vision even before I came to Vilnius.[23]

35 Oh, if only I had had a spiritual director from the beginning, then I would not have wasted so many of God's graces. A confessor can help a soul a great deal, but he can also cause it a lot of harm. Oh, how careful confessors should be about the work of God's grace in their penitents' souls! This is a matter of great importance. By the graces given to a soul, one can recognize the degree of its intimacy with God.

36 **(14)**Once I was summoned to the judgment [seat] of God. I stood alone before the Lord. Jesus appeared such as we know Him during His Passion. After a moment, His wounds disappeared except for five, those in His hands, His feet and His side. Suddenly I saw the complete condition of my soul as God sees it. I could clearly see all that is displeasing to God. I did not know that even the smallest transgressions will have to be accounted for. What a moment! Who can describe it? To stand before the Thrice-Holy God! Jesus asked me, **Who are you?** I answered, "I am Your servant, Lord." **You are guilty of one day of fire in purgatory.** I wanted to throw myself immediately into the flames of purgatory, but Jesus stopped me and said, **Which do you prefer, suffer now for one day in purgatory or for a short while on earth?** I replied, "Jesus, I want to suffer in purgatory, and I want to suffer also the greatest pains on earth, even if it were until the end of the world." Jesus said, **One** [of the two] **is enough; you will go back to earth, and there you will suffer much, but not for long; you will accomplish My will and My desires, and a faithful servant of Mine will help you to do this. Now, rest your head on My bosom, on My heart, and draw from it strength and power for these sufferings, because**

you will find neither relief nor help nor comfort anywhere else. Know that you will have much, much to suffer, but don't let this frighten you; I am with you.

37 Soon afterwards I became ill.[24] Physical weakness was for me a school of patience. Only Jesus knows how many efforts of will I had to make to fulfill my duty.[25]

38 In order to purify a soul, Jesus uses whatever instruments He likes. My soul underwent a complete abandonment on the part of creatures; often my best intentions were misinterpreted by the sisters,[26] a type of suffering which is most painful; but God allows it, and we must accept it because in this way we become more like Jesus. There was one thing which I could not understand for a long time: Jesus ordered me to tell everything to my Superiors, but my Superiors did not believe what I said and treated me with pity as though I were being deluded or were imagining things.

Because of this, believing myself to be deluded, I resolved to avoid God interiorly for fear of these illusions. **(15)** But the grace of God pursued me at every step, and God spoke to me when I least expected it.

39 + One day Jesus told me that He would cause a chastisement to fall upon the most beautiful city in our country [probably Warsaw]. This chastisement would be that with which God had punished Sodom and Gomorrah.[27] I saw the great wrath of God and a shudder pierced my heart. I prayed in silence. After a moment, Jesus said to me, **My child, unite yourself closely to Me during the Sacrifice and offer My Blood and My Wounds to My Father in expiation for the sins of that city. Repeat this without interruption throughout the entire Holy Mass. Do this for seven days.** On the seventh day I saw Jesus in a bright cloud and began to beg Him to look upon the city and upon our whole country. Jesus looked [down] graciously. When I saw the kindness of Jesus, I began to beg His blessing. Immediately Jesus

said, **For your sake I bless the entire country.** And He made a big sign of the cross over our country. Seeing the goodness of God, a great joy filled my soul.

40   +The year 1929. Once during Holy Mass, I felt in a very special way the closeness of God, although I tried to turn away and escape from Him. On several occasions I have run away from God because I did not want to be a victim of the evil spirit; since others have told me, more than once, that such is the case. And this incertitude lasted for quite some time. During Holy Mass, before Communion, we had the renewal of vows. When we had left our kneelers and had started to recite the formula for the vows, Jesus appeared suddenly at my side clad in a white garment with a golden girdle around His waist, and He said to me, **I give you eternal love that your purity may be untarnished and as a sign that you will never be subject to temptations against purity.** Jesus took off His golden cincture and tied it around my waist.

Since then I have never experienced any attacks against this virtue, either in my heart or in my mind. I later understood that this was one of the greatest graces which the Most Holy Virgin Mary had obtained for me, as for many years I had been asking this grace of Her. Since that time I have experienced an increasing devotion to the Mother of God. She has taught me how to love God interiorly and also how to carry out His holy will in all things. O Mary, You are joy, because through You God descended to earth [and] into my heart.

41   **(16)**On one occasion I saw a servant of God in the immediate danger of committing a mortal sin. I started to beg God to deign to send down upon me all the torments of hell and all the sufferings He wished if only this priest would be set free and snatched from the occasion of committing a sin. Jesus heard my prayer

and, that very instant, I felt a crown of thorns on my head. The thorns penetrated my head with great force right into my brain. This lasted for three hours; the servant of God was set free from this sin, and his soul was strengthened by a special grace of God.

42 +Once, on Christmas Day [1928], I felt the omnipotence and the presence of God surrounding me. And once more I fled from this interior meeting with the Lord. I asked Mother Superior for permission to go to Jozefinek[28] to visit the sisters there. The Superior gave us permission, and we started to get ready right after lunch. The other sisters were already waiting for me at the door of the convent while I ran to my cell to get my cloak. On my way back, as I was passing close to the little chapel, I saw Jesus standing in the doorway. He said to me, **Go ahead, but I am taking your heart.** Suddenly I felt that I had no heart in my chest. But the sisters were scolding me for lingering behind, saying that it was already getting late, so I quickly went along with them. But a sense of uneasiness troubled me, and a strange longing invaded my soul, though no one knew what was happening except God.

After we had been at Jozefinek for only a few minutes, I said to the sisters, "Let's go back home." The sisters asked for at least a moment's rest, but my spirit could find no peace. I explained that we must return before dark; and in as much as we had quite a distance to go, we immediately returned home. When Mother Superior met us in the hallway she asked me, "Haven't the sisters gone yet, or have they already returned?" I said that we had already returned because I did not want to be returning in the evening. I took off my cloak and immediately went to the little chapel. As soon as I entered Jesus said to me, **Go to Mother Superior and tell her that you came back, not in order to reach home before dark, but because I had taken your heart.** Even though this was very difficult for me, I went **(17)** to the Superior, and I told her frankly the real reason why I had come back so soon, and I asked pardon of the Lord for everything that had displeased Him. And then Jesus filled me with great joy. I understood that apart from God there is no contentment anywhere.

43 On one occasion I saw two sisters who were about to enter hell. A terrible agony tore my soul; I prayed to God for them, and Jesus said to me, **Go to Mother Superior and tell her that those two sisters are in danger of committing a mortal sin.** The next day I told this to the Superior. One of them had already repented with great fervor and the other was going through a great struggle.

44 One day Jesus said to me, **I am going to leave this house... because there are things here which displease Me.** And the Host came out of the tabernacle and came to rest in my hands and I, with joy, placed it back in the tabernacle. This was repeated a second time, and I did the same thing. Despite this, it happened a third time, but the Host was transformed into the living Lord Jesus, who said to me, **I will stay here no longer!** At this, a powerful love for Jesus rose up in my soul. I answered, "And I, I will not let You leave this house, Jesus!" And again Jesus disappeared while the Host remained in my hands. Once again I put it back in the chalice and closed it up in the tabernacle. And Jesus stayed with us. I undertook to make three days of adoration by way of reparation.

45 Once Jesus said to me, **Tell Mother General** [Michael] **that in this house ... such and such a thing is being committed ... which displeases Me and offends Me greatly.** I did not tell this to Mother right away, but the uneasiness which the Lord made me feel did not permit me to wait a minute longer, and I wrote immediately to Mother General, and peace returned to my soul.

46 I often felt the Passion of the Lord Jesus in my body, although this was imperceptible [to others], and I rejoiced in it because Jesus wanted it so. But this lasted for only a short time. These sufferings set my soul afire with love for God and for immortal souls. Love endures everything, love is stronger than death, love fears nothing...

(18)+February 22, 1931

47 In the evening, when I was in my cell, I saw the Lord Jesus clothed in a white garment. One hand [was] raised in the gesture of blessing, the other was touching the garment at the breast. From beneath the garment, slightly drawn aside at the breast, there were emanating two large rays, one red, the other pale. In silence I kept my gaze fixed on the Lord; my soul was struck with awe, but also with great joy. After a while, Jesus said to me, **Paint an image according to the pattern you see, with the signature: Jesus, I trust in You. I desire that this image be venerated, first in your chapel, and** [then] **throughout the world.**

48 **I promise that the soul that will venerate this image will not perish. I also promise victory over** [its] **enemies already here on earth, especially at the hour of death. I Myself will defend it as My own glory.**

49 When I told this to my confessor,[29] I received this for a reply: "That refers to your soul." He told me, "Certainly, paint God's image in your soul." When I came out of the confessional, I again heard words such as these: **My image already is in your soul. I desire that there be a Feast of Mercy. I want this image, which you will paint with a brush, to be solemnly blessed on the first Sunday after Easter; that Sunday is to be the Feast of Mercy.**

50 +**I desire that priests proclaim this great mercy of Mine towards souls of sinners. Let the sinner not be afraid to approach Me. The flames of mercy are burning Me— clamoring to be spent; I want to pour them out upon**

these souls.

Jesus complained to me in these words, **Distrust on the part of souls is tearing at My insides. The distrust of a chosen soul causes Me even greater pain; despite My inexhaustible love for them they do not trust Me. Even My death is not enough for them. Woe to the soul that abuses these** [gifts].

51 **(19)**When I spoke about this to Mother Superior [Rose,[30] telling her] that God had asked this of me, she answered that Jesus should give some sign so that we could recognize Him more clearly.

When I asked the Lord Jesus for a sign as a proof "that You are truly my God and Lord and that this request comes from You," I heard this interior voice, **I will make this all clear to the Superior by means of the graces which I will grant through this image.**

52 When I tried to run away from these interior inspirations, God said to me that on the day of judgment He would demand of me a great number of souls.

Once, exhausted because of these various difficulties that had befallen me because of what Jesus had said to me and what He had demanded of me for the painting of this image, I made up my mind to approach Father Andrasz[31] before my perpetual vows, and to ask him to dispense me from all these interior inspirations and from the duty of painting this image. After having heard my confession, Father Andrasz gave me this answer: "I will dispense you from nothing, Sister; it is not right for you to turn away from these interior inspirations, but you must absolutely—and I say, absolutely—speak about them to your confessor; otherwise you will go astray despite the great graces you are receiving from God.

53 For the present you are coming to me for confession, but understand, Sister, that you must have a permanent

confessor; that is to say, a spiritual director."

I was very upset by this. I thought that I would get myself free from everything, and it turned out quite the opposite—an explicit command to follow the requests of Jesus. And now, still another torment, as I had no permanent confessor. Even if I went to the same confessor for a certain period of time, I could not open my soul to him in respect to these graces, and this caused me ineffable pain. So I asked Jesus to give these graces to someone else, because I did not know how to make use of them and was only wasting them. "Jesus, have mercy on me; do not entrust such great things to me, as You see that I am a bit of dust and completely inept."

But the goodness of Jesus is infinite; He had promised me visible help here on earth, and a little while later I received it **(20)** in Vilnius, in the person of Father Sopocko. I had already known him before coming to Vilnius, thanks to an interior vision. One day I saw him in our chapel between the altar and the confessional and suddenly heard a voice in my soul say, **This is the visible help for you on earth. He will help you carry out My will on earth.**

54   +One day, tired out with all these uncertainties, I asked Jesus, "Jesus, are You my God or some kind of phantom? Because my Superiors say that there are all sorts of illusions and phantoms. If You are my Lord, I beg You to bless me." Then Jesus made a big sign of the cross over me and I, too, signed myself. When I asked pardon of Jesus for this question, He replied that I had in no way displeased Him by this question and that my confidence pleased Him very much.

55   1933.   Spiritual Counsel Given Me
                  by Father Andrasz, S.J.

First: You must not turn away from these interior inspirations, but always tell everything to your confessor. If you recognize that these interior inspirations refer to your own self; that is to say, they are for the good of your soul or for the good of other souls, I urge you to follow them; and you must not neglect them, but always do so in consultation with your confessor.

Second: If these inspirations are not in accord with the faith or the spirit of the Church, they must be rejected immediately as coming from the evil spirit.

Third: If these inspirations do not refer to souls, in general, nor specifically to their good, you should not take them too seriously, and it would be better to even ignore them.

But you should not make this decision by yourself, either one way or the other, as you can easily be led astray despite these great favors from God. Humility, humility, and ever humility, as we can do nothing of ourselves; all is purely and simply God's grace.

You say to me that God demands great trust from souls; well then, you be the first to show this trust. And one more word—accept all this with serenity.

(21) Words of one of the confessors: "Sister, God is preparing many special graces for you, but try to make your life as clear as crystal before the Lord, paying no attention to what anyone else thinks about you. Let God suffice you; He alone."

Toward the end of my novitiate, a confessor [perhaps Father Theodore] told me: "Go through life doing good, so that I could write on its pages: 'She spent her life doing good.' May God bring this about in you."

Another time the confessor said to me, "Comport yourself before God like the widow in the Gospel; although the coin she dropped into the box was of little value, it counted far more before God than all the big offerings of others."

On another occasion the instruction I received was this:

"Act in such a way that all those who come in contact with you will go away joyful. Sow happiness about you because you have received much from God; give, then, generously to others. They should take leave of you with their hearts filled with joy, even if they have no more than touched the hem of your garment. Keep well in mind the words I am telling you right now."

Still another time he gave me the following recommendation: "Let God push your boat out into the deep waters, toward the unfathomable depths of the interior life."

Here are a few words from a conversation I had with the Mother Directress [Mary Joseph] toward the end of my novitiate: "Sister, let simplicity and humility be the characteristic traits of your soul. Go through life like a little child, always trusting, always full of simplicity and humility, content with everything, happy in every circumstance. There, where others fear, you will pass calmly along, thanks to this simplicity and humility. Remember this, Sister, for your whole life: as waters flow from the mountains down into the valleys, so, too, do God's graces flow only into humble souls."

56 O my God, I understand well that You demand this spiritual childhood[32] of me, because You are constantly asking it of me through Your representatives.

(22)At the beginning of my religious life, suffering and adversities frightened and disheartened me. So I prayed continuously, asking Jesus to strengthen me and to grant me the power of His Holy Spirit that I might carry out His holy will in all things, because from the beginning I have been aware of my weakness. I know very well what I am of myself, because for this purpose Jesus has opened the eyes of my soul; I am an abyss of misery, and hence I understand that whatever good there is in my soul consists solely of His holy grace. The knowledge of my own misery allows me, at the same time, to know the immensity of Your mercy. In my own interior life, I am looking with one eye at the abyss of my misery and baseness, and with the other, at the abyss of Your mercy, O God.

57 O my Jesus, You are the life of my life. You know only too well that I long for nothing but the glory of Your Name and that souls come to know Your goodness. Why do souls avoid You, Jesus?—I don't understand that. Oh, if I could only cut my heart into tiny pieces and in this way offer to You, O Jesus, each piece as a heart whole and entire, to make up in part for the hearts that do not love You! I love You, Jesus, with every drop of my blood, and I would gladly shed my blood for You to give You a proof of the sincerity of my love. O God, the more I know You the less I can comprehend You, but this "non-comprehension" lets me realize how great You are! And it is this impossibility of comprehending You which enflames my heart anew for You, O Lord. From the moment when You let me fix the eyes of my soul on You, O Jesus, I have been at peace and desired nothing else. I found my destiny at the moment when my soul lost itself in You, the only object of my love. In comparison with you, everything is nothing. Sufferings, adversities, humiliations, failures and suspicions that have come my way are splinters that keep alive the fire of my love for You, O Jesus.

My desires are mad and unattainable. I wish to conceal from You that I suffer. I want **(23)** never to be rewarded for my efforts and my good actions. You yourself, Jesus, are my only reward; You are enough, O Treasure of my heart! I want to share compassionately in the sufferings of my neighbors and to conceal my own sufferings, not only from them, but also from You, Jesus.

Suffering is a great grace; through suffering the soul becomes like the Savior; in suffering love becomes crystallized; the greater the suffering, the purer the love.

58 +One night, a sister who had died two months previously came to me. She was a sister of the first choir. I saw her in a terrible condition, all in flames with her face painfully distorted. This lasted only a short time, and then she disappeared. A shudder went through my soul because I did not know whether she was suffering in purgatory or in hell. Nevertheless I redoubled my prayers for her. The next night she came again, but I saw her in an even more horrible state, in the midst of flames which were even more intense, and despair was written all over her face. I was astonished to see her in a worse condition after the prayers I had offered for her, and I asked, "Haven't my prayers helped you?" She answered that my prayers had not helped her and that nothing would help her. I said to her, "And the prayers which the whole community has offered for you, have they not been any help to you?" She said no, that these prayers had helped some other souls. I replied, "If my prayers are not helping you, Sister, please stop coming to me." She disappeared at once. Despite this, I kept on praying.

After some time she came back again to me during the night, but already her appearance had changed. There were no longer any flames, as there had been before, and her face was radiant, her eyes beaming with joy. She told me that I had a true love for my neighbor and that many other souls had profited from my prayers. She urged me not to cease praying for the souls in purgatory, and she added that she herself would not remain there much longer. How astounding are the decrees of God!

59 (24)1933. On one occasion I heard these words in my soul, **Make a novena for your country. This novena will consist of the recitation of the Litany of the Saints. Ask your confessor for permission** [probably Father Sopocko or Father Andrasz].

60 I received permission at my next confession and began the novena that very evening. Towards the end of the

litany I saw a great radiance and, in the midst of it, God the Father. Between this radiance and the earth I saw Jesus, nailed to the Cross in such a way that when God wanted to look at the earth, He had to look through the wounds of Jesus. And I understood that it was for the sake of Jesus that God blesses the earth.

61 O Jesus, I thank you for this great grace; namely, that You yourself have deigned to choose a confessor for me, and that You had made him known to me in a vision even before I had met him [Father Sopocko]. When I went to confession to Father Andrasz, I thought that I would be released from following these interior inspirations. Father replied that he could not dispense me from this, "but pray, Sister, that you be given a spiritual director."

After a short but fervent prayer, I saw Father Sopocko for a second time, in our chapel, between the confessional and the altar. I was in Cracow at that time. These two visions bolstered up my spirit, all the more when I found him to be just as I had seen him in the visions, once at Warsaw during my third probation, and a second time at Cracow. O Jesus, I thank you for this great gift! And now when I hear people sometimes say that they have no confessor; that is to say, a director, fear takes hold of me, because I know very well how much harm I myself experienced when I did not have this help. It is so easy to go astray when one has no guide!

62 O life so dull and monotonous, how many treasures you contain! When I look at everything with the eyes of faith, no two hours are alike, and the dullness and monotony disappear. The grace which is given me in this hour will not be repeated in the next. It may be given me again, but it will not be the same grace. Time goes on, never to return again. Whatever is enclosed in it will never change; it seals with a seal for eternity.

63 (25)+Father Sopocko must be well loved by God. I say

this because I myself have experienced how much God defends him at certain moments. When I see this, I rejoice greatly that God has such chosen ones.

1929. The Trip to Calvary.[33]

64   When I came to Vilnius for two months to replace a sister who had gone for her third probation [Sister Peter, who worked in the kitchen], I stayed a little longer than two months. One day, the Mother Superior [Irene[34]], wanting to give me a bit of pleasure, gave me permission to go, together with another sister,[35] to Calvary to "walk the paths," as they say. I was delighted. Although it was not very far, it was Mother Superior's wish that we should go by boat. That evening Jesus said to me, **I want you to stay home.** I answered, "Jesus, everything is ready for us to leave tomorrow morning; what am I to do now?" The Lord answered, **This trip will be harmful to your soul.** I replied to Jesus, "You can find a way out. Arrange things in such a way that Your will may be done." At that moment the bell announced the time for sleep. I gave Jesus a parting glance and went to my cell.

Next morning the weather was beautiful, and my companion was filled with joy at the prospect of the great pleasure we would have in getting to see everything. But as for me, I was sure we would not go, even though there were no obstacles so far.

We were to receive Holy Communion earlier and leave right after the thanksgiving. But during the time of Communion, all of a sudden, the weather changed. Clouds covered the sky, and the rain came down in torrents. Everyone was astounded at such a sudden change in the weather.

(26) Mother Superior said to me, "I am so sorry you

cannot go, Sisters!" I answered, "Dear Mother, it doesn't really matter that we cannot go; it was God's will that we stay home." However, no one knew that it was Jesus' express desire that I stay home. I spent the whole day in recollection and meditation, thanking the Lord for having kept me home. That day, God granted me many heavenly consolations.

65 One time during the novitiate, when Mother Directress sent me to work in the wards' kitchen, I was very upset because I could not manage the pots, which were very large. The most difficult task for me was draining the potatoes,and sometimes I spilt half of them with the water. When I told this to Mother Directress, she said that with time I would get used to it and gain the necessary skill. Yet the task was not getting any easier, as I was growing weaker every day. So I would move away when it was time to drain the potatoes. The sisters noticed that I avoided this task and were very much surprised. They did not know that I could not help in spite of all my willingness to do this and not spare myself. At noon, during the examination of conscience, I complained to God about my weakness. Then I heard the following words in my soul, **From today on you will do this easily; I shall strengthen you.**

That evening, when the time came to drain off the water from the potatoes, I hurried to be the first to do it, trusting in the Lord's words. I took up the pot with ease and poured off the water perfectly. But when I took off the cover to let the potatoes steam off, I saw there in the pot, in the place of the potatoes, whole bunches of red roses, beautiful beyond description. I had never seen such roses before. Greatly astonished and unable to understand the meaning of this, I heard a voice within me saying, **I change such hard work of yours into bouquets of most beautiful flowers, and their perfume rises up to My throne.** From then on I have tried to drain the potatoes myself, not only during my week when it was my turn to cook, **(27)** but also in replacement of other sisters when it was their turn. And not only do I do this, but I try to be the first to help in any other burdensome task, because I have experienced how much this pleases God.

66 O inexhaustible treasure of purity of intention which makes all our actions perfect and so pleasing to God!

O Jesus, You know how weak I am; be then ever with me; guide my actions and my whole being, You who are my very best Teacher! Truly, Jesus, I become frightened when I look at my own misery, but at the same time I am reassured by Your unfathomable mercy, which exceeds my misery by the measure of all eternity. This disposition of soul clothes me in Your power. O joy that flows from the knowledge of one's self! O unchanging Truth, Your constancy is everlasting!

67 When I fell sick [probably the beginning of consumption] after my first vows and when, despite the kind and solicitous care of my Superiors and the efforts of the doctor, I felt neither better nor worse, remarks began to reach my ears which inferred that I was making believe. With that, my suffering was doubled, and this lasted for quite a long time. One day I complained to Jesus that I was being a burden to the sisters. Jesus answered me, **You are not living for yourself but for souls, and other souls will profit from your sufferings. Your prolonged suffering will give them the light and strength to accept My will.**

68 The heaviest suffering for me was that it seemed to me that neither my prayers nor my good works were pleasing to God. I did not dare lift up my eyes to heaven. This caused me such great suffering during the community exercises in the chapel that one day Mother Superior [Raphael] called me aside after the exercises and said to me, "Sister, ask God for grace and consolation, because I can see for myself **(28)** and the

sisters keep telling me that the very sight of you evokes pity. I really do not know what to do with you, Sister. I command you to stop tormenting yourself for no reason."

But all these conferences with Mother Superior brought me no relief, nor did they clarify anything for me. Rather, even greater darkness hid God from me. I looked for help in the confessional, but not even there did I find it. A saintly priest wanted to help me, but I was so miserable that I couldn't even define my trouble, and that vexed me even more. A deathly sadness penetrated my soul to such an extent that I was unable to hide it, and it was apparent to those around me. I lost hope. The night was growing darker and darker. The priest to whom I went to confession said to me, "I see very special graces in you, Sister, and I am not worried about you at all; why are you torturing yourself in this way?" But at that time I did not understand at all what he was saying and was extremely surprised when, by way of penance, I was ordered to say the *Te Deum* or the *Magnificat,* or to run fast around the garden in the evening, or else to laugh out loud ten times a day. These penances were very surprising to me; but even with that the priest was not able to give me much help. Evidently, God wanted me to give Him glory through suffering.

That priest consoled me, saying that in my present situation I was more pleasing to God than if I were filled with the greatest consolations. "It is a very great grace, Sister," he told me, "that in your present condition, with all the torments of soul you are experiencing, you not only do not offend God, but you even try to practice virtues. I am looking into your soul, and I see God's great plans and special graces there; and seeing this, I give thanks to the Lord." But despite all that, my soul was in a state of torture; and in the midst of unspeakable torments, I imitated the blind man who entrusts himself to his guide, holding his hand firmly, not giving up

obedience for a single moment, and this was my only
safety in this fiery trial.

69 **(29)** +O Jesus, eternal Truth, strengthen my feeble forces;
You can do all things, Lord. I know that without You all
my efforts are in vain. O Jesus, do not hide from me, for
I cannot live without You. Listen to the cry of my soul.
Your mercy has not been exhausted, Lord, so have pity
on my misery. Your mercy surpasses the understanding
of all Angels and people put together; and so, although
it seems to me that You do not hear me, I put my trust in
the ocean of Your mercy, and I know that my hope will
not be deceived.

70 Only Jesus knows how burdensome and difficult it is to
accomplish one's duties when the soul is so interiorly
tortured, the physical powers so weakened and the mind
darkened. In the silence of my heart I kept saying to
myself, "O Christ, may delights, honor and glory be
Yours, and suffering be mine. I will not lag one step
behind as I follow You, though thorns wound my feet."

71 I was sent for treatment to our house in Plock, and there
I had the privilege of decorating the chapel with flowers.
That was at Biala.[36] Sister Thecla did not always have
time for this, so I often decorated the chapel by myself.
One day, I had picked the prettiest roses to decorate the
room of a certain person. When I was approaching the
porch, I saw Jesus standing there. In a kindly way He
asked me, **My daughter, to whom are you taking these
flowers?** My silence was my reply to the Lord, because I
recognized immediately that I had a very subtle
attachment to this person,[37] which I had not noticed
before. Suddenly Jesus disappeared. At the same
moment I threw the flowers on the ground and went
before the Blessed Sacrament, my heart filled with
gratitude for the grace of knowing myself.

O Divine Sun, in Your rays the soul sees the tiniest
specks of dust which displease You.

72 **(30)**O Jesus, eternal Truth, our Life, I call upon You and I beg Your mercy for poor sinners. O sweetest Heart of my Lord, full of pity and unfathomable mercy, I plead with You for poor sinners. O Most Sacred Heart, Fount of Mercy from which gush forth rays of inconceivable graces upon the entire human race, I beg of You light for poor sinners. O Jesus, be mindful of Your own bitter Passion and do not permit the loss of souls redeemed at so dear a price of Your most precious Blood. O Jesus, when I consider the great price of Your Blood, I rejoice at its immensity, for one drop alone would have been enough for the salvation of all sinners. Although sin is an abyss of wickedness and ingratitude, the price paid for us can never be equalled. Therefore, let every soul trust in the Passion of the Lord, and place its hope in His mercy. God will not deny His mercy to anyone. Heaven and earth may change, but God's mercy will never be exhausted. Oh, what immense joy burns in my heart when I contemplate Your incomprehensible goodness, O Jesus! I desire to bring all sinners to Your feet that they may glorify Your mercy throughout endless ages.

73 O my Jesus, despite the deep night that is all around me and the dark clouds which hide the horizon, I know that the sun never goes out. O Lord, though I cannot comprehend You and do not understand Your ways, I nonetheless trust in Your mercy. If it is Your will, Lord, that I live always in such darkness, may You be blessed. I ask You only one thing, Jesus: do not allow me to offend You in any way. O my Jesus, You alone know the longings and the sufferings of my heart. I am glad I can suffer for You, however little. When I feel that the suffering is more than I can bear, I take refuge in the Lord in the Blessed Sacrament, and I speak to Him with profound silence.

(31) The Confession of One of Our Wards.

74 One day I felt driven to take steps to see to it that the

Feast of Mercy be instituted and the image of the Merciful Jesus be painted, and I could find no peace. Something was pervading my whole being, and yet I feared being deluded. However, these doubts always came from outside, because in the depths of my soul I felt it was the Lord who was penetrating my being. The priest to whom I was going to confession at that time told me that one can often have illusions, and I felt that he was somewhat afraid to hear my confession. This was a torture for me. Seeing that I was getting very little help from people, I turned all the more to Jesus, the best of all teachers. At one time, when I was filled with doubts as to whether the voice I heard came from the Lord or not, I began to speak to Jesus interiorly without forming any words. Suddenly an inner force took hold of me and I said, "If You who commune with me and talk to me are truly my God, I beg You, O Lord, to make this ward go this very day to confession; this sign will give me reassurance." At that very moment, the girl asked to go to confession.

The Mother in charge of the class was surprised at this sudden change in her, but she undertook to call a priest immediately, and this person made her confession with great compunction. At the same time, I heard a voice within me say, **Do you believe Me now?** And once again a strange power pervaded my soul, strengthening and reassuring me to such a degree that I myself was surprised that I had allowed myself to doubt even for a moment.

75 But these doubts always come from without, a fact which inclined me to close myself up more and more within myself. When, during confession, I sense uncertainty on the part of the priest, I do not open my soul to its depths, but only accuse myself of my sins. A priest who is not at peace with himself will not be able to inspire peace in another soul.

O priests, you bright candles enlightening human souls, let your brightness never be dimmed. I understood that at that time it was not God's will that I uncover my soul completely. Later on, God did give me this grace.

76 **(32)** O my Jesus, direct my mind, take possession of my whole being, enclose me in the depths of Your heart, and protect me against the assaults of the enemy. My only hope is in You. Speak through my mouth when I, wretchedness itself, find myself with the mighty and wise, so that they will know that this undertaking is Yours and comes from You.

Darkness and Temptations

77 My mind became dimmed in a strange way; no truth seemed clear to me. When people spoke to me about God, my heart was like a rock. I could not draw from it a single sentiment of love for Him. When I tried, by an act of the will, to remain close to Him, I experienced great torments, and it seemed to me that I was only provoking God to an even greater anger. It was absolutely impossible for me to meditate as I had been accustomed to do in the past. I felt in my soul a great void, and there was nothing with which I could fill it. I began to suffer from a great hunger and yearning for God, but I saw my utter powerlessness. I tried to read slowly, sentence by sentence, and to meditate in this way, but this also was of no avail. I understood nothing of what I had read.

The abyss of my misery was constantly before my eyes. Every time I entered the chapel for some spiritual exercise, I experienced even worse torments and temptations. More than once, all through Holy Mass, I had to struggle against blasphemous thoughts which were forcing themselves to my lips. I felt an aversion for the Holy Sacraments, and it seemed to me that I was not profiting from them in any way. It was only out of obedience to my confessor that I frequented them, and this blind obedience was for me the only path I could follow and my very last hope of survival. The priest explained to me that these were trials sent by God and that, in the situation I was in, not only was I not offending God, but I was most pleasing to Him. **(33)** "This is a sign," he told me, "that God loves you very much and that He has great confidence in you, since He is sending you such trials." But these words brought me no comfort; it seemed to me that they did not apply to me at all.

One thing did surprise me: it often happened that, at the time when I was suffering greatly, these terrible torments would disappear suddenly just as I was approaching the confessional; but as soon as I had left the confessional, all these torments would again seize me with even greater ferocity. I would then fall on my face before the Blessed Sacrament repeating these words: "Even if You kill me, still will I trust in You!" [cf. Job 13:15] It seemed to me that I would die in these agonies. But the most terrible thought for me was the conviction that I had been rejected by God. Then other thoughts came to me: why strive to acquire virtues and do good works? why mortify and annihilate yourself? what good is it to take vows? to pray? to sacrifice and immolate yourself? why sacrifice myself all the time? what good is it—if I am already rejected by God? why all these efforts? And here, God alone knew what was going on in my heart.

78 Once when I was being crushed by these dreadful sufferings, I went into the chapel and said from the bottom of my soul, "Do what You will with me, O Jesus; I will adore You in everything. May Your will be done in me, O my Lord and my God, and I will praise Your infinite mercy." Through this act of submission, these terrible torments left me. Suddenly I saw Jesus, who said to me, **I am always in your heart.** An inconceivable joy entered my soul, and a great love of God set my heart aflame. I see that God never tries us beyond what we are able to suffer. Oh, I fear nothing; if God sends such great

suffering to a soul, He upholds it with an even greater grace, although we are not aware of it. One act of trust at such moments gives greater glory to God than whole hours passed in prayer filled with consolations. Now I see that if God wants to keep a soul in darkness, no book, no confessor can bring it light.

79 **(34)**O Mary, my Mother and my Lady, I offer You my soul, my body, my life and my death, and all that will follow it. I place everything in Your hands. O my Mother, cover my soul with Your virginal mantle and grant me the grace of purity of heart, soul and body. Defend me with Your power against all enemies, and especially against those who hide their malice behind the mask of virtue. O lovely lily! You are for me a mirror, O my Mother!

80 O Jesus, Divine Prisoner of Love, when I consider Your love and how You emptied Yourself for me, my senses fail me. You hide Your inconceivable majesty and lower Yourself to miserable me. O King of Glory, though You hide Your beauty, yet the eye of my soul rends the veil. I see the angelic choirs giving You honor without cease, and all the heavenly Powers praising You without cease, and without cease they are saying: Holy, Holy, Holy.

Oh, who will comprehend Your love and Your unfathomable mercy toward us! O Prisoner of Love, I lock up my poor heart in this tabernacle, that it may adore You without cease night and day. I know of no obstacle in this adoration, and even though I be physically distant, my heart is always with You. Nothing can put a stop to my love for You. No obstacles exist for me. O my Jesus, I will console You for all the ingratitude, the blasphemies, the coldness, the hatred of the wicked, the sacrileges. O Jesus, I want to burn as a pure offering and to be consumed before the throne of Your hiddenness. I plead with You unceasingly for poor dying sinners.

81 O Holy Trinity, One and Indivisible God, may You be blessed for this great gift and testament of mercy. My Jesus, to atone for blasphemers I will keep silent when unjustly reprimanded and in this way make partial amends to You. I am singing within my soul an unending hymn to You, and no one will suspect or understand this. The song of my soul is known to You alone, O my Creator and Lord!

82 **(35)** I will not allow myself to be so absorbed in the whirlwind of work as to forget about God. I will spend all my free moments at the feet of the Master hidden in the Blessed Sacrament. He has been tutoring me from my most tender years.

83 **Write this: before I come as the just Judge, I am coming first as the King of Mercy. Before the day of justice arrives, there will be given to people a sign in the heavens of this sort:**

All light in the heavens will be extinguished, and there will be great darkness over the whole earth. Then the sign of the cross will be seen in the sky, and from the openings where the hands and the feet of the Savior were nailed will come forth great lights which will light up the earth for a period of time. This will take place shortly before the last day.

84 O Blood and Water, which gushed forth from the Heart of Jesus as a fount of mercy for us, I trust in You!

Vilnius, August 2, 1934.

85 On Friday, after Holy Communion, I was carried in spirit before the throne of God. There I saw the heavenly Powers which incessantly praise God. Beyond the throne I saw a brightness inaccessible to creatures, and there only the Incarnate Word enters as Mediator. When Jesus entered this light, I heard these words, **Write down at once what you hear: I am the Lord in My essence and am immune to orders or needs. If I call**

creatures into being—that is the abyss of My mercy.
And at that very moment I found myself, as before, in
our chapel at my kneeler, just as Mass had ended. I
already had these words written.

86 + [Once] when I saw how much my confessor [probably
Father Sopocko] was to suffer because of this work
which God was going to carry out through him, fear
seized me for the moment, and I said to the Lord,
"Jesus, this is Your affair, so why are You acting this
way **(36)** toward him? It seems to me that You are
making difficulties for him while at the same time
ordering him to act."

**Write that by day and by night My gaze is fixed upon
him, and I permit these adversities in order to increase
his merit. I do not reward for good results but for the
patience and hardship undergone for My sake.**

Vilnius, October 26, 1934.

87 On Friday at ten minutes to six, when I and some of our
wards[38] were coming in from the garden to supper, I saw
the Lord Jesus above our chapel, looking just as He did
the first time I saw Him and just as He is painted in the
image. The two rays which emanated from the Heart of
Jesus covered our chapel and the infirmary, and then
the whole city, and spread out over the whole world.
This lasted about four minutes and disappeared. One of
the girls, who was walking with me a little behind the
others, also saw these rays, but she did not see Jesus, and
she did not know where these rays were coming from.
She was overwhelmed and told the other girls.They
began to laugh at her, suggesting that she was imagining
things or that perhaps it was light reflected by a passing
airplane. But she persisted in her conviction, saying that
never had she seen such rays before. When the others
suggested that it might have been a searchlight, she
replied that she knew very well what a searchlight was
like, but never had she seen rays such as these.

After supper the girl approached me and told me she
had been so moved by these rays that she could not keep
silent, but wanted to tell everyone about them. Yet she
had not seen Jesus. She kept telling me about these rays,
and this put me in an awkward situation, as I could not
tell her that I had seen the Lord Jesus. I prayed for her,
asking the Lord to give her those graces of which she
had such need. My heart rejoiced in the fact that Jesus
takes the initiative to make Himself known, even though
the occasion of such action on His part causes me
annoyance. For Jesus, one can bear anything.

88 **(37)**+During adoration I felt God close to me. A moment
later I saw Jesus and Mary. At the sight of them I was
filled with joy, and I asked the Lord, "What is Your will,
Jesus, concerning the matter about which my confessor
told me to ask You?" Jesus replied, **It is My will that he
should remain here and that he should not take the
initiative of dispensing himself.** I asked Jesus whether
the inscription could be: "Christ King of Mercy." He
answered, **I am King of Mercy,** but He did not say
"Christ." **I desire that this image be displayed in public
on the first Sunday after Easter. That Sunday is the
Feast of Mercy. Through the Word Incarnate I make
known the bottomless depth of My mercy.**

89 +Strangely, all things came about just as the Lord had
requested. In fact, it was on the first Sunday after Easter
[April, 1935] that the image was publicly honored by
crowds of people for the first time. For three days it was
exposed and received public veneration. Since it was
placed at the very top of a window at Ostra Brama
[Shrine of Our Lady above the "Eastern Gate" to the
city of Vilnius], it could be seen from a great distance. At
Ostra Brama, during these three days, the closing of the
Jubilee of the Redemption of the World was being
celebrated, marking the nineteen hundred years that
have passed since the Passion of our Savior. I see now

that the work of Redemption is bound up with the work of mercy requested by the Lord.

90 One day, I saw interiorly how much my confessor would have to suffer: friends will desert you while everyone will rise up against you and your physical strength will diminish. I saw you as a bunch of grapes chosen by the Lord and thrown into the press of suffering. Your soul, Father, will at times be filled with doubts about this work and about me.

I saw that God himself seemed to be opposing [him], and I asked the Lord why He was acting in this way toward him, as though He were placing obstacles in the way of his doing what He himself had asked him to do. And the Lord said, **I am acting thus with him to give testimony that this work is Mine. Tell him(38)not to fear anything; My gaze is on him day and night. There will be as many crowns to form his crown as there will be souls saved by this work. It is not for the success of a work, but for the suffering that I give reward.**

91 O my Jesus, You alone know what persecutions I suffer, and this only because I am being faithful to You and following Your orders. You are my strength; sustain me that I may always carry out what You ask of me. Of myself I can do nothing, but when You sustain me, all difficulties are nothing for me. O my Lord, I can see very well that from the time when my soul first received the capacity to know You, my life has been a continual struggle which has become increasingly intense.

Every morning during meditation, I prepare myself for the whole day's struggle. Holy Communion assures me that I will win the victory; and so it is. I fear the day when I do not receive Holy Communion. This Bread of the Strong gives me all the strength I need to carry on my mission and the courage to do whatever the Lord asks of me. The courage and strength that are in me are not of me, but of Him who lives in me—it is the Eucharist.

O my Jesus, the misunderstandings are so great; sometimes, were it not for the Eucharist, I would not have the courage to go any further along the way You have marked out for me.

92 Humiliation is my daily food. I understand that the bride must herself share in everything that is the groom's; and so His cloak of mockery must cover me, too. At those times when I suffer much, I try to remain silent, as I do not trust my tongue which, at such moments, is inclined to talk for itself, while its duty is to help me praise God for all the blessings and gifts which He has given me. When I receive Jesus in Holy Communion, I ask Him fervently to deign to heal my tongue so that I would offend neither God nor neighbor by it. I want my tongue to praise God without cease. Great are the faults committed by the tongue. The soul will not attain sanctity if it does not keep watch over its tongue.

93 (39)+A Short Version of the Catechism of the Vows[39]

Q. What is a vow?
A. A vow is a voluntary promise made to God, to carry out a more perfect act.

Q. Is a vow binding in a matter which is the object of a commandment?
A. Yes. The carrying out of an act which is the object of a commandment has a double value and merit; and the neglect of such an act is a double transgression and evil, because by breaking such a vow we add to the sin against the commandment, the sin of sacrilege.

Q. Why do religious vows have such value?
A. Because they are the foundation of the religious life approved by the Church, in which the members

bound together in a religious community undertake to strive always for perfection by means of the three religious vows of poverty, chastity and obedience, observed according to the rules.

Q. What is the meaning of the words, "strive for perfection?"

A. To strive for perfection means that the religious life does not in itself demand that perfection be already attained, but obliges, under the pain of sin, that we work daily to attain it. Therefore, a religious who does not want to become perfect neglects his principal duty of state.

Q. What are "solemn" religious vows?

A. "Solemn" religious vows are so absolute that, in extraordinary cases, only the Holy Father can dispense from them.

Q. What are simple religious vows?

A. These are vows which are less absolute—the Holy See dispenses from perpetual and annual vows.

(40) Q. What is the difference between a vow and a virtue?

A. A vow pertains only to that which is commanded under pain of sin; the virtue goes beyond this and helps in the carrying out of the vow; on the other hand, by breaking the vow we fail in the virtue and do it damage.

Q. To what do the religious vows oblige us?

A. The religious vows oblige us to strive to acquire the virtues and to submit ourselves completely to our Superiors and to the Rules which are in force; thus the religious gives his own person to the Community, renouncing every right over himself and his actions, which he sacrifices to the service of God.

The Vow of Poverty

The vow of poverty is the voluntary renunciation of the right over property or to the use of such property with the purpose of pleasing God.

Q. What objects does the vow of poverty concern?

A. All those goods and those objects which appertain to the Community. We have no longer any right over anything that has been given to us, once it has been accepted, whether an article or money. All these donations and presents, which may have been given us out of gratitude or in any other way, belong by right to the Community. We cannot make use, without violating the vow, of any wages we may receive for work or even any annuity.

Q. When do we break or violate the vow in a matter which entails the seventh commandment?

A. We break or violate it when, without permission, we take for ourselves anything that belongs to the house; when, without permission, we retain something in order to appropriate it; and when, without authorization, we sell or exchange something that belongs to the Community. When we make use of an object for some other purpose than that intended by the Superior. When we give to, or accept from another, anything whatsoever without permission. When by negligence we destroy or damage something. When, in going from one house to another, we take something with us without permission. In a situation where the vow is broken, the religious **(41)** is bound to restitution to the Community.

The Virtue of Poverty

This is an evangelical virtue which impels the heart to detach itself from temporal things; the religious, in virtue of his profession, is strictly obliged to it.

Q. When do we sin against the virtue of poverty?
A. When we desire something, contrary to this virtue. When we become attached to something, and when we make use of superfluous things.

Q. How many degrees of poverty are there and what are they?
A. There are, in practice, four degrees of poverty for one who is a professed religious: to dispose of nothing without the consent of the Superiors (the strict matter of the vow); to avoid superfluities and be content with necessities (this pertains to the virtue); to readily content oneself with things of inferior quality in what concerns one's cell, clothing, nourishment, etc., and to experience this contentment interiorly; to rejoice in extreme poverty.

The Vow of Chastity

Q. To what does this vow oblige us?
A. To renounce marriage and to avoid everything that is forbidden by the sixth and ninth commandments.

Q. Is a fault against the virtue a violation of the vow?
A. Every fault against the virtue is at the same time a violation of the vow, because here there is no difference, as in the case of poverty and obedience, between the vow and the virtue. (42)

Q. Is every bad thought a sin?
A. No, every bad thought is not a sin; it becomes so only when the acquiescence of the will and consent are joined to the consideration of the mind.

Q. Is there anything, over and above sins against chastity, which is detrimental to the virtue?
A. Lack of custody of the senses, of the imagination, of

the feelings; familiarity and sentimental friendships are detrimental to the virtue.

Q. What are the means by which this virtue may be preserved?

A. To conquer interior temptations with the thought of the presence of God, and moreover to fight without fear. And for exterior temptations, to avoid occasions. There are, in all, seven principal means: to guard the senses, to avoid occasions, to avoid idleness, to remove temptations promptly, to remove oneself from all — and especially particular friendships, the spirit of mortification, and to reveal all these temptations to one's confessor.

Besides this, there are also five means of preserving this virtue: humility, the spirit of prayer, modesty of the eyes, fidelity to the rule, a sincere devotion to the Blessed Virgin Mary.

The Vow of Obedience

The vow of obedience is superior to the first two. It is, to tell the truth, a holocaust, and it is more necessary because it forms and animates the monastic body.

Q. To what does the vow of obedience oblige us?

A. By the vow of obedience, the religious promises to God to be obedient to his legitimate superiors in everything that they will ordain in virtue of the rule. The vow of obedience makes the religious dependent on his superior in virtue of these rules for his whole life and in all his affairs. A religious commits a grave sin against the vow every time he disobeys an order given **(43)** in virtue of obedience and of these rules.

The Virtue of Obedience

The virtue of obedience goes further than the vow; it embraces the rules, the regulations and even the counsels of the superiors.

Q. Is the virtue of obedience indispensable for a religious?

A. The virtue of obedience is so indispensable to a religious that, even if he were to perform good actions contrary to obedience, these would be evil and without merit.

Q. Can we sin gravely against the virtue of obedience?

A. We sin gravely when we scorn the authority or the order of the superior, or when spiritual or temporal harm to the community results from our disobedience.

Q. What faults endanger the vow?

A. To be prejudiced against the superior, or to harbor an antipathy for him—murmuring and criticism, tardiness and negligence.

The Degrees of Obedience

Prompt and complete fulfillment—the obedience of the will, when the will persuades the intellect to submit to the advice of the superior. To facilitate obedience, Saint Ignatius suggests, moreover, three means: always to see God in our superior, whoever he might be; to justify in itself the order or advice of the superior; to accept each order as an order from God, without examining it or reflecting on it. General means: humility. Nothing is difficult for the humble.

94 **(44)**O my Lord, inflame my heart with love for You, that my spirit may not grow weary amidst the storms, the sufferings and the trials. You see how weak I am. Love can do all.

95 +A Deeper Knowledge of God and the Terror of the
Soul.

In the beginning, God lets himself be known as Holiness,
Justice, Goodness—that is to say, Mercy. The soul does
not come to know this all at once, but piecemeal, in
flashes; that is to say, when God draws near. And this
does not last for long, because the soul could not bear
such light. During prayer the soul experiences flashes of
this light which make it impossible to pray as before.
Try as it may to force itself to pray as it did before, all is
in vain; it becomes completely impossible for it to
continue to pray as it did before it received this light.
This light which has touched the soul is alive within it,
and nothing can either quench or diminish it. This flash
of the knowledge of God draws the soul and enkindles
its love for Him.

But this same flash, at the same time, allows the soul to
know itself as it is; the soul sees its whole interior in a
superior light, and it rises up alarmed and terrified. Still,
it does not remain under the effects of terror, but it
begins to purify itself, to humble and abase itself before
the Lord. These lights become stronger and more
frequent; the more the soul is crystallized, the more
these lights penetrate it. However, if the soul has
responded faithfully and courageously to these first
graces, God fills it with His consolations and gives
himself to it in a perceptible manner. At certain
moments, the soul, as it were, enters into intimacy with
God and greatly rejoices in this; it believes that it has
already reached the degree of perfection destined for it,
because its defects and faults are asleep within it, and
this makes it think that they no longer exist. Nothing
seems difficult for it; it is ready for everything. It begins
to plunge itself into God and taste the divine delights. It
is carried along by grace and does not take account of

the fact that the time of trial and testing may come. And, in fact, this state does not last long. Other moments will soon come. I should add here, however, that the soul will respond more faithfully to divine grace if it has a well-informed confessor to whom it can confide everything.

96 **(45)**+Trials sent by God to a soul which is particularly loved by Him. Temptations and darkness; Satan.

The soul's love [for God] is still not such as God would have it. The soul suddenly loses the tangible perception of God's presence. Various defects and imperfections rise up within it, and it must fight them furiously. All her faults lift up their heads, but the soul's vigilance is great. The former awareness of the presence of God gives place to coldness and spiritual dryness; the soul has no taste for spiritual exercises; it cannot pray, either in the old way, or in the manner in which it had just begun to pray. It struggles this way and that, but can find no satisfaction. God has hidden himself from it, and it can find no consolation in creatures, nor can any of these creatures find a way of consoling it. The soul craves passionately for God, but sees its own misery; it begins to sense God's justice; it seems to it that it has lost all the gifts that God had given it; its mind is dimmed, and darkness fills it; unspeakable torment begins. The soul tries to explain its state to the confessor, but it is not understood and is assailed by an even greater unrest. Satan begins his work.

97 Faith staggers under the impact; the struggle is fierce. The soul tries hard to cling to God by an act of will. With God's permission, Satan goes even further: hope and love are put to the test. These temptations are terrible. God supports the soul in secret, so to speak. The soul is not aware of this, but otherwise it would be impossible

to stand firm; and God knows very well how much He can allow to befall a soul. The soul is tempted to unbelief in respect to revealed truths and to insincerity toward the confessor. Satan says to it, "Look, no one understands you; why speak about all this?" Words that terrify it sound in its ears, and it seems to the soul that it is uttering these against God. It sees what it does not want to see. It hears what it does not want to hear. And, oh, it is a terrible thing at times like these not to have an experienced confessor! The soul carries the whole burden alone. However, one should make every effort to find, if it is at all possible, a well-informed confessor, for the soul can collapse under the burden and come to the very edge of the precipice. **(46)** All these trials are heavy and difficult. God does not send them to a soul which has not already been admitted to a deeper intimacy with Him and which has not yet tasted the divine delights. Besides, in this God has His own plans, which for us are impenetrable. God often prepares a soul in this way for His future designs and great works. He wants to try it as pure gold is tried. But this is not yet the end of the testing; there is still the trial of trials, the complete abandonment of the soul by God.

+ The Trial of Trials,
Complete Abandonment—Despair

98 When the soul comes out victorious from the preceding trials, even though it may stumble here and there, it fights on valiantly, humbly calling upon God, "Save me, I am perishing!" And it is still able to fight on.

At this point, however, the soul is engulfed in a horrible night. It sees within itself only sin. It feels terrible. It sees itself completely abandoned by God. It feels itself to be the object of His hatred. It is but one step away from despair. The soul does its best to defend itself; it tries to stir up its confidence; but prayer is an even greater torment for it, as this prayer seems to arouse God to an even greater anger. The soul finds itself poised on the summit of a lofty mountain on the very brink of a precipice.

The soul is drawn to God, but feels repulsed. All other sufferings and tortures in the world are as nothing compared with this sensation into which it has been plunged; namely, that of being rejected by God. No one can bring it any relief; it finds itself completely alone; there is no one to defend it. It raises its eyes to heaven, but is convinced that this is not for her—for her all is lost. It falls deeper and deeper from darkness to darkness, and it seems to it that it has lost forever the God it used to love so dearly. This thought is torture beyond all description. But the soul does not agree to it and tries to lift its gaze toward heaven, but in vain! And this makes the torture even more intense.

(47)If God wishes to keep the soul in such darkness, no one will be able to give it light. It experiences rejection by God in a vivid and terrifying manner. From its heart burst forth painful moans, so painful that no priest will comprehend it, unless he himself has been through these trials. In the midst of this, the evil spirit adds to the soul's suffering, mocking it: "Will you persist in your faithfulness? This is your reward; you are in our power!" But Satan has only as much influence over the soul as God allows him, and God knows how much we can bear. "What have you gotten out of your mortifications," says Satan, "and out of your fidelity to the rule? What use are all these efforts? You have been rejected by God!" This word, *rejected,* becomes a fire which penetrates every nerve to the marrow of the bone. It pierces right through her entire being. The ordeal reaches its climax. The soul no longer looks for help anywhere. It shrinks into itself and loses sight of everything; it is as though it has accepted the torture of being abandoned. This is a moment for which I have no words. This is the agony of the soul.

99   When for the first time this moment was drawing near, I
was snatched from it by virtue of holy obedience. The
Directress of Novices, alarmed by my appearance, sent
me off to confession, but the confessor did not
understand me, and I experienced no relief whatsoever.
O Jesus, give us experienced priests!

When I told this priest I was undergoing infernal
tortures, he answered that he was not worried about my
soul, because he saw in it a great grace of God. But I
understood nothing of this, and not even the least
glimmer of light broke through to my soul.

100 Then my physical strength began to fail me, and I could
no longer carry out my duties. Nor could I any longer
hide my sufferings. Although I did not say a word about
them, the look of pain on my face betrayed me. The
Superior told me that the sisters had come to her saying
that, when they look at me in the chapel, they are moved
to pity because I look so terrible. Yet, despite all efforts,
the soul is unable to conceal such suffering.

101 Jesus, You alone know how the soul, engulfed in
darkness, moans in the midst of these torments and,
despite all this, thirsts for God as burning lips thirst for
water. It dies and withers; it dies a death without death;
that is to say, it cannot die. All its efforts come to
nothing; it is under a powerful hand. **(48)** Now the soul
comes under the power of the Just One. All exterior
temptations cease; all that surrounds it becomes silent,
like a dying person who loses contact with everything
around it: the person's entire soul is in the hand of the
Just God, the Thrice-Holy God,—rejected for all
eternity! This is the culminating moment, and God
alone can test a soul in this way, because He alone
knows what the soul can endure.

When the soul has been saturated through and through
by this infernal fire, it is, as it were, cast headlong into

great despair. My soul experienced this moment when I was all alone in my cell. When my soul began to sink into this despair, I felt that the end was near. But I seized my little crucifix and clutched it tightly in my hand. And now I felt my body separate itself from my soul; and though I wanted to go to my Superiors, I no longer had the physical strength. I uttered my last words: "I trust in Your Mercy!"—and it seemed to me that I provoked God to an even greater anger. And now I was drowned in despair, and all that was left me was a moan of unadulterated pain which, from time to time, tore itself from my soul. The soul is in agony—and it seemed to me that I would remain in this state, because by my own strength I could not emerge from it. Every recollection of God opened up an unspeakable ocean of suffering, and yet despite this there is something within the soul which is drawn to Him, though it seems to her for this only—that she suffer more. The memory of the love with which God formerly surrounded it is still another kind of suffering. His gaze pierces it, and everything within the soul is burned by this gaze.

102   After some time, one of the sisters came into the cell and found me almost dead. She was frightened and went to find the Directress of Novices who, in the name of holy obedience ordered me to get up from the ground. My strength returned immediately, and I got up, trembling. The Directress recognized immediately the state of my soul and spoke to me about the inscrutable mercy of God, saying, "Do not be distressed about anything, Sister. I command this of you in virtue of obedience." Then she said to me, "I see now, Sister, that God is calling you to a high degree of holiness; the Lord wants to draw you very close to Himself since He has allowed these things to happen to you so soon. Be faithful to God, Sister, because this is a sign that He wants you to have a high place in heaven." However, I did not understand anything of these words. **(49)** When I went

into the chapel, I felt as though my soul had been set free from everything, as though I had just come forth from the hand of God. I perceived the inviolability of my soul; I felt that I was a tiny child.

103 Suddenly I saw the Lord interiorly, and He said to me, **Fear not, My daughter; I am with you.** In that single moment, all the darkness and torments vanished, my senses were inundated with unspeakable joy, [and] the faculties of my soul filled with light.

104 I want to add that, although my soul was already in the rays of His love, traces of my past tortures remained on my body for two days: a deathly pale face and bloodshot eyes. Jesus alone knows what I suffered. What I have written is very poor compared to the reality. I cannot put it in words; it seemed to me that I had come back from the other world. I feel an aversion for everything that is created; I snuggle to the heart of God like a baby to its mother's breast. I see everything differently now. I am conscious of what the Lord, by one single word, has done in my soul, and I live by it. I shudder at the recollection of this past torture. I would not have believed that one could suffer so, if I had not gone through it myself. This is a completely spiritual suffering.

105 However, in all these sufferings and struggles, I was not omitting Holy Communion. When it seemed to me that I should not communicate, I went, before Holy Communion, to the Directress and told her that I could not approach the Sacrament, because it seemed to me that I should not do so. But she would not permit me to omit Holy Communion, so I went, and I understand now that it was only obedience that saved me.

The Directress herself told me later that my trials had passed quickly, "and this solely because you were obedient, Sister; and it was through the power of obedience that you struggled through this so bravely." It is true that it was the Lord himself who brought me out of this torment, but my fidelity to obedience did please Him.

106 Though these are frightening things, the soul should not be too fearful, because God will never test us beyond what we are able to bear. On the other hand, He may never send us such sufferings, but I write this because, if it pleases the Lord to let a soul pass **(50)** through such sufferings, it should not be afraid but, insofar as this depends on the soul itself, it should remain faithful to God. God will do a soul no harm, because He is Love itself, and in this unfathomable love has called it into being. However, when I was so tormented, I myself did not understand this.

107 O my God, I have come to know that I am not of this earth; You, O Lord, have poured this profound awareness into my soul. My communion is more with heaven than with earth, though I in no way neglect my duties.

108 During those times, I had no spiritual director; I was without any kind of guidance whatever. I begged the Lord, but He did not give me a director. Jesus himself has been my Master from the days of my infancy up to the present moment. He accompanied me across all the deserts and through all dangers. I see clearly that God alone could have led me through such great perils unharmed, with my soul untarnished and passing victoriously through all difficulties, immense though they were. Going out [...] Later on, the Lord did give me a director.

109 After such sufferings the soul finds itself in a state of great purity of spirit and very close to God. But I should add that during these spiritual torments it is close to God, but it is blind. The soul's vision is plunged into darkness, and though God is nearer than ever to the soul which is suffering, the whole secret consists in the fact that it knows nothing of this. The soul in fact declares

that, not only has God abandoned it, but it is the object of His hatred. With how great a malady are they eyes of the soul afflicted! When struck by divine light, the soul affirms that this light does not exist, although it is precisely because this divine light is so bright that it is blinded. Yet despite all, I learned later that God is closer to a soul at such moments than at others, because it would not be able to endure these trials with the help of ordinary grace alone. God's omnipotence and an extraordinary grace must be active here, for otherwise the soul would succumb at the first blow.

110 O Divine Master, what happens in my soul is Your work alone! You, O Lord, are not afraid to place the soul on the edge of a terrible precipice where it stands, alarmed and filled with fright, and then You call it back again to Yourself. These are Your imponderable mysteries.

111 **(51)**When, in the midst of these interior torments, I tried to accuse myself in confession of the smallest trifles, the priest was surprised that I had not committed graver faults, and he said to me, "If you are as faithful as this to God during these sufferings, this in itself is evidence to me that God is sustaining you, Sister, with a special grace, and it is a good thing that you do not understand this." It is a strange thing, nevertheless, that confessors could neither understand me nor set my mind at peace concerning these matters, until I met Father Andrasz and, later on, Father Sopocko.

112 +A few words about confession and confessors. I shall speak only of what I have experienced and gone through within my own soul. There are three things which hinder the soul from drawing profit from confession in these exceptional moments.

The first thing: when the confessor has little knowledge of extraordinary ways and shows surprise if a soul discloses to him the great mysteries worked in it by God. Such surprise frightens a sensitive soul, and it notices that the confessor hesitates to give his opinion; and if it does notice this, it will not be set at peace, but will have even more doubts after confession than before, because it will sense that the confessor is trying to set it at peace while he himself is uncertain. Or else, as has happened to me, a confessor, unable to penetrate some of the soul's mysteries, refuses to hear the confession, showing a certain fear when the soul approaches the confessional.

How can a soul in this state obtain peace in the confessional when it has become so oversensitive to every word of the priest? In my opinion, at times of such special trials sent by God to a soul, the priest, if he does not understand the soul, should direct it to some other experienced and well-instructed confessor. Or else he himself should seek light in order to give the soul what it needs, instead of downrightly denying it confession. For in this way he is exposing the soul to a great danger; and more than one soul may well leave the road along which God wanted it to journey. This is a matter of great importance, for I have experienced it myself. I myself began to waver; despite special gifts from God, and even though God himself reassured me, I have nevertheless always wanted to have the Church's seal as well.

(52) The second thing: the confessor does not allow the soul to express itself frankly, and shows impatience. The soul then falls silent and does not say everything [it has to say] and, by this, profits nothing. It profits even less when the confessor, without really knowing the soul, proceeds to put it to the test. Instead of helping the soul, he does it harm. The soul is aware that the confessor does not know it, because he did not allow it to lay itself open fully as regards both its graces and its misery. And so the test is ill-adapted. I have been submitted to some tests at which I have had to laugh.

I will express this better thus: The confessor is the doctor of the soul, but how can a doctor prescribe a suitable remedy if he does not know the nature of the sickness? Never will he be able to do so. For either the remedy will not produce the desired effect, or else it will be too strong and will aggravate the illness, and sometimes—God forbid—even bring about death. I am speaking from my own experience because, in certain instances, it was the Lord himself who directly sustained me.

The third thing: it also happens sometimes that the confessor makes light of little things. There is nothing little in the spiritual life. Sometimes a seemingly insignificant thing will disclose a matter of great consequence and will be for the confessor a beam of light which helps him to get to know the soul. Many spiritual undertones are concealed in little things.

A magnificent building will never rise if we reject the insignificant bricks. God demands great purity of certain souls, and so He gives them a deeper knowledge of their own misery. Illuminated by light from on high, the soul can better know what pleases God and what does not. Sin depends upon the degree of knowledge and light that exists within the soul. The same is true of imperfections. Although the soul knows that it is only sin in the strict sense of the term which pertains to the sacrament of penance, yet these petty things are of great importance to a soul which is tending to sanctity, and the confessor must not treat them lightly. The patience and kindness of the confessor open the way to the innermost secrets of the soul. The soul, unconsciously as it were, reveals its abysmal depth and feels stronger and more resistant; it fights with greater courage and tries to do things better because it knows it must give an account of them.

(53) I will mention one more thing regarding the confessor. It is his duty to occasionally put to the test, to try, to exercise, to learn whether he is dealing with straw, with iron or with pure gold. Each of these three types of souls needs different kinds of training. The confessor must—and this is absolutely necessary—form a clear judgment of each soul in order to know how heavy a burden it can carry at certain times, in certain circumstances, or in particular situations. As for myself, it was only later on, after many [negative] experiences, that, when I saw that I was not understood, I no longer laid bare my soul or allowed my peace to be disturbed. But this happened only when all these graces had already been submitted to the judgement of a wise, well-instructed and experienced confessor. Now I know what to go by in certain cases.

113   And again, I would like to say three words to the soul that is determined to strive for sanctity and to derive fruit; that is to say, benefit from confession.

First word—complete sincerity and openness. Even the holiest and wisest confessor cannot forcibly pour into the soul what he desires if it is not sincere and open. An insincere, secretive soul risks great dangers in the spiritual life, and even the Lord Jesus Himself does not give Himself to such a soul on a higher level, because He knows it would derive no benefit from these special graces.

Second word—humility. A soul does not benefit as it should from the sacrament of confession if it is not humble. Pride keeps it in darkness. The soul neither knows how, nor is it willing, to probe with precision the depths of its own misery. It puts on a mask and avoids everything that might bring it recovery.

Third word—obedience. A disobedient soul will win no victory, even if the Lord Jesus himself, in person, were to hear its confession. The most experienced confessor will be of no help whatsoever to such a soul. The disobedient soul exposes itself to great misfortunes; it will make no progress toward perfection, nor will it succeed in the spiritual life. God lavishes His graces most generously upon the soul, but it must be an obedient soul.

114 **(54)** +Oh, how pleasing are the hymns flowing from a suffering soul! All heaven delights in such a soul, especially when it is tested by God. It mournfully sings out its longing for Him. Great is its beauty, because it comes from God. The soul walks through the jungle of life, wounded by God's love. With one foot only it touches the ground.

115 + When a soul has come out of these tribulations, it is deeply humble. Its purity of soul is great. It knows better without need of reflecting, as it were, what it ought to do at a given moment and what to forbear. It feels the lightest touch of grace and is very faithful to God. It recognizes God from afar and continuously rejoices in Him. It discovers God very quickly in other souls and in its environment in general. The soul has been purified by God himself. God, as Pure Spirit, introduces the soul to a life which is purely spiritual. God himself has first prepared and purified the soul; that is, He has made it capable of close communion with himself. The soul, in a state of loving repose, communes spiritually with the Lord. It speaks to God without the need of expressing itself through the senses. God fills it with His light.

The enlightened mind sees clearly and distinguishes the various degrees of the spiritual life. It recognizes [that state] when its union with God was imperfect: where the senses were involved, and the spirit was linked with the senses in a manner—exalted and special, to be sure— but not yet perfect. There is a higher and more perfect union with God; namely, intellectual union. Here, the soul is safer from illusions; its spirituality is purer and more profound. In a life where the senses are involved, there is more danger of illusion. Both for the soul and for its confessor, prudence must play a greater part. There are moments when God introduces the soul to a purely spiritual state. The senses dim and are seemingly dead. The soul is most closely united to God; it is immersed in the Deity; its knowledge is complete and perfect, not sporadic as before, but total and absolute. It rejoices in this. But I want to say more about those moments of trial; at those times the confessor must have patience with such a soul. But the soul must have even greater patience with itself.

116 **(55)**My Jesus, You know what my soul goes through at the recollection of these sufferings. I have often marvelled that the angels and saints hold their peace at the sight of a soul suffering like that. Yet they have special love for us at such moments. My soul has often cried out after God, as a little child who cries as loudly as he can when his mother covers her face and he cannot recognize her. O my Jesus, honor and glory to You for these trials of love! Great and incomprehensible is your mercy. All that You intended for my soul, O Lord, is steeped in Your mercy.

117 I will mention here that those who live with such a person should not add external sufferings; for indeed, when the soul's cup is full, the little drop we may add to it may be the one drop too much, and the cup of bitterness will overflow. And who will answer for such a soul? Let us beware of adding to the suffering of others, because that is displeasing to the Lord. If the sisters or the superiors knew or even suspected that a soul was suffering such trials, and they nevertheless added still other sufferings, they would be sinning gravely, and God himself would demand an account of them on behalf of such a soul. I am not speaking here of instances which of their very nature are sinful, but of things which in other circumstances would not be sinful. Let us be on our guard against having the weight of such a soul on our conscience. This is a grave and common defect in religious life; namely, that when one sees a suffering soul, one always wants to add even more suffering. I do

not say that everyone acts like this, but there are some. We take the liberty of passing all sorts of judgments, and we repeat them when we would do better to remain silent.

118 The tongue is a small member, but it does big things. A religious who does not keep silence will never attain holiness; that is, she will never become a saint. Let her not delude herself—unless it is the Spirit of God who is speaking through her, for then she must not keep silent. But, in order to hear the voice of God, one has to have silence in one's soul and to keep silence; not a gloomy silence, but an interior silence; that is to say, recollection in God. One can speak a great deal without breaking silence and, on the contrary, one can speak little and be constantly breaking silence. Oh, what irreparable damage is done by the breach (56) of silence! We cause a lot of harm to our neighbor, but even more to our own selves.

In my opinion, and according to my experience, the rule concerning silence should stand in the very first place. God does not give himself to a chattering soul which, like a drone in a beehive, buzzes around but gathers no honey. A talkative soul is empty inside. It lacks both the essential virtues and intimacy with God. A deeper interior life, one of gentle peace and of that silence where the Lord dwells, is quite out of the question. A soul that has never tasted the sweetness of inner silence is a restless spirit which disturbs the silence of others. I have seen many souls in the depths of hell for not having kept their silence; they told me so themselves when I asked them what was the cause of their undoing. These were souls of religious. My God, what an agony it is to think that not only might they have been in heaven, but they might even have become saints! O Jesus, have mercy!

119 I tremble to think that I have to give an account of my tongue. There is life, but there is also death in the

tongue. Sometimes we kill with the tongue: we commit real murders. And we are still to regard that as a small thing? I truly do not understand such consciences. I have known a person who, when she learned from someone that a certain thing was being said about her, fell seriously ill. She lost a good deal of blood and shed many tears, and the outcome was very sad. It was not the sword that did all this, but the tongue. O my silent Jesus, have mercy on us!

120 I have wandered onto the subject of silence. But this is not what I wanted to speak about, but rather about the soul's life with God and about its response to grace. When a soul has been cleansed, and the Lord is on intimate terms with it, it begins to apply all its inner force in striving after God. Yet the soul cannot do anything of itself. God alone arranges everything. The soul knows this and is mindful of it. It is still in exile and understands well that there may yet come cloudy and rainy days, but it must now look upon things differently from what it had up to now. It does not seek reassurance in a false peace, but makes ready for battle. It knows it comes from a warrior race. It is now much more aware of everything. It knows that it is of royal stock. It is concerned with all that is great and holy.

121 (57)+There is a series of graces which God pours into the soul after these trials by fire. The soul enjoys intimate union with God. It has many visions, both corporeal and intellectual. It hears many supernatural words, and sometimes distinct orders. But despite these graces, it is not self-sufficient. In fact it is even less so as a result of God's graces, because it is now open to many dangers and can easily fall prey to illusions. It ought to ask God for a spiritual director; but not only must it pray for one, it must also make every effort to find a leader who is an expert in these things, just as a military leader must know the ways along which he will lead [his followers] into battle. A soul that is united with God must be

prepared for great and hard-fought battles.

+After these purifications and tears, God abides in the
soul in a special way, but the soul does not always
cooperate with these graces. Not that the soul itself is
not willing to work, but it encounters so many interior
and exterior difficulties that it really takes a miracle to
sustain the soul on these summits. In this, it absolutely
needs a director. People have often sown doubt in my
soul, and I myself have sometimes become frightened at
the thought that I was, after all, an ignorant person and
did not have knowledge of many things, above all,
spiritual things. But when my doubts increased, I sought
light from my confessor or my superiors. Yet I did not
obtain what I desired.

122   When I opened myself up to my superiors, one of them
[probably Mother Michael or Mother Mary Joseph]
understood my soul and the road God intended for me.
When I followed her advice, I made quick progress
towards perfection. But this did not last long. When I
opened up my soul still more deeply, I did not obtain
what I desired; it seemed to my superior that these
graces [of which I was the object] were unlikely, and so I
could not draw any further help from her. She told me it
was impossible that God should commune with His
creatures in such a way: "I fear for you, Sister; isn't this
an illusion of some sort! (58)You'd better go and seek
the advice of a priest." But the confessor did not
understand me and said, "You'd better go, Sister, and
talk about these matters with your superiors." And so I
would go from the superiors to the confessor and from
the confessor to the superiors, and I found no peace.
These divine graces became a great suffering for me.
And more than once I said to the Lord directly, "Jesus, I
am afraid of You; could You not be some kind of a
ghost?" Jesus always reassured me, but I still continued
to be incredulous. It is a strange thing however: the
more I became incredulous, the more Jesus gave me

proofs that these things came from Him.

123 +When I saw that my mind was not being set at rest by
my superiors, I decided to say nothing [to them] of these
purely interior matters. Exteriorly I tried, as a good nun
should, to tell everything to my superiors, but as for the
needs of my soul, I spoke about these only in the
confessional. For many very good reasons, I learned
that a woman is not called to discern such mysteries. I
laid myself open to much unnecessary suffering. For
quite a long time I was regarded as one possessed by the
evil spirit, and I was looked upon with pity, and the
superior took certain precautionary actions in my
respect. It reached my ears that the sisters also regarded
me as such. And the sky grew dark around me. I began
to shun these divine graces, but it was beyond my power
to do so. Suddenly I would be enveloped in such
recollection that, against my will, I was immersed in
God, and the Lord kept me completely dependent upon
Himself.

124 In the initial moments my soul is always a little
frightened, but later it is filled with a strange peace and
strength.

125 +All these things could still be endured. But when the
Lord demanded that I should paint that picture, they
began to speak openly about me and to regard me as a
hysteric and a fantasist, and the rumors began to grow
louder. One of the sisters came to talk to me in private.
She began by pitying me and said, "I've heard them say
that you are a fantasist, Sister, and that you've been
having visions. My poor Sister, defend yourself in this
matter." (59) She was a sincere soul, and she told me
sincerely what she had heard. But I had to listen to such
things every day. God only knows how tiring it was.

126 Yet, I resolved to bear everything in silence and to give
no explanations when I was questioned. Some were

irritated by my silence, especially those who were more curious. Others, who reflected more deeply, said, "Sister Faustina must be very close to God if she has the strength to bear so much suffering." It was as if I were facing two groups of judges. I strove after interior and exterior silence. I said nothing about myself, even though I was questioned directly by some sisters. My lips were sealed. I suffered like a dove, without complaint. But some sisters seemed to find pleasure in vexing me in whatever way they could. My patience irritated them. But God gave me so much inner strength that I endured it calmly.

127 + I learned that I would have help from no one at such moments, and I started to pray and beg the Lord for a confessor. My only desire was that some priest would say this one word to me, "Be at peace, you are on the right road," or "Reject all this for it does not come from God." But I could not find such a priest who was sufficiently sure of himself to give me a definite opinion in the name of the Lord. And so the uncertainty continued. O Jesus, if it is Your will that I live in such uncertainty, may Your Name be blessed! I beg You, Lord, direct my soul yourself and be with me, for of myself I am nothing.

128 Thus I have already been judged from all sides. There is no longer anything in me that has escaped the sisters' judgment. But it seems now to have worn itself out, and they have begun to leave me in peace. My tormented soul has had some rest, and I have learned that the Lord has been closest to me in times of such persecutions. This [truce] lasted for only a short time. A violent storm broke out again. And now the old suspicions became, for them, as if true facts, and once again I had to listen to the same old songs. The Lord would have it that way. But then, strangely enough, even exteriorly I began to experience **(60)** various failures. This brought down on me many sufferings of all sorts, known to God alone.

But I tried as best I could to do everything with the purest of intentions. I could now see that everywhere I was being watched like a thief: in the chapel; while I was carrying out my duties; in my cell.[40] I was now aware that, besides the presence of God, I had always close to me a human presence as well. And I must say that, more than once, this human presence bothered me greatly. There were times when I wondered whether I should undress to wash myself or not. Indeed, even that poor bed of mine was checked many times.[41] More than once I was seized with laughter when I learned they would not even leave my bed alone. One of the sisters herself told me that she came to observe me in my cell every evening to see how I behave in it.

Still, superiors are always superiors. And although they humiliated me personally and, on occasions, filled me with all kinds of doubts, they always allowed me to do what the Lord demanded. Though not in the way I asked, but in some other way, they fulfilled the Lord's demands and gave me permission for all the rigors and mortifications [He asked of me].

One day, one of the Mothers [probably Mother Jane] poured out so much of her anger on me and humiliated me so much that I thought I would not be able to endure it. She said to me, "You queer, hysterical visionary, get out of this room; go on with you, Sister!" She continued to pour out upon my head everything she could think of. When I got to my cell, I fell on my face before the cross, and then looked at Jesus; but I could no longer say a single word. Yet I concealed everything from the others and pretended that nothing had happened between us.

129 Satan always takes advantage of such moments; thoughts of discouragement began to rise to the surface—for your faithfulness and sincerity—this is your reward. How can one be sincere when one is so misunderstood? Jesus, Jesus, I cannot go on any longer. Again I fell to the ground under this weight, and I broke out in a sweat,

and fear began to overcome me. I had no one to lean on interiorly. Suddenly I heard a voice within my soul, **Do not fear; I am with you.** And an unusual light illumined my mind, and I understood that I should not give in to such sorrows. I was filled with a certain strength and left my cell with new courage to suffer.

130 **(61)**Nevertheless, I began to grow a bit negligent. I did not pay attention to these interior inspirations and tried to distract myself. But despite the noise and the distraction, I could see what was going on in my soul. The word of God is clear, and nothing can stifle it. I began to avoid encounters with the Lord in my soul because I did not want to fall prey to illusions. However, in a sense, the Lord kept pursuing me with His gifts; and truly I experienced, alternately, torture and joy. I make no mention here of the various visions and graces God granted me during this time, because I've written this down elsewhere.[42]

131 But I will simply mention here that these various sufferings had come to a peak, and I resolved to put an end to these doubts of mine before my perpetual vows. Throughout my probation, I prayed for light for the priest to whom I was to open up my soul to its depths. I asked God that He himself would help me and grant me the grace to be able to express even the most secret things that exist between me and Him and to be so disposed that, whatever the priest would decide, I would accept as coming from Jesus himself. No matter what judgment he would pass on me, all I wanted was the truth and a decisive answer to certain questions. I put myself completely in God's hands, and [all] my soul desired was the truth. I could not go on living in doubt any longer although, in the depths of my soul, I was so very sure that these things came from God, that I would lay down my life for this. However, I placed the confessor's opinion above all, and I made up my mind to do as he thought best and to act according to the advice

that he would give me. I looked forward to that moment which would decide the course of my actions for the rest of my life. I knew that everything would depend on this. It mattered little whether what he would say to me would be in accord with my inspirations or quite the contrary; this no longer mattered to me. I wanted to know the truth and follow it.

Jesus, You can help me! From this moment, I have begun anew. I conceal all the graces within my soul and await whomsoever the Lord will send me. With no doubt in my heart, I asked the Lord himself to deign to help me during these moments, and a courage of sorts entered my soul.

132 **(62)**I must again mention that there are some confessors who seem to be true spiritual fathers, but only as long as things go well. When the soul finds itself in greater need, they become perplexed, and either cannot or will not understand the soul. They try to get rid of the person as soon as possible. But if the soul is humble, it will always profit in some little way or other. God himself will sometimes cast a shaft of light into the depths of the soul, because of its humility and faith. The confessor will sometimes say something he had never intended to say, without even realizing it himself. Oh, let the soul believe that such words are the words of the Lord himself! Though indeed we ought to believe that every word spoken in the confessional is God's, what I have referred to above is something that comes directly from God. And the soul perceives that the priest is not master of himself, that he is saying things that he would rather not say. This is how God rewards faith.

I have experienced this many times myself. A certain very learned and respected priest [probably Father Wilkowski, the sisters' confessor at Plock], to whom I sometimes happened to go to confession, was always severe and opposed to these matters [which I brought up to him]. But on one occasion he replied to me, "Bear in mind, Sister, that if God is asking this of you, you should not oppose Him. God sometimes wants to be praised in just this way. Be at peace; what God has started, He will finish. But I say this to you: faithfulness to God and humility. And once again: humility. Bear well in mind what I have told you today." I was delighted, and I thought that perhaps this priest had understood me. But it so turned out that I never went to confession to him again.

133 +Once, one of the older Mothers [probably Mother Jane[43]] summoned me, and it was as if fiery bolts from the blue were coming down upon my head, so much so that I could not even discover what it was all about. But after a while I understood that it was about a matter over which I had no control whatsoever. She said to me, "Get it out of your head, Sister, that the Lord Jesus might be communing in such an intimate way with such a miserable bundle of imperfections as you! Bear in mind that it is only with holy souls that the Lord Jesus communes in this way!" I acknowledged that she was right, because I am indeed a wretched person, but still I trust in God's mercy. When I met the Lord I humbled myself and said, "Jesus, it seems that You do not associate intimately with such wretched people as I." **Be at peace, My daughter, it is precisely through such misery that I want to show the power of My mercy.** I understood that this Mother had merely wanted to subject me to a [salutary] humiliation.

134 (63) + O my Jesus, You have tested me so many times in this short life of mine! I have come to understand so many things, and even such that now amaze me. Oh, how good it is to abandon oneself totally to God and to give Him full freedom to act in one's soul!

135 During the third probation, the Lord gave me to understand that I should offer myself to Him so that He could do with me as He pleased. I was to remain

standing before Him as a victim offering. At first, I was quite frightened, as I felt myself to be so utterly miserable and knew very well that this was the case. I answered the Lord once again, "I am misery itself; how can I be a hostage [for others]? **You do not understand this today. Tomorrow, during your adoration, I will make it known to you.** My heart trembled, as did my soul, so deeply did these words sink into my soul. The word of God is living.

When I came to the adoration, I felt within my soul that I had entered the temple of the living God, whose majesty is great and incomprehensible. And He made known to me what even the purest spirits are in His sight. Although I saw nothing externally, God's presence pervaded me. At that very moment my intellect was strangely illumined. A vision passed before the eyes of my soul; it was like the vision Jesus had in the Garden of Olives. First, the physical sufferings and all the circumstances that would increase them; [then] the full scope of the spiritual sufferings and those that no one would know about. Everything entered into the vision: false suspicions, loss of good name. I've summarized it here, but this knowledge was already so clear that what I went through later on was in no way different from what I had known at that moment. My name is to be: "sacrifice."

When the vision ended, a cold sweat bathed my forehead. Jesus made it known to me that, even if I did not give my consent to this, I could still be saved; and He would not lessen His graces, but would still continue to have the same intimate relationship with me, so that even if I did not consent to make this sacrifice, God's generosity would not lessen thereby.

136 And the Lord gave me to know that the whole mystery depended on me, on my free consent to the sacrifice given with full use of my faculties. In this free and

conscious act lies the whole power and value before His
Majesty. Even if none of these things for which I offered
myself would ever happen to me, before the Lord
everything was as though it had already been **(64)**
consummated.

At that moment, I realized I was entering into
communion with the incomprehensible Majesty. I felt
that God was waiting for my word, for my consent.
Then my spirit immersed itself in the Lord, and I said,
"Do with me as You please. I subject myself to Your
will. As of today, Your holy will shall be my
nourishment, and I will be faithful to Your commands
with the help of Your grace. Do with me as You please. I
beg You, O Lord, be with me at every moment of my
life."

137 Suddenly, when I had consented to the sacrifice with all
my heart and all my will, God's presence pervaded me.
My soul became immersed in God and was inundated
with such happiness that I cannot put in writing even the
smallest part of it. I felt that His Majesty was enveloping
me. I was extraordinarily fused with God. I saw that
God was well pleased with me and, reciprocally, my
spirit drowned itself in Him. Aware of this union with
God, I felt I was especially loved and, in turn, I loved
with all my soul. A great mystery took place during that
adoration, a mystery between the Lord and myself. It
seemed to me that I would die of love [at the sight of] His
glance. I spoke much with the Lord, without uttering a
single word. And the Lord said to me, **You are the
delight of My Heart; from today on, every one of your
acts, even the very smallest, will be a delight to My eyes,
whatever you do.** At that moment I felt transconsecrated.
My earthly body was the same, but my soul was
different; God was now living in it with the totality of
His delight. This is not a feeling, but a conscious reality
that nothing can obscure.

138 A great mystery has been accomplished between God

and me. Courage and strength have remained in my soul. When the time of adoration came to an end, I came out and calmly faced everything I had feared so much before. When I came out into the corridor, a great suffering and humiliation, at the hands of a certain person, was awaiting me. I accepted it with submission to a higher will and snuggled closely to the Most Sacred Heart of Jesus, letting Him know that I was ready for that for which I had offered myself.

Suffering seemed to spring out of the ground. Even Mother Margaret herself was surprised. For others, many things passed unnoticed, for indeed it wasn't worth paying any attention to them; but in my case, nothing passed unnoticed; each word was analyzed, each step watched. One sister said to me, "Get ready, **(65)** Sister, to receive a small cross at the hands of Mother Superior. I feel sorry for you." But as for me, I rejoiced at this in the depths of my soul and had been ready for it for a long time. When she saw my courage, she was surprised. I see now that a soul cannot do much of itself, but with God it can do all things. Behold what God's grace can do. Few are the souls that are always watchful for divine graces, and even fewer of such souls who follow those inspirations faithfully.

139 Still, a soul which is faithful to God cannot confirm its own inspirations; it must submit them to the control of a very wise and learned priest; and until it is quite certain, it should remain distrustful. It should not, on its own initiative alone, put its trust in these inspirations and all other higher graces, because it can thus expose itself to great losses.

Even though a soul may immediately distinguish between false inspirations and those of God, it should nevertheless be careful, because many things are uncertain. God is pleased and rejoices when a soul distrusts Him for His own sake; because it loves Him, it is prudent and itself asks and searches for help to make certain that it is really God who is acting within it. And once a well-instructed confessor has confirmed this, the soul should be at peace and give itself up to God, according to His directions; that is, according to the directions of the confessor.

140 Pure love is capable of great deeds, and it is not broken by difficulty or adversity. As it remains strong in the midst of great difficulties, so too it perseveres in the toilsome and drab life of each day. It knows that only one thing is needed to please God: to do even the smallest things out of great love—love, and always love.

Pure love never errs. Its light is strangely plentiful. It will not do anything that might displease God. It is ingenious at doing what is more pleasing to God, and no one will equal it. It is happy when it can empty itself and burn like a pure offering. The more it gives of itself, the happier it is. But also, no one can sense dangers from afar as can love; it knows how to unmask and also knows with whom it has to deal.

141 **(66)+** But my torments are coming to an end. The Lord is giving me the promised help. I can see it in two priests; namely, Father Andrasz and Father Sopocko. During the retreat before my perpetual vows,[44] I was set completely at peace for the first time [by Father Andrasz[45]], and afterwards I was led in the same direction by Father Sopocko. This was the fulfilment of the Lord's promise.

142 When I was set at peace and taught how to follow God's paths, my spirit rejoiced in the Lord, and it seemed to me that I was running, not walking. My wings were spread for flight; I soared into the very heat of the sun, and I will not descend until I rest in Him, in whom my soul has lost itself forever. And I subjected myself totally to the action of grace. God stoops very low to my soul. I do not draw back, nor do I resist Him, but I lose myself in Him as my only treasure. I am one with the Lord. It is

as if the gulf between us, Creator and creature, disappears. For a few days, my soul was in a state of continuous ecstasy. God's presence did not leave me for a single moment. And my soul remained in a continuous loving union with the Lord. But this in no way interfered with the performance of my duties. I felt I was transformed into love; I was all afire, but without being burned up. I lost myself in God unceasingly; God drew me to himself so strongly and powerfully that sometimes I was not aware of being on earth. I had impeded and feared God's grace for so long, and now God himself, through Father Andrasz, has removed all difficulties. My spirit has been turned towards the Sun and has blossomed in His rays for Him alone; I understand no more... [The sentence breaks off here and begins a completely new thought in the next line.]

143 +I have wasted many of God's graces because I was always afraid of being deluded. God drew me to himself so powerfully that often it was not in my power to resist his grace when I was suddenly immersed in him. At these moments, Jesus filled me with such great peace that, later on, even when I tried to become uneasy, I could not do so. And then, I heard these words in my soul: **In order that you may be assured that it is I who am demanding all these things of you, I will give you such profound peace (67) that even if you wanted to feel troubled and frightened, it would not be in your power to do so today, but love will flood your soul to the point of self-oblivion.**

144 Later Jesus gave me another priest [Father Sopocko], before whom He ordered me to reveal my soul. At first I did so with a bit of hesitation, but a severe reprimand from Jesus brought about a deep humility within my soul. Under his direction, my soul made quick progress in the love of God, and many wishes of the Lord were carried out externally.[46] Many a time have I been astounded at his courage and his profound humility.

145 Oh, how wretched my soul is for having wasted so many
graces! I was running away from God, and He pursued
me with his graces. I most often experienced God's
graces when I least expected them. From the moment
He gave me a spiritual director, I have been more
faithful to grace. Thanks to the director and his
watchfulness over my soul, I have learned what guidance
means and how Jesus looks at it. Jesus warned me of the
least fault and stressed that He himself judges the matter
that I present to my confessor; and [He told me] that ...
**any transgressions against the confessor touch Me
myself.**

When under his direction my soul began to experience
deep recollection and peace, I often heard these words in
my soul: **Strengthen yourself for combat**—repeated
over and over at various times.

+Jesus often makes known to me what He does not like
in my soul, and He has more than once rebuked me for
what seemed to be trifles, but which were, in fact, things
of great importance. He has warned me and tried me
like a Master. For many years He himself educated me,
until the moment when He gave me a spiritual director.
Previously, He himself had made clear to me what I did
not understand; but now, He tells me to ask my
confessor about everything and often says, **I will answer
you through his mouth. Be at peace. (68)** It has never
happened to me that I have received an answer which
was contrary to what the Lord wanted of me, when I
presented it to the spiritual director [Father Sopocko].
It sometimes happens that Jesus first asks certain things
of me, about which no one knows anything, and then,
when I kneel at the confessional, my confessor gives me
the same order—however, this is infrequent.

+When, over a long period of time, a soul has received
much light and many inspirations, and when the
confessors have confirmed the source of these

inspirations and set the soul at peace; if its love is great, Jesus now makes it known that it is time to put into action what it has received. The soul recognizes that God is counting on it, and this knowledge fortifies it. It knows that to be faithful it will often have to face various difficulties, but it trusts in God and, thanks to this trust, it reaches that point to which God is calling it. Difficulties do not terrify it; they are its daily bread, as it were. They do not frighten or terrify the soul, just as a warrior who is constantly in battle is not terrified by the roar of the cannon. Far from being frightened, it listens to determine from which side the enemy is launching his attack, in order to defeat him. It does nothing blindly, but examines and ponders everything deeply and, not counting on itself, it prays fervently and asks advice of other warriors who are experienced and wise. When the soul acts in this way, it nearly always wins.

There are attacks when a soul has no time to think or seek advice; then it must enter into a life-or-death struggle. Sometimes it is good to flee for cover in the wound of the Heart of Jesus, without answering a single word. By this very act the enemy is already defeated.

In time of peace, as well, the soul continues making efforts, just as in time of battle. It must exercise itself, and do so with energy; otherwise it has no chance of attaining victory. I regard the time of peace as a time of preparation for victory. The soul must be ever watchful; watchfulness and again, watchfulness. The soul that reflects receives much light. A distracted soul runs the risk of a fall, and let it not be surprised when it does fall. O Spirit of God, Director of the soul, wise is he whom You have trained! But for the Spirit of God to act in the soul, peace and recollection are needed.

146   **(69)**Prayer.—A soul arms itself by prayer for all kinds of combat. In whatever state the soul may be, it ought to pray. A soul which is pure and beautiful must pray, or

else it will lose its beauty; a soul which is striving after this purity must pray, or else it will never attain it; a soul which is newly converted must pray, or else it will fall again; a sinful soul, plunged in sins, must pray so that it might rise again. There is no soul which is not bound to pray, for every single grace comes to the soul through prayer.

147   I recall that I have received most light during adoration which I made lying prostrate before the Blessed Sacrament for half an hour every day throughout Lent. During that time I came to know myself and God more profoundly. And yet, even though I had the superiors' permission to do so, I encountered many obstacles to praying in such a way. Let the soul be aware that, in order to pray and persevere in prayer, one must arm oneself with patience and cope bravely with exterior and interior difficulties. The interior difficulties are discouragement, dryness, heaviness of spirit and temptations. The exterior difficulties are human respect and time; one must observe the time set apart for prayer. This has been my personal experience because, when I did not pray at the time assigned for prayer, later on I could not do it because of my duties; or if I did manage to do so, this was only with great difficulty, because my thoughts kept wandering off to my duties. I also experienced this difficulty: when a soul has prayed well and left prayer in a state of profound interior recollection, others resist its recollection; and so, the soul must be patient to persevere in prayer. It often happened to me that when my soul was more deeply immersed in God, and I had derived greater fruit from prayer, and God's presence accompanied me during the day, and at work there was more recollection and greater precision and effort at my duty, this was precisely when I received the most rebukes for being negligent in my duty and indifferent to everything; because less recollected souls want others to be like

them, for they are a constant [source of] remorse to them.

148 **(70)**+A noble and delicate soul, even the most simple, but one of delicate sensibilities, sees God in everything, finds Him everywhere, and knows how to find Him in even the most hidden things. It finds all things important, it highly appreciates all things, it thanks God for all things, it draws profit for the soul from all things, and it gives all glory to God. It places its trust in God and is not confused when the time of ordeals comes. It knows that God is always the best of Fathers and makes little of human opinion. It follows faithfully the faintest breath of the Holy Spirit; it rejoices in this Spiritual Guest and holds onto Him like a child to its mother. Where other souls come to a standstill and fear, this soul passes on without fear or difficulty.

149 When the Lord himself wants to be close to a soul and to lead it, He will remove everything that is external. When I fell ill and was taken to the infirmary, I suffered much unpleasantness because of this. There were two of us sick in the infirmary. Sisters would come to see Sister N., but no one came to visit me. It is true that there was only one infirmary, but each one had her own cell. The winter nights were long, and Sister N. had the light and the radio headphones, while I could not even prepare my meditation for lack of a light.

When nearly two weeks had passed in this way, I complained to the Lord one evening that I was suffering so much and that I could not even prepare my meditation because there was no light. And the Lord said that He would come every evening and give me the points for the next day's meditation. These points always concerned His sorrowful Passion. He would say, **Consider My sufferings before Pilate.** And thus, point by point, I meditated upon His sorrowful Passion for one week. From that moment, a great joy entered my soul, and I no longer wanted either the visitors or the light; Jesus sufficed me for everything. The superiors were indeed very solicitous for the sick, but the Lord ordained that I should feel forsaken. This best of masters withdraws every created thing in order that He himself might act. Many a time, I have experienced such sufferings and persecutions that Mother M. [probably Mother Margaret] herself said to me, "Sister, along your path, sufferings just spring up out of the ground. I look upon you, (71) Sister, as one crucified. But I can see that Jesus has a hand in this. Be faithful to the Lord."

150 +I want to write down a dream that I had about Saint Therese of the Child Jesus. I was still a novice at the time and was going through some difficulties which I did not know how to overcome. They were interior difficulties connected with exterior ones. I made novenas to various saints, but the situation grew more and more difficult. The sufferings it caused me were so great that I did not know how to go on living, but suddenly the thought occurred to me that I should pray to Saint Therese of the Child Jesus. I started a novena to this Saint, because before entering the convent I had had a great devotion to her. Lately I had somewhat neglected this devotion, but in my need I began again to pray with great fervor.

On the fifth day of the novena, I dreamed of Saint Therese, but it was as if she were still living on earth. She hid from me the fact that she was a saint and began to comfort me, saying that I should not be worried about this matter, but should trust more in God. She said, "I suffered greatly, too," but I did not quite believe her and said, "It seems to me that you have not suffered at all." But Saint Therese answered me in a convincing manner that she had suffered very much indeed and said to me, "Sister, know that in three days the difficulty will come to a happy conclusion." When I was not very willing to believe her, she revealed to me that she was a saint. At that moment, a great joy filled my soul, and I said to her, "You are a saint?" "Yes," she answered, "I am a saint.

Trust that this matter will be resolved in three days."
And I said, "Dear sweet Therese, tell me, shall I go to
heaven?" And she answered, "Yes, you will go to
heaven, Sister." "And will I be a saint?" To which she
replied, "Yes, you will be a saint." "But, little Therese,
shall I be a saint as you are, raised to the altar?" And she
answered, "Yes, you will be a saint just as I am, but you
must trust in the Lord Jesus." I then asked her if my
mother and father would go to heaven, will [unfinished
sentence] (72) And she replied that they would. I further
asked, "And will my brothers and sisters go to heaven?"
She told me to pray hard for them, but gave me no
definite answer. I understood that they were in need of
much prayer.

This was a dream. And as the proverb goes, dreams are
phantoms; God is faith. Nevertheless, three days later
the difficulty was solved very easily, just as she had said.
And everything in this affair turned out exactly as she
said it would. It was a dream, but it had its significance.

151 +Once, when I was in the kitchen with Sister N.,[47] she got
a little upset with me and, as a punishment, ordered me
to sit on the table while she herself continued to work
hard, cleaning and scrubbing. And while I was sitting
there, the sisters came along and were astounded to find
me sitting on the table, and each one had her say. One
said that I was a loafer and another, "What an
eccentric!" I was a postulant at the time. Others said,
"What kind of a sister will she make?" Still, I could not
get down because sister had ordered me to sit there by
virtue of obedience[48] until she told me to get down.
Truly, God alone knows how many acts of self-denial it
took. I thought I'd die of shame. God often allowed such
things for the sake of my inner formation, but He
compensated me for this humiliation by a great
consolation. During Benediction I saw Him in great
beauty. Jesus looked at me kindly and said, **My
daughter, do not be afraid of sufferings; I am with you.**

152 Once, I had night duty,[49] and I was suffering greatly in spirit because of the painting of the image, and I no longer knew which way to turn because they were constantly trying to convince me that the whole thing was an illusion. On the other hand, one priest said that perhaps God wanted to be worshiped through this image and therefore I ought to try to get it painted. Meanwhile, my soul was becoming extremely exhausted. When I entered the little chapel, I brought my head close to the tabernacle, knocked **(73)** and said, "Jesus, look at the great difficulties I am having because of the painting of this image." And I heard a voice from the tabernacle, **My daughter, your sufferings will not last much longer.**

153 One day, I saw two roads. One was broad, covered with sand and flowers, full of joy, music and all sorts of pleasures. People walked along it, dancing and enjoying themselves. They reached the end without realizing it. And at the end of the road there was a horrible precipice; that is, the abyss of hell. The souls fell blindly into it; as they walked, so they fell. And their number was so great that it was impossible to count them. And I saw the other road, or rather, a path, for it was narrow and strewn with thorns and rocks; and the people who walked along it had tears in their eyes, and all kinds of suffering befell them. Some fell down upon the rocks, but stood up immediately and went on. At the end of the road there was a magnificent garden filled with all sorts of happiness, and all these souls entered there. At the very first instant they forgot all their sufferings.

154 Once, when there was adoration at the convent of the Sisters of the Holy Family,[50] I went there in the evening with one of our sisters. As soon as I entered the chapel, the presence of God filled my soul. I prayed as I do at certain times, without saying a word. Suddenly, I saw the Lord, who said to me, **Know that if you neglect the matter of the painting of the image and the whole work of mercy, you will have to answer for a multitude of**

souls on the day of judgment. After these words of Our Lord, a certain fear filled my soul, and alarm took hold of me. Try as I would, I could not calm myself. These words kept resounding in my ears: So, I will not only have to answer for myself on the day of judgment, but also for the souls of others. These words cut deep into my heart. When I returned home, I went to the little Jesus,[51] fell on my face before the Blessed Sacrament and said to the Lord, "I will do everything in my power, but I beg You to be always with me and to give me strength to do Your holy will; for You can do everything, while I can do nothing of myself."

155 **(74)**+It has happened to me for some time now that I immediately sense in my soul when someone is praying for me; and I likewise sense it in my soul when some soul asks me for prayer, even though they do not speak to me about it. The feeling is one of certain disquiet, as if someone were calling me; and when I pray I obtain peace.

156 +Once, I desired very much to receive Holy Communion, but I had a certain doubt, and I did not go. I suffered greatly because of this. It seemed to me that my heart would burst from the pain. When I set about my work, my heart full of bitterness, Jesus suddenly stood by me and said, **My daughter, do not omit Holy Communion unless you know well that your fall was serious; apart from this, no doubt must stop you from uniting yourself with Me in the mystery of My love. Your minor faults will disapper in My love like a piece of straw thrown into a great furnace. Know that you grieve Me much when you fail to receive Me in Holy Communion.**

157 +In the evening, when I entered the small chapel, I heard these words in my soul: **My daughter, consider these words: "And being in agony, he prayed more earnestly."** When I started to think about them more deeply, much light streamed into my soul. I learned how much we need perseverance in prayer and that our salvation often

depends on such difficult prayer.

158 +When I was at Kiekrz [1930] to replace one of the sisters[52] for a short time, I went across the garden one afternoon and stopped on the shore of the lake; I stood there for a long time, contemplating my surroundings. Suddenly, I saw the Lord Jesus near me, and He graciously said to me, **All this I created for you, My spouse; and know that all this beauty is nothing compared to what I have prepared for you in eternity.** My soul was inundated with such consolation that I stayed there until evening, and it seemed to me like a brief moment. That was my free day, set apart for a one-day retreat,[53] **(75)** so I was quite free to devote myself to prayer. Oh, how the infinitely good God pursues us with His goodness! It often happens that the Lord grants me the greatest graces when I do not at all expect them.

159 +O Blessed Host, in golden chalice enclosed for me,
   That through the vast wilderness of exile
   I may pass—pure, immaculate, undefiled;
   Oh, grant that through the power of Your love
      this might come to be.

   O Blessed Host, take up Your dwelling within my soul,
   O Thou my heart's purest love!
   With Your brilliance the darkness dispel.
   Refuse not Your grace to a humble heart.

   O Blessed Host, enchantment of all heaven,
   Though Your beauty be veiled
   And captured in a crumb of bread,
   Strong faith tears away that veil.

160 +The crusade day,[54] which is the fifth of the month, happened to fall on the First Friday of the month. This was my day for keeping watch before the Lord Jesus. It was my duty to make amends to the Lord for all offenses and acts of disrespect and to pray that, on this day, no sacrilege be committed. This day, my spirit was set

aflame with special love for the Eucharist. It seemed to me that I was transformed into a blazing fire. When I was about to receive Holy Communion, a second Host fell onto the priest's sleeve, and I did not know which host I was to receive. After I had hesitated for a moment, the priest made an impatient gesture with his hand to tell me I should receive the Host. When I took the Host he gave me, the other one fell onto my hands. The priest went along the altar rail to distribute Communion, and I held the Lord Jesus in my hands all that time. When the priest approached me again, I raised the Host for him to put it back into the chalice, because when I had first received Jesus I could not speak before consuming the Host, and so could not tell him that the other had fallen. But while I was holding the Host **(76)** in my hand, I felt such a power of love that for the rest of the day I could neither eat nor come to my senses. I heard these words from the Host: **I desired to rest in your hands, not only in your heart.** And at that moment I saw the little Jesus. But when the priest approached, I saw once again only the Host.

161 O Mary, Immaculate Virgin,
Pure crystal for my heart,
You are my strength, O sturdy anchor!
You are the weak heart's shield and protection.

O Mary you are pure, of purity incomparable;
At once both Virgin and Mother,
You are beautiful as the sun, without blemish,
And your soul is beyond all comparison.

Your beauty has delighted the eye of the Thrice-Holy
     One.
He descended from heaven, leaving His eternal throne,
And took Body and Blood of your heart
And for nine months lay hidden in a Virgin's Heart.

O Mother, Virgin, purest of all lilies,
Your heart was Jesus' first tabernacle on earth.

Only because no humility was deeper than yours
Were you raised above the choirs of Angels and above
   all Saints.

O Mary, my sweet Mother,
I give you my soul, my body and my poor heart.
Be the guardian of my life,
Especially at the hour of death, in the final strife.

162 **(77)**J.M.J.   Jesus, I trust in You.   January 1, 1937

Chart of internal control of the soul. Particular examen—to be united with the merciful Christ. Practice: inner silence, strict observance of silence.

The Conscience

January: God and the soul; silence. Victories 41, falls 4.
               Exclamatory Prayer: But Jesus remained silent.

February: God and the soul; silence. Victories 36, falls 3.
               Exclamatory Prayer: Jesus, I trust in You.

March: God and the soul; silence. Victories 51, falls 2.
               Exclamatory Prayer: Jesus, enkindle my heart with love.

April: God and the soul; silence. Victories 61, falls 4.
               Exclamatory Prayer: With God, I can do all things.

May: God and the soul; silence. Victories 92, falls 3.
               Exclamatory Prayer: In His Name is my strength.

June: God and the soul; silence. Victories 64, falls 1.
              Exclamatory Prayer: All for Jesus.

July: God and the soul; silence. Victories 62, falls 8.
              Exclamatory Prayer: Jesus, rest in my heart.

August: God and the soul; silence. Victories 88, falls 7.
              Exclamatory Prayer: Jesus, You know...

September: God and the soul; silence. Victories 99, falls 1.
              Exclamatory Prayer: Jesus, hide me in Your Heart.

October: God and the soul; silence. Victories 41, falls 3.
              Exclamatory Prayer: Mary, unite me with Jesus.

November: God and the soul; silence. Victories, falls.
              Exclamatory Prayer: O my Jesus, have mercy!

December: God and the soul; silence. Victories, falls.
              Exclamatory Prayer: Hail, living Host!

163 (78)JMJ   The Year 1937

General Exercises

+O Most Holy Trinity! As many times as I breathe, as many times as my heart beats, as many times as my blood pulsates through my body, so many thousand times do I want to glorify Your mercy.

+I want to be completely transformed into Your mercy and to be Your living reflection, O Lord. May the greatest of all divine attributes, that of Your unfathomable mercy, pass through my heart and soul to my neighbor.

Help me, O Lord, that my eyes may be merciful, so that I may never suspect or judge from appearances, but look for what is beautiful in my neighbors' souls and come to their rescue.

Help me, that my ears may be merciful, so that I may give heed to my neighbors' needs and not be indifferent to their pains and moanings.

Help me, O Lord, that my tongue may be merciful, so that I should never speak negatively of my neighbor, but have a word of comfort and forgiveness for all.

Help me, O Lord, that my hands may be merciful and filled with good deeds, so that I may do only good to my neighbors and take upon myself the more difficult and toilsome tasks.

Help me, that my feet may be merciful, so that I may hurry to assist my neighbor, overcoming my own fatigue and weariness. My true rest is in the service of my neighbor.

Help me, O Lord, that my heart may be merciful so that I myself may feel all the sufferings of my neighbor. I will refuse my heart to no one. I will be sincere even with those who, I know, will abuse my kindness. And I will lock myself up in the most merciful Heart of Jesus. I will bear my own suffering in silence. May Your mercy, O Lord, rest upon me.

+You yourself command me to exercise the three degrees of mercy. The first: the act of mercy, of whatever kind. The second: the word of mercy—if I cannot carry out a work of mercy, I will assist by my words. The third: prayer—if I cannot show mercy by deeds or words, I can always do so by prayer. My prayer reaches out even there where I cannot reach out physically.

O my Jesus, transform me into Yourself, for you can do all things.

[four pages left blank][55]

164 **(83)**+JMJ   Warsaw, 1933.

Probation Before Perpetual Vows[56]

When I learned I was to go for probation, my heart beat with joy at the thought of such an immense grace, that of the perpetual vows. I went before the Blessed Sacrament; and when I immersed myself in a prayer of thanksgiving, I heard these words in my soul: **My child you are My delight, you are the comfort of My Heart. I grant you as many graces as you can hold. As often as you want to make Me happy, speak to the world about My great and unfathomable mercy.**

165 A few weeks before I was told about the probation, I entered the chapel for a moment and Jesus said to me, **At this very moment the superiors are deciding which sisters are going to take perpetual vows. Not all of them will be granted this grace, but this is their own fault. He who does not take advantage of small graces will not receive great ones. But to you, my child, this grace is being given.** My soul was seized with joyful surprise, because a few days earlier one of the sisters had said to me, "Sister, you will not be going for the third probation. I myself will see to it that you will not be permitted to make your vows." I said nothing to the sister, but felt great pain which I tried to conceal as best I could.

O Jesus, how strange are Your ways! I now see that people can do very little on their own, for I did make my probation, as Jesus had told me.

166   In prayer I always find light and strength of spirit, although there are moments so trying and hurtful, that it is sometimes difficult to imagine that these things can happen in a convent. Strangely, God sometimes allows them, but always in order to manifest or develop virtue in a soul. That is the reason for trials.

167   **(84)**Today [November, 1932], I arrived in Warsaw for the third probation. After a cordial meeting with the dear Mothers, I went into the small chapel for a moment. Suddenly God's presence filled my soul, and I heard these words, **My daughter, I desire that your heart be formed after the model of My merciful Heart. You must be completely imbued with My mercy.**

Dear Mother Directress [Margaret]

at once asked me whether I had had a retreat that year, and I said no. "Then you must first have a retreat of at least three days."

Thanks be to God there was at Walendow[57] an eight-day retreat in which I could take part. But difficulties arose in regard to my leaving for this retreat. A certain person opposed my going very much, and it already [appeared that] I was not to go. After dinner, I went into the chapel for a five-minute adoration. Suddenly I saw the Lord Jesus, who said to me, **My daughter, I am preparing many graces for you, which you will receive during this retreat which you will begin tomorrow.** I answered, "Jesus, the retreat has already begun, and I am not supposed to go." And He said to me, **Get ready for it, because you will begin the retreat tomorrow. And as for your departure, I will arrange that with the superiors.** And in an instant, Jesus disappeared.

I began to wonder how this was going to happen. But after a moment I rejected all such thoughts and devoted the time I had to prayer, begging the Holy Spirit for light to see the whole misery that I am. After a short while, I left the little chapel to go about my duties. Soon Mother General [Michael] called me and said, "Sister, you will go to Walendow today with Mother Valeria so that you can start the retreat tomorrow. Fortunately, Mother Valeria happens to be here and you can go together." Within two hours I was already in Walendow. I reflected for a moment within myself and recognized that only Jesus can arrange things in such a way.

168 **(85)**When the person who so strongly opposed my participation in the retreat saw me, she showed surprise and dissatisfaction. Paying no heed to this, I greeted her affectionately and went to visit the Lord, in order to learn how I should conduct myself during the retreat.

169 My conversation with the Lord Jesus before the retreat. Jesus told me that this retreat would be a little different from others. **You shall strive to maintain a profound peace in respect to your communings with Me. I will remove all doubts in this regard. I know that you are at peace now as I speak to you, but the moment I stop talking you will start looking for doubts. But I want you to know that I will affirm your soul to such a degree that even if you wanted to be troubled, it will not be within your power. And as a proof that it is I who am speaking to you, you will go to confession on the second day of the retreat to the priest who is preaching the retreat; you will go to him as soon as he has finished his conference and will present to him all your doubts concerning Me. I will answer you through his lips, and then your fears will end. During this retreat, observe such strict silence that it will be as though nothing exists around you. You shall speak only to Me and to your confessor; you will ask your superiors only for penances.** I felt immense joy that the Lord would show me such kindness and lower himself so much for my sake.

170 The first day of the retreat. I tried to be the first in the chapel in the morning; before the meditation I had a bit of time for prayer to the Holy Spirit and to Our Lady. I

earnestly begged the Mother of God to obtain for me the grace of fidelity to these inner inspirations and of faithfully carrying out God's will, whatever it might be. I began this retreat with a very special kind of courage.

171 **(86)**Struggle to keep silence. As usual, sisters from various houses came to the retreat. One of the sisters whom I had not seen for a long time, came to my cell and said she had something to tell me. I did not answer her, and she saw that I did not want to break silence. She said to me, "I didn't know you were such an eccentric, sister," and she went away. I was well aware that she had no other business with me than to satisfy her own curious self-love. O God, preserve me in faithfulness.

172 The father[58] who preached the retreat came from America. He had come to Poland for only a short time, and it so happened that he conducted our retreat. A deep interior life was reflected from his person. His bearing testified to the greatness of his spirit. Mortification and recollection characterized this priest. But despite these great virtues, I experienced much difficulty in revealing my soul to him in regard to graces received; as for sins, it is always easy to do so, but in respect to graces I really have to make a great effort, and even then I do not tell everything.

173 Satan's temptations during meditation. I felt a strange fear that the priest would not understand me, or that he would have no time to hear everything I would have to say. How am I going to tell him all this? If it were Father Bukowski I could do it more easily, but this Jesuit whom I am seeing for the first time... Then I remembered Father Bukowski's advice that I should at least take brief notes of the lights sent to me by God during the retreats and give him at least a brief report on them. My God, for a day and a half all has gone well, and now a life and death struggle is beginning. The conference is to start in a half hour, and then I am to go to confession.

Satan tried to persuade me into believing that if my superiors have told me that my inner life is an illusion, why should I ask again**(87)**and trouble the confessor? Didn't M.X. [probably Mother Jane] tell you that the Lord Jesus does not commune with souls as miserable as yours? This confessor is going to tell you the same thing. Why speak to him about all this? These are not sins, and Mother X. told you that all this communing with the Lord Jesus was daydreaming and pure hysteria. So why tell it to this confessor? You would do better to dismiss all this as illusions. Look how many humiliations you have suffered because of them, and how many more are still awaiting you, and all the sisters know that you are a hysteric. "Jesus!" I called out with all the strength of my soul.

174 At that moment the priest came in and began the conference. He spoke for a short time, as if he were in a hurry. After the conference, he went over to the confessional. Seeing that none of the sisters were going there, I sprang from my kneeler, and in an instant was in the confessional. There was no time to deliberate. Instead of telling the father about the doubts that had been sown in me in respect to my dealings with the Lord Jesus, I began to speak about these temptations I have just described above. The confessor immediately understood my situation and said, "Sister, you distrust the Lord Jesus because He treats you so kindly. Well, Sister, be completely at peace. Jesus is your Master, and your communing with Him is neither daydreaming nor hysteria nor illusion. Know that you are on the right path. Please try to be faithful to these graces; you are not free to shun them. You do not need at all, Sister, to tell your superiors about these interior graces, unless the Lord Jesus instructs you clearly to do so, and even then you should first consult with your confessor. But if the Lord Jesus demands something external, in this case, after consulting your confessor, you should carry out

what He asks of you, even if this costs you greatly. On the other hand, you must tell your confessor everything. There is absolutely no other course for you to take, Sister. Pray that**(88)**you may find a spiritual director, or else you will waste these great gifts of God. I repeat once again, be at peace; you are following the right path. Take no heed of anything else, but always be faithful to the Lord Jesus, no matter what anyone says about you. It is with just such miserable souls that the Lord Jesus communes in this intimate way. And the more you humble yourself, the more the Lord Jesus will unite Himself with you."

175 When I left the confessional, ineffable joy filled my soul, so that I withdrew to a secluded spot in the garden to hide myself from the sisters to allow my heart to pour itself out to God. God's presence penetrated me and, in an instant, all my nothingness was drowned in God; and at the same moment I felt, or rather discerned, the Three Divine Persons dwelling in me. And I had such great peace in my soul that I myself was surprised that I could have had so many misgivings.

176 +Resolution: Faithfulness to inner inspirations, even though I would have no idea how much I would have to pay for it. I must do nothing on my own without first consulting the confessor.

177 +Renewal of vows. From the moment I woke up in the morning, my spirit was totally submerged in God, in that ocean of love. I felt that I had been completely immersed in Him. During Holy Mass, my love for Him reached a peak of intensity. After the renewal of vows and Holy Communion, I suddenly saw the Lord Jesus, who said to me with great kindness, **My daughter, look at My merciful Heart.** As I fixed my gaze on the Most Sacred Heart, the same rays of light, as are represented in the image as blood and water, came forth from it, and I understood how great is the Lord's mercy. And again Jesus said to me with kindness, **My daughter, speak to**

priests about this inconceivable mercy of Mine. The flames of mercy are burning Me—clamoring to be spent; I want to keep pouring them out upon souls; souls just don't want to believe in My goodness. Suddenly Jesus disappeared. But throughout that whole day my spirit remained immersed**(89)**in God's tangible presence, despite the buzz and chatter that usually follow a retreat. It did not disturb me in the least. My spirit was in God, although externally I took part in the conversations and even went to visit Derdy.[59]

178 Today we are beginning the third probation. All three of us met at Mother Margaret's, as the other sisters were having their probation in the novitiate. Mother Margaret began with a prayer, explained to us what the third probation consists of, and then spoke on how great is the grace of the perpetual vows. Suddenly I began to cry out loud. In an instant all God's graces appeared before the eyes of my soul, and I saw myself so wretched and ungrateful toward God. The sisters began to rebuke me, saying, "Why did she break out crying?" But Mother Margaret came to my defense, saying that she was not surprised.

At the end of the hour, I went before the Blessed Sacrament and, like the greatest and most miserable of wretches, I begged for His mercy that He might heal and purify my poor soul. Then I heard these words, **My daughter, all your miseries have been consumed in the flame of My love, like a little twig thrown into a roaring fire. By humbling yourself in this way, you draw upon yourself and upon other souls an entire sea of My mercy.** I answered, "Jesus, mold my poor heart according to Your divine delight."

179 Throughout the third probation it was my duty to help the sister in the vestiary.[60] This duty gave me many occasions to practice virtues. Sometimes I had to take linen to certain sisters three times and still one could not

satisfy them. But I also came to recognize the great virtues of some sisters who always asked**(90)**for the poorest things from the vestiary. I admired their spirit of humility and mortification.

180 +During Advent, a great yearning for God arose in my soul. My spirit rushed toward God with all its might. During that time, the Lord gave me much light to know His attributes.

The first attribute which the Lord gave me to know is His holiness. His holiness is so great that all the Powers and Virtues tremble before Him. The pure spirits veil their faces and lose themselves in unending adoration, and with one single word they express the highest form of adoration; that is—Holy... The holiness of God is poured out upon the Church of God and upon every living soul in it, but not in the same degree. There are souls who are completely penetrated by God, and there are those who are barely alive.

The second kind of knowledge which the Lord granted me concerns His justice. His justice is so great and penetrating that it reaches deep into the heart of things, and all things stand before Him in naked truth, and nothing can withstand Him.

The third attribute is love and mercy. And I understood that the greatest attribute is love and mercy. It unites the creature with the Creator. This immense love and abyss of mercy are made known in the Incarnation of the Word and in the Redemption [of humanity], and it is here that I saw this as the greatest of all God's attributes.

181 Today I was cleaning the room of one of the sisters. Although I was trying to clean it with utmost care, she kept following me all the time and saying, "You've left a speck of dust here and a spot on the floor there." At each of her remarks I did each place over a dozen times **(91)** just to satisfy her. It is not work that makes me tired, but all this talking and excessive demands. My whole day's

martyrdom was not enough for her, so she went to the Directress and complained, "Mother, who is this careless sister who doesn't know how to work quickly?" The next day, I went again to do the same job, without trying to explain myself. When she started driving me, I thought, "Jesus, one can be a silent martyr; it is not the work that wears you out, but this kind of martyrdom."

182   I learned that certain people have a special gift for vexing others. They try you as best they can. The poor soul that falls into their hands can do nothing right; her best efforts are maliciously criticized.

+Christmas Eve.
Today I was closely united with the Mother of God. I relived her interior sentiments. In the evening, before the ceremony of the breaking of the wafer, I went into the chapel to break the wafer, in spirit, with my loved ones, and I asked the Mother of God for graces for them. My spirit was totally steeped in God. During the Midnight Mass ["Pasterka" or Shepherds' Mass], I saw the Child Jesus in the Host, and my spirit was immersed in Him. Although He was a tiny Child, His majesty penetrated my soul. I was permeated to the depths of my being by this mystery, this great abasement on the part of God, this inconceivable emptying of Himself. These sentiments remained vividly alive in my soul all through the festive season. Oh, we shall never comprehend this great self-abasement on the part of God; the more I think of it, [unfinished thought].

183   One morning after Holy Communion, I heard this voice, **I desire that you accompany Me when I go to the sick.** I answered that I was quite willing, but after a moment of reflection I started wondering how I was going to do so; the sisters of the second choir[61] do not accompany the Blessed Sacrament. It is always the sister-directresses who go. **(92)**I thought to myself: Jesus will find a way. Shortly afterwards, Mother Raphael sent for me and

said, "Sister, you will accompany the Lord Jesus when the priest goes to visit the sick." And all through the time of my probation I carried the light, accompanying the Lord and, as a knight of Jesus, I always tried to gird myself with an iron belt,[62] for it would not be proper to accompany the King in everyday dress. And I offered this mortification for the sick.

184 +Holy Hour. During this hour, I tried to meditate on the Lord's Passion. But my soul was filled with joy, and suddenly I saw the Child Jesus. But His majesty penetrated me to such an extent that I said, "Jesus, You are so little, and yet I know that You are my Creator and Lord." And Jesus answered me, **I am, and I keep company with you as a child to teach you humility and simplicity.**

I gathered all my sufferings and difficulties into a bouquet for Jesus for the day of our perpetual betrothal. Nothing was difficult for me, when I remembered it was for my Betrothed as proof of my love for Him.

185 +My silence for Jesus. I strove after great silence for Jesus. Amidst the greatest din, Jesus always found silence in my heart, although it sometimes cost me a lot. But what can be too great for Jesus, for Him whom I love with all the strength of my heart?

186 +Today Jesus said to me, **I desire that you know more profoundly the love that burns in My Heart for souls, and you will understand this when you meditate upon My Passion. Call upon My mercy on behalf of sinners; I desire their(93)salvation. When you say this prayer, with a contrite heart and with faith on behalf of some sinner, I will give him the grace of conversion. This is the prayer:**

187 **"O Blood and Water, which gushed forth from the Heart of Jesus as a fount of Mercy for us, I trust in You."**

188 During the last days of the carnival, when I was making a Holy Hour, I saw how the Lord Jesus suffered as He was being scourged. Oh, such an inconceivable agony! How terribly Jesus suffered during the scourging! O poor sinners, on the day of judgment how will you face the Jesus whom you are now torturing so cruelly? His blood flowed to the ground, and in some places His flesh started to fall off. I saw a few bare bones on His back. The meek Jesus moaned softly and sighed.

189 On one occasion, Jesus gave me to know how pleasing to Him is the soul that faithfully keeps the rule. A soul will receive a greater reward for observing the rule than for penances and great mortifications. The latter will be rewarded also if they are undertaken over and above the rule, but they will not surpass the rule.

190 Once during an adoration, the Lord demanded that I give myself up to Him as an offering, by bearing a certain suffering in atonement, not only for the sins of the world in general, but specifically for transgressions committed in this house. Immediately I said, "Very good; I am ready." But Jesus gave me to see what I was going to suffer, and in one moment the whole passion unfolded itself before my eyes. Firstly, my intentions will not be recognized; there will be all kinds of suspicion and distrust as well as various kinds of humiliations and adversities. I will not mention everything here. (94)All these things stood before my soul's eye like a dark storm from which lightning was ready to strike at any moment, waiting only for my consent. For a moment, my nature was frightened. Then suddenly the dinner bell rang. I left the chapel, trembling and undecided. But the sacrifice was ever present before me, for I had neither decided to accept it, nor had I refused the Lord. I wanted to place myself completely in His will. If the Lord Jesus himself were to impose it on me, I was ready. But Jesus gave me to know that I myself was to give my free consent and accept it with full

consciousness, or else it would be meaningless. Its whole power was contained in my free act before God. But at the same time, Jesus gave me to understand that the decision was completely within my power. I could do it or not do it. And so I then answered immediately, "Jesus, I accept everything that You wish to send me; I trust in Your goodness." At that moment, I felt that by this act I glorified God greatly. But I armed myself with patience. As soon as I left the chapel, I had an encounter with reality. I do not want to describe the details, but there was as much of it as I was able to bear. I would not have been able to bear even one drop more.

191 +One morning I heard these words in my soul: **Go to Mother General [Michael] and tell her that this thing displeases Me in such and such a house.** I cannot mention what the thing was nor the house in question, but I did tell it to Mother General, although it cost me very much.

192 Once, I took upon myself a terrible temptation which one of our students in the house at Warsaw was going through. It was the temptation of suicide. For seven days I suffered; and after the seven days Jesus granted her the grace which was being asked, and then my suffering also ceased. It was a great suffering. I often take upon myself the torments of our students. Jesus permits me to do this, and so do my confessors.

193 **(95)** My heart is a permanent dwelling place for Jesus. No one but Jesus has access to it. It is from Jesus that I derive strength to fight difficulties and oppositions. I want to be transformed into Jesus in order to be able to give myself completely to souls. Without Jesus I would not get near to souls, because I know what I am of myself. I absorb God into myself in order to give Him to souls.

194 +March 27.   I desire to struggle, toil and empty myself

for our work of saving immortal souls. It does not matter if these efforts should shorten my life; it is no longer mine, but belongs to the Community. I want to be useful to the whole Church by being faithful to my Community.

195 O Jesus, today my soul is as though darkened by suffering. Not a single ray of light. The storm is raging, and Jesus is asleep. O my Master, I will not wake You; I will not interrupt Your sweet sleep. I believe that You fortify me without my knowing it.

Throughout the long hours I adore You, O living Bread, amidst the great drought in my soul. O Jesus, pure Love, I do not need consolations; I am nourished by Your will, O Mighty One! Your will is the goal of my existence. It seems to me that the whole world serves me and depends on me. You, O Lord, understand my soul with all its aspirations.

Jesus, when I myself cannot sing You the hymn of love, I admire the singing of the Seraphim, they who are so dearly loved by You. I desire to drown myself in You as they do. Nothing will stem such love, for no might has power over it. It is like lightning that illuminates the darkness,**(96)**but does not remain in it. O my Master, shape my soul according to Your will and Your eternal designs!

196 A certain person seems to have made it her task to try out my virtue in all sorts of ways. One day, she stopped me in the corridor and began by saying that she had no grounds for rebuking me, but she ordered me to stand there opposite the small chapel[63] for half an hour and to wait for Mother Superior, who was to pass by there after recreation,[64] and I was to accuse myself of various things which she had told me to say. Although I had no idea of these things being on my soul, I was obedient and waited for Mother Superior for a full half hour. Each sister who passed by looked at me with a smile. When I

accused myself before Mother Superior [Raphael], she sent me to my confessor. When I made my confession, the priest saw immediately that this was something that did not come from my own soul and that I had not the faintest idea of such things. He was very surprised that this person had dared to take upon herself to give such orders.

197 O Church of God, you are the best mother, you alone can rear a soul and cause it to grow. Oh, how great is my love and respect for the Church, that best of all mothers!

198 On one occasion the Lord said to me, **My daughter, your confidence and love restrain My justice, and I cannot inflict punishment because you hinder Me from doing so.** Oh, how great is the power of a soul filled with confidence!

199 When I think of my perpetual vows and Who it is that wants to be joined with me, for hours I become absorbed in the thought of Him. How can this be; You are God and I—I am Your creature. You, the Immortal King and I, a beggar and misery itself! But now all is clear to me;**(97)**Your grace and Your love, O Lord, will fill the gulf between You, Jesus, and me.

200 O Jesus, how deeply it hurts the soul when it is always trying to be sincere and they accuse it of hypocrisy and behave with mistrust toward it. O Jesus, You also suffered like this to make satisfaction to Your Father.

201 I want to hide myself so that no creature might know my heart. Jesus, You alone know my heart and possess it whole and entire. No one knows our secret. We understand each other mutually with one look. From the moment we came to know each other I have been happy. Your greatness is my fullness. O Jesus, when I am in the last place, lower than the postulants, even the youngest of them, then I feel that I am in my proper place. I did not know that the Lord had put so much happiness in these drab little corners. Now I understand

that even in prison there can burst forth from a pure heart the fullness of love for You, O Lord! External things mean nothing to pure love; it cuts through them all. Neither prison doors nor the gates of heaven are strong enough to stop it. It reaches God himself, and nothing can quench it. It knows no obstacles; it is free like a queen and has free access to all places. Death itself must bow its head before it....

202 My sister [Wanda[65]] came to see me today. When she told me of her plans, I was horror-stricken. How is such a thing possible? Such a beautiful little soul before the Lord, and yet great darkness had come over her, and she did not know how to help herself. She had a dark view of everything. The good God entrusted her to my care, and for two weeks I was able to work with her. But how many sacrifices this soul cost me is known only to God. For no other soul did I bring so many sacrifices and sufferings and prayers before the throne of God as I did for her soul. **(98)**I felt that I had forced God to grant her grace. When I reflect on all this, I see that it was truly a miracle. Now I can see how much power intercessory prayer has before God.

203 Now, during this Lent, I often experience the Passion of the Lord Jesus in my own body. I experience deeply in my heart all that Jesus suffered, although no exterior sign betrays these sufferings of mine. Only my confessor knows about them.

204 A short conversation with Mother Directress [Margaret]. When I asked her about some particulars concerning progress in the spiritual life, this holy Mother answered everything with great clarity. She said to me, "If you continue cooperating with God's grace in this way, Sister, you will be only one step away from close union with God. You understand what I mean by this. This means that your characteristic trait should be faithfulness to the grace of the Lord. God does not lead

all souls along such a path."

205 +The Resurrection. Today, during the [Mass of the] Resurrection, I saw the Lord Jesus in the midst of a great light. He approached me and said, **Peace be to you, My children,** and He lifted up His hand and gave His blessing. The wounds in His hands, feet and side were indelible and shining. When He looked at me with such kindness and love, my whole soul drowned itself in Him. And He said to me, **You have taken a great part in My Passion; therefore I now give you a great share in My joy and glory.** The whole time of the Resurrection [Mass] seemed like only a minute to me. A wondrous recollection filled my soul and lasted throughout the whole festal season. The kindness of Jesus is so great that I cannot express it.

206 (99)The next day, after Communion, I heard the voice saying, **My daughter, look into the abyss of My mercy and give praise and glory to this mercy of Mine. Do it in this way: Gather all sinners from the entire world and immerse them in the abyss of My mercy. I want to give Myself to souls; I yearn for souls, My daughter. On the day of My feast, the Feast of Mercy, you will go through the whole world and bring fainting souls to the spring of My mercy. I shall heal and strengthen them.**

207 I prayed today for a soul in agony, who was dying without the Holy Sacraments, although she desired them. But it was already too late. It was a relative of mine, my uncle's wife. She was a soul pleasing to God. There was no distance between us at that moment.

208 O you small, everyday sacrifices, you are to me like wild flowers which I strew over the feet of my beloved Jesus. I sometimes compare these trifles to the heroic virtues, and that is because their enduring nature demands heroism.

209 In my sufferings, I do not seek help from creatures, but God is everything to me. And yet, it often seems that

even the Lord does not hear me. I arm myself with patience and silence, like a dove that does not complain and feels no bitterness when its children are being taken away from it. I want to soar into the very heat of the sun, and I do not want to stop in its vapors. I will not grow weary, because it is on You that I am leaning—O You, my Strength!

210 I fervently beg the Lord to strengthen my faith, so that in my drab, everyday life I will not be guided by human dispositions, but by those of the spirit. Oh, how everything drags man towards the earth! But lively faith maintains the soul in the higher regions and assigns self-love its proper place; that is to say, the lowest one.

211 **(100)**+Once again, a terrible darkness envelops my soul. It seems to me that I am falling prey to illusions. When I went to confession to obtain some light and peace, I did not find these at all. The confessor[66] left me with even more doubts than I had before. He said to me, "I cannot discern what power is at work in you, Sister; perhaps it is God and perhaps it is the evil spirit." When I left the confessional, I started to think about his words. The longer I did so, the deeper my soul sank into darkness. "Jesus, what am I to do?" When Jesus approached me with kindness, I was frightened. "Are you really Jesus?" On the one hand, I am drawn by love and, on the other, by fear. What torture! I cannot describe it!

212 When I went to confession again, I got the answer, "I do not understand you, Sister. It would be better if you did not come to me for confession." O my God!... I have to do such violence to myself before I say anything about my spiritual life, and here I am getting this answer: "Sister, I do not understand you"!

213 When I left the confessional, a multitude of torments oppressed me. I went before the Blessed Sacrament and said, "Jesus, save me; You see how weak I am!" Then I

heard these words, **I will give you help during the retreat before the vows.** Encouraged by these words, I began to go forward without asking anyone's advice. But I distrusted myself so much that I made up my mind to put an end to the doubts once and for all. I therefore looked forward with special eagerness to the retreat before perpetual vows. But even for many days before the retreat, I kept on asking God to give light to the priest who would hear my confession, so that he could say, once and for all, either yes or no. And I thought to myself, "I'll be set at peace once and for all." But I continued to worry whether anyone would be willing to hear me out concerning all these matters. And yet again, I decided not to think about all this and to put my trust in the Lord. The words that continued to ring in my ears were: "during the retreat."

214 **(101)**Everything is now ready. Tomorrow morning we are leaving for Cracow, for the retreat. Today I entered the chapel to thank the Lord for the countless graces He has bestowed on me during these five months. My heart was deeply touched at the thought of so many graces and so much care on the part of the superiors.

215 **My daughter, be at peace; I am taking all these matters upon Myself. I will arrange all things with your superiors and with the confessor. Speak to Father Andrasz with the same simplicity and confidence with which you speak to Me.**

216 We have come to Cracow today [April 18, 1933]. What a joy it is to find myself again where I took my first steps in the spiritual life! Dear Mother Directress [Mary Joseph] is ever the same, cheerful and full of love of neighbor. I entered the chapel for a moment and joy filled my soul. In a flash I recalled the whole ocean of graces that had been given me as a novice here.

217 And today we gathered together to go for an hour's visit to the novitiate. The Mother Directress, Mary Joseph,

gave us a short talk and outlined the program of the retreat. As she spoke these few words to us, I saw before my eyes all the good things this dear Mother had done for us. I felt in my soul such profound gratitude toward her. My heart grieved at the thought that this was the last time I would be in the novitiate. Now I must battle together with Jesus, work with Jesus, suffer with Jesus; in a word, live and die with Jesus. Mother Directress will no longer be at my heels to teach me here, warn me there, or to admonish, encourage or reproach me. I am so afraid of being on my own. Jesus, do something about this. I will always have a superior, that's true; but now a person is left more on her own.

(102)   Cracow, April 21, 1933

+ For the Greater Glory of God.

The Eight-day Retreat before Perpetual Vows.

218 I am beginning the retreat today. Jesus, my Master, guide me. Govern me according to Your will, purify my love that it may be worthy of You, do with me as Your most merciful Heart desires. Jesus, there will be just the two of us during these days until the moment of our union. Keep me, Jesus, in a recollected spirit!

219 In the evening, the Lord said to me, **My daughter, let nothing frighten or disconcert you. Remain deeply at peace. Everything is in My hands. I will give you to understand everything through Father Andrasz. Be like a child towards him.**

A Moment Before the Blessed Sacrament.

220 O my eternal Lord and Creator, how am I going to thank You for this great favor; namely, that You have deigned to choose miserable me to be Your betrothed and that

You are to unite me to yourself in an eternal bond? O dearest Treasure of my heart, I offer You all the adoration and thanksgiving of the Saints and of all the choirs of Angels, and I unite myself in a special way with Your Mother. O Mary, my Mother, I humbly beg of You, cover my soul with Your virginal cloak at this very important moment of my life, so that thus I may become dearer to Your Son and may worthily praise Your Son's mercy before the whole world and throughout all eternity.

221 **(103)**I could not understand the meditation today. My spirit was so extraordinarily immersed in God. I could not force myself to think about what the priest was saying during the retreat [conferences]. I am often unable to think according to the points; my spirit is with the Lord, and that is my meditation.

222 A few words from my conference with Mother Directress, Mary Joseph. She clarified many things for me, and she set me at peace as regards my spiritual life, reassuring me that I was on the right path. I thanked the Lord Jesus for this great favor, for she is the first of the superiors who did not cause me any doubts in this regard. Oh, how infinitely good God is!

223 O living Host, my one and only strength, fountain of love and mercy, embrace the whole world, fortify faint souls. Oh, blessed be the instant and the moment when Jesus left us His most merciful Heart!

224 To suffer without complaining, to bring comfort to others and to drown my own sufferings in the most Sacred Heart of Jesus!

I will spend all my free moments at the feet of [Our Lord in] the Blessed Sacrament. At the feet of Jesus, I will seek light, comfort and strength. I will show my gratitude unceasingly to God for His great mercy towards me, never forgetting the favors He has bestowed on me, especially the grace of a vocation.

I will hide myself among the sisters like a little violet among lilies. I want to blossom for my Lord and Maker, to forget about myself, to empty myself totally for the sake of immortal souls—this is my delight.

(104) +A few of my thoughts.

225 As regards Holy Confession, I shall choose what costs and humiliates me most. Sometimes a trifle costs more than something greater. I will call to mind the Passion of Jesus at each confession, to arouse my heart to contrition. Insofar as possible with the grace of God, I will always practice perfect contrition. I will devote more time to this contrition. Before I approach the confessional, I shall first enter the open and most merciful Heart of the Savior. When I leave the confessional, I shall rouse in my soul great gratitude to the Holy Trinity for this wonderful and inconceivable miracle of mercy that is wrought in my soul. And the more miserable my soul is, the more I feel the ocean of God's mercy engulfing me and giving me strength and great power.

226 The rules that I most often fail to obey: sometimes I break silence; disobedience to the signal of the bell; sometimes I meddle in other people's affairs. I will do my very best to improve.

I will avoid sisters who grumble, and if they cannot be avoided, I will at least keep silent before them, thus letting them know how sorry I am to hear such things.

I must take no heed of the opinion of others, but obey the evidence of my own conscience and take God to be the witness of all my actions. I must do everything and act in all matters now as I would like to do and act at the hour of my death. For this reason, in every action I must be mindful of God.

Avoid presumed permissions.[67] I must report [even] small things to my superiors, and do so in as much detail as is possible. I must be faithful in my spiritual exercises; I must not easily ask to be dispensed from them. I must keep silence outside the time of recreation, and avoid jokes and witty words that make others laugh and break silence. I must have great appreciation(105)for even the most minute rules. I must not let myself become absorbed in the whirl of work, [but] take a break to look up to heaven. Speak little with people, but a good deal with God. Avoid familiarity. I must pay little attention as to who is for me and who is against me. I must not tell others about those things I have had to put up with. I must avoid speaking out loud to others during work. I must maintain peace and equanimity during times of suffering. In difficult moments I must take refuge in the wounds of Jesus; I must seek consolation, comfort, light and affirmation in the wounds of Jesus.

227   +In the midst of trials I will try to see the loving hand of God. Nothing is as constant as suffering—it always faithfully keeps the soul company. O Jesus, I will let no one surpass me in loving You!

+O Jesus, hidden in the Blessed Sacrament,

228   You see that in pronouncing my perpetual vows I am leaving the novitiate[68] today. Jesus, You know how weak and little I am, and so from today on, I am entering Your novitiate in a very special way. I continue to be a novice, but Your novice, Jesus, and You will be my Master to the last day. Daily I will attend lectures at Your feet. I will not do the least thing by myself, without consulting You first as my Master. Jesus, how happy I am that You yourself have drawn me and taken me into Your novitiate; that is to say, into the tabernacle. In making my perpetual vows, I have by no means become a perfect nun. No, no! I am still a weak little novice of Jesus, and I must strive to acquire perfection as I did in the first days of the novitiate, and I will make every effort to keep the same disposition of soul which I had

on that first day the convent gate opened to admit me.

With the trust and simplicity of a small child, I give myself to You today, O Lord Jesus, my Master. I leave You complete freedom in directing my soul. Guide me along the paths You wish. I won't question them. I will follow You trustingly. Your merciful Heart can do all things!

The little novice of Jesus—Sister Faustina.

229 **(106)**+At the beginning of the retreat, Jesus told me, **During this retreat, I myself will direct your soul. I want to confirm you in peace and love.** And so the first few days passed by. On the fourth day, doubts began to trouble me: Is not this tranquillity of mine false? Then I heard these words, **My daughter, imagine that you are the sovereign of all the world and have the power to dispose of all things according to your good pleasure. You have the power to do all the good you want, and suddenly a little child knocks on your door, all trembling and in tears and, trusting in your kindness, asks for a piece of bread lest he die of starvation. What would you do for this child? Answer Me, my daughter.** And I said, "Jesus, I would give the child all it asked and a thousand times more." And the Lord said to me, **That is how I am treating your soul. In this retreat I am giving you, not only peace, but also such a disposition of soul that even if you wanted to experience uneasiness you could not do so. My love has taken possession of your soul, and I want you to be confirmed in it. Bring your ear close to My Heart, forget everything else, and meditate upon My wondrous mercy. My love will give you the strength and courage you need in these matters.**

230 Jesus, living Host, You are my Mother, You are my all! It is with simplicity and love, with faith and trust that I will always come to You, O Jesus! I will share everything with You, as a child with its loving mother, my joys and

sorrows—in a word, everything.

231 No one can comprehend what my heart feels when I meditate on the fact that God unites me with himself through the vows. God makes known to me, even now, the immensity of the love He already had for me before time began; and as for me, I have just begun to love Him, in time. His love was [ever] great, pure and disinterested, and my love for Him comes from the fact that I am beginning to know Him. The more I come to know Him, the more**(107)**ardently, the more fiercely I love Him, and the more perfect my acts become. Meanwhile, each time I call to mind that in a few days I am to become one with the Lord through perpetual vows, a joy beyond all description floods my soul. From the very first time that I came to know the Lord, the gaze of my soul became drowned in Him for all eternity. Each time the Lord draws close to me and my knowledge of Him grows deeper, a more perfect love grows within my soul.

232 +Before confession, I heard these words in my soul, **My daughter, tell him everything and reveal your soul to him as you do before Me. Do not fear anything. It is to keep you in peace that I place this priest between your soul and Myself. The words he will speak to you are My words. Reveal to him your soul's greatest secrets. I will give him light to know your soul.**

233 When I approached the confessional, I felt so much at ease in my soul about speaking of everything that, later on, I myself was astounded. His answers brought a great peace into my soul. His words were, are, and always will be pillars of fire which enlightened and will go on enlightening my soul in its pursuit of the greatest sanctity.

The directions I received from Father Andrasz I have noted on another page in this notebook [cf. Diary no. 55].

234 When I finished this confession, my spirit was immersed in God, and I prayed for three hours, but it seemed to me like only a few minutes. Since then, I have placed no obstacles in the way of grace working in my soul. Jesus knew why I had been afraid to commune intimately with Him and was not at all offended. From the moment the priest assured me that what I had experienced was not an illusion, but the grace of God, I have tried to be faithful to God in everything. I can see now that there are few such priests who understand the full depth of God's work in the soul. Since then, my wings have been set free for flight, and I yearn to soar into the very fire of the sun. My flight will not come to an end until I rest in Him forever. When we fly very high, all the vapors, mists and**(108)**clouds are beneath our feet, and our whole carnal being is necessarily subject to the spirit.

235 O Jesus, I long for the salvation of immortal souls. It is in sacrifice that my heart will find free expression, in sacrifice which no one will suspect. I will burn and be consumed unseen in the holy flames of the love of God. The presence of God will help my sacrifice to be perfect and pure.

236 Oh, how misleading are appearances, and how unjust the judgments. Oh, how often virtue suffers only because it remains silent. To be sincere with those who are incessantly stinging us demands much self-denial. One bleeds, but there are no visible wounds. O Jesus, it is only on the last day that many of these things will be made known. What joy—none of our efforts will be lost!

237 Holy Hour. During this hour of adoration, I saw the abyss of my misery; whatever there is of good in me is Yours, O Lord. But because I am so small and wretched, I have a right to count on Your boundless mercy.

238 Evening. O Jesus, tomorrow morning I am to make my perpetual vows. I had asked heaven and earth and had

called upon all beings to thank God for this immense and inconceivable favor of His when suddenly I heard these words, **My daughter, your heart is My heaven.** Just a few moments of prayer and I have to run, as they drive us out of everywhere; because every place—the chapel, the refectory, the recreation room and the kitchen—is being made ready for tomorrow, and we are to go to**(109)**bed. However, sleep is out of the question. Joy has driven sleep away. I thought: What is it going to be like in heaven, if already here in exile God so fills my soul."

239 Prayer during the Mass on the day of the perpetual vows. Today I place my heart on the paten where Your Heart has been placed, O Jesus, and today I offer myself together with You to God, Your Father and mine, as a sacrifice of love and praise. Father of Mercy, look upon the sacrifice of my heart, but through the wound in the Heart of Jesus.

May 1, 1933. First Day.

Union with Jesus on the day of perpetual vows. Jesus, from now on Your Heart is mine, and mine is Yours alone. The very thought of Your Name, Jesus, is the delight of my heart. I truly would not be able to live without You, even for a moment, Jesus. Today my soul has lost itself in You, my only treasure. My love knows no obstacles in giving proof of itself to its Beloved.

The words of Jesus during my perpetual vows: **My spouse, our hearts are joined forever. Remember to Whom you have vowed**... everything cannot be put into words.

My petition while we were lying prostrate under the pall.[69] I begged the Lord to grant me the grace of never consciously and deliberately offending Him by even the smallest sin or imperfection.

Jesus, I trust in You! Jesus, I love You with all my heart!

When times are most difficult, You are my Mother.

For love of You, O Jesus, I die completely to myself today and begin to live for the greater glory of Your Holy Name.

(110)+Love, it is for love of You, O Most Holy Trinity, that I offer myself to You as an oblation of praise, as a holocaust of total self-immolation. And through this self-immolation, I desire the exaltation of Your Name, O Lord. I cast myself as a little rosebud at Your feet, O Lord, and may the fragrance of this flower be known to You alone.

240   Three requests on the day of my perpetual vows. Jesus, I know that today You will refuse me nothing.

First request: Jesus, my most beloved Spouse, I beg You for the triumph of the Church, particularly in Russia and in Spain; for blessings on the Holy Father, Pius XI, and on all the clergy; for the grace of conversion for impenitent sinners. And I ask You for a special blessing and for light, O Jesus, for the priests before whom I will make my confessions throughout my lifetime.

Second request: I beg Your blessings on our Congregation, and may it be filled with great zeal. Bless, O Jesus, our Mother General and our Mother Directress, all the novices and all the superiors. Bless my dearest parents. Bestow Your grace, O Jesus, on our wards; strengthen them so powerfully by Your grace so that those who leave our houses will no longer offend You by any sin. Jesus, I beg You for my homeland; protect it against the assaults of its enemies.

Third request: Jesus, I plead with You for the souls that are most in need of prayer. I plead for the dying; be merciful to them. I also beg You, Jesus, to free all souls from purgatory.

Jesus, I commend to You these particular persons: My confessors, persons recommended to my prayers, a certain person..., Father Andrasz, Father Czaputa, and the priest I met in Vilnius [Father Sopocko], who is to be my confessor, a certain soul... **(111)**a certain priest, a certain religious[70] to whom You know how much I owe, Jesus, and all the people who have been recommended to my prayer. Jesus, on this day You can do everything for those for whom I am pleading. For myself I ask, Lord, transform me completely into Yourself, maintain in me a holy zeal for Your glory, give me the grace and spiritual strength to do Your holy will in all things.

Thank You, o my dearest Bridegroom, for the dignity You have conferred on me, and in particular for the royal coat-of-arms which will adorn me from this day on and which even the Angels do not possess; namely, the cross, the sword and the crown of thorns. But above all, O my Jesus, I thank You for Your Heart—it is all I need.

Mother of God, Most Holy Mary, my Mother, You are my Mother in a special way now because Your beloved Son is my Bridegroom, and thus we are both Your children. For Your Son's sake, You have to love me. O Mary, my dearest Mother, guide my spiritual life in such a way that it will please Your Son.

+Holy and Omnipotent God, at this moment of immense grace by which You are uniting me with Yourself forever, I, mere nothingness, with the utmost gratitude, cast myself at Your feet like a tiny, unknown flower and, each day, the fragrance of that flower of love will ascend to Your throne.

In times of struggle and suffering, of darkness and storm, of yearning and sorrow, in times of difficult trials, in times when nobody will understand me, when I will even be condemned and scorned by everyone, I will remember the day of my perpetual vows, the day of God's incomprehensible grace.

(112) J.M.J.

Special Resolutions of the Retreat, May 1, 1933

241 Love of neighbor. First: Helpfulness towards the sisters. Second: Do not speak about those who are absent, and defend the good name of my neighbor. Third: Rejoice in the success of others.

242 +O God, how much I desire to be a small child.[71] You are my Father, and You know how little and weak I am. So I beg You, keep me close by Your side all my life and especially at the hour of my death. Jesus, I know that Your goodness surpasses the goodness of a most tender mother.

243 I will thank the Lord Jesus for every humiliation and will pray specially for the person who has given me the chance to be humiliated. I will immolate myself for the benefit of souls. I will not count the cost of any sacrifice. I will cast myself beneath the feet of the sisters, like a carpet on which they can not only tread, but also wipe their feet. My place is under the feet of the sisters. I will make every effort to obtain that place unnoticed by others. It is enough that God sees this.

244 Now a gray, ordinary day has begun. The solemn hours of the perpetual vows have passed, but God's great grace has remained in my soul. I feel I am all God's; I feel I am His child, I feel I am wholly God's property. I experience this in a way that can be physically sensed. I am completely at peace about everything, because I know it is the Spouse's business to look after me. I have forgotten about myself completely. My trust placed in His Most Merciful Heart has no limit. I am continuously united with Him. It seems to me as though Jesus could not be happy without me, nor could I without Him. Although I understand that, being God, He is happy in himself and has absolutely no need of any creature, still, His goodness compels Him to give himself to the

creature, and with a generosity which is beyond understanding.

245 **(113)**My Jesus, I will now strive to give honor and glory to Your Name, doing battle till the day on which You yourself will say, enough! Every soul You have entrusted to me, Jesus, I will try to aid with prayer and sacrifice, so that Your grace can work in them. O great lover of souls, my Jesus, I thank You for this immense confidence with which You have deigned to place souls in our care. O you days of work and of monotony, you are not monotonous to me at all, for each moment brings me new graces and opportunity to do good.

+ [April] 25, 1933

Monthly Permissions[72]

246 To enter the chapel when I pass near it.
To pray in my moments of leisure.
To accept, give or lend small things.
To have a mid-morning and an afternoon snack.
Sometimes I will not be able to take part in recreation.
Sometimes I will not be able to take part in community exercises.
Sometimes I will not be able to take part in evening and morning prayers.
Sometimes to remain at work a little longer after nine or to make my spiritual exercises after nine.
To write down something or take notes when I have a free moment.
To telephone.
To go out of the house.
To visit a church when I am in town.
To enter other sisters' cells in case of need.
To take a drink of water occasionally outside the prescribed times.

Small Mortifications

To recite the Chaplet of The Divine Mercy with outstretched arms.
On Saturday, to say five decades of the Rosary with outstretched arms.
To sometimes recite a prayer [while] lying prostrate.
On Thursdays, a Holy Hour.
On Fridays, some greater mortification for dying sinners.

247 **(114)**Jesus, Friend of a lonely heart, You are my haven, You are my peace. You are my salvation, You are my serenity in moments of struggle and amidst an ocean of doubts. You are the bright ray that lights up the path of my life. You are everything to a lonely soul. You understand the soul even though it remains silent. You know our weaknesses, and like a good physician, You comfort and heal, sparing us sufferings—expert that You are.

248 The words of the Bishop [Rospond[73]], spoken at the ceremony of the taking of perpetual vows: "Accept this candle as a sign of heavenly light and of burning love."

While giving the ring: "I betroth you to Jesus Christ, the Son of the Father Most High; may He keep you unblemished. Take this ring as a sign of the eternal covenant you are making with Christ, the Spouse of Virgins. May it be for you the ring of faith and the sign of the Holy Spirit, that you may be called the bride of Christ and, if you serve Him faithfully, be crowned [as such] for all eternity.

249 +Jesus, I trust in You; I trust in the ocean of your mercy. You are a Mother to me.

250 +This year, 1933, is for me an especially solemn year, because in this Jubilee Year of the Lord's Passion, I have taken my perpetual vows. I have joined my sacrifice in a special way to the sacrifice of the crucified Jesus, in order to thus become more pleasing to God. I do all things with Jesus, through Jesus, in Jesus.

251 After perpetual vows, I stayed in Cracow throughout the month of May, because it was undecided whether I was to go to Rabka or to Vilnius. Once Mother General [Michael] asked me, "Why are you sitting here so quietly and not getting ready to go somewhere, Sister?" I answered, "I want to do God's pure will; wherever you bid me to go, dear Mother, I will know God's pure will for me will be there, without any admixture on my part."

(115) Mother General replied to this, "Very well!" The next day she summoned me and said, "You wanted to have God's pure will, Sister; very well, then; you are going to Vilnius." I thanked her and awaited the day when I would be told to go. However, my soul was filled with a certain joy and fear, at one and the same time. I felt that God was preparing great graces for me there, but also great sufferings. Yet, I stayed on in Cracow until the 27th of May. As I had no regular duties, I only went to help in the garden. And as it happened that I worked all alone for the whole month, I was able to make a Jesuit retreat.[74] Although I went to community recreation, I still managed to make the Jesuit retreat. I received much light from God during this time.

252 +It was four days after my perpetual vows. I was trying to make a Holy Hour. It was the first Thursday of the month. As soon as I entered the chapel, God's presence enveloped me. I was distinctly aware that the Lord was near me. After a moment, I saw the Lord, all covered with wounds; and He said to me, **Look at whom you have espoused.** I understood the meaning of these words and answered the Lord, "Jesus, I love You more when I see You wounded and crushed with suffering like this than if I saw You in majesty." Jesus asked, **Why?** I replied, "Great majesty terrifies me, little nothing that I am, and Your wounds draw me to Your Heart and tell me of Your great love for me." After this conversation there was silence. I fixed my gaze upon His sacred

wounds and felt happy to suffer with Him. I suffered, and yet I did not suffer, because I felt happy to know the depth of His love, and the hour passed like a minute.

253 +I must never judge anyone, but look at others with leniency and at myself with severity. I must refer everything to God and, in my own eyes, recognize myself for what I am: utter misery and nothingness. In suffering, I must be patient and quiet, knowing that everything passes in time.

254 **(116)**+The moments I lived through when I was taking my perpetual vows are better left unsaid.

I am in Him, and He in me. As the Bishop [Rospond] was putting the ring on my finger, God pervaded my whole being, and since I cannot express that moment, I will be silent about it. My relationship with God, since perpetual vows, has been more intimate than it had ever been before. I sense that I love God and that He loves me. Having once tasted God, my soul could not live without Him. One hour spent at the foot of the altar in the greatest dryness of spirit is dearer to me than a hundred years of worldly pleasures. I prefer to be a lowly drudge in the convent than a queen in the world.

255 +I will hide from people's eyes whatever good I am able to do so that God himself may be my reward. I will be like a tiny violet hidden in the grass, which does not hurt the foot that treads on it, but diffuses its fragrance and, forgetting itself completely, tries to please the person who has crushed it underfoot. This is very difficult for human nature, but God's grace comes to one's aid.

256 +Thank You, Jesus, for the great favor of making known to me the whole abyss of my misery. I know that I am an abyss of nothingness and that, if Your holy grace did not hold me up, I would return to nothingness in a moment. And so, with every beat of my heart, I thank You, my God, for Your great mercy towards me.

257 Tomorrow I am to leave for Vilnius. Today, I went to

confession to Father Andrasz, this priest who is so filled with the spirit of God, who untied my wings so that I could soar to the highest summits. He reassured me in everything and told me to believe in Divine Providence. "Have confidence and walk ahead with courage." An extraordinary, divine power came over me after that confession. **(117)**Father stressed that I must be faithful to God's grace and said, "No harm will come to you if, in the future, you continue to keep this same simplicity and obedience. Have confidence in God; you are on the right path and in good hands, in God's hands."

258 +That evening, I remained in the chapel a little longer. I talked to the Lord about a certain soul. Encouraged by His goodness, I said, "Jesus, you gave me this Father who understands my inspirations, and now You are taking him away from me again. What am I going to do in this Vilnius? I don't know anyone there, and even the dialect of the people there is foreign to me." And the Lord said to me, **Do not fear; I will not leave you to yourself.** My soul drowned itself in a prayer of thanksgiving for all the graces that the Lord had granted me through the mediation of Father Andrasz.

Suddenly I remembered the vision in which I had seen that priest between the confessional and the altar, trusting that I would meet him some day. And the words I had heard came back vividly: **He will help you to fulfill my will here on earth.**

259 Today, 27 [May 1933], I am leaving for Vilnius. When I came out of the house, I looked at the garden and the house, and when I cast a glance at the novitiate, tears suddenly ran down my cheeks. I remembered all the blessings and graces bestowed on me by the Lord. Then, suddenly and unexpectedly, I saw the Lord by the flower bed, and He said to me, **Do not weep; I am with you always.** God's presence, which enveloped me as Jesus was speaking, accompanied me throughout the journey.

260 I had permission to visit Czestochowa while on my journey. I saw the Mother of God [image] for the first time, when I went to attend the unveiling of the image at five in the morning. I prayed without interruption until eleven, and it seemed to me that I had just come. The superior of the house there [Mother Serafin[75]] sent a sister for me, to tell me to come to breakfast and said she was worried(118)that I would miss my train. The Mother of God told me many things. I entrusted my perpetual vows to Her. I felt that I was her child and that She was my Mother. She did not refuse any of my requests.

261 +I am already in Vilnius today. A few scattered tiny huts make up the convent. It seems a bit strange to me after the large buildings of Jozefow. There are only eighteen sisters here. The house is small, but the community life is more intimate. All the sisters received me very warmly, which was for me a great encouragement to endure the hardships that lay ahead. Sister Justine had even scrubbed the floor in anticipation of my arrival.

262 +When I went to Benediction, Jesus enlightened me on how I was to conduct myself in respect to certain persons. I clung with all my might to the most sweet Heart of Jesus, knowing how much I would be exposed to external distractions because of the work I would be doing here in the garden, where I necessarily would be in close contact with lay persons.

263 +The week for confession came and, to my great joy, I saw the priest I had known before coming to Vilnius. [That is to say,] I had known him by seeing him in a vision. At that moment, I heard these words in my soul: **This is My faithful servant; he will help you to fulfill My will here on earth.** Yet, I did not open myself to him as the Lord wished. And for some time I struggled against grace. During each confession, God's grace penetrated me in a very special way, yet I did not reveal my soul

before him, and I had the intention of not going to confession to that priest. After this decision, a terrible anxiety entered my soul. God reproached me severely. When I did lay bare my soul completely to this priest, Jesus poured an ocean of graces into it. Now I understand what it means to be faithful to a particular grace. That one grace draws down a whole series of others.

264 **(119)**+O my Jesus, keep me near to You! See how weak I am! I cannot go a step forward by myself; so You, Jesus, must stand by me constantly like a mother by a helpless child—and even more so.

265 Days of work, of struggle and of suffering have begun. Everything continued according to the convent routine. One is always a novice, having to learn many things and to get to know about many things, because although the rule is the same, each house has its own customs; and thus, each change is a little novitiate.

August 5, 1933. The Feast of Our Lady of Mercy.

266 Today I received a great and incomprehensible grace, a purely interior one, for which I will be grateful to God throughout this life and in eternity...

267 Jesus told me that I please Him best by meditating on His sorrowful Passion, and by such meditation much light falls upon my soul. He who wants to learn true humility should reflect upon the Passion of Jesus. When I meditate upon the Passion of Jesus, I get a clear understanding of many things I could not comprehend before. I want to resemble You, O Jesus,—You crucified, tortured and humiliated. Jesus, imprint upon my heart and soul Your own humility. I love You, Jesus, to the point of madness, You who were crushed with suffering as described by the prophet [cf. Isaiah 53:2-9], as if he could not see the human form in You because of Your

great suffering. It is in this condition, Jesus, that I love You to the point of madness. O eternal and infinite God, what has love done to You?...

268 October 11, 1933.—Thursday.—I tried to make a Holy Hour, but began it with great difficulty. A certain yearning started to tear at my heart. My mind was dimmed so that I could not understand the simplest forms of prayer. And so passed by an hour of prayer, or rather of struggle. I resolved to pray for a second hour, but my inner sufferings increased—great**(120)** dryness and discouragement. I resolved to pray for a third hour. In the third hour, which I resolved to spend kneeling without any support, my body started to clamor for rest. But I in no way relented. I stretched out my arms and, though I spoke no words, I persisted by sheer will. After a while, I took the ring off my finger and asked Jesus to look at the ring, that sign of our eternal union, and I offered Jesus the feelings I had had on the day of perpetual vows. After a while, I feel my heart inundated with a wave of love. A sudden recollection of spirit, the senses quiet down, and God's presence pervades my soul. I know only this: that it is Jesus and I. I saw Him just as He had appeared to me in that instant after my perpetual vows, when I was likewise making a Holy Hour. Jesus was suddenly standing before me, stripped of His clothes, His body completely covered with wounds, His eyes flooded with tears and blood, His face disfigured and covered with spittle. The Lord then said to me, **The bride must resemble her Betrothed.** I understood these words to their very depth. There is no room for doubt here. My likeness to Jesus must be through suffering and humility. **See what love of human souls has done to Me. My daughter, in your heart I find everything that so great a number of souls refuses Me. Your heart is My repose. I often wait with great graces until towards the end of prayer.**

269 Once, when I had finished a novena to the Holy Spirit

for the intention of my confessor [Father Sopocko], the Lord answered, **I made him known to you even before your superiors had sent you here. As you will act towards your confessor, so I will act toward you. If you conceal something from him, even though it be the least of My graces, I too will hide myself from you, and you will remain alone.** And so I followed God's wish, and a deep peace filled my soul. Now I understand how the Lord defends confessors and how He protects them.

(121)Advice of the Rev. Dr. Sopocko.

270 Without humility, we cannot be pleasing to God. Practice the third degree of humility;[76] that is, not only must one refrain from explaining and defending oneself when reproached with something, but one should rejoice at the humiliation.

If the things you are telling me really come from God, prepare your soul for great suffering. You will encounter disapproval and persecution. They will look upon you as a hysteric and an eccentric, but the Lord will lavish His graces upon you. True works of God always meet opposition and are marked by suffering. If God wants to accomplish something, sooner or later He will do so in spite of the difficulties. Your part, in the meantime, is to arm yourself with great patience.

271 When the Rev. Dr. Sopocko went to the Holy Land, Father Dabrowski, S.J., was the community's confessor. During one confession he asked me if I was aware of the high degree of [spiritual] life that was present in my soul. I answered that I was aware of it and knew what was going on within me. To this the Father replied, "You must not destroy what is going on in your soul, Sister, nor must you change anything on your own. It is not in every soul that the beautiful gift of a higher interior life is manifest as it is in your case, Sister, for it is manifest in an immense degree. Be careful not to waste these great

graces of God; a great..."[Here the thought breaks off.]

272 But previously, this priest had put me through many trials. When I told him that the Lord wanted these things of me [that is, the painting of the image, the establishing of a feast of The Divine Mercy, and the founding of a new community], he laughed at me and told me to come to confession at eight in the evening. When I came at eight, a brother was already locking the church. When I told him that Father had ordered me to come at that time**(122)** and asked him to let Father know I was there, the good brother went to let him know. Father told him to tell me that priests do not hear confessions at that time of day. I returned home empty-handed and did not go to confession to him again, but I made a whole hour's adoration and took on certain mortifications for him, that he might obtain light from God in order to know souls. But when Father Sopocko left, and he substituted for him, I was forced to go to confession to him. Yet, while previously he had been unwilling to acknowledge these inner inspirations, he now put me under obligation to be faithful to them. God lets such things happen sometimes, but may He be glorified in everything. Still, it requires much grace not to falter.

Annual Retreat. January 10, 1934.

273 My Jesus, again the moment approaches when I will be alone with You. Jesus, I ask You with all my heart, let me know what there is in me that displeases You and also let me know what I should do to become more pleasing to You. Do not refuse me this favor and be with me. I know that without You, Lord, all my efforts will not amount to much. Oh, how I rejoice at Your greatness, O Lord! The more I come to know You, the more ardently I yearn for You and sigh after You!

274 Jesus gave me the grace of knowing myself. In this divine

light I see my principal fault; it is pride which takes the form of my closing up within myself and of a lack of simplicity in my relations with Mother Superior [Irene].

The second light concerns speaking. I sometimes talk too much. A thing could be settled in one or two words, and as for me, I take too much time about it. But Jesus wants me to use that time to say some short indulgenced prayers for the souls in purgatory. And the Lord says that every word will be weighed on the day of judgment.

(123)The third light concerns our rules. I have not sufficiently avoided the occasions that lead to breaking the rules, especially that of silence. I will act as if the rule were written just for me; it should not affect me at all how anyone else might act, as long as I myself act as God wishes.

Resolution. Whatever Jesus demands of me regarding external things, I will immediately go and tell my superiors. I shall strive for childlike openness and frankness in my relations with the superior.

275 Jesus loves hidden souls. A hidden flower is the most fragrant. I must strive to make the interior of my soul a resting place for the Heart of Jesus. In difficult and painful moments, O my Creator, I sing You a hymn of trust, for bottomless is the abyss of my trust in You and in Your mercy!

276 From the moment I came to love suffering, it ceased to be a suffering for me. Suffering is the daily food of my soul.

277 I will not speak with a certain person, because I know that Jesus does not like it and that she does not profit by it.

278 At the feet of the Lord. Hidden Jesus, Eternal Love, our Source of Life, Divine Madman, in that You forget yourself and see only us. Before creating heaven and earth, You carried us in the depths of Your Heart. O

Love, O depth of Your abasement, O mystery of happiness, why do so few people know You? Why is Your love not returned? O Divine Love, why do You hide Your beauty? O Infinite One beyond all understanding, the more I know You the less I comprehend You; but because I cannot comprehend You, I better comprehend Your greatness. I do not envy the Seraphim their fire, for I have a greater gift deposited in my heart. **(124)**They admire You in rapture, but Your Blood mingles with mine. Love is heaven given us already here on earth. Oh, why do You hide in faith? Love tears away the veil. There is no veil before the eye of my soul, for You yourself have drawn me into the bosom of secret love forever. Praise and glory be to You, O Indivisible Trinity, One God, unto ages of ages!

279 God made known to me what true love consists in and gave light to me about how, in practice, to give proof of it to Him. True love of God consists in carrying out God's will. To show God our love in what we do, all our actions, even the least, must spring from our love of God. And the Lord said to me, **My child, you please Me most by suffering. In your physical as well as your mental sufferings, My daughter, do not seek sympathy from creatures. I want the fragrance of your suffering to be pure and unadulterated. I want you to detach yourself, not only from creatures, but also from yourself. My daughter, I want to delight in the love of your heart, a pure love, virginal, unblemished, untarnished. The more you will come to love suffering, My daughter, the purer your love for Me will be.**

280 Jesus commanded me to celebrate the Feast of God's Mercy on the first Sunday after Easter. [This I did] through interior recollection and exterior mortification, wearing the belt for three hours and praying continuously for sinners and for mercy on the whole world. And Jesus said to me, **My eyes rest with pleasure**

upon this house today.

281 I feel certain that my mission will not come to an end upon my death, but will begin. O doubting souls, I will draw aside for you the veils of heaven to convince you of God's goodness, so that you will no longer continue to wound with your distrust the sweetest Heart of Jesus. God is Love and Mercy.

282 **(125)**Once the Lord said to me, **My Heart was moved by great mercy towards you, My dearest child, when I saw you torn to shreds because of the great pain you suffered in repenting for your sins. I see your love, so pure and true that I give you first place among the virgins. You are the honor and glory of My Passion. I see every abasement of your soul, and nothing escapes my attention. I lift up the humble even to my very throne, because I want it so.**

God, One in the Holy Trinity.

283 I want to love You as no human soul has ever loved You before; and although I am utterly miserable and small, I have nevertheless cast the anchor of my trust deep down into the abyss of Your mercy, O my God and Creator! In spite of my great misery I fear nothing, but hope to sing You a hymn of glory for ever. Let no soul, even the most miserable, fall prey to doubt; for, as long as one is alive, each one can become a great saint, so great is the power of God's grace. It remains only for us not to oppose God's action.

284 O Jesus, if only I could become like mist before Your eyes, to cover the earth so that You would not see its terrible crimes. Jesus, when I look at the world and its indifference towards You, again and again it brings tears to my eyes; but when I look at a cold soul of a religious, my heart bleeds.

285 1934. Once, when I returned to my cell, I was so tired that I had to rest a moment before I started to undress,

and when I was already undressed, one of the sisters asked me to fetch her some hot water. Although I was tired, I dressed quickly and brought her the water she **(126)**wanted, even though it was quite a long walk from the cell to the kitchen, and the mud was ankle-deep. When I re-entered my cell, I saw the ciborium with the Blessed Sacrament, and I heard this voice, **Take this ciborium and bring it to the tabernacle.** I hesitated at first, but when I approached and touched it, I heard these words, **Approach each of the sisters with the same love with which you approach Me; and whatever you do for them, you do it for Me.** A moment later, I saw that I was alone.

286 +Once, after an adoration for our country, a pain pierced my soul, and I began to pray in this way: "Most merciful Jesus, I beseech You through the intercession of Your Saints, and especially the intercession of Your dearest Mother who nurtured You from childhood, bless my native land. I beg You, Jesus, look not on our sins, but on the tears of little children, on the hunger and cold they suffer. Jesus, for the sake of these innocent ones, grant me the grace that I am asking of You for my country." At that moment, I saw the Lord Jesus, His eyes filled with tears, and He said to me, **You see, My daughter, what great compassion I have for them. Know that it is they who uphold the world.**

287 +My Jesus, when I look at this life of souls, I see that many of them serve You with some mistrust. At certain times, especially when there is an opportunity to show their love for God, I see them running away from the battlefield. And once Jesus said to me, **Do you, my child, also want to act like that?** I answered the Lord, "Oh, no, my Jesus, I will not retreat from the battlefield, even if mortal sweat breaks out on my brow; I will not let the sword fall from my hand until I rest at the feet of the Holy Trinity!" Whatever I do, I do not rely on my own strength, but on God's grace. With God's grace a

soul can overcome the greatest difficulties.

288 **(127)**+Once when I was having a long talk with Jesus about our students, encouraged by His kindness, I asked Him, "Do You have among our students any who are a comfort to Your Heart?" The Lord answered [that] He has, **but their love is weak, and so I put them in your special care—pray for them.**

O great God, I admire Your goodness! You are the Lord of heavenly hosts, and yet You stoop so low to Your miserable creatures. Oh, how ardently I desire to love You with every beat of my heart! The whole extent of the earth is not enough for me, heaven is too small, and boundless space is nothing; You alone are enough for me, Eternal God! You alone can fill the depths of my soul.

289 My happiest moments are when I am alone with my Lord. During these moments I experience the greatness of God and my own misery.

Once, Jesus said to me, **Do not be surprised that you are sometimes unjustly accused. I myself first drank this cup of undeserved suffering for love of you.**

290 Once, when I was deeply moved by the thought of eternity and its mysteries, my soul became fearful; and when I pondered about these a little longer, I started to be troubled by various doubts. Then Jesus said to me, **My child, do not be afraid of the house of your Father. Leave these vain inquiries to the wise of this world. I want to see you always as a little child. Ask your confessor about everything with simplicity, and I will answer you through his lips.**

291 On a certain occasion, I saw a person about to commit a mortal sin. I asked the Lord to send me the greatest torments so that that soul could be saved. **(128)**Then I suddenly felt the terrible pain of a crown of thorns on my head. It lasted for quite a long time, but that person remained in the Lord's grace. O my Jesus, how very easy

it is to become holy; all that is needed is a bit of good will. If Jesus sees this little bit of good will in the soul, He hurries to give himself to the soul, and nothing can stop Him, neither shortcomings nor falls—absolutely nothing. Jesus is anxious to help that soul, and if it is faithful to this grace from God, it can very soon attain the highest holiness possible for a creature here on earth. God is very generous and does not deny His grace to anyone. Indeed He gives more than what we ask of Him. Faithfulness to the inspirations of the Holy Spirit—that is the shortest route.

292 +When a soul loves God sincerely, it ought not fear anything in the spiritual life. Let it subject itself to the action of grace, and let it not impose any restraints on itself in communing with the Lord.

293 +When Jesus ravished me by His beauty and drew me to Himself, I then saw what in my soul was displeasing to Him and made up my mind to remove it, cost what it may; and aided by the grace of God I did remove it at once. This magnanimity pleased the Lord, and from that moment God started granting me higher graces. In my interior life I never reason; I do not analyze the ways in which God's Spirit leads me. It is enough for me to know that I am loved and that I love. Pure love enables me to know God and understand many mysteries. My confessor is an oracle for me. His word is sacred to me—I am speaking about the spiritual director [Father Sopocko].

294 +Once the Lord said to me, **Act like a beggar who does not back away when he gets more alms [than he asked for], but offers thanks the more fervently. You too should not back away and say that you are not worthy of receiving greater graces when I give them to you. I know you are unworthy, but rejoice all the more and take as many (129) treasures from My Heart as you can carry, for then you will please Me more. And I will tell**

you one more thing:Take these graces not only for yourself, but also for others; that is, encourage the souls with whom you come in contact to trust in My infinite mercy. Oh, how I love those souls who have complete confidence in Me. I will do everything for them.

295 +At that moment Jesus asked me, **My child, how is your retreat going?** I answered, "But Jesus, You know how it is going." **Yes, I know, but I want to hear it from your own lips and from your heart.** "O my Master, when You are leading me, everything goes smoothly, and I ask You, Lord, to never leave my side." And Jesus said, **Yes, I will be with you always, if you always remain a little child and fear nothing. As I was your beginning here, so I will also be your end. Do not rely on creatures, even in the smallest things, because this displeases Me. I want to be alone in your soul. I will give light and strength to your soul, and you will learn from My representative that I am in you, and your uncertainty will vanish like mist before the rays of the sun.**

296 +O Supreme Good, I want to love You as no one on earth has ever loved You before! I want to adore You with every moment of my life and unite my will closely to Your holy will. My life is not drab or monotonous, but it is varied like a garden of fragrant flowers, so that I don't know which flower to pick first, the lily of suffering or the rose of love of neighbor or the violet of humility. I will not enumerate these treasures in which my every day abounds. It is a great thing to know how to make use of the present moment.

297 +Jesus, Supreme Light, grant me the grace of knowing myself, and pierce my dark soul with Your light, and fill the abyss of my soul with Your own self, for You alone [...]

298 O my Jesus, the Life, the Way and the Truth, I beg You to keep me close to You as a mother holds a baby to her bosom, for I am not only a helpless child, but an

accumulation of misery and nothingness.

(130)+The Mystery of the Soul. Vilnius, 1934

299 When, on one occasion, my confessor told me to ask the Lord Jesus the meaning of the two rays in the image,[77] I answered, "Very well, I will ask the Lord."

During prayer I heard these words within me: **The two rays denote Blood and Water. The pale ray stands for the Water which makes souls righteous. The red ray stands for the Blood which is the life of souls...**

These two rays issued forth from the very depths of My tender mercy when My agonized Heart was opened by a lance on the Cross.

These rays shield souls from the wrath of My Father. Happy is the one who will dwell in their shelter, for the just hand of God shall not lay hold of him. I desire that the first Sunday after Easter be the Feast of Mercy.

300 +**Ask of my faithful servant** [Father Sopocko] **that, on this day, he tell the whole world of My great mercy; that whoever approaches the Fount of Life on this day will be granted complete remission of sins and punishment.**

+**Mankind will not have peace until it turns with trust to My mercy.**

+**Oh, how much I am hurt by a soul's distrust! Such a soul professes that I am Holy and Just, but does not believe that I am Mercy and does not trust in My Goodness. Even the devils glorify My Justice but do not believe in My Goodness.**

My Heart rejoices in this title of Mercy.

301 **Proclaim that mercy is the greatest attribute of God. All the works of My hands are crowned with mercy.**

302 **(131)**+O Eternal Love, I want all the souls You have created to come to know You. I would like to be a priest, for then I would speak without cease about Your mercy to sinful souls drowned in despair. I would like to be a

missionary and carry the light of faith to savage nations
in order to make You known to souls, and to be
completely consumed for them and to die a martyr's
death, just as You died for them and for me. O Jesus, I
know only too well that I can be a priest, a missionary, a
preacher, and that I can die a martyr's death by
completely emptying myself and denying myself for love
of You, O Jesus, and of immortal souls.

303 Great love can change small things into great ones, and it
is only love which lends value to our actions. And the
purer our love becomes, the less there will be within us
for the flames of suffering to feed upon, and the
suffering will cease to be a suffering for us; it will become
a delight! By the grace of God, I have received such a
disposition of heart that I am never so happy as when I
suffer for Jesus, whom I love with every beat of my
heart.

Once when I was suffering greatly, I left my work and
escaped to Jesus and asked Him to give me His strength.
After a very short prayer I returned to my work filled
with enthusiasm and joy. Then, one of the sisters
[probably Sister Justine] said to me, "You must have
many consolations today, Sister; you look so radiant.
Surely, God is giving you no suffering, but only
consolations." "You are greatly mistaken, Sister," I
answered, "for it is precisely when I suffer much that my
joy is greater; and when I suffer less, my joy also is less."
However, that soul was letting me recognize that she
does not understand what I was saying. I tried to explain
to her that when we suffer much we have a great chance
to show God that we love Him; but when we suffer little
we have less occasion to show God our love; and when
we do not suffer at all, our love is then neither great nor
pure. By the grace of God, we can attain a point where
suffering will become a delight to us, for love can work
such things in pure souls.

304 **(132)**+O my Jesus, my only hope, thank You for the book which You have opened before my soul's eyes. That book is Your Passion which You underwent for love of me. It is from this book that I have learned how to love God and souls. In this book there are found for us inexhaustible treasures. O Jesus, how few souls understand You in Your martyrdom of love! Oh, how great is the fire of purest love which burns in Your Most Sacred Heart! Happy the soul that has come to understand the love of the Heart of Jesus!

305 It is my greatest desire that souls should recognize You as their eternal happiness, that they should come to believe in Your goodness and glorify Your infinite mercy.

306 I asked the Lord to grant me the grace that my nature be immune and resist the influences that sometimes try to draw me away from the spirit of our rule and from the minor regulations. These minor transgressions are like little moths that try to destroy the spiritual life within us, and they surely will destroy it if the soul is aware of these minor transgressions and yet disregards them as small things. I can see nothing that is small in the religious life. Little matter if I am sometimes the object of vexation and jeers, as long as my spirit remains in harmony with the spirit of the rules, the vows and the religious statutes.

O my Jesus, delight of my heart, You know my desires. I should like to hide from people's sight so as to be like one alive and yet not living. I want to live pure as a wild flower; I want my love always to be turned to You, just as a flower that is always turning to the sun. I want the fragrance and the freshness of the flower of my heart to be always preserved for You alone. I want to live beneath Your divine gaze, for You alone are enough for me. When I am with You, Jesus, I fear nothing, for nothing can do me harm.

307 **(133)** + 1934. Once during Lent, I saw a great light and a great darkness over house and chapel. I saw the struggle of these two powers...

308 1934, Holy Thursday. Jesus said to me, **I desire that you make an offering of yourself for sinners and especially for those souls who have lost hope in God's mercy.**

God and Souls. An Act of Oblation.

309 Before heaven and earth, before all the choirs of Angels, before the Most Holy Virgin Mary, before all the Powers of heaven, I declare to the One Triune God that today, in union with Jesus Christ, Redeemer of souls, I make a voluntary offering of myself for the conversion of sinners, especially for those souls who have lost hope in God's mercy. This offering consists in my accepting, with total subjection to God's will, all the sufferings, fears and terrors with which sinners are filled. In return, I give them all the consolations which my soul receives from my communion with God. In a word, I offer everything for them: Holy Masses, Holy Communions, penances, mortifications, prayers. I do not fear the blows, blows of divine justice, because I am united with Jesus. O my God, in this way I want to make amends to You for the souls that do not trust in Your goodness. I hope against all hope in the ocean of Your mercy. My Lord and my God, my portion—my portion forever, I do not base this act of oblation on my own strength, but on the strength that flows from the merits of Jesus Christ. I will daily repeat this act of self-oblation by pronouncing the following prayer which You yourself have taught me, Jesus:

"O Blood and Water which gushed forth from the Heart of Jesus as a Fount of Mercy for us, I trust in You!"

S. M. Faustina of the Blessed Sacrament
Holy Thursday, during Holy Mass, March 29, 1934.

310 **(134) — I am giving you a share in the redemption of mankind. You are solace in My dying hour.**

311 When I received permission from my confessor [Father Sopocko] to make this act of oblation, I soon learned that it was pleasing to God, because I immediately began to experience its effects. In a moment my soul became like a stone—dried up, filled with torment and disquiet. All sorts of blasphemies and curses kept pressing upon my ears. Distrust and despair invaded my heart. This is the condition of the poor people, which I have taken upon myself. At first, I was very much frightened by these horrible things, but during the first [opportune] confession, I was set at peace.

312 +Once when I went outside the convent to go to confession [St. Michael's Church], I chanced upon my confessor [Father Sopocko] saying Mass just then. After a while I saw the Child Jesus on the altar, joyfully and playfully holding out His hands to him. But a moment later the priest took the beautiful Child into his hands, broke Him up and ate Him alive. At the first instant I felt a dislike for the priest for having done this to Jesus, but I was immediately enlightened in the matter and understood that this priest was very pleasing to God.

313 +Once, when I was visiting the artist [Eugene Kazimirowski] who was painting the image, and saw that it was not as beautiful as Jesus is, I felt very sad about it, but I hid this deep in my heart. When we had left the artist's house, Mother Superior [Irene] stayed in town to attend to some matters while I returned home alone. I went immediately to the chapel and wept a good deal. I said to the Lord, "Who will paint You as beautiful as You are?" Then I heard these words: **Not in the beauty of the color, nor of the brush lies the greatness of this image, but in My grace.**

314 +When I went to the garden one afternoon, my Guardian

Angel said to me, "Pray for the dying." And so I began at once to pray the rosary with the gardeners for the dying. After the rosary, we said various prayers for the dying. After the prayers, the wards began to chat gayly among themselves. **(135)** In spite of the noise they were making, I heard these words in my soul: "Pray for me!" But as I could not understand these words very well, I moved a few steps away from the wards, trying to think who it could be who was asking me to pray. Then I heard the words: "I am Sister ...."[78] This sister was in Warsaw while I was, at the time, in Vilnius. "Pray for me until I tell you to stop. I am dying." Immediately, I began to pray fervently for her, [addressing myself] to the expiring Heart of Jesus. She gave me no respite, and I kept praying from three [o'clock] until five. At five, I heard the words: "Thank you!" and I understood that she had died. But during Holy Mass on the following day, I continued to pray fervently for her soul. In the afternoon, a postcard came saying that Sister ... had died at such and such a time. I understood that it was at the same hour when she had said to me, "Pray for me."

315 +Mother of God, Your soul was plunged into a sea of bitterness; look upon Your child and teach her to suffer and to love while suffering. Fortify my soul that pain will not break it. Mother of grace, teach me to live by [the power of] God.

316 Once, the Mother of God came to visit me. She was sad. Her eyes were cast down. She made it clear that She wanted to say something, and yet, on the other hand, it was as if She did not want to speak to me about it. When I understood this, I began to beg the Mother of God to tell me and to look at me. Just then Mary looked at me with a warm smile and said, *You are going to experience certain sufferings because of an illness and the doctors; you will also suffer much because of the image, but do not be afraid of anything.* The next day I fell ill and

suffered a great deal, just as the Mother of God had told me. But my soul was ready for the sufferings. Suffering is a constant companion of my life.

317 O my God, my only hope, I have placed all my trust in You, and I know I shall not be disappointed.

318 **(136)**I often feel God's presence after Holy Communion in a special and tangible way. I know God is in my heart. And the fact that I feel Him in my heart does not interfere with my duties. Even when I am dealing with very important matters which require attention, I do not lose the presence of God in my soul, and I am closely united with Him. With Him I go to work, with Him I go for recreation, with Him I suffer, with Him I rejoice; I live in Him and He in me. I am never alone, because He is my constant companion. He is present to me at every moment. Our intimacy is very close, through a union of blood and of life.

319 August 9, 1934. Night adoration on Thursdays.[79] I made my hour of adoration from eleven o'clock till midnight. I offered it for the conversion of hardened sinners, especially for those who have lost hope in God's mercy. I was reflecting on how much God had suffered and on how great was the love He had shown for us, and on the fact that we still do not believe that God loves us so much. O Jesus, who can understand this? What suffering it is for our Savior! How can He convince us of His love if even His death cannot convince us? I called upon the whole of heaven to join me in making amends to the Lord for the ingratitude of certain souls.

320 Jesus made known to me how very pleasing to Him were prayers of atonement. He said to me, **The prayer of a humble and loving soul disarms the anger of My Father and draws down an ocean of blessings.** After the adoration, half way to my cell, I was surrounded by a pack of huge black dogs who were jumping and howling

and trying to tear me to pieces. I realized that they were not dogs, but demons. One of them spoke up in a rage, "Because you have snatched so many souls away from us this night, we will tear you to pieces." I answered, "If that is the will of the most merciful God, tear me to pieces, for I have justly deserved it, because I am the most miserable of all sinners, and God is ever holy, just, and infinitely merciful." To these words all the demons answered as one, "Let us flee, for she is not alone; the Almighty is with her!" And they vanished like dust, like the noise of the road, while I continued on my way to my cell undisturbed, finishing my *Te Deum* and pondering the infinite and unfathomable mercy of God.

(137) August 12, 1934.

321   A sudden illness—a mortal suffering. It was not death, that is to say, a passing over to real life, but a taste of the sufferings of death. Although it gives us eternal life, death is dreadful. Suddenly, I felt sick, I gasped for breath, there was darkness before my eyes, my limbs grew numb—and there was a terrible suffocation. Even a moment of such suffocation is extremely long.... There also comes a strange fear, in spite of trust. I wanted to receive the last sacraments, but it was extremely difficult to make a confession even though I desired to do so. A person does not know what he is saying; not finishing one thing, he begins another.

Oh, may God keep every soul from delaying confession until the last hour! I understood the great power of the priest's words when they are poured out upon the sick person's soul. When I asked my spiritual father whether I was ready to stand before the Lord and whether I could be at peace, I received the reply, "You can be completely at peace, not only right now but after each weekly confession." Great is the divine grace that accompanies these words of the priest. The soul feels power and courage for battle.

322 O my Congregation, my mother, how sweet it is to live in you, but it is even better to die in you!

323 After I received the last sacraments, there was a definite improvement. I remained alone. This lasted for half an hour and then came another attack; but this one was not so strong, as the doctor intervened.

I united my sufferings with the sufferings of Jesus and offered them for myself and for the conversion of souls who do not trust in the goodness of God. Suddenly, my cell was filled with black figures full of anger and hatred for me. One of them said, "Be damned, you and He who is within you, for you are beginning to torment us even in hell." As soon as I said, "And the Word was made flesh and dwelt among us," the figures vanished in a sudden whir.

324 The next day, I felt very weak, but experienced no further suffering. After Holy Communion, I saw the Lord Jesus just as I had seen Him during one adoration. The Lord's gaze pierced my soul through and through, and not even the least speck of dust escaped His notice. And I said to Jesus, "Jesus, I thought You were going to take me." And Jesus answered, **My will has not yet been fully accomplished in you; you will still remain on earth, but not for long. I am well pleased with your trust, but your love should be more ardent. (138)Pure love gives the soul strength at the very moment of dying. When I was dying on the cross, I was not thinking about Myself, but about poor sinners, and I prayed for them to My Father. I want your last moments to be completely similar to Mine on the cross. There is but one price at which souls are bought, and that is suffering united to My suffering on the cross. Pure love understands these words; carnal love will never understand them.**

325 1934. On the day of the Assumption of the Mother of God, I did not assist at Holy Mass. The woman doctor[80] did not allow me; but I prayed fervently in my cell. After

a short time, I saw the Mother of God, unspeakably beautiful. She said to me, *My daughter, what I demand from you is prayer, prayer, and once again prayer, for the world and especially for your country. For nine days receive Holy Communion in atonement and unite yourself closely to the Holy Sacrifice of the Mass. During these nine days you will stand before God as an offering; always and everywhere, at all times and places, day or night, whenever you wake up, pray in the spirit. In spirit, one can always remain in prayer.*

326 Once, Jesus said to me, **My gaze from this image is like My gaze from the cross.**

327 Once, my confessor [Father Sopocko] asked me where the inscription should be placed, because there was not enough space in the picture for everything. I answered, "I will pray and give you an answer next week." When I left the confessional and was passing before the Blessed Sacrament, I received an inner understanding about the inscription. Jesus reminded me of what He had told me the first time; namely, that these three words must be clearly in evidence: "Jesus, I trust in You." ["Jezu, Ufam Tobie."] I understood that Jesus wanted the whole formula to be there, but He gave no direct orders to this effect as He did for these three words.

I am offering people a vessel with which they are to keep coming for graces to the fountain of mercy. That vessel is this image with the signature: "Jesus, I trust in You."

328 O purest Love, rule in all Your plenitude in my heart and help me to do Your holy will most faithfully!

329 **(139)**Toward the end of a three-day retreat, I saw myself walking along a rough path. I kept stumbling continually, and I saw following me the figure of a person who kept supporting me. I was not happy with this and asked the person to leave me alone, as I wanted

to walk on my own. But the figure, whom I could not recognize, did not leave me for a moment. I got impatient and turned around and pushed the person away from me. At that moment I saw that it was Mother Superior [Irene], and at the same moment I saw that it was not Mother Superior, but the Lord Jesus who looked deeply into me and gave me to understand how painful it was to Him when I did not, even in the smallest things, do my superior's will, **which is My will,** [He said]. I asked pardon of the Lord and took the warning very much to heart.

330 +Once, the confessor told me to pray for his intention, and I began a novena to the Mother of God. This novena consisted in the prayer, "Hail, Holy Queen," recited nine times. Toward the end of the novena I saw the Mother of God with the Infant Jesus in Her arms, and I also saw my confessor kneeling at Her feet and talking with Her. I did not understand what he was saying to Her, because I was busy talking with the Infant Jesus, who came down from His Mother's arms and approached me. I could not stop wondering at His beauty. I heard a few of the words that the Mother of God spoke to him [i.e., my confessor] but not everything. The words were: *I am not only the Queen of Heaven, but also the Mother of Mercy and your Mother.* And at that moment She stretched out her right hand, in which She was clasping her mantle, and She covered the priest with it. At that moment, the vision vanished.

331 Oh, how great a grace it is to have a spiritual director! One makes more rapid progress in virtue, sees the will of God more clearly, fulfills it more faithfully, and follows a road that is sure and free of dangers. The director knows how to avoid the rocks against which the soul could be shattered. The Lord gave me this grace rather late, to be sure, but I rejoice in it greatly, seeing how God inclines His will to my director's wishes. I will mention just one incident out of a thousand that have happened

to me. As I usually do, I asked the Lord Jesus one evening to give me the points for next day's meditation. I received the answer: **Meditate on the Prophet Jonah and his mission.** I thanked the Lord, but began to think within myself of how different that subject was **(140)** from the others. But with all my soul I strove to meditate about it, and I recognized myself in the person of the prophet, in the sense that often I, too, try to make excuses to the Lord, claiming that someone else would do His holy will better [than I could], and not understanding that God can do all things and that His omnipotence will be all the more manifest if the tool is poorer. God made this clear to me in the following way. That afternoon, there was confession for the community. When I presented to the director of my soul the fear that seized me because of this mission for which God was using me, clumsy tool that I was, my spiritual father answered that, willing or not, we must carry out the will of God, and he gave me the Prophet Jonah as an example. After the confession, I wondered how the confessor knew that God had told me to meditate about Jonah; surely I myself had not told him. Then I heard these words: **When the priest acts in my place, he does not act of himself, but I act through him. His wishes are Mine.** I can see how Jesus defends His representatives. He himself enters into their actions.

332 +Thursday. When I started the Holy Hour, I wanted to immerse myself in the agony of Jesus in the Garden of Olives. Then I heard a voice in my soul: **Meditate on the mystery of the Incarnation.** And suddenly the Infant Jesus appeared before me, radiant with beauty. He told me how much God is pleased with simplicity in a soul. **Although My greatness is beyond understanding, I commune only with those who are little. I demand of you a childlike spirit.**

333 I now see clearly how God acts through the confessor and how faithfully He keeps His promises. Two weeks

ago, my confessor told me to reflect upon this spiritual childhood. It was somewhat difficult at first, but my confessor, disregarding my difficulties, told me to continue to reflect upon spiritual childhood. "In practice, this spiritual childhood," [he said,] "should manifest itself in this way: a child does not worry about the past or the future, but makes use of the present moment. I want to emphasize that spiritual childlikeness in you, Sister, and I place great stress upon it." I can see how God bows down to my confessor's wishes; He does not show himself to me at this time as a Teacher in the fullness of His strength and human adulthood, but as a little Child. The God who is beyond all understanding stoops to me under the appearance of a little Child.

334　But the eye of my soul does not stop at this appearance. Although You take the form of a little Child, I see in You the immortal, infinite Lord of lords, whom pure spirits adore,(141)day and night, and for whom the hearts of the Seraphim burn with the fire of purest love. O Christ, O Jesus, I want to surpass them in my love for You! I apologize to you, O pure spirits, for my boldness in comparing myself to you. I, this chasm of misery, this abyss of misery; and You, O God, who are the incomprehensible abyss of mercy, swallow me up as the heat of the sun swallows up a drop of dew! A loving look from You will fill up any abyss. I feel immensely happy at the greatness of God. Seeing God's greatness is more than enough to make me happy throughout all eternity!

335　Once, when I saw Jesus in the form of a small child, I asked, "Jesus, why do you now take on the form of a child when You commune with me? In spite of this, I still see in You the infinite God, my Lord and Creator. Jesus replied that until I learned simplicity and humility, He would commune with me as a little child.

336　+1934. During Holy Mass, when the Lord Jesus was exposed in the Blessed Sacrament, before Holy Communion I saw two rays coming out from the

Blessed Host, just as they are painted in the image, one of them red and the other pale. And they were reflected on each of the sisters and wards, but not on all in the same way. On some of them the rays were barely visible. It was the last day of the children's retreat.

337 November 22, 1934. +On one occasion, my spiritual director [Father Sopocko] told me to look carefully into myself and to examine whether I had any attachment to some particular object or creature, or even to myself, or whether I engaged in useless chatter, "for all these things," [he said,] "get in the way of the Lord Jesus, who wants complete freedom in directing your soul. God is jealous of our hearts and wants us to love Him alone."

338 When I started to look deep within myself, I did not find any attachment to anything, but as in all things that concern me, so also in this matter, I was afraid and distrustful of myself. Tired out by this detailed self-examination, I went before the Blessed Sacrament and asked Jesus with all my heart, "Jesus, my Spouse, Treasure of my heart, **(142)** You know that I know You alone and that I have no other love but You; but, Jesus, if I were about to become attached to anything that is not You, I beg and entreat You, Jesus, by the power of Your mercy, let instant death descend upon me, for I prefer to die a thousand times than to be unfaithful to You once in even the smallest thing."

339 At that moment, Jesus suddenly stood before me, coming I know not from where, radiant with unbelievable beauty, clothed in a white garment, with uplifted arms, and He spoke these words to me, **My daughter, your heart is My repose; it is My delight. I find in it everything that is refused Me by so many souls. Tell this to My representative.** And an instant later, I saw nothing, but a whole ocean of consolations entered my soul.

340 I know now that nothing can put a stop to my love for You, Jesus, neither suffering, nor adversity, nor fire nor

the sword, nor death itself. I feel stronger than all these things. Nothing can compare with love. I see that the smallest things done by a soul that loves God sincerely have an enormous value in His Holy eyes.

341 November 5, 1934. One morning, when it was my duty to open the gate to let out our people who deliver baked goods, I entered the little chapel to visit Jesus for a minute and to renew the intentions of the day. Today, Jesus, I offer You all my sufferings, mortifications and prayers for the intentions of the Holy Father, so that he may approve the Feast of Mercy. But, Jesus, I have one more word to say to You: I am very surprised that You bid me to talk about this Feast of Mercy, for they tell me that there is already such a feast[81] and so why should I talk about it? And Jesus said to me, **And who knows anything about this feast? No one! Even those who should be proclaiming My mercy and teaching people about it often do not know about it themselves. That is why I want the image to be solemnly blessed on the first Sunday after Easter, and I want it to be venerated publicly so that every soul may know about it.**

Make a novena for the Holy Father's intention. It should consist of thirty-three acts; that is, repetition that many times of the short prayer—which I have taught you—to The Divine Mercy.

342 **(143)**Suffering is the greatest treasure on earth; it purifies the soul. In suffering, we learn who our true friend is.

343 True love is measured by the thermometer of suffering. Jesus, I thank You for the little daily crosses, for opposition to my endeavors, for the hardships of communal life, for the misinterpretation of my intentions, for humiliations at the hands of others, for the harsh way in which we are treated, for false suspicions, for poor health and loss of strength, for self-denial, for dying to myself, for lack of recognition in everything, for the upsetting of all my plans.

Thank You, Jesus, for interior sufferings, for dryness of spirit, for terrors, fears and incertitudes, for the darkness and the deep interior night, for temptations and various ordeals, for torments too difficult to describe, especially for those which no one will understand, for the hour of death with its fierce struggle and all its bitterness.

I thank You, Jesus, You who first drank the cup of bitterness before You gave it to me, in a much milder form. I put my lips to this cup of Your holy will. Let all be done according to Your good pleasure; let that which Your wisdom ordained before the ages be done to me. I want to drink the cup to its last drop, and not seek to know the reason why. In bitterness is my joy, in hopelessness is my trust. In You, O Lord, all is good, all is a gift of Your paternal Heart. I do not prefer consolations over bitterness or bitterness over consolations, but thank You, O Jesus, for everything! It is my delight to fix my gaze upon You, O incomprehensible God! My spirit abides in these mysterious dwelling places, and there I am at home. I know very well the dwelling place of my Spouse. I feel there is not a single drop of blood in me that does not burn with love for You.

O Uncreated Beauty, whoever comes to know You once cannot love anything else. I can feel the bottomless abyss of my soul, and nothing will fill it but God himself. I feel that I am drowned in Him like a single grain of sand in a bottomless ocean.

(144)   December 20, 1934.

344 One evening as I entered my cell, I saw the Lord Jesus exposed in the monstrance under the open sky, as it seemed. At the feet of Jesus I saw my confessor, and behind him a great number of the highest ranking ecclesiastics, clothed in vestments the like of which I had never seen except in this vision; and behind them, groups of religious from various orders; and further still

I saw enormous crowds of people, which extended far beyond my vision. I saw the two rays coming out from the Host, as in the image, closely united but not intermingled; and they passed through the hands of my confessor, and then through the hands of the clergy and from their hands to the people, and then they returned to the Host... and at that moment I saw myself once again in the cell which I had just entered.

345   December 22, 1934. When it was possible for me to go to confession during the week, I happened to get there when my confessor was saying Holy Mass. During the third part of the Mass I saw the Infant Jesus, a little smaller than usual and with this difference, that He was wearing a violet tunic. He usually has a white one.

346   December 24, 1934. The Vigil of Christmas. During the morning Mass, I felt the closeness of God. Though I was hardly aware of it, my spirit was drowned in God. Suddenly, I heard these words: **You are My delightful dwelling place; My Spirit rests in you.** After these words, I felt the Lord looking into the depths of my heart; and seeing my misery, I humbled myself in spirit and admired the immense mercy of God, that the Most High Lord would approach such misery.

During Holy Communion, joy filled my soul. I felt that I am closely united to the Godhead. His omnipotence enveloped my whole being. Throughout the whole day I felt the closeness of God in a special manner; and although my duties prevented me throughout the whole day from going to chapel even for a moment, there was not a moment when I was not united with God. I felt Him within **(145)** me more distinctly than ever. Unceasingly greeting the Mother of God and entering into Her spirit, I begged Her to teach me true love of God. And then I heard these words: *I will share with you the secret of My happiness this night during Holy Mass.*

We had supper before six o'clock. Despite all the joy

and the external noise accompanying the sharing of the wafer and the mutual exchange of good wishes, I did not for a moment lose the awareness of God's presence. After supper we hurried away to finish our work, and at nine I was able to go to the chapel for adoration. I was allowed to stay up and wait for the Midnight Mass. I was delighted to have free time from nine until midnight. From nine to ten o'clock I offered my adoration for my parents and my whole family. From ten to eleven, I offered it for the intention of my spiritual director, in the first place thanking God for granting me this great visible help here on earth, just as He had promised me, and I also asked God to grant him the necessary light so that he could get to know my soul and guide me according to God's good pleasure. And from eleven to twelve I prayed for the Holy Church and the clergy, for sinners, for the missions and for our houses. I offered the indulgences for the souls in purgatory.

Twelve O'clock, December 25, 1934

347 Midnight Mass. As Holy Mass began, I immediately felt a great interior recollection; joy filled my soul. During the offertory, I saw Jesus on the altar, incomparably beautiful. The whole time the Infant kept looking at everyone, stretching out His little hands. During the elevation, the Child was not looking towards the chapel but up to heaven. After the elevation He looked at us again, but just for a short while, because He was broken up and eaten by the priest in the usual manner. His pinafore was now white. The next day I saw the same thing, and on the third day as well. It is difficult for me to express the joy of my soul. (146)The vision was repeated at the three Masses in the same way as in the first ones.

1934.

348 The first Thursday after Christmas. I completely forgot

it was Thursday and so did not make my adoration. At nine o'clock I went directly to the dormitory with the other sisters. But strangely enough, I could not fall asleep. It seemed to me that I had not yet done something that I was supposed to do. Mentally, I reviewed all my duties, and could not recollect anything. This lasted until ten o'clock. At ten, I saw the Sorrowful Face of Jesus. Then Jesus spoke these words to me: **I have been waiting to share My suffering with you, for who can understand My suffering better than My spouse?** I asked pardon of Jesus for my coldness. Ashamed and not daring to look at the Lord Jesus, but with a contrite heart, I asked Him to give me one thorn from His crown. He answered that He would grant me this favor, but not until tomorrow, and immediately the vision disappeared.

349 In the morning, during meditation, I felt a painful thorn in the left side of my head. The suffering continued all day. I meditated continually about how Jesus had been able to endure the pain of so many thorns which made up His crown. I joined my suffering to the sufferings of Jesus and offered it for sinners. At four o'clock when I came for adoration, I saw one of our wards offending God greatly by sins of impure thoughts. I also saw a certain person who was the cause of her sin. My soul was pierced with fear, and I asked God, for the sake of Jesus' pain, to snatch her from this terrible misery.

350 Jesus answered that He would grant her that favor, not for her sake, but for the sake of my request. Now I understood how much we ought to pray for sinners, and especially for our wards.

Our life is truly apostolic; I cannot imagine a religious living in one of our houses; that is, in our Community, and not having an apostolic spirit. Zeal for the salvation of souls should burn in our hearts.

351 **(147)**O my God, how sweet it is to suffer for You, suffer

in the most secret recesses of the heart, in the greatest hiddenness, to burn like a sacrifice noticed by no one, pure as crystal, with no consolation or compassion. My spirit burns in active love. I waste no time in dreaming. I take every moment singly as it comes, for this is within my power. The past does not belong to me; the future is not mine; with all my soul I try to make use of the present moment.

January 4, 1935. The first chapter[82] of Mother Borgia.[83]

352 At the chapter, Mother [Borgia] stressed a life of faith and fidelity in small things. Half way through the chapter, I heard these words: **I desire that you would all have more faith at the present time. How great is My joy at the faithfulness of My spouse in the smallest things.** Then I looked at the crucifix and saw that Jesus' head was turned towards the refectory, and His lips were moving.

When I told Mother Superior about it, she answered, "You see, Sister, how Jesus demands that our life be a life of faith."

353 When Mother left for the chapel and I stayed to set the room in order, I heard these words: **Tell all the sisters that I demand that they live in the spirit of faith towards the superiors at this present time.** I begged my confessor to release me from this duty.

354 As I was talking to a certain person[84] who was to paint the image but, for certain reasons, was not painting it, I heard this voice in my soul: **I want her to be more obedient.** I understood that our efforts, no matter how great, are not pleasing to God if they do not bear the seal of obedience; I am speaking about a religious soul. O God, how easy it is to know Your will in the convent! We religious have God's will set clearly before our eyes from morning till night, and in moments of uncertainty we have our superiors through whom God speaks.

355 **(148)**1934—1935. New Year's Eve. I was given

permission not to go to sleep, but rather pray in the chapel. One of the sisters had asked me to offer an hour of adoration for her. I said yes, and prayed for her for an hour. During the hour, God gave me to understand how very pleasing this soul was to Him.

I offered the second hour of adoration for the conversion of sinners, and I tried especially to offer expiation to God for the insults that were being committed against Him at this present moment. How greatly God is being offended!

I offered the third hour for my spiritual director. I fervently prayed for light for him in a particular matter.

Finally the clock struck twelve, the last hour of the year. I finished it in the Name of the Holy Trinity, and I also started the first hour of the New Year in the Name of the Holy Trinity. I asked each of the Three Persons to bless me and, with great confidence, looked toward the New Year which certainly would not be sparing of suffering.

356 O Blessed Host, in whom is contained the testament of God's mercy for us, and especially for poor sinners.

O Blessed Host, in whom is contained the Body and Blood of the Lord Jesus as proof of infinite mercy for us, and especially for poor sinners.

O Blessed Host, in whom is contained life eternal and of infinite mercy, dispensed in abundance to us and especially to poor sinners.

O Blessed Host, in whom is contained the mercy of the Father, the Son and the Holy Spirit toward us, and especially toward poor sinners.

(149)O Blessed Host, in whom is contained the infinite price of mercy which will compensate for all our debts, and especially those of poor sinners.

O Blessed Host, in whom is contained the fountain of living water which springs from infinite mercy for us, and especially for poor sinners.

O Blessed Host, in whom is contained the fire of purest love which blazes forth from the bosom of the Eternal Father, as from an abyss of infinite mercy for us, and especially for poor sinners.

O Blessed Host, in whom is contained the medicine for all our infirmities, flowing from infinite mercy, as from a fount, for us and especially for poor sinners.

O Blessed Host, in whom is contained the union between God and us through His infinite mercy for us, and especially for poor sinners.

O Blessed Host, in whom are contained all the sentiments of the most sweet Heart of Jesus toward us, and especially poor sinners.

O Blessed Host, our only hope in all the sufferings and adversities of life.

O Blessed Host, our only hope in the midst of darkness and of storms within and without.

O Blessed Host, our only hope in life and at the hour of our death.

O Blessed Host, our only hope in the midst of adversities and floods of despair.

O Blessed Host, our only hope in the midst of falsehood and treason.

O Blessed Host, our only hope in the midst of the darkness and godlessness which inundate the earth.

O Blessed Host, our only hope in the longing and pain in which no one will understand us.

(150)O Blessed Host, our only hope in the toil and monotony of everyday life.

O Blessed Host, our only hope amid the ruin of our hopes and endeavors.

O Blessed Host, our only hope in the midst of the ravages of the enemy and the efforts of hell.

O Blessed Host, I trust in You when the burdens are beyond my strength and I find my efforts are fruitless.

O Blessed Host, I trust in You when storms toss my heart about and my fearful spirit tends to despair.

O Blessed Host, I trust in You when my heart is about to tremble and mortal sweat moistens my brow.

O Blessed Host, I trust in You when everything conspires against me and black despair creeps into my soul.

O Blessed Host, I trust in You when my eyes will begin to grow dim to all temporal things and, for the first time, my spirit will behold the unknown worlds.

O Blessed Host, I trust in You when my tasks will be beyond my strength and adversity will become my daily lot.

O Blessed Host I trust in You when the practice of virtue will appear difficult for me and my nature will grow rebellious.

O Blessed Host, I trust in You when hostile blows will be aimed against me.

O Blessed Host, I trust in You when my toils and efforts will be misjudged by others.

O Blessed Host, I trust in You when Your judgments will resound over me; it is then that I will trust in the sea of Your mercy.

357 +Most Holy Trinity, I trust in Your infinite mercy. God is my Father and so I, His child, have every claim to His divine Heart; and the greater the darkness, the more complete our trust should be.

358 I do not understand how it is possible not to trust in Him who can do all things. With Him, everything; without Him, nothing. He is Lord. He will not allow those who have placed all their trust in Him to be put to shame.

359 **(151)**January 10, 1935. +Thursday. In the evening during benediction,[85] such thoughts as these began to distress me: Is not perhaps all this that I am saying about God's great mercy just a lie or an illusion...? And I wanted to think about this for a while, when I heard a strong and clear inner voice saying, **Everything that you say about My goodness is true; language has no adequate expression to extol My goodness.** These words were so filled with power and so clear that I would give my life in declaring they came from God. I can tell this by the profound peace that accompanied them at that time and that still remains with me. This peace gives me such great strength and power that all difficulties, adversities, sufferings, and death itself are as nothing. This light gave me a glimpse of the truth that all my efforts to bring souls to know the mercy of the Lord are very pleasing to God. And from this springs such great joy in my soul that I do not know whether it could be any greater in heaven. Oh, if souls would only be willing to listen, at least a little, to the voice of conscience and the voice— that is, the inspirations—of the Holy Spirit! I say "at least a little," because once we open ourselves to the influence of the Holy Spirit, He himself will fulfill what is lacking in us.

+New Year 1935

360 Jesus likes to intervene in the smallest details of our life, and He often fulfills secret wishes of mine that I sometimes hide from Him, although I know that from Him nothing can be hidden.

There is a custom among us of drawing by lot, on New Year's Day, special Patrons for ourselves for the whole year. In the morning during meditation, there arose within me a secret desire that the Eucharistic Jesus be my special Patron for this year also, as in the past. But, hiding this desire from my Beloved, I spoke to Him about everything else but that. When we came to refectory for breakfast, we blessed ourselves and began drawing our patrons. When I approached the holy cards on which the names of the patrons were written, without hesitation I took one, but I didn't read the name immediately **(152)** as I wanted to mortify myself for a few minutes. Suddenly, I heard a voice in my soul: **I am your patron. Read.** I looked at once at the inscription and read, "Patron for the Year 1935—the Most Blessed Eucharist." My heart leapt with joy, and I slipped quietly away from the sisters and went for a short visit before the Blessed Sacrament, where I poured out my heart. But Jesus sweetly admonished me that I should be at that moment together with the sisters. I went immediately in obedience to the rule.

Holy Trinity, One God,

361 incomprehensible in the greatness of Your mercy for creatures, and especially for poor sinners, You have made known the abyss of Your mercy, incomprehensible and unfathomable [as it is] to any mind, whether of man or angel. Our nothingness and our misery are drowned in Your greatness. O infinite goodness, who can ever praise You sufficiently? Can there be found a soul that understands You in Your love? O Jesus, there are such souls, but they are few.

362 +One day, during the morning meditation, I heard this voice: **I myself am your director; I was, I am, and I will be. And since you asked for visible help, I chose and gave you a director even before you had asked, for My work required this. Know that the faults you commit against him wound My Heart. Be especially on your guard against self-willfulness; even the smallest thing should bear the seal of obedience.**

With a crushed and humbled heart I begged forgiveness of Jesus for these faults. I also begged pardon of my spiritual director and resolved to do nothing rather than to do many things wrongly.

363 O good Jesus, thank You for the great grace of making known to me what I am of myself: misery and sin, and nothing more. I can do only one thing of myself, and that is to offend You, O my God, because misery can do no more of itself than offend You, O infinite Goodness!

364 **(153)** +Once I was asked to pray for a certain soul. I decided at once to make a novena to the Merciful Lord to which I added a mortification; namely, that I would wear chains[86] on both legs throughout Holy Mass. I had been doing this already for three days when I went to confession and told my spiritual director that I had undertaken this mortification, presuming permission to do so. I had thought he would not object, but I heard the contrary; that is, that I should do nothing without permission. O my Jesus, so it was willfulness again! But my falls do not discourage me; I know very well that I am misery [itself]. Because of the condition of my health I did not receive this permission, and my spiritual director was surprised that I had been allowing myself greater mortifications without his permission. I asked pardon for my self-willfulness, or rather for having presumed permission, and I asked him to change this mortification for another one.

365 My spiritual director replaced it with an interior mortification; namely, throughout Holy Mass I was to meditate on why the Lord Jesus had submitted to being baptized. The meditation was no mortification for me, for thinking about God is a delight and not a mortification; but there was a mortification of the will in that I was not doing [simply] what I like, but what I was told to do, and it is in this that interior mortification consists. When I left the confessional and started to recite my penance, I heard these words: **I have granted the grace you asked for on behalf of that soul, but not because of the mortification you chose for yourself. Rather, it was because of your act of complete obedience**

to My representative that I granted this grace to that soul for whom you interceded and begged mercy. Know that when you mortify your own self-will, then Mine reigns within you.

366   O my Jesus, be patient with me. I will be more careful in the future. I will rely, not upon myself, but upon Your grace and Your very great goodness to miserable me.

367   **(154)** +On one occasion, Jesus gave me to know that when I pray for intentions which people are wont to entrust to me, He is always ready to grant His graces, but souls do not always want to accept them: **My Heart overflows with great mercy for souls, and especially for poor sinners. If only they could understand that I am the best of Fathers to them and that it is for them that the Blood and Water flowed from My Heart as from a fount overflowing with mercy. For them I dwell in the tabernacle as King of Mercy. I desire to bestow My graces upon souls, but they do not want to accept them. You, at least, come to Me as often as possible and take these graces they do not want to accept. In this way you will console My Heart. Oh, how indifferent are souls to so much goodness, to so many proofs of love! My Heart drinks only of the ingratitude and forgetfulness of souls living in the world. They have time for everything, but they have no time to come to Me for graces.**

So I turn to you, you—chosen souls, will you also fail to understand the love of My Heart? Here, too, My Heart finds disappointment; I do not find complete surrender to My love. So many reservations, so much distrust, so much caution. To comfort you, let Me tell you that there are souls living in the world who love Me dearly. I dwell in their hearts with delight. But they are few. In convents too, there are souls that fill My Heart with joy. They bear My features; therefore the Heavenly Father looks upon them with special pleasure. They will be a marvel to Angels and men. Their number is very small. They are a defense for the world before the justice

of the Heavenly Father and a means of obtaining mercy for the world. The love and sacrifice of these souls sustain the world in existence. The infidelity of a soul specially chosen by Me wounds My Heart most painfully. Such infidelities are swords which pierce My Heart.

368 **(155)** January 29, 1935. This Tuesday morning during meditation, I had an interior vision of the Holy Father saying Mass. After the Pater Noster, he talked to Jesus about that matter which Jesus had ordered me to tell him. Although I have not spoken to the Holy Father personally, this matter was taken care of by someone else [Father Sopocko[87]]; at this moment, however, I knew by interior knowledge that the Holy Father was considering this matter, which will soon come to pass in accordance with the desires of Jesus.

369 Before the eight-day retreat, I went to my spiritual director and asked him for certain mortifications for the time of the retreat. However, I did not receive permission for everything I asked for, but for some things only. I received permission for one hour of meditation on the Passion of the Lord Jesus and for a certain humiliation. But I was a little dissatisfied at not receiving permission for everything I had asked. When we returned home, I dropped into the chapel for a moment, and then I heard this voice in my soul: **There is more merit to one hour of meditation on My sorrowful Passion than there is to a whole year of flagellation that draws blood; the contemplation of My painful wounds is of great profit to you, and it brings Me great joy. I am surprised that you still have not completely renounced your self-will, but I rejoice exceedingly that this change will be accomplished during the retreat.**

370 That same day, when I was in church waiting for confession, I saw the same rays issuing from the monstrance and spreading throughout the church. This lasted all through the service. After the Benediction,

[the rays shone out] to both sides and returned again to the monstrance. Their appearance was bright and transparent like crystal. I asked Jesus that He deign to light the fire of His love in all souls that were cold. Beneath these rays a heart will grow warm even if it were like a block of ice; even if it were hard as a rock, it will crumble into dust.

+

(156) J.M.J.   Vilnius, February 4, 1935

Eight-day retreat.

371   Jesus, King of Mercy, again the time has come when I am alone with You. Therefore I beg You, by all the love with which Your Heart burns, to destroy completely within me my self-love and, on the other hand, to enkindle in my heart the fire of Your purest love.

372   In the evening, after the conference, I heard these words: **I am with you. During this retreat, I will strengthen you in peace and in courage so that your strength will not fail in carrying out My designs. Therefore you will cancel out your will absolutely in this retreat and, instead, My complete will shall be accomplished in you. Know that it will cost you much, so write these words on a clean sheet of paper: "From today on, my own will does not exist," and then cross out the page. And on the other side write these words: "From today on, I do the will of God everywhere, always, and in everything." Be afraid of nothing; love will give you strength and make the realization of this easy.**

373   In the fundamental meditation about the goal; that is, of choosing love: the soul must love; it has need of loving. The soul must divert the stream of its love, but not into the mud or into a vacuum, but into God. How I rejoice when I reflect on this, for I feel clearly that He himself is in my heart. Just Jesus alone! I love creatures insofar as they help me to become united with God. I love all people because I see the image of God in them.

374 **(157)** J.M.J.   Vilnius, February 4, 1935

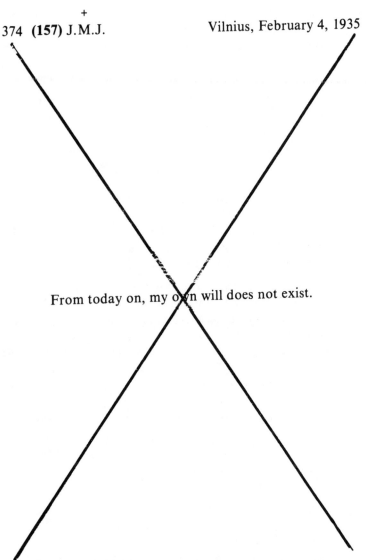

From today on, my own will does not exist.

The moment I knelt down to cross out my own will, as the Lord had bid me to do, I heard this voice in my soul: **From today on, do not fear God's judgment, for you will not be judged.**

+
(158) J.M.J.   Vilnius, February 4, 1935

From today on, I do the Will of God

everywhere, always, and in everything.[88]

+

(159) J.M.J.   Vilnius, February 8, 1935

375 Particular interior practice; that is, the examination of
conscience. Self-denial, denial of my own will.

I. The denial of my reason. Subjecting it to the reason
of those who represent God to me here on earth.

II. The denial of my will. Doing the will of God, which
is revealed in the will of those who represent God
to me and which is contained in the rule of our
order.

III. The denial of my judgment. Accepting immediately
and without reflection, analysis or reasoning all
orders given by those who represent God to me.

IV. The denial of my tongue. I will not give it the least
bit of freedom; but in one case only I will give it
complete freedom; that is, in proclaiming the glory
of God. Whenever I receive Holy Communion, I
will ask Jesus to fortify and cleanse my tongue that
I may not injure my neighbor with it. That is why I
have the greatest respect for the rule which speaks
about silence.

376 My Jesus, I trust that Your grace will help me to carry
out these resolutions. Although the above points are
contained in the vow of obedience, I want to practice
these things in a special way, because this is the essence
of the religious life. Merciful Jesus, I beg You fervently
to enlighten my mind so that I may come to know You
better, You who are the Infinite Being, and that I may
get to know myself better, who am nothingness itself.

377 **(160)** Concerning Holy Confession. We should derive
two kinds of profit from Holy Confession:

1. We come to confession to be healed;

2. We come to be educated—like a small child, our
soul has constant need of education.

O my Jesus, I understand these words to their very

depths, and I know from my own experience that, on its own strength, the soul will not go far; it will exert itself greatly and will do nothing for the glory of God; it will err continually, because our mind is darkened and does not know how to discern its own affairs. I shall pay special attention to two things: firstly, I will choose, in making my confession, that which humiliates me most, even if it be a trifle, but something that costs me much, and for that reason I will tell it; secondly, I will practice contrition, not only during confession, but during every self-examination, and I will arouse within myself an act of perfect contrition, especially when I am going to bed. One more word: a soul which sincerely wants to advance in perfection must observe strictly the advice given by the spiritual director. There is as much holiness as there is dependence.

378   Once as I was talking with my spiritual director, I had an interior vision—quicker than lightning—of his soul in great suffering, in such agony that God touches very few souls with such fire. The suffering arises from this work. There will come a time when this work, which God is demanding so very much, will be as though utterly undone. And then God will act with great power, which will give evidence of its authenticity. It will be a new splendor for the Church, although it has been dormant in it from long ago. That God is infinitely merciful, no one can deny. He desires everyone to know this before He comes again as Judge. He wants souls to come to know Him first as King of Mercy. When this triumph comes, we shall already have entered the new life in which there is no suffering. But before this, your soul [of the spiritual director] will be surfeited with bitterness at the sight of the destruction of your efforts. However, this will only appear to be so, because what God has once decided upon, He does not change. But although this destruction **(161)** will be such only in outward appearance, the suffering will be real. When will this

happen? I do not know. How long will it last? I do not know.[89] But God has promised a great grace especially to you and to all those... **who will proclaim My great mercy. I shall protect them Myself at the hour of death, as My own glory. And even if the sins of soul are as dark as night, when the sinner turns to My mercy he gives Me the greatest praise and is the glory of My Passion. When a soul praises My goodness, Satan trembles before it and flees to the very bottom of hell.**

379 During one of the adorations, Jesus promised me that: **With souls that have recourse to My mercy and with those that glorify and proclaim My great mercy to others, I will deal according to My infinite mercy at the hour of their death.**

My Heart is sorrowful, Jesus said, **because even chosen souls do not understand the greatness of My mercy. Their relationship [with Me] is, in certain ways, imbued with mistrust. Oh, how much that wounds My Heart! Remember My Passion, and if you do not believe My words, at least believe My wounds.**

380 I make no movement, no gesture after my own liking, because I am bound by grace; I always consider what is more pleasing to Jesus.

381 When meditating once on obedience, I heard these words: **In this meditation, the priest[90] is speaking particularly for you. Know that I am borrowing his lips.** I tried to listen most attentively to everything and to apply everything to my own heart, as in every meditation. When the priest said that an obedient soul was filled with the power of God... **Yes, when you are obedient I take away your weakness and replace it with My strength. I am very surprised that souls do not want to make that exchange with Me.** I said to the Lord, "Jesus, enlighten my heart, or else I, too, will not understand much from these words."

382 **(162)** I know that I live, not for myself, but for a great

number of souls. I know that graces granted me are not for me alone, but for souls. O Jesus, the abyss of Your mercy has been poured into my soul, which is an abyss of misery itself. Thank You, Jesus, for the graces and the pieces of the Cross which You give me at each moment of my life.

383 At the beginning of the retreat, I saw, on the ceiling of the chapel, Jesus nailed to the Cross. He was looking at the sisters with great love, but not at all of them. There were three sisters at whom Jesus looked severely, for what reasons I do not know. I only know what a terrible thing it is to meet with such a look, which is the look of a severe Judge. That look was not directed at me, and yet I was paralyzed with terror. I still tremble as I write these words. I did not dare to say so much as a single word to Jesus. My physical strength failed me, and I thought I would not live to the end of the conference. The next day, I saw the same thing again, just as I had seen it the first time, and this time I dared to speak these words: "Jesus, how great is Your mercy!"

On the third day, that gaze of great kindness upon all the sisters, except the three, was again repeated. I gathered up my courage, which drew its force from love of neighbor, and I said to the Lord, "You, who are Mercy Itself, as You yourself told me, I beg You by the power of Your mercy, to look then with kindness at these three sisters as well. And if this is not in accord with Your wisdom, I ask You for an exchange: turn to them the kind look meant for my soul, and let Your severe gaze at their souls be turned on me." Jesus then said to me these words: **My daughter, for the sake of your sincere and generous love, I grant them many graces although they are not asking Me for them. But I am doing so because of the promise I have made to you.** And at that moment, He turned a merciful look towards those three sisters as well. My heart leapt with joy to see the goodness of God.

384 **(163)** When I stayed for adoration from nine to ten o'clock, four other sisters stayed, too. When I approached the altar and began to meditate on the Passion of the Lord Jesus, a terrible pain immediately filled my soul because of the ingratitude of so many souls living in the world; but particularly painful was the ingratitude of souls especially chosen by God. There is no notion or comparison [which can describe it]. At the sight of this blackest ungratefulness I felt as though my heart were torn open; my strength failed me completely, and I fell on my face, not attempting to hide my loud cries. Each time I thought of God's great mercy and of the ingratitude of souls, pain stabbed at my heart, and I understood how painfully it wounded the sweetest Heart of Jesus. With a burning heart, I renewed my act of self-oblation on behalf of sinners.

385 With joy and longing I have pressed my lips to the bitterness of the cup which I receive each day at Holy Mass. It is the share which Jesus has allotted to me for each moment, and I will not relinquish it to anyone. I will comfort the most sweet Eucharistic Heart continuously and will play harmonious melodies on the strings of my heart. Suffering is the most harmonious melody of all. I will assiduously search out that which will make Your Heart rejoice today!

The days of my life are not monotonous. When dark clouds cover the sun, like the eagle I will try to brave the billows and make known to others that the sun is not dying out.

386 I feel that God will let me draw aside the veils [of heaven] so that the earth will not doubt His goodness. God is not subject to eclipse or change. He is forever one and the same; nothing can contradict His will. I feel within myself a power greater than human. I feel courage and strength thanks to the grace that dwells in me. I understand souls who are suffering against hope, for I have gone through that fire myself. But God will not

give [us anything] beyond our strength. Often have I lived hoping against hope, and have advanced my hope to complete trust in God. Let that which He has ordained from all ages happen to me.

(164) A general principle.

387 It would be a very ugly thing for a religious to seek relief from suffering.

388 See what grace and reflection made out of the greatest criminal. He who is dying has much love: "Remember me when You are in paradise." Heartfelt repentance immediately transforms the soul. The spiritual life is to be lived earnestly and sincerely.

389 Love must be reciprocal. If Jesus tasted the fullness of bitterness for me, then I, His bride, will accept all bitterness as proof of my love for Him.

390 He who knows how to forgive prepares for himself many graces from God. As often as I look upon the cross, so often will I forgive with all my heart.

391 Through Holy Baptism, we entered into union with other souls. Death tightens the bonds of love. I ought always to be of help to others. If I am a good religious, I will be useful, not only to the Order, but to the whole Country as well.

392 The Lord God grants His graces in two ways: by inspiration and by enlightenment. If we ask God for a grace, He will give it to us; but let us be willing to accept it. And in order to accept it, self-denial is needed. Love does not consist in words or feelings, but in deeds. It is an act of the will; it is a gift; that is to say, a giving. The reason, the will, the heart—these three faculties must be exercised during prayer. I will rise from the dead in Jesus, but first I must live in Him. If I do not separate myself from the Cross, then the Gospel will be revealed in me. Jesus in me makes up for all my deficiencies. His grace operates without ceasing. The Holy Trinity grants

me Its life abundantly, by the gift of the Holy Spirit. The Three Divine Persons live in me. When God loves, He loves with all His Being, with all the power of His Being. If God has loved me in this way, how should I respond— I, His spouse?

393 **(165)** During one conference, Jesus said to me, **You are a sweet grape in a chosen cluster; I want others to have a share in the juice that is flowing within you.**

394 During the renewal of the vows,[91] I saw the Lord Jesus on the Epistle side [of the altar], wearing a white garment with a golden belt and holding a terrible sword in His hand. This lasted until the moment when the sisters began to renew their vows. Then I saw a resplendence beyond compare and, in front of this brilliance, a white cloud in the shape of a scale. Then Jesus approached and put the sword on one side of the scale, and it fell heavily towards the ground until it was about to touch it. Just then, the sisters finished renewing their vows. Then I saw Angels who took something from each of the sisters and placed it in a golden vessel somewhat in the shape of a thurible. When they had collected it from all the sisters ánd placed the vessel on the other side of the scale, it immediately outweighed and raised up the side on which the sword had been laid. At that moment, a flame issued forth from the thurible, and it reached all the way to the brilliance. Then I heard a voice coming from the brilliance: **Put the sword back in its place; the sacrifice is greater.** Then Jesus gave us His blessing, and all I had seen vanished. The sisters had already begun to receive Holy Communion. When I received Holy Communion, my soul was filled with such great joy that I am unable to describe it.

395 [February] 15, 1935. A few days' visit at my parents' home[92] to see my dying mother.

When I learned that my mother was seriously ill and near death, and that she had asked that I come home, as she wanted to see me once more before dying, a host of emotions were awakened in my heart. As a child who sincerely loves its mother, I wanted very much to fulfill her wish. But I left this to God and resigned myself completely to His will. Paying no heed to the ache in my heart, I followed God's will. On the morning of my name day, February fifteen, **(166)** Mother Superior gave me a second letter from my family and granted me permission to go to my parents' home to fulfill the wish and request of my dying mother. I began at once to make the necessary preparations for the journey and left Vilnius in the evening. I offered the whole night for my seriously ill mother, that God might grant her the grace of losing none of the merits of her suffering.

396 My traveling companions were very kind; several women of the Sodality of Mary were in the same compartment with me. I sensed that one of them was suffering greatly and fighting a difficult battle in her soul. I began to pray in spirit for this soul. At eleven o'clock these women went to another compartment for a chat, leaving only the two of us behind in the carriage. I could feel that my prayer was causing this soul's struggle to become even fiercer. I did not console her, but prayed all the more fervently. Finally, the lady turned to me and asked if she was obliged to fulfill a certain promise which she had made to God. At that moment, I received inner knowledge of the promise and replied, "You are absolutely obliged to keep it, or else you will be miserable for the rest of your life. This thought will pursue you everywhere and give you no peace." Surprised at my answer, she opened her soul to me.

She was a schoolteacher. When she was about to take her examinations, she had promised God that if she did well in her examinations she would devote herself to His service; that is, enter a religious congregation. She passed the examinations very well. "But," she said, "when I entered into the hustle and bustle of the world, I no longer wanted to enter a convent. However, my conscience has given me no peace, and despite amusements I am always unhappy."

After a lengthy conversation, she was completely changed and told me that she would immediately take steps to enter a convent. She asked me to pray for her, and I felt that God would be generous with His grace.

397 That morning I arrived in Warsaw, and at eight o'clock that evening I was already at home. What a joy it was for my parents and for the whole family! It is difficult to describe it. (167) My mother's health had improved a bit, but the doctor gave no hope of complete recovery. After greeting each other, we knelt down to thank God for the grace of being able to be together once again in this life.

398 When I saw how my father prayed, I was very much ashamed that, after so many years in the convent, I was not able to pray with such sincerity and fervor. And so I never cease thanking God for such parents.

399 Oh, how everything had changed beyond recognition during those ten years! The garden had been so small, and now I could not recognize it. My brothers and sisters had still been children, and now they were all grown up. I was surprised that I did not find them as they had been when we parted. Stanley accompanied me to church every day. I felt that he was very pleasing to God.

400 On the last day, when everyone had left the church, I went before the Blessed Sacrament with him, and together we recited the *Te Deum*. After a moment of silence, I offered his soul to the Sweetest Heart of Jesus. How easy it was to pray in that little church! I remembered all the graces that I had received there, and which I had not understood at the time and had so often abused. I wondered how I could have been so blind. And as I was thus regretting my blindness, I suddenly

saw the Lord Jesus, radiant with unspeakable beauty, and He said to me with kindness, **My chosen one, I will give you even greater graces that you may be the witness of My infinite mercy throughout all eternity.**

401 The days at home passed in much company, as everybody wanted to see me and talk with me. Often I could count as many as twenty-five people there. They listened with great interest to my accounts of the lives of the saints. It seemed to me that our house was truly the house of God, as each evening we talked about nothing but God. When, tired from these talks and yearning for solitude and silence, I quietly slipped out into the garden in the evening so I could converse with God alone, even in this I was unsuccessful; immediately my brothers and sisters came and took me into the house and, once again, I had to talk, with all those eyes fixed on me. **(168)** But I struck on one way of getting some respite; I asked my brothers to sing for me. inasmuch as they had lovely voices; and besides, one played the violin and another, the mandolin. And during this time I was able to devote myself to interior prayer without shunning their company.

What also cost me a lot was that I had to kiss the children. The women I knew came with their children and asked me to take them in my arms, at least for a moment, and kiss them. They regarded this as a great favor, and for me it was a chance to practice virtue, since many of the children were quite dirty. But in order to overcome my feelings and show no repugnance, I would kiss such a dirty child twice. One of these friends came with a child whose eyes were diseased and filled with pus, and she said to me, "Sister, take it in your arms for a moment, please." My nature recoiled, but not paying attention to anything, I took the child and kissed it twice, right on the infection, asking God to heal it.

I had many opportunities to practice virtue. I listened to people pour out their grievances, and I saw that no heart was joyful, because no heart truly loved God; and this did not surprise me at all. I was very sorry not to have seen two of my sisters. I felt interiorly that their souls were in great danger. Pain gripped my heart at the thought of them. Once, when I felt very close to God, I fervently asked the Lord to grant them grace, and the Lord answered me, **I am granting them not only necessary graces, but special graces as well.** I understood that the Lord would call them to a greater union with Him. I rejoice immensely that such great love reigns in our family.

402 As I was taking leave of my parents and asking for their blessing, I felt the power of the grace of God being poured out upon my soul. My father, my mother and my godmother blessed me with tears in their eyes, wished me the greatest faithfulness to God's graces, and begged me never to forget how many graces God had granted me in calling me to the religious life. They asked me to pray for them. **(169)** Although everyone was crying, I did not shed a single tear; I tried to be brave and comforted them as best I could, reminding them of heaven where there would be no more parting. Stanley walked me to the car. I told him how much God loves pure souls and assured him God was satisfied with him. When I was telling him about the goodness of God and of how He thinks of us, he burst out crying like a little child, and I was not surprised, for this was a pure soul and, as such, more capable of recognizing God.

403 Once I was in the car, I let my heart have its way, and I, too, cried like a baby, for joy that God was granting our family so many graces, and I became steeped in a prayer of thanksgiving.

By evening I was already in Warsaw. Firstly, I greeted the Lord of the house [Jesus in the Eucharist], and then I went to greet the whole community.

404 When I entered the chapel to say goodnight to the Lord before retiring, and apologized for having talked so

little to Him when I was at home, I heard a voice within my soul, **I am very pleased that you had not been talking with Me, but were making My goodness known to souls and rousing them to love Me.**

405 Mother Superior [Mary Joseph] said to me, "We are both going to Jozefinek tomorrow, Sister, and you will have a chance to talk with Mother General [Michael]." I was delighted. Mother General was ever the same, full of goodness, peace and the Spirit of God. I had a long talk with her. We attended the afternoon service. The Litany of the Sacred Heart of Jesus was sung. The Lord Jesus was exposed in the monstrance.

406 After a short while, I saw the little Jesus, who came out from the Host and rested in my hands. This lasted for a moment; immense joy flooded my soul. The Child Jesus had the same appearance as He had the time we entered the Chapel with Mother Superior—my former Directress, Mary Joseph. The next day I was already back in my beloved Vilnius.

407 Oh, how happy I felt to be back in our convent! I felt as though I was entering the convent for the second time. I took unending delight in the silence and peace in which the soul can so easily immerse itself in God, helped by everyone and disturbed by no one.

(170) The Great Lent

408 When I become immersed in the Lord's Passion, I often see the Lord Jesus, during adoration, in this manner: after the scourging, the torturers took the Lord and stripped Him of His own garment, which had already adhered to the wounds; as they took it off, His wounds reopened; then they threw a dirty and tattered scarlet cloak over the fresh wounds of the Lord. The cloak, in some places, barely reached His knees. They made Him sit on a piece of beam. And then they wove a crown of thorns, which they put on His sacred head. They put a reed in His hand and made fun of Him, bowing to Him

as to a king. Some spat in His face, while others took the reed and struck Him on the head with it. Others caused him pain by slapping Him; still others covered His face and struck Him with their fists. Jesus bore all this with meekness. Who can comprehend Him—comprehend His suffering? Jesus' eyes were downcast. I sensed what was happening in the most sweet Heart of Jesus at that time. Let every soul reflect on what Jesus was suffering at that moment. They tried to outdo each other in insulting the Lord. I reflected: Where does such malice in man come from? It is caused by sin. Love and sin have met.

409   When I was attending Mass in a certain church with another sister, I felt the greatness and majesty of God; I felt the church was permeated by God. His majesty enveloped me and, though it terrified me, it filled me with peace and joy. I knew that nothing could oppose His will. Oh, if only all souls knew who is living in our churches, there would not be so many outrages and so much disrespect in these holy places!

410   O eternal and incomprehensible Love, I beg You for one grace: enlighten my mind with light from on high; help me to know and appreciate all things according to their value. I feel the greatest joy in my soul when I come to know the truth.

411   **(171)** March 21, 1935. Often during Mass, I see the Lord in my soul; I feel His presence which pervades my being. I sense His divine gaze; I have long talks with Him without saying a word; I know what His divine Heart desires, and I always do what will please Him the most. I love Him to distraction, and I feel that I am being loved by God. At those times when I meet with God deep within myself, I feel so happy that I do not know how to express it. Such moments are short, for the soul could not bear it for long, as separation from the body would be inevitable. Though these moments are very short,

their power, however, which is transmitted to the soul, remains with it for a very long time. Without the least effort, I experience the profound recollection which then envelops me—and it does not diminish even if I talk with people, nor does it interfere with the performance of my duties. I feel the constant presence of God without any effort of my soul. I know that I am united with Him as closely as a drop of water is united with the bottomless ocean.

Last Thursday, toward the end of my prayers, I felt this grace, and it lasted for an unusually long time, for it was throughout Mass, so that I thought I would die of joy. At such times, my knowledge of God and His attributes becomes more acute, and also I know my own self and my misery much better. I am amazed at the Lord's great condescension to such a miserable soul as mine. After Holy Mass, I felt completely immersed in God and am still conscious of His every glance into the depth of my heart. About midday I entered the chapel for a moment, and again the power of grace struck my heart. As I continued in a state of recollection, Satan took a flowerpot and angrily hurled it to the ground with all his might. I saw all his rage and his jealousy.

412   There was no one in the chapel, so I got up, picked up the pieces of the flowerpot, repotted the flower and tried to do all this before anyone came in. But I did not manage to do so, as Mother Superior [Borgia] came in at that moment together with the sister sacristan[93] and several other sisters. Mother Superior was surprised that I had been touching something on the altar and **(172)** thus caused the flowerpot to fall. Sister sacristan showed her displeasure, and I did my best not to explain or excuse myself. But towards evening I felt very exhausted and could not make my Holy Hour, so I asked Mother Superior to allow me to go to bed early. I fell asleep as soon as I lay down, but at about eleven o'clock Satan shook my bed. I awoke instantly, and I started to pray

peacefully to my Guardian Angel. Then I saw the souls who were doing penance in purgatory. They appeared like shadows, and among them I saw many demons. One of these tried to vex me; taking the form of a cat, he kept throwing himself onto my bed and on my feet, and he was quite heavy, as if [weighing] a ton.

I kept praying the rosary all the while, and toward dawn these beings vanished, and I was able to get some sleep. When I entered the chapel in the morning I heard a voice in my soul, **You are united to Me; fear nothing. But know, my child, that Satan hates you; he hates every soul, but he burns with a particular hatred for you, because you have snatched so many souls from his dominion.**

Holy Thursday, April 18.

413 This morning I heard these words: **From today until the** [celebration of the] **Resurrection, you will not feel My presence, but your soul will be filled with great longing.** And immediately a great longing filled my soul; I felt a separation from my beloved Jesus, and when the moment for Holy Communion came, I saw the suffering Face of Jesus in every Host [contained] in the chalice. From that moment, I felt a more intense yearning in my heart.

414 On Good Friday, at three o'clock in the afternoon, when I entered the chapel, I heard these words: **I desire that the image be publicly (173) honored.** Then I saw the Lord Jesus dying on the Cross amidst great suffering, and out of the Heart of Jesus came the same two rays as are in the image.

415 Saturday. During Vespers I saw the Lord Jesus radiant as the sun, in a bright garment, and He said to me, **May your heart be joyful.** And great joy flooded me, and I was penetrated with God's presence, which for the soul is a treasure beyond words.

416 When the image was displayed,[94] I saw a sudden movement of the hand of Jesus, as He made a large sign of the cross. In the evening of the same day, when I had gone to bed, I saw the image going over the town, and the town was covered with what appeared to be a mesh and nets. As Jesus passed, He cut through all the nets and finally made a large sign of the cross and disappeared. I saw myself surrounded by a multitude of malicious figures burning with hatred for me. Various threats came from their lips, but none of them touched me. After a moment, this apparition vanished, but for a long time I could not get to sleep.

417 [April] 26. On Friday, when I was at Ostra Brama to attend the ceremony during which the image was displayed, I heard a sermon given by my confessor [Father Sopocko]. This sermon about Divine Mercy was the first of the things that Jesus had asked for so very long ago. When he began to speak about the great mercy of the Lord, the image came alive and the rays pierced the hearts of the people gathered there, but not all to the same degree. Some received more, some less. Great joy filled my soul to see the grace of God.

(174) Then I heard the words, **You are a witness of My mercy. You shall stand before My throne forever as a living witness to My mercy.**

418 When the sermon was over, I did not wait for the end of the service, as I was in a hurry to get back home. When I had taken a few steps, a great multitude of demons blocked my way. They threatened me with terrible tortures, and voices could be heard: "She has snatched away everything we have worked for over so many years!" When I asked them, "Where have you come from in such great numbers?" the wicked forms answered, "Out of human hearts; stop tormenting us!"

419 Seeing their great hatred for me, I immediately asked my Guardian Angel for help, and at once the bright and

radiant figure of my Guardian Angel appeared and said to me, "Do not fear, spouse of my Lord; without His permission these spirits will do you no harm." Immediately the evil spirits vanished, and the faithful Guardian Angel accompanied me, in a visible manner, right to the very house. His look was modest and peaceful, and a flame of fire sparkled from his forehead.

O Jesus, I would like to toil and wear myself out and suffer all my life for that one moment in which I saw Your glory, O Lord, and profit for souls.

Sunday, [April] 28, 1935.

420 Low Sunday; that is, the Feast of The Divine Mercy, the conclusion of the Jubilee of Redemption. When we went to take part in the celebrations, my heart leapt with joy that the two solemnities were so closely united. I asked God for mercy on the souls of sinners. Toward the end of the service, when the priest took the Blessed Sacrament to bless the people, I saw the Lord Jesus as He is represented in the image. The Lord gave His blessing, and the rays extended over the whole world. Suddenly, I saw an impenetrable brightness in the form of a crystal dwelling place, woven together from waves of a brilliance unapproachable **(175)** to both creatures and spirits. Three doors led to this resplendence. At that moment, Jesus, as He is represented in the image, entered this resplendence through the second door to the Unity within. It is a triple Unity, which is incomprehensible—which is infinity. I heard a voice, **This Feast emerged from the very depths of My mercy, and it is confirmed in the vast depths of My tender mercies. Every soul believing and trusting in My mercy will obtain it.** I was overjoyed at the immense goodness and greatness of my God.

April 29, 1935.

421 On the eve of the exposition of the image, I went with our Mother Superior to visit our confessor [Father Sopocko]. When the conversation touched upon the image, the confessor asked for one of the sisters to help make some wreaths. Mother Superior replied, "Sister Faustina will help." I was delighted at this, and when we returned home, I immediately set about preparing some greens, and with the help of one of our wards brought them over. Another person, who works at the church, also helped. Everything was ready by seven o'clock that evening, and the image was already hanging in its place. However, some ladies saw me standing around there, for I was more a bother than a help, and on the next day they asked the sisters what this beautiful image was and what was its significance. Surely these sisters would know, [they thought] as one of them had helped adorn it the day before. The sisters were very surprised as they knew nothing about it; they all wanted to see it and immediately they began to suspect me. They said, "Sister Faustina must certainly know all about it."

When they began asking me, I was silent, since I could not tell the truth. My silence increased their curiosity, and I was even more on my guard not to tell a lie and not to tell the truth, since I had no permission [to do so]. Then they started to show their displeasure and reproached me openly saying, "How is it that **(176)** outsiders know about this and we, nothing?" Various judgments were being made about me. I suffered much for three days, but a special power took over in my soul. I was happy to suffer for God and for the souls that have been granted His mercy during these days. Seeing that so many souls have been granted divine mercy these days, I regard as nothing even the greatest suffering and toil, even if they were to continue till the end of the world; for they will come to an end, while these souls have been saved from torments that are without end. It was a great joy for me to see others returning to the source of happiness, the bosom of The Divine Mercy.

422 Seeing Father Sopocko's sacrifice and efforts for this work, I admired his patience and humility. This all cost a great deal, not only in terms of toil and various troubles, but also of money; and Father Sopocko was taking care of all the expenses. I can see that Divine Providence had prepared him to carry out this work of mercy before I had asked God for this. Oh, how strange are Your ways, O God! And how happy are the souls that follow the call of divine grace!

423 Praise the Lord, my soul, for everything, and glorify His mercy, for His goodness is without end. Everything will pass, but His mercy is without limit or end. And although evil will attain its measure, in mercy there is no measure.

O my God, even in the punishments You send down upon the earth I see the abyss of Your mercy, for by punishing us here on earth You free us from eternal punishment. Rejoice, all you creatures, for you are closer to God in His infinite mercy than a baby to its mother's heart. O God, You are compassion itself for the greatest sinners who sincerely repent. The greater the sinner, the greater his right to God's **(177)** mercy.

A Certain Moment, May 12, 1935

424 In the evening, I just about got into bed, and I fell asleep immediately. Though I fell asleep quickly, I was awakened even more quickly. A little child came and woke me up. The child seemed about a year old, and I was surprised it could speak so well, as children of that age either do not speak or speak very indistinctly The child was beautiful beyond words and resembled the Child Jesus, and he said to me, **Look at the sky.** And when I looked at the sky I saw the stars and the moon shining. Then the child asked me, **Do you see this moon and these stars?** When I said yes, he spoke these words to

me, **These stars are the souls of faithful Christians, and the moon is the souls of religious. Do you see how great the difference is between the light of the moon and the light of the stars? Such is the difference in heaven between the soul of a religious and the soul of a faithful Christian.** And he went on to say that, **True greatness is in loving God and in humility.**

425 Then I saw a soul which was being separated from its body amid great torment. O Jesus, as I am about to write this, I tremble at the sight of the horrible things that bear witness against him.... I saw the souls of little children and those of older ones, about nine years of age, emerging from some kind of a muddy abyss. The souls were foul and disgusting, resembling the most terrible monsters and decaying corpses. But the corpses were living and gave loud testimony against the dying soul. And the soul I saw dying was a soul full of the world's applause and honors, the end of which are emptiness and sin. Finally a woman came out who was holding something like tears in her apron, and she witnessed very strongly against him.

426 O terrible hour, **(178)** at which one is obliged to see all one's deeds in their nakedness and misery; not one of them is lost, they will all accompany us to God's judgment. I can find no words or comparisons to express such terrible things. And although it seems to me that this soul is not damned, nevertheless its torments are in no way different from the torments of hell; there is only this difference: that they will someday come to an end.

427 A moment later, I again saw the child who had awakened me. It was of wondrous beauty and repeated these words to me, **True greatness of the soul is in loving God and in humility.** I asked the child, "How do you know that true greatness of the soul is in loving God and in humility? Only theologians know about such things and you haven't even learned the catechism. So how do

you know?" To this he answered, **I know; I know all things.** And with that, He disappeared.

428 But I could no longer get to sleep; my mind became exhausted by thinking about the things I had seen. O human souls, how late you learn the truth! O abyss of God's mercy, pour yourself out as quickly as possible over the whole world, according to what You yourself have said.

May, 1935. A Certain Moment.

429 When I became aware of God's great plans for me, I was frightened at their greatness and felt myself quite incapable of fulfilling them, and I began to avoid interior conversations with Him, filling up the time with vocal prayer. I did this out of humility, but I soon recognized it was not true humility, but rather a great temptation from the devil. When, on one occasion, instead of interior prayer, I took up a book of spiritual reading, I heard these words spoken distinctly and forcefully within my soul, **You will prepare the world for My final coming.** These words moved me deeply, and although I pretended **(179)** not to hear them, I understood them very well and had no doubt about them. Once, being tired out from this battle of love with God, and making constant excuses on the grounds that I was unable to carry out this task, I wanted to leave the chapel, but some force held me back and I found myself powerless. Then I heard these words, **You intend to leave the chapel, but you shall not get away from Me, for I am everywhere. You cannot do anything of yourself, but with me you can do all things.**

430 When, in the the course of the week, I went to see my confessor [Father Sopocko], and revealed the condition of my soul to him, especially the fact that I was avoiding interior conversation with God, I was told that I must not shrink from interior conversation with God, but should listen intently to the words He speaks to me.

431 I followed my confessor's advice, and at the first meeting with the Lord, I fell at Jesus' feet and, with a grief-stricken heart, apologized for everything. Then Jesus lifted me up from the ground and sat me beside Him and let me put my head on His breast, so that I could better understand and feel the desires of His most sweet Heart. Then He spoke these words to me, **My daughter, have fear of nothing; I am always with you. All your adversaries will harm you only to the degree that I permit them to do so. You are my dwelling place and my constant repose. For your sake I will withhold the hand which punishes; for your sake I bless the earth.**

432 At that very moment, I felt some kind of fire in my heart. I feel my senses deadening and have no idea of what is going on around me. I feel the Lord's gaze piercing me through and through. I am very much aware of His greatness and my misery. An extraordinary suffering pervades my soul, together with a joy I cannot compare to anything. I feel powerless in the embrace of God. I feel that I am in Him and that I am dissolved in Him like a drop of water in the ocean. I cannot express what takes place within me; after such interior prayer, I feel strength and power to practice the most difficult virtues. I feel dislike for all things that the world holds in esteem. With all my soul I desire silence and solitude.

433 **(180)** May, 1935. During Forty Hours' Devotion I saw the face of the Lord Jesus in the Sacred Host which was exposed in the monstrance. Jesus was looking with kindness at everyone.

434 I often see the Child Jesus during Holy Mass. He is extremely beautiful. He appears to be about one year old. Once, when I saw the same Child during Mass in our chapel, I was seized with a violent desire and an irresistible longing to approach the altar and take the Child Jesus. At that moment, the Child Jesus was standing by me on the side of my kneeler, and He leaned with His two little hands against my shoulder, gracious

and joyful, His look deep and penetrating. But when the priest broke the Host, Jesus was once again on the altar, and was broken and consumed by the priest.

After Holy Communion, I saw Jesus in the same way in my heart and felt Him physically in my heart throughout the day. Unconsciously, a most profound recollection took possession of me, and I did not exchange a word with anyone. I avoided people as much as I could, always answering questions regarding my duties, but beyond that, not a word.

June 9, 1935. Pentecost.

435   As I was walking in the garden in the evening, I heard these words: **By your entreaties, you and your companions shall obtain mercy for yourselves and for the world.** I understood that I would not remain in the Congregation in which I am at the present time.[95] I saw clearly that God's will regarding me was otherwise. But I kept making excuses before God, telling Him that I was unable to carry out this task. "Jesus, You know very well what I am" [I said], and I started enumerating my weaknesses to the Lord, hiding behind them so that He would agree that I was unable to carry out **(181)** His plans. Then I heard these words: **Do not fear; I myself will make up for everything that is lacking in you.** But these words penetrated me to my depths and made me even more aware of my misery, and I understood that the word of the Lord is living and that it penetrates to the very depths. I understood that God demands a more perfect way of life of me. However, I kept using my incompetence as an excuse.

436   June 29, 1935. When I talked to my spiritual director [Father Sopocko] about various things that the Lord was asking of me, I thought he would tell me that I was incapable of accomplishing all those things, and that the Lord Jesus did not use miserable souls like me for the works He wanted done. But I heard words [to the effect]

that it was just such souls that God chooses most frequently to carry out His plans. This priest is surely guided by the Spirit of God; he has penetrated the secrets of my soul, the deepest secrets which were between me and God, about which I had not yet spoken to him, because I had not understood them myself, and the Lord had not clearly ordered me to tell him. The secret is this: God demands that there be a Congregation which will proclaim the mercy of God to the world and, by its prayers, obtain it for the world. When the priest asked me if I had not had any such inspirations, I replied that I had not had any clear orders; but at that instant a light penetrated my soul, and I understood that the Lord was speaking through him.

437 In vain had I defended myself by saying I had not received any clear orders, for at the end of our conversation I saw the Lord Jesus on the threshold, as He is represented in the image, and He said to me, **I desire that there be such a Congregation.**[96] This lasted only a moment. **(182)** Yet I did not tell him about it right away, as I was in a hurry to get back home, and I kept repeating to the Lord, "I am unable to carry out Your plans, O Lord!" But, strangely enough, Jesus paid no attention to my appeals, but gave me to see and understand how pleasing this work was to Him. He took no account of my weakness, but gave me to know how many difficulties I must overcome. And I, His poor creature, could say nothing but "I am incapable of it, O my God!"

438 June 30, 1935. At the very beginning of Holy Mass on the following day, I saw Jesus in all His unspeakable beauty. He said to me that He desired that **such a Congregation be founded as soon as possible, and you shall live in it together with your companions. My Spirit shall be the rule of your life. Your life is to be modeled on Mine, from the crib to My death on the Cross. Penetrate My mysteries, and you will know the abyss of**

My mercy towards creatures and My unfathomable goodness—and this you shall make known to the world. Through your prayers, you shall mediate between heaven and earth.

439 Then came the moment to receive Holy Communion, and Jesus disappeared, and I saw a great brightness. Then I heard these words: **We give Our blessing,** and at that moment a bright ray issued from that light and pierced my heart; an extraordinary fire was enkindled in my soul—I thought I would die of joy and happiness. I felt the separation of my spirit from my body. I felt totally immersed in God, I felt I was snatched up by the Almighty, like a particle of dust, into unknown expanses.

Trembling with joy in the embrace of the Creator, I felt He himself was supporting me so that I could bear this great happiness and gaze at His Majesty. I know now that, if He himself had not **(183)** first strengthened me by His grace, my soul would not have been able to bear the happiness, and I would have died in an instant. Holy Mass came to an end I know not when, for it was beyond my power to pay attention to what was going on in the chapel. But when I recovered my senses, I felt the strength and courage to do God's will; nothing seemed difficult to me; and whereas I had previously been making excuses to the Lord, I now felt the Lord's courage and strength within me, and I said to the Lord, "I am ready for every beck and call of Your will!" Interiorly, I had gone through everything that I was going to experience in the future.

440 O my Creator and Lord, my entire being is Yours! Dispose of me according to Your divine pleasure and according to Your eternal plans and Your unfathomable mercy. May every soul know how good the Lord is; may no soul fear to commune intimately with the Lord; may no soul use unworthiness as an excuse, and may it never postpone [accepting] God's invitations, for that is not

pleasing to the Lord. There is no soul more wretched than I am, as I truly know myself, and I am astounded that divine Majesty stoops so low. O eternity, it seems to me that you are too short to extol [adequately] the infinite mercy of the Lord!

441 Once, the image was being exhibited over the altar during the Corpus Christi procession [June 20, 1935]. When the priest exposed the Blessed Sacrament, and the choir began to sing, the rays from the image pierced the Sacred Host and spread out all over the world. Then I heard these words: **These rays of mercy will pass through you, just as they have passed through this Host, and they will go out (184) through all the world.** At these words, profound joy invaded my soul.

442 Once when my confessor [Father Sopocko] was saying Mass, I saw, as usual, the Child Jesus on the altar, from the time of the Offertory. However, a moment before the Elevation, the priest vanished from my sight, and Jesus alone remained. When the moment of the Elevation approached, Jesus took the Host and the chalice in His little hands and raised them together, looking up to heaven, and a moment later I again saw my confessor. I asked the Child Jesus where the priest had been during the time I had not seen him. Jesus answered, **In My Heart.** But I could not understand anything more of these words of Jesus.

443 On one occasion I heard these words, **I desire that you live according to My will, in the most secret depths of your soul.** I reflected on these words, which spoke very much to my heart. This was on the day of confessions for the community. When I went to confession and had accused myself of my sins, the priest [Father Sopocko] repeated to me the same words that the Lord had previously spoken.

444 The priest spoke these profound words to me, "There are three degrees in the accomplishment of God's will: in the first, the soul carries out all rules and statutes pertaining

to external observance; in the second degree, the soul accepts interior inspirations and carries them out faithfully; in the third degree, the soul, abandoned to the will of God, allows Him to dispose of it freely, and God does with it as He pleases, and it is a docile tool in His hands." And the priest said that I was at the second degree in the accomplishment of God's will and that I had not yet reached the **(185)** third degree, but that I should strive to attain it. These words pierced my soul. I see clearly that God often gives the priest knowledge of what is going on in the depths of my soul. This does not surprise me at all; indeed, I thank God that He has such chosen persons.

Thursday, Nocturnal Adoration.

445 When I came for adoration, an inner recollection took hold of me immediately, and I saw the Lord Jesus tied to a pillar, stripped of His clothes, and the scourging began immediately. I saw four men who took turns at striking the Lord with scourges. My heart almost stopped at the sight of these tortures. The Lord said to me, **I suffer even greater pain than that which you see.** And Jesus gave me to know for what sins He subjected himself to the scourging: these are sins of impurity. Oh, how dreadful was Jesus' moral suffering during the scourging! Then Jesus said to me, **Look and see the human race in its present condition.** In an instant, I saw horrible things: the executioners left Jesus, and other people started scourging Him; they seized the scourges and struck the Lord mercilessly. These were priests, religious men and women, and high dignitaries of the Church, which surprised me greatly. There were lay people of all ages and walks of life. All vented their malice on the innocent Jesus. Seeing this, my heart fell as if into a mortal agony. And while the executioners had been scourging Him, Jesus had been silent and looking into the distance; but when those other souls I mentioned scourged Him,

Jesus closed His eyes, and a soft, but most painful moan escaped from His Heart. And Jesus gave me to know in detail the gravity of the malice of these ungrateful souls: **You see, this is a torture greater than My death.** Then my lips too fell silent, and I began to experience **(186)** the agony of death, and I felt that no one would comfort me or snatch me from that state but the One who had put me into it. Then the Lord said to me, **I see the sincere pain of your heart which brought great solace to My Heart. See and take comfort.**

446 Then I saw the Lord Jesus nailed to the cross. When He had hung on it for a while, I saw a multitude of souls crucified like Him. Then I saw a second multitude of souls, and a third. The second multitude were not nailed to [their] crosses, but were holding them firmly in their hands. The third were neither nailed to [their] crosses nor holding them firmly in their hands, but were dragging [their] crosses behind them and were discontent. Jesus then said to me, **Do you see these souls? Those who are like Me in the pain and contempt they suffer will be like Me also in glory. And those who resemble Me less in pain and contempt will also bear less resemblance to Me in glory.**

Among the crucified souls, the most numerous were those of the clergy. I also saw some crucified souls whom I knew, and this gave me great joy. Then Jesus said to me, **In your meditation tomorrow, you shall think about what you have seen today.** And immediately Jesus disappeared on me.

447 Friday. I was ill and could not attend Holy Mass. At seven o'clock in the morning I saw my confessor celebrating Holy Mass, during which I saw the Child Jesus. Toward the end of Mass, the vision disappeared, and I found myself back in my cell as before. Indescribable joy took hold of me because, although I could not go to Mass in our own chapel, I had assisted at

it in a church which was far distant. Jesus has a remedy for everything.

(187) July 30, 1935.

448 Feast of St. Ignatius. I prayed fervently to this Saint, reproaching him for looking on and not coming to my aid in such important matters as doing the will of God. I said to him, "You, our Patron, who were inflamed with the fire of love and zeal for the greater glory of God, I humbly beg you to help me to carry out God's designs."[97] This was during Holy Mass. Then I saw Saint Ignatius at the left side of the altar, with a large book in his hand. And he spoke these words to me, "My daughter, I am not indifferent to your cause. This rule can be adapted, and it can be adapted to this Congregation." And gesturing with his hand toward the big book, he disappeared. I rejoiced greatly at the fact of how much the saints think of us and of how closely we are united with them. Oh, the goodness of God! How beautiful is the spiritual world, that already here on earth we commune with the saints! All day long, I could feel the presence of this dear Patron Saint.

August 5, 1935. The Feast of Our Lady of Mercy.

449 I prepared for this feast with greater zeal than in previous years. On the morning of the feast itself, I experienced an inner struggle at the thought that I must leave this Congregation which enjoys such special protection from Mary. This struggle lasted through the meditation and through the first Mass as well. During the second Mass, I turned to our Holy Mother, telling Her that it was difficult for me to separate myself from this Congregation... "which is under Your special protection, O Mary." Then I saw the Blessed Virgin, unspeakably beautiful. She came down from the altar to my kneeler, held me close to herself and said to me, *I am Mother to you all, thanks to the unfathomable mercy of*

God. Most pleasing to Me is that soul which faithfully carries out the will of God. She gave me to understand that I had faithfully fulfilled the will **(188)** of God and had thus found favor in His eyes. *Be courageous. Do not fear apparent obstacles, but fix your gaze upon the Passion of My Son, and in this way you will be victorious.*

Nocturnal Adoration.

450 I was suffering very much, and it seemed to me I would not be able to make my adoration, but I gathered up all my will power and, although I collapsed in my cell, I paid no attention to what ailed me, for I had the Passion of Jesus before my eyes. When I entered the chapel, I received an inner understanding of the great reward that God is preparing for us, not only for our good deeds, but also for our sincere desire to perform them. What a great grace of God this is!

Oh, how sweet it is to toil for God and souls! I want no respite in this battle, but I shall fight to the last breath for the glory of my King and Lord. I shall not lay the sword aside until He calls me before His throne; I fear no blows, because God is my shield. It is the enemy who should fear us, and not we him. Satan defeats only the proud and the cowardly, because the humble are strong. Nothing will confuse or frighten a humble soul. I have directed my flight at the very center of the sun's heat, and nothing can lower its course. Love will not allow itself to be taken prisoner; it is free like a queen. Love attains God.

451 Once after Holy Communion, I heard these words: **You are Our dwelling place.** At that moment, I felt in my soul the presence of the Holy Trinity, the Father, the Son and the Holy Spirit. I felt that I was the temple of God. I felt I was a child of the Father. I cannot explain all this, but the spirit understands it well. O infinite Goodness, how low You stoop to Your miserable creature!

452 If only souls would become recollected, God would speak to them at once, for dissipation drowns out the word of the Lord.

453 **(189)** On one occasion, the Lord said to me, **Why are you fearful and why do you tremble when you are united to Me? I am displeased when a soul yields to vain terrors. Who will dare to touch you when you are with Me? Most dear to Me is the soul that strongly believes in My goodness and has complete trust in Me. I heap My confidence upon it and give it all it asks.**

454 Once, the Lord said to me, **My daughter, take the graces that others spurn; take as many as you can carry.** At that moment, my soul was inundated with the love of God. I feel that I am united with the Lord so closely that I cannot find words to express that union; in this state I suddenly feel that all the things God has, all the goods and treasures, are mine, although I set little store by them, for He alone is enough for me. In Him I see my everything; without Him—nothing.

I look for no happiness beyond my own interior where God dwells. I rejoice that God dwells within me; here I abide with Him unendingly; it is here that my greatest intimacy with Him exists; here I dwell with Him in safety; here is a place not probed by the human eye. The Blessed Virgin encourages me to commune with God in this way.

455 When some suffering afflicts me, it no longer causes me any bitterness, nor do great consolations carry me away. I am filled with the peace and equanimity that flow from the knowledge of the truth.

How can living surrounded by unfriendly hearts do me any harm when I enjoy full happiness within my soul? Or how can having kind hearts around me help me when I do not have God within me? When God dwells within me, who can harm me?

+
(190) J.M.J.   Vilnius, August 12, 1935
Three-day Retreat.

456 On the evening of the introductory day of the retreat, as I listened to the points for the meditation, I heard these words: **During this retreat I will speak to you through the mouth of this priest to strengthen you and assure you of the truth of the words which I address to you in the depths of your soul. Although this is a retreat for all the sisters, I have you especially in mind, as I want to strengthen you and make you fearless in the midst of all the adversities which lie ahead. Therefore, listen intently to his words and meditate upon them in the depths of your soul.**

457 Oh, how astonished I was, for everything the Father said about union with God and the obstacles to this union I had experienced literally in my soul and heard from Jesus, who speaks to me in the depths of my soul. Perfection consists in this close union with God.

458 During the ten-o'clock meditation, Father [Rzyczkowski[98]] spoke about divine mercy and about God's goodness to us. He said that as we review the history of mankind, we can see this great goodness of God at every step. All the attributes of God, such as omnipotence and wisdom, serve to reveal to us the greatest of His attributes; namely, His goodness. God's goodness is the greatest of God's attributes. Many souls striving for perfection, however, are not aware of this great goodness of God. Everything that Father said in the course of the meditation about the goodness of God, was exactly what Jesus had said to me concerning **(191)** the Feast of Mercy. I have now come to understand clearly what the Lord has promised me, and I have no doubt about anything; God's language is clear and distinct.

459 Throughout that entire meditation I saw the Lord Jesus on the altar, in a white garment, His hand holding the notebook in which I write these things. Throughout the entire meditation Jesus kept turning the pages of the notebook and remained silent; however, my heart could not bear the fire that was enkindled in my soul. Despite the great effort of my will to take control of myself and not let others see what was going on in my soul, toward the end of the meditation I felt that I was completely beyond my own control. Then Jesus said to me, **You have not written everything in the notebook about My goodness towards humankind; I desire that you omit nothing; I desire that your heart be firmly grounded in total peace.**

460 O Jesus, my heart stops beating when I think of all You are doing for me! I am amazed at You, Lord, that You would stoop so low to my wretched soul! What inconceivable means You take to convince me!

461 This is the first time in my life that I have made such a retreat. I understand in a special and clear way every single word that Father speaks, for I have first experienced it all in my soul. I now see that Jesus will not leave in doubt any soul that loves Him sincerely. Jesus wants the soul that is in close communion with Him to be filled with peace, despite sufferings and adversities.

462 Now I understand well that what unites our soul most closely to God is self-denial; that is, joining our will to the will of God. This is what makes the soul truly free, contributes to profound recollection of the spirit, and makes all life's burdens light, and death sweet.

463 **(192)** Jesus told me that if I should have any doubts regarding the feast or the founding of the Congregation,—**or regarding anything else about which I have spoken in the depths of your soul, I will reply immediately through the mouth of this priest.**

464 During a meditation on humility, an old doubt returned: that a soul as miserable as mine could not carry out the task which the Lord was demanding [of me]. Just as I was analyzing this doubt, the priest who was conducting the retreat interrupted his train of thought and spoke about the very thing I was having doubts about; namely, that God usually chooses the weakest and simplest souls as tools for His greatest works; that we can see that this is an undeniable truth when we look at the men He chose to be His apostles; or again, when we look at the history of the Church and see what great works were done by souls that were the least capable of accomplishing them; for it is just in this way that God's works are revealed for what they are, the works of God. When my doubt had completely disappeared, the priest resumed his conference on humility.

Jesus was standing, as He usually did during each conference, on the altar and said nothing to me, but with His kindly gaze pierced my poor soul which no longer had any excuse.

465 Jesus, my Life, how well I feel that You are transforming me into Yourself, in the secrecy of my soul where the senses can no longer perceive much. O my Savior, conceal me completely in the depths of Your Heart and shield me with Your rays against everything that is not You. I beg You, Jesus, let the two rays that have issued from Your most merciful Heart continuously nourish my soul.

466 **(193)**   Time of Confession.

My confessor [Father Sopocko] asked me if at that moment Jesus was there and if I could see Him. "Yes, He is here, and I can see Him." He then told me to ask Jesus about certain persons. Jesus did not answer me, but looked at him. However, after the confession, when I was reciting my penance, Jesus spoke these words to me: **Go and console him on my behalf.** Not understanding the meaning of these words, I immediately repeated to him what Jesus had told me to do.

467   Throughout the whole retreat, I was in uninterrupted communion with Jesus and entered into an intimate relationship with Him with all the might of my heart.

468   The day of the renewal of vows. At the beginning of Holy Mass, I saw Jesus in the usual way. He blessed us and then entered the tabernacle. Then I saw the Mother of God in a white garment and blue mantle, with Her head uncovered. She approached me from the altar, touched me with Her hands and covered me with Her mantle, saying, *Offer these vows for Poland. Pray for her.* This was on August fifteen.

469   On the evening of that same day, I felt in my soul a great yearning for God. I do not see Him at this moment with my bodily eyes as I have on other occasions, but I sense His presence and yet do not grasp Him [with my mind]. This causes me great yearning and torment beyond words. I am dying from the desire to possess Him, to be drowned in Him forever. My spirit pursues Him with all its might; there is nothing in the world that could comfort me. O Love Eternal, now I understand in what close intimacy my heart was with You! For what else can satisfy me in heaven or on earth except You, O my God, in Whom my soul is drowned.

470   **(194)** One evening, as I looked up from my cell to the sky and saw the beautiful star-strewn firmament and the moon, an inconceivable fire of love for my Creator welled up within my soul and, unable to bear the yearning for Him that arose within my soul, I fell on my face, humbling myself in the dust. I glorified Him for all His works and, when my heart could no longer bear what was going on within it, I wept aloud. Then my Guardian Angel touched me and spoke to me these words: "The Lord orders me to tell you to rise from the

ground." I did so immediately, but felt no consolation in my soul. The yearning for God grew even stronger in me.

471   One day, when I was at adoration, and my spirit seemed to be dying for Him, and I could no longer hold back my tears, I saw a spirit of great beauty who spoke these words to me: "Don't cry—says the Lord." After a moment I asked, "Who are you?" He answered me, "I am one of the seven spirits who stand before the throne of God day and night and give Him ceaseless praise." Yet this spirit did not soothe my yearning, but roused me to even greater longing for God. This spirit is very beautiful, and his beauty comes from close union with God. This spirit does not leave me for a single moment, but accompanies me everywhere.

On the following day during Holy Mass, before the Elevation, this spirit began to sing these words: "Holy, Holy, Holy." His voice was like that of a thousand voices; it is impossible to put it into words. Suddenly my spirit was united with God, and in that instant I saw the grandeur and the inconceivable holiness of God and, at the same time, I realized **(195)** the nothingness I am of myself.

472   I knew, more distinctly than ever before, the Three Divine Persons, the Father, the Son and the Holy Spirit. But their being, their equality and their majesty are one. My soul is in communion with these Three; but I do not know how to express this in words; yet my soul understands it well. Whoever is united to One of the Three Persons is thereby united to the whole Blessed Trinity, for this Oneness is indivisible. This vision, or rather, this knowledge filled my soul with unimaginable happiness, because God is so great. What I am describing I did not see with my eyes, as on previous occasions, but in a purely interior manner, in a purely spiritual way,

independent of the senses. This continued until the end of Holy Mass.

This now happens often to me, and not only in the chapel, but also at work and at times when I least expect it.

473 When our confessor [Father Sopocko] was away, I confessed to the Archbishop [Romuald Jalbrzykowski [99]]. When I revealed my soul to him, I received this reply: "My daughter, arm yourself with great patience; if these things come from God, they will be realized sooner or later. So be completely at peace. I understand you very well in this matter, my daughter. And now, as regards your leaving the Congregation and thinking of another one, do not entertain such thoughts, for this would be a serious interior temptation." After this confession, I said to the Lord Jesus, "Why do You command me to do such things and yet do not make it possible to accomplish them?" Then I saw the Lord Jesus after Holy Communion in the same little chapel where I had gone to confession, in the same way in which He is represented in the image. The Lord said to me, **Do not be sad. I will give him to understand the things I am asking of you.** When we were leaving, **(196)** the Archbishop was very busy, but he told us to return and wait a bit. When we entered the chapel again, I heard these words in my soul: **Tell him what you have seen in this chapel.** At that very moment the Archbishop came in and asked if we did not have something to tell him. But although I had been commanded to tell him, I could not do so because I was in the company of one of the sisters.

One more word from the Holy Confession: "To entreat mercy for the world is a great and beautiful idea. Pray much, Sister, pray for mercy upon sinners, but do it in your own convent."

The following day, Friday, September 13, 1935.

474 In the evening, when I was in my cell, I saw an Angel, the executor of divine wrath. He was clothed in a dazzling robe, his face gloriously bright, a cloud beneath his feet. From the cloud, bolts of thunder and flashes of lightning were springing into his hands; and from his hand they were going forth, and only then were they striking the earth. When I saw this sign of divine wrath which was about to strike the earth, and in particular a certain place, which for good reasons I cannot name, I began to implore the Angel to hold off for a few moments, and the world would do penance. But my plea was a mere nothing in the face of the divine anger. Just then I saw the Most Holy Trinity. The greatness of Its majesty pierced me deeply, and I did not dare to repeat my entreaties. At that very moment I felt in my soul the power of Jesus' grace, which dwells in my soul. When I became conscious of this grace, I was instantly snatched up before the Throne of God. Oh, how great is our Lord and God and how incomprehensible His holiness! I will make no attempt to describe this greatness, because before long we shall all see Him as He is. I found myself pleading with **(197)** God for the world with words heard interiorly.

As I was praying in this manner, I saw the Angel's helplessness: he could not carry out the just punishment which was rightly due for sins. Never before had I prayed with such inner power as I did then.

475 The words with which I entreated God are these: **Eternal Father, I offer You the Body and Blood, Soul and Divinity of Your dearly beloved Son, Our Lord Jesus Christ for our sins and those of the whole world; for the sake of His sorrowful Passion, have mercy on us.**

476 The next morning, when I entered chapel, I heard these words interiorly: **Every time you enter the chapel, immediately recite the prayer which I taught you yesterday.** When I had said the prayer, in my soul I

heard these words: **This prayer will serve to appease My wrath. You will recite it for nine days, on the beads of the rosary, in the following manner: First of all, you will say one OUR FATHER and HAIL MARY and the I BELIEVE IN GOD. Then on the OUR FATHER beads you will say the following words: "Eternal Father, I offer You the Body and Blood, Soul and Divinity of Your dearly beloved Son, Our Lord Jesus Christ, in atonement for our sins and those of the whole world." On the HAIL MARY beads you will say the following words: "For the sake of His sorrowful Passion have mercy on us and on the whole world." In conclusion, three times you will recite these words: "Holy God, Holy Mighty One, Holy Immortal One, have mercy on us and on the whole world."**[100]

477 Silence is a sword in the spiritual struggle. A talkative soul will will never attain sanctity. The sword of silence will cut off everything that would like to cling to the soul. We are sensitive to words and quickly want to answer back, without taking any regard as to whether it is God's will that we should speak. A silent soul is strong; no adversities will harm it if it perseveres in silence. The silent **(198)** soul is capable of attaining the closest union with God. It lives almost always under the inspiration of the Holy Spirit. God works in a silent soul without hindrance.

478 O my Jesus, You know, You alone know well that my heart knows no other love but You! All my virginal love is drowned eternally in You, O Jesus! I sense keenly how Your divine Blood is circulating in my heart; I have not the least doubt that Your most pure love has entered my heart with Your most sacred Blood. I am aware that You are dwelling in me, together with the Father and the Holy Spirit, or rather I am aware that it is I who am living in You, O incomprehensible God! I am aware that I am dissolving in You like a drop in an ocean. I am aware that You are within me and all about me, that

You are in all things that surround me, in all that happens to me. O my God, I have come to know You within my heart, and I have loved You above all things that exist on earth or in heaven. Our hearts have a mutual understanding, and no one of humankind will comprehend this.

479 My second confession to the Archbishop [Jalbrzykowski]. "Know, my daughter, that if this is the will of God, it will take place sooner or later, for God's will must be done. Love God in your heart, have..." [unfinished thought].

480 September 29. The Feast of Saint Michael the Archangel. I have become interiorly united with God. His presence penetrates me to my very depths and fills me with peace, joy and amazement. After such moments of prayer, I am filled with strength and an extraordinary courage to suffer and struggle. Nothing terrifies me, even if the whole world should turn against me. All adversities touch only the surface, but they have no entry **(199)**to the depths, because God, who strengthens me, who fills me, dwells there. All the snares of the enemy are crushed at His footstool. During these moments of union, God sustains me with His might. His might passes on to me and makes me capable of loving Him. A soul never reaches this state by its own efforts. At the beginning of this interior grace, I was filled with fright, and I started to give in to it; but very quickly, the Lord let me know how much this displeases Him. But it is also He, Himself, who set my fears at rest.

481 Almost every feast of the Church gives me a deeper knowledge of God and a special grace. That is why I prepare myself for each feast and unite myself closely with the spirit of the Church. What a joy it is to be a faithful child of the Church! Oh, how much I love Holy Church and all those who live in it! I look upon them as living members of Christ, who is their Head. I burn with

love with those who love; I suffer with those who suffer. I am consumed with sorrow at the sight of those who are cold and ungrateful; and I then try to have such a love for God that it will make amends for those who do not love Him, those who feed their Savior with ingratitude at its worst.

482 O my God, I am conscious of my mission in the Holy Church. It is my constant endeavor to plead for mercy for the world. I unite myself closely with Jesus and stand before Him as an atoning sacrifice on behalf of the world. God will refuse me nothing when I entreat Him with the voice of His Son. My sacrifice is nothing in itself, but when I join it to the sacrifice of Jesus Christ, it becomes all-powerful and has the power to appease divine wrath. God loves us in His Son; the painful Passion of the Son of God constantly turns aside the wrath of God.

483 **(200)** O God, how I desire that souls come to know You and to see that You have created them because of Your unfathomable love. O my Creator and Lord, I feel that I am going to remove the veil of heaven so that earth will not doubt Your goodness.

Make of me, Jesus, a pure and agreeable offering before the Face of Your Father. Jesus, transform me, miserable and sinful as I am, into Your own self (for You can do all things), and give me to Your Eternal Father. I want to become a sacrificial host before You, but an ordinary wafer to people. I want the fragrance of my sacrifice to be known to You alone. O Eternal God, an unquenchable fire of supplication for Your mercy burns within me. I know and understand that this is my task, here and in eternity. You yourself have told me to speak about this great mercy and about Your goodness.

484 On a certain occasion, I understood how very displeased God is with an act, however commendable, that does not bear the stamp of a pure intention. Such deeds incite

God to punishment rather than to reward. May such deeds be as few as possible in our lives; indeed, in religious life, there should be none at all.

485 I accept joy or suffering, praise or humiliation with the same disposition. I remember that one and the other are passing. What does it matter to me what people say about me? I have long ago given up everything that concerns my person. My name is host—or sacrifice, not in words but in deeds, in the emptying of myself and in becoming like You on the Cross, O good Jesus, my Master!

486 **(201)** Jesus, when You come to me in Holy Communion, You who together with the Father and the Holy Spirit have deigned to dwell in the little heaven of my heart, I try to keep You company throughout the day, I do not leave You alone for even a moment. Although I am in the company of other people or with our wards, my heart is always united to Him. When I am asleep I offer Him every beat of my heart; when I awaken I immerse myself in Him without saying a word. When I awaken I adore the Holy Trinity for a short while and thank God for having deigned to give me yet another day, that the mystery of the incarnation of His Son may once more be repeated in me, and that once again His sorrowful Passion may unfold before my eyes. I then try to make it easier for Jesus to pass through me to other souls. I go everywhere with Jesus; His presence accompanies me everywhere.

487 In the sufferings of soul or body, I try to keep silence, for then my spirit gains the strength that flows from the Passion of Jesus. I have ever before my eyes His sorrowful Face, abused and disfigured, His divine Heart pierced by our sins and especially by the ingratitude of chosen souls.

488 Twice I was exhorted to make myself ready for sufferings awaiting me in Warsaw. The first warning was given

interiorly by a voice I heard, and the second took place during Holy Mass. Before the elevation, I saw the Lord Jesus on the Cross and He said to me, **Prepare yourself for sufferings.** I thanked the Lord for the grace of this warning and said to Him, "I am certainly not going to suffer more than You, my Savior." However, I took this to heart and kept strengthening myself through prayer and little sufferings so that I would be able to endure it when the greater ones come.

(202) October 19, 1935.

Trip from Vilnius to Cracow for an Eight-day Retreat.

489 On Friday evening during the rosary, when I was thinking about tomorrow's journey and about the importance of the matter which I was to present to Father Andrasz,[101] fear seized me at the sight of my misery and incapability, and of the greatness of God's work. Crushed by this suffering, I submitted myself to the will of God. At that moment, I saw Jesus, in a bright garment, near my kneeler. He said, **Why are you afraid to do My will? Will I not help you as I have done thus far? Repeat every one of My demands to those who represent Me on earth, but do only what they tell you to do.** At that, a certain strength entered my soul.

490 The next morning, I saw my Guardian Angel, who accompanied me throughout the journey as far as Warsaw. He disappeared when we entered the convent gate. Just as we were passing the little chapel on the way to greet the superiors, God's presence took hold of me, and the Lord filled me with the fire of His love. At such moments, I always have a better understanding of the greatness of His majesty.

When we took our seats on the train from Warsaw to Cracow, I once again saw my Guardian Angel at my side. He was absorbed in prayer and in contemplating God, and I followed him with my thoughts. When we arrived at the convent entrance, he disappeared.

491 When I entered the chapel, once again the majesty of God overwhelmed me. I felt that I was immersed in God, totally immersed in Him and penetrated by Him, being aware of how much the heavenly Father loves us. Oh, what great happiness fills my heart from knowing God and the divine life! It is my desire to share this happiness with all people. I cannot keep this happiness locked in my own heart alone, for His flames burn me and cause my bosom and my entrails to burst asunder. I desire to go throughout the whole world and speak to souls about the great mercy of God. Priests, help me in this; use the strongest words [at your disposal] to proclaim His mercy, for every word falls short of how merciful He really is.

+

(203) J.M.J. Cracow, October 20, 1935.

Eight-day Retreat.

492 Eternal God, Goodness itself, whose mercy is incomprehensible to every intellect, whether human or angelic, help me, your feeble child, to do Your holy will as You make it known to me. I desire nothing but to fulfill God's desires. Lord, here are my soul and my body, my mind and my will, my heart and all my love. Rule me according to Your eternal plans.

493 After Holy Communion, my soul was again flooded with God's love. I rejoiced in His greatness. Here I see distinctly His will, which I am to carry out, and at the same time my own weakness and misery; I see how I can do nothing without His help.

Second Day of Retreat.

494 When I was about to go to the parlor to see Father Andrasz, I felt frightened because the secret is binding only in the confessional. This was a groundless fear. One word from Mother Superior set me at ease about it. Meanwhile, when I entered the chapel, I heard these

words in my soul: **I want you to be open and simple as a child with My representative just as you are with Me; otherwise I will leave you and will not commune with you.**

Truly, God gave me the great grace of complete confidence, and after the conversation, God granted me the grace of deep peace and light concerning these matters.

495 Jesus, Eternal Light, enlighten my mind, strengthen my will, inflame my heart and be with me as You have promised, for without You I am nothing. You know, Jesus, how weak I am. I do not need to tell You this, for You yourself know perfectly well how wretched I am. It is in You that all my strength lies.

496 **(204)**   Confession Day.

From early morning, the turmoil in my soul was more violent than anything I had ever experienced before. Complete abandonment by God; I felt the utter weakness that I was. Thoughts bore in upon me: why should I leave this convent where I am loved by the sisters and superiors, where life is so tranquil; [where I am] bound by perpetual vows and carry out my duties without difficulty; why should I listen to the voice of my conscience; why follow an inspiration coming from who knows where; wouldn't it be better to carry on like all the other sisters? Perhaps the Lord's words could be stifled, not taken heed of; maybe God will not demand an account of them on the day of judgment. Where will this inner voice lead me? If I follow it, what tremendous difficulties, tribulations and adversities are in store for me. I fear the future, and I am agonizing in the present.

This suffering continued with the same intensity throughout the whole day. When, in the evening, my turn came for confession, I could not make a full confession, even though I had been preparing for a long time. I received absolution and left, not knowing what was going on within me. When I went to bed, the suffering grew even worse; or rather, it changed into a fire which penetrated all the faculties of my soul like lightning, piercing me to the marrow, and to the most secret recesses of my heart. In the midst of this suffering, I was unable to bring myself to do anything. "Your will be done, Lord." At times I could not even think these words. Truly, a deadly fear had taken hold of me, and the flames of hell were touching me. Toward morning, silence set in, and my tribulations disappeared in the twinkling of an eye, but I felt so frightfully exhausted that I could not even move. During my conversation with Mother Superior, my strength returned bit by bit, but God alone knows how I felt throughout that whole day.

497 O Eternal Truth, Word Incarnate, who most faithfully fulfilled Your Father's will, today I am becoming a martyr of Your inspirations, since I cannot carry them out because I have no will of my own, though interiorly I see Your will clearly. **(205)** I submit in everything to the will of my superiors and my confessor. I will follow Your will insofar as You will permit me to do so through Your representative. O my Jesus, it cannot be helped, but I give priority to the voice of the Church over the voice with which You speak to me.

After Holy Communion

498 I saw Jesus in the usual way, and He spoke these words to me: **Lay your head on my shoulder, rest and regain your strength. I am always with you. Tell the friend of My Heart that I use such feeble creatures to carry out My work.** After a while my spirit was strengthened with great power. **Tell him that I had let him see your weakness during your confession to show him what you are of yourself.**

499 Each battle valiantly fought brings me joy, peace, light, experience and courage for the future; honor and glory

to God; and in the end, for me, a reward.

Today is the Feast of Christ the King.
[October 27, 1935]

500 During Holy Mass I prayed fervently that Jesus might
become King of all hearts and that divine grace might
shine in every soul. Then I saw Jesus as He is depicted in
the image, and He said to me, **My daughter, you give Me
the greatest glory by faithfully fulfilling My desires.**

501 Oh, how great is Your beauty, Jesus my Spouse! Living
Flower enclosing life-giving dew for a thirsting soul! My
soul is drowned in You. You alone are the object of my
desires and strivings. Unite me as closely as possible to
Yourself, to the Father and to the Holy Spirit. Let me
live and die in You.

502 Only love has meaning; it raises up our smallest actions
into infinity.

503 My Jesus, truly I would not know how to live without
You—my spirit is welded to Yours. No one can really
understand this; one must first live in You in order to
recognize You in others.

(206)   Cracow, October 25, 1935.

Retreat Resolutions.

504 Not to do anything without the permission of my
confessor and the consent of my superiors in all things,
but especially regarding these inspirations and demands
of the Lord.

All my free time I will spend with the Divine Guest
within my soul; I will safeguard my interior and exterior
silence so that Jesus can rest in my heart.

My sweetest repose will be in serving and obliging the
sisters, in forgetting about myself and thinking of how
to please the sisters.

I will not offer explanations on my own behalf or seek to

vindicate myself when criticized; I will let others judge me as they will.

I have only one trusted Friend in whom I confide everything, and that is Jesus—the Eucharist, and His representative—my confessor.

In the midst of all sufferings, both physical and spiritual, as well as in darkness and desolation, I will remain silent, like a dove, and not complain.

I will empty myself continually at His feet in order to obtain mercy for poor souls.

505 All my nothingness is drowned in the sea of Your mercy. With the confidence of a child, I throw myself into Your arms, O Father of Mercy, to make up for the unbelief of so many souls who are afraid to trust in You. Oh, how very few souls really know You! How ardently I desire that the Feast of Mercy be known by souls! Mercy is the crown of Your works; You provide for all with the love of a most tender mother.

+

(207) J.M.J.   Cracow, October 27, 1935.

Father Andrasz—Spiritual Counsel.

506 "Do nothing without the consent of the superiors. One must think this matter over thoroughly and pray much. One must be very careful about these things because, in your present situation, Sister, the will of God is certain and clear, for you are in fact bound to this Congregation by vows, and perpetual vows at that; so there should be no doubt. What you are experiencing interiorly, Sister, are only the glimmerings of a project. God can make some alterations, but such things are very rare. Don't be in a hurry, Sister, until you have received more precise knowledge. The works of God proceed slowly, but if they are of Him, you will surely recognize them clearly. If they are not, they will disappear; and you, by being obedient, will not go astray. Speak frankly about

everything to your confessor and obey him blindly.

"For the present, Sister, there is nothing more for you to do than accept the suffering until the time when everything will become clear; that is, all things will be resolved. You are well disposed as regards these matters, and so continue in this simplicity and spirit of obedience; this is a good sign. If you continue in this attitude, God will not allow you to fall into error. Still, as much as is possible, keep far away from these things, but if despite that they still come your way, receive them calmly and do not fear anything. You are in the good hands of a very good God. In all that you have told me, I do not see any illusion or anything contrary to faith. These are things which are good in themselves, and it would indeed be good if there were a group of souls pleading with God for the world, as we all are in need of prayer. You have a good director; stay with him and be at peace. Be faithful to God's will and carry it out. As to your duties, always do what you are told to do and as you are told to do it, no matter how humiliating or toilsome it might be. Always choose the last place, and then they themselves will say to you, 'Go up higher.' In spirit and in your demeanor, consider yourself the least in the whole house and in the entire Congregation. In everything and at all times, be most faithful to God."

507 **(208)** I desire, O my Jesus, to suffer and burn with the flame of Your love in all the circumstances of my life. I am Yours, completely Yours, and I wish to disappear in You, O Jesus, I wish to be lost in Your divine beauty. You pursue me with Your love, O Lord; You penetrate my soul like a ray of the sun and change its darkness into Your light. I feel very vividly that I am living in You as one small spark swallowed up by the incomprehensible fire with which You burn, O inconceivable Trinity! No greater joy is to be found than that of loving God. Already here on earth we can taste the happiness of those in heaven by an intimate union with God, a union

that is extraordinary and often quite incomprehensible to us. One can attain this very grace through simple faithfulness of soul.

508 When a reluctance and a monotony as regards my duties begins to take possession of me, I remind myself that I am in the house of the Lord, where nothing is small and where the glory of the Church and the progress of many a soul depend on this small deed of mine, accomplished in a divinized way. Therefore there is nothing small in a religious congregation.

509 In the adversities that I experience, I remind myself that the time for doing battle has not yet come to an end. I arm myself with patience, and in this way I defeat my assailant.

510 In no way do I seek perfection inquisitively, but I probe into the spirit of Jesus and fix my eyes on His deeds as summarized in the Gospel. Even if I lived a thousand years, I would not exhaust what is contained there.

511 When my intentions are not recognized, but rather condemned, I am not too much surprised, for I know that it is only God who scrutinizes my heart. Truth will not die; the wounded heart will regain peace in due time, and my spirit is strengthened through adversities. I do not always listen to what my heart tells me, but I keep asking God for light; and when I feel I have regained my equilibrium, then I say more.

512 **(209)** The day of the renewal of vows. The presence of God flooded my soul. During Holy Mass I saw Jesus, and He said to me, **You are my great joy; your love and your humility make Me leave the heavenly throne and unite myself with you. Love fills up the abyss that exists between My greatness and your nothingness.**

513 Love is flooding my soul; I am plunged into an ocean of love. I feel that I am swooning and becoming completely lost in Him.

514 Jesus, make my heart like unto Yours, or rather transform it into Your own Heart that I may sense the needs of other hearts, especially those who are sad and suffering. May the rays of mercy rest in my heart.

515 In the evening, when I was walking in the garden saying my rosary and came to the cemetery,[102] I opened the gate a little and began to pray for a while, and I asked them interiorly, "You are very happy are you not?" Then I heard the words, "We are happy in the measure that we have fulfilled God's will"—and then silence as before. I became introspective and reflected for a long time on how I am fulfilling God's will and how I am profiting from the time that God has given me.

516 On the evening of that same day, when I had already gone to bed, a certain soul came to me, woke me up by tapping on the night table and asked me to pray for her. I wanted to ask who she was, but I mortified my curiosity and joined this little mortification to my prayer and offered them for her.

517 Once, when visiting a sick sister[103] who was eighty-four and known for many virtues, I asked her, "Sister, you are surely ready to stand before the Lord, are you not?" She answered, "I have been preparing myself all my life long for this last hour." And then she added, "Old age does not dispense one from the combat."

518 (210) + Before All Souls' Day, I went to the cemetery at dusk. Although it was locked, I managed to open the gate a bit and said, "If you need something, my dear little souls, I will be glad to help you to the extent that the rule permits me." I then heard these words, "Do the will of God; we are happy in the measure that we have fulfilled God's will."

519 In the evening, these souls came and asked me to pray for them, and I did pray very much for them. In the evening, when the procession was returning from the cemetery, I saw a great multitude of souls walking with us into the

chapel and praying with us. I prayed a good deal, for I had my superiors' permission[104] to do so.

520 During the night, a soul I had already seen before visited me. However, it did not ask for prayer, but reproached me, saying that I used to be very haughty and vain... "and now you are interceding for others while you yourself still have certain vices." I answered that I indeed had been vain and haughty, but that I had confessed this and had done penance for my stupidity, and that I trusted in the goodness of my God, and that if I still fell occasionally, this was indeliberate and never premeditated, even in the smallest things. Still, the soul continued to reproach me, saying, "Why are you unwilling to recognize my greatness? Why do you alone not glorify me for my great deeds as all others do?" Then I saw that this was Satan under the assumed appearance of this soul and I said, "Glory is due to God alone; begone Satan!" And in an instant this soul fell into an abyss, horrible beyond all description. And I said to the wretched soul that I would tell the whole Church about this.

521 On Saturday we left Cracow and returned to Vilnius. On the way we visited Czestochowa. When I was praying before the miraculous picture, I felt that ... are pleasing ... [unfinished thought].

[End of Notebook I]

The Mercy of the Lord I Will Sing Forever

Divine Mercy in my soul.

Sr. M. Faustina

Diary

Notebook II

(1)+
J.M.J.

522 +The mercy of the Lord I will sing forever,
     Before all the people will I sing it,
     For it is God's greatest attribute
     And for us an unending miracle.

         You gush forth from the Divine Trinity,
         But from one single womb filled with love.
         The mercy of the Lord will be revealed in the soul
         In all its fullness, when the veil falls.

     From the fountain of Your mercy, O Lord,
     Flows all happiness and life,
     And thus, all creatures and the whole of creation
     Sing out in ecstasy a song of mercy.

         The bowels of God's mercy are opened for us
         Through the life of Jesus, stretched on the Cross.
         O sinner, you must not doubt or despair,
         But trust in mercy, for you also can become holy.

     Two streams in the form of rays
     Have gushed forth from the Heart of Jesus,
     Not for Angels, nor Cherubim, nor Seraphim,
     But for the salvation of sinful man.

(2)   +
         J.M.J.

523   O will of God,
                                          be my love.

My Jesus, You know that of myself I would not have
written a single letter, and if I do write, it is only because
of a clear command of holy obedience.

God and Souls

S. M. Faustina
of the Blessed Sacrament[105]

524   + O Jesus, hidden God,
                          My heart perceives You
                          Though veils hide You;
                          You know that I love you.

(3)   +   Vilnius, November 24, 1935.
         J.M.J.   + Notebook Two

                    Blessed Be God!

525 O Holy Trinity, in whom is contained the inner life of
     God, the Father, the Son, and the Holy Spirit, eternal
     joy, inconceivable depth of love, poured out upon all
     creatures and constituting their happiness, honor and
     glory be to Your holy name forever and ever. Amen.

     When I consider Your greatness and beauty, O my God,
     I rejoice exceedingly that the Lord I serve is so great.
     With love and joy I carry out His will, and the more I
     come to know Him, the more I desire to love Him. I
     burn with the desire to love Him ever more and more.

526 **(4)** + The 14th. This Thursday, when we were having nocturnal adoration, at first I could not pray; a sort of dryness engulfed me. I could not meditate on Jesus' sorrowful Passion. So I lay prostrate and offered the most sorrowful Passion of the Lord Jesus to the heavenly Father in reparation for the sins of all the world. When I got to my feet after this prayer and walked to my kneeler, I suddenly saw Jesus next to it. The Lord Jesus appeared as He was during the scourging. In His hands He was holding a white garment with which He clothed me and a cord with which He girded me, and He covered me with a red cloak like the one He was clothed with during His Passion and a veil of the same color, and He said to me, **This is how you and your companions are going to be clothed. My life from birth to death on the Cross will be the rule for you. Fix your eyes upon Me and live according to what you see. I desire that you penetrate into My spirit more deeply and understand (5) that I am meek and humble of heart.**

527 On one occasion, I felt an urge to set to work and fulfill whatever God is demanding of me. I entered the chapel for a moment and heard a voice in my soul saying, **Why are you afraid? Do you think that I will not have enough omnipotence to support you?** At that moment, my soul felt extraordinary strength, and all the adversities that could befall me in carrying out God's will seemed as nothing to me.

528 On Friday during Mass when my soul was flooded with God's happiness, I heard these words in my soul: **My mercy has passed into souls through the divine-human Heart of Jesus as a ray from the sun passes through crystal.** I felt in my heart and understood that every approach to God is brought about by Jesus, in Him and through Him.

529 **(6)** On the evening of the last day [November 15] of the novena at Ostra Brama, after the singing of the litany,

one of the priests exposed the Blessed Sacrament in the monstrance. When he placed it on the altar, I immediately saw the Infant Jesus, stretching out His little arms, first of all toward His Mother, who at that time had taken on a living appearance. When the Mother of God was speaking to me, Jesus stretched out His tiny hands toward the congregation. The Blessed Mother was telling me to accept all that God asked of me like a little child, without questioning; otherwise it would not be pleasing to God. At that moment, the Infant Jesus vanished, and the Mother of God was again lifeless, and Her picture was the same as it had been before. But my soul was filled with great joy and gladness, and I said to the Lord, "Do with me as You please; I am ready for everything, but You, O Lord, must not abandon me even for a moment."

(7) +

J.M.J.

530   To the Glory of the Holy Trinity.

I asked Mother Superior [Borgia] to permit me to make a forty-day fast, taking once a day a piece of bread and a glass of water. However, following the advice of my confessor [Father Sopocko], Mother Suyperior did not agree to forty days, but to seven. "I cannot take you away from your duties completely, Sister, because of the other sisters who might notice something. I give you my permission to devote yourself to prayer and to note down some of these things, but it will be very difficult for me to protect you as regards the fasting. Really, I can think of no solution to this," and she said, "Go now, Sister, and perhaps some light will come to me." On Sunday morning, I understood that when Mother Superior assigned me as portress during mealtime, she was doing so with the thought of giving me the opportunity to fast. In the morning, I did not go to breakfast, but, a little while later, I went (8) to Mother Superior and asked her whether I had been assigned as portress in view of making it possible for me to fast unnoticed. Mother replied, "When I assigned you,[106] Sister, it was with this in mind." I then saw that this was the same thought that I had had interiorly.

531   November 24, 1935. Sunday, first day. I went at once before the Blessed Sacrament and offered myself with Jesus, present in the Most Holy Sacrament, to the Everlasting Father. Then I heard these words in my soul: **Your purpose and that of your companions is to unite yourselves with Me as closely as possible; through love You will reconcile earth with heaven, you will soften the just anger of God, and you will plead for mercy for the world. I place in your care two pearls very precious to My Heart: these are the souls of priests and religious. You will pray particularly for them; their power will come from your diminishment. You will join prayers, fasts, mortifications, labors (9) and all sufferings to My prayer, fasting, mortification, labors and sufferings and then they will have power before My Father.**

532   After Holy Communion, I saw the Lord Jesus, who said these words to me: **Today, penetrate into the spirit of My poverty and arrange everything in such a way that the most destitute will have no reason to envy you. I find pleasure, not in large buildings and magnificent structures, but in a pure and humble heart.**

533   When I was by myself, I began to reflect on the spirit of poverty. I clearly saw that Jesus, although He is Lord of all things, possessed nothing. From a borrowed manger He went through life doing good to all, but himself having no place to lay His head. And on the Cross, I see the summit of His poverty, for He does not even have a garment on himself. O Jesus, through a solemn vow of poverty I desire to become like You; poverty will be my mother. **(10)** As exteriorly we should possess nothing and have nothing to dispose of as our own; so interiorly we should desire nothing. And in the Most Blessed

Sacrament, how great is Your poverty! Has there ever been a soul as abandoned as You were on the Cross, Jesus?

534   Chastity. There is no need to explain that this vow forbids all those things prohibited by the sixth and ninth commandments: deeds, thoughts, words, feelings... I understand that a solemn vow differs from a simple vow; I understand this in all its implications. While reflecting upon this, I heard these words in my soul: **You are My spouse forever; your chastity should be greater than that of the Angels, for I call no angel to such intimacy as I do you. The smallest act of My spouse is of infinite value. A pure soul has inconceivable power before God.**

535   **(11)** Obedience. **I have come to do My Father's will. I obeyed My parents, I obeyed My tormentors and now I obey the priests.** I understand, O Jesus, the spirit of obedience and in what it consists. It includes not only external performance, but also the reason, the will and judgment. Obeying our superiors, we obey God. It makes no difference whether it is an angel or a man who, acting in God's stead, gives me orders; I must always obey. I am not going to write much about the vows; they are clear and specific. I will rather put down a few general thoughts about this congregation.

+ General Summary.

536   There will never be any splendid houses, but only a small church with a small community consisting of a few souls, not more than ten, plus two externs to look after the external affairs **(12)** of the community and the church. These two sisters will not wear the habit, but secular dress; they will take simple vows, and they will depend strictly on the superior who will be cloistered. They will share in all the spiritual benefits of the congregation. There must never be more than two and, preferably, only one. Each house will be independent of

the others, although they will be closely united by the rule, the vows and the spirit. In exceptional cases, however, a sister from one community may be tranferred to another and also, if there is question of founding a new house, some sisters may be transferred, if need be, from another house. Each house will depend on the local ordinary.

537 Each sister will have a separate cell, but life will be communal as regards prayer, meals and recreation. Each nun, after her profession, **(13)** will no longer see the world, even through a grill, as this will be covered with a dark cloth, and even the conversations will be strictly limited. She will be as if dead, not understood by the world and not understanding the world. She is to stand between heaven and earth, begging God constantly for mercy on the world and that priests be empowered so that their words be not empty and that they, in their extraordinary dignity and so exposed to risks, might keep themselves completely stainless. Though these souls will not be numerous, they will be heroic souls. There will be no room for cowardly or effeminate souls.

538 There will be no distinction between the sisters, no mothers,[107] no reverends, no venerables, but all will be equal, even though there might be great differences in their parentage. We know who Jesus was, and yet how He humbled himself and with whom He associated. Their habit will be like that worn by Jesus during His Passion, and they will not simply wear the robe [He wore]; **(14)** they must also seal themselves with the marks He bore: suffering and scorn. Each one will strive for the greatest self-denial and have a love of humility, and she who will distinguish herself most in this latter virtue will be the one who is capable of leading the others.

539 As God has made us sharers in His mercy and even more than that, dispensers of that mercy, we should therefore have great love for each soul, beginning with the elect

and ending with the soul that does not yet know God. By prayer and mortification, we will make our way to the most uncivilized countries, paving the way for the missionaries. We will bear in mind that a soldier on the front line cannot hold out long without support from the rear forces that do not actually take part in the fighting but provide for all his needs; and that such is the role of prayer, and that therefore each one of us is to be distinguished by an apostolic spirit.

540 **(15)** In the evening when I was writing, I heard a voice in my cell which said, "Do not leave this Congregation; have mercy upon yourself, such great sufferings are in store for you." When I looked in the direction of the voice, I saw nothing, and I continued to write. Suddenly I heard a noise and the words: "When you leave, we will destroy you. Do not torture us." I glanced around and saw many ugly monsters. So I mentally made the sign of the Cross and they disappeared immediately. How terribly ugly Satan is! The poor damned souls that have to keep him company! Just the sight of him is more disgusting than all the torments of hell.

541 A short time later, I heard this voice in my soul: **Do not fear anything; nothing will happen to you against My will.** After these words of the Lord, a strange power entered my soul. I rejoiced greatly that God is so good.

542 **(16)** Postulancy.[108] Age of admission: any person between the ages of fifteen and thirty. Firstly, the spirit with which the candidate is imbued and her character are to be taken into consideration, whether she has a strong will and the courage to follow in Jesus' footsteps with joy and gladness, as God loves a cheerful giver. She must despise the world and herself. The lack of a dowry will never be an obstacle to admission. All formalities concerning the candidate must be clear; no complicated cases should be admitted.

Melancholy persons, those disposed to sadness, those

suffering from contagious diseases, those of an unstable character and those who are inclined to be suspicious of others are not adaptable to the religious life and must not be admitted. Members should be selected with greatest care, as one ill-fitting member is enough to throw the whole convent into confusion.

543 The duration of the postulancy. The postulancy will last one year. **(17)** During this time, the candidate should examine whether she is attracted to this type of life and whether it is suitable to her. The directress should also diligently consider whether or not the person in question is suitable for this type of life. After a year, if the postulant shows evidence of a stable will and an earnest desire to serve God, she should be admitted to the novitiate.

544 The novitiate[109] is to last one year, without any interruption. At this time the novice should be taught about the virtues relating to the vows and about the importance of the vows. The directress should do her utmost to provide a solid formation. Let her train the novices in the practice of humility, because only a humble heart keeps the vows easily and experiences the great joys that God pours out upon the faithful soul.

The novices should not be burdened with duties that entail responsibilities, so that they may be free to devote themselves to their own perfection. They are obliged to observe the rules and statutes strictly, as are the postulants.

545 **(18)** After a year of novitiate, if the novice proves faithful, she may be admitted to make her profession for one year. This is to be repeated for three years. She may then be given duties of responsibility. However, she will still belong to the novitiate, and once a week she must attend conferences together with the novices, and she will spend the last six months entirely in the novitiate in order to prepare well for her solemn profession.[110]

546 Meals. We will have no meat. Our meals shall be such that not even the poor will have any reason to envy us. Still, feast days may differ slightly from regular days. The sisters will eat three times a day. Fasts, especially the two great ones, will be observed strictly, according to the original spirit. The food should be the same for all the nuns without **(19)** exception so that communal life may be kept pure. This refers not only to food but to clothing and the furnishing of cells as well. However, if a sister should fall ill, she should receive every consideration.

547 Prayers. One hour of meditation, Holy Mass and Holy Communion, prayers, two examinations of conscience, office,[111] rosary, spiritual reading, one hour of prayer during the night. As to the horarium, it is better to draw it up after we have begun to live this type of life.

548 Suddenly I heard these words in my soul: **My daughter, I assure you of a permanent income on which you will live. Your duty will be to trust completely in My goodness, and My duty will be to give you all you need. I am making Myself dependent upon your trust: if your trust is great, then My generosity will be without limit.**

549 **(20)** Work. As poor persons, the nuns themselves will do all the work in the convent. Each one should be glad when she is given some work which is humbling or which goes against her nature, as that will greatly help her interior formation. The superior will often change the sisters' duties, and in this way help them to detach themselves completely from the little details to which women have a great attachment. Truly, I often find it amusing to see with my own eyes souls who have forsaken really great things only to attach themselves to fiddle faddle; that is, trifles. Each sister, including even the superior, shall work in the kitchen for a month. Every one should take a turn at every chore which is to be done in the convent.

550 And always and in everything, their intention should be pure, for every sort of mixed motive is displeasing to God. They should accuse themselves of all external transgressions, **(21)** and ask the superior for a penance. They should do this in a spirit of humility.

They should love one another with a sublime love, with a pure love, seeing God's likeness in every sister. Love should be the special characteristic of this little community, so they must not close up their hearts, but embrace the whole world, rendering mercy to every soul through prayer, according to their calling. If we live in this spirit of mercy, we ourselves will obtain mercy.

551 How great should each one's love for the Church be! As a good child prays for the mother it loves, so also should every Christian soul pray for the Church, its Mother. What then should be said of us religious who have especially committed ourselves to praying for the Church? How great, then, is our apostolate, hidden though it be. All our little daily nothings will be placed at the feet of the Lord Jesus as a propitiatory offering for the world; but in order that **(22)** our offering may be pleasing to God, it must be pure. And for it to be pure, the heart must be freed of all natural attachments, and all its affections must be directed towards the Creator, loving all creatures in Him and according to His will; and, acting thus, each with a zealous spirit will bring joy to the Church.

552 In addition to the vows, I see one rule as most important. Although all the rules are important, I put this one in first place, and it is silence. Truly, if this rule were to be observed strictly, I would not worry about the others. Women are very fond of talking, but the Holy Spirit does not speak to a soul that is distracted and garrulous. He speaks by His quiet inspirations to a soul that is recollected, to a soul that knows how to keep silence. If silence were strictly observed, there would not be any grumbling, bitterness, slandering, or gossip, and charity

would not be tarnished. **(23)** In a word, many wrongs would not be done. Silent lips are pure gold and bear witness to holiness within.

553   But I want to speak immediately of a second rule; that is, speech. Keeping silent when one ought to speak is an imperfection and sometimes even a sin. And so, let all the sisters take part in recreation, and the superior should not dispense them from this except for a matter of great importance. Recreation is an opportunity for getting to know one another. Let each sister speak her mind in all simplicity for the edification of the others and not in a spirit of superiority nor, God forbid, in a quarrelsome manner, for that would not be in keeping with perfection and the spirit of our vocation, which should be especially characterized by love. Twice a day, there will be a recreation of one half hour. But if a sister breaks silence outside that time, **(24)** she must accuse herself before the superior at once and ask for a penance, and the superior should punish these offenses with public penances, or else she will answer for this before the Lord.

554   Enclosure.[112] No one may enter the enclosure without the special permission of the Ordinary and under very special circumstances, such as the administration of the Sacraments to the ill in order to prepare them for death, and for the burial rites. There also may be need of letting in a workman to do some repairs, but for this a specific permission will be required. The door to the enclosure will always be locked and only the superior will have the key.

555   The use of the parlor. None of the sisters will make use of the parlor without special permission of the superior, and the superior should not permit frequent visits. **(25)** Those who have died to the world should not be going back to it, not even through conversations. But if the superior thinks it right to permit some sister to go to the

parlor, let her observe the following directions. She herself should accompany the sister, and if she cannot do so, she should arrange to be replaced by a sister who will be bound to confidence and must not repeat what she has heard, but who is to inform the superior of everything. Conversations ought to be short, unless there is permission for extra time for the sake of the person who has come for the visit. However, the curtain is not to be drawn aside, except for very special cases, as for example when a mother or father urgently asks that this be done.

556 Letters. Every sister may write sealed letters to the Ordinary to whom the house is subject. For any other letter, permission is required, and the sister shall hand the letter unsealed to the superior. The superior is to be guided by the spirit of love (26) and prudence, and has the right to send or withhold the letter, in the light of whatever is for the greater glory of God. However, I would like very much that such communications be as rare as possible. Let us help people by prayer and mortification, and not by correspondence.

557 Confession. Both the regular and the extraordinary confessors for the community will be appointed by the Ordinary [Bishop].[113] There will be one regular confessor, and he will hear the sisters' confessions once a week. The extraordinary confessor will come once every three months, and each sister is obliged to see him, even if she makes no confession. The two confessors will hold their posts in the convent for three years. Then there will be a secret vote, and the superior will submit the results to the Ordinary. The confessor can be re-appointed for an additional three years and even a third three-year term. (27) The sisters will make their confession through a locked grille. The conferences to the community will also be given through a grille, covered with a dark curtain. The sisters will never talk among themselves about confession or the confessors; rather, let them pray

for them that God may give them the light to direct their souls.

558 Holy Communion. The sisters should never talk about who goes more and who goes less frequently to Holy Communion. They should refrain from passing judgment on this subject which does not concern them. All judgments in this matter belong exclusively to the confessor. The superior may speak to a sister, not to inquire why she is not going to Communion, but simply to make confession available to her. The superiors should never dare to enter into the domain of the sisters' consciences. The superior may sometimes arrange that the community offer **(28)** Communion for a certain intention. Each sister should strive for the greatest purity of soul, so that she might receive the Divine Visitor every day.

559 On one occasion, when I entered the chapel, I saw the walls of a building in a state of disrepair [a torn down building].[114] The windows were without panes, and the doors had only frames with no paneling. Then I heard these words in my soul: **This is where the convent will be.** I was a little disappointed that these ruins were to be the convent.

560 Thursday. I felt urged to undertake as soon as possible the task which the Lord was asking of me. While making my confession, I was holding to my own opinion over that of the confessor. At first, I did not realize this, but when I was making my Holy Hour I saw the Lord Jesus **(29)** as He appears in the Image, and He told me that I must repeat to my confessor and my superiors everything He says to me or asks of me... **and do only what you receive permission to do.** And He gave me to know how displeased He was with persons who are self-willed, and I recognized that I was one of these. I saw this shadow of self-will in myself, and I threw myself in the dust[115] before His Majesty and, with a broken heart, begged His pardon. But Jesus did not let me remain in this state

for long. His divine gaze filled my heart with such joy that I have no words to express it. And Jesus gave me to know that I should ask Him more questions and seek His advice. Truly, how sweet is the look of my Lord; His eyes penetrate my soul to its most secret depths. My spirit communicates with God without any word being spoken. I am aware that He is living in me and I in Him.

561 **(30)** All at once, I saw the image in some small chapel and at that moment I saw that the chapel became an enormous and beautiful temple. And in this temple I saw the Mother of God with the Infant in Her arms. And a moment later, the Infant Jesus disappeared from the arms of His Mother, and I saw the living image of Jesus Crucified. The Mother of God told me to do what She had done, that, even when joyful, I should always keep my eyes fixed on the cross, and She told me that the graces God was granting me were not for me alone, but for other souls as well.

562 When I see the Infant Jesus during Holy Mass, it is not always the same: sometimes He is very joyous, and sometimes He is not even looking at the chapel. At present, He is often very joyful when our confessor [Father Sopocko] offers Holy Mass. I was greatly surprised that the Infant Jesus loves him so much. Sometimes I see Him dressed in a colorful pinafore.[116]

563 **(31)** Before I came to Vilnius and met this confessor, I once saw a rather small church and near it, this congregation.[117] The convent had twelve cells: each nun was to live separately. I saw the priest [Father Sopocko] who was helping me to prepare the convent and whom I was to meet some years later, but whom I already knew from the vision. I saw how he was arranging everything in the convent with great care, assisted by another priest [probably Father Wantuchowski[118]] whom I have not yet met. I saw the iron grating, covered with a dark curtain, and the sisters did not go out to the church.

564 On the feast day of the Immaculate Conception of the
Mother of God, during Holy Mass, I heard the rustling
of garments and saw the most holy Mother of God in a
most beautiful radiance. Her white garment was girdled
with a blue (32) sash. She said to me, *You give Me great
joy when you adore the Holy Trinity for the graces and
privileges which were accorded Me.* And She
immediately disappeared.

Penances and Mortification.

565 Interior mortifications take the first place, but besides
this, we must practice exterior mortifications, strictly
determined, so that all can practice them. These are: on
three days a week, Wednesday, Friday and Saturday,
there will be a strict fast; each Friday, all the sisters—
each one in her own cell—will take the discipline[119] for
the length of the recitation of Psalm 50, and all will do
this at the same time; namely, three o'clock; and this will
be offered for dying sinners. During the two great
fasts,[120] ember days[121] and vigils,[122] the food will consists
of a piece of bread and some water, once a day.

Let each sister try to observe these mortifications which
are prescribed (33) for all. But if anyone desires to do
something more, she should ask the superior for
permission. One more general mortification: no sister is
allowed to enter the cell of another without special
permission from the superior, but the superior should
sometimes unexpectedly enter the cells of the sisters, not
in order to spy, but in the spirit of love and the
responsibility which she has before God. None of the
sisters will lock anything; the rule will be the general key
for all.

566 One day, after Holy Communion, I suddenly saw the
Infant Jesus standing by my kneeler and holding on to it
with His two little hands. Although He was but a little
Child, my soul was filled with awe and fear, for I see in
Him my Judge, my Lord, and my Creator, before whose

holiness the Angels tremble. At the same time, my soul was flooded with such unspeakable **(34)** love that I thought I would die under its influence. I now see that Jesus first strengthens my soul and makes it capable of abiding with Him, for otherwise I would not be able to bear what I experience at such a moment.

Relationship of Sisters with the Superior.

567   All the sisters should respect the superior as the Lord Jesus himself, as I mentioned when speaking about the vow of obedience. They should behave toward her with childlike trust, and should never murmur or find fault with her commands, as this is very displeasing to God. Let each be guided by a spirit of faith in her realtionship to superiors; let her ask with simplicity for all that she needs. God forbid that it ever happen or be repeated that any of the sisters would be a cause of sorrow or tears to the superior. Let each one know that as the fourth commandment obliges a child to honor its parents, in like manner is the religious bound to respect her superior. Only a bad **(35)** religious would take the liberty of judging her superior. Let the sisters be sincere with the superior, telling her about everything and about their needs with childlike simplicity.

The sisters will address the superior thus: "With your leave, Sister Superior." They shall never kiss her hand, but whenever they meet her in the corridor or enter her cell, they should say, "Praised be Jesus Christ," bowing their heads slightly.

They shall address each other as "Sister," adding the proper name. Their relationship toward the superior should be marked by a spirit of faith and not by sentimentality or flattery, as these are unworthy of a religious and would degrade her very much. A religious should be as free as a queen, and will be such only when she lives in the spirit of faith. We should obey and respect the superior, not because she is good, holy or prudent, but solely because she represents God, and by obeying her we are obeying God himself.

(36) Relationship of the Superior to the Sisters.

568 The superior should be distinguished by humility and love toward each sister without exception. She must not let herself be led by likes and dislikes, but by the spirit of Christ alone. Let her be aware that God will demand of her an account for each sister. She should not moralize to the sisters, but rather set them an example of profound humility and self-denial; this will be the most efficacious lesson she can give her subjects. She should be firm, but never harsh. She should be patient when bothered with the same questions. Even if she has to give the same answer a hundred times over, she should do so with equanimity. Let her strive to anticipate the sisters' needs rather than wait till they ask for this or that, for people vary in disposition.

If the superior notices that a sister is sad or is suffering, she should try her very best to help and comfort her. She should pray much and ask for light **(37)** in order to know how to deal with each sister, for each soul is a world of its own. God has various ways of communicating with souls, ways that are often beyond our comprehension and notice. Therefore the superior should be careful not to hinder God's action in a soul. She should never reprimand a sister when irritated; rather, reprimands should always be seasoned with encouragement. The person is to be helped to recognize and acknowledge her error, but she should not be crushed.

The superior should be outstanding for a love for her sisters which shows itself in actions. She should take upon herself all burdens so as to ease the burdens of the sisters. She should not demand any services from them, but should respect them as brides of Jesus and be always ready to serve them, day and night. Let her ask rather than order. Her heart should be open to the sufferings of the sisters, and she herself should look closely at, and learn from, the open book; namely, Jesus Crucified. Let her pray fervently for light, especially when she has some important dealing with a **(38)** sister. She should be on her guard lest she interfere with the sisters' consciences, for only a priest has this grace. But it may happen that a sister may feel the necessity to pour out her soul to the superior, in which case the superior may listen to this outpouring, but she is bound to secrecy, as nothing hurts a person so much as to have something she has said in confidence or in secret talked about with others. Women usually have weak heads in this respect; it is rarely that one finds a woman with a man's mind. The superior should strive for deep union with God, and God will govern through her. The most holy Mother will be the superioress[123] of the convent, and we shall be Her faithful daughters.

569 December 15, 1935. From early morning, today, a strange power has been pushing me to action, not giving me a moment's peace. A strange ardor has been lit in my heart, urging me to action, and I cannot stop it. This is a secret martyrdom known only to God, but let Him do **(39)** with me as He pleases; my heart is ready for anything. O Jesus, my dearest Master, do not abandon me, not even for a moment. Jesus, You know well how weak I am of myself; that is why I know that it is my weakness that forces You to be with me constantly.

570 On one occasion, I saw Jesus in a bright garment; this was in the greenhouse. [He said to me,] **Write what I say to you. My delight is to be united with you. With great desire, I wait and long for the time when I shall take up My residence sacramentally in your convent. My spirit will rest in that convent and I will bless its neighborhood in a special way. Out of love for you all, I will avert any punishments which are rightly meted out by My Father's justice. My daughter, I have inclined My heart to your requests. Your assignment and duty here on earth is to**

beg for mercy for **(40)** the whole world. **No soul will be justified until it turns with confidence to My mercy, and this is why the first Sunday after Easter is to be the Feast of Mercy. On that day, priests are to tell everyone about My great and unfathomable mercy. I am making you the administrator of My mercy. Tell the confessor that the Image is to be on view in the church and not within the enclosure in that convent. By means of this Image I shall be granting many graces to souls; so let every soul have access to it.**

571   O my Jesus, Eternal Truth, I fear nothing, neither hardships nor sufferings; I fear only one thing, and that is to offend You. My Jesus, I would rather not exist than make You sad. Jesus, You know that my love knows no one but You. My soul is absorbed in You.

572   **(41)** Oh, how great should be the ardor of every soul who will live in that convent, since God desires to come and live with us! Let everyone remember that if we religious do not intercede before God, who will? Each of us should burn like a pure sacrifice before the majesty of God, but to be pleasing to God, each one should unite herself closely to Jesus. It is only with Him, in Him and through Him that we can be pleasing to God.

573   December 21, 1935. One day my confessor [Father Sopocko] told me to go and look at a certain house to see whether it was the same house I had seen in my vision. When I went with my confessor to see that house, or rather those ruins, at a glance I recognized that they were the same as I had seen in my vision. The moment I touched the boards which had been nailed together in place of the doors, a strength pervaded my soul like a flash, giving me **(42)** unshakable certitude. I went away quickly from that place, my heart full of joy, for it seemed to me that there was a certain force chaining me to that place.

I am very happy to see that everything agrees perfectly

with what I saw in the vision. When the confessor spoke to me about the arrangement of the cells and other things, I recognized everything to be the same as had been told to me by Jesus. I am delighted that God is acting in this way through my confessor, but I am not surprised that God is giving him so much light; since God, who is Light itself, lives in a pure and humble heart, and all sufferings and adversities serve but to reveal the soul's holiness. When I returned home, I went immediately to our chapel to rest a while. Then suddenly I heard these words in my soul: **Do not fear anything. I am with you. These matters are in My hands and I will bring them to fruition according to My mercy, for nothing can oppose My will.**

(43)   Christmas Eve, 1935.

574 From early morning, my spirit was immersed in God. His presence pervaded my whole being. In the evening, before supper, I went to the chapel for a minute to share the wafer, at the feet of Jesus, with those who are far away and whom Jesus loves greatly and to whom I owe so much. Just as I was spiritually sharing the wafer with a certain person [probably Father Sopocko], I heard these words within me: **His heart is for Me a heaven on earth.** When I was leaving the chapel, in an instant, God's omnipotence enveloped me. I understood how greatly God loves us. Oh, if people could at least partly comprehend and understand this!

Christmas Day.

575 Midnight Mass. During Holy Mass, I again saw the little Infant Jesus, extremely beautiful, joyfully stretching out His little arms to me. **(44)** After Holy Communion, I heard the words: **I am always in your heart; not only when you receive Me in Holy Communion, but always.** I spent these holydays in great joy.

576 O Holy Trinity, Eternal God, my spirit is drowned in Your beauty. The ages are as nothing in Your sight. You

are always the same. Oh, how great is Your majesty. Jesus, why do You conceal Your majesty, why have You left Your heavenly throne and dwelt among us? The Lord answered me, **My daughter, love has brought Me here, and love keeps Me here. My daughter, if you knew what great merit and reward is earned by one act of pure love for Me, you would die of joy. I am saying this that you may constantly unite yourself with Me through love, for this is the goal of the life of your soul. This act is an act of the will. Know that a pure soul is humble. (45) When you lower and empty yourself before My majesty, I then pursue you with My graces and make use of My omnipotence to exalt you.**

577 Once, when my confessor told me to say "Glory be to the Father" as my penance, it took me a very long time; and I began many times, but did not finish, because my spirit became united with God, and I could not stick to the prayer. Quite frequently, I am unwittingly enveloped by God's omnipotence and become entirely plunged in Him through love, and then I do not know what is going on around me. When I told my confessor that this short prayer often takes very much of my time and that sometimes I cannot even finish it, he told me to say it right away, there, at the confessional. However, my spirit became immersed in God and, in spite of my efforts, I could not think as I wished. And so the confessor said, "Please repeat after me." **(46)** I repeated every word, but while I was pronouncing each word, my spirit would be steeped in the Person I was naming.

578 On one occasion, Jesus told me, concerning a certain priest [probably Father Sopocko], that these present years would be the adornment of his priestly life. The days of suffering always seem longer, but they too will pass, though they pass so slowly that it seems they are moving backwards. However, their end is near, and then will come endless and inconceivable joy. Eternity! Who can understand this one word which comes from

You, O incomprehensible God, this one word: eternity!

579 I know that the graces given me by God are often meant exclusively for certain souls. Awareness of this fills me with great joy; I always rejoice at the good of other souls as if it were my own.

580 **(47)** On a certain occasion, the Lord said to me, **I am more deeply wounded by the small imperfections of chosen souls than by the sins of those living in the world.** It made me very sad that chosen souls make Jesus suffer, and Jesus told me, **These little imperfections are not all. I will reveal to you a secret of My Heart: what I suffer from chosen souls. Ingratitude in return for so many graces is My Heart's constant food, on the part of [such] a chosen soul. Their love is lukewarm, and My Heart cannot bear it; these souls force Me to reject them. Others distrust My goodness and have no desire to experience that sweet intimacy in their own hearts, but go in search of Me, off in the distance, and do not find Me. This distrust of My goodness hurts Me very much. If My death has not convinced you of My love, what will? Often a soul wounds Me mortally, and then no one can comfort Me. (48) They use My graces to offend Me. There are souls who despise My graces as well as all the proofs of My love. They do not wish to hear My call, but proceed into the abyss of hell. The loss of these souls plunges Me into deadly sorrow. God though I am, I cannot help such a soul because it scorns Me; having a free will, it can spurn Me or love Me. You, who are the dispenser of My mercy, tell all the world about My goodness, and thus you will comfort My Heart.**

581 **I will tell you most when you converse with Me in the depths of your heart. Here, no one can disturb My actions. Here, I rest as in a garden enclosed.**

582 The interior of my soul is like a large and magnificent world in which God and I live. Except for God, no one is allowed there. At the beginning of this life with God,

(49) I was dazzled and overcome with awe. His radiance blinded me, and I thought He was not in my heart; and yet those were the moments when God was working in my soul. Love was becoming purer and stronger, and the Lord brought my will into the closest union with His own holy Will. No one will understand what I experience in that splendid palace of my soul where I abide constantly with my Beloved. No exterior thing hinders my union with God. Even if I used the most forceful words, they would not express even a shadow of how my soul revels in happiness and inexplicable love, as great and pure as the spring from which it flows; that is, God himself. My spirit is so prevaded with God that I feel it physically, and the body partakes of these joys. Although it happens that God's touches vary in the same soul, they come, however, from the same source.

583 **(50)** On one occasion, I saw Jesus thirsting and fainting, and He said to me, **I thirst.** When I gave Him water, He took it, but did not drink and immediately disappeared. He was clothed as He was during His Passion.

584 **When you reflect upon what I tell you in the depths of your heart, you profit more than if you had read many books. Oh, if souls would only want to listen to My voice when I am speaking in the depths of their hearts, they would reach the peak of holiness in a short time.**

585 January 8, 1936. When I went to see the Archbishop [Jalbrzykowski], I told him that Jesus was asking that I pray for God's mercy upon the world and that there be a religious congregation which would entreat the mercy of God for the world. I asked his permission for all the Lord Jesus was demanding of me. The Arch **(51)** bishop answered me in these words: "As for prayer, I give my permission and even encourage you, Sister, to pray as much as possible for the world and to beg God's mercy, as mercy is what we all need; and I presume that your confessor certainly does not forbid you to pray for this

intention. But as regards this congregation, wait a while, Sister, so that all things may arrange themselves more favorably. This thing is good in itself, but there is no need to hurry. If it is God's will, it will be done, whether it be a little sooner or a little later. Why shouldn't it be? There are so many different kinds of congregations; this one too will come to be if God so wills. Be completely at peace. The Lord Jesus can do all things. Strive for a close union with God and do not lose heart." These words filled me with great joy.

586 When I left the Archbishop's house, I heard the following words in my soul: **To confirm your spirit, (52) I speak through My representatives in accordance with what I demand of you, but know that this will not always be so. They will opppose you in many things, and through this My grace will be manifest in you, and it will be evident that this matter is My doing. But as for you, fear nothing; I am always with you. And know this, too, My daughter: all creatures, whether they know it or not, and whether they want to or not, always fulfill My will.**

587 Once, I suddenly saw Jesus in great majesty, and He spoke these words to me: **My daughter, if you wish, I will this instant create a new world, more beautiful than this one, and you will live there for the rest of your life.** I answered, "I don't want any worlds. I want You, Jesus. I want to love You, with the same love that You have for me. I beg You for only one thing: to make my heart capable of loving you. (53) I am very much surprised at Your offer, my Jesus; what are those worlds to me? Even if You gave me a thousand of them, what are they to me? You know very well, Jesus, that my heart is dying of longing for You. Everything that is not You is nothing to me." —At that moment, I could no longer see anything, but a strange force took over my soul, a strange fire sprang up in my heart, and I entered into a kind of agony for Him. Then I heard these words: **With no other soul do I unite myself as closely and in such a**

way as I do with you, and this because of the deep humility and ardent love which you have for Me.

588 On one occasion, I heard these words within me: **Every movement of your heart is known to me. Know, My daughter, that one glance of yours directed at someone else would wound Me (54) more than many sins committed by another person.**

589 Love casts out fear. Since I came to love God with my whole being and with all the strength of my heart, fear has left me. Even if I were to hear the most terrifying things about God's justice, I would not fear Him at all, because I have come to know Him well. God is love, and His Spirit is peace. I see now that my deeds which have flowed from love are more perfect than those which I have done out of fear. I have placed my trust in God and fear nothing. I have given myself over to His holy will; let Him do with me as He wishes, and I will still love Him.

590 When I receive Holy Communion, I entreat and beg the Savior to heal my tongue, that I may never fail in love of neighbor.

591 **(55)** Jesus, You know how ardently I desire to hide so that no one may know me but Your sweetest Heart. I want to be a tiny violet, hidden in the grass, unknown in a magnificent enclosed garden in which beautiful lilies and roses grow. The beautiful rose and the lovely lily can be seen from afar, but in order to see a little violet, one has to bend low; only its scent gives it away. Oh, how happy I am to be able to hide myself in this way! O my divine Bridegroom, the flower of my heart and the scent of my pure love are for You. My soul has drowned itself in You, Eternal God. From the moment when You yourself drew me to yourself, O my Jesus, the more I have known You, the more ardently I have desired You.

592 I learned in the Heart of Jesus that in heaven itself there is a heaven to which not all, but only chosen souls, have

access. Incomprehensible is the happiness in which the soul will be immersed. O my God, oh, that I could describe this, even in some little degree. **(56)** Souls are penetrated by His divinity and pass from brightness to brightness, an unchanging light, but never monotonous, always new though never changing. O Holy Trinity, make yourself known to souls!

593 O my Jesus, nothing is better for the soul than humiliations. In contempt is the secret of happiness, when the soul recognizes that, of itself, it is only wretchedness and nothingness, and that whatever it possesses of good is a gift of God. When the soul sees that everything is given it freely and that the only thing it has of itself is its own misery, this is what sustains it in a continual act of humble prostration before the majesty of God. And God, seeing the soul in such a disposition, pursues it with His graces. As the soul continues to immerse itself more deeply into the abyss of its nothingness and need, God uses His omnipotence to exalt it. If there is a truly happy soul upon earth, it can only be **(57)** a truly humble soul. At first, one's self-love suffers greatly on this account, but after a soul has struggled courageously, God grants it much light by which it sees how wretched and full of deception everything is. God alone is in its heart. A humble soul does not trust itself, but places all its confidence in God. God defends the humble soul and lets Himself into its secrets, and the soul abides in unsurpassable happiness which no one can comprehend.

594 One evening, one of the deceased sisters, who had already visited me a few times, appeared to me. The first time I had seen her, she had been in great suffering, and then gradually these sufferings had diminished; this time she was radiant with happiness, and she told me she was already in heaven. She told me that God had tried **(58)** our house with tribulation because Mother General [Michael] had given in to doubts, not believing what I

had said about this soul. And further, as a sign that she only now was in heaven, God would bless our house. Then she came closer to me, embraced me sincerely and said, "I must go now." I understood how closely the three stages of a soul's life are bound together; that is to say, life on earth, in purgatory and in heaven [the Communion of Saints].

595 I have noticed many times that God tries certain people on account of those things about which He spoke to me, for mistrust displeases Jesus. Once, when I saw that God had tried a certain Archbishop [Jalbrzykowski] because he was opposed to the cause and distrustful of it, I felt sorry for him and pleaded with God for him, and God relieved his suffering. God is very displeased with lack of trust in Him, and this is why some souls lose many graces. Distrust **(59)** hurts His most sweet Heart, which is full of goodness and incomprehensible love for us. A priest should sometimes be distrustful in order to better ascertain the genuineness of gifts bestowed on a given soul; and when he does so in order to direct the soul to deeper union with God, his will be a great and incomprehensible reward indeed. But there is a great difference between this and disrespect and distrust of divine graces in a soul simply because one cannot comprehend and penetrate these things with one's mind, and this latter is displeasing to the Lord. I greatly pity souls who encounter inexperienced priests.

596 Once, a certain priest [Father Sopocko[124]] asked me to pray for him. I promised to pray, and asked for a mortification. When I received permission for **(60)** a certain mortification, I felt a great desire to give up all the graces that God's goodness would intend for me that day in favor of that priest, and I asked the Lord Jesus to deign to bestow on me all the sufferings and afflictions, both exterior and spiritual, that the priest would have had to suffer during that day. God partially answered my request and, at once, all sorts of difficulties and

adversities sprang up out of nowhere, so much so that one of the sisters remarked out loud that the Lord Jesus must have a hand in this because everyone was trying Sister Faustina. The charges made were so groundless that what some sisters put forward, others denied, while I offered all this in silence on behalf of the priest.

But that was not all; I began to experience interior sufferings. First, I was seized by depression and aversion towards the sisters, then a kind of uncertainty began **(61)** to trouble me. I could not recollect myself during prayer, and various things would take hold of my mind. When, tired out, I entered the chapel, a strange pain seized my soul, and I began to weep softly. Then I heard in my soul a voice, saying, **My daughter, why are you weeping? After all, you yourself offered to undertake these sufferings. Know that what you have taken upon yourself for that soul is only a small portion. He is suffering much more.** And I asked the Lord, "Why are You treating him like that?" The Lord answered me that it was for the triple crown meant for him: that of virginity, the priesthood and martyrdom. At that moment, a great joy flooded my soul at the sight of the great glory that is going to be his in heaven. Right away I said the *Te Deum*[125] for this special grace of God; namely, of learning how God treats those He intends to have close to himself. Thus, all sufferings are nothing in comparison with what awaits us in heaven.

597 **(62)** One day, after our Mass, I suddenly saw my confessor [Father Sopocko] saying Mass in Saint Michael's Church, in front of the picture of the Mother of God. It was at the time of the Offertory, and I saw the Infant Jesus clinging to him as if fleeing from something and seeking refuge in him. But when the time came for Holy Communion, He disappeared as usual. Suddenly, I saw the Blessed Mother, who shielded him with Her cloak and said, *Courage, My son, courage.* She said something else which I could not hear.

598   Oh, how ardently I desire that every soul would praise
Your mercy. Happy is the soul that calls upon the mercy
of the Lord. It will see that the Lord will defend it as His
glory, as He said. And who would dare fight against
God? All you souls, praise the Lord's mercy **(63)** by
trusting in His mercy all your life and especially at the
hour of your death. And fear nothing, dear soul,
whoever you are; the greater the sinner, the greater his
right to Your mercy, O Lord. O incomprehensible
goodness! God is the first to stoop to the sinner. O Jesus,
I wish to glorify Your mercy on behalf of thousands of
souls. I know very well, O my Jesus, that I am to keep
telling souls about Your goodness, about Your
incomprehensible mercy.

599   On one occasion, after a person had asked me for prayer,
when I met the Lord I said to Him, "Jesus, I especially
love those souls whom You love." And Jesus answered,
**And as for Me, I bestow special graces on those souls for
whom you intercede.**

600   How wondrously Jesus defends me; truly this is a great
grace of God which I have experienced for a long time
now.

601   **(64)** Once, when one of our sisters[126] became fatally ill
and all the community[127] was gathered together, there
was also a priest[128] there who gave the sister absolution.
Suddenly, I saw many spirits of darkness. Then,
forgetting that I was with the sisters, I seized the holy-
water sprinkler and sprinkled the spirits, and they
disappeared at once. However, when the sisters came to
the refectory, Mother Superior [Borgia] remarked that I
should not have sprinkled the sick sister in the presence
of the priest, as this was his duty. I accepted the
admonition in the spirit of penance, but holy water is
indeed of great help to the dying.

602   My Jesus, You see how weak I am of myself. Therefore,
You yourself direct my affairs. And know, Jesus, that

without You I will not budge for any cause, but with You I will take on the most difficult things.

603 **(65)** January 29, 1936. In the evening, when I was in my cell, I suddenly saw a great light and a dark gray cross high up within the light. Suddenly, I found myself caught up close to the cross. I gazed at it intently, but could not understand anything, and so I prayed, asking what it could mean. At that moment I saw the Lord Jesus, and the cross disappeared. The Lord Jesus was sitting in a great light, and His legs, up to the knees, were drowned in the light so that I could not see them. Jesus bent toward me, looked at me kindly and spoke to me about the will of the Heavenly Father. He told me that the most perfect and holy soul is the one that does the will of the Father, but there are not many such, and that He looks with special love upon the soul who lives His will. And Jesus told me that I was doing the will of God perfectly... **and for this reason I am uniting Myself with you and communing with you in a special and intimate way.**

God embraces with His incomprehensible love the soul who **(66)** lives by His will. I understood how much God loves us, how simple He is, though incomprehensible, and how easy it is to commune with Him, despite His great majesty. With no one do I feel as free and as much at ease as with Him. Even a mother and her truly loving child do not understand each other so well as God and I do. When I was in that state of communion with God, I saw two particular persons, and their sad interior condition was revealed to me. They were in a sorrowful state, but I trust that they, too, will glorify the mercy of God.

604 At the same time, I saw a certain person [Father Sopocko] and, in part, the condition of his soul and the ordeals God was sending him. His sufferings were of the mind and in a form so acute that I pitied him and said to

the Lord, "Why do you treat him like that?" And the Lord answered, **For the sake of his triple crown.** And the Lord also gave me to understand what unimaginable glory awaits the person who resembles the **(67)** suffering Jesus here on earth. That person will resemble Jesus in His glory. The Heavenly Father will recognize and glorify our soul to the extent that He sees in us a resemblance to His Son. I understood that this assimilation into Jesus is granted to us while we are here on earth. I see pure and innocent souls upon whom God has exercised His justice; these souls are the victims who sustain the world and who fill up what is lacking in the Passion of Jesus. They are not many in number. I rejoice greatly that God has allowed me to know such souls.

605   O Holy Trinity, Eternal God, I thank You for allowing me to know the greatness and the various degrees of glory to which souls attain. Oh, what a great difference of depth in the knowledge of God there is between one degree and another! Oh, if people could only know this! O my God, if I were thereby able to attain one more degree, I would gladly suffer all the torments of the martyrs put together. **(68)** Truly, all those torments seem as nothing to me compared with the glory that is awaiting us for all eternity. O Lord, immerse my soul in the ocean of Your divinity and grant me the grace of knowing You; for the better I know You, the more I desire You, and the more my love for You grows. I feel in my soul an unfathomable abyss which only God can fill. I lose myself in Him as a drop does in the ocean. The Lord has inclined himself to my misery like a ray of the sun upon a barren and rocky desert. And yet, under the influence of His rays, my soul has become covered with verdure, flowers, and fruit, and has become a beautiful garden for His repose.

606   My Jesus, despite Your graces, I see and feel all my misery. I begin my day with battle and end it with battle.

As soon as I conquer one obstacle, ten more appear **(69)** to take its place. But I am not worried, because I know that this is the time of struggle, not peace. When the burden of the battle becomes too much for me, I throw myself like a child into the arms of the heavenly Father and trust I will not perish. O my Jesus, how prone I am to evil, and this forces me to be constantly vigilant. But I do not lose heart. I trust God's grace, which abounds in the worst misery.

607 In the midst of the worst difficulties and adversities, I do not lose inner peace or exterior balance, and this discourages my adversaries. Patience in adversity gives power to the soul.

608 February 2, [1936]. In the morning, when the bell awoke me, I was so overcome by drowsiness which I could not shake off that I jumped into cold water, and after two minutes the sleepiness left me. When I came to meditation **(70)** a host of absurd thoughts swarmed into my head, so much so that I had to struggle throughout the whole meditation. It was the same during prayer time, but when Mass began, a strange silence and joy filled my heart. Just then, I saw Our Lady with the Infant Jesus, and the Holy Old Man [St. Joseph] standing behind them. The most holy Mother said to me, *Take My Dearest Treasure,* and She handed me the Infant Jesus. When I took the Infant Jesus in my arms, the Mother of God and Saint Joseph disappeared. I was left alone with the Infant Jesus.

609 I said to Him, "I know that You are my Lord and Creator even though You are so tiny." Jesus stretched His little arms out to me and looked at me with a smile. My spirit was filled with incomparable joy. Then suddenly Jesus disappeared, and it was time for Holy Communion. I went with the other sisters to the Holy Table, my soul deeply moved. After Holy Communion, **(71)** I heard these words in my soul: **I am in your heart, I whom you had in your arms.** I then pleaded with Jesus

for a certain soul [Father Sopocko], asking the Lord to grant him the grace to fight, and to take this trial from him. **As you ask, so shall it be, but his merit will not be lessened.** Joy reigned in my soul that God is so good and merciful; God grants everything that we ask of Him with trust.

610 After each conversation with the Lord, my soul is extraordinarily strengthened, and a profound tranquility prevails therein and gives me such courage that I do not fear anything in the world, but fear only lest I make Jesus sad.

611 O my Jesus, I implore You by the goodness of Your most sweet Heart, let Your anger diminish and show us Your mercy. May Your wounds be our shield against Your Father's **(72)** justice. I have come to know You, O God, as the source of mercy that vivifies and nourishes every soul. Oh, how great is the mercy of the Lord; it surpasses all His other qualities! Mercy is the greatest attribute of God; everything that surrounds me speaks to me of this. Mercy is the life of souls; His compassion is inexhaustible. O Lord, look on us and deal with us according to Your countless mercies, according to Your great mercy.

612 One time, I was in doubt as to whether what had happened to me had seriously offended the Lord Jesus or not. As I could not solve this doubt, I made up my mind not to go to Communion before first going to confession, although I immediately made an act of contrition, as it is my habit to ask for forgiveness after the slightest transgression. During those days when I did not receive Holy Communion, **(73)** I did not feel the presence of God. This caused me unspeakable pain, but I took it as a punishment for sin. However, at the time of Holy Confession I was reproached for not going to Holy Communion, because what had happened to me was not an obstacle to receiving Holy Communion. After confession, I received Holy Communion, and I saw the

Lord Jesus who said to me, **Know, My daughter, that you caused Me more sorrow by not uniting yourself with Me in Holy Communion than you did by that small transgression.**

613 One day, I saw a small chapel in which six sisters were receiving Holy Communion from our confessor [Father Sopocko], who was wearing a surplice and stole.[129] There were no decorations and no kneelers in the chapel. After Holy Communion, I saw the Lord Jesus as He is represented in the image. Jesus was walking away, and I called to Him, "How can You pass me by and not say anything to me, Lord? Without You, **(74)** I shall do nothing; You must stay with me and bless me, and this community and my country as well." Jesus made the sign of the cross and said, **Do not fear anything; I am always with you.**

614 On the last two days before Lent we had an hour of propitiatory adoration with the girls.[130] During both hours I saw the Lord Jesus as He was after the scourging. My soul felt such great pain that it seemed to me that I was experiencing all those torments in my own body and in my own soul.

615 March 1, 1936. Today during Holy Mass I experienced a strange force and urge to start realizing God's wishes. I had such a clear understanding of the things the Lord was asking of me that truly if I were to say **(75)** that I do not understand what God is demanding from me, I would be lying, because the Lord is making His will known to me so clearly and distinctly that I do not have the least shadow of a doubt about them. I realized that it would be the greatest ingratitude to delay any longer this undertaking which the Lord wishes to bring to fulfillment for His glory and the benefit of a great number of souls. And He is using me as a miserable tool through which to realize His eternal plans of mercy. Truly, how ungrateful my soul would be to resist God's

will any longer. Nothing will stop me any longer, be it persecution, sufferings, sneers, threats, entreaties, hunger, cold, flattery, friendships, adversities, friends or enemies; be it things I am experiencing now or things that will come in the future or even the hatred of hell— nothing will deter me from doing the will of God.

(76) I am not counting on my own strength, but on His omnipotence for, as he gave me the grace of knowing His holy will, He will also grant me the grace of fulfilling it. I cannot fail to mention how much my own lower nature resists this thing, manifesting its own desires, and there results within my soul a great struggle, like that of Jesus in the Garden of Olives. And so I too cry out to God, the Eternal Father, "If it is possible, take this cup from me, but, nevertheless, not my will, but Yours be done, O Lord; may Your will be done." What I am about to go through is no secret to me, but with full knowledge I accept whatever You send me, O Lord. I trust in You, O merciful God, and I wish to be the first to manifest to You that confidence which You demand of souls. O Eternal Truth, help me and enlighten me along the roadways of life, and grant that Your will be accomplished in me.

(77) My God, I desire nothing but the fulfillment of Your will. It does not matter whether it will be easy or difficult. I feel an extraordinary force driving me to action. One thing alone holds me back, and that is holy obedience. O my Jesus, You urge me on the one hand and hold me back and restrain me on the other. In this, too, O my Jesus, may Your holy will be done.

I continued in this state, without a break, for many days. My physical strength declined, and though I did not speak to anyone about it, nevertheless Mother Superior [Borgia] noticed my pain and remarked that I had changed in appearance and was very pale. She told me to go to bed earlier and to sleep longer, and she had a cup of hot milk brought to me in the evening. She had a motherly heart, full of care, and tried to help me. But in the case of spiritual sufferings, **(78)** external things have no influence, and they do not bring much relief. It was from the confessional that I drew my strength and the consolation of knowing that it would not be long before I could begin to act.

616 On Thursday, when I went to my cell, I saw over me the Sacred Host in great brightness. Then I heard a voice that seemed to be coming from above the Host: **In the Host is your power; it will defend you.** After these words, the vision disappeared, but a strange power entered my soul, and a strange light as to what our love for God consists in; namely, in doing His will.

617 O Holy Trinity, Eternal God, I want to shine in the crown of Your mercy as a tiny gem whose beauty depends on the ray of Your **(79)** light and of Your inscrutable mercy. All that is beautiful in my soul is Yours, O God; of myself, I am ever nothing.

618 At the beginning of Lent, I asked my confessor for some mortification for this time of fast. I was told not to cut down on my food but, while eating, to meditate on how the Lord Jesus, on the Cross, accepted vinegar and gall. This would be my mortification. I did not know that this would be so beneficial to my soul. The benefit is that I am meditating constantly on His sorrowful Passion and so, while I am eating, I am not preoccupied with what I am eating, but am reflecting on my Lord's death.

619 At the beginning of Lent, I also asked to have the subject of my particular examen changed, and I was told to do everything with the pure intention of reparation for poor sinners. **(80)** This keeps me in continual union with God, and this intention perfects my actions, because everything I do is done for immortal souls. All hardships and fatigue are as nothing when I think that they reconcile sinful souls with God.

620 Mary is my Instructress, who is ever teaching me how to

live for God. My spirit brightens up in Your gentleness and Your humility, O Mary.

621 On one occasion, when I dropped by the chapel for a five-minute adoration and was praying for a certain soul, I came to understand that God does not always accept our petitions for the souls we have in mind, but directs these to other souls. Hence, although we do not relieve the souls we intended to relieve in their purgatorial suffering, still our prayer is not lost.

622 **(81)** Intimate communion of a soul with God. God approaches a soul in a special way known only to himself and to the soul. No one perceives this mysterious union. Love presides in this union, and everything is achieved by love alone. Jesus gives himself to the soul in a gentle and sweet manner, and in His depths there is peace. He grants the soul many graces and makes it capable of sharing His eternal thoughts. And frequently, He reveals to it His divine plans.

623 Father Andrasz told me that it would be a good thing to have in God's Church a group of souls who would beg for His mercy, because in fact we are all in need of that mercy. After these words, an extraordinary light filled my soul. Oh, how good is the Lord!

624 **(82)** March 18, 1936. Once, I asked the Lord Jesus to take the first step by bringing about some change or some external event, or by letting them expel me, as I found it impossible to leave the Congregation on my own initiative. And I was in an agony over this for more than three hours. I could not pray, but kept submitting my will to the will of God.

The next morning, Mother Superior [Borgia] told me that Mother General [Michael] was transferring me to Warsaw. I answered Mother that perhaps I should not go but leave [the Congregation] directly from here. I regarded this to be the external sign for which I had been asking God. Mother Superior made no reply, but after some time she called me again and said, "You know what, Sister: go anyway and don't worry about wasting a trip, even if you should return immediately." I answered, "All right, I will go," although my heart was seized with pain because I knew **(83)** that by this trip this matter would be delayed. However, I try always to be obedient, despite everything.

625 In the evening, when I was praying, the Mother of God told me, *Your lives must be like Mine: quiet and hidden, in unceasing union with God, pleading for humanity and preparing the world for the second coming of God.*

626 In the evening, during Benediction, my soul was for some time in communion with God the Father. I felt I was in His hand like a little child, and I heard these words in my soul: **Do not fear anything, My daughter; all the adversaries will be shattered at My feet.** At these words, a deep peace and a great interior calm entered my soul.

627 **(84)** When I complained to the Lord that He was taking my help away and that I would be alone again and would not know what to do, I heard these words: **Do not be afraid; I am always with you.** After these words, a deep peace once again entered my soul. His presence penetrated me completely in a way that could be sensed. My spirit was flooded with light, and my body participated in this as well.

628 On the evening of the last day before my departure from Vilnius, an elderly sister[131] revealed the condition of her soul to me. She said that she had already been suffering interiorly for several years, that it seemed to her that all her confessions had been bad, and that she had doubts as to whether the Lord Jesus had forgiven her. I asked her if she had ever told her confessor about this. She answered that she had spoken many **(85)** times about this to her confessors and... "the confessors are always telling me to be at peace, but still I suffer very much, and

nothing brings me relief, and it constantly seems to me that God has not forgiven me." I answered, "You should obey your confessor, Sister, and be fully at peace, because this is certainly a temptation."

But she entreated me with tears in her eyes to ask Jesus if He had forgiven her and whether her confessions had been good or not. I answered forcefully, "Ask Him yourself, Sister, if you don't believe your confessors!" But she clutched my hand and did not want to let me go until I gave her an answer, and she kept asking me to pray for her and to let her know what Jesus would tell me about her. Crying bitterly, she would not let me go and said to me, "I know that the Lord Jesus speaks to you, Sister." Since she was clutching my hand and I could not wrench myself away, I promised her **(86)** I would pray for her. In the evening, during Benediction, I heard these words in my soul: **Tell her that her disbelief wounds My heart more than the sins she committed.** When I told her this, she began to cry like a child, and great joy entered her soul. I understood that God wanted to console this soul through me. Even though it cost me a good deal, I fulfilled God's wish.

629 When I entered the chapel for a moment that same evening, to thank God for all the graces He had bestowed on me in this house, suddenly God's presence enveloped me. I felt like a child in the hands of the best of fathers, and I heard these words: **Do not fear anything. I am always with you.** His love penetrated my whole being. I felt I was entering into such close intimacy with Him that **(87)** I cannot find words to express it.

630 Then I saw one of the seven spirits near me, radiant as at other times, under a form of light. I constantly saw him beside me when I was riding on the train. I saw an angel standing on every church we passed, but surrounded by a light which was paler than that of the spirit who was

accompanying me on the journey, and each of these spirits who were guarding the churches bowed his head to the spirit who was near me.

When I entered the convent gate at Warsaw, the spirit disappeared. I thanked God for His goodness, that He gives us angels for companions. Oh, how little people reflect on the fact that they always have beside them such a guest, and at the same time a witness to everything! Remember, sinners, that you likewise have a witness to all your deeds.

631 O my Jesus, Your goodness surpasses all understanding, and no one will exhaust Your mercy. Damnation is for the **(88)** soul who wants to be damned; but for the one who desires salvation, there is the inexhaustible ocean of the Lord's mercy to draw from. How can a small vessel contain the unfathomable ocean?

632 As I was taking leave of the sisters and was about to depart, one of them[132] apologized much to me for having helped me so little in my duties, and not only for having neglected to help me, but also for having tried to make things more difficult for me. However, in my own heart, I regarded her as a great benefactress, because she had exercised me in patience to such an extent that one of the elder sisters had once said, "Sister Faustina must be either a fool or a saint, for truly, an ordinary person would not tolerate having someone constantly do such things out of spite." However, I had **(89)** always approached her with good will. That particular sister had tried to make my work more difficult to the point that, despite my efforts, she had sometimes succeeded in spoiling what had been well done, as she herself admitted to me at our parting, and for which she begged my pardon. I had not wanted to probe her intentions, but took it as a trial from God...

633 I am greatly surprised at how one can be so jealous. When I see someone else's good, I rejoice at it as if it

were mine. The joy of others is my joy, and the suffering
of others is my suffering, for otherwise I would not dare
to commune with the Lord Jesus. The spirit of Jesus is
always simple, meek, sincere; all malice, envy, and
unkindness disguised under a smile of good will are
clever little devils. A severe word flowing from sincere
love does not wound the heart.

634 **(90)** March 22, [1936]. When I arrived at Warsaw, I went
into the small chapel for a moment to thank the Lord for
a safe journey, and I asked the Lord to give me the
assistance and the grace necessary for everything that
was in store for me here. I submitted myself in all things
to His holy will. I heard these words: **Fear nothing; all
difficulties will serve for the fulfillment of My will.**

635 March 25. In the morning, during meditation, God's
presence enveloped me in a special way, as I saw the
immeasurable greatness of God and, at the same time,
His condescension to His creatures. Then I saw the
Mother of God, who said to me, *Oh, how pleasing to
God is the soul that follows faithfully the inspirations of
His grace! I gave the Savior to the world; as for you, you
have to speak to the world about His great mercy and
prepare the world for the Second* **(91)** *Coming of Him
who will come, not as a merciful Savior, but as a just
Judge. Oh, how terrible is that day! Determined is the
day of justice, the day of divine wrath. The angels
tremble before it. Speak to souls about this great mercy
while it is still the time for* [granting] *mercy. If you keep
silent now, you will be answering for a great number of
souls on that terrible day. Fear nothing. Be faithful to
the end. I sympathize with you.*

636 When I arrived at Walendow, one of the sisters[133] gave
me this welcome: "Sister, now that you have come to us
here, everything is going to be all right." I said to her,
"Why do you say that, Sister?" She answered that she
felt this in her soul. This particular person is full of

simplicity and very pleasing to the Heart of Jesus. The house really was in dire straits [financially]. ...I shall not mention all of that here.

637 **(92)** Confession. As I was preparing for confession, I said to Jesus, hidden in the Blessed Sacrament, "Jesus, I beg You to speak to me through the mouth of this priest. And this will be a sign to me, because he does not know at all that You want me to establish that Congregation of Mercy. Let him say something to me about this mercy."

When I approached the confessional and started my confession, the priest interrupted me and started telling me about the great mercy of God, and he spoke more forcefully about it than I had ever heard anyone speak before. And he asked me, "Do you know that the mercy of the Lord is greater than all His works, that it is the crown of His works?" And I listened attentively to these words which the Lord was speaking through the mouth of the priest. Although I believe that it is always God who speaks through the lips of the priest in the confessional, I experienced it in a special way on that occasion. **(93)**

Although I did not reveal anything of the divine life which is in my soul and only accused myself of my offenses, the priest himself told me very much of what was in my soul and put me under obligation to be faithful to the inspirations of God. He said to me, "You are going through life with the Mother of God, who faithfully responded to every divine inspiration." O my Jesus, who can ever comprehend Your goodness?

638 Jesus, drive away from me the thoughts that are not in accord with Your will. I know that nothing now binds me to this earth but this work of mercy.

639 Thursday. During the evening adoration, I saw Jesus scourged and tortured. He said to me, **My daughter, I**

desire that even in the smallest things, you rely on your confessor. Your greatest sacrifices do not please Me if you practice them without the confessor's (94) permission; on the other hand, the smallest sacrifice finds great value in My eyes, if it is done with his permission. The greatest works are worthless in My eyes if they are done out of self-will, and often they are not in accord with My will and merit punishment rather than reward. And on the other hand, even the smallest of your acts, done with the confessor's permission is pleasing in My eyes and very dear to Me. Hold firmly to this always. Be constantly on the watch, for many souls will turn back from the gates of hell and worship My mercy. But fear nothing, as I am with you. Know that of yourself you can do nothing.

640 On the First Friday of the month, before Communion, I saw a large ciborium (95) filled with sacred hosts. A hand placed the ciborium in front of me, and I took it in my hands. There were a thousand living hosts inside. Then I heard a voice, **These are hosts which have been received by the souls for whom you have obtained the grace of true conversion during this Lent.** That was a week before Good Friday. I spent the day in great interior recollection, emptying myself for the sake of souls.

641 Oh, what joy it is to empty myself for the sake of immortal souls! I know that the grain of wheat must be destroyed and ground between millstones in order to become food. In the same way, I must become destroyed in order to be useful to the Church and souls, even though exteriorly no one will notice my sacrifice. O Jesus, outwardly I want to be hidden, just like this little wafer wherein the eye perceives nothing, and yet I am a host consecrated to You.

642 (96) Palm Sunday. This Sunday, I experienced in a special way the sentiments of the most sweet Heart of Jesus. My spirit was there where Jesus was. I saw Jesus

riding on a donkey's foal, and the disciples and a great multitude with branches in their hands joyfully accompanying the Lord Jesus. Some strewed them before His feet where He was riding, while others raised their branches in the air, leaping and jumping before the Lord and not knowing what to do for joy. And I saw another crowd which came out to meet Jesus, likewise with joyful faces and with branches in their hands, and they were crying out unceasingly with joy. There were little children there also. But Jesus was very grave, and the Lord gave me to know how much He was suffering at the time. And at that moment, I saw nothing but only Jesus, whose Heart was saturated with ingratitude.

643 **(97)** Quarterly confession. Father Bukowski. When some inner force urged me again not to put off this matter, I was unable to find peace. I told the confessor, Father Bukowski, that I could not wait any longer. Father answered me, "Sister, this is an illusion. The Lord Jesus cannot be demanding this. You have made your perpetual vows. All this is an illusion. You are inventing some sort of heresy!" And he was shouting at me, almost at the top of his voice. I asked him whether all of this was an illusion, and He said, "Everything." "Then please tell me what course I must take." "Well, Sister, you must not follow any inspiration. You should get your mind off all this. You should pay no attention to what you hear in your soul and try to carry out your exterior duties well. Give no thought to these things and put them completely out of your mind." I answered, "Good, **(98)** up to now, I have been following my conscience, but now that you direct me, Father, to pay no heed to my interior, I will cease to do so." Then he said, "If the Lord Jesus tells you something again, please let me know, but you must take no action." I answered, "Very well; I will try to be obedient." I do not know why Father was being so severe.

644 When I left the confessional, a multitude of thoughts oppressed my soul. Why be sincere? What I have told is no sin, so I have no duty to tell it to the confessor. And again, what a relief that I do not have to heed my interior any more as long as things are all right on the outside. I do not have to pay attention to anything or to follow the inner voices that have often cost me so much humiliation. From now on, I will be free. And again, **(99)** a strange pain seized my soul: can I not, then, commune with the One whom I desire so greatly? The One who is the whole strength of my soul? I began to cry out, "To whom shall I go, O Jesus?" But from the moment of the confessor's prohibition, great darkness fell upon my soul. I feared lest I hear some inner voice, which would occasion the breaking of my confessor's prohibition. And then again, I die of longing for God. My interior is torn asunder, not having any will of its own, since it has been turned over completely to God.

That was on Wednesday of Holy Week. The suffering intensified on Holy Thursday. When I came to make my meditation, I entered into a kind of agony. I did not feel the presence of God, but all the justice of God weighed heavily upon me. I saw myself as if knocked down for the sins of the world. Satan began to mock me, "See, now you will no longer strive to win souls; look how you've been paid! Nobody will **(100)** believe you that Jesus demands this. See how much you are suffering now, and how much more you are going to suffer! After all, the confessor has now released you from all these things." Now I can live as I like, as long as things are all right outwardly. These dreadful thoughts tormented me throughout the whole hour.

When it was almost time for Holy Mass, my heart was seized with pain; am I, then, to leave the Congregation? And since Father has told me that this is a kind of heresy, am I to fall away from the Church? I cried out to the Lord with a sorrowful interior cry, "Jesus, save me!"

Still, not a single ray of light entered my soul, and I felt my strength failing, as if the body were separating itself from the soul. I submitted to the will of God and repeated, "O God, let whatever You have decided upon happen to me. Nothing in me is any longer my own." Then, suddenly, God's presence enveloped me and penetrated me through and through. **(101)** This was just as I was receiving Holy Communion. A moment after Holy Communion, I lost all awareness of everything around me and of my whereabouts.

645 Then I saw the Lord Jesus, as He is represented in the image, and He said to me, **Tell the confessor that this work is Mine and that I am using you as a lowly instrument.** And I said, "Jesus, I can no longer do anything You command me to do, because my confessor has told me that all this is an illusion, and that I am not allowed to obey any of Your commands. I will do nothing that You will tell me to do now. I am sorry, my Lord, but I am not allowed to do anything, and I must obey my confessor. Jesus, I most earnestly ask Your pardon. You know how much I suffer because of this, but it can't be helped, Jesus. The confessor has forbidden me to follow Your orders." Jesus listened to my arguments and complaints with kindness and satisfaction. I thought **(102)** the Lord Jesus would be grievously offended but, on the contrary, He was pleased and said to me kindly, **Always tell your confessor about everything I say to you and command you to do, and do only that for which you obtain permission. Do not be upset, and fear nothing; I am with you.** My soul was filled with joy, and all those oppressive thoughts vanished. Certitude and courage entered my soul.

646 But after a short while, I entered into the sufferings which Jesus underwent in the Garden of Olives. This lasted until Friday morning. On Friday, I experienced the Passion of Jesus but, this time, in a different way. On

that day, Father Bukowski came from Derdy. Some strange power pushed me to go to confession and tell him about everything that had happened to me and about what Jesus had said to me. When I told Father, he was quite different and he said **(103)** to me, "Sister, don't be afraid of anything; you will come to no harm, for the Lord Jesus will not allow it. If you are obedient and persevere in this disposition, you need not worry about anything. God will find a way to bring about His work. You should always have this simplicity and sincerity and tell everything to Mother General. What I said to you was said as a warning, because illusions may afflict even holy persons, and Satan's insinuations may play a part in this, and sometimes this comes from our own selves, so one has to be careful. And so continue as you have thus far. You can see, Sister, that the Lord is not angered by this. And Sister, you can repeat these things that have happened to you at present to your regular confessor [Father Sopocko]."

647 From this, I came to understand one thing: that I must pray much for each of my confessors, that he might obtain the light of the Holy **(104)** Spirit, for when I approach the confessional without first praying fervently, the confessor does not understand me very well. Father encouraged me to pray fervently for these intentions, that God would give better knowledge and understanding of the things He is asking of me. "Make novena after novena, Sister, and God will not refuse the graces."

648 Good Friday. At three o'clock, I saw the Lord Jesus, crucified, who looked at me and said, **I thirst.** Then I saw two rays issue from His side, just as they appear in the image. I then felt in my soul the desire to save souls and to empty myself for the sake of poor sinners. I offered myself, together with the dying Jesus, to the Eternal Father, for the salvation of the whole world. With Jesus, through Jesus **(105)** and in Jesus is my

communion with You, Eternal Father. On Good Friday, Jesus suffered in His soul in a way which was different from [His suffering on] Holy Thursday.

649 Mass of the Resurrection. [April 12, 1936]. When I entered the chapel, my spirit was immersed in God, its only treasure. His presence flooded me.

650 O my Jesus, my Master and Director, strengthen and enlighten me in these difficult moments of my life. I expect no help from people; all my hope is in You. I feel alone in the face of Your demands, O Lord. Despite the fears and qualms of my nature, I am fulfilling Your holy will and desire to fulfill it as faithfully as possible throughout my life and in my death. Jesus, with You I can do all things. Do with me as You please; only give me Your merciful Heart and that is enough for me.

(106) O Jesus my Lord, help me. Let what You have planned before all ages happen to me. I am ready at each beckoning of Your holy will. Enlighten my mind that I may know Your will. O God, You who pervade my soul, You know that I desire nothing but Your glory.

O Divine Will, You are the delight of my heart, the food of my soul, the light of my intellect, the omnipotent strength of my will; for when I unite myself with Your will, O Lord, Your power works through me and takes the place of my feeble will. Each day, I seek to carry out God's wishes.

651 O incomprehensible God, how great is Your mercy! It surpasses the combined understanding of all men and angels. All the angels (107) and all humans have emerged from the very depths of Your tender mercy. Mercy is the flower of love. God is love, and mercy is His deed. In love it is conceived; in mercy it is revealed. Everything I look at speaks to me of God's mercy. Even God's very justice speaks to me about His fathomless mercy, because justice flows from love.

652 There is one word I heed and continually ponder; it alone is everything to me; I live by it and die by it, and it is the holy will of God. It is my daily food. My whole soul listens intently to God's wishes. I do always what God asks of me, although my nature often quakes and I feel that the magnitude of these things is beyond my strength. I know well what I am of myself, but I also know what the grace of God is, which supports me.

653 **(108)** April 25, 1936. Walendow. On that day, the suffering in my soul was more severe than ever before. From early morning, I felt as if my body and soul had separated. I felt that God's presence had penetrated my whole being; I felt all the justice of God within me; I felt I stood alone before God. I thought: one word from my spiritual director would set me entirely at peace; but what can I do?—he is not here. However, I decided to seek light in holy confession. When I uncovered my soul to the priest,[134] he was afraid to continue hearing my confession, and that caused me even greater suffering. When I see that a priest is fearful, I do not obtain any inner peace. So I have decided that only to my spiritual director will I open my soul in all matters, from the greatest to the least, and that I will follow his directions strictly.

654 Now I understand that confession is only the confessing **(109)** of one's sins, and spiritual guidance is a different thing altogether. But this is not what I want to speak about. I want to tell about a strange thing that happened to me for the first time. When the confessor started talking to me, I did not understand a single word. Then I saw Jesus Crucified and He said to me, **It is in My Passion that you must seek light and strength.** After the confession, I meditated on Jesus' terrible Passion, and I understood that what I was suffering was nothing compared to the Savior's Passion, and that even the smallest imperfection was the cause of this terrible suffering. Then my soul was filled with very great

contrition, and only then I sensed that I was in the sea of the unfathomable mercy of God. Oh, how few words I have to express what I am experiencing! I feel I am like a drop of dew engulfed in the depths of the bottomless ocean of divine mercy.

655 **(110)** + May 11, 1936. I came to Cracow. I was happy that at last I shall be able to carry out all that the Lord Jesus was demanding.

Once, when I was speaking with Father A.... [Andrasz] and had told him everything, I received this answer: "Sister, pray till the day of the Feast of the Most Sacred Heart and add some mortification to the prayer, and on the Feast of the Sacred Heart I will give you an answer." But one day, I heard this voice in my soul: **Fear nothing; I am with you.** After these words, I felt such an urgency within me that, without waiting for the Feast of the Sacred Heart, I said during confession that I was going to leave the Congregation immediately. Father answered, "Sister, since you have made the decision by yourself, then take the responsibility for yourself. Go." I was happy to be leaving.

The following morning, God's presence suddenly left me. **(111)** A great darkness came over my soul. I could not pray. Because of this sudden loss of the presence of God, I decided to postpone the matter for a while, until I had talked with Father.

Father A. [Andrasz] answered that such changes in souls were frequent, and that this was not an obstacle to action.

656 When I talked to Mother General [Michael] about everything that had happened to me, she said, "Sister, I am locking you in the tabernacle with the Lord Jesus; wherever you go from there, that will be the will of God."

657 June 19. When we went to the Jesuits' place for the

procession of the Sacred Heart, during Vespers I saw the same rays coming forth from the Sacred Host, just as they are painted in the image. My soul was filled with great longing for God.

(112) June, 1936. Conversation with Father A. [Andrasz]

658 "Know that these are hard and difficult things. Your principal spiritual director is the Holy Spirit. We can only give direction to these inspirations, but your real director is the Holy Spirit. If you yourself have decided to leave, Sister, I neither prohibit nor order you to do so. You take the responsibility for yourself. I say this to you, Sister: you can begin to take action. You are capable of doing so, and therefore you *can* do so. These things are indeed probable; all you have told me up to now [before perpetual vows in Cracow in 1933] speaks in favor of taking action. Still, you have to be very careful in all this. Pray much and ask that I be given light."

659 During Holy Mass, offered by Father Andrasz, I saw the little Infant Jesus, who told me that I was to depend on him for everything; **no action undertaken on your own, even though you (113) put much effort into it, pleases Me.** I understood this [need of] dependence.

660 O my Jesus, on the day of the last judgment, You will demand from me an account of this work of mercy. O just Judge, but my Spouse as well, help me to do Your holy will. O mercy, O divine virtue!

O most merciful Heart of Jesus, my Betrothed, make my heart like unto Yours.

661 July 16. I spent this whole night in prayer. I meditated upon the Lord's Passion, and my soul was crushed by the burden of God's justice. The Hand of the Lord touched me.

662 July 17. O my Jesus, You know how much adversity I

encounter in this matter, how much reproach I must put up with, how many ironic smiles I must take with equanimity. Oh, alone I would not **(114)** be able to survive this, but with You, my Master, I can do all things. Oh, how painfully an ironic smile wounds, especially when one [appears to] speak with great sincerity.

663 July 22. O my Jesus, I know that a person's greatness is evidenced by his deeds and not by his words or feelings. It is the works that have come from us that will speak about us. My Jesus, do not allow me to daydream, but give me the courage and strength to fulfill Your holy will.

Jesus, if You wish to leave me in uncertainty, even to the end of my life, may Your Holy Name be blessed.

June.

664 + O my Jesus, how immensely I rejoice at the assurance You have given me that the Congregation will come into being. I no longer have the least shadow of a doubt about this, and I see how great is the glory which it will give to God. It will be the reflection of God's greatest attribute; that is, His divine mercy. Unceasingly, **(115)** they will intercede for divine mercy for themselves and for the whole world. And every act of mercy will flow from God's love, that love with which they will be filled to overflowing. They will strive to make their own this great attribute of God, and to live by it and to bring others to know it and to trust in the goodness of the Lord. This Congregation of Divine Mercy will be in God's Church like a beehive in a magnificent garden, hidden and meek. The sisters will work like bees to feed their neighbors' souls with honey, while the wax will flame for the glory of God.

+ June 29, 1936.

665 Father Andrasz told me to make a novena for the intention of knowing better the will of God. I prayed

ardently, adding a certain bodily mortification. Towards the end of the novena, I received an inner light and the assurance that the Congregation will come into being and that it is pleasing to God. Despite the difficulties **(116)** and adversities, complete peace and strength entered my soul from on high. I understood that nothing could resist or nullify the will of God. I understood that I must carry out this will of God despite obstacles, persecution and sufferings of all kinds, and despite natural repugnance and fear.

666 I understood that all striving for perfection and all sanctity consist in doing God's will. Perfect fulfillment of God's will is maturity in sanctity; there is no room for doubt here. To receive God's light and recognize what God wants of us and yet not do it is a great offense against the majesty of God. Such a soul deserves to be competely forsaken by God. It resembles Lucifer, who had great light, but did not do God's will. An extraordinary peace entered my soul when I reflected on the fact that, despite great difficulties, I had always faithfully followed God's will **(117)** as I knew it. O Jesus, grant me the grace to put Your will into practice as I have come to know it, O God.

667 July 14. I received a letter at three o'clock [from Father Sopocko[135]]. O Jesus, You alone know what I suffer, but I will keep silent and will not say anything about it to any creature, because I know that no one will comfort me. You are everything to me, O God, and Your holy will is my nourishment. I am living now on what I will live on in eternity.

I have great reverence for Saint Michael the Archangel; he had no example to follow in doing the will of God, and yet he fulfilled God's will faithfully.

668 + July 15. During Holy Mass, I offered myself completely to the heavenly Father through the sweetest Heart of Jesus; let Him do as He pleases with me. Of myself I am

nothing, and in my misery I have nothing of worth; so I abandon myself into the ocean of Your mercy, O Lord.

669 **(118)** July 16. I am learning how to be good from Jesus, from Him who is goodness itself, so that I may be called a daughter of the heavenly Father. This morning, when someone hurt my feelings, I tried, in that suffering, to unite my will to the will of God, and I praised God by my silence. In the afternoon, I went for a five-minute adoration, when suddenly I saw the crucifix I have on my breast come alive. Jesus said to me, **My daughter, suffering will be a sign to you that I am with you.** My soul was greatly moved by these words.

670 O Jesus, my Master and my Director, it is only with You that I can converse. With no one else is it so easy to talk as with You, O God.

671 In my spiritual life, I will always hold on to the priest's hand. About my soul's life and its needs, I will speak only with my confessor.

672 **(119)** + August 4, 1936. Inner torment for more than two hours. Agony.... Suddenly, God's presence pervades me and I feel as though I am coming under the power of the just God. His justice pervades me to the marrow; outwardly I lose strength and consciousness. With this, I come to know the great holiness of God and my own great misery. A great torment afflicts my soul; the soul perceives its deeds to be not without blemish. Then the strength of trust is awakened in the soul, which longs for God with all its might. Yet it sees how miserable it is and what utter vanity everything that surrounds it. And face to face with such holiness, Oh, poor soul....

August 13.

673 I was tormented by terrible temptations all day; blasphemies thrust themselves upon my lips, and I felt an aversion for everything that is holy and godlike. Yet I struggled throughout the day. In the evening, my mind

became oppressed: what's the use of telling this to the confessor? **(120)** He will ridicule it. A feeling of aversion and discouragement filled my soul, and it seemed to me that I could by no means receive Holy Communion in that condition. At the thought of not receiving Communion, such a terrible pain seized my soul that I almost cried aloud in the chapel. But I suddenly realized that the sisters were there and decided to go to the garden and hide myself there so as to be able to at least cry out loud. Then suddenly, Jesus stood by me and said, **Where are you intending to go?**

674   I gave no answer to Jesus, but poured out all my sorrow before Him, and Satan's attempts ceased. Jesus then said to me, **The inner peace that you have is a grace,** and suddenly He was gone. I felt happy and unaccountably peaceful. Really, for so much peace to return within a moment—that is a thing only Jesus can do, He, the most high Lord.

675   **(121)** + August 7, 1936.

When I received the article[136] about Divine Mercy with the image [on the cover], God's presence filled me in an extraordinary way. When I steeped myself in a prayer of thanksgiving, I suddenly saw the Lord Jesus in a great brightness, just as He is painted, and at His feet I saw Father Andrasz and Father Sopocko. Both were holding pens in their hands, and flashes of light and fire, like lightning, were coming from the tips of their pens and striking a great crowd of people who were hurrying I know not where. Whoever was touched by the ray of light immediately turned his back on the crowd and held out his hands to Jesus. Some returned with great joy, others with great pain and compunction. Jesus was looking at both priests with great kindness. After a while, I was left alone with Jesus, and I said, "Jesus, take me now, for Your will has already been accomplished." And Jesus answered, **(122) My will has not yet been**

completely accomplished in you; you will still suffer much, but I am with you; do not fear.

676   I have been talking much with the Lord about Father Andrasz and also about Father Sopocko. I know that whatever I ask of the Lord He will not refuse me, and He will give them that for which I ask. I sensed and I know how greatly Jesus loves them. I am not writing about this in detail, but I know this, and it makes me very happy.

August 15, 1936.

677   During a Mass celebrated by Father Andrasz, a moment before the Elevation, God's presence pervaded my soul, which was drawn to the altar. Then I saw the Mother of God with the Infant Jesus. The Infant Jesus was holding onto the hand of Our Lady. A moment later, the Infant Jesus ran with joy to the center of the altar, and the Mother of God said to me, *See with what assurance I entrust Jesus into his hands. In the same way, you are to* **(123)** *entrust your soul and be like a child to him.*

—After these words, my soul was filled with unusual trust. The Mother of God was clothed in a white dress, strangely white, transparent; on Her shoulders She had a transparent blue; that is, a blue-like mantle; with uncovered head [and] flowing hair, She was exquisite, and inconceivably beautiful. She was looking at Father with great tenderness, but after a moment, He broke up this beautiful Child, and living blood flowed forth. Father bent forward and received the true and living Jesus into himself. Had he eaten Him? I do not know how this took place. Jesus, Jesus, I cannot keep up with You, for in an instant, You become incomprehensible to me.

678   The essence of the virtues is the will of God. He who does the will of God faithfully, practices all the virtues. In all the events and circumstances of my life, I adore and bless the holy will of God. The holy will of God is the

object of my love. **(124)** In the most secret depths of my soul, I live according to His will. I act exteriorly according to what I recognize inwardly as the will of God. Sweeter to me are the torments, sufferings, persecutions and all manner of adversities by divine will than popularity, praise and esteem by my own will.

679   Good night, my Jesus; the bell is calling me to sleep. My Jesus, You see that I am dying from the desire to save souls. Good night, my Beloved; I rejoice at being one day closer to eternity. And if You let me wake up tomorrow, Jesus, I shall begin a new hymn to Your praise.

680 +   July 13. During meditation today, I came to understand that I should never speak about my own interior experiences, [but] that I should conceal nothing from my spiritual director; and I will especially ask God to enlighten my spiritual **(125)** director. I attach greater importance to the words of my confessor than to all the lights taken together that I receive interiorly.

681 + Amid the greatest torments, I fix the gaze of my soul upon Jesus Crucified; I do not expect help from people, but place my trust in God. In His unfathomable mercy lies all my hope.

682 + The more I feel that God is transforming me, the more I desire to immerse myself in silence. The love of God is doing its work in the depths of my soul. I see that the mission which the Lord has entrusted to me is beginning.

683 + Once, when I was praying fervently to the Jesuit Saints, I suddenly saw my Guardian Angel, who led me before the throne of God. I passed **(126)** through great hosts of saints, and I recognized many of them, whom I knew from their pictures. I saw many Jesuits, who asked me from what congregation I was. When I answered they asked, "Who is your spiritual director?" I answered that it was Father A.... When they wanted to say more, my Guardian Angel beckoned me to be silent, and I came

before the throne of God. I saw a great and inaccessible light, and I saw a place destined for me, close to God. But what it was like I do not know, because a cloud covered it. However, my Guardian Angel said to me, "Here is your throne, for your faithfulness in fulfilling the will of God."

684 + Holy Hour. —Thursday. During this hour of prayer, Jesus allowed me to enter the Cenacle, and I was a witness to what happened there. However, I was most deeply moved when, before the Consecration, Jesus raised **(127)** His eyes to heaven and entered into a mysterious conversation with His Father. It is only in eternity that we shall really understand that moment. His eyes were like two flames; His face was radiant, white as snow; His whole personage full of majesty, His soul full of longing. At the moment of Consecration, love rested satiated—the sacrifice fully consummated. Now only the external ceremony of death will be carried out—external destruction; the essence [of it] is in the Cenacle. Never in my whole life had I understood this mystery so profoundly as during that hour of adoration. Oh, how ardently I desire that the whole world would come to know this unfathomable mystery!

685 After the Holy Hour, when I went to my cell, I suddenly learned how greatly God was offended by a certain person, who was close to my heart. At the sight of this, my soul was pierced with pain, and I cast myself in the dust before the Lord, begging His mercy. For two hours, in tears, prayer and flagellation I prevented **(128)** the sin, and I learned that God's mercy had embraced that poor soul. Oh, the price of one single sin!

686 + September. First Friday. In the evening, I saw the Mother of God, with Her breast bared and pierced with a sword. She was shedding bitter tears and shielding us against God's terrible punishment. God wants to inflict terrible punishment on us, but He cannot because the Mother of God is shielding us. Horrible fear seized my

soul. I kept praying incessantly for Poland, for my dear Poland, which is so lacking in gratitude for the Mother of God. If it were not for the Mother of God, all our efforts would be of little use. I intensified my prayers and sacrifices for our dear native land, but I see that I am a drop before the wave of evil. How can a drop stop a wave? O yes! A drop is nothing of itself, but with You, Jesus, I shall stand up bravely to the whole wave of evil and even **(129)** to the whole of hell. Your omnipotence can do all things.

687   Once, as I was going down the hall to the kitchen, I heard these words in my soul: **Say unceasingly the chaplet that I have taught you. Whoever will recite it will receive great mercy at the hour of death. Priests will recommend it to sinners as their last hope of salvation. Even if there were a sinner most hardened, if he were to recite this chaplet only once, he would receive grace from My infinite mercy. I desire that the whole world know My infinite mercy. I desire to grant unimaginable graces to those souls who trust in My mercy.**

688   Jesus, Life and Truth, my Master, guide every step of my life, that I may act according to Your holy will.

689   **(130)** + On one occasion, I saw the throne of the Lamb of God and before the throne three Saints: Stanislaus Kostka, Andrew Bobola and Prince Casimir, who were interceding for Poland. All at once I saw a large book which stands before the throne, and it was given to me to read. The book was written in blood. Still, I could not read anything but the name, Jesus. Then I heard a voice which said to me, **Your hour has not yet come.** Then the book was taken away from me, and I heard these words: **You will bear witness to My infinite mercy. In this book are written the names of the souls that have glorified My mercy.** I was overwhelmed with joy at the sight of such great goodness of God.

690 + On one occasion, I came to know of the condition of two religious sisters who were grumbling interiorly about an order the superior had given them, and for this reason God had withheld many special graces from them. **(131)** My heart ached at this sight. How sad it is, O Jesus, when we ourselves are the cause of the loss of graces. Whoever understands this is always faithful.

691 + Thursday. Although I was very tired today, I nevertheless resolved to make a Holy Hour. I could not pray, nor could I remain kneeling, but I remained in prayer for a whole hour and united myself in spirit with those souls who are already worshiping God in the perfect way. But towards the end of the hour, I suddenly saw Jesus, who looked at me penetratingly and said with ineffable sweetness, **Your prayer is extremely pleasing to Me.** After these words, an unusual power and spiritual joy entered my soul. God's presence continued to pervade my soul. Oh, what happens to a soul that meets the Lord face to face, no pen has ever expressed or ever will express!

692 **(132)** + O Jesus, I understand that Your mercy is beyond all imagining, and therefore I ask You to make my heart so big that there will be room in it for the needs of all the souls living on the face of the earth. O Jesus, my love extends beyond the world, to the souls suffering in purgatory, and I want to exercise mercy toward them by means of indulgenced prayers. God's mercy is unfathomable and inexhaustible, just as God himself is unfathomable. Even if I were to use the strongest words there are to express this mercy of God, all this would be nothing in comparison with what it is in reality. O Jesus, make my heart sensitive to all the sufferings of my neighbor, whether of body or of soul. O my Jesus, I know that You act toward us as we act toward our neighbor.

My Jesus, make my heart like unto Your merciful

Heart. Jesus, help me to go through life doing good to everyone.

693 **(133)** September 14, [1936]. The Archbishop [Jalbrzykowski] of Vilnius visited us. Although he stayed with us for a very short time, I still had a chance to talk with this worthy priest about the work of mercy. He showed himself very favorably disposed to this cause of mercy: "Sister, be completely at peace; if this is within the plans of divine providence, it will come about. In the meantime, Sister, pray for a clearer outward sign. Let the Lord Jesus give you a clearer knowledge of this. I beg you to wait a little while longer. The Lord Jesus will arrange the circumstances in such a way that everything will turn out all right."

694 September 19, 1936. When we left the doctor's[137] [office] and stepped into the sanatorium chapel for a moment, I heard these words in my soul: **My child, just a few more drops in your chalice; it won't be long now.** Joy **(134)** filled my soul; this was the first call from my beloved Spouse and Master. My heart melted, and there was a moment when my soul was immersed in the whole sea of God's mercy. I felt that my mission was beginning in all its fullness. Death destroys nothing that is good. I pray most of all for souls that are experiencing inner sufferings.

695 Once, I received light concerning two sisters. I understood that it is not possible for a person to act in the same manner towards everyone. There are some people who have a strange way of making friends with others. And then, as friends and under the pretext of that friendship, they manage to draw the person out, word by word. Then, when the right moment comes, they use those very same words to hurt that person. My Jesus, how strange is human frailty! Your love, Jesus, gives the soul this great prudence in its dealings with others.

696 **(135)** + September 24, 1936.

Mother Superior [Irene] ordered me to say one decade of the rosary in place of all the other exercises, and to go to bed at once. As soon as I lay down I fell asleep, for I was very tired. But a while later, I was awakened by suffering. It was such a great suffering that it prevented me from making even the slightest movement; I could not even swallow my saliva. This lasted for about three hours. I thought of waking up the novice sister[128] who shared my room, but then I thought, "She cannot give me any help, so let her sleep. It would be a pity to wake her." I resigned myself completely to the will of God and thought that the day of my death, so much desired, had come. It was an occasion for me to unite myself with Jesus, suffering on the Cross. Beyond that, I was unable to pray. When the suffering ceased, I began **(136)** to perspire. But I still could not move, as the pain would return at each attempt. In the morning, I felt very tired, though I felt no further physical pain. Still, I could not get up to attend Mass. I thought to myself, if after such suffering death does not come, then how great the sufferings of death must be!

697 Jesus, You know that I love suffering and want to drain the cup of suffering to the last drop; and yet, my nature experienced a slight shudder and fear. Quickly, however, my trust in the infinite mercy of God was awakened in all its force, and everything else had to give way before it, like a shadow retreating before the sun's rays. O Jesus, how great is Your goodness! Your infinite goodness, so well known to me, enables me to bravely look death itself in the eye. I know that nothing will happen to me without God's permission. I desire to glorify Your infinite mercy during my life, at the hour of death, in the resurrection and throughout eternity.

(137) + My Jesus, my strength, my peace, my repose; my soul bathes daily in the rays of Your mercy. There is not

a moment in my life when I do not experience Your
mercy, O God. I count on nothing in my whole life, but
only on Your infinite mercy. It is the guiding thread of
my life, O Lord. My soul is filled with God's mercy.

698 + Oh, how sorely Jesus is hurt by the ingratitude of a
chosen soul! What a martyrdom it is for His unspeakable
love! God loves us with the entire infinite Being that He
is; and imagine, a miserable particle of dust scorns that
love! My heart bursts with pain when I see this
ingratitude.

699 On one occasion, I heard these words: **My daughter, tell
the whole world about My inconceivable (138) mercy. I
desire that the Feast of Mercy[129] be a refuge and shelter
for all souls, and especially for poor sinners. On that day
the very depths of My tender mercy are open. I pour out
a whole ocean of graces upon those souls who approach
the fount of My mercy. The soul that will go to
Confession and receive Holy Communion shall obtain
complete forgiveness of sins and punishment. On that
day all the divine floodgates through which grace flow
are opened. Let no soul fear to draw near to Me, even
though its sins be as scarlet. My mercy is so great that no
mind, be it of man or of angel, will be able to fathom it
throughout all eternity. Everything that exists has come
forth from the very depths of My most tender mercy.
Every soul in its relation to Me will contemplate My
love and mercy throughout eternity. The Feast of Mercy
emerged from My very depths of tenderness. (139) It is
My desire that it be solemnly celebrated on the first
Sunday after Easter. Mankind will not have peace until
it turns to the Fount of My Mercy.**

700 + Once, when I was very tired and in much pain, I told
Mother Superior [Irene] about it and received the
answer that I should get used to suffering. I listened to
everything that Mother told me, and then I went out.
Our Mother Superior has great love of neighbor and

especially great love for the sick sisters, as everyone knows. And yet, as regards me, it is extraordinary that the Lord Jesus has permitted that she not understand me and that she test me much in this respect.

701 On this particular day, when I was feeling so bad and still went to work, every now and then I would feel sick. It was so very hot that, even without working, a person felt terrible, **(140)** not to mention what it was like when one had to work while suffering. So, before noon, I straightened up from my work, looked up to the sky with great trust and said to the Lord, "Jesus, cover the sun, for I cannot stand this heat any longer." And, O wonder, at that very moment a white cloud covered the sun and, from then on, the heat became less intense. When a little while later I began to reproach myself that I did not bear the heat, but begged for relief, Jesus himself put me at ease.

702 August 13, 1936. Tonight God's presence is pervading me, and in an instant I come to know the great holiness of God. Oh, how the greatness of God overwhelms me! I then come to know the whole depth of my nothingness. This is a great torment, for this knowledge is followed by love. The soul bounds forward vehemently toward God, and the two loves come face to face: the Creator and the creature; **(141)** one little drop seeks to measure itself with the ocean. At first, the little drop wants to enclose the infinite ocean within itself; but at the same moment, it knows itself to be just one small drop, and thus it is vanquished, and it passes completely into God like a drop into the ocean. At first, this moment is a torment, but so sweet that, on experiencing it, the soul is happy.

703 At present, the topic of my particular examen is my union with the Merciful Christ. This practice gives me unusual strength; my heart is always united with the One it desires, and its actions are regulated by mercy, which flows from love.

704 I spend every free moment at the feet of the hidden God. He is my Master; I ask Him about everything; I speak to Him about everything. Here I obtain strength and light; here I learn everything; here I am given light on how to act toward my neighbor. From the time **(142)** I left the novitiate, I have enclosed myself in the tabernacle together with Jesus, my Master. He himself drew me into the fire of living love on which everything converges.

705 September 25. I suffer great pain in my hands, feet and side, the places where Jesus' body was pierced. I experience these pains particularly when I meet with a soul who is not in the state of grace. Then I pray fervently that the mercy of God will embrace that soul.

706 [September] 29. On the Feast of Saint Michael the Archangel, I saw by my side that great Leader, who spoke these words to me: "The Lord has ordered me to take special care of you. Know that you are hated by evil; but do not fear—'Who is like God!'" And he disappeared. But I feel his presence and assistance.

707 **(143)** October 2, 1936. The First Friday of the month. After Holy Communion, I suddenly saw the Lord Jesus, who spoke these words to me: **Now I know that it is not for the graces or gifts that you love me, but because My will is dearer to you than life. That is why I am uniting myself with you so intimately as with no other creature.**

708 At that moment, Jesus disappeared. My soul was filled with the presence of God. I know that the gaze of the Mighty One rests upon me. I plunged myself completely in the joy that flows from God. I continued throughout the whole day without interruption, thus immersed in God. In the evening, I fell as if into a faint and a strange sort of agony. My love wants to equal the love of the Mighty One. It is drawn to Him so vehemently that it is impossible, without some special grace from God, to bear the vastness of such a grace in this life. But I see clearly that Jesus himself is sustaining me and

strengthening me and making me capable of communing with Him. In all this, the soul is particularly active.

709 **(144)** October 3, 1936. During the rosary today, I suddenly saw a ciborium with the Blessed Sacrament. The ciborium was uncovered and quite filled with hosts. From the ciborium came a voice: **These hosts have been received by souls converted through your prayer and suffering.** At this point, I felt God's presence as a child would; I felt strangely like a child.

710 When one day I felt I would be unable to carry on till nine and asked S.N.[140] for something to eat, because I was going to bed earlier as I was not feeling well, S.N. answered, "But you are not ill, Sister; they only wanted you to have some rest, so they made up the illness." O my Jesus, my illness is so far advanced[141] that the doctor has separated me from the sisters to prevent them from becoming infected, and yet one is judged in this way. But that's good; all this is for You, my Jesus. I do not want to write much about external matters, for they are not the reason for my writing; **(145)** I want in particular to note the graces granted me by the Lord, because these are not only for me, but for many other souls as well.

711 October 5, [1936]. Today I received a letter from Father Sopocko. I learned that he intends to publish a holy card of the Merciful Christ. He asked me to send him a certain prayer[142] which he wants to put on the back, if he receives the Archbishop's approbation. Oh, what great joy fills my heart that God has let me see this work of His mercy! How great is this work of the Most High God! I am but His instrument. Oh, how ardently I desire to see this Feast of the Divine Mercy which God is demanding through me. But if it is the will of God that it be celebrated solemnly only after my death, even so I rejoice in it already, and I celebrate it interiorly with my confessor's permission.

712 **(146)** + I saw Father Andrasz today, kneeling and

engulfed in prayer, and suddenly Jesus stood by him and, holding out both hands over his head, He said to me:—**He will lead you through; do not fear.**

713 October 11. This evening, as I was writing about this great mercy of God and its great advantage to souls, Satan rushed into my room with great anger and fury. He seized the screen and began to break and crush it. I was a little frightened at first, but I immediately made the sign of the cross with my little crucifix, and the beast fell quiet and disappeared at once. Today, I did not see this hideous figure but only his anger. Satan's anger is terrible, and yet the screen was not shattered or broken, and I went on writing quietly. I know well that the wretch will not touch me without God's willing it, but what is he up to? He is beginning to attack me openly **(147)** and with such great fury and hate, but he does not disturb my peace for a moment, and this composure of mine makes him furious.

714 + The Lord said to me today: **Go to the Superior and tell her that I want all the sisters and wards to say the chaplet which I have taught you. They are to say it for nine days in the chapel in order to appease My Father and to entreat God's mercy for Poland.** I answered the Lord that I would tell her, but that I must first speak about this with Father Andrasz, and I resolved that as soon as Father comes I will speak to him at once about this matter. When Father arrived, the circumstances were such that they prevented me from seeing him, but I should not have paid any attention to the circumstances and should have gone and settled the matter. I thought to myself, "Well, I'll do it when he comes again."

715 Oh, how much **(148)** that displeased God! In one moment, the presence of God left me, that great presence of God which is continuously within me in a distinctly felt way. At that moment, however, it completely left me. Darkness dominated my soul to

such an extent that I did not know whether I was in the state of grace or not. Therefore, I did not receive Holy Communion for four days, after which I saw Father Andrasz and told him everything. He comforted me, saying, "You have not lost the grace of God, but all the same, be true to Him." The moment I left the confessional, God's presence enveloped me as before. I understood that God's grace must be received just as God sends it, in the way He wants, and one must receive it in that form under which God sends it to us.

716 O my Jesus, I am making at this very moment a firm and eternal resolution by virtue of Your grace and mercy, fidelity to the tiniest grace of Yours.

717 **(149)** All night long, I was preparing to receive Holy Communion, since I could not sleep because of physical suffering. My soul was flooded with love and repentance.

718 After Holy Communion, I heard these words:—**You see what you are of yourself, but do not be frightened at this. If I were to reveal to you the whole misery that you are, you would die of terror. However, be aware of what you are. Because you are such great misery, I have revealed to you the whole ocean of My mercy. I seek and desire souls like yours, but they are few. Your great trust in Me forces Me to continuously grant you graces. You have great and incomprehensible rights over My Heart, for you are a daughter of complete trust. You would not have been able to bear the magnitude of the love which I have for you if I had revealed it to you fully here on earth. I often give you a glimpse of it, but know that this is only an exceptional grace from Me. My love and mercy knows no bounds.**

719 **(150)** Today, I heard these words: **Know, my child, that for your sake I grant blessings to this whole vicinity. But you ought to thank Me on their behalf, as they do not thank Me for the kindnesses I extend to them. For the sake of your gratitude, I will continue to bless them.**

720 O my Jesus, You know how difficult community life is, how many misunderstandings and misconceptions, despite at times the most sincere good will on both sides. But that is Your mystery, O Lord. We shall know it in eternity; however, our judgments should always be mild.

721 It is a great, an immeasurably great grace of God to have a spiritual director. I feel now that, without him, I would not be able to journey alone in my spiritual life. Great is the power of a priest. I thank God unceasingly for giving me a spiritual director.

722 **(151)** + Today, I heard these words: **You see how weak you are, so when shall I be able to count on you?** I answered, "Jesus, be always with me, for I am Your little child. Jesus, You know what little children do."

723 + Today, I heard these words: **The graces I grant you are not for you alone, but for a great number of other souls as well... And your heart is My constant dwelling place, despite the misery that you are. I unite Myself with you, take away your misery and give you My mercy. I perform works of mercy in every soul. The greater the sinner, the greater the right he has to My mercy. My mercy is confirmed in every work of My hands. He who trusts in My mercy will not perish, for all his affairs are Mine, and his enemies will be shattered at the base of My footstool.**

724 **(152)** On the eve of the retreat, I started to pray that the Lord Jesus might give me just a little health so that I could take part in the retreat, because I was feeling so ill that I thought perhaps it might be my last. However, as soon as I had started praying I felt a strange dissatisfaction. I interrupted the prayer of supplication and began to thank the Lord for everything He sends me, submitting myself completely to His holy will. Then I felt profound peace of soul.

+ Faithful submission to the will of God, always and everywhere, in all events and circumstances of life, gives great glory to God. Such submission to the will of God carries more weight with Him than long fasts, mortifications and the most severe penances. Oh, how great is the reward for one act of loving submission to the will of God! As I write, my soul is enraptured at the thought of how much God loves it and of the peace that my soul already enjoys, here on earth.

+

(153) J.M.J.   Cracow, 1936

O Divine Will, be my love!

725   + Eight-day Retreat, October 20, 1936.

My Jesus, I am going into the wilderness today to speak only with You, my Master and my Lord. Let the earth be silent, and You alone speak to me, Jesus. You know that I understand no other voice but Yours, O Good Shepherd. In the dwelling of my heart is that wilderness to which no creature has access. There, You alone are King.

726 +When I entered the chapel for a five-minute adoration, I asked the Lord Jesus how I should conduct myself during this retreat. Then I heard this voice in my soul: **I desire that you be entirely transformed into love and that you burn ardently as a pure victim of love...**

727 **(154)** Eternal Truth, give me a ray of Your light that I may come to know You, O Lord, and worthily glorify Your infinite mercy. And at the same time, grant me to know myself, the whole abyss of misery that I am.

728 + I have chosen Saint Claude de la Colombiere and Saint Gertrude as my patron saints for this retreat, that they may intercede for me before the Mother of God and the merciful Savior.

729 During the meditation on creation... at a certain point, my soul became closely united to its Lord and Creator.

In this union, I recognized the purpose and destiny of my life. My purpose is to become closely united to God through love, and my destiny is to praise and glorify God's mercy.

The Lord has allowed me to know and experience this in a distinct and even physical way. I become lost in admiration when I recognize and experience this incomprehensible love of God with which God loves me. Who is God—and what am I? **(155)** I cannot meditate on this any further. Only love can understand this meeting of two spirits, namely, God-who-is-Spirit and the soul-who-is-creature. The more I know Him, the more completely with all the strength of my being I drown in Him.

730 + **In this retreat, I shall keep you continually close to My Heart, that you may better know My mercy, that mercy which I have for people and especially for poor sinners.**

731 On the initial day of the retreat, I was visited by one of the sisters[143] who had come to make her perpetual vows. She confided to me that she had no trust in God and became discouraged at every little thing. I answered her, "It is well that you have told me this, Sister; I will pray for you." And I spoke a few words to her about how much distrust hurts the Lord Jesus, especially distrust on the part of a chosen soul. She told me that, beginning with her perpetual vows, she would practice trust. Now I know that even [some] souls that are chosen and well-advanced **(156)** in the religious life or the spiritual life do not have the courage to entrust themselves completely to God. And this is so because few souls know the unfathomable mercy of God and His great goodness.

732 + The great majesty of God which pervaded me today and still pervades me awoke in me a great fear, but a fear filled with respect, and not the fear of a slave, which is quite different from the fear of respect. This fear

animated by respect arose in my heart today because of love and the knowledge of the greatness of God, and that is a great joy to the soul. The soul trembles before the smallest offense against God; but that does not trouble or darken its happiness. There, where love is in charge, all is well.

733 It sometimes happens, while I am listening to the meditation, that one word puts me in very close union with the Lord, and I no longer know what Father [144] is saying. I know that I am close to the most merciful Heart of Jesus; my whole spirit is entirely plunged in Him, and in one moment **(157)** I learn more than during long hours of intellectual inquiry and meditation. These are sudden lights which permit me to know things as God sees them, regarding matters of both the interior and the exterior world.

734 I see that Jesus himself is acting in my soul during this retreat. And as for me, I try only to be faithful to His grace. I have submitted my soul completely to the influence of God. This Mighty Ruler of Heaven has taken entire possession of my soul. I feel that I am being lifted up above earth and heaven into the inner life of God, where I come to know the Father, the Son and the Holy Spirit, but always in the unity of majesty.

735 + I will enclose myself in the chalice of Jesus so that I may comfort Him continually. I will do everything within my power to save souls, and I will do it through prayer and suffering.

(158)+I try always to be a Bethany for Jesus, so that He may rest here after all His labors. In Holy Communion, my union with Jesus is so intimate and incomprehensible that even if I wanted to describe it in writing I could not do so, because I lack the words.

736 This evening, I saw the Lord Jesus just as He was during His Passion. His eyes were raised up to His Father, and He was praying for us.

737 + Although I was ill, I made up my mind to make a Holy Hour today as usual. During that hour, I saw the Lord Jesus being scourged at the pillar. In the midst of this frightful torture, Jesus was praying. After a while, He said to me, **There are few souls who contemplate My Passion with true feeling; I give great graces to souls who meditate devoutly on My Passion.**

738 + **Without special help from Me, you are not even capable of accepting My graces. You know who you are.**

739 **(159)** After Holy Communion today, I spoke at length to the Lord Jesus about people who are special to me. Then I heard these words: **My daughter, don't be exerting yourself so much with words. Those whom you love in a special way, I too love in a special way, and for your sake, I shower My graces upon them. I am pleased when you tell Me about them, but don't be doing so with such excessive effort.**

740 + O Savior of the world. I unite myself with Your mercy. My Jesus, I join all my sufferings to Yours and deposit them in the treasury of the Church for the benefit of souls.

741 Today, I was led by an Angel to the chasms of hell. It is a place of great torture; how awesomely large and extensive it is! The kinds of tortures I saw: the first torture that constitutes hell is the loss of God; the second is perpetual remorse of conscience; the third is that one's condition will never change;**(160)**the fourth is the fire that will penetrate the soul without destroying it—a terrible suffering, since it is a purely spiritual fire, lit by God's anger; the fifth torture is continual darkness and a terrible suffocating smell, and, despite the darkness, the devils and the souls of the damned see each other and all the evil, both of others and their own; the sixth torture is the constant company of Satan; the seventh torture is horrible despair, hatred of God, vile words, curses and blasphemies. These are the tortures suffered by all the

damned together, but that is not the end of the sufferings. There are special tortures destined for particular souls. These are the torments of the senses. Each soul undergoes terrible and indescribable sufferings, related to the manner in which it has sinned. There are caverns and pits of torture where one form of agony differs from another. I would have died at the very sight of these tortures if the omnipotence of God had not supported me. Let the sinner know that he will be tortured throughout all eternity, in those senses which he made use of to sin. **(161)**I am writing this at the command of God, so that no soul may find an excuse by saying there is no hell, or that nobody has ever been there, and so no one can say what it is like.

I, Sister Faustina, by the order of God, have visited the abysses of hell so that I might tell souls about it and testify to its existence. I cannot speak about it now; but I have received a command from God to leave it in writing. The devils were full of hatred for me, but they had to obey me at the command of God. What I have written is but a pale shadow of the things I saw. But I noticed one thing: that most of the souls there are those who disbelieved that there is a hell. When I came to, I could hardly recover from the fright. How terribly souls suffer there! Consequently, I pray even more fervently for the conversion of sinners. I incessantly plead God's mercy upon them. O my Jesus, I would rather be in agony until the end of the world, amidst the greatest sufferings, than offend You by the least sin.

+

(162) J.M.J.

742 **My daughter, if I demand through you that people revere My mercy, you should be the first to distinguish yourself by this confidence in My mercy. I demand from you deeds of mercy, which are to arise out of love for Me. You are to show mercy to your neighbors always**

and everywhere. You must not shrink from this or try to excuse or absolve yourself from it.

I am giving you three ways of exercising mercy toward your neighbor: the first—by deed, the second—by word, the third—by prayer. In these three degrees is contained the fullness of mercy, and it is an unquestionable proof of love for Me. By this means a soul glorifies and pays reverence to My mercy. Yes, the first Sunday after Easter is the Feast of Mercy, but there must also be acts of mercy, and I demand the worship of My mercy through the solemn celebration of the Feast and through the veneration of the image which is painted. By means of this image I shall grant many graces to souls. It is to be a reminder of the demands of My mercy, because even the strongest(163) faith is of no avail without works. O my Jesus, You yourself must help me in everything, because You see how very little I am, and so I depend solely on Your goodness, O God.

+ Particular Examen

Union with the merciful Christ. With my heart I encompass the whole world, especially countries which are uncivilized or where there is persecution. I am praying for mercy upon them.

743 Two general resolutions:

First: To strive after inner silence and to observe the rule of silence strictly.

Second: Faithfulness to interior inspirations; to bring them into my life and actions according to the advice of my spiritual director.

In this present illness, I desire to glorify the will of God. I will try, as far as I am able, to take part(164)in all the community exercises. I will give the Lord God fervent thanks for every sorrow and suffering.

744 + I often feel that, apart from Jesus, I get no help from

anyone, although sometimes I am very much in need of clarifications concerning the demands of the Lord.

This evening, I suddenly received light from God regarding a certain matter. For twelve years, I have been reflecting on a certain matter and could not understand it. Today, Jesus gave me to know how much that had pleased Him.

The Feast of Christ the King. [October 25, 1936]

745 During Holy Mass, I was so enveloped in the great interior fire of God's love and the desire to save souls that I do not know how to express it. I feel I am all aflame. I shall fight all evil with the weapon of mercy. I am being burned up by the desire to save souls. I traverse the world's length and breadth **(165)**and venture as far as its ultimate limits and its wildest lands to save souls. I do this through prayer and sacrifice. I want every soul to glorify the mercy of God, for each one experiences the effects of that mercy on himself. The Saints in heaven worship the mercy of the Lord. I want to worship it even now, here on earth, and to spread devotion to it in the way that God demands of me.

746 I have understood that at certain and most difficult moments I shall be alone, deserted by everyone, and that I must face all the storms and fight with all the strength of my soul, even with those from whom I expected to get help.

But I am not alone, because Jesus is with me, and with Him I fear nothing. I am well aware of everything, and I know what God is demanding of me. Suffering, contempt, ridicule, persecution and humiliation will be my constant lot. I know no other way. For sincere love—ingratitude; this is my path, marked out by the footprints of Jesus.

(166) My Jesus, my strength and my only hope, in You alone is all my hope. My trust will not be frustrated.

747 The day of renewal of vows [Friday, October 30, 1936].
     God's presence pervades my soul, not only in a spiritual
     way, but I feel it in a physical way also.

748 November 2, [1936]. In the evening after Vespers, I went
     to the cemetery [in the sisters' park]. I had been praying
     for a while when I saw one of our sisters, who said to me,
     "We are in the chapel." I understood that I was to go to
     the chapel and there pray and gain the indulgences. The
     next day, during Holy Mass, I saw three white doves
     soaring from the altar toward heaven. I understood that
     not only the three souls that I saw had gone to heaven,
     but also many others who had died beyond the confines
     of our institute. Oh, how good and merciful is the Lord!

749 **(167)** Conversation with Father Andrasz, at the end of
     the retreat. I was greatly surprised by one thing that I
     noticed during each conversation in the course of which
     I had asked advice and direction of Father Andrasz, and
     it is this: I noticed that Father Andrasz answered all my
     questions about things which the Lord has asked of me
     so clearly and with such assurance that it was as though
     he were experiencing it all himself. O my Jesus, if only
     there were more spiritual directors of this kind, souls
     under such guidance would very quickly reach the
     summits of sanctity and would not waste such great
     graces! I give unceasing thanks to God for so great a
     grace; namely, that in His great goodness He has
     deigned to place these pillars of light along the path of
     my spiritual life. They light my way so that I do not go
     astray or become delayed in my journey toward close
     union with the Lord. I have a great love for the Church,
     which educates souls and leads them to God.

750 **(168)** October 31, 1936. Conversation with Mother
     General [Michael].

     When I was talking to Mother General about the
     question of my leaving the Order, I received this answer:
     "If Jesus demands of you that you leave this

Congregation, let Him give me some sign that this is His will. Sister, pray for such a sign, because I am worried lest you should fall prey to some illusion. On the other hand, I would not want to hinder or oppose the will of God, for I too want to do the will of God." And so, we agreed that I will still remain just as I am, until such time as the Lord will let Mother General know that He demands that I leave this Congregation. And so the matter was put off for a while.

751   And so You see, Jesus, that everything is now up to You. I am perfectly at peace, despite these great urgings. For my part, I have done everything, and it is now Your turn, my Jesus, and in this way **(169)** Your cause will be made apparent. I am totally in accord with Your will; do with me as You please, O Lord, but only grant me the grace of loving You more and more ardently. This is what is most precious to me. I desire nothing but You, O Love Eternal! It matters not along what paths You will lead me, paths of pain or paths of joy. I want to love You at every moment of my life. If You tell me to leave, O Jesus, in order to carry out Your will, I will leave. If You tell me to stay, I will stay. It matters not what I will suffer, in the one instance or the other. O my Jesus, if I leave, I know what I shall have to suffer and endure. I agreed to this with full awareness, and I have already accepted it by an act of the will. It does not matter what the chalice holds for me. It is enough for me to know that it has been given to me by the loving hand of God. If you tell me to turn back and stay, I will stay in spite of all the interior urgings. If You still keep them **(170)** in my soul and leave me in this inner agony even to the end of my life, I accept this in the full consciousness of my will and in loving submission to You, O my God. If I stay, I shall hide myself in Your mercy, my God, so deeply that no human eye will see me. Throughout my life, I want to be a thurible filled with hidden fire, and may the smoke rising up to You, O Living Host, be pleasing to You. I

feel in my own heart that every little sacrifice arouses the fire of my love for You, but in such a silent and secret way that no one will detect it.

752 When I told Mother General that the Lord wanted the Congregation to say the chaplet in order to propitiate God's anger, Mother told me that at present she could not introduce new prayers that had not yet been approved... "But give me the chaplet, Sister, [she said;] perhaps it can be said during an adoration. We **(171)** shall see. It would be good if Father Sopocko could publish a pamphlet with the chaplet; then it would be better and easier to recite it in the Congregation, for it is a bit difficult to do so now."

753 The mercy of the Lord is praised by the holy souls in heaven who have themselves experienced that infinite mercy. What these souls do in heaven, I already will begin to do here on earth. I will praise God for His infinite goodness, and I will strive to bring other souls to know and glorify the inexpressible and incomprehensible mercy of God.

754 +The Lord's Promise: **The souls that say this chaplet will be embraced by My mercy during their lifetime and especially at the hour of their death.**

755 O my Jesus, teach me to open the bosom of mercy and love to everyone who asks for it. Jesus, my Commander, teach me so that all my prayers and deeds may bear the seal of Your mercy.

756 **(172)** November 18, 1936. Today, I tried to make all my exercises before Benediction, because I was feeling more ill than usual. So I went to bed directly after Benediction. But when I entered the bedroom, I suddenly knew interiorly that I should go to the cell of S.N.,[145] because she was in need of help. I entered her cell at once, and S.N. said to me, "Oh, how good it is that God has brought you here, Sister!" And her voice was so faint

that I could hardly hear her. She said to me, "Sister, please bring me some tea with lemon, because I am terribly thirsty, and I cannot move because I am in such pain." And truly, she was suffering very much and had a high fever. I made her more comfortable, and she was able to quench her thirst with the little bit of tea that I brought her. When I entered my own cell, my soul was engulfed by the great love of God, and I understood that we should take great heed of our interior inspirations and follow them faithfully, and that faithfulness to one grace draws down others.

757 **(173)** November 19, [1936]. During Mass today, I saw the Lord Jesus, who said to me, **Be at peace, My daughter; I see your efforts, which are very pleasing to Me.** And the Lord disappeared, and it was time for Holy Communion. After I received Holy Communion, I suddenly saw the Cenacle and in it Jesus and the Apostles. I saw the institution of the Most Blessed Sacrament. Jesus allowed me to penetrate His interior, and I came to know the greatness of His majesty and, at the same time, His great humbling of Himself. The extraordinary light that allowed me to see His majesty revealed to me, at the same time, what was in my own soul.

758 Jesus gave me to know the depth of His meekness and humility and to understand that He clearly demanded the same of me. I felt the gaze of God in my soul. This filled me with unspeakable love, but I understood that the Lord was looking with love on my virtues and my heroic efforts, and I knew that this was what was drawing God into my heart. It is from this that I have come to understand that it is not enough for me to strive only for the ordinary virtues, but that I must try to exercise **(174)** the heroic virtues. Although exteriorly a thing may be quite ordinary, it is the different manner [in which it is carried out] that only the eye of God

catches. O my Jesus, what I have written is just a pale shadow of what I understand in my soul; these are purely spiritual things, but in order to write something of what the Lord gives me to know, I must use words with which I am totally dissatisfied, because they do not express the reality.

759   When I experienced these sufferings for the first time, it was like this: after the annual vows,[146] on a certain day, during prayer, I saw a great brilliance and, issuing from the brilliance, rays which completely enveloped me. Then suddenly, I felt a terrible pain in my hands, my feet and my side and the thorns of the crown of thorns. I experienced these sufferings during Holy Mass on Friday, but this was only for a brief moment. This was repeated for several Fridays, and later on I did not experience any sufferings up to the present time; that is, up to the end of September **(175)** of this year. In the course of the present illness, during Holy Mass one Friday, I felt myself pierced by the same sufferings, and this has been repeated on every Friday and sometimes when I meet a soul that is not in the state of grace. Although this is infrequent, and the suffering lasts a very short time, still it is terrible, and I would not be able to bear it without a special grace from God. There is no outward indication of these sufferings. What will come later, I do not know. All this, for the sake of souls...

760   November 21, [1936]. Jesus, You see that I am neither gravely ill nor in good health. You fill my soul with enthusiasm for action, and I have no strength. The fire of Your love burns in me, and for what I cannot accomplish by physical strength, love will compensate.

761   Jesus, my spirit yearns for You, and I desire very much to be united with You, but Your works hold me back. The number of souls that I am to bring to You is not yet complete. I desire toil and suffering; let everything You have planned **(176)** before the ages be fulfilled in me, O my Creator and Lord! It is only Your word that I

understand; it alone gives me strength. Your Spirit, O
Lord, is the Spirit of Peace; and nothing troubles my
depths because You dwell there, O Lord.

I know that I am under Your special gaze, O Lord. I do
not examine with fear Your plans regarding me; my task
is to accept everything from Your hand. I do not fear
anything, although the storm is raging, and frightful
bolts strike all around me, and I then feel quite alone.
Yet, my heart senses You, and my trust grows, and I see
all Your omnipotence which upholds me. With You,
Jesus, I go through life, amid storms and rainbows, with
a cry of joy, singing the song of Your mercy. I will not
stop singing my song of love until the choir of Angels
picks it up. There is no power that can stop me in my
flight toward God. I see that even the superiors do not
always understand the road along which God is leading
me, and I am not surprised at this.

762 **(177)** Once, I saw Father Sopocko praying as he was
reflecting on these matters. Then I saw how a ring of
light appeared suddenly above his head. Although
distance separates us, I often see him, especially as he
works at his desk, despite his fatigue.

763 November 22, [1936]. Today during confession, the
Lord Jesus spoke to me through the lips of a certain
priest. This priest did not know my soul, and I only
accused myself of my sins; yet he spoke these words to
me: "Accomplish faithfully everything that Jesus asks of
you, despite the difficulties. Know that, although people
may be angry with you, Jesus is not angry and never will
be angry with you. Pay no attention to human opinion."
This instruction surprised me at first; but I understood
that the Lord was speaking through him without his
realizing it. O holy mystery, what great treasures are
contained in you! O holy faith, you are my guidepost!

764 **(178)** November 24. Today, I received a letter from
Father Sopocko.[147] I learned from it that God himself is

conducting this whole affair. And as the Lord has begun it, so will He continue to carry it along. And the greater the difficulties which I see, the more am I at peace. Oh, if in this whole matter the glory of God and the profit to souls were not greatly served, Satan would not be opposing it so much. But he senses what he is going to lose because of it. I have now learned that Satan hates mercy more than anything else. It is his greatest torment. Still, the word of God will not pass away; God's utterance is living; difficulties will not suppress the works of God, but show that they are God's...

765 On one occasion, I saw the convent of the new congregation.[148] As I walked about, inspecting everything, I suddenly saw a crowd of children who seemed to be no older than five to eleven years of age. When they saw me they surrounded me and began to cry out, "Defend us from evil," **(179)** and they led me into the chapel which was in this convent. When I entered the chapel, I saw the distressful Lord Jesus. Jesus looked at me graciously and said that He was gravely offended by children: **You are to defend them from evil.** From that moment, I have been praying for children, but I feel that prayer alone is not enough.

766 O my Jesus, you know what efforts are needed to live sincerely and unaffectedly with those from whom our nature flees, or with those who, deliberately or not, have made us suffer. Humanly speaking, this is impossible. At such times more than at others, I try to discover the Lord Jesus in such a person and for this same Jesus, I do everything for such people. In such acts, love is pure, and such practice of love gives the soul endurance and strength. I do not expect anything from creatures, and therefore I am not disappointed. I know that a creature is poor of itself, **(180)** so what can one expect from it? God is everything for me; I want to evaluate everything according to God's ways.

767 + My communion with the Lord is now purely spiritual. My soul is touched by God and wholly absorbs itself in Him, even to the complete forgetfulness of self. Permeated by God to its very depths, it drowns in His beauty; it completely dissolves in Him—I am at a loss to describe this, because in writing I am making use of the senses; but there, in that union, the senses are not active; there is a merging of God and the soul; and the life of God to which the soul is admitted is so great that the human tongue cannot express it.

When the soul returns to its habitual form of life, it then sees that this life is all darkness and mist and dreamlike confusion, an infant's swaddling clothes. In such moments the soul only receives from God, for of itself it does nothing; it does not make even the slightest effort; all in her is wrought by God. But when the soul returns to its ordinary state, it sees that it is not **(181)** within its power to continue in this union.

These moments are short, but their effects are lasting. The soul cannot remain long in this state; or else it would be forcibly freed of the bonds of the body forever. Even as it is, it is sustained by a miracle of God. God allows the soul to know in a clear way how much He loves it, as though it were the only object of His delight. The soul recognizes this clearly and without a veil, so to speak. It reaches out for God with all its might, but it feels like a baby; it knows that this is not within its power. Therefore, God descends to the soul and unites it to himself in a way that... here, I must be silent, for I cannot describe what the soul experiences.

768 It is a strange thing that although the soul which experiences this union with God cannot find words and expressions to describe it, nevertheless, when it meets a similar soul, the two understand each other extra-ordinarily well in regard to these matters, even though they speak but little with each other. A soul united with

God in this way easily recognizes a similar soul, even if **(182)** the latter has not revealed its interior [life] to it, but merely speaks in an ordinary way. It is a kind of spiritual kinship. Souls united with God in this way are few, fewer than we think.

769 I have noticed that the Lord grants this grace to souls for two purposes. The first is when the soul is to do some great work which is, humanly speaking, absolutely beyond its power. In the second case, I have noticed that the Lord grants it in order that kindred souls might be guided and set at peace, although the Lord can grant this grace as He pleases and to whomever He pleases. However, I have noticed this grace in three priests, one of whom is a secular priest [probably Father Sopocko] and the other two, religious priests [probably Father Elter and Father Andrasz], and also in two religious sisters [probably Mother Michael and Sister Mary Joseph], but not in the same degree.

770 As for myself, I received this grace for the first time, and that for only a brief moment, in the eighteenth[149] year of my life, within the octave of Corpus Christi [June 18-25, 1925], during Vespers, when I made to the Lord Jesus the vow of perpetual chastity. **(183)**I was still living in the world, but I entered the convent soon afterwards. The grace lasted for a very brief moment, but its power was great. After this grace, there was a long interval. It is true that I received many graces from the Lord during this interval, but they were of a different order. It was a time of trials and purification. The trials were so painful that my soul felt as though it was being totally abandoned by God and it was steeped in profound darkness. I became aware and understood that no one would be able to bring me out of those torments or even understand me.

There were two occasions when my soul was plunged into despair, once for half an hour, and the second time for three quarters of an hour. Just as I cannot describe the greatness of the graces, so too with these ordeals sent by the Lord; whatever words I might use, they are only a pale shadow [of the reality]. However, just as the Lord plunged me into these torments, so too He brought me out of them. Only this lasted for a few years, after which I again received this extraordinary grace of union **(184)** which has continued to this day. Still, during this second period of union, there also have been short interruptions. But for some time now, I have not experienced any interruption at all; on the contrary, I am more and more deeply steeped in God. The great light which illumines the mind gives me a knowledge of the greatness of God; but it is not as if I were getting to know the individual attributes, as before—no, it is different now: in one moment, I come to know the entire essence of God.

771 In that same moment, the soul drowns entirely in Him and experiences a happiness as great as that of the chosen ones in heaven. Although the chosen ones in heaven see God face to face and are completely and absolutely happy, still their knowledge of God is not the same. God has given me to understand this. This deeper knowledge begins here on earth, depending on the grace [given], but to a great extent it also depends on our faithfulness to that grace.

However, the soul receiving this unprecedented grace of union with God cannot say that it sees God face to face, because even here there is a very thin veil of faith, but so very**(185)** thin that the soul can say that it sees God and talks with Him. It is "divinized." God allows the soul to know how much He loves it, and the soul sees that better and holier souls than itself have not received this grace. Therefore, it is filled with holy amazement, which maintains it in deep humility, and it steeps itself in its own nothingness and holy astonishment; and the more it humbles itself, the more closely God unites himself with it and descends to it.

The soul, at this moment is, as it were, hidden; its senses are inactive; in one moment, it knows God and drowns in Him. It knows the whole depth of the Unfathomable One, and the deeper this knowledge, the more ardently the soul desires Him.

772 Great is the mutual exchange between the soul and God. When the soul leaves its concealment, the senses get a taste of what the soul has delighted in. Although this also is a great grace from God, it is not a purely spiritual one, for in the first moments the senses do not take part. Every grace gives the soul power and strength to act, and courage to suffer. The soul knows very well what God is asking of it, and it carries out **(186)** His holy will despite adversities.

773 Yet, the soul cannot proceed on its own in these matters. It must follow the advice of an enlightened confessor, for otherwise it could go astray or gain no profit.

774 + O my Jesus, I understand well that, just as illness is measured with a thermometer, and a high fever tells us of the seriousness of the illness, so also, in the spiritual life, suffering is the thermometer which measures the love of God in a soul.

775 + My goal is God... and my happiness is in accomplishing His will, and nothing in the world can disturb this happiness for me: no power, no force of any kind.

776 The Lord visited my cell today and said to me, **My daughter, I will not leave you in this community for much longer. I am telling you this so that you will be more diligent in taking advantage of the graces which I grant you.**

777 **(187)** November 27, [1936]. Today I was in heaven, in spirit, and I saw its inconceivable beauties and the happiness that awaits us after death. I saw how all creatures give ceaseless praise and glory to God. I saw

how great is happiness in God, which spreads to all creatures, making them happy; and then all the glory and praise which springs from this happiness returns to its source; and they enter into the depths of God, contemplating the inner life of God, the Father, the Son, and the Holy Spirit, whom they will never comprehend or fathom.

This source of happiness is unchanging in its essence, but it is always new, gushing forth happiness for all creatures. Now I understand Saint Paul, who said, "Eye has not seen, nor has ear heard, nor has it entered into the heart of man what God has prepared for those who love Him."

778 And God has given me to understand that there is but one thing that is of infinite value in His eyes, and that is love of God; love, love and once again, love; and nothing can compare with a single act of pure **(188)**love of God. Oh, with what inconceivable favors God gifts a soul that loves Him sincerely! Oh, how happy is the soul who already here on earth enjoys His special favors! And of such are the little and humble souls.

779 The sight of this great majesty of God, which I came to understand more profoundly and which is worshiped by the heavenly spirits according to their degree of grace and the hierarchies into which they are divided, did not cause my soul to be stricken with terror or fear; no, no, not at all! My soul was filled with peace and love, and the more I come to know the greatness of God, the more joyful I become that He is as He is. And I rejoice immensely in His greatness and am delighted that I am so little because, since I am little, He carries me in His arms and holds me close to His Heart.

780 O my God, how I pity those people who do not believe in eternal life; how I pray for them that a ray of mercy would envelop them too, and that God would clasp them to His fatherly bosom.

781 O Love, O queen! Love knows no **(189)** fear. It passes through all the choirs of angels that stand on guard before His throne. It will fear no one. It reaches God and is immersed in Him as in its sole treasure. The Cherubim who guards paradise with flaming sword, has no power over it. O pure love of God, how great and unequalled you are! Oh, if souls only knew your power!

782 + I am very weak today. I cannot even make my meditation in the chapel, but must lie down. O my Jesus, I love You, and I want to worship You with my very weakness, submitting myself entirely to Your holy will.

783 + I must be on my guard, especially today, because I am becoming over-sensitive to everything. Things I would not pay any attention to when I am healthy bother me today. O my Jesus, my shield and my strength, grant me Your grace that I may emerge victorious from these combats. O my Jesus, transform me into Yourself by the power of Your love, that I may be a worthy tool in proclaiming Your mercy.

784 **(190)** + I thank God for this illness and these physical discomforts, because I have time to converse with the Lord Jesus. It is my delight to spend long hours at the feet of the hidden God, and the hours pass like minutes as I lose track of time. I feel that a fire is burning within me, and I understand no other life but that of sacrifice, which flows from pure love.

785 November 29, [1936]. The Mother of God has taught me how to prepare for the Feast of Christmas. I saw Her today, without the Infant Jesus. She said to me: *My daughter, strive after silence and humility, so that Jesus, who dwells in your heart continuously, may be able to rest. Adore Him in your heart; do not go out from your inmost being. My daughter, I shall obtain for you the grace of an interior life which will be such that, without ever leaving that interior life, you will be able to carry out all your external duties with even greater care. Dwell*

*with Him continuously in your own heart. He will be
your strength. Communicate with creatures only in so
far as is necessary* **(191)** *and is required by your duties.
You are a dwelling place pleasing to the living God; in
you He dwells continuously with love and delight. And
the living presence of God, which you experience in a
more vivid and distinct way, will confirm you, my
daughter, in the things I have told you. Try to act in this
way until Christmas Day, and then He himself will
make known to you in what way you will be communing
and uniting yourself with Him.*

786 November 30, [1936]. During Vespers today, an unusual
pain pierced my soul. I see that, in every respect, this
work is beyond my strength. I am a little child before the
immensity of the task, and it is only at the Lord's clear
command that I am setting about to carry it out. On the
other hand, even these great graces are a burden for me,
and I am barely able to carry them. I see my superiors'
disbelief and doubts of all kinds and, for this reason,
their apprehensive behavior towards me. My Jesus, I see
that even such great graces can be [a source of] suffering.
And yet, it is so; **(192)** not only may they be a cause of
suffering, but they must be such, as a sign of God's
action. I understand well that if God himself did not
strengthen the soul in these various ordeals, the soul
would not be able to master the situation. Thus God
himself is its shield.

As I continued Vespers, meditating on this mixture of
suffering and grace, I heard the voice of Our Lady:
*Know, My daughter, that although I was raised to the
dignity of Mother of God, seven swords of pain pierced
My heart. Don't do anything to defend yourself; bear
everything with humility; God himself will defend you.*

December 1, [1936]. One-day retreat.

787 Today, during the morning meditation, the Lord gave
me to see and understand clearly that His demands are

unchangeable. I see clearly that no one can release me from the duty of doing the known will of God. A great lack of health and physical strength is not a sufficient reason and does not release me **(193)** from this work that the Lord himself is carrying out through me. I am to be just a tool in His hands. And so, O Lord, here I am to carry out Your will. Command me according to Your eternal plans and desires. Only give me the grace that I may always be faithful to You.

788 As I was conversing with the hidden God, He gave me to see and understand that I should not be reflecting so much and building up fear of the difficulties which I might encounter. **Know that I am with you; I bring about the difficulties, and I overcome them; in one instant, I can change a hostile disposition to one which is favorable to this cause.** The Lord explained many things to me in today's dialogue, although I am not putting everything in writing.

789 Always and in all circumstances, yield the first place to others; especially during recreation listen quietly, without interrupting, even if someone tells me the same thing ten times. I will never ask questions about something that interests me very much.

790 **(194)** Resolution: still the same; namely, to unite myself with the Merciful Christ.

General resolution: interior calm, silence.

791 Hide me, Jesus, in the depths of Your mercy, and then let my neighbor judge me as he pleases.

792 I must never speak of my own experiences. In suffering, I must seek relief in prayer. In doubts, even the smallest, I must seek only the advice of my confessor. I must always have a heart which is open to receive the sufferings of others, and drown my own sufferings in the Divine Heart so that they would not be noticed on the outside, in so far as possible.

I must always strive for equanimity, no matter how stormy the circumstances might be. I must not allow anything to disturb my interior calm and silence. Nothing can compare with peace of soul. When I am wrongfully accused of something, I will not explain myself; if the superior wants to know **(195)** the truth, whether I was in the right or not, let her find out from others rather than from me. My concern is to accept everything with a humble inner disposition.

I will spend this Advent in accordance with the directions of the Mother of God: in meekness and humility.

793 I am reliving these moments with Our Lady. With great longing, I am waiting for the Lord's coming. Great are my desires. I desire that all humankind come to know the Lord. I would like to prepare all nations for the coming of the Word Incarnate. O Jesus, make the fount of Your mercy gush forth more abundantly, for humankind is seriously ill and thus has more need than ever of Your compassion. You are a bottomless sea of mercy for us sinners; and the greater the misery, the more right we have to Your mercy. You are a fount which makes all creatures happy by Your infinite mercy.

794 **(196)** Today [December 9, 1936], I am leaving for Pradnik, just outside Cracow, to undergo treatment. I am to stay there for three months. I am being sent there through the great solicitude of my superiors, especially that of our dear Mother General [Michael], who is so solicitous for the sisters who are ill.

795 I have accepted the favor of this treatment, but I am fully resigned to the will of God. Let God do with me as He pleases. I desire nothing but the fulfillment of His holy will. I am uniting myself with the Mother of God, and I am leaving Nazareth and going to Bethlehem. I will spend Christmas there among strangers, but with Jesus, Mary and Joseph, because such is the will of God. I am striving to do the will of God in all things. I do not desire

a return to health more than death. I entrust myself completely to His infinite mercy and, as a little child, I am living in the greatest peace. I am trying only to make my love for Him deeper and purer, to be a delight to His divine glance...

796 **(197)** The Lord told me to say this chaplet for nine days before the Feast of Mercy. It is to begin on Good Friday. **By this novena, I will grant every possible grace to souls.**

797 When I was somewhat overcome by the fear that I was to be outside the community for so long a time alone, Jesus said to me, **You will not be alone, because I am with you always and everywhere. Near to My Heart, fear nothing. I myself am the cause of your departure. Know that My eyes follow every move of your heart with great attention. I am bringing you into seclusion so that I myself may form your heart according to My future plans. What are you afraid of? If you are with Me, who will dare touch you? Nevertheless, I am very pleased that you confide your fears to Me, My daughter. Speak to Me about everything in a completely simple and human way; by this you will give Me great joy. I understand you because I am God-Man. (198) This simple language of your heart is more pleasing to Me than the hymns composed in My honor. Know, My daughter, that the simpler your speech is, the more you attract Me to yourself. And now, be at peace close to My Heart. Lay your pen aside and get ready to leave.**

798 December 9, 1936. This morning, I left for Pradnik. Sister Chrysostom drove me here. I have a private room to myself; I am very much like a Carmelite. When Sister Chrysostom had left and I was alone, I steeped myself in prayer, entrusting myself to the special protection of the Mother of God. She alone is always with me. She, like a good Mother, watches over all my trials and efforts.

799 Suddenly, I saw the Lord Jesus, who said to me, **Be at**

peace, My child. See, you are not alone. My Heart watches over you. Jesus filled me with strength concerning a certain person. I feel strength within my soul.

(199) A moral principle.

800 If one does not know what is better, one must reflect, consider and seek advice, because one must not act with an uncertain conscience. When uncertain, say to yourself: "Whatever I do will be good. I have the intention of doing good." The Lord God accepts what we consider good, and the Lord God also accepts and considers it as good. One should not worry if, after some time, one sees that these things are not good. God looks at the intention with which we begin, and will reward us accordingly. This is a principle which we ought to follow.

801 Today, I still managed to pay a short visit to the Lord [in the Eucharist] before going to bed. My spirit was immersed in Him as in its only treasure. My heart rested a while near the Heart of my Spouse. I received light as to how I should behave toward those around me, and then I returned to my solitude. The doctor is taking good care of me; all those around me are very kind to me.

802 **(200)** December 10, [1936]. I got up earlier today and made my meditation before Holy Mass. Holy Mass is at six o'clock here. After Holy Communion my spirit was drowned in the Lord as in the sole object of its love. I felt absorbed by His omnipotence. When I came back to my private room, I felt sick and had to lie down at once. The sister[150] brought me some medication, but I felt bad all day. In the evening, I tried to make a Holy Hour, but I could not do so; all I could do was unite myself with the suffering Jesus.

803 My room is next to the men's ward. I didn't know that men were such chatterboxes. From morning till late at night, there is talk about various subjects. The women's

ward is much quieter. It is women who are always
blamed for this; but I have had occasion to be convinced
that the opposite is true. It is very difficult for me to
concentrate on my prayer in the midst of these jokes and
this laughter. They do not disturb me when the grace of
God takes complete possession of me, **(201)** because
then I do not know what is going on around me.

804   My Jesus, how little these people talk about You. They
talk about everything but You, Jesus. And if they talk so
little [about You], it is quite probable that they do not
think about You at all. The whole world interests them;
but about You, their Creator, there is silence. Jesus, I
am sad to see this great indifference and ingratitude of
creatures. O my Jesus, I want to love You for them and
to make atonement to You, by my love.

Immaculate Conception of the Mother of God.

805   From early morning, I felt the nearness of the Blessed
Mother. During Holy Mass, I saw Her, so lovely and so
beautiful that I have no words to express even a small
part of this beauty. She was all [in] white, with a blue
sash around Her waist. Her cloak was also blue, and
there was a crown on Her head. Marvelous light
streamed forth from Her whole figure. *I am the Queen
of heaven and earth, but especially the Mother of your
[Congregation].* She pressed me to Her heart and said, *I
feel constant compassion for you.* I felt **(202)** the force of
Her Immaculate Heart which was communicated to my
soul. Now I understand why I have been preparing for
this feast for two months and have been looking forward
to it with such yearning. From today onwards, I am
going to strive for the greatest purity of soul, that the
rays of God's grace may be reflected in all their
brilliance. I long to be a crystal in order to find favor in
His eyes.

806   + That same day, I saw a certain priest [probably Father
Sopocko or Father Andrasz] who was surrounded by

the light which flowed from Her; evidently, this soul loves the Immaculate One.

807 An extraordinary yearning fills my soul. I am surprised that it does not separate the soul from the body. I desire God; I want to become immersed in Him. I understand that I am in a terrible exile; my soul aspires for God with all its might. O you inhabitants of my fatherland, be mindful of this exile! When will the veils be lifted for me as well? Although I see **(203)** and feel to a certain extent how very thin is the veil separating me from the Lord, I long to see Him face to face; but let everything be done according to Your will.

808 December 11. I could not assist at the whole Mass today; I assisted at only the most important parts, and after receiving Holy Communion I immediately returned to my solitude. The presence of God suddenly enveloped me, and at the same moment I felt the Passion of the Lord, for a very short while. During that moment, I attained a more profound knowledge of the work of mercy.

809 During the night, I was suddenly awakened and knew that some soul was asking me for prayer, and that it was in much need of prayer. Briefly, but with all my soul, I asked the Lord for grace for her.

810 The following afternoon, when I entered the ward, I saw someone dying, and learned that the agony had started during the night. When I verified it—it had been at the time when **(204)** I had been asked for prayer. And just then, I heard a voice in my soul: **Say the chaplet which I taught you.** I ran to fetch my rosary and knelt down by the dying person and, with all the ardor of my soul, I began to say the chaplet. Suddenly the dying person opened her eyes and looked at me; I had not managed to finish the entire chaplet when she died, with extraordinary peace. I fervently asked the Lord to fulfill the promise He had given me for the recitation of the

chaplet. The Lord gave me to know that the soul had been granted the grace He had promised me. That was the first soul to receive the benefit of the Lord's promise. I could feel the power of mercy envelop that soul.

811 When I entered my solitude, I heard these words: **At the hour of their death, I defend as My own glory every soul that will say this chaplet; or when others say it for a dying person, the indulgence is the same. When (205) this chaplet is said by the bedside of a dying person, God's anger is placated, unfathomable mercy envelops the soul, and the very depths of My tender mercy are moved for the sake of the sorrowful Passion of My Son.**

Oh, if only everyone realized how great the Lord's mercy is and how much we all need that mercy, especially at that crucial hour!

812 + Today I have fought a battle with the spirits of darkness over one soul. How terribly Satan hates God's mercy! I see how he opposes this whole work.

813 + O merciful Jesus, stretched on the cross, be mindful of the hour of our death. O most merciful Heart of Jesus, opened with a lance, shelter me at the last moment of my life. O Blood and Water, which gushed forth from the Heart of Jesus as a fount of unfathomable mercy for me at the hour of my death, O dying Jesus, Hostage of mercy, avert the Divine wrath at the hour of my death.

814 **(206)** + December 12, [1936]. Today, I only received Holy Communion and stayed for a few moments of the Mass. All my strength is in You, O Living Bread. It would be difficult for me to live through the day if I did not receive Holy Communion. It is my shield; without You, Jesus, I know not how to live.

815 Jesus, my Love, today gave me to understand how much He loves me, although there is such an enormous gap between us, the Creator and the creature; and yet, in a

way, there is something like equality: love fills up the gap. He himself descends to me and makes me capable of communing with Him. I immerse myself in Him, losing myself as it were; and yet, under His loving gaze, my soul gains strength and power and an awareness that it loves and is especially loved. It knows that the Mighty One protects it. Such prayer, though short, benefits the soul greatly, and whole hours of ordinary prayer do not give the soul that light which is given by a brief moment of this higher form of prayer.

816 **(207)** + This afternoon, I had my first open-air rest [on the sunny veranda at the sanatorium]. Sister Felicia[151] visited me today and brought a few necessary things and some lovely apples and words of greeting from our beloved Mother Superior and dear sisters.

December 13, [1936]. Confession before Jesus.

817 When I reflected that I had not been to confession for more than three weeks, I wept seeing the sinfulness of my soul and certain difficulties. I had not gone to confession because the circumstances made it impossible. On the day of confessions, I had been confined to bed. The following week, confessions were in the afternoon, and I had left for the hospital that morning. This afternoon, Father Andrasz came into my room and sat down to hear my confession. Beforehand, we did not exchange a single word. I was delighted because I was extremely anxious to go to confession. As usual, I unveiled my whole soul. Father gave a reply to each little detail. I felt unusually happy to be able **(208)** to say everything as I did. For penance, he gave me the Litany of the Holy Name of Jesus. When I wanted to tell him of the difficulty I have in saying this litany, he rose and began to give me absolution. Suddenly his figure became diffused with a great light, and I saw that it was not Father A., but Jesus. His garments were bright as snow, and He disappeared immediately. At first, I was a little uneasy, but after a while a kind of peace entered my

soul; and I took note of the fact that Jesus heard the confession in the same way that confessors do; and yet something was wondrously transpiring in my heart during this confession; I couldn't at first understand what it signified.

818 December 16, [1936]. I have offered this day for Russia. I have offered all my sufferings and prayers for that poor country. After Holy Communion, Jesus said to me, **I cannot suffer that country any longer. Do not tie my hands, My daughter. (209)** I understood that if it had not been for the prayers of souls that are pleasing to God, that whole nation would have already been reduced to nothingness. Oh, how I suffer for that nation which has banished God from its borders!

819 + O inexhaustible spring of Divine Mercy, pour yourself out upon us! Your Goodness knows no limits. Confirm, O Lord, the power of Your mercy over the abyss of my misery, for You have no limit to Your mercies. Wonderful and matchless is Your mercy, astonishing the human and angelic mind.

820 My Guardian Angel told me to pray for a certain soul, and in the morning I learned that it was a man whose agony had begun that very moment. The Lord Jesus makes it known to me in a special way when someone is in need of my prayer. I especially know when my prayer is needed by a dying soul. This happens more often now than it did in the past.

821 **(210)** The Lord Jesus gave me to know how very pleasing to Him is a soul who lives in accordance with the will of God. It thereby gives very great glory to God...

822 I have come to understand today that even if I did not accomplish any of the things the Lord is demanding of me, I know that I shall be rewarded as if I had fulfilled everything, because He sees the intention with which I begin, and even if He called me to himself today, the

work would not suffer at all by that, because He himself is the Lord of both the work and the worker. My part is to love Him to folly; all works are nothing more than a tiny drop before Him. It is love that has meaning and power and merit. He has opened up great horizons in my soul—love compensates for the chasms.

823 December 17, [1936]. I have offered this day for priests. I have suffered more today than ever before, both interiorly and exteriorly. I did not know it was possible to suffer (211) so much in one day. I tried to make a Holy Hour, in the course of which my spirit had a taste of the bitterness of the Garden of Gethsemane. I am fighting alone, supported by His arm, against all the difficulties that face me like unassailable walls. But I trust in the power of His name and I fear nothing.

824 In this seclusion, Jesus himself is my Master. He himself educates and instructs me. I feel that I am the object of His special action. For His inscrutable purposes and unfathomable decrees, He unites me to Himself in a special way and allows me to penetrate His incomprehensible mysteries. There is one mystery which unites me with the Lord, of which no one—not even angels—may know. And even if I wanted to tell of it, I would not know how to express it. And yet, I live by it and will live by it for ever. This mystery distinguishes me from every other soul here on earth or in eternity.

825 (212) + O bright and clear day on which all my dreams will be fulfilled; O day so eagerly desired, the last day of my life! I look forward with joy to the last stroke the Divine Artist will trace on my soul, which will give my soul a unique beauty that will distinguish me from the beauty of other souls. O great day, on which divine love will be confirmed in me. On that day, for the first time, I shall sing before heaven and earth the song of the Lord's fathomless mercy. This is my work and the mission which the Lord has destined for me from the beginning of the world. That the song of my soul may be pleasing

to the Holy Trinity, do You, O Spirit of God, direct and form my soul yourself. I arm myself with patience and await Your coming, O merciful God, and as to the terrible pains and fear of death, at this moment more than at any other time, I trust in the abyss of Your **(213)** mercy and am reminding You, O merciful Jesus, sweet Savior, of all the promises You have made to me.

826 This morning I had an adventure. My watch had stopped, and I did not know when to get up, and I thought of what a misfortune it would be to miss Holy Communion. It was still dark, so I had no way of knowing whether it was time to get up. I dressed, made my meditation and went to the chapel, but everything was still locked, and silence reigned everywhere. I steeped myself in prayer, especially for the sick. I now see how much the sick have need of prayer. Finally, the chapel was opened. I found it difficult to pray because I was already feeling very exhausted, and immediately after Holy Communion I returned to my room. Then I saw the Lord, who said to me, **Know, My daughter, that the ardor of your heart is pleasing to Me. And just as you desire ardently to become united with Me in Holy Communion, so too do I desire to give Myself wholly to you; and as a (214) reward for your zeal, rest on My Heart.** At that moment, my spirit was immersed in His Being, like a drop in a bottomless ocean. I drowned myself in Him as in my sole treasure. Thus I came to recognize that the Lord allows certain difficulties for His greater glory.

827 December 18, [1936]. Today I felt bad that a week had gone by and no one had come to visit me.[152] When I complained to the Lord, He answered, **Isn't it enough for you that I visit you every day?** I apologized to the Lord and the hurt vanished. O God, my strength, You are sufficient for me.

828 This evening, I learned that a certain soul was in need of

my prayer. I prayed fervently, but felt that this was still not enough, so I continued to pray for a longer time. On the following day, I learned that the agony of a certain soul had started at just that time and had continued until morning. I recognized what struggles it had gone through. **(215)** In a strange way, the Lord Jesus makes known to me that a dying soul has need of my prayer. I feel vividly and clearly that spirit who is asking me for prayer. I was not aware that souls are so closely united, and often it is my Guardian Angel who tells me.

829 During Holy Mass, the little Infant Jesus brings joy to my soul. Often, distance does not exist—I see a certain priest who brings Him down. I am awaiting Christmas with great yearning; I am living in expectation together with the Most Holy Mother.

830 O Light Eternal, who come to this earth, enlighten my mind and strengthen my will that I may not give up in times of great affliction. May Your light dissipate all the shadows of doubt. May Your omnipotence act through me. I trust in You, O uncreated Light! You, O Infant Jesus, are a model for me in accomplishing Your Father's will, You, who said, "Behold, I come to do Your will." Grant that I also **(216)** may do God's will faithfully in all things. O Divine Infant, grant me this grace!

831 O my Jesus, my soul was yearning for the days of trial, but do not leave me alone in the darkness of my soul. Rather, do You hold me firmly, close to Yourself. Set a guard over my lips, so that the fragrance of my sufferings may be known and pleasing to You alone.

832 O merciful Jesus, how longingly You hurried to the Upper Room to consecrate the Host that I am to receive in my life. Jesus, You desired to dwell in my heart. Your living Blood unites with mine. Who can understand this close union? My heart encloses within itself the Almighty, the Infinite One. O Jesus, continue to grant

me Your divine life. Let Your pure and noble Blood
throb with all its might in my heart. I give You my whole
(217) being. Transform me into Yourself and make me
capable of doing Your holy will in all things and of
returning Your love. O my sweet Spouse, You know
that my heart knows no one but You. You have opened
up in my heart an insatiable depth of love for You. From
the very first moment it knew You, my heart has loved
You and has lost itself in You as its one and only object.
May Your pure and omnipotent love be the driving
force of all my actions. Who will ever conceive and
understand the depth of mercy that has gushed forth
from Your Heart?

833 I have experienced how much envy there is, even in
religious life. I see that there are few truly great souls,
ready to trample on everything that is not God. O soul,
you will find no beauty outside of God. Oh, how fragile
is the foundation of those who elevate themselves at the
expense of others! What a loss!

834 **(218)** December 19, [1936]. This evening, I felt in my soul
that a certain person had need of my prayer.
Immediately, I began to pray. Suddenly, I realize
interiorly and am aware of who the spirit is who is
asking this of me; I pray until I feel at peace. There is
great help for the dying in this chaplet. I often pray for
an intention that I have learned of interiorly. I always
pray until I experience in my soul that the prayer has
had its effect.

835 Especially now, while I am in this hospital, I experience
an inner communion with the dying who ask me for
prayer when their agony begins. God has given me a
wondrous contact with the dying! Since this has been
happening more frequently, I have been able to verify it,
even to the exact hour.

Today I was awakened suddenly at eleven o'clock at
night and clearly felt the presence near me of some spirit

who was asking me for prayer. Some force simply compelled me to pray. My vision is purely spiritual, by means of a sudden light **(219)** that God grants me at that moment. I keep on praying until I feel peace in my soul, and not always for an equally long time; because sometimes it happens that with one "Hail Mary" I am already at peace, and then I say the *De Profundis* and pray no longer. And sometimes it happens that I pray the entire chaplet and only then feel at peace. I have also discovered that if I feel constrained to pray for a longer time; that is to say, I experience interior unrest, the soul is undergoing a greater struggle and is going through a longer final agony.

This is how I have verified the exact time: I have a watch, and I look to see what time it is. On the following day, when they tell me about that person's death, I ask them about the time, and it exactly corresponds, as does the length of the person's last agony. They say to me, "Such and such a person died today, but she passed away quickly and peacefully." It sometimes happens that the dying person is in the second or third building away, yet for the spirit, space does not **(220)** exist. It sometimes happens that I know about a death occurring several hundred kilometers away. This has happened several times with regard to my family and relatives and also sisters in religion, and even souls whom I have not known during their lifetime.

O God of fathomless mercy, who allow me to give relief and help to the dying by my unworthy prayer, be blessed as many thousand times as there are stars in the sky and drops of water in all the oceans! Let Your mercy resound throughout the orb of the earth, and let it rise to the foot of Your throne, giving praise to the greatest of Your attributes; that is, Your incomprehensible mercy. O God, this unfathomable mercy enthralls anew all the holy souls and all the spirits of heaven. These pure spirits are immersed in holy amazement as they glorify this inconceivable mercy of God, which in turn arouses even greater admiration in them, and their praise is carried out in a perfect manner. O eternal God, how ardently I desire to glorify this greatest of Your **(221)** attributes; namely, Your unfathomable mercy. I see all my littleness, and cannot compare myself to the heavenly beings who praise the Lord's mercy with holy admiration. But I, too, have found a way to give perfect glory to the incomprehensible mercy of God.

836   O most sweet Jesus, who have deigned to allow miserable me to gain a knowledge of Your unfathomable mercy; O most sweet Jesus, who have graciously demanded that I tell the whole world of Your incomprehensible mercy, this day I take into my hands the two rays that spring from Your merciful Heart; that is, the Blood and the Water; and I scatter them all over the globe so that each soul may receive Your mercy and, having received it, may glorify it for endless ages. O most sweet Jesus who, in Your incomprehensible kindness, have deigned to unite my wretched heart to Your most merciful Heart, it is with Your own Heart that I glorify God, our Father, as no soul has ever glorified Him before.

837   **(222)** December 21, [1936]. The radio is always playing in the afternoon, so I feel the loss of silence. All morning long, there is ceaseless talk and noise. My God, I was looking forward to being in silence, happy that I should be talking only with the Lord, and here it is just the opposite. Yet, nothing disturbs me now, neither the talking nor the radio. In a word—nothing. By the grace of God, when I am praying I do not even know where I am; I know only that my soul is united with the Lord. And thus I pass my days in this hospital.

838   + I marvel at how many humiliations and sufferings that priest accepts in this whole matter.[153] I see this at particular times, and I support him with my unworthy prayers. Only God can give one such courage; otherwise

one would give up. But I see with joy that all these adversities contribute to God's greater glory. The Lord has few such souls. O infinite eternity, you will make manifest the efforts of heroic souls, because the earth rewards their efforts with hatred and ingratitude. Such souls do not have friends; they are solitary. **(223)** And in this solitude, they gain strength; they draw their strength from God alone. With humility, but also with courage, they stand firmly in the face of all the storms that beat upon them. Like high-towering oaks, they are unmoved. And in this there is just this one secret: that it's from God that they draw this strength, and everything whatsoever they have need of, they have for themselves and for others. They not only carry their own burden, but also know how to take on, and are capable of taking on, the burdens of others. They are pillars of light along God's ways; they live in light themselves and shed light upon others. They themselves live on the heights, and know how to show the way to lesser ones and help them attain those heights.

839 + My Jesus, You see that I do not know how to write well and, on top of that, I don't even have a good pen. And often it scratches so badly that I must put sentences together, letter by letter. And that is not all. I also have the difficulty of keeping secret from the sisters the things I write down, and so I often have to shut my notebook every few minutes and listen patiently to someone's story, **(224)** and then the time set aside for writing is gone. And when I shut the notebook suddenly, the ink smears. I write with the permission of my superiors and at the command of my confessor. It is a strange thing: sometimes the writing goes quite well, but at other times, I can hardly read it myself.

840 December 23, [1936]. I am spending this time with the Mother of God and preparing myself for the solemn moment of the coming of the Lord Jesus. The Mother of God is instructing me in the interior life of the soul with

Jesus, especially in Holy Communion. It is only in eternity that we shall know the great mystery effected in us by Holy Communion. O most precious moments of my life!

841 O my Creator, I long for You! You understand me, O Lord of mine! All that is on earth seems to me like a pale shadow. It is You I long for and desire. Although You do so inconceivably much for me, for You yourself visit me in a special way, yet those visits do not soothe the wound of the heart, but make me long all the more **(225)** for You, O Lord. Oh, take me to Yourself, Lord, if such is Your will! You know that I am dying, and I am dying of longing for You; and yet, I cannot die. Death, where are you? You draw me into the abyss of Your divinity, and You veil yourself with darkness. My whole being is immersed in You, yet I desire to see You face to face. When will this come about for me?

842 Sister Chrysostom[154] came to visit me today. She brought some lemons and apples and a tiny Christmas tree. I was delighted with them. Through Sister Chrysostom, Mother Superior asked the doctor [Adam Silberg] to let me come home for Christmas, and he readily agreed. I was very happy and burst into tears like a little child. Sister Chrysostom was surprised that I looked so bad and had changed so much, and she told me, "You know, Little Faustina, probably you will die. You must be suffering a great deal, Sister." I answered that I was suffering more that day than on other days, but that it was nothing and that, for the salvation of souls, it was not too much. O merciful Jesus, give me the souls of sinners!

843 **(226)** December 24, [1936]. During Holy Mass today, I was united in a particular way with God and His Immaculate Mother. The humility and love of the Immaculate Virgin penetrated my soul. The more I imitate the Mother of God, the more deeply I get to

know God. Oh, what infinite longing envelops my soul! Jesus, how can You still leave me in this exile? I am dying of longing for You. Every touch of my soul by You wounds me immensely. Love and suffering go together; yet I would not exchange this pain caused by You for any treasure, because it is the pain of incomprehensible delights, and these wounds of the soul are inflicted by a loving hand.

844 Sister C.[155] came in the afternoon and took me home for the holydays. I was happy to be reunited with the community. As we were riding through the city [Cracow], I imagined it was the town of Bethlehem. As I watched all those people hurrying about, I thought: who is meditating today, in recollection and silence, on this inconceivable mystery? O pure Virgin, You are traveling today, and so am I. I feel that **(227)** today's journey has its symbolism. O radiant Virgin, pure as crystal, all immersed in God, I offer You my spiritual life; arrange everything that it may be pleasing to Your Son. O my Mother, how ardently I desire that You give me the Infant Jesus during the Midnight Mass. And I felt such a living presence of God in the depths of my soul, that it was only by sheer will-power that I restrained my joy in order not to show outwardly what was going on in my soul.

845 Before the vigil supper, I entered the chapel for a moment to break the wafer spiritually with those dear to my heart. I presented them all, by name, to Jesus and begged for graces on their behalf. But that wasn't all. I commended to the Lord all those who are being persecuted, those who are suffering, those who do not know His Name, and especially poor sinners. O little Jesus, I fervently ask You, enclose them all in the ocean of Your incomprehensible mercy. O sweet little Jesus, here is my heart; let it be a little cozy dwelling place for Yourself. O Infinite Majesty, with what sweetness You drew close to us. **(228)** Here, there is no dread of the

thunderbolts of the great Jehovah; here, there is the sweet little Jesus. Here, no soul is afraid, although Your majesty has not lessened, but only concealed itself. After supper, I felt very tired and was in pain. I had to lie down. But I kept vigil with the Most Holy Mother, awaiting the arrival of the little Child.

846   December 25, [1936]. Midnight Mass. During Mass, God's presence pierced me through and through. A moment before the Elevation I saw the Mother of God and the Infant Jesus and the good Old Man [St. Joseph]. The Most Holy Mother spoke these words to me: *My daughter, Faustina, take this most precious Treasure,* and she gave me the Infant Jesus. When I took Jesus in my arms, my soul felt such unspeakable joy that I am unable to describe it. But, strange thing, after a short while Jesus became awful, horrible-looking, grown up and suffering; and then the vision vanished, and soon it was time to go to Holy Communion. When I received the Lord Jesus in Holy Communion, my soul trembled under the influence of God's presence. The next day, **(229)** I saw the Divine Infant for a brief moment during the Elevation.

847   On the second day of the Feast, Father Andrasz came to celebrate Mass for us, and during Mass I again saw the little Jesus. In the afternoon, I went to confession. Father did not give an answer to some of my questions that concerned this work. He said, "When you recover, we shall talk about it in concrete terms; and now, try to recover completely. As for the rest, you know what guidance to follow and what direction to take in these matters." As penance, Father told me to say the chaplet that Jesus had taught me.

848   While I was saying the chaplet, I heard a voice which said, **Oh, what great graces I will grant to souls who say this chaplet; the very depths of My tender mercy are**

stirred for the sake of those who say the chaplet. Write down these words, My daughter. Speak to the world about My mercy; let all mankind recognize My unfathomable mercy. It is a sign for the end times; after it will come (230) the day of justice. While there is still time, let them have recourse to the fount of My mercy; let them profit from the Blood and Water which gushed forth for them.

O human souls, where are you going to hide on the day of God's anger? Take refuge now in the fount of God's mercy. O what a great multitude of souls I see! They worshiped the Divine Mercy and will be singing the hymn of praise for all eternity.

849 December 27. Today, I returned to my place of solitude [her private room at the sanatorium]. I had a pleasant trip as I travelled with a certain person[156] who was taking her baby to be baptized. We gave her a lift as far as the Church in Podgorze.[157] In order to get out, she put the baby in my arms. When I took it, I offered it, with an ardent prayer, to God so that some day it might give Him special glory. I felt in my soul that the Lord was looking in a special way on that little soul. When we arrived on Pradnik, Sister N.[158] helped me to carry my bundle. When we entered my room, we saw a beautiful paper angel with the inscription, "Gloria in...." I think it is from (231) the sick sister to whom I sent the Christmas tree.[159]

850 And so, the holydays are over. Nothing can still the yearning of my soul. I long for You, O my Creator and eternal God! Neither celebrations nor beautiful hymns soothe my soul; rather, they make me yearn all the more. At the very mention of Your Name, my spirit springs toward You, O Lord.

851 December 28, [1936]. Today I have started a novena to The Divine Mercy. That is, I place myself in spirit before the image and recite the chaplet which the Lord has

taught me. On the second day of the novena, I saw the image, as it were, come alive, adorned with numberless votive lamps, and I saw great crowds of people coming there, and many of them were filled with happiness. O Jesus, with what great joy did my heart beat! I am making the novena for the intention of two people; namely, the Archbishop [Jalbrzykowski] and Father Sopocko. I am earnestly asking the Lord to inspire the Archbishop to approve the chaplet, which is so pleasing to God, and also the image, and that he may not put off or delay this work....

852 **(232)** Today the Lord's gaze shot through me suddenly, like lightning. At once, I came to know the tiniest specks in my soul, and knowing the depths of my misery, I fell to my knees and begged the Lord's pardon, and with great trust I immersed myself in His infinite mercy. Such knowledge does not depress me nor keep me away from the Lord, but rather it arouses in my soul greater love and boundless trust. The repentance of my heart is linked to love. These extraordinary flashes from the Lord educate my soul. O sweet rays of God, enlighten me to the most secret depth, for I want to arrive at the greatest possible purity of heart and soul.

853 In the evening, a great longing took possession of my soul. I took the pamphlet with the Image of the Merciful Jesus on it and pressed it to my heart, and the following words burst forth from my soul: "Jesus, Eternal Love, I live for You, I die for You, and I want to become united with You." Suddenly I saw the Lord in His inexpressible beauty. He looked at me graciously and said, **(233) My daughter, I too came down from heaven out of love for you; I lived for you, I died for you, and I created the heavens for you.** And Jesus pressed me to His Heart and said to me, **Very soon now; be at peace, My daughter.** When I was alone, my soul was set afire with the desire to suffer until the moment when the Lord would say, "Enough." And even if I were to live for thousands of

years, I see in the light of God that that is but one moment. Souls...[unfinished thought].

854 December 29, [1936]. Today after Holy Communion, I heard a voice in my soul: **My daughter, stand ready, for I will come unexpectedly.** Jesus, You do not want to tell me the hour I am looking forward to with such longing? **My daughter, it is for your own good. You will learn it, but not now; keep watch.** O Jesus, do with me as You please. I know You are the merciful Savior and You will not change towards me at the hour of my death. If at this time you are showing me so much special love, and are condescending to unite Yourself with me is such an intimate way and with such great kindness, I expect even **(234)** more at the hour of my death. You, my Lord-God, cannot change. You are always the same. Heaven can change, as well as everything that is created; but You, Lord, are ever the same and will endure forever. So come as You like and when You like. Father of infinite mercy, I, Your child, wait longingly for Your coming. O Jesus, You said in the Holy Gospel, "Out of your mouth do I judge you." Well, Jesus, I am always speaking of Your inconceivable mercy, so I trust that You will judge me according to Your unfathomable mercy.

855 December 30, 1936. The year is coming to an end. I took today as the day of the monthly retreat. My spirit engrossed itself in the benefits that God has lavished on me throughout this whole year. My soul trembled at the sight of this immensity of God's graces. From my soul there burst forth a hymn of thanksgiving to the Lord. For a whole hour, I remained steeped in adoration and thanksgiving, contemplating, one by one, the benefits I had received from God and also my own minor shortcomings. **(235)** All that this year contained has gone into the abyss of eternity. Nothing is lost. I am glad that nothing gets lost.

December 30, [1936]. One-day retreat.

856   During the morning meditation, I felt an aversion and a
      repugnance for all created things. Everything pales
      before my eyes; my spirit is detached from all things. I
      desire only God himself, and yet I must live. This is a
      martyrdom beyond description. God imparts himself to
      the soul in a loving way and draws it into the infinite
      depths of His divinity, but at the same time He leaves it
      here on earth for the sole purpose that it might suffer
      and die of longing for Him. And this strong love is so
      pure that God himself finds pleasure in it; and self-love
      has no access to its deeds, for here everything is totally
      saturated with bitterness, and thus is totally pure. Life is
      a continuous dying, painful and terrible, and at the same
      time it is the depth of true life and of inconceivable
      happiness and the strength of the soul; and because of
      this, [the soul] is capable of great deeds for the sake of
      God.

857   **(236)** + In the evening, I prayed for a few hours, first for
      my parents and relatives, for Mother General and for
      the whole Congregation, for our students, and for three
      priests [probably Archbishop Jalbrzykowski, Father
      Sopocko, and Father Andrasz] to whom I owe very
      much. I ran the length and breadth of the whole world
      and thanked the unfathomable mercy of God for all the
      graces granted to people, and I begged pardon for
      everything by which they have offended Him.

858   During Vespers, I saw the Lord Jesus, who looked
      sweetly and profoundly into my soul. **My daughter,
      have patience; it won't be long now.** That profound look
      and those words filled my soul with strength and power,
      courage and extraordinary trust that I would carry out
      everything He was demanding of me, despite such
      tremendous difficulties, and [filled me with] a special
      conviction that the Lord is with me and that with Him I
      can do all things. All the powers on earth and in hell are

as nothing to me. Everything must fall before the power of His Name. I entrust everything into Your hands, O my Lord and God. Sole Commander of my soul, direct me according to Your eternal desires.

+

859 **(237)** J.M.J.   Cracow, Pradnik, January 1, 1937.

Jesus, I trust in You.

+ Today, at midnight, I bid good-bye to the old year 1936, and welcomed the year 1937. It was with fear and trembling that, in this first hour of the year, I faced this new period of time. Merciful Jesus, with You I go boldly and courageously into conflicts and battles. In Your Name, I will accomplish everything and overcome everything. My God, Infinite Goodness, I beg of You, let Your infinite mercy accompany me always and in all things.

As I enter this year, fear of life overwhelms me, but Jesus brings me out of this fear and lets me know what great glory this work of mercy will bring Him.

860 There are times in life when the soul finds comfort only in profound prayer. Would that souls knew how to persevere in prayer at such times. This is very important.

+

(238)J.M.J.   Jesus, I trust in You.

+ Resolutions for the year 1937, day 1, month 1.

861 Particular examen: remains the same; namely, to unite myself with the Merciful Christ (that is; what would Christ do in such and such a case?) and, in spirit, to embrace the whole world, especially Russia and Spain.

General resolutions.

I.   Strict observance of silence - interior silence.

II.   To see the image of God in every sister; all love of neighbor must flow from this motive.

III.   To do the will of God faithfully at every moment of my life and to live by this.

IV.   To give a faithful account of everything to the spiritual director and not to undertake anything of importance without a clear understanding with him. I shall try to clearly lay bare to him the most secret depths of my soul, bearing in mind**(239)**that I am dealing with God himself, and that His representative is just a human being, and so I must pray daily that he be given light.

V.   During the evening examination of conscience, I am to ask myself the question: What if He were to call me today?

VI.   Not to look for God far away, but within my own being to abide with Him alone.

VII.   In sufferings and torments, to take refuge in the tabernacle and to be silent.

VIII.   To join all sufferings, prayers, works and mortifications to the merits of Jesus in order to obtain mercy for the world.

IX.   To use free moments, however short, for prayers for the dying.

X.   There must not be a day in my life when I do not recommend to the Lord the works of our Congregation. Never have regard for what others think of you [for human respect].

XI.   Have no familiar relationships with anyone. Gentle firmness toward the girls, boundless patience; punish them severely but with such punishments as these: prayer and self-sacrifice. The strength that is in the emptying of myself for their sake is for **(240)** them a [source of] constant remorse and the softening of their obdurate hearts.

XII.   The presence of God is the basis of all my thoughts, words and deeds.

XIII. To take advantage of all spiritual help. To always put self-love in its proper place; namely, the last. To perform my spiritual exercises as though I were doing them for the last time in my life, and in like manner to carry out all my duties.

862 January 2, [1937]. The Name of Jesus. Oh, how great is Your Name, O Lord! It is the strength of my soul. When my strength fails, and darkness invades my soul, Your Name is the sun whose rays give light and also warmth, and under their influence the soul becomes more beautiful and radiant, taking its splendor from Your Name. When I hear the sweetest name of Jesus, my heartbeat grows stronger, and there are times when, hearing the Name of Jesus, I fall into a swoon. My spirit eagerly strains toward Him. **(241)**

863 This is a particularly important day for me. On this day I made my first visit connected with the painting of the Image.[160] On this day the Divine Mercy received special external honor for the first time, although it has been known for a long time, but here it was in the form that the Lord had requested. This day of the sweet Name of Jesus reminds me of many special graces.

864 January 3. The Mother Superior of the Congregation that serves this hospital visited me today, together with one of her sisters.[161] For a long while, we talked about spiritual matters. I recognized in her a great ascetic, and so our conversation was pleasing to God.

Today a girl came to see me. I saw that she was suffering, but not so much in body as in soul. I comforted her as much as I could, but my words of consolation were not enough. She was a poor orphan with a soul plunged in bitterness and pain. She opened her soul to me and told me everything. I understood **(242)** that, in this case, simple words of consolation would not be enough. I fervently interceded with the Lord for that soul and offered Him my joy so that He would give it to her and take all feeling of joy away from me. And the Lord heard my prayer: I was left only with the consolation that she had been consoled.

865 Adoration. First Sunday of the month. During adoration, I felt so strongly urged to act that I burst into tears and said to the Lord, "Jesus, do not urge me, but give this inspiration to those who You know are delaying the work." And I heard these words: **My daughter, be at peace; it will not be long now.**

866 During Vespers, I heard these words: **My daughter, I want to repose in your heart, because many souls have thrown Me out of their hearts today. I have experienced sorrow unto death.** I tried to comfort the Lord, by offering Him my love a thousand times over. I felt, within my soul, a great disgust for sin.

867 **(243)** + My heart is steeped in continual bitterness, because I want to go to You, Lord, into the fullness of life. O Jesus, what a dreadful wilderness this life seems to me! There is on this earth no nourishment for either my heart or my soul. I suffer because of my longing for You, O Lord. You have left me the Sacred Host, O Lord, but it enkindles in my soul an even greater longing for You, O my Creator and Eternal God! Jesus, I yearn to become united with You. Deign to hear the sighs of Your dearly beloved. Oh, how I suffer because I am still unable to be united with You. But let it be done according to Your wishes.

868 January 5, 1937. This evening, I saw a certain priest [probably Father Sopocko] who was in need of prayer for a certain matter. I prayed fervently because the

matter is very close to my heart as well. Thank You, Jesus, for this kindness.

869 O Jesus, have mercy! Embrace the whole world and press me to Your Heart.... O Lord, let my soul repose in the sea of Your unfathomable mercy.

870 **(244)** January 6, 1937. Today during Holy Mass, I was unwittingly absorbed in the infinite majesty of God. The whole immensity of God's love flooded my soul. At that particular moment, I became aware of how much God abases himself for my sake. He, the Lord of Lords—and what am I, miserable being that I am, that You would commune thus with me? The wonder that took hold of me after this special grace continued very vividly throughout the entire day. Taking advantage of the intimacy to which the Lord was admitting me, I interceded before Him for the whole world. At such moments I have the feeling that the whole world is depending on me.

871 + My Master, cause my heart never to expect help from anyone, but I will always strive to bring assistance, consolation and all manner of relief to others. My heart is always open to the sufferings of others; and I will not close my heart to the sufferings of others, even though because of this I have been scornfully nicknamed "dump"; that is, [because] everyone dumps **(245)** his pain into my heart. [To this] I answered that everyone has a place in my heart and I, in return, have a place in the Heart of Jesus. Taunts regarding the law of love will not narrow my heart. My soul is always sensitive on this point, and Jesus alone is the motive for my love of neighbor.

872 January 7. During the Holy Hour, the Lord allowed me to taste His Passion. I shared in the bitterness of the suffering that filled His soul to overflowing. Jesus gave me to understand how a soul should be faithful to prayer despite torments, dryness and temptations;

because oftentimes the realization of God's great plans depends mainly on such prayer. If we do not persevere in such prayer, we frustrate what the Lord wanted to do through us or within us. Let every soul remember these words: "And being in anguish, He prayed longer." I always prolong such prayer as much as is in my power and in conformity with my duty.

873   **(246)** January 8. On Friday morning, as I was going to the chapel to attend Holy Mass, I suddenly saw a huge juniper tree on the pavement and in it a horrible cat who, looking angrily at me, blocked my way to the chapel. One whisper of the name of Jesus dissipated all that. I offered the whole day for dying sinners. During Holy Mass, I felt the closeness of the Lord in a special way. After Holy Communion, I turned my gaze with trust toward the Lord and told him, "Jesus, I so much desire to tell You something." And the Lord looked at me with love and said, **And what is it that you desire to tell Me?**
"Jesus, I beg You, by the inconceivable power of Your mercy, that all the souls who will die today escape the fire of hell, even if they have been the greatest sinners. Today is Friday, the memorial of Your bitter agony on the Cross; because Your mercy is inconceivable, the Angels will not be surprised at this." Jesus pressed me to His Heart and said, **My beloved (247) daughter, you have come to know well the depths of My mercy. I will do what you ask, but unite yourself continually with My agonizing Heart and make reparation to My justice. Know that you have asked Me for a great thing, but I see that this was dictated by your pure love for Me; that is why I am complying with your requests.**

874   Mary, Immaculate Virgin, take me under Your special protection and guard the purity of my soul, heart and body. You are the model and star of my life.

875   Today, I experienced a great suffering during the visit of

our sisters. I learned of something that hurt me terribly, but I controlled myself so that the sisters didn't notice anything. For some time, the pain was tearing my heart apart, but all that is for the sake of poor sinners.... O Jesus, for poor sinners.... Jesus, my strength, stay close to me, help me....

876 **(248)** January 10, 1937. I asked the Lord today to give me strength in the morning so that I could go to receive Holy Communion. My Master, I ask You with all my thirsting heart to give me, if this is according to Your holy will, any suffering and weakness that You like—I want to suffer all day and all night—but please, I fervently beg You, strengthen me for the one moment when I am to receive Holy Communion. You see very well, Jesus, that here they do not bring Holy Communion to the sick; so, if You do not strengthen me for that moment so that I can go down to the chapel, how can I receive You in the Mystery of Love? And You know how much my heart longs for You. O my sweet Spouse, what's the good of all these reasonings? You know how ardently I desire You, and if You so choose You can do this for me.

On the following morning, I felt as if I were perfectly well; the faintings and the weaknesses ceased. But as soon as I returned from the chapel, all the sufferings and weaknesses immediately returned, as if they had been waiting for me. But I had no fear of them **(249)** at all, because I had been nourished by the Bread of the Strong. I boldly look at everything; even death itself I look straight in the eye.

877 + O Jesus concealed in the Host, my sweet Master and faithful Friend, how happy my soul is to have such a Friend who always keeps me company. I do not feel lonely even though I am in isolation. Jesus-Host, we know each other—that is enough for me.

878 January 12, 1937. Today, when the doctor [Adam

Silberg] making his rounds came to see me, he somehow didn't like the way I looked. Naturally, I was suffering more, and so my temperature had gone up considerably. Consequently, he decided I must not go down for Holy Communion until my temperature dropped to normal. I said, "All right," although pain seized my heart; but I said I would go only if I had no fever. So he agreed to that. When the doctor left, I said to the Lord, "Jesus, now it is up to You whether I shall go or not," and I didn't think about it anymore, although the thought kept coming to my mind: I am not **(250)** to have Jesus— no, that's impossible—and not just once but for several days, until my temperature drops. But in the evening, I said to the Lord, "Jesus, if my Communions are pleasing to You, I beg You humbly, grant that I have not one degree of fever tomorrow morning."

In the morning, as I was taking my temperature, I thought to myself, "If there is even one degree, I will not get up because that would be contrary to obedience." But when I looked at the thermometer, there wasn't even one degree of fever. I jumped to my feet at once and went to Holy Communion. When the doctor came and I told him that I had had not even one degree of fever, and so had gone to Holy Communion, he was surprised. I begged him not to make it difficult for me to go to Holy Communion, for it would have an adverse effect on the treatment. The doctor answered, "For peace of conscience and at the same time to avoid difficulties for yourself, Sister, let us make the following agreement: when the weather is fine, and it isn't raining, and you feel all right, then, Sister, please go; but you must weigh these matters in your conscience." It made me very happy that the doctor was being so considerate **(251)** for my sake. You see, Jesus, that I have already done whatever was up to me; now I am counting on You and am quite at peace.

879 I saw Father Andrasz as he was saying Holy Mass today.

Before the Elevation, I saw the Infant Jesus with His hands spread out, and He was very joyous; then, after a moment, I saw nothing more. I was in my room and I continued making my thanksgiving. But later on, I thought to myself, "Why was the Infant Jesus so merry? After all, He is not always so merry when I see Him." Then I heard these words interiorly: **Because I am very much at home in his heart.** And I was not at all surprised at this, because I know he loves Jesus very much.

880 My union with the dying is still as close as ever. Oh, how incomprehensible is God's mercy that the Lord allows me, by my unworthy prayer, to come to the aid of the dying. I try to be at the side of every dying person whenever I can. Have confidence in God, for He is good and inconceivable. His mercy surpasses our understanding.

881 **(252)** January 14, 1937. Today, Jesus entered my room wearing a bright robe and girded with a golden belt, His whole figure resplendent with great majesty. He said, **My daughter, why are you giving in to thoughts of fear?** I answered, "O Lord, You know why." And He said, **Why?** "This work frightens me. You know that I am incapable of carrying it out." And He said, **Why?** "You see very well that I am not in good health, that I have no education, that I have no money, that I am an abyss of misery, that I fear contacts with people. Jesus, I desire only You. You can release me from this." And the Lord said to me, **My daughter, what you have said is true. You are very miserable, and it pleased Me to carry out this work of mercy precisely through you who are nothing but misery itself. Do not fear; I will not leave you alone. Do whatever you can in this matter; I will accomplish everything that is lacking in you. You know what is within your power to do; do that.** The Lord looked into the depth of my being with great kindness; I thought I would die for joy under that gaze. The Lord disappeared, and joy, **(253)** strength and power to act

remained in my soul. But I was surprised that the Lord did not want to release me and that He is not changing anything He has once said. And despite all these joys, there is always a shadow of sorrow. I see that love and sorrow go hand in hand.

882 I rarely have such visions. But I more often commune with the Lord in a more profound manner. My senses sleep and, although not in a visible way, all things become more real and clearer to me than if I saw them with my eyes. My intellect learns more in one moment than during long years of thinking and meditation, both as regards the essence of God and as regards revealed truths, and also as regards the knowledge of my own misery.

883 Nothing disturbs my union with the Lord, neither conversation with others nor any duties; even if I am to go about settling very important matters, this does not disturb me. My spirit is with God, and my interior being is filled with God, so I do not look for Him **(254)** outside myself. He, the Lord, penetrates my soul just as a ray from the sun penetrates clear glass. When I was enclosed in my mother's womb, I was not so closely united with her as I am with my God. There, it was an unawareness; but here, it is the fullness of reality and the consciousness of union. My visions are purely interior, but the more I understand them, the less I am able to express them in words.

884 Oh, how beautiful is the world of the spirit! And so real that, by comparison, the exterior life is just a vain illusion and powerlessness.

885 Jesus, give me the strength and wisdom to get through this terrible wilderness, that my heart may bear patiently this longing for You, O my Lord! I always remain in holy amazement when I sense that You are approaching me, You, the Lord of the awesome throne; that You descend to this miserable exile and visit this poor beggar

who has nothing but misery! I do not know how to entertain You, my Royal Prince, but You know that I love You with every beat of my heart. I see how You lower yourself, but nevertheless Your majesty does not **(255)** diminish in my eyes. I know that You love me with the love of a bridegroom, and that is enough for me. Although we are separated by a great chasm, for You are the Creator and I am Your creature, nevertheless, love alone explains our union. Without it, all is incomprehensible. Only love makes it possible to understand these incomprehensible intimacies with which You visit me. O Jesus, Your greatness terrifies me, and I would be in constant astonishment and fear, if You yourself did not set me at peace. You make me capable of communing with You before each approach.

886 January 15, 1937. Sorrow will not establish itself in a heart which loves the will of God. My heart, longing for God, feels the whole misery of exile. I keep going forward bravely—though my feet become wounded—to my homeland and, on the way, I nourish myself on the will of God. It is my food. Help me, happy inhabitants of the heavenly homeland, so that your sister may not falter on the way. Although the desert is fearful, I walk with lifted head and eyes fixed on the sun; that is to say, on the merciful Heart of Jesus.

887 **(256)** January 19, 1937. My life at present flows on in peaceful awareness of God. My silent soul lives on Him, and this conscious life of God in my soul is for me a source of happiness and strength. I do not look for happiness outside the depths of my soul in which God dwells; of this I am aware. I feel a certain need to share myself with others. I have discovered a fountain of happiness in my soul, and it is God. O my God, I see that everything that surrounds me is filled with God, and most of all my own soul, which is adorned with the grace of God. Already now, I will begin to live on that on which I shall live for all eternity.

888 Silence is so powerful a language that it reaches the throne of the living God. Silence is His language, though secret, yet living and powerful.

889 Jesus, You have given me to know and understand in what a soul's greatness consists: not in great deeds but in great love. Love has its worth, and it confers greatness on all our deeds. Although our actions are small and ordinary in themselves, because of love they become great and powerful before God.

890 **(257)** Love is a mystery that transforms everything it touches into things beautiful and pleasing to God. The love of God makes a soul free. She is like a queen; she knows no slavish compulsion; she sets about everything with great freedom of soul, because the love which dwells in her incites her to action. Everything that surrounds her makes her know that only God himself is worthy of her love. A soul in love with God and immersed in Him approaches her duties with the same dispositions as she does Holy Communion and carries out the simplest tasks with great care, under the loving gaze of God. She is not troubled if, after some time, something turns out to be less successful. She remains calm, because at the time of the action she had done what was in her power. When it happens that the living presence of God, which she enjoys almost constantly, leaves her, she then tries to continue living in lively faith. Her soul understands that there are periods of rest and periods of battle. Through her will, she is always with God. Her soul, like a knight, is well trained in battle; from afar it sees where the foe is hiding and is ready **(258)** for battle. She knows she is not alone—God is her strength.

891 January 21, [1937]. Since early morning today, I have been wondrously united with the Lord. In the evening, the hospital chaplain visited me. After we had talked for a while, I felt my spirit beginning to immerse itself in God, and I began to lose all sense of what was happening

around me. I ardently implored Jesus, "Give me the ability to talk." And the Lord granted that I could talk freely with him. But there was a moment when I could not understand what the priest was saying. I heard his voice, but it was impossible for me to understand him, and I apologized for not understanding him although I could hear his voice. This is a moment of the grace of union with God, but imperfect, because exteriorly the senses are acting imperfectly too. There is no total immersion in God; that is, suspension of the senses, as often happens when one neither sees nor hears anything exteriorly, the whole soul being freely absorbed in God. When such a grace visits me, I want to be alone, and I ask Jesus to **(259)** protect me from the eyes of creatures. I was really very embarrassed before the priest, but I was reassured, because he got to know a little of my soul in confession.

892 Today the Lord gave me to know, in spirit, about the Convent of Divine Mercy. I saw a great spirit in this convent, but everything was poor and very scanty. O my Jesus, you are allowing me to live in spirit with these souls, but perhaps I shall never set foot there; but may Your Name be blessed, and whatever You have intended, may it be done.

893 January 22, [1937]. Today is Friday. My soul is in a sea of suffering. Sinners have taken everything away from me. But that is all right; I have given everything away for their sake that they might know that You are good and infinitely merciful. I shall be faithful to You, come rain or shine.

894 Today the doctor decided that I am not to go to Mass, but only to Holy Communion. I wanted very much to assist at Mass, but my confessor,[162] in agreement with the doctor, told me to obey. "It is God's will, Sister, that you should get **(260)** well, and you must not undertake mortifications of any kind. Be obedient, Sister, and God

will reward you for it." I felt that the confessor's words were Jesus' words, and although it made me sad to miss Holy Mass, during which God had been granting me the grace of seeing the Infant Jesus; nevertheless, I placed obedience above everything else.

I became absorbed in prayer and said my penance. Then I suddenly saw the Lord, who said to me, **My daughter, know that you give Me greater glory by a single act of obedience than by long prayers and mortifications.** Oh, how good it is to live under obedience, to live conscious of the fact that everything I do is pleasing to God!

895   January 23, [1937]. I did not feel like writing today. Then I heard a voice in my soul: **My daughter, you do not live for yourself but for souls; write for their benefit. You know that My will as to your writing has been (261) confirmed many times by your confessors. You know what is pleasing to Me, and if you have any doubts about what I am saying, you also know whom you are to ask. I grant him light to pronounce judgment on my case. My eye watches over him. My daughter, you are to be like a child towards him, full of simplicity and candor. Put his judgment above all My demands. He will guide you according to My will. If he doesn't allow you to carry out My demands, be at peace; I will not judge you, but the matter will remain between Me and him. You are to be obedient.**

896   January 25, 1937. Today my soul is steeped in bitterness. O Jesus, O my Jesus, today everyone can add to my cup of bitterness. It makes no difference whether they be friend or foe, they can all inflict suffering on me. And You, O Jesus, are bound to give me strength and power in these difficult moments. O Blessed Host, support me and seal my lips against all murmuring and complaint. When I am silent, I know I shall be victorious.

897   **(262)** January 27, 1937. I feel considerable improvement in my health. Jesus is bringing me from the gates of

death to life, because there was so little left but for me to die, and lo, the Lord grants me the fullness of life. Although I am still to remain in the sanatorium, I am almost completely well. I see that the will of God has not yet been fulfilled in me, and that is why I must live, for I know that if I fulfill everything the Lord has planned for me in this world, He will not leave me in exile any longer, for heaven is my home. But before we go to our Homeland, we must fulfill the will of God on earth; that is, trials and struggles must run their full course in us.

898   O my Jesus, You are giving me back my health and life; give me also strength for battle, because I am unable to do anything without You. Give me strength, for You can do all things. You see that I am a frail child, and what can I do?

I know the full power of Your mercy, and I trust that You will give me everything Your feeble child needs.

899   (263) I have desired death so much! I do not know whether I shall ever again in my life experience such great longing for God. There have been times when I fell into a swoon for Him. Oh, how ugly the earth when one knows heaven! I must do violence to myself in order to live. O will of God, you are my nourishment.

900   Oh, how drab and full of misunderstandings is this life! My patience is exercised, and after it comes experience. I understand and learn many things each day and see that I know very little, and I am constantly discovering faults in my conduct. Still, I am not discouraged by this, but thank God that He deigns to grant me His light that I may know myself.

901   + There is a certain person [Stanislava Kwietniewska[163]] who tests my patience. I must devote much time to her. When I talk with her, I feel that she is lying, and this, continually. And because she tells me about things far away which I cannot verify, she is able to get away with the lie. But I am inwardly convinced that there is no

(264) truth in what she says. When it occurred to me once that I might be mistaken and that she might be telling the truth, I asked the Lord Jesus to give me the following sign: if she is really lying, let her admit to me herself that she has lied about any one of the things concerning which I am inwardly convinced that she is lying. And if she is telling the truth, let the Lord Jesus take this conviction away from me. A little later, she came to me again and said, "Sister, I beg your forgiveness, but I have lied about such and such a thing," and I understood that the inner light concerning that person had not misled me.

902   January 29, 1937. I overslept today. A little longer, and I would have been too late for Holy Communion because the chapel is a good distance from our section.[164] When I went outdoors, the snow was knee-deep. But before it occurred to me that the doctor would not have allowed me to go out in such snow, I had already come**(265)**to the Lord in the chapel. I received Holy Communion and was back in no time. I heard these words in my soul: **My daughter, rest close to My Heart. Known to Me are your efforts.** My soul is more joyful when I am close to the Heart of my God.

January 30, 1937. One-day retreat.

903   I am coming to know God's greatness more and more and to rejoice in Him. I remain unceasingly with Him in the depths of my heart. It is in my own soul that I most easily find God.

904   During my meditation, I heard these words: **My daughter, you give Me most glory by patiently submitting to My will, and you win for yourself greater merit than that which any fast or mortification could ever gain for you. Know, My daughter, that if you submit your will to Mine, you draw upon yourself My special delight. This sacrifice is pleasing to Me and full of sweetness. I take great pleasure in it; there is power in it.**

905 **(266)** + Examination of conscience: continuation of the same, to unite myself to the Merciful Christ. Practice: interior silence; that is, strict observance of silence.

906 + In difficult moments, I will fix my gaze upon the silent Heart of Jesus, stretched upon the Cross, and from the exploding flames of His merciful Heart, will flow down upon me power and strength to keep fighting.

907 An extraordinary thing, [that] in winter a canary comes to my window and sings beautifully for a while. I have tried to check whether there is a canary in a cage somewhere around, but there is none anywhere, not even in the neighboring ward. One of the other patients also heard it, but only once, and wondered how a canary could be singing in this freezing season of the year.

908 + O Jesus, how sorry I feel for poor sinners. Jesus, grant them contrition and repentance. Remember Your own sorrowful Passion. I know Your infinite mercy and cannot bear it that a soul that has cost You so much should perish. Jesus, give me the souls **(267)** of sinners; let Your mercy rest upon them. Take everything away from me, but give me souls. I want to become a sacrificial host for sinners. Let the shell of my body conceal my offering, for Your Most Sacred Heart is also hidden in a Host, and certainly You are a living sacrifice.

Transform me into Yourself, O Jesus, that I may be a living sacrifice and pleasing to You. I desire to atone at each moment for poor sinners. The sacrifice of my spirit is hidden under the veil of the body; the human eye does not perceive it, and for that reason it is pure and pleasing to You. O my Creator and Father of great mercy, I trust in You, for You are Goodness Itself. Souls, do not be afraid of God, but trust in Him, for He is good, and His mercy is everlasting.

909 + We know each other mutually, O Lord, in the dwelling of my heart. Yes, now it is I who am receiving You as a Guest in the little home of my heart, but the time is

coming when You will call me to Your dwelling place, which You have prepared for me from the beginning of the world. Oh, what am I compared to You, O Lord?

910 **(268)** The Lord is leading me into a world unknown to me. He makes known to me His great grace, but I am afraid of it and will not submit to its influence in so far as it may be in my power, until I am assured by my spiritual director as to what this grace is.

911 On one occasion, God's presence pervaded my whole being, and my mind was mysteriously enlightened in respect to His Essence. He allowed me to understand His interior life. In spirit, I saw the Three Divine Persons, but Their Essence was One. He is One, and One only, but in Three Persons; none of Them is either greater or smaller; there is no difference in either beauty or sanctity, for They are One. They are absolutely One. His Love transported me into this knowledge and united me with Himself. When I was united to One, I was equally united to the Second and to the Third in such a way that when we are united with One, by that very fact, we are equally united to the two Persons in the same way as with the One. Their will is One, one God, though in Three Persons. When One of the Three Persons communicates with a soul, **(269)** by the power of that one will, it finds itself united with the Three Persons and is inundated in the happiness flowing from the Most Holy Trinity, the same happiness that nourishes the saints. This same happiness that streams from the Most Holy Trinity makes all creation happy; from it springs that life which vivifies and bestows all life which takes its beginning from Him. In these moments, my soul experienced such great divine delights that I find this difficult to express.

912 Then I heard the following words spoken thus: **I want you to be My spouse.** Fear pierced my soul, but I calmly continued to reflect on what sort of an espousal this could be. However, each time fear would invade my

soul, a power from on high would give it peace.

After all, I have taken perpetual vows, and I have taken them of my own completely free will. And so I continued to reflect on what this could mean. I sensed, and came to realize, that this was some special kind of grace. Whenever I think about it, I feel faint for God, but in this swooning, my mind is clear and penetrated with light. When I am united **(270)** to Him, I faint from an abundance of happiness, but my mind is bright and clear and free from all shadows. You abase Your majesty to dwell with a poor creature. Thank you, O Lord, for this great grace that makes it possible for me to commune with You. Jesus, Your Name is my delight, I have a presentiment of my Beloved from afar, and my languishing soul rests in His embrace; I don't know how to live without Him. I would rather be with Him in afflictions and suffering than without Him in the greatest heavenly delights.

913 February 2, 1937. Today, from early morning, Divine absorption penetrates my soul. During Mass, I thought I would see the little Jesus, as I often do; however, today during Holy Mass I saw the Crucified Jesus. Jesus was nailed to the cross and was in great agony. His suffering pierced me, soul and body, in a manner which was invisible, but nevertheless most painful.

914 Oh, what awesome mysteries take place during Mass! A great mystery is accomplished in the Holy Mass. **(271)** With what great devotion should we listen to and take part in this death of Jesus. One day we will know what God is doing for us in each Mass, and what sort of gift He is preparing in it for us. Only His divine love could permit that such a gift be provided for us. O Jesus, my Jesus, with what great pain is my soul pierced when I see this fountain of life gushing forth with such sweetness and power for each soul, while at the same time I see souls withering away and drying up through their own fault. O Jesus, grant that the power of mercy embrace these souls.

915 + O Mary, today a terrible sword has pierced Your holy soul. Except for God, no one knows of Your suffering. Your soul does not break; it is brave, because it is with Jesus. Sweet Mother, unite my soul to Jesus, because it is only then that I will be able to endure all trials and tribulations, and only in union with Jesus will my little sacrifices be pleasing to God. Sweetest Mother, continue to teach me about the interior life. May the sword of suffering never break me. O pure Virgin, pour courage into my heart and guard it.

916 **(272)** This day is so special for me; even though I encountered so many sufferings, my soul is overflowing with great joy. In a private room next to mine, there was a Jewish woman who was seriously ill. I went to see her three days ago and was deeply pained at the thought that she would soon die without having her soul cleansed by the grace of Baptism. I had an understanding with her nurse, a [religious] Sister, that when her last moment would be approaching, she would baptize her. There was this difficulty however, that there were always some Jewish people with her. However, I felt inspired to pray before the image which Jesus had instructed me to have painted. I have a leaflet with the Image of the Divine Mercy on the cover. And I said to the Lord, "Jesus, You yourself told me that You would grant many graces through this image. I ask You, then, for the grace of Holy Baptism for this Jewish lady. It makes no difference who will baptize her, as long as she is baptized.

After these words, I felt strangely at peace, and I was quite sure that, despite the difficulties, the waters of Holy Baptism would be poured upon her soul. That night, **(273)** when she was very low, I got out of bed three times to see her, watching for the right moment to give her this grace. The next morning, she seemed to feel a little better. In the afternoon her last moment began to approach. The Sister who was her nurse said that

Baptism would be difficult because they were with her. The moment came when the sick woman began to lose consciousness, and as a result, in order to save her, they began to run about; some [went] to fetch the doctor, while others went off in other directions to find help.

And so the patient was left alone, and Sister baptized her, and before they had all rushed back, her soul was beautiful, adorned with God's grace. Her final agony began immediately, but it did not last long. It was as if she fell asleep. All of a sudden, I saw her soul ascending to heaven in wondrous beauty. Oh, how beautiful is a soul with sanctifying grace! Joy flooded my heart that before this image I had received so great a grace for this soul.

917 Oh, how great is God's mercy; let every soul praise it. O my Jesus, that soul for all eternity will be singing You a hymn of mercy. **(274)** I shall not forget the impression this day has made on my soul. This is the second great grace which I have received here for souls before this image.

Oh, how good the Lord is, and how full of compassion; Jesus, how heartily I thank You for these graces.

918 February 5, 1937. My Jesus, in spite of everything, I desire very much to unite myself to You. Jesus, if this be possible, take me to Yourself, for it seems to me that my heart will burst of longing for You!

Oh, how very much I feel that I am in exile! When will I find myself in the house of our Father, delighting in the happiness that streams from the Most Holy Trinity? But, if it is Your will that I still go on living and suffering, then I desire what You have destined for me. Keep me here on earth for as long as You wish, even though this be until the end of the world. O will of my Lord, be my delight and the rapture of my soul. Although the earth is so filled with people, I feel all alone, and the earth is a terrible desert to me. O Jesus,

Jesus, You know and understand the fervors of my heart; You, O Lord, alone can fill me.

919 **(275)** + Today, when I warned a certain young lady that she should not be standing for hours in the corridor with the men, because it was unbecoming for a well-bred young lady to do so, she apologized and promised to correct herself. She began to cry when she became aware of her thoughtlessness. As I was saying these few things to her concerning moral behavior, all the men from the ward came over and listened to my words of advice. The Jewish people even heard a few things about themselves. A certain person told me afterwards that they put their ears against the wall and listened attentively. I somehow felt they were listening, but I said what I had to say. The walls are so thin here that one can be heard, even when speaking in a low voice.

920 +There is a woman here[165] who was once one of our students. Naturally, she puts my patience to the test. She comes to see me several times a day. After each of these visits I am tired out, but I see that the Lord Jesus has sent that soul to me. Let everything glorify You, O Lord. Patience gives glory to God. O how poor the souls are!

921 **(276)** February 6, [1937]. Today, the Lord said to me, **My daughter, I am told that there is much simplicity in you, so why do you not tell Me about everything that concerns you, even the smallest details? Tell Me about everything, and know that this will give Me great joy.** I answered, "But You know about everything, Lord." And Jesus replied to me, **Yes, I do know; but you should not excuse yourself with the fact that I know, but with childlike simplicity talk to Me about everything, for My ears and heart are inclined towards you, and your words are dear to Me.**

922 + When I began this big novena for three intentions, I saw a tiny insect on the ground and thought: how did it

get here in the middle of winter? Then I heard the following words in my soul: **You see, I am thinking of it and sustaining it, and what is it compared to you? Why was your soul fearful for a moment?** I apologized to the Lord for that moment. Jesus wants me to always be a child and to leave all care to Him, and to submit blindly to His holy will. He took everything upon Himself.

923 **(277)** February 7, [1937]. Today, the Lord said to me, **I demand of you a perfect and whole-burnt offering; an offering of the will. No other sacrifice can compare with this one. I myself am directing your life and arranging things in such a way that you will be for Me a continual sacrifice and will always do My will. And for the accomplishment of this offering, you will unite yourself with Me on the Cross. I know what you can do. I myself will give you many orders directly, but I will delay the possibility of their being carried out and make it depend on others. But what the superiors will not manage to do, I myself will accomplish directly in your soul. And in the most hidden depths of your soul, a perfect holocaust will be carried out, not just for a while, but know, My daughter, that this offering will last until your death. But there is time, so that I the Lord will fulfill all your wishes. I delight in you as in a living host; let nothing terrify you; I am with you.**

924 Today, I received a note from Mother Superior forbidding me to go to the bedside of the dying. And so, I will send to the dying obedience in place of self, and it will support the souls **(278)** who are dying. Such is God's will, and that is enough for me. That which I cannot understand now I will learn later.

925 February 7, 1937. Today, I prayed more fervently than ever for the Holy Father [Pius XI] and three priests[166] that God would inspire them as to what He is asking of me, for the realization of this depends on them. Oh, how happy I am that the Holy Father's health is improving. Today I heard him addressing the Eucharistic

Congress,[167] and I went there in spirit to receive the Apostolic Blessing.

926 February 9, [1937]. Shrove Tuesday. During the last two days of the carnival, I experienced the overwhelming flood of chastisements and sins. In one instant the Lord gave me a knowledge of the sins committed throughout the whole world during these days. I fainted from fright, and even though I know the depth of God's mercy, I was surprised that God allows humanity to exist. And the Lord gave me to know who it is that upholds the existence of mankind: it is the chosen souls. When the number of the chosen ones is complete, the world will cease to exist.

927 On these two days, I received Holy Communion **(279)** as an act of reparation, and I said to the Lord, "Jesus, I offer everything today for sinners. Let the blows of Your justice fall on me, and the sea of Your mercy engulf the poor sinners." And the Lord heard my prayer: many souls returned to the Lord, but I was in agony under the yoke of God's justice. I felt I was the object of the anger of the Most High God. By evening my sufferings had reached such a stage of interior desolation that moans welled up involuntarily from my breast. I locked the door of my room and began an adoration; that is to say, a Holy Hour. Interior desolation and an experience of God's justice—that was my prayer; and the moans and pain that welled up from my soul took the place of a sweet conversation with the Lord.

928 Then suddenly I saw the Lord, who clasped me to His Heart and said to me, **My daughter, do not weep, for I cannot bear your tears. I will grant you everything you ask for, but stop crying.** And I was filled with great **(280)** joy, and my spirit, as usual, was drowned in Him as in its only treasure. Today, encouraged by His kindness, I conversed with Jesus at greater length.

929 When I had rested near His sweetest Heart, I told Him,

"Jesus, I have so much to tell You." And the Lord said to me with great love, **Speak, My daughter.** And I started to enumerate the pains of my heart; that is, how greatly concerned I am for all mankind, that "they all do not know You, and those who do know You do not love You as You deserve to be loved. I also see how terribly sinners offend You; and then again, I see how severely the faithful, especially Your servants, are oppressed and persecuted. And then, too, I see many souls rushing headlong into the terrible abyss of hell. You see, Jesus, this is the pain that gnaws at my heart and bones. And, although You show me special love and inundate my heart with streams of Your joys, nevertheless, this does not appease the sufferings I have just mentioned, but rather they penetrate my poor heart **(281)** all the more acutely. Oh, how ardently I desire that all mankind turn with trust to Your mercy. Then, seeing the glory of Your name, my heart will be comforted."

Jesus listened to these outpourings of my heart with gravity and interest, as if He had known nothing about them, and this seemed to make it easier for me to talk. And the Lord said to me, **My daughter, those words of your heart are pleasing to Me, and by saying the chaplet you are bringing humankind closer to Me.** After these words, I found myself alone, but the presence of God is always in my soul.

930 + O my Jesus, although I will go to You, and You will fill me with Yourself, and that will make my happiness complete, I will nevertheless not forget about humanity. I desire to draw aside the veils of heaven, so that the earth would have no doubts about The Divine Mercy. My repose is in proclaiming Your mercy. The soul gives the greatest glory to its Creator when it turns with trust to The Divine Mercy.

931 **(282)** February 10, [1937]. Today is Ash Wednesday.

During Holy Mass, I felt for a short time the Passion of

Jesus in my members. Lent is a very special time for the work of priests. We should assist them in rescuing souls.

932   A few days ago, I wrote to my director [probably Father Andrasz[168]], asking permission for some little mortifications during Lent. As I did not have the doctor's permission to go to town, I had to do this by letter. But Ash Wednesday is already here, and I still have no answer. This morning after Holy Communion, I asked Jesus to inspire my director with His light so that he would answer me, and I knew in my soul that Father was not against my practicing these mortifications for which I had asked permission, and that he would give his permission. So, in peace, I began to undertake these practices. That same afternoon I received a letter from Father, saying that he readily gives me permission to undertake those practices for which I had asked **(283)** permission. I was very pleased that my interior knowledge was in agreement with my spiritual Father's opinion.

933   Then I heard the following words in my soul: **You will receive a greater reward for your obedience and subjection to your confessor than you will for the practices which you will be carrying out. Know this, My daughter, and act accordingly: anything, no matter how small it be, that has the seal of obedience to My representative is pleasing to Me and great in My eyes.**

934   Small practices for Lent. Although I wish and desire to do so, I cannot practice big mortifications as before, because I am under the strict surveillance of the doctor. But I can practice little things: first—sleep without a pillow; keep myself a little hungry; every day, with my arms outstretched, say the chaplet which the Lord taught me; occasionally, with arms outstretched, for an indefinite period of time **(284)** pray informally. Intention: to beg divine mercy for poor sinners, and for priests, the power to bring sinful hearts to repentance.

935 My contact with the dying is, just as it has been in the past, very close. I often accompany a person who is dying far away, but my greatest joy is when I see the promise of mercy fulfilled in these souls. The Lord is faithful; what He once ordains—He fulfills.

936 + A certain person in our ward was beginning to die. Amidst terrible tortures, she was dying for three days, sometimes regaining consciousness. Everyone in the ward was praying for her. I longed to go to her, but Mother Superior had forbidden me to go to visit the dying, so I prayed for that poor soul in my room. But when I heard that she was still in agony, and there was no saying how long it was going to take, I suddenly felt inspired in my soul and said to the Lord, "Jesus, if all I do is pleasing to You, **(285)** I ask You, as evidence, to let that soul stop suffering and pass on immediately to her happy eternity." A few minutes later I learned that the person had passed away so peacefully and quickly that they did not even have time to light the candle.

937 + I will say a word more about my spiritual director [Father Andrasz or Father Sopocko[169]]. It is strange that there are so few priests who know how to pour power, strength and courage into a soul so that it can make constant progress without getting tired. Under such direction a soul, even of lesser strength, can do much for the glory of God. And here I discovered a secret; namely, that the confessor, or rather the spiritual director, does not make light of the trifles that the soul brings to him. And when the soul notices that it is being controlled in this, it begins to exert itself and does not omit the slightest opportunity to practice virtue and also avoids the smallest faults. And from these efforts, as with little stones, there rises within the soul a most beautiful temple. **(286)** On the contrary, if the soul notices that the confessor neglects these little things, it likewise neglects them and ceases to give an account of them to the confessor and, worse still, will begin to grow

negligent in little things. Thus, instead of going forward, it gradually retreats backward and becomes aware of the situation only when it has already fallen into some serious trouble. Here, a serious question poses itself: who is at fault, the soul in question or the confessor; that is to say, the director? It seems to me that all the blame should be put on the imprudent director; the soul's only fault is to have taken upon itself the choice of a director. The director could well have led the soul along the road of God's will to sanctity.

938 The soul should have prayed ardently and at greater length for a director and should have asked the Lord himself to choose a spiritual director for it. What begins in God will be godly, and what begins in a purely human manner will remain human. God is so merciful that, in order to **(287)** help a soul He himself chooses the spiritual guide and will enlighten the soul concerning the one before whom it should uncover the most hidden depths of its soul just as it sees itself before the Lord Jesus himself. And when the soul considers and recognizes that God has been arranging all this, it should pray fervently for the confessor that he might have the divine light to know it well. And let it not change such a director except for a serious reason. Just as it had prayed fervently and at great length in order to learn God's will before choosing a director, so too should it pray fervently and at great length to discern whether it is truly God's will that he leave this director and choose another. If God's will is not absolutely clear, he should not make this change, for a person will not go far by himself, and Satan wants just this: to have the person who is aspiring for sanctity direct himself because then, without doubt, he will never attain it.

939 There is an exception [to this], and that is when God himself directs the person, but the director **(288)** will immediately recognize that the person in question is being guided by God himself. God will allow him to

know this clearly and distinctly, and such a person should be even more under the director's control than anyone else. In this case, the director does not so much guide and point out the road along which the soul is to journey; but rather, he judges and confirms that the soul is following the right path and is being led by a good spirit.

In this situation, the director should be not only holy, but also experienced and prudent, and the soul should give priority to his opinion over that of God himself, for then the soul will be safe from illusions and deviations. A soul that will not fully submit its inspirations to the strict control of the Church; that is, to the director, clearly shows by this that a bad spirit is guiding it. The director should be extremely prudent in such cases and test the soul's obedience. Satan can even clothe himself in a cloak of humility, but he does not know how to wear the cloak of obedience **(289)** and thus his evil designs will be disclosed. But the director should not be overly afraid of such a soul, because if God puts that special soul in his care, He will also give him great divine light regarding it, for otherwise how could he deal wisely with the great mysteries which take place between the soul and God.

940 I myself suffered a great deal and was much tried in this respect. Therefore, I am writing only about what I myself have experienced. It was only after many novenas, prayers and penances that God sent me a priest who understood my soul. Oh, there would be many more saintly souls if there were more experienced and saintly confessors. Many a soul, earnestly striving for sanctity, cannot manage by itself during times of trial and abandons the road to perfection.

941 O Jesus, give us fervent and holy priests! Oh, how great is the dignity of the priest, but at the same time, how great is his responsibility! Much has been given you, O priest, but much will also be demanded of you....

942 **(290)** February 11, [1937]. Today is Friday. During Mass, I suffered pain in my body: in my hands, my feet and my side. Jesus is sending me this kind of suffering that I may make reparation for sinners. The pain is brief, but very severe. I do not suffer for more than a couple of minutes, but the impression remains for a long time and is very vivid.

943 + Today, I feel such desolation in my soul that I do not know how to explain it even to myself. I would like to hide from people and cry endlessly. No one understands a heart wounded by love, and when such a heart feels itself abandoned interiorly, no one can comfort it. O souls of sinners, you have taken the Lord away from me, but all right, all right; you get to know how sweet the Lord is, and let the whole sea of bitterness flood my heart. I have given all my divine comforts to you.

944 + There are moments when I mistrust myself, when I feel my own weakness and wretchedness in the most profound depths of my own being, and I have noticed that I can endure such moments only by trusting in the infinite mercy **(291)** of God. Patience, prayer and silence—these are what give strength to the soul. There are moments when one should be silent, and when it would be inappropriate to talk with creatures; these are the moments when one is dissatisfied with oneself, and when the soul feels as weak as a little child. Then the soul clings to God with all its might. At such times, I live solely by faith, and when I feel strengthened by God's grace, then I am more courageous in speaking and communicating with my neighbors.

945 In the evening, the Lord said to me, **My child, rest on My Heart; I see that you have worked hard in My vineyard.** And my soul was flooded with divine joy.

946 February 12, [1937]. Today, the presence of God is piercing me through and through, like a ray from the sun. My soul is longing for God so intensely that I fall

into a swoon every now and then. I feel Eternal Love touching my heart, and my littleness cannot bear it, **(292)** and this causes me to swoon. Still, my interior strength is great, and my soul wants to match the Love with which it is loved. The soul at such moments has a very deep knowledge of God, and the more it comes to know Him, the purer and more fervent does its love for Him become. How unfathomable are the mysteries of the soul and God!

947 Sometimes there are whole hours when my soul is lost in wonder at seeing the infinite majesty of God abasing Itself to the level of my soul. Unending is my interior astonishment that the Most High Lord is pleased in me and tells me so Himself. And I immerse myself even deeper in my nothingness, because I know what I am of myself. Still I must say that I, in return, love my Creator to folly with every beat of my heart and with every nerve; my soul unconsciously drowns, drowns... in Him. I feel that nothing will separate me from the Lord, neither heaven nor earth, neither the present nor the future. Everything may change, but love never, never; it is always the same. **(293)** He, the Immortal Mighty One, makes His will known to me that I may love Him very specially, and He himself makes my soul capable of the kind of love with which He wants me to love Him. I bury myself more and more in Him, and I fear nothing.

Love has overtaken my whole heart, and even if I were to be told of God's justice and of how even the pure spirits tremble and cover their faces before Him, saying endlessly, "Holy," which would seem to suggest that my familiarity with God would be to the detriment of His honor and majesty, [I would reply,] "O no, no, and once again, no!" In pure love, there is room for everything: the highest praise and the deepest adoration, yet the soul is immersed in Him in deepest peace through love; and the words of people, speaking from the exterior, have no effect upon that soul. What they tell the soul about God is but a pale shadow in comparison to its own experience of Him; and it is often surprised how other people can be struck with admiration at what someone else says about God when, for this soul, it is nothing special, as it knows that what can be put into words **(294)** is not yet that great. So this soul listens to everything with respect, but has its own special life in God.

948 February 13, [1937]. Today, during the Passion Service,[170] I saw Jesus being tortured and crowned with thorns and holding a reed in His hand. Jesus was silent as the soldiers were bustling about, vying with each other in torturing Him. Jesus said nothing, but just looked at me, and in that gaze I felt His pain, so terrible that we have not the faintest idea of how much He suffered for us before He was crucified. My soul was filled with pain and longing; in my soul, I felt great hatred for sin, and even the smallest infidelity on my part seemed to me like a huge mountain for which I must expiate by mortification and penance. When I see Jesus tormented, my heart is torn to pieces, and I think: what will become of sinners if they do not take advantage of the Passion of Jesus? In His Passion, I see a whole sea of mercy.

+

(295) J.M.J.   February 12, 1937

+ The Love of God is the flower—Mercy the fruit.

949 Let the doubting soul read these considerations on Divine Mercy and become trusting.[171]

Divine Mercy, gushing forth from the bosom of the Father, I trust in You.

Divine Mercy, greatest attribute of God, I trust in You.

Divine Mercy, incomprehensible mystery, I trust in You.

Divine Mercy, fount gushing forth from the mystery of the Most Blessed Trinity, I trust in You.

Divine Mercy, unfathomed by any intellect, human or angelic, I trust in You.

Divine Mercy, from which wells forth all life and happiness, I trust in You.

Divine Mercy, better than the heavens, I trust in You.

Divine Mercy, source of miracles and wonders, I trust in You.

Divine Mercy, encompassing the whole universe, I trust in You.

Divine Mercy, descending to earth in the Person of the Incarnate Word, I trust in You.

(296) Divine Mercy, which flowed out from the open wound of the Heart of Jesus, I trust in You.

Divine Mercy, enclosed in the Heart of Jesus for us, and especially for sinners, I trust in You.

Divine Mercy, unfathomed in the institution of the Sacred Host, I trust in You.

Divine Mercy, in the founding of Holy Church, I trust in You.

Divine Mercy, in the Sacrament of Holy Baptism, I trust in You.

Divine Mercy, in our justification through Jesus Christ, I trust in You.

Divine Mercy, accompanying us through our whole life, I trust in You.

Divine Mercy, embracing us especially at the hour of death, I trust in You.

Divine Mercy, endowing us with immortal life, I trust in You.

Divine Mercy, accompanying us every moment of our life, I trust in You.

Divine Mercy, shielding us from the fire of hell, I trust in You.

Divine Mercy, in the conversion of hardened sinners, I trust in You.

Divine Mercy, astonishment for Angels, incomprehensible to Saints, I trust in You.

Divine Mercy, unfathomed in all the mysteries of God, I trust in You.

Divine Mercy, lifting us out of every misery, I trust in You.

Divine Mercy, source of our happiness and joy, I trust in You.

Divine Mercy, in calling us forth from nothingness to existence, I trust in You.

Divine Mercy, embracing all the works of His hands, I trust in You.

Divine Mercy, crown of all of God's handiwork, I trust in You.

(297) Divine Mercy, in which we are all immersed, I trust in You.

Divine Mercy, sweet relief for anguished hearts, I trust in You.

Divine Mercy, only hope of despairing souls, I trust in You.

Divine Mercy, repose of hearts, peace amidst fear, I trust in You.

Divine Mercy, delight and ecstasy of holy souls, I trust in You.

Divine Mercy, inspiring hope against all hope, I trust in You.

950   + Eternal God, in whom mercy is endless and the treasury of compassion inexhaustible, look kindly upon us and increase Your mercy in us, that in difficult moments we might not despair nor become despondent, but with great confidence submit ourselves to Your holy will, which is Love and Mercy itself.

951   + O incomprehensible and limitless Mercy Divine,
To extol and adore You worthily, who can?
Supreme attribute of Almighty God,
You are the sweet hope for sinful man.

Into one hymn yourselves unite, stars, earth and sea, and in one accord, thankfully and fervently sing of the incomprehensible Divine Mercy.

952 **(298)** My Jesus, You see that Your holy will is everything to me. It makes no difference to me what You do with me. You command me to set to work—and I begin calmly, although I know that I am incapable of it; through Your representatives, You order me to wait— so I wait patiently; You fill my soul with enthusiasm— but You do not make it possible for me to act; You attract me to yourself in heaven—and You leave me in this world; You pour into my soul a great yearning for yourself—and You hide yourself from me. I am dying of the desire to be united with You forever, and You do not let death come near me. O will of God, you are the nourishment and delight of my soul. When I submit to the holy will of my God, a deep peace floods my soul.

O my Jesus, You do not give a reward for the successful performance of a work, but for the good will and the labor undertaken. Therefore, I am completely at peace, even if all my undertakings and efforts should be thwarted or should come to naught. If I do **(299)** all that is in my power, the rest is not my business. And therefore the greatest storms do not disturb the depths of my peace; the will of God dwells in my conscience.

953 + February 15, 1937. Today my suffering increased somewhat: I not only feel greater pain all through my lungs, but also some strange pains in my intestines. I am suffering as much as my weak nature can bear, all for immortal souls, to plead the mercy of God for poor sinners and to beg for strength for priests. Oh, how much reverence I have for priests; and I am asking Jesus, the High Priest, to grant them many graces.

954 Today after Holy Communion, the Lord told me, **My daughter, My delight is to unite myself with you. It is when you submit yourself to My will that you give Me the greatest glory and draw down upon yourself a sea of blessings. I would not take such special delight in you if you were not living by my will.** O my sweet Guest, I am prepared for all sacrifices for Your sake, but You know

(300) that I am weakness itself. Nevertheless, with You I can do all things. O my Jesus, I beseech You, be with me at each instant.

955   February 15, 1937. Today, I heard these words in my soul: **Host pleasing to My Father, know, My daughter, that the entire Holy Trinity finds Its special delight in you, because you live exclusively by the will of God. No sacrifice can compare with this.**

956   + After these words, the knowledge of God's will came to me; that is to say, I now see everything from a higher point of view and accept all events and things, pleasant and unpleasant, with love, as tokens of the heavenly Father's special affection.

957   The pure offering of my will will burn on the altar of love. That my sacrifice may be perfect, I unite myself closely with the sacrifice of Jesus on the cross. When great sufferings will cause my nature to tremble, and my physical and spiritual strength will diminish, then will I hide myself deep in the open wound of the Heart **(301)** of Jesus, silent as a dove, without complaint. Let all my desires, even the holiest, noblest and most beautiful, take always the last place and Your holy will, the very first. The least of Your desires, O Lord, is more precious to me than heaven, with all its treasures. I know very well that people will not understand me; that is why my sacrifice will be purer in Your eyes.

958   Some days ago, a certain person came to me and asked me to pray for her intention, as she had some urgent and important business. All of a sudden, I felt in my soul that this matter was not pleasing to God, and I replied that I would not pray for this intention, "but I will pray for you, in general"[I added]. A few days later, this lady came back to me and thanked me for not having prayed for her intention, but rather for her, because she had been motivated by a spirit of revenge toward a certain person to whom she owed respect and veneration in

virtue **(302)** of the fourth commandment. The Lord Jesus had changed her interior [dispositions], and she herself acknowledged her guilt; but was, however, surprised that I had penetrated her secret.

959 + Today I received a letter from Father Sopocko, who sent me greetings for my feast day [February 15]. His greetings gave me joy, but his poor health made me sad. I had known about this by interior intuition, but had not quite believed it. But it seems to me that if he himself wrote that this was so, then the other things about which he did not write are also true, and my interior knowledge has not deceived me. He requested me to underline all that I know does not come from me; that is to say, all that Jesus tells me which I hear in my soul.[172] He has already asked me to do this several times, but I did not have the time and, to tell the truth, I was in no hurry to do so. But how does he know that I have not done this? I was very surprised; but now I am setting about this work with all my heart. O my Jesus, Your representative's will is clearly Your holy will, without a shadow of a doubt.

960 **(303)** February 16, 1937. Today I entered a neighboring room by mistake and so, for a while, I talked with the person who was there. When I returned to my own room, I thought about that person for a few moments. Then suddenly, Jesus stood by my side and said, **My daughter, what are you thinking about right now?** Without thinking, I snuggled close to His heart, because I realized that I had been thinking too much about creatures.

961 + This morning after completing my spiritual exercises, I began at once to crochet. I sensed a stillness in my heart; I sensed that Jesus was resting in it. That deep and sweet consciousness of God's presence prompted me to say to the Lord, "O Most Holy Trinity dwelling in my heart, I beg You: grant the grace of conversion to as many souls as the [number of] stitches that I will make today with

this crochet hook." Then I heard these words in my soul: **My daughter, too great are your demands.** "Jesus, You know that for You it is easier to grant much rather than a little." **That is so, it is less difficult for Me to grant a soul much rather than a little, but every conversion of a sinful soul demands sacrifice.** "Well, Jesus, I offer You **(304)** this whole-hearted work of mine; this offering does not seem to me to be too small for such a large number of souls; You know, Jesus, that for thirty years You were saving souls by just this kind of work. And since holy obedience forbids me to perform great penances and mortifications, therefore I ask You, Lord: accept these mere nothings stamped with the seal of obedience as great things." Then I heard a voice in my soul: **My dear daughter, I comply with your request.**

962 + I often see a certain person dear to God. The Lord has great love for him, not only because he is striving to spread the veneration of God's mercy, but also because of the love he has for the Lord God, although he does not always feel this love in his own heart and is almost always in Gethsemane. However, this person is always pleasing to God, and his great patience will overcome all difficulties.

963 + Oh, if only the suffering soul knew how it is loved by God, it would die of joy and excess of happiness! Some day, we will know the value of suffering, but then we will no longer be able to suffer. The present moment is ours.

964 **(305)** February 17, 1937. This morning during Holy Mass, I saw the Suffering Jesus, His Passion was imprinted on my body in an invisible manner, but no less painfully.

965 Jesus looked at me and said, **Souls perish in spite of My bitter Passion. I am giving them the last hope of salvation; that is, the Feast of My Mercy.**[255] **If they will not adore My mercy, they will perish for all eternity. Secretary of My mercy, write, tell souls about this great**

mercy of Mine, because the awful day, the day of My justice, is near.

966 + Today, I heard in my soul these words: **My daughter, it is time for you to take action; I am with you. Great persecutions and sufferings are in store for you, but be comforted by the thought that many souls will be saved and sanctified by this work.**

967 + When I set to work at underlining the Lord's words and thus was going through everything in sequence, I reached the page where I had marked down Father Andrasz's advice and directions. I did not know what to do, to underline or not to underline, and then I heard these words in my soul: **Underline, because these words are Mine; I have borrowed the lips (306) of the friend of My Heart in order to speak to you and reassure you. You are to observe these directions until your death. It would not please Me at all if you were to disobey these directions. Know that it is I who have placed him between Myself and your soul. I am doing this to set you at peace and so that you may not err.**

968 **Since I have placed you in this priest's special care, you are thus exempted from giving a detailed account to your superiors concerning My relationship with you. In all other matters, be as a child with your superiors, but whatever I do in the depths of your soul is to be told, with all frankness, only to the priests.**

And I have noticed that, from the time God gave me a spiritual director, He has not required me to report everything to the superiors, as was the case before, but only that which concerns external matters; apart from this, only the director knows my soul. To have a spiritual director is a special grace of God. Oh, how few have received it! The soul remains in constant peace amidst the greatest difficulties. Every day after Holy Communion, I thank the Lord Jesus for this grace, and every **(307)** day I ask the Holy Spirit to enlighten him. I have truly experienced in my soul what power the director's words have. Blessed be God's mercy for this grace!

969 +Today, I went to meditate before the Blessed Sacrament [in the sanatorium chapel]. When I approached the altar, God's presence pervaded my soul, I was plunged into the ocean of His divinity, and Jesus said to me, **My daughter, all that exists is yours.** I answered the Lord, "My heart wants nothing but You alone, O Treasure of my heart. For all the gifts You give me, thank you, O Lord, but I desire only Your Heart. Though the heavens are immense, they are nothing to me without You. You know very well, O Jesus, that I am constantly swooning because of my longing for You." **Know this, My daughter, that you are already tasting now what other souls will obtain only in eternity.**

970 And all of a sudden, my soul was flooded with the light of the knowledge of God. Oh, would that I could express even a little of what my soul experiences when resting near the Heart of the incomprehensible **(308)** Majesty! I cannot put it into words. Only a soul who has experienced such a grace at least once in his life, will recognize it. When I returned to my room, it seemed to me that I was coming from real life to death. When the doctor came to take my pulse, he was surprised: "Sister, what happened? You have never had a pulse like this! I would like to know what has speeded it up so much." What could I tell him, when I myself did not know that my pulse was so rapid. I only know that I am dying of yearning for God, but this I did not tell him, for how can medicine help in this instance?

971 February 19, 1937. Contact with the dying. They ask me for prayer, and I can pray, as the Lord grants me an extraordinary spirit of prayer. I am constantly united with Him, and I am fully aware that I live for souls in order to bring them to Your mercy, O Lord. In this

matter, no sacrifice is too insignificant.

972 **(309)** Today, the doctor decided that I am to stay here until April. It is God's will, even though I did want to be back in the company of my sisters.

973 I learned today about the death of one of our sisters[173] who died in Plock, but she visited me even before they told me about her death.

974 February 22, 1937. Today, there began in our chapel a retreat for the hospital attendants, although anyone who wishes may take part in it. There is one conference a day. Father Bonaventure[174] speaks for a whole hour, and he speaks directly to souls. I took part in this retreat, as I very much desire to know God more deeply and to love Him more ardently, for I have understood that the greater the knowledge, the stronger the love.

975 Today I heard these words: **Pray for souls that they be not afraid to approach the tribunal of My mercy. Do not grow weary of praying for sinners. You know what a burden their souls are to My Heart. Relieve My deathly sorrow; dispense My mercy.**

976 **(310)** February 24, 1937. Today during Holy Mass, I saw the dying Jesus. The sufferings of the Lord pierced my soul and body in an invisible manner. The pain is enormous, though it lasts a very short time.

977 During the singing of the Lenten Lamentations, I am so taken up with His Passion that I cannot withhold my tears. I would like to hide somewhere in order to give myself freely to the sorrow which flows from the consideration of His Passion.

978 When I was praying for the intention of Father Andrasz, I learned how very pleasing he is to God. Since then, I have had even greater respect for him, as for a saint. This has given me great joy, and I thank God fervently for it.

979 Today at Benediction, I saw Jesus, and He spoke these

words to me: **Be obedient to your director in everything; his word is My will. Be certain in the depths of your soul that it is I who am speaking through his lips, and I desire that you reveal the state of your soul to him with the same simplicity (311) and candor as you have with Me. I say it again, My daughter: know that his word is My will for you.**

980 Today, I saw the Lord in great beauty, and He said to me, **My loving host, pray for priests, especially during this time of harvest. My Heart is pleased with you, and for your sake I am blessing the earth.**

981 I understood that these two years of interior suffering which I have undergone in submission to God's will in order to know it better have advanced me further in perfection than the previous ten years. For two years now, I have been on the cross between heaven and earth. That is to say, I am bound by the vow of obedience and must obey the superior as God himself. And on the other hand, God makes His will known to me directly, and so my inner torture is so great that no one **(312)** will either understand or imagine these spiritual sufferings. It seems to me that it would be easier to give up my life than to go again and again through one hour of such pain. I am not even going to write much about this matter, because one cannot describe what it is like to know God's will directly and at the same time to be perfectly obedient to the divine will as expressed indirectly through the superiors. Thanks be to God that He has given me a director; otherwise, I would not have advanced one single step.

982 + I recently received a lovely letter from my dear seventeen-year-old sister [Wanda[175]]. She is begging and entreating me to help her enter the convent. She is ready for any sacrifices for God. I can tell from her letter that the Lord himself is guiding her, and I rejoice in God's great mercy.

983 + Today, the Majesty of God enveloped and transpierced my soul to its very depths. The greatness of God is pervading my being and flooding me so that I am completely drowning in His greatness. I am dissolving and disappearing entirely in Him as in my life-source, as in perfect life.

984 **(313)** My Jesus, I understand well that my perfection consists not in the fact that You command me to carry out these great works of Yours—Oh no!—the soul's greatness does not consist in this, but in great love for You. O Jesus, in the depths of my soul I understand that the greatest achievements cannot compare with one act of pure love for You. I desire to be faithful to You and to do Your bidding. I am making use of my strength and my reason to carry out all You are asking of me, O Lord, but I have not the least shadow of attachment to all this. I do it all because such is Your will. All my love is drowned, not in Your works, but in You yourself, O my Creator and Lord!

985 February 25, 1937. I prayed earnestly for a happy death on behalf of a certain soul who was suffering much. For two weeks, she had remained between life and death. I was touched with pity for her and said to the Lord, "Sweet Jesus, if the works I am undertaking for Your glory are pleasing to You, then please take her to Yourself **(314)** and let her rest in Your mercy." I was strangely reassured; and, after a short while, they came to tell me that the person who had been suffering so much had just died.

986 I saw a certain priest [probably Father Sopocko] in need and prayed for him until Jesus looked upon him with kindness and granted him His strength.

987 Today, I came to know that a member of my family is offending God and is in great peril of death. This knowledge pierced my soul with such great pain that I thought I would not survive that offense against God. I

begged God's pardon, but I saw His great anger.

988 I was praying for a certain priest [probably Father Sopocko], asking God to help him in certain matters when I suddenly saw Jesus Crucified. His eyes were closed, and He was immersed in torture. I worshiped His five wounds, each one separately, and asked His blessing for him. Jesus gave me to know interiorly how dear that soul was to Him, **(315)** and I felt that grace was flowing from Jesus' wounds upon that soul who, like Jesus, is also stretched upon the cross.

989 My Lord and my God, You know that it is You alone whom my soul has come to love. My soul is entirely drowned in You, O Lord. Even if I did not accomplish any of the things that You have made known to me, O Lord, I would be completely at peace because I would have done what I could.

990 I know well, O Lord, that You have no need of our works; You demand love. Love, love and once again, love of God—there is nothing greater in heaven or on earth. The greatest greatness is to love God; true greatness is in loving God; real wisdom is to love God. All that is great and beautiful is in God; there is no beauty or greatness outside of Him. O you sages of the world and you great minds, recognize that true greatness is in loving God! Oh, how astonished I am that some people deceive themselves, saying: There is no eternity!

991 **(316)** February 26, 1937. Today, I saw how the Holy Mysteries were being celebrated without liturgical vestments and in private homes, because of a passing storm; and I saw the sun come out from the Blessed Sacrament, and all other lights went out, or rather, they were dimmed; and all the people were looking toward this [one] light. But at the present time I do not understand the meaning of this vision.[176]

992 + I am going forward through life amidst rainbows and storms, but with my head held high with pride, for I am

a royal child. I feel that the blood of Jesus is circulating in my veins, and I have put my trust in the great mercy of the Lord.

993 + I asked the Lord to have a certain person come to visit me today so that I could see her one more time, and that would be a sign for me that she was being called to the convent which Jesus is having me establish. And, O wonder, the person in question came, and I tried to form her a bit, spiritually. I began to show her the way of self-denial and sacrifice, which she readily accepted. However, I have placed this whole matter in the hands of the Lord, that He may direct everything according to His good pleasure.

994 **(317)** Today, when I heard the hymn, "Good night, Holy Head of My Jesus," on the radio, my spirit was suddenly drowned in God, and divine love flooded my soul; I dwelt for a moment with the heavenly Father.

995 + Although it is not easy to live in constant agony,
To be nailed to the cross of various pains,
Still, I am inflamed with love by loving,
And like a Seraph I love God, though I am but weakness.

Oh, great is the soul that, midst suffering,
Stands faithfully by God and does His will
And remains uncomforted midst great rainbows and storms,
For God's pure love sweetens her fate.

It is no great thing to love God in prosperity
And thank Him when all goes well,
But rather to adore Him midst great adversities
And love Him for His own sake and place one's hope in Him.

When the soul is in the shadows of Gethsemane,
All alone in the bitterness of pain,
(318) It ascends toward the heights of Jesus,
And though ever drinking bitterness—it is not sad.

When the soul does the will of the Most High God,
Even amidst constant pain and torments,
Having pressed its lips to the chalice proferred,
It becomes mighty, and nothing will daunt it.

> Though tortured, it repeats: Your will be done,
> Patiently awaiting the moment of its transfiguration,
> For, though in deepest darkness, it hears the voice of
>   Jesus: You are Mine,
> And this it will know fully when the veil falls.

996 February 28, 1937. Today, I was undergoing the Passion of Jesus for a longer time, and thus I saw that many souls were in need of prayer. I feel that I am being completely transformed into prayer in order to beg God's mercy for every soul. O my Jesus, I am receiving You into my heart as a pledge of mercy for souls.

997 This evening, when I heard the hymn, "Good night, Holy Head of my Jesus," on the radio, my spirit was suddenly swept away to God's mysterious bosom, and I knew **(319)** in what the greatness of a soul consists and what matters to God: love, love, and once again, love. And I understood how all that exists is saturated with God, and such a love of God inundated my soul that I am at a loss to describe it. Happy the soul that knows how to love unreservedly, for in this lies its greatness.

998 Today, I took part in a one-day retreat. When I was at the last conference,[177] the priest was speaking of how much the world needs God's mercy, and that this seems to be a special time when people have great need of prayer and God's mercy. Then I heard a voice in my soul: **These words are for you. Do all you possibly can for this work of My mercy. I desire that My mercy be worshiped, and I am giving mankind the last hope of salvation; that is, recourse to My mercy. My Heart rejoices in this feast.** After these words, I understood that nothing can dispense me from the obligation which the Lord demands from me.

999 Last night I was in such pain that I thought it was the end. The doctors could not diagnose what the sickness was. **(320)** I felt as if my entrails had been torn to shreds, but after a few hours of such sufferings I am all right. All this is for sinners. Let Your mercy descend upon them, O Lord.

1000 In the terrible desert of life,
O my sweetest Jesus,
Protect souls from disaster,
For You are the Fountain of Mercy.

Let the resplendence of Your rays,
O sweet Commander of our souls,
Let mercy change the world.
And you who have received this grace, serve Jesus.

Steep is the great highway I must travel,
But I fear nothing,
For the pure fount of mercy is flowing for my sake,
And, with it, strength for the humble soul.

I am exhausted and worn out,
But my conscience bears me witness
That I do all for the greater glory of the Lord,
The Lord who is my repose and my heritage.

[End of Notebook Two of the Diary.]

Sister Faustina of the Blessed Sacrament

Congregation

of the Sisters of Our Lady of Mercy

I shall Sing the Lord's Mercy

Notebook III

(1)+
J.M.J.

1001   Thank You, O Lord, my Master,
That You have transformed me entirely into Yourself,
And accompany me through life's toils and labors;
I fear nothing when I have You in my heart.

+

J.M.J.

1002 The Lord's Supper is laid,
Jesus sits down at table with His Apostles,
His Being all transformed into love,
For such was the Holy Trinity's counsel.

With great desire, I desire to eat with you,
Before I suffer death.
About to leave you, love holds Me in your midst.
He sheds His Blood, gives His life, for He loves
immensely.

Love hides beneath the appearance of bread,
Departing, He remains with us.
Such self-abasement was not needed,
Yet burning love hid Him under these species.

Over the bread and wine He says these words:
"This is My Blood, this is My Body."
Although mysterious, these are words of love.
Then He passes the Cup among His disciples.

Jesus grew deeply troubled within
And said, "One of you will betray his Master."
They fell silent, with a silence as of the tomb,
And John inclined his head on His breast.

The supper is ended.
Let us go to Gethsemane.
Love is satisfied,
And there the traitor is waiting.

(2) +
J.M.J.

1003 O Divine Will, You are my nourishment, You are my
delight. Hasten, O Lord, the Feast of Mercy that souls
may recognize the fountain of Your goodness.

God and souls.

Sister M. Faustina
of the Blessed Sacrament.
Cracow, March 1, 1937.

1004 O will of the Omnipotent God,
You are my delight,
You are my joy.
Whatever the hand of my Lord holds out to me
I will accept with gladness, submission and love.

Your holy will is my repose;
In it is contained all my sanctity,
And all my eternal salvation,
For doing God's will is the greatest glory.

The will of God—those are His various wishes
Which my soul carries out without reserve,
Because such are His divine desires,
In those moments when God shares His confidences
with me.

Do with me as You will, Lord.
I place no obstacles, I make no reservations.
For You are my whole delight and the love of my
soul,
And to You, in turn, I pour out the confidences of my
heart.

+
(3) J.M.J.   Cracow, March 1, 1937.
                                      + Third Notebook

God and Souls.

1005 Let the glory and praise to The Divine Mercy rise from every creature throughout all ages and times.

1006 + O my Lord and God, You command me to write about the graces You grant me. O my Jesus, were it not for a clear command from my confessors,[178] that I am to write down what goes on in my soul, I would not, of my own choice, write a single word. And so, if I do write about myself, it is at the formal command of holy obedience.

1007 + Praise and glory be to You, O Holy Trinity, Eternal God. May the mercy springing from Your very bowels protect us from Your just anger. Let the praise of Your incomprehensible mercy resound everywhere. All Your works bear the seal of Your unfathomable mercy, O God.

1008 March 1, 1937. The Lord gave me to know how displeased He is with a talkative soul. **I find no rest in such a soul. The constant din tires Me, and in the midst of it the soul cannot discern My voice.**

1009 Today I asked the Lord Jesus to let me meet with a certain person, and this would be a sign for me that He is calling her to this convent [which I am to found]. And I did meet her and understood that this soul has a vocation, and I asked the Lord to deign to form her Himself. I have talked to her often about a vocation; the Lord will do the rest.

1010 **(4)** + March 5, 1937. Today, I experienced the Passion of the Lord Jesus in my own body for a long while. The pain is very great, but all this is for the sake of immortal souls.

1011 Today, the Lord visited me, pressed me to His Heart and said, **Rest, My little child. I am always with you.**

1012 + March 8, 1937. Today, as I was praying for the intention of Father Andrasz, I suddenly understood how intimately this soul communed with God and how pleasing he was to the Lord. It gave me immense joy, because I desire intensely that all souls be united with God as closely as possible.

1013 + During prayer today, my soul was overcome with such a strong desire to begin the work, that I could not restrain my enthusiasm. Oh, how ardently I desire that the souls in this Congregation present themselves before the throne of God and continuously implore His incomprehensible mercy on behalf of the whole world, praising and glorifying this unfathomable mercy of God. A mysterious force is driving me to action.

1014 March 12, 1937. I saw the weariness of a certain priest [probably Father Sopocko] for whom the Lord has traced out a hard and difficult road; but the fruits of his work are alive. May God give us many such souls, capable of loving Him in the midst of the greatest torments.

1015 + I felt today how greatly a certain dying soul desired prayers. I prayed until I felt she had died. Oh, dying souls are in such great need of prayer! O Jesus, inspire souls to pray often for the dying.

1016 **(5)** March 15, 1937. Today, I entered into the bitterness of the Passion of the Lord Jesus. I suffered in a purely spiritual way. I learned how horrible sin was. God gave me to know the whole hideousness of sin. I learned in the depths of my soul how horrible sin was, even the smallest sin, and how much it tormented the soul of Jesus. I would rather suffer a thousand hells than commit even the smallest venial sin.

1017 The Lord said to me, **I want to give myself to souls and to fill them with My love, but few there are who want to accept all the graces My love has intended for them. My**

grace is not lost; if the soul for whom it was intended does not accept it, another soul takes it.

1018   I frequently feel that certain persons are praying for me. I experience this suddenly in my soul, but I do not always know which person is interceding for me. I also know when some person has trouble because of something that has to do with me; of this too I am inwardly aware, even though the distance [that separates us] is very great.[179]

1019   March 18, 1937. I have come to know that I have received a certain grace that brings me into great intimacy and communion with the Lord. He gives me to know this by means of an interior light. He allows me to know His greatness and holiness and how graciously He lowers himself to me. He gives me an exclusive knowledge of His love for me, and of how He is Lord of absolutely all things, and also of how He gives himself to a soul while suspending all the laws of nature. He acts as He wills.

1020   I understand the spiritual espousal of a soul with God, which has no exterior manifestation. It is a purely interior act between the soul and God. This grace has drawn me into the very burning center of God's love. I have come to understand His Trinitarian Quality and the absolute Oneness of His Being. This grace is different from all other graces. It is so extremely spiritual that my inaccurate description knows not how to express even a shade of it.

1021   **(6)** + I have such a strong desire to hide myself that I would like to live as though I did not exist. I feel a strange inner urge to hide myself as deeply as possible so as to be known only to the Heart of Jesus. I want to be a quiet little dwelling place for Jesus to rest in. I shall admit nothing that might awaken my Beloved. My concealment gives me a chance to commune constantly and exclusively with my Bridegroom. I commune with creatures in so far as it is pleasing to Him. My heart has come to love the Lord with the full force of love, and I know no other love, because it is from the beginning that my soul has sunk deeply in the Lord as in its only treasure.

1022 + Although outwardly I meet with many sufferings and various adversities, this does not, however, lessen my interior life for a moment nor disturb my inner silence. I do not fear at all being abandoned by creatures because, even if all abandoned me, I would not be alone, for the Lord is with me. And even if the Lord were to hide, love will know how to find Him. For love knows no gates or guards; even the keen-eyed Cherub himself, with his flaming sword, will not stop love; it will work its way through wilderness and scorching heat, through storm, thunder and darkness, and will reach the source from which it came, and there it will endure forever. All things will come to an end; but love, never.

1023 + Today, I received some oranges. When the sister had left, I thought to myself, "Should I eat the oranges instead of doing penance and mortifying myself during Holy Lent? After all, I am feeling a bit better." Then I heard a voice in my soul: **My daughter, you please Me more by eating the oranges out of obedience and love of Me than by fasting and mortifying yourself of your own will. A soul that loves Me very much must, ought to live by My will. I know your heart, and I know that it will not be satisfied by anything but My love alone.**

1024 **(7)** + I would not know how to live without the Lord. Jesus often visits me in this seclusion, teaches me, reassures me, rebukes me, and admonishes me. He himself forms my heart according to His divine wishes and likings, but always with much goodness and mercy. Our hearts are fused as one.

1025 March 19, 1937. Today, I united myself in spirit with the

Adoration that is taking place in our house [40-hour adoration in Cracow], but my soul was full of torments, and some strange kind of apprehension was piercing my heart. Because of this, I redoubled my prayers. Suddenly I saw the gaze of God reaching into the depths of my heart.

1026 As I sat down to a very tasty breakfast, I said to the Lord, "Thank you for these gifts, but my heart is dying of longing for You, and nothing earthly is tasty to me. I desire the food of Your love."

1027 Today I was drawn by some mysterious force to act. I must resist this attraction, or else I would follow it at once.

1028 March 21, 1937. Palm Sunday. During Mass, my soul was steeped in the bitterness and suffering of Jesus. Jesus gave me to understand how much He had suffered in that triumphal procession. "Hosanna" was reverberating in Jesus' heart as an echo of "Crucify." Jesus allowed me to feel this in a special way.

1029 The doctor did not allow me to go to the chapel to attend the Passion Service, although I had a great desire for it; however, I prayed in my own room. Suddenly I heard the bell in the next room, and I went in and rendered a service to a seriously sick person. **(8)** When I returned to my room, I suddenly saw the Lord Jesus, who said, **My daughter, you gave Me greater pleasure by rendering Me that service than if you had prayed for a long time.** I answered, "But it was not to You, Jesus, but to that patient that I rendered this service." And the Lord answered me, **Yes, My daughter, but whatever you do for your neighbor, you do for Me.**

1030 + O my Jesus, give me wisdom, give me a mind great and enlightened by Your light, and this only, that I may know You better, O Lord. For the better I get to know You, the more ardently will I love You, the sole object of my love. In You my soul drowns, in You my heart dissolves. I know not how to love partially, but only with the full strength of my soul and the total ardor of my heart. You yourself, O Lord, have enkindled this love of mine for You; in You my heart has drowned forever.

1031   March 22, 1937. As I was talking, today, to a certain person, I recognized that she was suffering greatly in spirit, although exteriorly she pretended that she was very happy and was not suffering at all. I felt inspired to tell her that what was troubling her was a temptation. When I disclosed to her what was torturing her, she burst into tears and told me that she had come to see me precisely to speak to me, because she felt that it would bring her relief. The suffering was of such a kind that the soul was being attracted by God's grace on the one hand and by the world on the other. She was going through a terrible struggle that brought her to the point of weeping like a little child. But she went away soothed and set at peace.

1032   + During Holy Mass, I saw the Lord Jesus nailed upon the cross amidst great torments. A soft moan issued from His Heart. After some time, He said, **I thirst. I thirst for the salvation of souls. Help Me, My daughter, to save souls. Join your sufferings to My Passion and offer them to the heavenly Father for sinners.**

1033   **(9)** + When I see that the burden is beyond my strength, I do not consider or analyze it or probe into it, but I run like a child to the Heart of Jesus and say only one word to Him: "You can do all things." And then I keep silent, because I know that Jesus himself will intervene in the matter, and as for me, instead of tormenting myself, I use that time to love Him.

1034   Monday of Holy Week. I asked the Lord to let me take part in His Sorrowful Passion that I might experience in soul and body, to the extent that this is possible for a creature, His bitter Passion. I asked to experience all the bitterness, in so far as this was possible. And the Lord answered that He would give me this grace, and that on Thursday, after Holy Communion, He would grant this in a special way.

1035 + This evening, a certain young man was dying; he was suffering terribly. For his intention, I began to say the chaplet which the Lord had taught me. I said it all, but the agony continued. I wanted to start the Litany of the Saints, but suddenly I heard the words, **Say the chaplet.** I understood that the soul needed the special help of prayers and great mercy. And so I locked myself in my room and fell prostrate before God and begged for mercy upon that soul. Then I felt the great majesty of God and His great justice. I trembled with fear, but did not stop begging the Lord's mercy for that soul. Then I took the cross off my breast, the crucifix I had received when making my vows,[180] and I put it on the chest of the dying man and said to the Lord, "Jesus, look on this soul with the same love with which You looked on my holocaust on the day of my perpetual vows, and by the power of the promise which You made to me in respect to the dying and those who would invoke Your mercy on them, [grant this man the grace of a happy death]." His suffering then ceased, and he died peacefully. Oh, how much we should pray for the dying! Let us take advantage of mercy while there is still time for mercy.

1036 **(10)** + I realize more and more how much every soul needs God's mercy throughout life and particularly at the hour of death. This chaplet mitigates God's anger, as He himself told me.

1037 + I find myself so weak that were it not for Holy Communion I would fall continually. One thing alone sustains me, and that is Holy Communion. From it I draw my strength; in it is all my comfort. I fear life on days when I do not receive Holy Communion. I fear my own self. Jesus concealed in the Host is everything to me. From the tabernacle I draw strength, power, courage and light. Here, I seek consolation in time of anguish. I would not know how to give glory to God if I did not have the Eucharist in my heart.

1038 + My beloved native land, Poland, if you only knew how many sacrifices and prayers I offer to God for you! But be watchful and give glory to God, who lifts you up and singles you out in a special way. But know how to be grateful.

1039 + I suffer great pain at the sight of the sufferings of others. All these sufferings are reflected in my heart. I carry their torments in my heart so that it even wears me out physically. I would like all pains to fall upon me so as to bring relief to my neighbor.

1040 Amid terrible torments, I fix my eyes on You, my God, and though a storm is gathering over my head, I know that the sun is not extinguished. Nor do I wonder at the deceitfulness of creatures, but I accept in advance whatever may happen. My lips are silent, while my ears are satiated with derision. I strive for silence in my heart amidst the greatest sufferings, and I protect myself against all attacks with the shield of Your Name.

1041 **(11)** An ardent desire for this Feast[181] is burning up my whole soul. In fervent prayer for the hastening of the Feast I find some relief, and I have begun a novena for the intention of certain priests that God may grant them light and inspiration to apply for the promulgation of this Feast, and that the Spirit of God inspire the Holy Father regarding the entire matter.

The novena consists of an hour of adoration before the Blessed Sacrament. I have implored God to hasten this Feast and have asked the Holy Spirit to inspire certain people regarding this whole matter. I am finishing this novena on Holy Thursday.

1042 + March 23, 1937. Today is the seventh day of the novena. I have received a great and inconceivable grace: the Most Merciful Jesus has promised that I will be present at the celebration of this solemn Feast.

1043 This day, the 23rd, that is, Tuesday of Holy Week, is a day on which the Lord has granted me many graces.

1044 Suddenly, God's presence took hold of me, and at once I saw myself in Rome, in the Holy Father's chapel and at the same time I was in our chapel. And the celebration of the Holy Father and the entire Church was closely connected with our chapel and, in a very special way, with our Congregation. And I took part in the solemn celebration simultaneously here and in Rome, for the celebration was so closely connected with Rome that, even as I write, I cannot distinguish the two but I am writing it down as I saw it. I saw the Lord Jesus in our chapel, exposed in the monstrance on the high altar. The chapel was adorned as for a feast, and on that day anyone who wanted to come was allowed in.[182] The crowd was so enormous that the eye could not take it all in. Everyone was participating in the celebrations with great joy, and many of them obtained what they desired. **(12)** The same celebration was held in Rome, in a beautiful church, and the Holy Father, with all the clergy, was celebrating this Feast, and then suddenly I saw Saint Peter, who stood between the altar and the Holy Father. I could not hear what Saint Peter said but I saw that the Holy Father understood his words....

1045 Then some clergymen whom I did not know began to examine me and to humiliate me,[183] or rather, what I had written; but I saw how Jesus himself was defending me and giving them to understand what they did not know.

1046 Then suddenly, I saw how the two rays, as painted in the image, issued from the Host and spread over the whole world. This lasted only a moment, but it seemed as though it had lasted all day, and our chapel was overcrowded all day long, and the whole day abounded in joy.

1047   Then suddenly I saw on our altar the living Lord Jesus, just as He is depicted in the image. Yet I felt that the sisters and all the people did not see the Lord Jesus as I saw Him. Jesus looked with great kindness and joy at the Holy Father, at certain priests, at the entire clergy, at the people and at our Congregation.

1048   Then, in an instant, I was caught up to stand near Jesus, and I stood on the altar next to the Lord Jesus, and my spirit was filled with a happiness so great that I am unable to comprehend it or write about it. A profound peace as well as repose filled my soul. Jesus bent toward me and said with great kindness, **What is it you desire, My daughter?** And I answered, "I desire worship and glory be given to Your mercy." **I already am receiving worship by the institution and celebration of this Feast; what else do you desire?** I then looked at the immense crowd worshiping The Divine Mercy and I said to the Lord, "Jesus, bless all those who are gathered to give glory to You and to venerate Your infinite mercy." Jesus made a sign of the cross with His hand, and this blessing was reflected in the souls like a flash of light. **(13)** My spirit was engulfed in His love. I felt as if I had dissolved and disappeared completely in God. When I came to myself, a profound peace was flooding my soul, and an extraordinary understanding of many things was communicated to my intellect, an understanding that had not been granted me previously.

1049   I am immensely happy, although I am the least of all; and I would not change anything of what God has given me. I would not want to change places even with a Seraph, as regards the interior knowledge of God which He himself has given me. The intimate knowledge I have of the Lord is such as no creature can comprehend, particularly, the depth of His mercy that envelops me. I am happy with everything You give me.

1050   March 24, 1937. Wednesday of Holy Week. My heart is languishing for God. I desire to become united with

Him. A faint fear pierces my soul and at the same time a kind of flame of love sets my heart on fire. Love and suffering are united in my heart.

1051 I have felt great sufferings in my body, but I feel the Lord is upholding me, for otherwise I would not be able to bear it.

1052 O my Jesus, I beg You on behalf of the whole Church: Grant it love and the light of Your Spirit, and give power to the words of priests so that hardened hearts might be brought to repentance and return to You, O Lord. Lord, give us holy priests; You yourself maintain them in holiness. O Divine and Great High Priest, may the power of Your mercy accompany them everywhere and protect them from the devil's traps and snares which are continually being set for the souls of priests. May the power of Your mercy, O Lord, shatter and bring to naught all that might tarnish the sanctity of priests, for You can do all things.

1053 **(14)** March 25, 1937. Holy Thursday. During Holy Mass, I saw the Lord, who said to me, **Lean your head on My breast and rest.** The Lord pressed me to His Heart and said, **I shall give you a small portion of My Passion, but do not be afraid, be brave; do not seek relief, but accept everything with submission to My will.**

1054 When Jesus was taking leave of me, such great pain filled my soul that it is impossible to express it. Physical strength left me; I left the chapel quickly and went to bed. I was oblivious of what was going on around me. My soul was filled with longing for the Lord, and all the bitterness of His Divine Heart was imparted to me. This lasted for about three hours. I asked the Lord to protect me from the eyes of those around me. Although I wanted to, I could not take any food all day, until evening.

I earnestly desired to spend the whole night with Jesus in the dark prison cell.[184] I prayed until eleven o'clock. At eleven, the Lord said to me, **Lie down and take your rest. I have let you experience in three hours what I suffered during the whole night.** And immediately I went to bed.

I had no physical strength left; the suffering had deprived me of it completely. Throughout all this time, I had been in a sort of swoon. Every beat of Jesus' Heart was reflected in my heart and pierced my soul. If these tortures had concerned me only, I would have suffered less; but as I looked at the One whom my heart has loved with all all its might and saw that He was suffering, and that I could not bring Him any relief, my heart dissolved in love and bitterness. I was dying with Him, and yet I could not die. But I would not have exchanged that martyrdom for all the pleasures in the whole world. In the course of this suffering, my love grew immeasurably. I know that the Lord was supporting me with His omnipotence, for otherwise I would not have been able to endure it for even a moment. Together with Him, I underwent, in a special way, all the various tortures. The world still has no idea of all that Jesus suffered. **(15)** I accompanied Him to the Garden of Gethsemane; I stayed with Him in the prison; I went with Him before the judges; I underwent with Him each of the tortures. Not a single one of His movements or looks escaped my notice. I came to know all the omnipotence of His love and of His mercy toward souls.

1055   March 26, 1937. Friday. In the morning, I at once felt the torture of His five wounds in my body. This suffering continued until three o'clock. Although there is no outward sign of it, the torture is no less painful. I am glad that Jesus is protecting me from people's eyes.

1056   At eleven o'clock Jesus said to me, **My host, you are refreshment for My tormented Heart.** I thought, after these words, that my heart would burn up. And He brought me into such close intimacy with Himself that my heart was espoused to His Heart in a loving union, and I could feel the faintest stir of His Heart and He, of mine. The fire of my created love was joined to the ardor of His eternal love. This one grace surpasses all others in its immensity. His Trinitarian Being enveloped me entirely, and I am totally immersed in Him. My littleness is, as it were, wrestling with this Immortal Mighty One. I am immersed in incomprehensible love and incomprehensible torture because of His Passion. All that concerns His Being is imparted to me also.

1057 Up to now, Jesus has been bringing me to know about, and to have a presentiment of, this grace, but today He granted it to me. I would not even dare to dream about it. My heart is in ceaseless ecstasy, as it were, although outwardly nothing disturbs my contacts with my neighbor or my attending to various matters. Nothing is capable of interrupting my ecstasy, nor can anyone suspect it, because I have asked God to protect me from detection by people. And, together with this grace, there entered my soul a whole ocean of light, enabling me to understand God and myself. Amazement overwhelms me entirely and leads me as if into a new ecstasy [aroused by the fact] that God has deigned to descend to me, who am so little.

1058 **(16)** + At three o'clock, I prayed prostrate, in the form of a cross, for the whole world. Jesus' mortal life was coming to an end. I heard His seven words; then He looked at me and said, **Beloved daughter of My Heart, you are My solace amidst terrible torments.**

1059 Jesus is commanding me to make a novena before the Feast of Mercy, and today I am to begin it for the conversion of the whole world and for the recognition of The Divine Mercy... **so that every soul will praise My goodness. I desire trust from My creatures. Encourage souls to place great trust in My fathomless mercy. Let the weak, sinful soul have no fear to approach Me, for**

even if it had more sins than there are grains of sand in the world, all would be drowned in the unmeasurable depths of My mercy.

1060 When Jesus had given up His last breath, my soul dissolved from the pain, and for a long time I could not come to myself. I found some relief in tears. The One whom my heart had come to love has died. Will anyone understand my grief?

1061 In the evening, over the radio, I heard hymns; that is, psalms, sung by priests.[185] I burst into tears, and all of the pain was renewed in my soul, and I wept sorrowfully, unable to find appeasement in this pain. Then I heard a voice in my soul: **Do not cry; I am not suffering any more. And for the faithfulness with which you accompanied Me in My sufferings and death, your own death will be a solemn one, and I will accompany you in that last hour. Beloved pearl of My Heart, I see your love so pure, purer than that of the angels, and all the more so because you keep fighting. For your sake I bless the world. I see your efforts to please Me, and they delight My Heart.**

After these words, I wept no more, but thanked the heavenly Father for having sent us His Son and for the work of the Redemption of mankind.

1062 **(17)** + I made an hour of adoration in thanksgiving for the graces which had been granted me and for my illness. Illness also is a great grace. I have been ill for four months, but I do not recall having wasted so much as a minute of it. All has been for God and souls; I want to be faithful to Him everywhere.

During this adoration, I realized the utter care and goodness that Jesus has been lavishing upon me and the protection He has given me against all evil. I thank You especially, Jesus, for visiting me in my solitude, and I thank You also for inspiring my superiors to send me for this treatment. Give them, Jesus, the omnipotence of

Your blessing and compensate them for all the losses incurred because of me.

1063 Today, Jesus is bidding me to comfort and reassure a certain soul who has opened herself to me and told me about her difficulties. This soul is pleasing to the Lord, but she is not aware of it. God is keeping her in deep humility. I have carried out the Lord's directives.

1064 + O my most sweet Master, good Jesus, I give You my heart. You shape and mold it after Your liking. O fathomless love, I open the calyx of my heart to You, like a rosebud to the freshness of dew. To You alone, my Betrothed, is known the fragrance of the flower of my heart. Let the fragrance of my sacrifice be pleasing to You. O Immortal God, my everlasting delight, already here on earth You are my heaven. May every beat of my heart be a new hymn of praise to You, O Holy Trinity! Had I as many hearts as there are drops of water in the ocean or grains of sand in the whole world, I would offer them all to You, O my Love, O Treasure of my heart! Whomever I shall meet in my life, no matter who they may be, I want to draw them all to love You, O my Jesus, my Beauty, my Repose, my sole Master, Judge, Savior and Spouse, all in one; I know that one title will modify the other—I have entrusted everything to Your mercy.

1065 **(18)** + My Jesus, support me when difficult and stormy days come, days of testing, days of ordeal, when suffering and fatigue begin to oppress my body and my soul. Sustain me, Jesus, and give me strength to bear suffering. Set a guard upon my lips that they may address no word of complaint to creatures. Your most merciful Heart is all my hope. I have nothing for my defense but only Your mercy; in it lies all my trust.

1066 March 27, 1937. Today, I returned from Pradnik, after nearly four months of treatment. For everything, I give great thanks to God. I have made use of every moment to glorify God. When I went into the chapel for a moment, I realized how much I would have to suffer and struggle, with regard to this whole matter. O Jesus, my strength, You alone can help me; grant me fortitude.

1067 March 28. Resurrection. During the Mass of Resurrection, I saw the Lord in beauty and splendor, and He said to me, **My daughter, peace be with you.** He blessed me and disappeared, and my soul was filled with gladness and joy beyond words. My heart was fortified for struggle and sufferings.

1068 Today, I had a conversation with Father [Andrasz] and he recommended great caution in the matter of these sudden appearances of the Lord Jesus. When he was speaking about divine mercy, some sort of strength and power entered my heart. My God, I want so much to express everything and am so very unable to do so. Father tells me that the Lord Jesus is very generous in communicating himself to souls and, on the other hand, He is, so to speak, stingy. "Although God's generosity is very great," said Father, "be careful anyway, because these sudden appearances arouse suspicion; although, personally, I do not see anything wrong here, or anything contrary to faith. Be a little more careful, and when Mother Superior comes, you can talk to her about these things."

1069 **(19)** March 29, 1937. During meditation today, I saw the Lord in great beauty, and He said to me, **Peace be to you, My daughter.** My whole soul trembled with love for Him and I said, "O Lord, although I love You with all my heart, please do not appear to me, because my spiritual director has told me that these sudden appearances of Yours arouse the suspicion that You could be an illusion. And although I love You more than my own life, and I know that You are my Lord and God, who are communing with me, I must above all be obedient to my confessor."

Jesus listened to my words with gravity and kindness and spoke these words to me: **Tell your confessor that I commune with your soul in such an intimate manner because you do not steal My gifts, and this is why I pour all these graces upon your soul, because I know that you will not hoard them for yourself. But as a sign that his prudence is agreeable to Me, you shall not see Me, and I will not appear to you in this way until you have given him an account of what I have just said.**

1070 + April 2, 1937. In the morning, during Mass, I heard these words: **Tell the superior that I want adoration to take place here for the intention of imploring mercy for the world.**

1071 O my Jesus, You alone know what my heart is going through. O my Strength, You can do all things, and though I expose myself to great sufferings, I shall always remain faithful to You because I am sustained by Your singular grace.

1072 + April 3, 1937. Today, the Lord said to me, **Tell the Reverend Professor** [probably Father Theodore[186]] **that I desire that on the Feast of My Mercy he deliver a sermon about My fathomless mercy.** I fulfilled God's wish, but the priest did not want to acknowledge the Lord's message. When I left the confessional, I heard these words: **Do as I tell you and be at peace; this matter is between him and Me. You will not be held responsible for this.**

1073 **(20)** April 4, 1937. Low Sunday; that is, the Feast of Mercy. In the morning, after Holy Communion, my soul was immersed in the Godhead. I was united to the Three Divine Persons in such a way that when I was united to Jesus, I was simultaneously united to the Father and to the Holy Spirit. My soul was flooded with joy beyond understanding, and the Lord gave me to experience the whole ocean and abyss of His fathomless mercy. Oh, if only souls would want to understand how much God loves them! All comparisons, even if they were the most tender and the most vehement, are but a mere shadow when set against the reality.

When I was united to the Lord, I came to know how many souls are glorifying God's mercy.

1074 When I went for adoration, I heard these words: **My beloved daughter, write down these words, that today My Heart has rested in this convent** [the Cracow house]. **Tell the world about My mercy and My love.**

The flames of mercy are burning me. I desire to pour them out upon human souls. Oh, what pain they cause Me when they do not want to accept them!

My daughter, do whatever is within your power to spread devotion to My mercy. I will make up for what you lack. Tell aching mankind to snuggle close to My merciful Heart, and I will fill it with peace.

Tell [all people], **My daughter, that I am Love and Mercy itself. When a soul approaches Me with trust, I fill it with such an abundance of graces that it cannot contain them within itself, but radiates them to other souls.**

1075 **Souls who spread the honor of My mercy I shield through their entire lives as a tender mother her infant, and at the hour of death I will not be a Judge for them, but the Merciful Savior.** (21) **At that last hour, a soul has nothing with which to defend itself except My mercy. Happy is the soul that during its lifetime immersed itself in the Fountain of Mercy, because justice will have no hold on it.**

1076 **Write this: Everything that exists is enclosed in the bowels of My mercy, more deeply than an infant in its mother's womb. How painfully distrust of My goodness wounds Me! Sins of distrust wound Me most painfully.**

1077 During Holy Mass, the Directress of Novices [Sister Callista[187]] played a beautiful hymn about the mercy of God. I then asked the Lord to give her a deeper knowledge of the abyss of this inconceivable mercy.

1078 + When I was saying good night to the Lord before retiring, I heard the words, **Host, dear to My Heart, for your sake I bless the earth.**

1079 April 7, 1937. Today, when a certain person entered the chapel, I felt a terrible pain in my hands, my feet and my side, just as Jesus did during His Passion. This lasted only for a brief moment. But in this way I recognized a soul who was not in God's grace.

1080 On one occasion I saw the Holy Father reflecting about this matter [presumably the establishment of the Feast of The Divine Mercy].

1081 April 10, 1937. Today, Mother Superior gave me an article about The Divine Mercy to read, and with it there was also a reproduction of the image that had been painted. The article appeared in the *Vilnius Weekly*[188] and was sent to us in Cracow by Father Michael Sopocko, that zealous apostle of The Divine Mercy. In this article are included words that the Lord Jesus has spoken to me, some of them quoted verbatim.

1082 When I took the issue of the *Weekly* into my hands, an arrow of love pierced my soul.—**For the sake of your (22) ardent desires, I am hastening the Feast of Mercy.** My spirit burst into such a powerful flame of love that it seemed to me that I was totally dissolved in God.

1083 + That beautiful soul who is spreading this work of divine mercy throughout the world is, by his deep humility, very pleasing to God.

1084 Before every major grace, my soul undergoes a test of patience, for I feel the grace, but do not yet possess it. My spirit burns with impatience, but the hour has not yet come. These moments are so very extraordinary that it is difficult to describe them.

1085   April 13, 1937. Today I must stay in bed all day. I had a violent fit of coughing, which left me so weak that I have no strength to walk. My spirit is eager to do God's work, but physical strength has left me. I cannot penetrate Your actions at this moment, O Lord; therefore, I keep repeating with a loving act of the will: do with me as You please.

1086   Although the temptations are strong, a whole wave of doubts beats against my soul, and discouragement stands by, ready to enter into the act, the Lord, however, strengthens my will, against which all the attempts of the enemy are shattered as if against a rock. I see how many actual graces God grants me; these support me ceaselessly. I am very weak, and I attribute everything solely to the grace of God.

1087   + When one day I resolved to practice a certain virtue, I lapsed into the vice opposed to that virtue ten times more frequently than on other days. In the evening, I was reflecting on why, today, I had lapsed so extraordinarily, and I heard the words: **You were counting too much on yourself and too little on Me.** And I understood the cause of my lapses.

1088   **(23)** Sudden return of health.

After I had written a letter to Father Sopocko on Sunday, April 11, I suddenly became so very ill that I did not send that letter, but waited for a clear sign of God's will. However, my health got so bad that I had to go to bed. The coughing racked me so much that it seemed to me that, if this repeats a few more times, it will surely be the end of me.

1089   On April 14, I felt so bad that I barely managed to get up to assist at Holy Mass. I felt much worse than I did at the time they sent me for treatment. There was wheezing, and there were rattling noises in my lungs and strange pains. When I received Holy Communion, I don't know why, but it was as if something were urging me to this prayer, and I began to pray in this manner: "Jesus, may Your pure and healthy blood circulate in my ailing organism, and may Your pure and healthy body transform my weak body, and may a healthy and vigorous life throb within me, if it is truly Your holy will that I should set about the work in question; and this will be a clear sign of Your holy will for me."

As I was praying in this way, I suddenly felt as if something were jolting my whole organism and, in an instant, I felt completely well. My breath is clear, as if there had never been anything the matter with my lungs, and I feel no pain, and this is a sign for me that I should set about the work.

1090   And this happened on the last day of my novena to the Holy Spirit. After this return to health, I found myself united with the Lord Jesus in a purely spiritual way. Jesus gave me strong assurances; that is, He confirmed me in respect to His demands. I remained close to the Lord Jesus all that day and talked with Him about the details concerning that congregation.

(24) Jesus infused my soul with power and courage to act. Now I understand that if the Lord demands something of a soul, He gives it the means to carry it out, and through grace He makes it capable of doing this. So, even if the soul be utterly miserable, at the Lord's command it can undertake things beyond its expectation, because this is the sign by which it can be known that the Lord is with that soul: if God's power and strength, which make the soul courageous and valiant, is manifest within it. As for myself, I am always at first a bit frightened at the Lord's greatness, but afterwards my soul is filled with profound peace which nothing can disturb, as well as an inner strength to do what the Lord is demanding at that particular moment....

1091 Then I heard these words: **Go tell the superior that you are in good health.**

I neither know, nor ask how long I will remain in good health. I only know that I am enjoying good health at present. The future does not belong to me. I asked for this health as evidence of God's will and not in order to seek relief from my suffering.

1092 April 16, 1937. Today, as God's Majesty swept over me, my soul understood that the Lord, so very great though He is, delights in humble souls. The more a soul humbles itself, the greater the kindness with which the Lord approaches it. Uniting himself closely with it, He raises it to His very throne. Happy is the soul whom the Lord himself defends. I have come to know that only love is of any value; love is greatness; nothing, no works, can compare with a single act of pure love of God.

1093 + O Jesus, shield me with Your mercy and also judge me leniently, or else Your justice may rightly damn me.

1094 **(25)** April 17. Today, during a catechetical lecture [by Father Theodore[189]], I was given a confirmation of what I had understood interiorly and lived by for quite some time; namely, that if a soul loves God sincerely and is intimately united with Him, then, even though such a soul may be living in the midst of difficult external circumstances, nothing can disturb its interior life; and in the midst of corruption, it can remain pure and unsullied; because the great love of God gives it strength for battle, and God also protects in a special way, even in a miraculous way, a soul that loves Him sincerely.

1095 When, one day, God gave me the inner knowledge that I had never lost my innocence, and that despite all dangers in which I had found myself, He himself had been guarding me so that the virginity of my soul and heart would remain intact, I spent the day in fervent interior thanksgiving. I thanked God that He had been pleased to protect me from evil, and also for this: that I had found favor in His eyes, that He himself had given me assurance of this.

1096   And a few years later, He deigned to confirm me in this grace, and since that time I have not experienced the rebellion of the senses against the soul. I have written this down in greater detail elsewhere in my diary [cf. paragraph no. 40]. As often as I recall this inconceivable grace, a fresh flame of love and gratitude to God bursts forth from my heart; and this same love leads me to complete forgetfulness of self.

1097   Since that time, I have been living under the virginal cloak of the Mother of God. She has been guarding me and instructing me. I am quite at peace, close to Her Immaculate Heart. Because I am so weak and inexperienced, I nestle like a little child close to Her heart.

1098   Although God has confirmed me in this virtue, I am, however, constantly on the watch and fear even my own shadow, but this only because I have come to love God intensely.

1099   (26) This grace from God was given to me precisely because I was the weakest of all people; this is why the Almighty has surrounded me with His special mercy.

1100   April 24. I can sense every major grace in advance; a strange longing and desire for God comes over me, and then I wait for the grace. And the greater the grace, the more distinct is the presentiment, and the fiercer is my struggle with the adversary of my salvation.

My soul is sometimes in such a condition that I can only describe it by means of a comparison: there are two great friends, and one of them is giving a great feast and has invited the other; both of them are looking forward to it; but the hour of the feast has been set. Well, the moments just before receiving the grace are so violent that it is difficult to describe them. They are marked by painful longing and the fire of love. I can feel the Lord is there, but I cannot be completely absorbed in Him, because the hour has been designated. Often, before such a moment of grace, I am utterly destitute in mind, will and heart. I am left all alone, and I wait for the One God. He himself effects this in me before His coming.

April 23, 1937. I have begun a three-day retreat today.[190]

1101 In the evening, I heard these words in my soul: **My daughter, know that I shall speak to you in a special way through this priest** [Father Plaza[191]] **so that you may not yield to doubt concerning My wishes.** Already in the first meditation my soul was struck by the following words of the priest: I must not oppose God's will and God's designs, whatever they might be; and as soon as I am convinced of the certitude and the authenticity of the will of God, I have the duty of carrying it out. No one can release me from this. Whatever **(27)** the will of God may be, once I have come to know it, I ought to carry it out. This is just a very short summary, but the whole meditation imprinted itself on my soul, and I have no doubts about anything. I know what God wants of me, and what I ought to do.

1102 There are, in my life, times and moments of spiritual insight; that is, divine illuminations, when the soul receives inward instruction about things it has not read in any book and has not been taught by any person. These are times of great inner knowledge which God himself imparts to the soul. These are great mysteries.... I often receive light and the knowledge of the interior life of God and of God's intimate disposition, and this fills me with unutterable trust and a joy that I cannot contain within myself; I desire to dissolve completely in Him....

1103 + The quintessence of love is sacrifice and suffering. Truth wears a crown of thorns. Prayer involves the intellect, the will, and the emotions.

1104 Today there was a beautiful teaching [by Father Plaza]

on the goodness and mercy of God. During this conference my soul experienced the flames of God's love, and I understood that God's word is a living word.

1105 My particular examen is still the same; namely, union with the merciful Christ, and silence.

The flower which I lay at the feet of the Mother of God for May is my practice of silence.

1106 **(28)** + Virtue without prudence is not virtue at all. We should often pray to the Holy Spirit for this grace of prudence. Prudence consists in discretion, rational reflection and courageous resolution. The final decision is always up to us. We must decide; we can and we ought to seek advice and light...

1107 Today during meditation, God gave me inner light and the understanding as to what sanctity is and of what it consists. Although I have heard these things many times in conferences, the soul understands them in a different way when it comes to know of them through the light of God which illumines it.

Neither graces, nor revelations, nor raptures, nor gifts granted to a soul make it perfect, but rather the intimate union of the soul with God. These gifts are merely ornaments of the soul, but constitute neither its essence nor its perfection. My sanctity and perfection consist in the close union of my will with the will of God. God never violates our free will. It is up to us whether we want to receive God's grace or not. It is up to us whether we will cooperate with it or waste it.

1108 In the last evening conference, which was a preparation for the renewal of vows, Father was speaking about the happiness that flows from the three vows, and about the reward that comes from observing them faithfully. Suddenly, my soul was thrown into great interior darkness. My soul was filled with bitterness instead of joy, and my heart was pierced with a sharp pain. I felt so miserable and unworthy of this grace and, conscious of my misery and unworthiness, I would not have dared to so much as approach the feet of the youngest postulant to kiss them. I saw the postulants, in spirit, beautiful and pleasing to the Lord; and myself, an abyss of misery. After **(29)** the conference, I flung myself at the feet of the hidden God, midst tears and pain. I threw myself into the sea of God's infinite mercy, and only there did I experience relief and feel that all of His omnipotent mercy was enveloping me.

1109 + 30. This is the day for the renewal of vows.

Immediately upon my awakening, God's presence enveloped me, and I felt I was a child of God. Divine love was poured into my soul, and God gave me to see how everything depended on His will. He spoke these words to me: **I want to grant a complete pardon to the souls that will go to Confession and receive Holy Communion on the Feast of My mercy.** Then He said to me, **My daughter, fear nothing. I am always with you, even if it seems to you that I am not. Your humility draws Me down from My lofty throne, and I unite myself closely with you.**

1110 29 [April 1937]. The Lord gave me to know about the disputes[192] that were going on in the Vatican concerning this Feast. The dignitary Pacelli did much work on this.

1111 Today is the renewal; that is, the profession of vows[193] in the course of a solemn celebration. As the sisters were making their vows, I heard angels singing in various tones, "Holy, Holy, Holy," with chanting so delightful that no human tongue could ever match it.

1112 In the afternoon, I talked with my beloved Mother Directress of Novices, Mother Mary Joseph. We walked once around the garden, and I was able to have a talk with her, although it was a rather general one. She is ever the same beloved Mother Directress of Novices, although she is in fact no longer the directress, but a Superior, and it is already ten years since I pronounced my vows. She told me that it is impossible for a religious to live without the cross. However, she revealed to me a certain suffering which I had experienced in Warsaw, although I had never told her **(30)** about it. All the graces which I had received during the novitiate came back vividly before the eyes of my soul. Oh, how grateful I am to her! When my soul was plunged in darkness, and it seemed to me that I was damned, she wrenched me from that abyss by the power of obedience.

1113   My soul is often burdened with suffering, and there is no human being who can understand these torments.

1114   May 1, 1937. Today I felt the nearness of my Mother, my heavenly Mother, although before every Holy Communion I earnestly ask the Mother of God to help me prepare my soul for the coming of Her Son, and I clearly feel Her protection over me. I entreat Her to be so gracious as to enkindle in me the fire of God's love, such as burned in Her own pure heart at the time of the Incarnation of the Word of God.

1115   May 4. Today I went to see Mother General [Michael] for a moment and asked her, "Dear Mother, have you had any inspiration regarding my leaving the convent?" Mother General answered, "Until the present, Sister, I have always restrained you, but now I leave you complete freedom to choose to do as you wish; you can leave the Congregation or you can stay." So I answered, "Very well." I thought of writing immediately to the Holy Father to ask him to release me from my vows.[194] When I had left Mother General, darkness once again descended upon my soul, as it had in the past. It is strange that, each time I ask permission to leave the Congregation, this darkness invades my soul, and I feel as though I have been left completely on my own. While experiencing this torment of the spirit, **(31)** I decided to go immediately to Mother and tell her about my strange torment and struggle. Mother answered, "That leaving of yours is a temptation." After talking to her for a while

I felt some relief, but the darkness persisted. "This Divine Mercy is a beautiful thing, and it must be a great work of the Lord, since Satan opposes it so much and wants to destroy it." Such were the words of our beloved Mother General.

1116 No one can understand or comprehend, nor can I myself describe, my torments. But there can be no sufferings greater than this. The sufferings of the martyrs are not greater because, at such times, death would be a relief for me. There is nothing to which I can compare these sufferings, this endless agony of the soul.

1117 May 5, [1937]. Today, I opened up my soul somewhat in confession, because it occurred to me that perhaps this is the real temptation: that at the time I ask to be allowed to leave the Congregation I experience such great suffering and darkness. To this the confessor replied that perhaps it was not the time appointed by God. "You must pray and wait patiently, but it is true that great sufferings are in store for you. You will have to bear many sufferings and overcome many difficulties; that much is certain. It would be better to wait and to pray much for deeper knowledge and for divine light. These are grave matters."

1118 My God! In these difficult moments my spiritual director [Father Andrasz] is away, for he has gone to Rome. Jesus, since You have taken him away from me, guide me Yourself, (32) because You alone know how much I can bear. I believe firmly that God cannot give me more than I can bear. I trust in His mercy.

1119 In the moments when I am between heaven and earth, I keep silent, because even if I did speak, who would understand what I say? Eternity will reveal many things about which I am now silent...

1120 When I went out into the garden, I saw how everything was breathing the joy of spring. The trees, adorned with flowers, gave off an intoxicating odor. Everything was throbbing with joy, and the birds were singing and chirping their adoration of God and said to me, "Rejoice and be happy, Sister Faustina"; but my soul remains in torment and darkness. My soul is so sensitive to the rustle of grace [that] it knows how to talk with all created things and with everything that surrounds me, and I know why God has adorned the earth in this way... But my heart cannot be joyful because my Beloved has hidden Himself from me, and I will not rest until I find Him... I do not know how to live without God, but I also feel that God, absolutely self-sufficient though He is, cannot be happy without me...

1121   May 6, [1937]. The Ascension of Our Lord.

Since early this morning, my soul has been touched by God. After Holy Communion, I communed for a while with the heavenly Father. My soul was drawn into the glowing center of love. I understood that no exterior works could stand comparison with pure love of God... I saw the joy of the Incarnate Word, and I was immersed in the Divine Trinity. When I came to myself, longing filled my soul, and I yearned to be united **(33)** with God. Such tremendous love for the heavenly Father enveloped me that I call this day an uninterrupted ecstasy of love. The whole universe seemed to me like a tiny drop in comparison with God. There is no greater happiness than when God gives me to know interiorly that every beat of my heart is pleasing to Him, and when He shows me that He loves me in a special way. This strong inner conviction, by which God assures me of His love for me and of how much my soul pleases Him, brings deep peace to my soul. Throughout this day I was unable to take any food; I felt gratified to the full with love.

1122   God of great mercy, who deigned to send us Your only-begotten Son as the greatest proof of Your fathomless love and mercy, You do not reject sinners; but in Your boundless mercy You have opened for them also Your treasures, treasures from which they can draw abundantly, not only justification, but also all the sanctity that a soul can attain. Father of great mercy, I desire that all hearts turn with confidence to Your infinite mercy. No one will be justified before You if he is not accompanied by Your unfathomable mercy. When You reveal the mystery of Your mercy to us, there will not be enough of eternity to properly thank You for it.

1123 Oh, how sweet it is to have in the depth of one's soul that which the Church tells us we must believe. When my soul is immersed in love, I solve the most intricate questions clearly and quickly. Only love is able to cross over precipices and mountain peaks. Love, once again, love.

1124 **(34)** + 12 [May 1937]. A strange darkness sometimes invades my intellect. I am submerged in nothingness against my will.

1125 May 20, 1937. When for a whole month I had been enjoying good health, it occurred to me that I did not know which was more pleasing to the Lord—my serving Him in illness or in the robust health for which I had asked Him—and I said to the Lord, "Jesus, do with me as You please," and Jesus returned me to my previous condition.

1126 Oh, how sweet it is to live in a convent among sisters, but I must not forget that these angels are in human bodies.

1127 On one occasion, I saw Satan hurrying about and looking for someone among the sisters, but he could find no one. I felt an interior inspiration to command him in the Name of God to confess to me what he was looking for among the sisters. And he confessed, though unwillingly, "I am looking for idle souls [cf. Si. 33:28; Pr. 12:11]." When I commanded him again in the Name of God to tell me to which souls in religious life he has the easiest access, he said, again unwillingly, "To lazy and idle souls." I took note of the fact that, at present, there were no such souls in this house. Let the toiling and tired souls rejoice.

1128 May 22, 1937. The heat is so intense today that it is difficult to bear. We are all thirsting for rain, and still it does not come. For several days the sky has been overcast, but there is no rain. When I looked at (35) the plants, thirsting for the rain. I was moved with pity, and I decided to say the chaplet until the Lord would send us rain. Before supper, the sky covered over with clouds, and a heavy rain fell on the earth. I had been saying this prayer without interruption for three hours. And the Lord let me know that everything can be obtained by means of this prayer.

[May] 23. The Feast of the Most Holy Trinity.

1129 During Holy Mass, I found myself suddenly united with the Most Holy Trinity. I recognized His majesty and greatness. I was united to the Three Persons. And once I was united to One of these Most Venerable Persons, I was at the same time united to the other Two Persons. The joy and happiness that my soul felt is beyond description. It grieves me that I am unable to put down in words that which has no words.

1130 I heard these words: **Tell the Superior General to count on you as the most faithful daughter in the Order.**[195]

1131 After these words, I received an inner understanding of what all created things are before God. Immense and incomprehensible is His majesty. And that He condescends toward us is the abyss of His mercy...

1132 All things will have an end in this vale of tears,
      Tears will run dry and pain will cease.
      Only one thing will remain—
      Love for You, O Lord.

          All things will have an end in this exile,
          The ordeals and wilderness of the soul.

And though she live in perpetual agony,
If God is with her, nothing can shake her.

1133 **(36)** 27 [May 1937]. Corpus Christi.

During prayer, I heard these words: **My daughter, let your heart be filled with joy. I, the Lord, am with you. Fear nothing. You are in My heart.** At that moment, I knew the great majesty of God, and I understood that nothing could be compared with one single perception of God. Outward greatness dwindles like a speck of dust before one act of a deeper knowledge of God.

1134 The Lord has poured such a depth of peace into my soul that nothing will disturb it any more. Despite everything that goes on around me, I am not deprived of my peace for a moment. Even if the whole world were crumbling, it would not disturb the depth of the silence which is within me and in which God rests. All events, all the various things which happen are under His foot.

1135 This deeper knowledge of God gives me full liberty and spiritual freedom, and nothing can disturb my close union with Him, not even the angelic powers. I feel that I am great when I am united to God. What happiness it is to have the consciousness of God in one's heart and to live in close intimacy with Him.

1136 When the procession from Borek[196] came to our house, carrying Him who was to be reposed in our chapel, I heard a voice coming from the Host: **Here is My repose.** During Benediction, Jesus gave me to know that soon a solemn moment would take place on this very spot. **I am pleased to rest in your heart and nothing will stop Me from granting you graces.** This greatness of God floods my soul, and I drown in Him, I lose myself in Him, I am melting away in Him...

1137 **(37)** May 30, [1937]. I am dying of yearning for God today. This longing fills all my soul. How very much I feel I am in exile. O Jesus, when will the longed-for moment come?

1138   May 31. My tormented soul finds aid nowhere but in You, O Living Host. I place all my trust in Your merciful heart. I am waiting patiently for Your word, Lord.

1139   Oh, what pain it causes my heart when I see a nun who has not the religious spirit! How can one be pleasing to God when one is inflated with pride and self-love under the pretense of striving for God's glory, while in fact one is seeking one's own glory? When I see such a thing, it gives me very great pain. How can such a soul be united closely with God? Union with the Lord is out of the question here.

1140   June 1, 1937. Today, the Corpus Christi procession[197] took place. At the first altar, a flame issued from the Host and pierced my heart, and I heard a voice, **Here is My resting place.** My heart was enflamed, and I felt that I was transformed completely into Him.

1141   In the evening, He gave me to understand how fleeting all earthly things are, and [how] everything that appears great disappears like smoke, and does not give the soul freedom, but weariness. Happy the soul that understands these things and with only one foot touches the earth. My repose is to be united with You; everything else tires me. Oh, how much I feel I am in exile! I see that no one understands my interior life. You alone understand me, You who are hidden in my heart and yet are eternally alive.

1142   **(38)** June 4. Today is the Feast of the Most Sacred Heart of Jesus. During Holy Mass, I was given the knowledge of the Heart of Jesus and of the nature of the fire of love with which He burns for us and of how He is an Ocean of Mercy. Then I heard a voice: **Apostle of My mercy, proclaim to the whole world My unfathomable mercy. Do not be discouraged by the difficulties you encounter in proclaiming My mercy. These difficulties that affect you so painfully are needed for your sanctification and as evidence that this work is Mine. My daughter, be**

diligent in writing down every sentence I tell you concerning My mercy, because this is meant for a great number of souls who will profit from it.

1143 + During Adoration, the Lord gave me a deeper knowledge of matters connected with this work.

1144 Today, I asked the Lord's pardon for all the offenses committed in our convents from which His divine Heart suffers.

1145 + June 6, [1937]. First Sunday of the month. Today I made my monthly retreat.

A light from the morning meditation: Whatever You do with me, Jesus, I will always love You, for I am Yours. Little matter whether You leave me here or put me somewhere else; I am always Yours.

It is with love that I abandon myself to Your most wise decrees, O God, and Your will, O Lord, is my daily nourishment. You, who know the beatings of my heart, know that it beats for You alone, my Jesus. Nothing can quench my longing for You. I am dying for You, Jesus. When will You take me into Your dwelling place [cf. Jn. 14:1-3]?

1146 **(39) [Let] the greatest sinners place their trust in My mercy. They have the right before others to trust in the abyss of My mercy. My daughter, write about My mercy towards tormented souls. Souls that make an appeal to My mercy delight Me. To such souls I grant even more graces than they ask. I cannot punish even the greatest sinner if he makes an appeal to My compassion, but on the contrary, I justify him in My unfathomable and inscrutable mercy. Write: before I come as a just Judge, I first open wide the door of My mercy. He who refuses to pass through the door of My mercy must pass through the door of My justice...**

1147 When once I felt hurt because of a certain thing and complained to the Lord, Jesus answered, **My daughter,**

why do you attach such importance to the teaching and the talk of people? I myself want to teach you; that is why I arrange things so that you cannot attend those conferences. In a single moment, I will bring you to know more than others will acquire through many years of toil.

1148   June 20, [1937]. We resemble God most when we forgive our neighbors. God is Love, Goodness, and Mercy...

Every soul, and especially the soul of every religious, should reflect My mercy. My Heart overflows with compassion and mercy for all. The heart of My beloved must resemble Mine; from her heart must spring the fountain of My mercy for souls; otherwise I will not acknowledge her as Mine.

1149   **(40)** + On several occasions, I have learned how some religious defend their own glory under the pretext of being concerned for the glory of God, whereas it is not a question of the glory of God, but of glory of self. O Jesus, how painful this has been for me! What secrets the day of Your judgment will bring to light! How can one steal God's gifts?

1150   Today, I experienced a good deal of sorrow because of a certain person, a lay person, that is. On the basis of one true thing, she said many things which were fictitious. And because they were taken to be true and spread around the whole house, when the news reached my ears, my heart felt a twinge of pain. How can one abuse the goodness of others like that? But I resolved not to say a word in my defense and to show even greater kindness toward that person. I became aware, however, that I was not strong enough to bear this calmly, because the matter lingered on for weeks. When I saw the storm building up and the wind beginning to blow sand straight into my eyes, I went before the Blessed Sacrament and said to the Lord, "Lord Jesus, I ask You to give me the strength of Your actual grace, because I feel that I will not manage to survive this struggle. Shield me with Your breast."

Then I heard the words, **Do not fear; I am with you.** When I left the altar, an extraordinary peace and power filled my soul, and the storm that was raging broke against my soul as against a rock; and the foam of the storm fell on those who had raised it. Oh, how good is the Lord, who will reward each one according to his deed! Let every soul beg for the help of actual grace, as sometimes ordinary grace is not enough.

1151 **(41)** + When pain overwhelms my soul,
And the horizon darkens like night,
And the heart is torn with the torment of suffering,
Jesus Crucified, You are my strength.

When the soul, dimmed with pain,
Exerts itself in battle without respite,
And the heart is in agony and torment,
Jesus Crucified, You are the hope of my salvation.

And so the days pass,
As the soul bathes in a sea of bitterness,
And the heart dissolves in tears,
Jesus Crucified, You shine for me like the dawn.

And when the cup of bitterness brims over,
And all things conspire against her,
And the soul goes down to the Garden of Olives,
Jesus Crucified, in You is my defense.

When the soul, conscious of its innocence,
Accepts these dispensations from God,
The heart can then repay hurts with love.
Jesus Crucified, transform my weakness into omnipotence.

1152 It is no easy thing to bear sufferings joyfully, especially those which are unmerited. Fallen nature rebels, and although the intellect and will are above suffering, because they are able to do good to those who inflict suffering on them, nevertheless the emotions raise a lot of noise and, like restless spirits, attack the intellect and will. But when they see they cannot do anything by themselves, they quiet down and submit to the intellect and will. Like some kind of hideousness,**(42)**they rush in and stir up a row, bent on making one obey them alone so long as they are not curbed by the intellect and will.

1153 June 23, [1937]. As I was praying before the Most Blessed Sacrament, my physical sufferings ceased suddenly, and I heard this voice in my soul: **You see, I can give you everything in one moment. I am not constrained by any law.**

June 24. After Holy Communion, I heard these words: **Know, My daughter, that in one moment I can give you everything that is needed for the fulfillment of this task.** After these words, an extraordinary light remained in my soul, and all God's demands seemed to me to be so simple that even a little child could carry them out.

1154 [June] 27. Today, I saw the convent of the new Congregation. It was a large and spacious building. I went from room to room, observing everything. I saw that God's Providence had provided for all that was necessary. The persons living in this convent were still wearing lay clothes, but a thoroughly religious spirit reigned there, and I was organizing everything just as the Lord wanted. All of a sudden, I heard a rebuke from one of our sisters, "Sister, how can you carry out such works?" I answered that it was not I, but the Lord working through me, and that I had the authorization for everything. During Mass, I received light and profound understanding concerning this whole work, and not a shadow of a doubt remained in my soul.

1155 **(43)** The Lord gave me knowledge of His will under three aspects, so to speak, but it all comes down to one.[198]

The first is that souls separated from the world will burn as an offering before God's throne and beg for mercy for the whole world... and by their entreaties they will obtain blessings for priests, and through their prayers prepare the world for the final coming of Jesus.

1156 The second is prayer joined to the act of mercy. In particular, they will defend the souls of children against the spirit of evil. Prayer and merciful deeds are all that will be required of these souls, and even the poorest persons can be admitted to their number. And in this egoistic world they will try to rouse up love, the mercy of Jesus.

1157 The third is prayer and deeds of mercy, without any obligation of taking vows. But by doing this, these persons will have a share in all the merits and privileges of the whole [congregation]. Everyone in the world can belong to this group.

1158 A member of this group ought to perform at least one act of mercy a day; at least one, but there can be many more, for such deeds can easily be carried out by anyone, even the very poorest. For there are three ways of performing an act of mercy: the merciful word, by forgiving and by comforting; secondly, if you can offer no word, then pray—that too is mercy; and thirdly, deeds of mercy. And when the Last Day comes, we shall be judged from this, and on this basis we shall receive the eternal verdict.

1159 God's floodgates have been opened for us. Let us want to take advantage of them before the day of God's justice arrives. And that will be a dreadful day!

1160 **(44)** When once I asked the Lord Jesus how He could tolerate so many sins and crimes and not punish them, the Lord answered me, **I have eternity for punishing** [these], **and so I am prolonging the time of mercy for the sake of** [sinners]. **But woe to them if they do not recognize this time of My visitation. My daughter, secretary of My mercy, your duty is not only to write about and proclaim My mercy, but also to beg for this grace for them, so that they too may glorify My mercy.**

1161 Today, my soul suffered such agony that I began to complain to the Lord Jesus, "Jesus, how can You leave me alone? I cannot take even one step forward by myself. You have taken my confessor away, and You yourself are hiding from me. Surely, You know, Jesus, that of myself I know nothing but how to waste Your graces. Jesus, You must arrange things so that Father Andrasz will return." But the anguish persisted.

1162 It occurred to me to go to some priest and tell him of my anguish as well as some various inspirations, that he might resolve them for me; and I shared this idea with Mother Superior [Irene]. Mother replied, "I understand, Sister, that you are going through a difficult time, but at present, I really do not know of any priest who would be suitable for you. At any rate, Father Andrasz will be returning soon. So, for now, go and tell everything to the Lord Jesus."

1163 When I went to talk with the Lord for a while, I heard a voice in my soul: **My—I will not give you the grace to reveal yourself to someone else, and even if you did bare yourself, I will not give that priest the grace needed to understand you. At this time, it is My desir that you put up with yourself patiently. (45) My daughter, it is not My will that you should tell everybody about the gifts I have granted you. I have entrusted you to the care of the friend of My Heart, and under his direction your soul will bloom. I have given him light to recognize My life in your soul.**

1164 **My daughter, when I was before Herod, I obtained a grace for you; namely, that you would be able to rise above human scorn and follow faithfully in My footsteps. Be silent when they do not want to acknowledge your truth, because it is then that you speak more eloquently.**

1165 **Know this, My daughter: if you strive for perfection you will sanctify many souls; and if you do not strive for** sanctity, by the same token, many souls will remain imperfect. **Know that their perfection will depend on your perfection, and the greater part of the responsibility for these souls will fall on you.**

1166 Then He said to me, **Do not fear, My child; but remain faithful only to My grace...**

1167 Satan has admitted to me that I am the object of his hatred. He said that "a thousand souls do me less harm than you do when you speak of the great mercy of the Almighty One. The greatest sinners regain confidence and return to God, and I lose everything. But what is more, you persecute me personally with that unfathomable mercy of the Almighty One." I took note of the great hatred Satan has for the Mercy of God. He does not want to acknowledge that God is good.

1168 **(46)** June 29, 1937. During breakfast today, Father Andrasz greeted the whole community by telephone. He is already back [from Rome], and this very afternoon he came to see us. The professed sisters, the novices, and both groups of students assembled in the quadrangle [the girls' playground in front of the building] and waited for our dear Father. The children welcomed him with songs and poems, and then we asked him to tell us about Rome and the many beautiful things he had seen there. He spoke for over two hours and, because of this, there was no time left to talk in private.

1169 Today, my soul entered into close union with the Lord. He made known to me how I should always abandon myself to His holy will: **In one moment, I can give you more than you are able to desire.**

1170 June 30, 1937. Today, the Lord said to me, **I have wanted to exalt this Congregation many times, but I am unable to do so because of its pride. Know, My daughter, that I do not grant My graces to proud souls, and I even take away from them the graces I have granted.**

1171 Today Sister Jolanta[199] asked me to make an agreement with her: she will pray for me, and I am to pray for the girls in her class in Vilnius. As for me, I always pray for our work, but I have resolved to pray for the class in Vilnius for two months, and Sister Jolanta will say three Hail Marys to the Incarnate Word every day for the intention that I might profit from God's grace. Our friendship has deepened.

1172 **(47)** July 1, 1937. The month of July.

Today during the Angelus, the Lord gave me an understanding of God's incomprehensible love for people. He lifts us up to His very Godhead. His only motives are love and fathomless mercy. Though You make known the mystery to us through an angel, You yourself carry it out.

1173 In spite of the profound peace my soul is enjoying, I am struggling continuously, and it is often a hard-fought battle for me to walk faithfully along my path; that is, the path which the Lord Jesus wants me to follow. And my path is to be faithful to the will of God in all things and at all times, especially by being faithful to inner inspirations in order to be a receptive instrument in God's hands for the carrying out of the work of His fathomless mercy.

1174 **(48)** July 4, 1937. First Sunday of the month.

Monthly retreat.

This evening, I prepared with great care and prayed long to the Holy Spirit that He might deign to grant me His light and take me under His special guidance; [I prayed] also to Our Lady, to my Guardian Angel, and to our patron saints.[200]

1175 Fruit of the meditation.

Whatever Jesus did, He did well. He went along, doing good. His manner was full of goodness and mercy. His steps were guided by compassion. Toward His enemies He showed goodness, kindness, and understanding, and to those in need help and consolation.

I have resolved to mirror faithfully these traits of Jesus in myself during this month, even if this costs me much.

1176 During Adoration, I heard a voice in my soul: **These efforts of yours, My daughter, are pleasing to Me; they are the delight of My Heart. I see every movement of your heart with which you worship Me.**

1177   Particular examen.

Continuation of the same: to unite myself with the merciful Christ. For the sake of His sorrowful Passion, I will entreat the heavenly Father for the whole world. A point of the rule: strict observance of silence.

I must probe the depth of my being and thank God for everything, uniting myself with Jesus. With Him, in Him, and through Him, I give glory to God.

1178 **(49)** O Lord, my Love, I thank You for this day on which You have allowed me to draw a wealth of graces from the fountain of Your unfathomable mercy. O Jesus, not only today, but at every moment, I draw from Your unfathomable mercy everything that the soul and body could want.

1179 July 7, 1937. In times of doubt; that is, when the soul is weak, let it ask Jesus himself to act. Although it knows that it should act by the grace of God, nevertheless, at certain times, it is better for it to leave all action to God.

1180 June [July] 15, 1937. Once, I learned that I was to be transferred to another house. My knowledge of this was purely interior. At the same time, I heard a voice in my soul: **Do not be afraid, My daughter; it is My will that you should remain here. Human plans will be thwarted, since they must conform to My will.**

1181 When I was close to the Lord, He said to me, **Why are you afraid to begin the work which I have commanded you to carry out?** I answered, "Why do You leave me on my own at such times, Jesus, and why do I not feel Your presence?" **My daughter, even though you do not perceive Me in the most secret depths of your heart, you still cannot say that I am not there. I only remove from you the awareness of My presence, and that should not be an obstacle to the carrying out of My will. I do this to achieve My unfathomable ends, which you will know of later on.**

My daughter, know without doubt, and once and for all, that only mortal sin drives Me out of a soul, and nothing else.

1182   **(50)** + Today the Lord said to me, **My daughter, My pleasure and delight, nothing will stop Me from granting you graces. Your misery does not hinder My mercy. My daughter, write that the greater the misery of a soul, the greater its right to My mercy; [urge] all souls to trust in the unfathomable abyss of My mercy, because I want to save them all. On the cross, the fountain of My mercy was opened wide by the lance for all souls—no one have I excluded!**

1183   O Jesus, I want to live in the present moment, to live as if this were the last day of my life. I want to use every moment scrupulously for the greater glory of God, to use every circumstance for the benefit of my soul. I want to look upon everything, from the point of view that nothing happens without the will of God.

God of unfathomable mercy, embrace the whole world and pour Yourself out upon us through the merciful Heart of Jesus.

1184   On an earlier occasion.

In the evening, I saw the Lord Jesus upon the cross. From His hands, feet and side, the Most Sacred Blood was flowing. After some time, Jesus said to me, **All this is for the salvation of souls. Consider well, My daughter, what you are doing for their salvation.** I answered, "Jesus, when I look at Your suffering, I see that I am doing next to nothing for the salvation of souls." And the Lord said to me, **Know, My daughter, that your silent day-to-day martyrdom in complete submission to My will ushers many souls into heaven. And when it seems to you that your suffering exceeds your strength, contemplate My wounds, (51) and you will rise above human scorn and judgment. Meditation on My Passion will help you rise above all things.** I understood many things I had been unable to comprehend before.

1185 July 9, 1937. This evening, one of the deceased sisters came and asked me for one day of fasting and to offer all my [spiritual] exercises on that day for her. I answered that I would.

1186 From early morning on the following day, I offered everything for her intention. During Holy Mass, I had a brief experience of her torment. I experienced such intense hunger for God that I seemed to be dying of the desire to become united with Him. This lasted only a short time, but I understood what the longing of the souls in purgatory was like.

1187 Immediately after Holy Mass, I asked Mother Superior's permission to fast, but I did not receive it because of my illness. When I entered the chapel, I heard these words: "If you had fasted, Sister, I would not have gotten relief until the evening, but for the sake of your obedience, which prevented you from fasting, I obtained this relief at once. Obedience has great power." After these words I heard: "May God reward you."

1188 I often pray for Poland, but I see that God is very angry with it because of its ingratitude.[201] I exert all the strength of my soul to defend it. I constantly remind God of the promises of His mercy. When I see His anger, I throw myself trustingly into the abyss of His mercy, and I plunge all Poland in it, and then He cannot use His justice. My country, how much you cost me! There is no day in which I do not pray for you.

1189 **(52)** (A sentence from Saint Vincent de Paul: "The Lord always sets His hand to a task when He removes all human means and orders us to do a thing that exceeds our strength.")

1190 + Jesus. —**From all My wounds, like from streams, mercy flows for souls, but the wound in My Heart is the fountain of unfathomable mercy. From this fountain spring all graces for souls. The flames of compassion burn Me. I desire greatly to pour them out upon souls. Speak to the whole world about My mercy.**

1191 As long as we live, the love of God grows in us. Until we die, we ought to strive for the love of God. I have learned and experienced that souls living in love are distinguished in this: that they are greatly enlightened concerning the things of God, both in their own souls and in the souls of others. And simple souls, without an education, are outstanding for their knowledge.

1192 At the fourteenth station. I get the strange feeling that Jesus is going into the ground.

When my soul is in anguish, I think only in this way: Jesus is good and full of mercy, and even if the ground were to give way under my feet, I would not cease to trust in Him.

1193 Today, I have heard these words: **My daughter, delight of My Heart, it is with pleasure that I look into your soul. I bestow many graces only because of you. I also withhold My punishments only because of you. You restrain Me, and I cannot vindicate the claims of My justice. You bind My hands with your love.**

1194 **(53)** July 13, 1937. Today, Jesus has given me light as to how I should behave toward one of the sisters, who had asked me about many spiritual matters concerning which she had doubts. But basically this was not the question; she only wanted to find out my opinion in these matters in order to have something to say about me to the other sisters. Oh, if at least she had repeated the same words that I had spoken to her without distortions and additions! Jesus put me on my guard in respect to her. I resolved to pray for her, because only prayer can enlighten that soul.

1195   O my Jesus, nothing can lower my ideals; that is, the love which I have for You. Although the path is very thorny, I do not fear to go ahead. Even if a hailstorm of persecutions covers me; even if my friends forsake me, even if all things conspire against me, and the horizon grows dark; even if a raging storm breaks out, and I feel I am quite alone and must brave it all; still, fully at peace, I will trust in Your mercy, O my God, and my hope will not be disappointed.

1196   Today, when a certain sister who was on duty approached me in the refectory [the sisters' dining room, where assigned sisters serve at the time of common meals], I experienced severe suffering in the places of the Wounds. I was given to know the state of her soul. I prayed much for her.

1197   Sudden calming of a storm. There was a terrible storm last night. I bowed my face low to the ground and started to say the Litany of the Saints. Towards the end of the Litany, such drowsiness came over me that I could in no way finish the prayer. Then I got up and said to the Lord, "Jesus, (54)calm the storm, for Your child is unable to pray any longer, and I am heavy with sleep." After these words, I threw the window wide open, not even securing it with hooks. Sister N. [probably Sister Fabiola Pawluk] then said to me, "Sister, what are you doing! The wind will surely tear the window loose!" I told her to sleep in peace, and at once the storm completely subsided. The next day, the sisters talked about the sudden calming of the storm, not knowing what this meant. I said nothing, but I merely thought within myself: Jesus and little Faustina know what it means...

1198 The 20th [of July, 1937]. I learned today that I am to go to Rabka.²⁰² I was not to leave until August 5, but I asked Mother Superior [Irene] to let me go at once. I have not seen Father Andrasz at all, and I asked her to let me leave as soon as possible. Mother Superior was a little surprised that I wanted to leave so soon, but I did not explain the reason for my wanting to do so. That will remain a secret forever. In these circumstances, I have made one resolution which I am going to keep.

1199 [July] 29. I am to leave for Rabka today. I went into the chapel and asked the Lord Jesus for a safe journey. But within my soul there was silence and darkness. I felt I was all alone and had no one [to turn to]. I asked Jesus to be with me. Then I felt a tiny ray of light in my soul as a sign that Jesus was with me but, after this grace, the darkness and shadows in my soul increased. Then I said, "Your will be done, for everything is possible to You." When I was on the train and gazed through the window at the beautiful countryside and the mountains, the torments of my soul grew even greater. As the sisters welcomed me and began to surround me with their warmth, my sufferings redoubled.

1200 I would have like to hide and rest for a while in solitude, in a word, **(55)** to be alone. At such moments, no creature is capable of giving me comfort, and even if I had wanted to say something about myself, I would have experienced new anguish. Therefore, I have kept silent at such moments and submitted myself, in silence, to the will of God—and that has given me relief. I demand nothing from creatures and communicate with them only in so far as is necessary. I will not take them into my confidence unless this is for the greater glory of God. My communing is with the angels [cf. Mt. 18:10; Ex. 23:20].

1201 I feel so unwell here, however, that I am obliged to stay in bed. I feel strange sharp pains all through my chest; I cannot even move my hand. One night, I had to lie quite motionless, as it seemed to me that if I budged, everything in my lungs would tear. The night was endless. I united myself to Jesus Crucified, and I implored the heavenly Father on behalf of sinners. It is said that maladies of the lungs do not cause such sharp pains, but I suffer these sharp pains constantly. My health has deteriorated so much here that I must remain in bed, and Sister N. [probably Sister Helen[203]] says I will not improve, because the climate of Rabka is not good for every sick person.

1202 I could not even go to Holy Mass or receive Holy Communion today but, amidst the sufferings of body and soul, I kept on repeating, "May the Lord's will be done. I know that Your bounty is without limit." Then I heard an angel who sang out my whole life history and everything it comprised. I was surprised, but also strengthened.

1203 Saint Joseph urged me to have a constant devotion to him. He himself told me to recite three prayers [the Our Father, Hail Mary, and Glory be] and the *Memorare*[204] once every day. He looked at me with great kindness and gave me to know how much he is supporting this work [of mercy]. He has promised me this special help and protection. I recite the requested prayers every day and feel his special protection.

(56) August 1, 1937. One-day retreat.

1204 A retreat of suffering. O Jesus, in these days of suffering, I am not capable of any kind of prayer. The oppression of my body and soul has increased. O my Jesus, You do see that Your child is on the decline. I am not forcing myself further, but simply submitting my will to the will of Jesus. O Jesus, You are always Jesus to me.

1205 When I went to confession, I did not even know how to confess. However, the priest [probably Father Casimir Ratkiewicz[205]] recognized the condition of my soul at once and said to me, "Despite everything, you are on the way to salvation; you are on the right path, but God may leave your soul in this darkness and obscurity until death, and the former light may never return. But in all things abandon yourself to the will of God."

1206   Today, I started a novena to Our Lady of the Assumption for three intentions: first, that I may see the Reverend Dr. Sopocko; second, that God would hasten this work; and third, for the intention of my country.

1207   August 10. Today I am returning to Cracow, in the company of one of the sisters. My soul is shrouded in suffering. I am continually uniting myself to Him by an act of the will. He is my power and strength.

1208   May You be blessed, O God, for everything You send me. Nothing under the sun happens without Your will. I cannot penetrate Your secrets with regard to myself, but I press my lips to the chalice You offer me.

1209   **(57)** Jesus, I trust in You.

Novena to The Divine Mercy[206]

which Jesus instructed me to write down and make before the Feast of Mercy. It begins on Good Friday.

I desire that during these nine days you bring souls to the fount of My mercy, that they may draw therefrom strength and refreshment and whatever graces they need in the hardships of life and, especially, at the hour of death.

On each day you will bring to My Heart a different group of souls, and you will immerse them in this ocean of My mercy, and I will bring all these souls into the house of My Father. You will do this in this life and in the next. I will deny nothing to any soul whom you will bring to the fount of My mercy. On each day you will beg My Father, on the strength of My bitter Passion, for graces for these souls.

I answered, "Jesus, I do not know how to make this novena or which souls to bring first into Your Most Compassionate Heart." Jesus replied that He would tell me which souls to bring each day into His Heart.

First Day

1210 Today, bring to Me all mankind, especially all sinners, and immerse them in the ocean of My mercy. In this way you will console Me in the bitter grief into which the loss of souls plunges Me.

1211 Most Merciful Jesus, whose very nature it is to have compassion on us and to forgive us, do not look upon our sins, but upon the trust which **(58)** we place in Your infinite goodness. Receive us all into the abode of Your Most Compassionate Heart, and never let us escape from It. We beg this of You by Your love which unites You to the Father and the Holy Spirit.

> Oh omnipotence of Divine Mercy,
> Salvation of sinful people,
> You are a sea of mercy and compassion;
> You aid those who entreat You with humility.

Eternal Father, turn Your merciful gaze upon all mankind and especially upon poor sinners, all enfolded in the Most Compassionate Heart of Jesus. For the sake of His sorrowful Passion, show us Your mercy, that we may praise the omnipotence of Your mercy forever and ever. Amen.

Second Day

1212 Today bring to Me the souls of priests and religious, and immerse them in My unfathomable mercy. It was they who gave Me the strength to endure My bitter Passion. Through them, as through channels, My mercy flows out upon mankind.

1213 Most Merciful Jesus, from whom comes all that is good, increase Your grace in us, that we may perform worthy works of mercy, and that all who see us may glorify the

Father of Mercy who is in heaven.

> The fountain of God's love
> Dwells in pure hearts,
> Bathed in the Sea of Mercy,
> Radiant as stars, bright as the dawn.

Eternal Father, turn Your merciful gaze **(59)** upon the company [of chosen ones] in Your vineyard—upon the souls of priests and religious; and endow them with the strength of Your blessing. For the love of the Heart of Your Son, in which they are enfolded, impart to them Your power and light, that they may be able to guide others in the way of salvation, and with one voice sing praise to Your boundless mercy for ages without end. Amen.

Third Day

1214 **Today bring to Me all devout and faithful souls, and immerse them in the ocean of My mercy. These souls brought Me consolation on the Way of the Cross. They were that drop of consolation in the midst of an ocean of bitterness.**

1215 Most Merciful Jesus, from the treasury of Your mercy, You impart Your graces in great abundance to each and all. Receive us into the abode of Your Most Compassionate Heart and never let us escape from It. We beg this of You by that most wondrous love for the heavenly Father with which Your Heart burns so fiercely.

> The miracles of mercy are impenetrable.
> Neither the sinner nor just one will fathom them.
> When You cast upon us an eye of pity,
> You draw us all closer to Your love.

Eternal Father, turn Your merciful gaze upon faithful souls, as upon the inheritance of Your Son. For the sake of His sorrowful Passion, grant them Your blessing and surround them with Your constant protection. Thus may they never fail in love or lose the treasure of the holy faith, but rather, with all the hosts of Angels and Saints, may they glorify Your boundless mercy for endless ages. Amen.

(60) Fourth Day

1216 **Today bring to Me the pagans and those who do not yet know me. I was thinking also of them during My bitter Passion, and their future zeal comforted My Heart. Immerse them in the ocean of My mercy.**

1217 Most Compassionate Jesus, You are the Light of the whole world. Receive into the abode of Your Most Compassionate Heart the souls of pagans who as yet do not know You. Let the rays of Your grace enlighten them that they, too, together with us, may extol Your wonderful mercy; and do not let them escape from the abode which is Your Most Compassionate Heart.

> May the light of Your love
> Enlighten the souls in darkness;
> Grant that these souls will know You
> And, together with us, praise Your mercy.

Eternal Father, turn Your merciful gaze upon the souls of pagans and of those who as yet do not know You, but who are enclosed in the Most Compassionate Heart of Jesus. Draw them to the light of the Gospel. These souls do not know what great happiness it is to love You. Grant that they, too, may extol the generosity of Your mercy for endless ages. Amen.

Fifth Day

1218 **Today bring to Me the souls of heretics and schismatics, and immerse them in the ocean of My mercy. During My bitter Passion they tore at My Body and Heart; that is, My Church. As they return to unity with the Church, My wounds heal, and in this way they alleviate My Passion.**

1219 Most Merciful Jesus, Goodness Itself, You do not refuse light to those who seek it of You. Receive into the abode of Your Most Compassionate Heart the souls of heretics and schismatics. Draw them by Your light into the unity of the Church, and do not let them escape from the abode of Your Most Compassionate Heart; but bring it about that they, too, come to adore the generosity of Your mercy.

> **(61)** Even for those who have torn the garment of Your unity,
>
> A fount of mercy flows from Your Heart.
> The omnipotence of Your mercy, Oh God.
> Can lead these souls also out of error.

Eternal Father, turn Your merciful gaze upon the souls of heretics and schismatics, who have squandered Your blessings and misused Your graces by obstinately persisting in their errors. Do not look upon their errors, but upon the love of Your own Son and upon His bitter Passion, which He underwent for their sake, since they, too, are enclosed in the Most Compassionate Heart of Jesus. Bring it about that they also may glorify Your great mercy for endless ages. Amen.

Sixth Day

1220 **Today bring to Me the meek and humble souls and the souls of little children, and immerse them in My mercy. These souls most closely resemble My Heart. They strengthened Me during My bitter agony. I saw them as earthly Angels, who would keep vigil at My altars. I pour out upon them whole torrents of grace. Only the humble soul is able to receive My grace. I favor humble souls with My confidence.**

1221 **(62)** Most Merciful Jesus, You Yourself have said, "Learn from Me for I am meek and humble of heart." Receive into the abode of Your Most Compassionate Heart all meek and humble souls and the souls of little children. These souls send all heaven into ecstasy, and they are the heavenly Father's favorites. They are a sweet-smelling bouquet before the throne of God; God himself takes delight in their fragrance. These souls have a permanent abode in Your Most Compassionate Heart, O Jesus, and they unceasingly sing out a hymn of love and mercy.

1222   A truly gentle and humble soul
        Already here on earth the air of paradise breathes,
        And in the fragrance of her humble heart
        The Creator Himself delights.

1223 Eternal Father, turn Your merciful gaze upon meek and humble souls, and upon the souls of little children, who are enfolded in the abode which is the Most Compassionate Heart of Jesus. These souls bear the closest resemblance to Your Son. Their fragrance rises from the earth and reaches Your very throne. Father of mercy and of all goodness, I beg You by the love You bear these souls and by the delight You take in them: bless the whole world, that all souls together may sing out the praises of Your mercy for endless ages. Amen.

Seventh Day

1224 **Today bring to Me the souls who especially venerate and glorify My mercy, and immerse them in My mercy. These souls sorrowed most over My Passion and entered most deeply into My Spirit. They are living images of My Compassionate Heart. These souls will shine with a special brightness in the next life. Not one of them will go into the fire of hell. I shall particularly defend each one of them at the hour of death.**

1225 (63) Most Merciful Jesus, whose Heart is Love Itself, receive into the abode of Your Most Compassionate Heart the souls of those who particularly extol and venerate the greatness of Your mercy. These souls are mighty with the very power of God Himself. In the midst of all afflictions and adversities they go forward, confident of Your mercy. These souls are united to Jesus and carry all mankind on their shoulders. These souls will not be judged severely, but Your mercy will embrace them as they depart from this life.

A soul who praises the goodness of her Lord
Is especially loved by Him.
She is always close to the living fountain
And draws graces from Mercy Divine.

Eternal Father, turn Your merciful gaze upon the souls who glorify and venerate Your greatest attribute, that of Your fathomless mercy, and who are enclosed in the Most Compassionate Heart of Jesus. These souls are a living Gospel; their hands are full of deeds of mercy, and their spirit, overflowing with joy, sings a canticle of mercy to You, O Most High! I beg You O God: Show them Your mercy according to the hope and trust they have placed in You. Let there be accomplished in them the promise of Jesus, who said to them, **I Myself will defend as My own glory, during their lifetime, and especially at the hour of their death, those souls who will venerate My fathomless mercy.**

Eighth Day

1226 **Today bring to Me the souls who are in the prison of Purgatory, and immerse them in the abyss of My mercy. Let the torrents of My Blood cool down their scorching flames. All these souls are greatly loved by Me. They are making retribution to My justice. It is in your power to bring them relief. Draw all the indulgences from the treasury (64) of My Church and offer them on their behalf. Oh, if you only knew the torments they suffer, you would continually offer for them the alms of the spirit and pay off their debt to My justice.**

1227 Most Merciful Jesus, You Yourself have said that You desire mercy; so I bring into the abode of Your Most Compassionate Heart the souls in Purgatory, souls who are very dear to You, and yet, who must make retribution to Your justice. May the streams of Blood and Water which gushed forth from Your Heart put out the flames of the purifying fire, that in that place, too, the power of Your mercy may be praised.

> From the terrible heat of the cleansing fire
> Rises a plaint to Your mercy,
> And they receive comfort, refreshment, relief
> In the stream of mingled Blood and Water.

Eternal Father, turn Your merciful gaze upon the souls suffering in Purgatory, who are enfolded in the Most Compassionate Heart of Jesus. I beg You, by the sorrowful Passion of Jesus Your Son, and by all the bitterness with which His most sacred Soul was flooded, manifest Your mercy to the souls who are under Your just scrutiny. Look upon them in no other way than through the Wounds of Jesus, Your dearly beloved Son; for we firmly believe that there is no limit to Your goodness and compassion.

Ninth Day

1228 **Today bring to Me souls who have become lukewarm, and immerse them in the abyss of My mercy. These souls wound My Heart most painfully. My soul suffered the most dreadful loathing in the Garden of Olives because of lukewarm souls. They were the reason I cried out: "Father, take this cup away from Me, if it be Your will." For them, the last hope (65) of salvation is to flee to My mercy.**

1229 Most Compassionate Jesus, You are Compassion Itself. I bring lukewarm souls into the abode of Your Most Compassionate Heart. In this fire of Your pure love let these tepid souls, who, like corpses, filled You with such deep loathing, be once again set aflame. O Most Compassionate Jesus, exercise the omnipotence of Your mercy and draw them into the very ardor of Your love; and bestow upon them the gift of holy love, for nothing is beyond Your power.

Fire and ice cannot be joined;
Either the fire dies, or the ice melts.
But by Your mercy, O God,
You can make up for all that is lacking.

Eternal Father, turn Your merciful gaze upon lukewarm
souls, who are nonetheless enfolded in the Most
Compassionate Heart of Jesus. Father of Mercy, I beg
You by the bitter Passion of Your Son and by His
three-hour agony on the Cross: Let them, too, glorify
the abyss of Your mercy....

1230 **(66)** O day of eternity, O day so long desired,
With thirst and longing, my eyes search you out.
Soon love will tear the veil asunder,
And you will be my salvation.

O day most beautiful, moment incomparable,
When for the first time I shall see my God,
The Bridegroom of my soul and Lord of lords,
And fear will not restrain my soul.

O day most solemn, O day of brightness,
When the soul will know God in His omnipotence
And drown totally in His love,
Knowing the miseries of exile are o'er.

O happy day, O blessed day,
When my heart will burn for You with fire eternal,
For even now I feel Your presence, though through
the veil.
Through life and death, O Jesus, You are my rapture
and delight.

O day, of which I dreamed through all my life,
Waiting long for You, O God,
For it is You alone whom I desire.
You are the one and only of my heart; all else is naught.

O day of delight, day of eternal bliss,
God of great majesty, my beloved Spouse,
You know that nothing will satisfy a virgin heart.
On Your tender Heart I rest my brow.

[End of Notebook Three]

Notebook Four

of the Diary of Sister Faustina

Notebook IV

(1)+
J.M.J.

1231 Today Jesus came to live in my heart,
He descended from His throne on high,
The great Lord, the Creator of all things;
And He came to me in the form of bread.

O Eternal God, in my bosom enclosed,
Possessing You, I possess all Heaven,
And with the Angels I sing to You: Holy,
I live for Your glory alone.

Not with a Seraph, do You unite yourself, O God,
But with a wretched man
Who can do nothing without You;
But to him You are ever merciful.

My heart is Your abode,
O King of Eternal Glory;
Rule in my heart and be Lord,
As in a palace of splendor untold.

O great, incomprehensible God,
Who have deigned to abase Yourself so,
Humbly I adore You
And beg You in Your goodness to save me.

(2)+
J.M.J.

1232 O sweet Mother of God,
I model my life on You;
You are for me the bright dawn;
In You I lose myself, enraptured.

O Mother, Immaculate Virgin,
In You the divine ray is reflected,
Midst storms, 'tis You who teach me to love the Lord,
O my shield and defense from the foe.

Cracow, August 10, 1937.

1233   Sr. Mary Faustina
                                  of the Blessed Sacrament

O Sacred Host, fountain of divine sweetness,
You give strength to my soul;
O You are the Omnipotent One, who took flesh of the
    Virgin,
You come to my heart, in secret,
Beyond reach of the groping senses.

(3)+
J.M.J.
                                  Cracow, August 10, 1937
                                         Notebook Four

1234 All for You, Jesus. I desire to adore Your mercy with
     every beat of my heart and, to the extent that I am able,
     to encourage souls to trust in that mercy, as You
     yourself have commanded me, O Lord.

1235 In my heart, in my soul, there is a dark night. My spirit
     has come up against an impenetrable wall that hides
     God from me. But this darkness is not of my doing.
     Strange indeed is this torture of which I fear to write in
     full. But even in this state, I am trying to be faithful to
     You, O my Jesus. Always and in all things, my heart
     beats for You alone.

1236 **(4)** August 10, 1937. I came back today from Rabka to
     Cracow. I feel very ill. Only Jesus knows how much I am
     suffering. During these days, I have very much
     resembled Jesus Crucified. I have armed myself with
     patience in order to explain to each sister why I was not
     able to stay there; that is, because my health had become
     worse, even though I knew very well that certain sisters
     would inquire, not out of sympathy for my sufferings,
     but in order to add to them.

1237 O Jesus, what darkness is enveloping me and what
     nothingness is penetrating me. But, my Jesus, do not

leave me alone; grant me the grace of faithfulness. Although I cannot penetrate the mystery of God's visitation, it is in my power to say: Your will be done.

1238 August 12. On passing through Cracow, Rev. Father Sopocko paid me a short visit today. I had wanted to see him, and God fulfilled my desire. **(5)** This priest is a great soul, entirely filled with God. My joy was very great, and I thanked God for this great grace, because it was for the greater glory of God that I wanted to see him.

1239 O living Host, O hidden Jesus. You see the condition of my soul. Of myself, I am unable to utter Your Holy Name. I cannot bring forth from my heart the fire of love but, kneeling at Your feet, I cast upon the Tabernacle the gaze of my soul, a gaze of faithfulness. As for You, You are ever the same, while within my soul a change takes place. I trust that the time will come when You will unveil Your countenance, and Your child will again see Your sweet face. I am astonished, Jesus, that You can hide yourself from me for so long and that You can restrain the enormous love You have for me. In the dwelling of my heart, I am listening and waiting for Your coming, O only Treasure of my heart!

1240 **(6)**The Lord Jesus greatly protects His representatives on earth. How closely He is united with them; and He orders me to give priority to their opinion over His. I have come to know the great intimacy which exists between Jesus and the priest. Jesus defends whatever the priest says, and often complies with his wishes, and sometimes makes His own relationship with a soul depend on the priest's advice. O Jesus, through a special grace, I have come to know very clearly to what extent You have shared Your power and mystery with them, more so than with the Angels. I rejoice in this, for it is all for my good.

1241 + O my Jesus, when someone is unkind and unpleasant

toward us, it is difficult enough to bear this kind of suffering. But this is very little in comparison to a suffering which I cannot bear; namely, that which I experience when someone exhibits kindness towards me and then lays snares at my feet at every step **(7)** I take. What great will power is necessary to love such a soul for God's sake. Many a time one has to be heroic in loving such a soul as God demands. If contact with that person were infrequent, it would be easier to endure, but when one lives in close contact with the person and experiences this at each step, this demands a very great effort.

1242   My Jesus, penetrate me through and through so that I might be able to reflect You in my whole life. Divinize me so that my deeds may have supernatural value. Grant that I may have love, compassion and mercy for every soul without exception. O my Jesus, each of Your saints reflects one of Your virtues; I desire to reflect Your compassionate heart, full of mercy; I want to glorify it. Let Your mercy, O Jesus, be **(8)** impressed upon my heart and soul like a seal, and this will be my badge in this and the future life. Glorifying Your mercy is the exclusive task of my life.

August 15, 1937. Father Andrasz's instructions.

1243   "These times of dryness and stark awareness of one's wretchedness, which God has permitted, allow the soul to know how little it can do by itself. They will teach you how much you should appreciate God's graces. Secondly, faithfulness in all exercises and duties, faithfulness in everything, just as in times of joy. Thirdly, as regards the matters in question, be absolutely obedient to the Archbishop [Jalbrzykowski] although, from time to time, the matter can be brought to his attention, but peacefully. **(9)** Sometimes, a little bitter truth is necessary."

At the end of the conversation, I asked the priest to

allow me to commune with Jesus as I had done formerly. He answered, "I cannot give orders to the Lord Jesus, but if He himself draws you to himself you may follow the attraction. However, always remember to show Him great reverence, for the Lord is great indeed. If you are truly seeking God's will in all this and desire to fulfill it, you can be at peace; the Lord will not allow any sort of error. As to the mortifications and sufferings, you will give me an account next time of how you carry them out. Place yourself in the hands of the Most Holy Mother."

1244 August 15, 1937. During meditation, God's presence pervaded me keenly, and I was aware of the Virgin Mary's joy at the moment of Her Assumption. Towards the end of the ceremony **(10)** carried out in honor of the Mother of God, I saw the Virgin Mary, and She said to me, *Oh, how very pleased I am with the homage of your love!* And at that moment She covered all the sisters of our Congregation with Her mantle. With Her right hand, She clasped Mother General Michael to herself, and with Her left hand She did so to me, while all the sisters were at Her feet, covered with Her mantle. Then the Mother of God said, *Everyone who perseveres zealously till death in My Congregation will be spared the fire of purgatory, and I desire that each one distinguish herself by the following virtues: humility and meekness; chastity and love of God and neighbor; compassion and mercy.* After these words, the whole Congregation disappeared from my sight, and I remained alone with the Most Holy Mother who instructed me about the will of God and how to **(11)** apply it to my life, submitting completely to His most holy decrees. It is impossible for one to please God without obeying His holy will. *My daughter, I strongly recommend that you faithfully fulfill all God's wishes, for that is most pleasing in His holy eyes. I very much desire that you distinguish yourself in this faithfulness in* *accomplishing God's will. Put the will of God before all sacrifices and holocausts.* While the heavenly Mother was talking to me, a deep understanding of this will of God was entering my soul.

1245 My Jesus, delight of my heart, when my soul is filled with Your divinity, I accept sweetness and bitterness with the same equanimity. One and the other will pass away. All that I keep in my soul is the love of God. For this I strive; all else is secondary.

1246 **(12)** 16 [August 1937]. After Holy Communion, I saw the Lord Jesus in all His majesty, and He said to me, **My daughter, during the weeks when you neither saw Me nor felt My presence, I was more profoundly united to you than at times** [when you experienced] **ecstasy. And the faithfulness and fragrance of your prayer have reached Me.** After these words, my soul became flooded with God's consolation. I did not see Jesus, and there was only one word I could utter and that was: "Jesus." And after pronouncing that Name, my soul was again filled with light and deeper recollection, which lasted uninterruptedly for three days. However, outwardly I could still carry out my usual duties.

My whole being was stirred to its most secret depths. God's greatness does not frighten me, but makes me happy. By giving Him glory, I myself am lifted up. On seeing His happiness, I myself am made happy, because **(13)** all that is in Him flows back upon me.

1247 I came to know of the condition of a certain soul and of what in that soul is displeasing to God. I learn it in the following way: I immediately feel pain in my hands, my feet and my side, in those places where the hands, feet and side of the Savior were pierced. At that same time, I receive knowledge of the soul's condition and of the nature of the sin committed.

1248 I experience a desire to make reparation to the Lord

Jesus in a way which corresponds [to the offense].
Today I wore a chain belt for seven hours in order to
obtain the grace of repentance for that soul. In the
seventh hour I felt relief as the soul experienced
interiorly the remission of its sin, although it had not yet
gone to confession. For sins of the flesh, I mortify the
body and fast to the degree that I am permitted. For sins
of pride, **(14)** I pray with my forehead touching the
floor. For sins of hatred, I pray and do some good deed
for a person whom I find difficult. And thus I make
amends according to the nature of the sin of which I am
aware.

1249   19 [August 1937]. Today during adoration, the Lord
gave me to know how much He desires a soul to
distinguish itself by deeds of love. And in spirit I saw
how many souls are calling out to us, "Give us God."
And the blood of the Apostles boiled up within me. I
will not be stingy with it; I will shed it all to the last drop
for immortal souls. Although perhaps God will not
demand that in the physical sense, in spirit it is possible
and no less meritorious.

1250   Today I realized that I was not to ask for a certain
permission, but that I was to respond to this matter as
the Mother of God would have me do. For the present,
no explanations are **(15)** necessary; peace has returned
to me. I received this inspiration just as I was on my way
to make my examination of conscience, and I was very
worried because I did not know how to go about it.
Divine light can do more in one moment than I,
fatiguing myself for several days.

1251   August 22. This morning Saint Barbara, Virgin, visited
me and recommended that I offer Holy Communion for
nine days on behalf of my country and thus appease
God's anger. This virgin was wearing a crown made of
stars and was holding a sword in her hand. The
brilliance of the crown was the same as that of the

sword. With her white dress and her flowing hair, she was so beautiful that if I had not already known the Virgin Mary I would have thought that it was She. Now I understand that each virgin has a special beauty all her own; a distinct beauty radiates from each of them.

1252 **(16)** + August 25, 1937. Today Reverend Father Sopocko arrived and will stay with us until the 30th. I was extremely glad, because only God knows how ardently I wished to see him for the sake of the Work God is doing through him, and this, even though the visit had some unpleasant aspects to it as well.

1253 + While he was celebrating Mass, I saw during the elevation the Crucified Lord Jesus, who was disengaging His right arm from the cross, and the light which was coming from the Wound was touching his arm. This happened in the course of three Masses, and I understood that God would give him strength to carry out this work despite difficulties and opposition. This soul, who is pleasing to God, is being crucified by numerous sufferings, but I am not at all surprised, for this is how God treats those He especially loves.

1254 **(17)** + Today, the 29th, I received permission[207] to have a longer conversation with Rev. Dr. Sopocko. I learned that, although there are difficulties, the work is moving ahead, and that the Feast of Mercy is already far advanced. It will not be long now before it becomes a reality, but much prayer is still needed to bring an end to certain difficulties.

1255 "As concerns yourself, Sister, it is good that you are remaining in a state of holy indifference in everything that pertains to the will of God, and that you are better maintaining a state of equilibrium. Please do your best to keep this equanimity. Now, as regards all these matters, you are to depend exclusively on Father Andrasz; I am in complete agreement with him. Do nothing on your own, Sister, but in all matters take counsel from your spiritual director. I beg you to keep your levelheadedness and as great a calm as possible.— One more thing—I am having printed **(18)** the chaplet which is to be on the back of the image, as well as the invocations that resemble a litany; these too will be placed on the back. Another large image has also been printed, and with it a few pages which contain the Novena to The Divine Mercy.[208] Pray, Sister, that this be approved."

1256 [August] 30. Reverend Father Sopocko left this morning. When I was steeped in a prayer of thanksgiving for the great grace that I had received from God; namely, that of seeing Father, I became united in a special way with the Lord who said to me, **He is a priest after My own Heart; his efforts are pleasing to Me. You see, My daughter, that My will must be done and that which I had promised you, I shall do. Through him I spread comfort to suffering and careworn souls. Through him it pleased Me to proclaim the worship of My mercy. (19) And through this work of mercy more souls will come close to Me than otherwise would have, even if he had kept giving absolution day and night for the rest of his life, because by so doing, he would have labored only for as long as he lived; whereas, thanks to this work of mercy, he will be laboring till the end of the world.**

1257 I had undertaken to make a novena for the intention of seeing him, but I did not even finish it before God granted me that grace.

1258 O my Jesus, how poorly I took advantage of this grace, but that did not depend on me, though from another point of view, it did so very much.

1259 + During this conversation, I came to know his anguished soul. This crucified soul resembles the Savior. Where he expects, with good reason, to find consolation, he finds the cross. He lives among many friends, but has no one but Jesus. This is how God strips the soul He especially loves.

1260 **(20)** Today I heard these words: **My daughter, be always like a little child towards those who represent Me, otherwise you will not benefit from the graces I bestow on you through them.**

1261 September 1, 1937. I saw the Lord Jesus, like a king in great majesty, looking down upon our earth with great severity; but because of His Mother's intercession He prolonged the time of His mercy.

1262 September 3. First Friday of the month. During Holy Mass, I became united with God. Jesus gave me to know that even the smallest thing does not happen on earth without His will. After having seen this, my soul entered into an unusual repose; I found myself completely at peace as to the work in its full extent. God can deal with me as He pleases, and I will bless Him for everything.

1263 **(21)** Up to now, I have been wondering, with some fear, where these inspirations would lead me. My fear increased when the Lord made known to me that I was to leave this Congregation. This is the third year passing by since that time, and my soul has felt, in turns, enthusiasm and an urge to act—and then I have a lot of courage and strength—and then again, when the decisive moment to undertake the work draws near, I feel deserted by God, and because of this an extraordinary fear pervades my soul, and I see that it is not the hour intended by God to initiate the work. These are sufferings about which I don't even know how to write. God alone knows what I put up with, day and night. It seems to me that the worst torments of the martyrs would be easier for me to bear than what I am going through, though without the shedding of a drop of blood. But all this is for souls, for souls, Lord....

1264 **(22)** Act of total abandonment to the will of God, which is for me, love and mercy itself.

Act of Oblation

Jesus-Host, whom I have this very moment received into my heart, through this union with You I offer myself to the heavenly Father as a sacrificial host, abandoning myself totally and completely to the most merciful and holy will of my God. From today onward, Your will, Lord, is my food. Take my whole being; dispose of me as You please. Whatever Your fatherly hand gives me, I will accept with submission, peace and joy. I fear nothing, no matter in what direction You lead me; helped by Your grace I will carry out everything You demand of me. I no longer fear any of Your inspirations nor **(23)** do I probe anxiously to see where they will lead me. Lead me, O God, along whatever roads You please; I have placed all my trust in Your will which is, for me, love and mercy itself.

Bid me to stay in this convent, I will stay; bid me to undertake the work, I will undertake it; leave me in uncertainty about the work until I die, be blessed; give me death when, humanly speaking, my life seems particularly necessary, be blessed. Should You take me in my youth, be blessed; should You let me live to a ripe old age, be blessed. Should You give me health and strength, be blessed; should You confine me to a bed of pain for my whole life, be blessed. Should you give only failures and disappointments in life, be blessed. Should You allow my purest intentions to be condemned, be blessed. Should You enlighten my mind, be blessed. Should You leave me in darkness and all kinds of **(24)** torments, be blessed.

From this moment on, I live in the deepest peace, because the Lord himself is carrying me in the hollow of His hand. He, Lord of unfathomable mercy, knows that I desire Him alone in all things, always and everywhere.

1265 Prayer. O Jesus, stretched out upon the cross, I implore You, give me the grace of doing faithfully the most holy will of Your Father, in all things, always and everywhere. And when this will of God will seem to me very harsh and difficult to fulfill, it is then I beg You, Jesus, may power and strength flow upon me from Your wounds, and may my lips keep repeating, "Your will be done, O Lord." O Savior of the world, Lover of man's salvation, who in such terrible torment and pain forget Yourself to think only of the salvation of souls, O most compassionate Jesus, grant me the grace to forget myself that I may live totally for souls, helping You in the work of salvation, according to the most holy will of Your Father....

1266 **(25)** August 5, [1937].[209] The Lord let me know how much our dear Mother Superior [Irene] is defending me against... not only by prayer but also by deed. Thank You, Jesus, for this grace. It will not go unrequited in my heart; when I am with Jesus, I do not forget about her.

1267 September 6, 1937. Today, I begin a new assignment. I go from the garden to the desert of the gate.[210] I went in to talk to the Lord for a while. I asked Him for a blessing and for graces to faithfully carry out the duties entrusted to me. I heard these words: **My daughter, I am always with you. I have given you the opportunity to practice deeds of mercy which you will perform according to obedience. You will give Me much pleasure if, each evening, you will speak to Me especially about this task.** I felt that Jesus had given me a new grace in relation to my new duties; but, despite this, I have locked myself deeper in His Heart.

1268 **(26)** Today I felt more ill, but Jesus has given me many more opportunities on this day to practice virtue. It so happened that I was busier than usual, and the sister in charge of the kitchen made it clear to me how irritated she was that I had come late for dinner, although it was quite impossible for me to have come sooner. At any rate, I felt so unwell that I had to ask Mother Superior to allow me to lie down. I went to ask Sister N. to take my place, and again I got a scolding: "What is this, Sister, you're so exhausted that you're going back to bed again! Confound you with all this lying in bed!" I put up with all that, but that wasn't the end. I still had to ask the sister who was in charge of the sick to bring me my meal. When I told her this, she burst out of the chapel into the corridor after me to give me a piece of her mind: "Why on earth are you going to bed, Sister, etc...." I asked her not to bother bringing me anything. (27) I am writing all this very briefly because it is not my intention to write about such things, and I am doing so merely to dissuade souls from treating others in this way, for this is displeasing to the Lord. In a suffering soul we should see Jesus Crucified, and not a loafer or burden on the community. A soul who suffers with submission to the will of God draws down more blessings on the whole convent than all the working sisters. Poor indeed is a convent where there are no sick sisters. God often grants many and great graces out of regard for the souls who are suffering, and He withholds many punishments solely because of the suffering souls.

1269 O my Jesus, when shall we look upon souls with higher motives in mind? When will our judgments be true? You give us occasions to practice deeds of mercy, and instead we use the occasions to pass judgment. In order to know whether the love of God flourishes in a convent, one must ask how they treat the sick, the disabled, and the infirm who are there.

1270 (28) September 10, [1937]. I learned in the course of meditation that the purer the soul, the greater her communion with God on the spiritual level. She pays little heed to the senses and their protests. God is a Spirit, and so I love Him in spirit and in truth.

1271 When I heard how dangerous it was to be at the gate

these days because of revolutionary disturbances and how many evil people have a hatred for convents, I went in and had a talk with the Lord and asked Him to so arrange it that no evil person would dare come to the gate. Then I heard these words: **My daughter, the moment you went to the gate I set a Cherub over it to guard it. Be at peace.** After returning from my conversation with the Lord, I saw a little white cloud and, in it, a Cherub with his hands joined. His gaze was like lightning, and I understood how the fire of God's love burns in that look....

1272 **(29)** September 14, 1937. Exaltation of the Holy Cross. Today I saw what great opposition this priest [Father Sopocko] is experiencing in regard to this whole matter. Even devout souls who are zealous for God's glory are opposing him. That he is not discouraged by all this is due to a special grace of God.

1273 Jesus: **My daughter, do you think you have written enough about My mercy? What you have written is but a drop compared to the ocean. I am Love and Mercy itself. There is no misery that could be a match for My mercy, neither will misery exhaust it, because as it is being granted—it increases. The soul that trusts in My mercy is most fortunate, because I myself take care of it.**

1274 I experience great torments of soul when I see God offended. Today I recognized that mortal sins were being committed not far from our door. It was evening. I prayed earnestly in the chapel, **(30)** and then I went to scourge myself. When I knelt down to pray, however, the Lord allowed me to experience how a soul rejected by God suffers. It seems to me that my heart was torn to pieces, and at the same time I understood how much such a soul wounds the most merciful Heart of Jesus. The poor creature does not want to accept God's mercy. The more God has pursued a soul with His mercy, the more just will He be towards it.

1275 **My Secretary, write that I am more generous toward sinners than toward the just. It was for their sake that I came down from heaven; it was for their sake that My Blood was spilled. Let them not fear to approach Me; they are most in need of My mercy.**

1276 September 16, 1937. I wanted very much to make a Holy Hour before the Blessed Sacrament today, but God's will was otherwise. At eight o'clock I was seized with such violent pains that **(31)** I had to go to bed at once. I was convulsed with pain for three hours; that is, until eleven o'clock at night. No medicine had any effect on me, and whatever I swallowed I threw up. At times, the pains caused me to lose consciousness. Jesus had me realize that in this way I took part in His Agony in the Garden, and that He himself allowed these sufferings in order to offer reparation to God for the souls murdered in the wombs of wicked mothers. I have gone through these sufferings three times now. They always start at eight o'clock in the evening and last until eleven. No medicine can lessen these sufferings. When eleven o'clock comes, they cease by themselves, and I fall asleep at that moment. The following day, I feel very weak.

This happened to me for the first time when I was at the sanatorium. The doctors couldn't get to the bottom of it, and no injection or medicine helped me at all **(32)** nor did I myself have any idea of what the sufferings were about. I told the doctor that never before in my life had I experienced such sufferings, and he declared he did not know what sort of pains they are. But now I understand the nature of these pains, because the Lord himself has made this known to me.... Yet when I think that I may perhaps suffer in this way again, I tremble. But I don't know whether I'll ever again suffer in this way; I leave that to God. What it pleases God to send, I will accept with submission and love. If only I could save even one soul from murder by means of these sufferings!

1277 On the day after these sufferings, I can sense the condition of souls and their disposition towards God; I am pervaded with true knowledge.

1278 I receive Holy Communion in the manner of the angels, so to speak. My soul is filled with God's light and nourishes itself from Him. (33) My feelings are as if dead. This is a purely spiritual union with God; it is a great predominance of spirit over nature.

1279 The Lord gave me knowledge of the graces which He has been constantly lavishing on me. This light pierced me through and through, and I came to understand the inconceivable favors that God has been bestowing on me. I stayed in my cell for a long act of thanksgiving, lying face down on the ground and shedding tears of gratitude. I could not rise from the ground because, whenever I tried to do so, God's light gave me new knowledge of His grace. It was only at the third attempt that I was able to get up. As His child, I felt that everything the heavenly Father possessed was equally mine. He himself lifted me from the ground up to His Heart. I felt that everything that existed was exclusively mine, but I had no desire for it all, because God alone is enough for me.

1280 (34) Today I learned with what aversion the Lord comes to a certain soul in Holy Communion. He goes to that heart as to a dark prison, to undergo torture and affliction. I kept begging His pardon and offering atonement for the offense.

1281 The Lord made known to me that I would see my brother [Stanley[211]], but I could not understand how this would happen or why he should come to visit me. I knew that God had given him the grace of a religious vocation, but why should he be coming to visit me? However, I put aside these thoughts and believed that if the Lord had given me to know he would come, that was enough for me. I fixed my thoughts on God, putting aside every preoccupation with creatures and entrusting everything to the Lord.

1282 + When the same poor people come to the gate a second time, I treat them with greater gentleness, and I do not let them **(35)** see that I know they have been here before; [I do this] in order not to embarrass them. And then they speak to me freely about their troubles and needs.

Although Sister N. tells me that is not the way to deal with beggars, and slams the door in their faces, when she is not there, I treat them as my Master would. Sometimes more is given when giving nothing, than when giving much in a rude manner.

1283 Often the Lord gives me interior knowledge concerning the persons I meet at the gate. One pitiable soul wanted to tell me a bit about herself. Taking advantage of the opportunity, I made her understand, in a delicate way, the miserable condition of her soul. She went away with a better disposition.

1284 September 17, [1937.] O Jesus, I see so much beauty scattered around me, beauty for which I give You **(36)** constant thanks. But I see that some souls are like stone, always cold and unfeeling. Even miracles hardly move them. Their eyes are always fixed on their feet, and so they see nothing but themselves.

1285 You have surrounded my life with Your tender and loving care, more than I can comprehend, for I will understand Your goodness in its entirety only when the veil is lifted. I desire that my whole life be but one act of thanksgiving to You, O God.

1286 + Thank You, O God, for all the graces
Which unceasingly You lavish upon me,
Graces which enlighten me with the brilliance of the sun,
For by them You show me the sure way.

Thank You, O Lord, for creating me,

For calling me into being from nothingness,
For imprinting Your divinity on my soul,
The work of sheer merciful love.

(37) Thank You, O God, for Holy Baptism
Which engrafted me into Your family,
A gift great beyond all thought or expression
Which transforms my soul.

Thank You, O Lord, for Holy Confession,
For that inexhaustible spring of great mercy,
For that inconceivable fountain of graces
In which sin-tainted souls become purified.

Thank You, O Jesus, for Holy Communion
In which You give us Yourself.
I feel Your Heart beating within my breast
As You cause Your divine life to unfold within me.

Thank You, O Holy Spirit, for the Sacrament of
    Confirmation,
Which dubs me Your knight
And gives strength to my soul at each moment,
Protecting me from evil.

Thank You, O God, for the grace of a vocation
For being called to serve You alone,
Leading me to make You my sole love,
An unequal honor for my soul.

(38) Thank You, O Lord, for perpetual vows,
For that union of pure love,
For having deigned to unite Your pure heart with
    mine
And uniting my heart to Yours in the purest of bonds.

Thank You, O Lord, for the Sacrament of Anointing
Which, in my final moments, will give me strength;
My help in battle, my guide to salvation,
Fortifying my soul till we rejoice forever.

Thank You, O God, for all the inspirations
That Your goodness lavishes upon me,

For the interior lights given my soul,
Which the heart senses, but words cannot express.

Thank You, O Holy Trinity, for the vastness of the graces
Which You have lavished on me unceasingly through life.
My gratitude will intensify as the eternal dawn rises,
When, for the first time, I sing to Your glory.

1287 + Despite the peace in my soul, I fight a continuous battle with the enemy of my soul. More and more, I am discovering his traps, and the battle flares up anew. **(39)** During interludes of calm, I exercise myself and keep watch, lest the enemy find me unprepared. And when I see his great fury, I stay inside the stronghold; that is, the Most Sacred Heart of Jesus.

1288 September 19, [1937]. Today, the Lord told me, **My daughter, write that it pains Me very much when religious souls receive the Sacrament of Love merely out of habit, as if they did not distinguish this food. I find neither faith nor love in their hearts. I go to such souls with great reluctance. It would be better if they did not receive Me.**

1289 Most sweet Jesus, set on fire my love for You and transform me into Yourself. Divinize me that my deeds may be pleasing to You. May this be accomplished by the power of the Holy Communion which I receive daily. Oh, how greatly I desire to be wholly transformed into You, O Lord!

1290 **(40)** September 19, 1937. Today, my own brother, Stanley, visited me. I rejoiced greatly in this beautiful soul, who also intends to devote himself to God's service. That is to say, God himself is drawing him to His love. We talked for a long time about God, about His goodness. During this conversation with him, I learned how pleasing his soul was to God. I received permission from Mother Superior to see him more often. When he asked my advice about entering religion, I replied, "Surely you know best what God is asking of you." I mentioned the Jesuit Order, but said, "Enter wherever you like." I promised to pray for him, and I decided to make a novena to the Sacred Heart through the intercession of Father Peter Skarga with the promise of having it announced in the *Messenger of the Sacred Heart*,[212] because he is having great difficulties in this matter. I understood that, in this case, prayer was more useful than advice.

1291 **(41)** September 21. Having awakened several times during the night, I thanked God briefly, but with all my heart, for all the graces He has given to me and to our Congregation, [and] I reflected on His great goodness.

1292 When I received Holy Communion, I said to Him, "Jesus, I thought about You so many times last night," and Jesus answered me, **And I thought of you before I called you into being.** "Jesus, in what way were You thinking about me?" **In terms of admitting you to My eternal happiness.** After these words, my soul was flooded with the love of God. I could not stop marveling at how much God loves us.

1293 It so happened that I fell again into a certain error, in spite of a sincere resolution not to do so—even though the lapse was a minor imperfection and rather involuntary—and at this I felt such acute pain in my soul that I interrupted my work and went **(42)** to the chapel for a while. Falling at the feet of Jesus, with love and a great deal of pain, I apologized to the Lord, all the more ashamed because of the fact that in my conversation with Him after Holy Communion this very morning I had promised to be faithful to Him. Then I heard these words: **If it hadn't been for this small imperfection, you wouldn't have come to Me. Know that as often as you come to Me, humbling yourself and**

asking My forgiveness, I pour out a superabundance of graces on your soul, and your imperfection vanishes before My eyes, and I see only your love and your humility. You lose nothing but gain much...

1294 The Lord has given me to know that when a soul does not accept the graces intended for it, another soul receives them immediately. O my Jesus, make me worthy of accepting Your graces because, of myself, I can do nothing. Without Your help, I cannot even utter Your Name worthily.

1295 **(43)** September 25, [1937.] When I learned how great are the difficulties in this whole work, I went to the Lord and said, "Jesus, don't You see how they are hindering Your work?" And I heard a voice in my soul: **Do as much as is in your power, and don't worry about the rest. These difficulties prove that this work is Mine. Be at peace so long as you do all that is in your power.**

1296 Today, I opened the gate for Mother Superior and knew interiorly that she was going to town on business regarding the work of the Divine Mercy. It is this superior who has contributed most to this whole work of mercy.

1297 Today I imprudently asked two poor children if they really had nothing to eat at home. The children, without answering me, walked away from the gate. I understood how difficult it was for them to speak about their poverty, so I went after them in a hurry and brought them back, **(44)** giving them as much as I had permission for.

1298 O God, show me Your mercy
According to the compassion of the Heart of Jesus.
Hear my sighs and entreaties,
And the tears of a contrite heart.

O Omnipotent, ever-merciful God,
Your compassion is never exhausted.

Although my misery is as vast as the sea,
I have complete trust in the mercy of the Lord.

O Eternal Trinity, yet ever-gracious God,
Your compassion is without measure.
And so I trust in the sea of Your mercy,
And sense You, Lord, though a veil holds me aloof.

May the omnipotence of Your mercy, O Lord,
Be glorified all over the world.
May its veneration never cease.
Proclaim, my soul, God's mercy with fervor.

1299 **(45)** September 27, [1937]. Today, Mother Superior and I went to see a certain gentleman[213] where they were printing and painting small holy cards of The Divine Mercy, and also the invocations and the chaplet, which have already received approbation. And we were also to see the improved larger image.[214] It very much resembles the original. This made me very happy.

1300 When I looked at this image, I was pierced with such a lively love for God that, for a moment, I did not know where I was. When we had finished our business, we went to the Church of the Most Holy Virgin Mary. We attended Holy Mass, during which the Lord gave me to know what a great number of souls would attain salvation through this work. Then I entered into an intimate conversation with the Lord, thanking Him for having condescended to grant me the grace of seeing how the veneration of His unfathomable mercy is spreading. I immersed myself in a profound prayer of thanksgiving. Oh, how great is God's generosity! Blessed be the Lord, who is faithful **(46)** in His promises...

1301 It is extraordinary how Mother Irene has so much light from God concerning this whole matter. She was the first to allow me to carry out the Lord's wishes, although it was not until two years after the revelation that she became my superior. And despite this fact, she was the first to go with me when the painting of the image was first undertaken. And now again, when some things concerning the Divine Mercy are being published, and small holy cards are being printed, again it is she who is going with me [to take care of] this matter. God has ordained all this in a mysterious way, because this was begun in Vilnius, and now God's will has so directed the circumstances that this matter is being continued in Cracow. I know how pleasing this superior is to God; I see how God is directing everything and wants me to be under her protection during these important times.... Thank You, Lord, for such superiors, who live in the love **(47)** and fear of God. That is why I pray for her most of all, because she has put herself out the most for the sake of this work of Divine Mercy....

1302   September 29, [1937]. Today, I have come to understand many of God's mysteries. I have come to know that Holy Communion remains in me until the next Holy Communion. A vivid and clearly felt presence of God continues in my soul. The awareness of this plunges me into deep recollection, without the slightest effort on my part. My heart is a living tabernacle in which the living Host is reserved. I have never sought God in some far-off place, but within myself. It is in the depths of my own being that I commune with my God.

1303   My God, despite all the graces, I long without cease to be eternally united with my God; and the better I know Him, the more ardently I desire Him.

+
(48) J.M.J.

1304   With longing I gaze into the starlit sky,
Into the sapphire of fathomless firmaments.
There the pure heart leaps out to find You, O God,
And yearns to be freed of the bonds of the flesh.

With great longing, I gaze upon you, my homeland,
When will this, my exile, come to an end?

O Jesus, such is the call of Your bride
Who suffers agony in her thirst for You.

With longing, I gaze at the footprints of the saints
Who crossed this wilderness on their way to the
fatherland.
They left me the example of their virtue and their
counsels,
And they say to me, "Patience, Sister, soon the fetters
will break."

But my longing soul hears not these words.
Ardently it yearns for its Lord and its God,
And it understands not human language,
Because it is enamored of Him alone.

My longing soul, wounded with love,
Forces its way through all created things
(49) And unites itself with infinite eternity,
With the Lord whom my heart has espoused.

Allow my longing soul, O God,
To be drowned in Your Divine Three-fold Essence.
Fulfill my desires, for which I humbly beg You,
With a heart brimming with love's fire.

1305   A certain person came to the door today and asked to be admitted as one of our students. But she could not be admitted. She was in great need of our house. During the conversation which I had with her, the Passion of Jesus was renewed in me. When she had gone, I undertook one of the severest mortifications. Nevertheless, the next time I will not let such a soul get away. For three days I suffered much on her account. How much I regret that our institutions are so small and that they cannot accommodate a greater number of souls. My Jesus, You know how much I grieve over every straying sheep....

1306   **(50)** + O humility, lovely flower, I see how few souls possess you. Is it because you are so beautiful and at the same time so difficult to attain? O yes, it is both the one and the other. Even God takes great pleasure in her. The floodgates of heaven are open to a humble soul, and a sea of graces flows down upon her. O how beautiful is a humble soul! From her heart, as from a censer, rises a varied and most pleasing fragrance which breaks through the skies and reaches God himself, filling His Most Sacred Heart with joy. God refuses nothing to such a soul; she is all-powerful and influences the destiny of the whole world. God raises such a soul up to His very throne, and the more she humbles herself, the more God stoops down to her, pursuing her with His graces and accompanying her at every moment with His omnipotence. Such a soul is most deeply united with God. O humility, strike deep roots in my whole being. O Virgin most pure, but also most humble, help me to attain deep **(51)** humility. Now I understand why there are so few saints; it is because so few souls are deeply humble.

1307 Eternal Love, Depth of Mercy, O Triune Holiness, yet One God, whose bosom is full of love for all, as a good Father You scorn no one. O Love of God, Living Fountain, pour Yourself out upon us, Your unworthy creatures. May our misery not hold back the torrents of Your love, for indeed, there is no limit to Your mercy.

1308 + Jesus, I have noticed that You seem to be less concerned with me. **Yes, My child, I am replacing Myself with your spiritual director** [Father Andrasz]. **He is taking care of you according to My will. Respect his every word as My own. He is the veil behind which I am hiding. Your director and I are one; his words are My words.**

1309 **(52)** When I make the Way of the Cross, I am deeply moved at the twelfth station. Here I reflect on the omnipotence of God's mercy which passed through the Heart of Jesus. In this open wound of the Heart of Jesus

I enclose all poor humans... and those individuals whom I love, as often as I make the Way of the Cross. From that Fount of Mercy issued the two rays; that is, the Blood and the Water. With the immensity of their grace they flood the whole world....

1310 When one is ill and weak, one must constantly make efforts to measure up to what others are doing as a matter of course. But even those matter-of-course things cannot always be managed. Nevertheless, thank You, Jesus, for everything, because it is not the greatness of the works, but the greatness of the effort that will be rewarded. What is done out of love is not small, O my Jesus, for Your eyes see everything. (53) I do not know why I feel so terribly unwell in the morning; I have to muster all my strength to get out of bed, sometimes even to the point of heroism. The thought of Holy Communion gives me back a little more strength. And so, the day starts with a struggle and ends with a struggle. When I go to take my rest, I feel like a soldier returning from the battlefield. You alone, my Lord and Master, know what this day has contained.

1311 Meditation. During meditation, the sister on the kneeler next to mine keeps coughing and clearing her throat, sometimes without a break. It occurred to me once that I might take another place for the time of the meditation, because Mass had already been offered. But then I thought that if I did change my place, the sister would notice this and might feel hurt that I had moved away from her. So I decided to continue in prayer in my usual place, (54) and to offer this act of patience to God. Toward the end of the meditation, my soul was flooded with God's consolation, and this to the limit of what my heart could bear; and the Lord gave me to know that if I had moved away from that sister I would have moved away also from those graces that flowed into my soul.

1312 + Jesus came to the main entrance today, under the guise of a poor young man. This young man, emaciated, barefoot and bareheaded, and with his clothes in tatters, was frozen because the day was cold and rainy. He asked for something hot to eat. So I went to the kitchen, but found nothing there for the poor. But, after searching around for some time, I succeeded in finding some soup, which I reheated and into which I crumbled some bread, and I gave it to the poor young man, who ate it. As I was taking the bowl from him, he gave me to know that He was the Lord of heaven and earth. When I saw Him as He was, He vanished from my sight. **(55)** When I went back in and reflected on what had happened at the gate, I heard these words in my soul: **My daughter, the blessings of the poor who bless Me as they leave this gate have reached My ears. And your compassion, within the bounds of obedience, has pleased Me, and this is why I came down from My throne—to taste the fruits of your mercy.**

1313 O my Jesus, now everything is clear to me, and I understand all that has just happened. I somehow felt and asked myself what sort of a poor man is this who radiates such modesty. From that moment on, there was stirred up in my heart an even purer love toward the poor and the needy. Oh, how happy I am that my superiors have given me such a task! I understand that mercy is manifold; one can do good always and everywhere and at all times. An ardent love of God sees all around itself constant opportunities to share itself through deed, word and prayer. Now I understand **(56)** the words which You spoke to me, O Lord, some time ago.

1314 + Oh, what great efforts I must make to carry out my duties well when my health is so poor! This will be known to You alone, O Christ.

1315 + In times of interior desolation I do not lose my peace, because I know that God never abandons a soul, except perhaps only when the soul itself breaks the bond of love by its unfaithfulness. However, all creatures without exception depend on the Lord and are maintained by His omnipotence. Some are under the rule of love, others under the rule of justice. It depends on us under which rule we want to live, because no one is refused the aid of sufficient grace. I am not frightened at all by my apparent abandonment. I examine myself more profoundly to discover whether this is due to my fault. If this is not the case—then may [the Lord] be blessed!

1316 **(57)** October 1, 1937. **Daughter, I need sacrifice lovingly accomplished, because that alone has meaning for Me. Enormous indeed are the debts of the world which are due to Me; pure souls can pay them by their sacrifice, exercising mercy in spirit.**

1317 I understand Your words, Lord, and the magnitude of the mercy that ought to shine in my soul. Jesus: **I know, My daughter, that you understand it and that you do everything within your power. But write this for the many souls who are often worried because they do not have the material means with which to carry out an act of mercy. Yet spiritual mercy, which requires neither permissions nor storehouses, is much more meritorious and is within the grasp of every soul. If a soul does not exercise mercy somehow or other, it will not obtain My mercy on the day of judgment. Oh, if only souls knew how to gather eternal treasure for themselves, they would not be judged, for they would forestall My judgment with their mercy.**

1318 **(58)** October 10, [1937]. O my Jesus, in thanksgiving for Your many graces, I offer You my body and soul, intellect and will, and all the sentiments of my heart. Through the vows, I have given myself entirely to You; I have then nothing more that I can offer You. Jesus said to me, **My daughter, you have not offered Me that which is really yours.** I probed deeply into myself and found that I love God with all the faculties of my soul and, unable to see what it was that I had not yet given to the Lord, I asked, "Jesus, tell me what it is, and I will give it to You at once with a generous heart." Jesus said to me with kindness, **Daughter, give Me your misery, because it is your exclusive property.** At that moment, a ray of light illumined my soul, and I saw the whole abyss of my misery. In that same moment I nestled close to the Most Sacred Heart of Jesus with so much trust that even if I had the sins of all the damned weighing on my conscience, I would not have doubted God's mercy **(59)** but, with a heart crushed to dust, I would have thrown myself into the abyss of Your mercy. I believe, O Jesus, that You would not reject me, but would absolve me through the hand of Your representative.

1319 You expired, Jesus, but the source of life gushed forth for souls, and the ocean of mercy opened up for the whole world. O Fount of Life, unfathomable Divine Mercy, envelop the whole world and empty Yourself out upon us.

1320 **At three o'clock, implore My mercy, especially for sinners; and, if only for a brief moment, immerse yourself in My Passion, particularly in My abandonment at the moment of agony. This is the hour of great mercy for the whole world. I will allow you to enter into My mortal sorrow. In this hour, I will refuse nothing to the soul that makes a request of Me in virtue of My Passion....**

   (60)+
   J.M.J.

1321 Hail, most merciful Heart of Jesus,
   Living Fountain of all graces,
   Our sole shelter, our only refuge;
   In You I have the light of hope.

Hail, most compassionate Heart of my God,
Unfathomable living Fount of Love
From which gushes life for sinful man
And the Spring of all sweetness.

Hail, open Wound of the Most Sacred Heart,
From which the rays of mercy issued forth
And from which it was given us to draw life
With the vessel of trust alone.

Hail, God's goodness, incomprehensible,
Never to be measured or fathomed,
Full of love and mercy, though always holy,
Yet, like a good mother, ever bent o'er us.

Hail, Throne of Mercy, Lamb of God,
Who gave Your life in sacrifice for me,
Before whom my soul humbles itself daily,
Living in faith profound.

[End of Notebook Four]

Sister Faustina

of the Blessed Sacrament

of the Congregation of the

Sisters of Our Lady of Mercy

Notebook V

+

(1) J.M.J.

1322 The barque of my life sails along
Amid darkness and shadows of night,
And I see no shore;
I am sailing the high seas.

> The slightest storm would drown me,
> Engulfing my boat in the swirling depths,
> If You yourself did not watch over me, O God,
> At each instant and moment of my life.

Amid the roaring waves
I sail peacefully, trustingly,
And gaze like a child into the distance without fear,
Because You, O Jesus, are my Light.

> Dread and terror is all about me,
> But within my soul is peace more profound than the
>   depths of the sea,
> For he who is with You, O Lord, will not perish;
> Of this Your love assures me, O God.

Though a host of dangers surround me,
None of them do I fear, for I fix my gaze on the starry
    sky,
And I sail along bravely and merrily,
As becomes a pure heart.

> And if the ship of my life sails so peacefully,
> This is due to but one thing above all:
> You are my helmsman, O God.
> This I confess with utmost humility.

+

(2) J.M.J.

1323   O my God, I love You.

Sister Faustina
of the Blessed Sacrament.

Cracow, October 20, 1937.

1324 + I bow down before You, O Bread of Angels,
     With deep faith, hope and love
     And from the depths of my soul I worship You,
     Though I am but nothingness.

       I bow down before You, O hidden God
       And love You with all my heart.
       The veils of mystery hinder me not at all;
       I love You as do Your chosen ones in heaven.

     I bow down before You, O Lamb of God
     Who take away the sins of my soul,
     Whom I receive into my heart each morn,
     You who are my saving help.

          +

     (3) J.M.J.

     Cracow, October 20, 1937.   Fifth Notebook

1325 O my God, let everything that is in me praise You, my
     Lord and Creator; and with every beat of my heart I
     want to praise Your unfathomable mercy. I want to tell
     souls of Your goodness and encourage them to trust in
     Your mercy. That is my mission, which You yourself
     have entrusted to me, O Lord, in this life and in the life
     to come.

1326 We are beginning an eight-day retreat today.[215] Jesus,
     my Master, help me to make these holy retreat exercises
     with the greatest fervor possible. May Your Spirit guide
     me, O God, into the most profound depths of knowledge
     of Yourself, and of my own self as well. For I shall love
     You only as much as I shall come to know You. And I
     shall despise myself only as much as I shall come to
     know my misery. I know, Lord, that You will not refuse
     me Your help. I desire to come out of this retreat a saint,
     even though human **(4)** eyes will not notice this, not
     even those of the superiors. I abandon myself entirely to
     the action of Your grace. Let Your will be accomplished
     entirely in me, O Lord.

1327 First day. Jesus: **My daughter, this retreat will be an uninterrupted contemplation. I will bring you into this retreat as into a spiritual banquet. Close to My merciful Heart, you will meditate upon all the graces your heart has received, and a deep peace will accompany your soul. I want the eyes of your soul to be always fixed on My holy will, since it is in this way that you will please Me most. No sacrifices can be compared to this. Throughout all the exercises you will remain close to My Heart. You shall not undertake any reforms, because I will dispose of your whole life as I see fit. The priest who will preach the retreat will not speak a single word which will trouble you.**

1328 My Jesus, I have already made two meditations, and I recognize, through them, that everything You have said is true. I am experiencing a profound peace, **(5)** and this peace flows from the witness of my conscience; that is to say, that I am always doing Your will, O Lord.

1329 In the meditation on the goal of man, I understood that this truth is deeply rooted in my soul, and that my deeds are therefore the more perfect. I know why I was created. All creatures taken together cannot take the place, for me, of my Creator. I know that God is my ultimate goal and so, in whatever I undertake, I take God into account.

1330 + Oh, how good it is to spend a retreat close to the most sweet heart of my God. I am in the wilderness with my Beloved. No one interrupts my sweet conversation with Him.

1331 Jesus, You yourself have deigned to lay the foundations of my sanctity, as my cooperation has not amounted to much. You have taught me to set no store on the use and choice of created things, because my heart is, of itself, so weak. And this is why I have asked You, O my Master, to take no heed of the pain of my heart, **(6)** but to cut away whatever might hold me back from the path of love. I did not understand You, Lord, in times of sorrow, when You were effecting Your work in my soul; but today I understand You and rejoice in my freedom of spirit. Jesus himself has seen to it that my heart has not been caught in the snares of any passion. I have come to know well from what dangers He has delivered me, and therefore my gratitude to my God knows no bounds.

1332 Second day. As I was meditating on the sin of the Angels and their immediate punishment, I asked Jesus why the Angels had been punished as soon as they had sinned. I heard a voice: **Because of their profound knowledge of God. No person on earth, even though a great saint, has such knowledge of God as an Angel has.** Nevertheless, to me who am so miserable, You have shown Your mercy, O God, and this, time and time again. You carry me in the bosom of Your mercy and forgive me every time that I ask Your forgiveness with a contrite heart.

1333 Profound silence engulfs my soul. Not a single cloud hides the sun from me. I lay myself **(7)** entirely open to its rays, that His love may effect a complete transformation in me. I want to come out of this retreat a saint, and this, in spite of everything; that is to say, in spite of my wretchedness, I want to become a saint, and I trust that God's mercy can make a saint even out of such misery as I am, because I am utterly in good will. In spite of all my defeats, I want to go on fighting like a holy soul and to comport myself like a holy soul. I will not be discouraged by anything, just as nothing can discourage a soul who is holy. I want to live and die like a holy soul, with my eyes fixed on You, Jesus, stretched out on the Cross, as the model for my actions. I used to look around me for examples and found nothing which sufficed, and I noticed that my state of holiness seemed to falter. But from now on, my eyes are fixed on You, O

Christ, who are for me the best of guides. I am confident that You will bless my efforts.

1334 + In the meditation on sin, the Lord gave me to know all the malice of sin and the ingratitude that is contained in it. I feel within my soul a great aversion for even the smallest sin. **(8)** However, the eternal truths I have been meditating on do not bring even a shadow of disturbance or unrest into my soul. And although I take them very much to heart, my contemplation is not thereby interrupted. In this contemplation, it is not transports of the heart that I experience, but a depth of peace and a wonderful silence. Although my love is great, I experience an extraordinary equilibrium. Even receiving the Eucharist causes no feeling, but brings me to a depth of union where my love and God's love are fused together as one.

1335 + Jesus has made known to me that I should pray for the sisters who are making the retreat. During prayer, I learned of the struggle that some are undergoing, and I redoubled my prayers.

1336 + In this profound silence, I am better able to judge the condition of my soul. My soul is like clear water in which I can see everything: both my misery and the vastness of God's graces. And owing to this true knowledge of itself, my spirit is strengthened in deep humility. I expose my heart to the action of Your grace like a crystal exposed to the rays of the sun. **(9)** May Your image be reflected in it, O my God, to the extent that it is possible to be reflected in the heart of a creature. Let Your divinity radiate through me, O You who dwell in my soul.

1337 As I was praying before the Blessed Sacrament and greeting the five wounds of Jesus, at each salutation I felt a torrent of graces gushing into my soul, giving me a foretaste of heaven and absolute confidence in God's mercy.

1338 As I write these words, I hear the cry of Satan: "She's writing everything, she's writing everything, and because of this we are losing so much! Do not write about the goodness of God; He is just!" And howling with fury, he vanished.

1339 O merciful God, You do not despise us, but lavish Your graces on us continuously. You make us fit to enter Your kingdom, and in Your goodness You grant that human beings may fill the places vacated by the ungrateful angels. O God of great mercy, who turned Your sacred gaze away from the rebellious angels and turned it upon contrite man, **(10)** praise and glory be to Your unfathomable mercy, O God who do not despise the lowly heart.

1340 My Jesus, despite these graces which You send upon me, I feel that my nature, ennobled thought it be, is not completely stilled; and so I keep a constant watch. I must struggle with many faults, knowing well that it is not the struggle which debases one, but cowardice and failure.

1341 When one's health is poor, there is much one has to bear. For when one is ill, but not in bed, one is not considered to be ill. For many reasons, therefore, there are constant occasions for sacrifices, and sometimes big ones. I understand now that only in eternity will many things be revealed. But I also understand that if God demands a sacrifice, He does not withhold His grace, but gives it to the soul in abundance.

1342 My Jesus, let my sacrifice burn before Your throne in all silence, but with the full force of love, as I beg You to have mercy on souls.

1343 **(11)** Third day. In the meditation on death, I prepared myself as if for real death. I examined my conscience and searched all my affairs at the approach of death and, thanks be to grace, my affairs were directed toward that ultimate goal. This filled my heart with great gratitude to God, and I resolved to serve my God even more faithfully in the future. One thing alone is necessary: to put my old self to death and to begin a new life. In the morning, I prepared to receive Holy Communion as if it were to be the last in my life, and after Holy Communion I brought before my imagination my actual death, and I said the prayers for the dying and then the *De Profundis* for my own soul. My body was lowered into the grave, and I said to my soul, "See what has become of your body, a heap of dirt teeming with vermin—that is your inheritance."

1344 O merciful God, who still allow me to live, give me strength that I may live a new life, the life of the spirit, over which death has no dominion. And with that, my heart was renewed, and I began a new life while still here on earth, a life of love of God. Nevertheless, I do not forget that **(12)** I am weakness itself, though I do not doubt even for a moment that I will obtain the help of Your grace, O God.

1345 + Fourth day. O Jesus, I have been feeling extraordinarily well, close to Your Heart, during this retreat. Nothing disturbs the depths of my peace. With one eye, I gaze on the abyss of my misery and with the other, on the abyss of Your mercy.

1346 During Holy Mass, which was celebrated by Father Andrasz, I saw the Infant Jesus who, with hands outstretched toward us, was sitting in the chalice being used at Holy Mass. After gazing at me penetratingly, He spoke these words: **As you see Me in this chalice, so I dwell in your heart.**

1347 + Holy Confession. After giving an account of my conscience, I was given the permissions I asked for: to wear the bracelet for half an hour every day during Holy Mass, and in times of difficulty, to wear the belt for two hours. [Father said,] "Sister, persevere in this great faithfulness to the Lord Jesus."

1348 **(13)** Fifth day. When I entered the chapel this morning, I learned that Mother Superior had had some trouble on my account. This hurt me very much. After Holy Communion, I leaned my head on the Most Sacred Heart of Jesus and said, "O my Lord, I beg You, let all the consolation that I am experiencing through Your presence in my heart be poured out into the soul of my dear Mother Superior, who has had some trouble because of me, and this involuntarily on my part."

1349 Jesus comforted me, saying that both our souls had benefited from this. But I begged the Lord to deign to spare me from being the occasion of anyone's suffering, as my heart could not bear this.

1350 O white Host, You preserve my soul in whiteness; I fear the day when I might forsake You. You are the Bread of Angels, and thus also the Bread of Virgins.

1351 Jesus, my most perfect model, with my eyes fixed on You, I will go through life in Your footsteps, adapting nature to grace, according to Your most holy will and Your light which illumines my soul, trusting completely in Your help.

+

(14) J.M.J.

1352   Chart of inner control[216]

Particular examen.

Unity with the merciful Christ. Because I am united to Jesus, I must be faithful always and everywhere, and I must be interiorly united with the Lord, while exteriorly observing fidelity to the rule, particularly that of silence.

1353	November	victories	- 53	defeats	- 2
	December	"	- 104		-
	January	"	- 78		- 1
	February	"	- 59		- 1
	March	"	- 50		
	April	"	- 61		
	May				
	June				
	July				
	August				
	September				
	October				

1354

When I hesitate on how to act in some situations, I always ask love. It advises best.

1355

(15)
Victories

General Examen of Conscience

October 25, 1937
Defeats

	Nov XI	Dec XII	Jan I	Feb II	Mar III	Apr IV	May V	Jun VI	Jul VII	Aug VIII	Sep IX	Oct X	Defeats
Commandments of God													
Vows-poverty													
Vows-chastity				9									
Vows-obedience		27		7									
Rules		7		7									
Love of neighbor	38	17	73	35	30	20							1,1,1,
Humility	7	39	23	34	56	25							2,3,1,1,6
Patience	23	56	50	17	80	50							
Silence	11	45	37	28	37	20							
Neighbor's good name		15	25	3	1								1,
Holy Mass and Communion		17	12	13	7	10							Holy Mass 6,2,1,12 / Holy Comm. 1,(12)
Meditation		6	5	10									1
Particular Examen		7	5	11									
Attitude-towards God and Confessor													
- Superiors		5		5									1,1
- Sisters		7											
and Students		4	7										
- Lay Persons	20	2											2,1

1356 **(16)** Sixth day. O my God, I am ready to accept Your will in every detail, whatever it may be. However You may direct me, I will bless You. Whatever You ask of me I will do with the help of Your grace. Whatever Your holy will regarding me might be, I accept it with my whole heart and soul, taking no account of what my corrupt nature tells me.

1357 Once, when I was passing by a group of people, I asked the Lord if they were all in the state of grace, because I did not feel His sufferings. **Because you do not feel My sufferings, it does not follow that they must all be in the state of grace. At times, I allow you to be aware of the condition of certain souls, and I give you the grace of suffering solely because I use you as the instrument of their conversion.**

1358 Where there is genuine virtue, there must be sacrifice as well; one's whole life must be a sacrifice. It is only by means of sacrifice that souls can become useful. It is my self-sacrifice which, in my relationship with my neighbor, can give glory to God, but God's love must flow through this sacrifice, because everything is concentrated in this love and takes its value from it.

1359 **(17) Bear in mind that when you come out of this retreat, I shall be dealing with you as with a perfect soul. I want to hold you in My hand as a pliant tool, perfectly adapted to the completion of My works.**

1360 O Lord, You who penetrate my whole being and the most secret depths of my soul, You see that I desire You alone and long only for the fulfillment of Your holy will, paying no heed to difficulties or sufferings or humiliations or to what others might think.

1361 **This firm resolution to become a saint is extremely pleasing to Me. I bless your efforts and will give you opportunities to sanctify yourself. Be watchful that you lose no opportunity that My providence offers you for sanctification. If you do not succeed in taking advantage**

of an opportunity, do not lose your peace, but humble yourself profoundly before Me and, with great trust, immerse yourself completely in My mercy. In this way, you gain more than you have lost, because more favor is granted to a humble soul than the soul itself asks for...

1362 **(18)** + Seventh day. I have come to a knowledge of my destiny; that is, an inward certainty that I will attain sanctity. This deep conviction has filled my soul with gratitude to God, and I have given back all the glory to God, because I know very well what I am of myself.

1363 I am coming out of this retreat thoroughly transformed by God's love. My soul is beginning a new life, earnestly and courageously; although outwardly my life will not change, and no one will notice it, nevertheless, pure love is [now] the guide of my life and, externally, it is mercy which is its fruit. I feel that I have been totally imbued with God and, with this God, I am going back to my everyday life, so drab, tiresome and wearying, trusting that He whom I feel in my heart will change this drabness into my personal sanctity.

In profound silence, close to Your merciful Heart, my soul is maturing during this retreat. In the clear rays of Your love, my soul has lost its tartness **(19)** and has become a sweet and ripe fruit.

1364 Now I can be wholly useful to the Church by my personal sanctity, which throbs with life in the whole Church, for we all make up one organism in Jesus. That is why I endeavor to make the soil of my heart bear good fruit. Although the human eye may perhaps never see it, there will nevertheless come a day when it will become apparent that many souls have been fed and will continue to be fed with this fruit.

1365 O Eternal Love, who enkindle a new life within me, a life of love and of mercy, support me with Your grace, so that I may worthily answer Your call, so that what You yourself have intended to accomplish in souls through me, might indeed be accomplished.

My God, I see the radiance of eternal dawn. My whole soul bounds toward You, O Lord; nothing any longer holds me back, nothing ties me to earth. Help me, O Lord, to bear the rest of my days with patience. The sacrifice of my love burns incessantly before Your Majesty, but so silently that only Your divine eye sees it, O God, and no other creature is capable of perceiving it.

1366 **(20)** O my Lord, although so many things occupy me, although I have this work at heart, although I desire the triumph of the Church and the salvation of souls, although all the persecutions of Your faithful ones affect me, although the fall of each soul is painful to me, yet, above and beyond all this, I still have a profound peace in my soul which neither triumphs nor desires nor adversities can disturb because, for me, You are above all dispensations, my Lord and my God.

1367 Eighth day. O my Lord, while calling to mind all Your blessings, in the presence of Your Most Sacred Heart, I have felt the need to be particularly grateful for so many graces and blessings from God. I want to plunge myself in thanksgiving before the Majesty of God and to continue in this prayer of thanksgiving for seven days and seven nights; and although I will outwardly carry out all my duties, my spirit will nonetheless stand continually before the Lord, and all my exercises will be imbued with the spirit of thanksgiving. Each evening, I will kneel for a half hour in my cell, alone with the Lord. As often as I shall awake at night, **(21)** I shall steep myself in a prayer of thanksgiving. In this way I want to repay, at least in some small way, for the immensity of God's blessings.

1368 However, in order to make all this more pleasing in the eyes of God and to remove the least shadow of doubt from my mind, I went to my spiritual director [Father Andrasz] and revealed these desires of my soul to him;

that is to say, the desire to be steeped in such thanksgiving. I received permission for everything, except that I should not force myself to pray at night should I awaken.

1369   With what great joy I returned to the convent! And on the next day I began this great act of thanksgiving by renewing my vows. My soul became thoroughly immersed in God, and there issued from my whole being but one single flame of gratitude and thanksgiving to God. There were not many words, because God's blessings, like a fierce fire, consumed my soul, and all sufferings and sorrows were like wood thrown into the flames, without which the fire would go out. I called upon all heaven and earth to join me in my act of thanksgiving.

1370   **(22)** The retreat has come to an end, those beautiful days of communing alone with the Lord Jesus. I made this retreat in the way Jesus wanted me to make it, and as He had told me to on the first day of the retreat; that is, in the deepest peace, I meditated on God's blessings. I have never made a retreat like this before. My soul was more profoundly strengthened by this peace than it would have been by any tremors or emotions. In the rays of love, I saw everything as it really is.

Coming out of this retreat, I feel thoroughly transformed by God's love.

1371   O Lord, deify my actions so that they will merit eternity; although my weakness is great, I trust in the power of Your grace, which will sustain me.

1372   My Jesus, You know that from my earliest years I have wanted to become a great saint; that is to say, I have wanted to love You with a love so great that there would be no soul who has hitherto loved You so. At first these desires of mine were kept secret, **(23)** and only Jesus knew of them. But today I cannot contain them within my heart; I would like to cry out to the whole world,

"Love God, because He is good and great is His mercy!"

1373 O humdrum days, filled with darkness, I look upon you with a solemn and festive eye. How great and solemn is the time that gives us the chance to gather merits for eternal heaven! I understand how the saints made use of it.

1374 October 30, 1937. Today, during the religious ceremonies[217] taking place during Mass, and the second day of thanksgiving, I saw the Lord Jesus in great beauty, and He said to me, **My daughter, I have not released you from taking action.** I answered, "Lord, my hand is too feeble for such work." **Yes, I know; but joined with My right hand you will accomplish everything. Nevertheless, be obedient, be obedient to the confessors. I will give them light on how to direct you.** "Lord, I already wanted to begin the work in Your Name, but Father S. keeps putting it off." Jesus answered me, **I know this; so do just what is within your power, but you must never withdraw your efforts.**

1375 **(24)** November 1, 1937.

After Vespers today, there was a procession to the cemetery. I could not go, because I was on duty at the gate. But that did not stop me at all from praying for the souls. As the procession was returning from the cemetery to the chapel, my soul felt the presence of many souls. I understood the great justice of God, how each one had to pay off the debt to the last cent.

1376 The Lord gave me an occasion to practice patience through a particular person with whom I have to carry out a certain task. She is slower than anyone I have ever seen. One has to arm oneself with great patience to listen to her tedious talk.

1377 November 5. This morning, five unemployed men came to the gate and insisted on being let in. When Sister N. had argued with them for quite a while and could not make them go away, she then came to the chapel **(25)** to find Mother [Irene], who told me to go. When I was still a good way from the gate I could hear them banging loudly. At first, I was overcome with doubt and fear, and I did not know whether to open the gate or, like Sister N., to answer them through the little window. But suddenly I heard a voice in my soul saying, **Go and open the gate and talk to them as sweetly as you talk to Me.**

I opened the gate at once and approached the most menacing of them and began to speak to them with such sweetness and calm that they did not know what to do with themselves. And they too began to speak gently and said, "Well, it's too bad that the convent can't give us work." And they went away peacefully. I felt clearly that Jesus, whom I had received in Holy Communion just an hour before, had worked in their hearts through me. Oh, how good it is to act under God's inspiration!

1378 I felt worse today, and I went to Mother Superior, intending to ask her for permission to go to bed. However, before I could ask for permission, **(26)** Mother Superior said to me, "Sister, you must somehow manage by yourself at the gate, because I am taking the girl to work at the cabbage, since there is no one else for the cabbage." I said—good, and left the room. When I got to the gate, I felt unusually strong, and I was at my post all day and felt well. I experienced the power of holy obedience.

1379 November 10, [1937]. When Mother [Irene] showed me the booklet with the chaplet, the litany and the novena, I asked her to let me look it over. As I was glancing through it, Jesus gave me to know interiorly: **Already there are many souls who have been drawn to My love by this image. My mercy acts in souls through this work.** I learned that many souls had experienced God's grace.

1380 I learned that Mother Superior would have quite a heavy cross to bear, together with physical suffering, but that it would not last long.[218]

1381 **(27)** + It occurred to me to take my medicine, not by the spoonful, but just a little at a time, because it was expensive. Instantly, I heard a voice, **My daughter, I do not like such conduct. Accept with gratitude everything I give you through the superiors, and in this way you will please Me more.**

1382 + When Sister Dominic[219] died at about one o'clock in the night, she came to me and gave me to know that she was dead. I prayed fervently for her. In the morning, the sisters told me that she was no longer alive, and I replied that I knew, because she had visited me. The sister infirmarian [Sister Chrysostom] asked me to help dress her. And then when I was alone with her, the Lord gave me to know that she was still suffering in purgatory. I redoubled my prayers for her. However, despite the zeal with which I always pray for our deceased sisters, I got mixed up as regards the days, and instead of offering three days of prayer, as the rule directs us to do, by mistake I offered only two days. On the fourth day, she gave me to know that I still owed her prayers, and that she was in need of them. I immediately **(28)** formed the intention of offering the whole day for her, and not just that day but much more, as love of neighbor dictated to me.

1383 Because Sister Dominic, after her death, gave the appearance of looking so well, some sisters said that perhaps she was only in a coma, and one of the sisters suggested to me that we ought to go and put a mirror to her mouth to see if it would mist, because it would if she were alive. I said all right, and we did as we said, but the mirror did not mist, although it seemed to us as if it had. Nevertheless, the Lord gave me to know how much this had displeased Him, and I was severely admonished never to act again against my inner convictions. I humbled myself profoundly before the Lord and asked His pardon.

1384 I see a certain priest [probably Father Sopocko] whom God loves greatly, but whom Satan hates terribly because he is leading many souls to a high degree of sanctity and has **(29)** regard only for God's glory. But I keep asking God that his patience with those who constantly oppose him might not run out. Where Satan himself can do no harm, he uses people.

1385 November 19. After Communion today, Jesus told me how much He desires to come to human hearts. **I desire to unite Myself with human souls; My great delight is to unite Myself with souls. Know, My daughter, that when I come to a human heart in Holy Communion, My hands are full of all kinds of graces which I want to give to the soul. But souls do not even pay any attention to Me; they leave Me to Myself and busy themselves with other things. Oh, how sad I am that souls do not recognize Love! They treat Me as a dead object.** I answered Jesus, "O Treasure of my heart, the only object of my love and entire delight of my soul, I want to adore You in my heart as You are adored on the throne of Your eternal glory. My love wants to make up to You **(30)** at least in part for the coldness of so great a number of souls. Jesus, behold my heart which is for You a dwelling place to which no one else has entry. You alone repose in it as in a beautiful garden.

1386 O my Jesus, farewell; I must go already to take up my tasks. But I will prove my love for You with sacrifice, neither neglecting nor letting any chance for practicing it slip by."

When I left the chapel, Mother Superior [Irene] said to me, "You will not go to the catechetical lecture, Sister, but will remain on duty." Very well, Jesus; I thus had, throughout the day, very many opportunities for sacrifice. I omitted none, owing to the strength of spirit I drew from Holy Communion.

1387 There are times in life when a soul is in such a state that it does not seem to understand human speech. Everything tires it, and nothing but ardent prayer will put it at ease. In fervent prayer the soul finds relief and, even if it wanted explanations from creatures, these would only make it more restless.

1388 **(31)** + During one time of prayer, I learned how pleasing to God was the soul of Father Andrasz. He is a true child of God. It is rare that divine sonship shines forth so clearly in a soul, and this because he has a special devotion to the Mother of God.

1389 O my Jesus, although I have such very strong impulsions, I am to act on them slowly, and this only in order not to spoil Your work with my haste. O my Jesus, You give me to know Your mysteries, and You want me to transmit them to other souls. Soon now it will be possible for me to act. At the moment of apparent absolute destruction, my mission, now no longer hindered by anything, will begin. Such is the will of God in this, and it will not change; although many persons will oppose it, nothing will change God's will.

1390 I see Father Sopocko, how his mind is busily occupied and working in God's cause in order to present the wishes of God to the officials of the Church. As a result of his efforts, a new **(32)** light will shine in the Church of God for the consolation of souls. Although for the present his soul is filled with bitterness, as though that were to be the reward for his efforts in the cause of the Lord, this will not however be the case. I see his joy, which nothing will diminish. God will grant him some of this joy already here on earth. I have never before come upon such great faithfulness to God as distinguishes this soul.

1391 During supper in the refectory today, I felt God's gaze in the depths of my heart. Such a vivid presence pervaded my soul that, for a while, I had no idea where I was. The sweet presence of God kept filling my soul and, at times, I could not understand what the sisters were saying to me.

1392   All the good that is in me is due to Holy Communion. I owe everything to it. I feel that this holy fire has transformed me completely. Oh, how happy I am to be a dwelling place for You, O Lord! My heart is a temple in which You dwell continually...

          +
     (33) J.M.J.

1393   Jesus, delight of my soul, Bread of Angels,
       My whole being is plunged in You,
       And I live Your divine life as do the elect in heaven,
       And the reality of this life will not cease, though I be laid in the grave.

          Jesus-Eucharist, Immortal God,
          Who dwell in my heart without cease,
          When I possess You, death itself can do me no harm.
          Love tells me that I will see You at life's end.

       Permeated by Your divine life,
       I gaze with assurance at the heavens thrown open for me,
       And death will shame-facedly go away, empty-handed,
       For Your divine life is contained within my soul.

          And although by Your holy will, O Lord,
          Death is to touch my body,
          I want this dissolution to come as quickly as possible,
          For through it I am entering eternal life.

       Jesus-Eucharist, life of my soul,
       You have raised me up to the eternal spheres,
       And this, by Your agony and death midst terrible tortures.

(34)26 [November 1937].

1394   Monthly one-day retreat.

In the course of this retreat, the Lord has given me the light to know His will more profoundly and to abandon myself completely to the holy will of God. This light has confirmed me in profound peace, making me understand that I should fear nothing except sin. Whatever God sends me, I accept with complete submission to His holy will. Wherever He puts me, I will try faithfully to do His holy will, as well as His wishes, to the extent of my power to do so, even if the will of God were to be as hard and difficult for me as was the will of the Heavenly Father for His Son, as He prayed in the Garden of Olives. I have come to see that if the will of the Heavenly Father was fulfilled in this way in His well-beloved Son, it will be fulfilled in us in exactly the same way: by suffering, persecution, abuse, disgrace. It is through all this that my soul becomes like unto Jesus. And the greater the sufferings, the more I see that I am becoming like Jesus. This is the surest way. If some other way were better, Jesus would have shown it to me. Sufferings in no way **(35)** take away my peace. On the other hand, although I enjoy profound peace, that peace does not lessen my experience of suffering. Although my face is often bowed to the ground, and my tears flow profusely, at the same time my soul is filled with profound peace and happiness...

1395 I want to hide myself in Your Most Merciful Heart as a dewdrop does in a flower blossom. Enclose me in this blossom against the frost of the world. No one can conceive the happiness which my heart enjoys in its solitude, alone with God.

1396 Today I heard a voice in my soul: **Oh, if sinners knew My mercy, they would not perish in such great numbers. Tell sinful souls not to be afraid to approach Me; speak to them of My great mercy.**

1397 The Lord said to me, **The loss of each soul plunges Me into mortal sadness. You always console Me when you (36) pray for sinners. The prayer most pleasing to Me is prayer for the conversion of sinners. Know, My daughter, that this prayer is always heard and answered.**

1398 Advent is approaching. I want to prepare my heart for the coming of the Lord Jesus by silence and recollection of spirit, uniting myself with the Most Holy Mother and faithfully imitating Her virtue of silence, by which She found pleasure in the eyes of God Himself. I trust that, by Her side, I will persevere in this resolution.

1399 When I entered the chapel for a moment in the evening, I felt a terrible thorn in my head. This lasted for a short time, but the pricking was so painful that in an instant my head dropped onto the communion rail. It seemed to me that the thorn had thrust itself into my brain. But all this is nothing; it is all for the sake of souls, to obtain God's mercy for them.

1400 I live from one hour to the next and am not able to get along in any other way. I want to make the best possible use of the present moment, faithfully accomplishing everything that it gives me. In all things, I depend on God with unwavering trust.

1401 **(37)** Yesterday I received a letter from Father Sopocko. I learned that God's work is progressing, however slowly. I am very happy about this, and I have redoubled my prayers for this entire work. I have come to learn that, for the present, so far as my participation in the work is concerned, the Lord is asking for prayer and sacrifice. Action on my part could indeed thwart God's plans, as Father Sopocko wrote in yesterday's letter. O my Jesus, grant me the grace to be an obedient instrument in Your hands. I have learned from this letter how great is the light which God grants to this priest. This confirms me in the conviction that God will carry out this work through him despite the mounting obstacles. I know well that the greater and the more beautiful the work is, the more terrible will be the storms that rage against it.

1402 God, in his unfathomable decrees, often allows it to be that those who have expended most effort in accomplishing some work do not enjoy its fruits here on earth; God reserves all their joy for eternity. But for all that, God sometimes lets them know how much their efforts please Him. **(38)** And such moments strengthen them for further struggles and ordeals. These are the souls that bear closest resemblance to the Savior who, in the work which He founded here on earth, tasted nothing but bitterness.

1403 O my Jesus, may You be blesssed for everything! I rejoice that Your most holy will is being accomplished. That is quite enough to make me happy.

1404 Hidden Jesus, in You lies all my strength. From my most tender years, the Lord Jesus in the Blessed Sacrament has attracted me to Himself. Once, when I was seven years old, at a Vesper Service, conducted before the Lord Jesus in the monstrance, the love of God was imparted to me for the first time and filled my little heart; and the Lord gave me understanding of divine things. From that day until this, my love for the hidden God has been growing constantly to the point of closest intimacy. All the strength of my soul flows from the Blessed Sacrament. I spend all my free moments in conversation with Him. He is my Master.

1405 **(39)** November 30, 1937. When I was going upstairs this evening, a strange dislike for everything having to do with God suddenly came over me. At that, I heard Satan who said to me, "Think no more about this work. God is not as merciful as you say He is. Do not pray for sinners, because they will be damned all the same, and by this work of mercy you expose your own self to damnation. Talk no more about this mercy of God with your confessor and especially not with Father Sopocko and

Father Andrasz." At this point, the voice took the appearance of my Guardian Angel, and at that moment I replied,

"I know who you are: the father of lies [cf. Jn. 8:44]." I made the sign of the cross, and the angel vanished with great racket and fury.

1406 Today, the Lord gave me to know interiorly that He would never abandon me. He gave me to know His majesty and His holiness as well as His love and mercy towards me; and He gave me a deeper knowledge of my own wretchedness. However, this great misery of mine does not deprive me of trust. On the contrary, the better I have come to know my own misery, the stronger has become my trust **(40)** in God's mercy. I have come to understand how all this depends on the Lord. I know that no one will touch a single hair of my head without His willing it.

1407 When I was receiving Holy Communion today, I noticed in the cup a Living Host, which the priest gave to me. When I returned to my place I asked the Lord, "Why was one Host alive, since You are equally alive under each of the species?" The Lord answered me, **That is so. I am the same under each of the species, but not every soul receives Me with the same living faith as you do, My daughter, and therefore I cannot act in their souls as I do in yours.**

1408 I was present at Holy Mass celebrated by Father Sopocko. During the Mass, I saw the Infant Jesus who, touching the priest's forehead with His finger, said to me, **His thought is closely united to Mine, so be at peace about what concerns My work. (41) I will not let him make a mistake, and you should do nothing without his permission.** This filled my soul with great peace as regards everything that has to do with this work.

1409 + Today the Lord Jesus is giving me an awareness of Himself and of His most tender love and care for me. He is bringing me to understand deeply how everything depends on His will, and how He allows certain difficulties precisely for our merit, so that our fidelity might be clearly manifest. And through this, I have been given strength for suffering and self-denial.

1410 Today [December 7, 1937] is the eve of the Feast of the Immaculate Conception of the Virgin Mary. During the midday meal, in an instant, God gave me to know the greatness of my destiny; that is, His closeness, which for all eternity will not be taken away from me, and He did this in such a vivid and clear fashion that I remained wrapped up in His living presence for a long time, humbling myself before His greatness.

+
(42) J.M.J.

1411 O Divine Spirit, Spirit of truth and of light,
Dwell ever in my soul by Your divine grace.
May Your breath dissipate the darkness,
And in this light may good deeds be multiplied.

O Divine Spirit, Spirit of love and of mercy,
Who pour the balm of trust into my heart,
Your grace confirms my soul in good,
Giving it the invincible power of constancy.

O Divine Spirit, Spirit of peace and of joy,
You invigorate my thirsting heart
And pour into it the living fountain of God's love,
Making it intrepid for battle.

O Divine Spirit, my soul's most welcome guest,
For my part, I want to remain faithful to You;
Both in days of joy and in the agony of suffering,
I want always, O Spirit of God, to live in Your presence.

O Divine Spirit, who pervade my whole being
And give me to know Your Divine Threefold Life,
Initiating me into Your Divine Essence,
Thus united to You, I will live a life without end.

1412 **(43)**+ It is with great zeal that I have prepared for the celebration of the Feast of the Immaculate Conception of the Mother of God. I have made an extra effort to keep recollected in spirit and have meditated on that unique privilege of Our Lady. And thus my heart was completely drowned in Her, thanking God for having accorded this great privilege to Mary.

1413 I prepared not only by means of the novena said in common by the whole community, but I also made a personal effort to salute Her a thousand times each day, saying a thousand "Hail Marys" for nine days in Her praise.

+ This is now the third time I have said such a novena to the Mother of God; that is, a novena made up of a thousand *Aves* each day. Thus the novena consists in nine thousand salutations. Although I have done this now three times in my life, and two of these while in the course of my duties, I have never failed in carrying out my tasks with the greatest exactitude. I have always said the novena outside the time of my exercises; that is to say, I have not said the *Aves* during Holy Mass or Benediction. Once, I made the novena while **(44)** lying ill in the hospital. Where there's a will, there's a way. Apart from recreation, I have only prayed and worked. I have not said a single unnecessary word during these days. Although I must admit that such a matter requires a good deal of attention and effort, nothing is too much when it comes to honoring the Immaculate Virgin.

1414 The Feast of the Immaculate Conception. Before Holy Communion I saw the Blessed Mother inconceivably beautiful. Smiling at me She said to me, *My daughter, at God's command I am to be, in a special and exclusive way your Mother; but I desire that you, too, in a special way, be My child.*

1415 *I desire, My dearly beloved daughter, that you practice the three virtues that are dearest to Me—and most*

*pleasing to God. The first is humility, humility, and
once again humility; the second virtue, purity; the third
virtue, love of God. As My daughter, you must especially
radiate with these virtues.* When the conversation
ended, She pressed me to Her Heart and disappeared.
When I regained the use of my senses, **(45)** my heart
became so wonderfully attracted to these virtues; and I
practice them faithfully. They are as though engraved in
my heart.

1416 This has been a great day for me. During this day I
remained as though in unceasing contemplation; the
very thought of this grace drew me into further
contemplation; and throughout the whole day I
continued in thanksgiving which I never stopped,
because each recollection of this grace caused my soul
ever anew to lose itself in God...

1417 O my Lord, my soul is the most wretched of all, and yet
You stoop to it with such kindness! I see clearly Your
greatness and my littleness, and therefore I rejoice that
You are so powerful and without limit, and so I rejoice
greatly at being so little.

1418 O suffering Christ, I am going out to meet You. As Your
bride, I must resemble You. Your cloak of ignominy
must cover me too. O Christ, You know how ardently I
desire to become like You. Grant that Your entire
Passion may be my lot. May all **(46)** Your sorrow be
poured into my heart. I trust that You will complete this
in me in the way You deem most fitting.

1419 + Today there was nocturnal adoration. I could not take
part in it because of my poor health, but before I fell
asleep I united myself with the sisters who were at
adoration. Between four and five o'clock, I was suddenly
awakened, and I heard a voice telling me to join those
who were adoring at that time. I understood that there
was among them a soul who was praying for me.

1420   When I steeped myself in prayer, I was transported in spirit to the chapel, where I saw the Lord Jesus, exposed in the monstrance. In place of the monstrance, I saw the glorious face of the Lord, and He said to me, **What you see in reality, these souls see through faith. Oh, how pleasing to Me is their great faith! You see, although there appears to be no trace of life in Me, in reality it is present in its fullness in each and every Host. But for Me to be able to act upon a soul, the soul must have faith. O how pleasing to Me is living faith!**

1421   Those taking part in adoration at that time **(47)** were Mother Superior and a few other sisters. But I recognized that it was Mother Superior's prayer which had moved heaven, and I rejoiced that there are souls so pleasing to God.

1422   When, during recreation the next day, I asked which sisters had been at adoration between four and five o'clock, one of the sisters cried out, "Why do you ask, Sister? Perhaps you had some revelation?" I fell silent and said no more; although I was asked by Mother Superior, I could not answer because it was not a suitable moment.

1423   On a certain occasion, one of the sisters [Sister Damian Ziolek[220]] confided to me that she wanted to choose a certain priest as her confessor. Very pleased, she shared the news with me and asked me to pray for that intention, and so I promised her to do so. During prayer, I learned that that soul would gain no spiritual profit from his direction. And then, the next time we met, she told me again of her great joy in being under his direction.

1424   I joined in her joy, but when she had **(48)** left I was severely rebuked. Jesus told me to tell her what He had given me to know during prayer, which I did at the first opportunity, although it cost me a great deal.

1425   Today, for a short while, I experienced the pain of the crown of thorns. I was praying for a certain soul before the Blessed Sacrament at the time. In an instant, I felt such a violent pain that my head dropped onto the altar rail. Although this moment was very brief, it was very painful.

1426 Christ, give me souls. Let anything You like happen to me, but give me souls in return. I want the salvation of souls. I want souls to know Your mercy. I have nothing left for myself, because I have given everything away to souls, with the result that on the day of judgment I will stand before You empty-handed, since I have given everything away to souls. Thus You will have nothing on which to judge me, and we shall meet on that day: Love and mercy...

+

(49) J.M.J.

1427 Hidden Jesus, life of my soul,
Object of my ardent desire,
Nothing will stifle Your love in my heart.
The power of our mutual love assures me of that.

Hidden Jesus, glorious pledge of my resurrection,
All my life is concentrated in You.
It is You, O Host, who empower me to love forever,
And I know that You will love me as Your child in return.

Hidden Jesus, my purest love,
My life with You has begun already here on earth,
And it will become fully manifest in the eternity to come,
Because our mutual love will never change.

Hidden Jesus, sole desire of my soul,
You alone are to me more than the delights of heaven.
My soul searches for You only, who are above all gifts and graces,
You who come to me under the form of bread.

Hidden Jesus, take at last to Yourself my thirsting
  heart
Which burns for You with the pure fire of the Seraphim.
I go through life in Your footsteps, invincible,
With head held high, like a knight, feeble maid though I
  be.

1428 **(50)** For a month now, I have been feeling worse. Every
time I cough, I feel my lungs disintegrating. It sometimes
happens that I feel the complete decay of my own
corpse. It is hard to express how great a suffering this is.
Although I fully agree to this with my will, it is
nevertheless a great suffering for nature, greater than
wearing a hairshirt or a flagellation to the point of
blood. I have felt it especially when I was going to the
refectory. It took great effort for me to eat anything
because food made me sick. I also started at this time to
suffer from pains in my intestines. All highly seasoned
dishes caused me such immense pain that I spent many
nights writhing in pain and in tears, for the sake of
sinners.

1429 However, I asked my confessor what to do: whether I
should continue to suffer this for the sake of sinners or
ask the superiors for an exception by way of milder
food. He decided that I should ask the superiors for
milder food. And thus I followed his directions, seeing
that this humiliation was more pleasing to God.

1430 **(51)** One day, I began to doubt as to how it was possible
to feel this continual decaying of the body and at the
same time to be able to walk and work. Perhaps this was
some kind of an illusion. Yet it cannot be an illusion,
because it causes me such terrible pains. As I was
thinking about this, one of the sisters came to converse
with me. After a minute or two, she made a terribly wry
face and said, "Sister, I smell a corpse here, as though it
were decaying. O how dreadful it is!" I said to her, "Do
not be frightened, Sister, that smell of a corpse comes

from me." She was very surprised and said she could not stand it any longer. After she had gone, I understood that God had allowed her to sense this so that I would have no doubt, but that He was no less than miraculously keeping the knowledge of this suffering from the whole community. O my Jesus, only You know the full depth of this sacrifice.

1431 Nevertheless, when in the refectory I still had to bear being the object of the frequent suspicion that I was being fussy [about my food]. At such times, as always, I hasten to the Tabernacle and bow before the ciborium **(52)** and there draw strength to accept God's will. That which I have written is not yet everything.

1432 Today during confession, breaking the wafer with me spiritually, he gave me the following wishes: "Be as faithful as you can to the grace of God; secondly, beg God's mercy for yourself and for the whole world, because we are all in great need of God's mercy."

1433 Two days before Christmas, these words were read in the refectory: "Tomorrow is the Birth of Jesus Christ according to the flesh."[221] At these words, my soul was pierced by the light and love of God, and I gained deeper knowledge of the Mystery of the Incarnation of the Son of God. How great is the mercy of God contained in the Mystery of the Incarnation of the Son of God!

1434 Today, the Lord gave me knowledge of His anger toward mankind which deserves to have its days shortened because of its sins. But I learned that the world's existence is maintained by chosen souls; that is, the religious orders. Woe to the world when there will be a lack of religious orders!

+

(53) J.M.J.

1435 I perform each deed in the face of death.
I do it now as I would want to see it in my last hour.

Although life, like the wind, will pass swiftly by,
No deed undertaken for God will perish.

I feel the complete decay of my organism,
Although I am still living and working.
Death will be no tragedy for me,
Because I have long felt it.

Although it is very unpleasant for nature
To constantly smell one's own corpse,
Yet it is not so terrible when the soul is filled with God's
light,
Because in it faith, hope, love and contrition are
awakened.

Daily I make great efforts
To take part in community life,
Thereby gaining graces for souls' salvation,
Shielding them by my sacrifice from the fire of hell.

For the salvation of even a single soul
Is worth the sacrifice of a lifetime
And the bearing of the greatest sacrifices and torments,
Seeing how great the glory it gives God.

1436 **(54)** + Lord, although You often make known to me the
thunders of Your anger, Your anger vanishes before
lowly souls. Although You are great, Lord, You allow
yourself to be overcome by a lowly and deeply humble
soul. O humility, the most precious of virtues, how few
souls possess you! I see only a semblance of this virtue
everywhere, but not the virtue itself. Lord, reduce me to
nothingness in my own eyes that I may find grace in
Yours.

1437 + Christmas Eve [1937]. After Holy Communion, the
Mother of God gave me to experience the anxious
concern she had in Her heart because of the Son of God.
But this anxiety was permeated with such fragrance of
abandonment to the will of God that I should call it
rather a delight than an anxiety. I understood how my

soul ought to accept the will of God in all things. It is a pity I cannot write this the way I experienced it. My soul was plunged in deep recollection all day long. Nothing could tear me away from this recollection, neither duties, nor the business I had with lay people.

1438 **(55)** Before supper, I went into the chapel for a moment to break the wafer spiritually with those beloved persons, so dear to my heart, though far away. First, I steeped myself in profound prayer and asked the Lord for graces for them all as a group and then for each one individually. Jesus gave me to know how much this pleased Him, and my soul was filled with even greater joy to see that God loves in a special way those whom we love.

1439 + After I had gone into the refectory, during the reading, my whole being found itself plunged in God. Interiorly, I saw God looking at us with great pleasure. I remained alone with the Heavenly Father. At that moment, I had a deeper knowledge of the Three Divine Persons, whom we shall contemplate for all eternity and, after millions of years, shall discover that we have just barely begun our contemplation. Oh, how great is the mercy of God, who allows man to participate in such a high **(56)** degree in His divine happiness! At the same time, what great pain pierces my heart [at the thought] that so many souls have spurned this happiness.

1440 When we began to share the wafer, a sincere and mutual love reigned among us. Mother Superior [Irene] expressed this wish to me: "Sister, the works of God proceed slowly, so do not be in a hurry." In general, the sisters sincerely wished me great love, which is that which I desire above all. I saw that these wishes truly came from their hearts, except for one sister, who had a concealed malice in her wishes, although this did not cause me much pain, for my soul was pervaded by God. Yet this enlightened me as to why God communicates so little with a soul of this kind, and I learned that such a soul is always seeking itself, even in holy things. Oh, how good the Lord is in not letting me go astray! I know that He will guard me, even jealously, but only as long as I remain little, because it is with such that the great Lord likes to commune. As to proud souls, He watches them from afar and opposes them.

1441 **(57)** Although I wanted to keep vigil for some time before the Midnight Mass,[222] I could not do so. I fell asleep at once, and I was even feeling very weak. But when they rang the bells for Midnight Mass, I jumped to my feet at once and dressed, though with great difficulty, because I felt sick again and again.

1442 + When I arrived at Midnight Mass, from the very beginning I steeped myself in deep recollection, during which time I saw the stable of Bethlehem filled with great radiance. The Blessed Virgin, all lost in the deepest of love, was wrapping Jesus in swaddling clothes, but Saint Joseph was still asleep. Only after the Mother of God put Jesus in the manger, did the light of God awaken Joseph, who also prayed. But after a while, I was left alone with the Infant Jesus who stretched out His little hands to me, and I understood that I was to take Him in my arms. Jesus pressed His head against my heart and gave me to know, by His profound gaze, how good He found it to be next to my heart. At that moment Jesus disappeared and the bell was ringing for Holy Communion.

1443 **(58)** My soul was languishing with joy. But toward the end of the Mass, I felt so weak that I had to leave the chapel and go to my cell, as I felt unable to take part in the community tea. But my joy throughout the whole Christmas Season was immense, because my soul was unceasingly united with the Lord. I have come to know that every soul would like to have divine comforts, but is by no means willing to forsake human comforts, whereas these two things cannot be reconciled.

1444 During this Christmas Season, I have sensed that certain souls have been praying for me. I rejoice that such spiritual union and knowledge exist already here on earth. O my Jesus, praise be to You for all this!

1445 In the greatest torments of soul I am always alone, but no—not alone, for I am with You, Jesus; but here I am speaking about [other] people. None of them understands my heart, but this does not surprise me anymore, whereas I used to be surprised when my intentions **(59)** were condemned and wrongly interpreted; no, this does not surprise me now at all. People do not know how to perceive the soul. They see the body, and they judge according to the body. But as distant as heaven is from earth, so distant are God's thoughts from our thoughts. I myself have experienced that quite often it happens that [...]

1446 The Lord said to me, **It should be of no concern to you how anyone else acts; you are to be My living reflection, through love and mercy.** I answered, "Lord, but they often take advantage of my goodness." **That makes no difference, My daughter. That is no concern of yours. As for you, be always merciful toward other people, and especially toward sinners.**

1447 **+Oh, how painful it is to Me that souls so seldom unite themselves to Me in Holy Communion. I wait for souls, and they are indifferent toward Me. I love them tenderly and sincerely, and they distrust Me. I want to lavish My graces on them, and they do not want to accept them. They treat Me as a dead object, whereas (60) My Heart is full of love and mercy. In order that you may know at least some of My pain, imagine the most tender of mothers who has great love for her children, while those children spurn her love. Consider her pain. No one is in a position to console her. This is but a feeble image and likeness of My love.**

1448 **Write, speak of My mercy. Tell souls where they are to** look for solace; that is, in the Tribunal of Mercy [the Sacrament of Reconciliation]. **There the greatest miracles take place [and] are incessantly repeated. To avail oneself of this miracle, it is not necessary to go on a great pilgrimage or to carry out some external ceremony; it suffices to come with faith to the feet of My representative and to reveal to him one's misery, and the miracle of Divine Mercy will be fully demonstrated. Were a soul like a decaying corpse so that from a human standpoint, there would be no [hope of] restoration and everything would already be lost, it is not so with God. The miracle of Divine Mercy restores that soul in full. Oh, how miserable are those who do not take advantage of the miracle of God's mercy! You will call out in vain, but it will be too late.**

+

(61) J.M.J.

The Year 1938

The First of January

1449   Welcome to you, New Year, in the course of which my perfection will be accomplished.[223] Thank You in advance, O Lord, for everything Your goodness will send me. Thank You for the cup of suffering from which I shall daily drink. Do not diminish its bitterness, O Lord, but strengthen my lips that, while drinking of this bitterness, they may know how to smile for love of You, my Master. I thank You for Your countless comforts and graces that flow down upon me each day like the morning dew, silently, imperceptibly, which no curious eye may notice, and which are known only to You and me, O Lord. For all this, I thank You as of today because, at the moment when You hand me the cup, my heart may not be capable of giving thanks.

1450   So today I submit myself completely and with loving consent to Your holy will, O Lord, and to Your most wise decrees, which are always full of clemency and mercy for me, though at times I can **(62)** neither understand nor fathom them. O my Master, I surrender myself completely to You, who are the rudder of my soul; steer it Yourself according to Your divine wishes. I enclose myself in Your most compassionate Heart, which is a sea of unfathomable mercy.

1451 + I am ending the old year with suffering and beginning the new one with suffering as well. Two days before the new year, I had to go to bed. I was feeling very bad, and a violent cough was weakening me. And together with this, a constant pain in my intestines and nausea had brought me to the point of exhaustion. Although I could not join in community prayer,[224] I united myself spiritually with the whole community. When the sisters got up at eleven o'clock at night to keep vigil and welcome the New Year, I had been writhing in agony since nightfall, and this lasted until midnight. I united my sufferings with the prayers of the sisters who were keeping vigil in the chapel and atoning to God for the offences of sinners.

1452 When the clock struck twelve, my soul immersed itself more deeply in recollection, and I heard a voice in my soul: **(63) Do not fear, My little child, you are not alone. Fight bravely, because My arm is supporting you; fight for the salvation of souls, exhorting them to trust in My mercy, as that is your task in this life and in the life to come.** After these words, I received a deeper understanding of divine mercy. Only that soul who wants it will be damned, for God condemns no one.

1453 Today is the Feast of the New Year. I felt so bad in the morning that I barely managed to go to the next cell to receive Holy Communion.[225] I could not go to Mass because I felt so sick, and I made my thanksgiving in bed too. I wanted so much to go to Mass and then to confession to Father Andrasz, but I felt so bad that I could go neither to Mass nor to confession. And because of this my soul suffered a good deal.

After breakfast, the Sister Infirmarian [Sister Chrysostom] came along and asked, "Sister, why didn't you go to Mass?" I answered that I couldn't. She shook her head disdainfully and said, "Such a great Feast Day, Sister, and you don't even go to Mass!" and she left my cell. I had been in bed for two days, writhing in pain, and she hadn't visited me; and when she did come, **(64)** on the third day, she did not even ask if I were able to get up, but asked irritably why I hadn't got up for Mass. When I was alone, I tried to get up, but I was seized again with sickness, and so I stayed in bed with a calm conscience. Yet my heart had plenty to offer the Lord, joining itself spiritually to Him during the second Mass. After the second Mass, Sister Infirmarian returned to me, but this time in her capacity as infirmarian, and with a thermometer. But I had no fever, although I was seriously ill and unable to rise. So there was another sermon to tell me that I should not capitulate to illness. I answered her that I knew that here one was regarded as seriously ill only when one was in one's last agony. However, knowing that she was about to give me a lecture, I replied that at the present time I was in no need of being incited to greater zeal. And once again, I remained alone in my cell.

My heart was crushed with sorrow, and bitterness flooded my soul, and I repeated these words: "Welcome, New Year; welcome, cup of bitterness." My Jesus, my heart is eager for You, and yet the gravity of my illness prevents me from participating physically **(65)** in the community prayers, and I am suspected of being lazy. My sufferings are becoming greater. After dinner, Mother Superior [Irene] looked in for a moment, but she left very soon. I intended to ask to have Father Andrasz come to my cell to hear my confession, but I restrained myself from making the request for two reasons: first, not to give occasion for murmuring, as had happened above in respect to Holy Mass; and secondly, because I would not even be able to make the confession, since I felt I would burst into tears like a little child. A while later, one of the sisters came along and again reproved me: "There's some milk with butter in the oven, Sister; why don't you drink it?" I answered that there was no one to bring it to me.

1454 + When night fell, the physical sufferings increased and were joined by moral sufferings. Night and suffering. The solemn silence of the night made it possible for me to suffer freely. My body was stretched on the wood of the cross. I writhed in terrible pain until eleven o'clock. I went in spirit to the Tabernacle and uncovered the ciborium, leaning my head on the rim of the cup, and all my tears **(66)** flowed silently toward the Heart of Him who alone understands what pain and suffering is. And I experienced the sweetness of this suffering, and my soul came to desire this sweet agony, which I would not have exchanged for all the world's treasures. The Lord gave me strength of spirit and love towards those through whom these sufferings came. This then was the first day of the year.

1455 Also on this day I felt the prayer of a beautiful soul [probably Father Sopocko or Father Andrasz] who was praying for me and giving me, in spirit, his priestly blessing. I answered in return with my own ardent prayer.

1456 + O most gracious Lord, how merciful it is on Your part to judge each one according to his conscience and his discernment, and not according to people's talk. My spirit delights and feeds more and more on Your wisdom, which I am getting to know more and more deeply. And in this, the vastness of Your mercy becomes more and more manifest to me. O my Jesus, the effect of all this knowledge on my soul is that I am being transformed into a flame of love towards You, my God.

1457 **(67)** + January 2, 1938. As I was preparing for Holy

Communion today, Jesus demanded that I should write more; not only about the graces which He grants me, but also about external matters, and this for the consolation of many souls.

1458 + After that night of suffering, when the priest [Father Matzänger[226]] entered my cell with the Lord Jesus, such fervor filled my whole being that I felt that if the priest had tarried a little longer, Jesus himself would have leaped out of his hand and come to me.

1459 After Holy Communion the Lord said to me, **If the priest had not brought Me to you, I would have come Myself under the same species. My daughter, your sufferings of this night obtained the grace of mercy for an immense number of souls.**

1460 + **My daughter, I have something to tell you.** I replied, "Speak, Jesus, for I thirst for Your words." **It displeases Me that, because the sisters were murmuring, you did not ask to have Father Andrasz hear your confession in your cell. Know that, because of this, you gave them even greater cause for murmuring. (68)** Very humbly I begged the Lord's forgiveness. O my Master, rebuke me; do not overlook my faults, and do not let me err.

1461 + O my Jesus, when I am misunderstood and my soul is in anguish, I want to stay a while alone with You. The words of mortals give me no comfort. Do not send me, O Lord, such messengers as speak only for themselves and say what their own nature dictates to them. Such consolers make me very tired.

1462 January 6, 1938. Today, when the chaplain [Father Theodore] brought the Lord Jesus, a light issued from the Host, its light striking my heart and filling me with a great fire of love. Jesus was letting me know that I should answer the inspirations of grace with more faithfulness, and that my vigilance should be more subtle.

1463 + The Lord also gave me to know that many bishops were considering the question of this Feast, as well as a certain lay person. Some were enthusiastic about this work of God, while others regarded it with disbelief; but in spite of everything, the result was great glory for the **(69)** work of God. Mother Irene and Mother Mary Joseph were giving some kind of a report to these dignitaries, but they were being questioned, not so much about the work, as about myself.[227] As regards the work itself, there was no doubt, since the glory of God was already being proclaimed.

1464 I feel much better today. I was glad I would be able to meditate more during the Holy Hour. Then I heard a voice: **You will not be in good health. Do not put off the Sacrament of Penance, because this displeases Me. Pay little attention to the murmurs of those around you.** This surprised me, because I am feeling better today, but I gave it no more thought. When the sister switched off the light, I began the Holy Hour. But after a while something went wrong with my heart. I suffered in silence until eleven o'clock, but then I began to feel so bad that I woke up Sister N. [probably Sister Fabiola], who is my roommate, and she gave me some drops, which brought me a little relief so that I could lie down. I now understand the Lord's warning. I decided to call any priest at all, the next day, and to open **(70)** the secrets of my soul to him. But that was not all, for while I was praying for sinners and offering all my sufferings for them, the Evil Spirit could not stand that.

1465 Taking the form of an apparition he said," Do not pray for sinners, but for yourself, for you will be damned." Paying no attention to Satan, I continued to pray with redoubled fervor for sinners. The Evil Spirit howled with fury, "Oh, if I had power over you!" and disappeared. I saw that my suffering and prayer shackled Satan and snatched many souls from his clutches.

1466 Jesus, lover of human salvation, draw all souls to the divine life. May the greatness of Your mercy be praised here on earth and in eternity. O great lover of souls, who in Your boundless compassion opened the salutary fountains of mercy so that weak souls may be fortified in this life's pilgrimage, Your mercy runs through our life like a golden thread and maintains in good order the contact of our being with God. For He does not need anything to make Him happy; so everything is **(71)** solely the work of His mercy. My senses are transfixed with joy when God grants me a deeper awareness of that great attribute of His; namely, His unfathomable mercy.

1467 January 7, 1938. First Friday of the month. This morning during Mass, for a brief while, I saw the suffering Savior. What struck me was that Jesus was so peaceful amidst His great sufferings. I understood that this was a lesson for me on what my outward behavior should be in the midst of my various sufferings.

1468 For quite a long while, I felt pain in my hands, feet and side. Then I saw a certain sinner who, profiting from my sufferings, drew near to the Lord. All this for starving souls that they may not die of starvation.

1469 + I went to confession to the chaplain [Father Theodore] today. Jesus comforted me through this priest. O my Mother, Church of God, you are a true Mother who understands her children...

1470 **(72)** Oh, how good it is that Jesus will judge us according to our conscience and not according to people's talk and judgments. O inconceivable goodness, I see You full of goodness in the very act of judgment.

1471 Although I am feeling weak, and my nature is clamoring for rest, I feel the inspiration of grace telling me to take hold of myself and write, write for the comfort of souls, whom I love so much and with whom I will share all eternity. And I desire eternal life for them so ardently that that is why I use all my free moments, no matter how short, for writing in the way that Jesus wishes of me.

1472 January 8. During Holy Mass, I had a moment of knowledge concerning Father S., that great glory is being given to God through our mutual efforts. And even though we are far from each other, we are often together, because we are united by a common goal.

1473 O my Jesus, my only desire, although I wanted to receive You today with greater fervor than ever, **(73)** nevertheless, precisely on this day, my soul is drier than ever. My faith grows in power, and so the fruit of Your coming, Lord, will be abundant. Although many a time You come without touching my senses and reign only in the loftier part of me, the senses too sometimes rejoice at Your coming.

1474 I often ask the Lord Jesus for an intellect enlightened by faith. I express this to the Lord in these words: "Jesus, give me an intellect, a great intellect, for this only, that I may understand You better; because the better I get to know You, the more ardently will I love You. Jesus, I ask You for a powerful intellect, that I may understand divine and lofty matters. Jesus, give me a keen intellect with which I will get to know Your Divine Essence and Your indwelling, Triune life. Give my intellect these capacities and aptitudes by means of Your special grace. Although I know that there is a capability through grace which the Church gives me, there is still a treasure of graces which You give us, O Lord, when we ask You for them. But if my request is not pleasing to You, then I beg You, do not give me the inclination to pray thus."

1475 **(74)** I strive for the greatest perfection possible in order to be useful to the Church. Greater by far is my bond to the Church. The sanctity or the fall of each individual soul has an effect upon the whole Church. Observing myself and those who are close to me, I have come to understand how great an influence I have on other souls, not by any heroic deeds, as these are striking in themselves, but by small actions like a movement of the hand, a look, and many other things too numerous to mention, which have an effect on and reflect in the souls of others, as I myself have noticed.

1476 Oh, how good it is that our rule demands strict silence in the dormitory [common bedrooms] and does not allow us to stay in them unless it is absolutely necessary. I have at present a little room in which two of us sleep, but at the time of my sickness when I had to stay in bed, I found out how bothersome it was if someone was sitting in the bedroom all the time. Sister N.[228] had some handwork to do and sat in the bedroom almost all of the time, **(75)** and another S.[229] would come to instruct her on how to do it. It's difficult to describe how much this tires one, especially when one is ill and has spent a night in pain. Every word has a repercussion somewhere in the brain, especially when the eyes are heavy with sleep. O rule, how much love there is in you...

1477 When, during Vespers, the Magnificat was being sung and they came to the words, "He has shown the strength of His arm," a profound spirit of recollection enveloped my soul, and I understood that the Lord would soon accomplish His work in my soul.[230] I am not surprised now that the Lord did not disclose everything to me at first.

1478 + Why are You sad today, Jesus? Tell me, who is the cause of Your sadness? And Jesus answered me, **Chosen souls who do not have My spirit, who live according to the letter [cf. 2 Cor. 3:6] and have placed the letter above My spirit, above the spirit of love.**

I have founded My whole law on love, and yet I do not see love, even in religious orders. This is why sadness fills My Heart.

+

(76) J.M.J.

1479 O my Jesus, in terrible bitterness and pain,
I yet feel the caress of Your Divine Heart.
Like a good mother, You press me to Your bosom,
And even now You give me to experience what the veil hides.

O my Jesus, in this wilderness and terror which surround me,
My heart still feels the warmth of Your gaze,
Which no storm can blot out from me,
As You give me the assurance of Your great love, O God.

O my Jesus, midst the great miseries of this life,
You shine like a star, O Jesus, protecting me from shipwreck.
And though my miseries be great,
I have great trust in the power of Your mercy.

O hidden Jesus, in the many struggles of my last hour,
May the omnipotence of Your grace be poured out upon my soul,
That at death's moment I may gaze upon You
And see You face to face, as do the chosen in heaven.

O my Jesus, midst the dangers which surround me,
I go through life with a cry of joy, my head raised proudly,
Because against Your Heart so filled with love, O Jesus,
All enemies will be crushed, all darkness dispelled.

1480 **(77)** + Jesus, hide me in Your mercy and shield me against everything that might terrify my soul. Do not let my trust in Your mercy be disappointed. Shield me with the omnipotence of Your mercy, and judge me leniently as well.

1481 Today[231] during Holy Mass, I saw the Infant Jesus near my kneeler. He appeared to be about one year old, and

He asked me to take Him in my arms. When I did take Him in my arms, He cuddled up close to my bosom and said, **It is good for Me to be close to your heart.** "Although You are so little, I know that You are God. Why do You take the appearance of such a little baby to commune with me?" **Because I want to teach you spiritual childhood. I want you to be very little, because when you are little, I carry you close to My Heart, just as you are holding Me close to your heart right now.** And with that, I was again alone, but no one can conceive the emotions of my soul, I was so fully plunged in God, like a sponge thrown into the sea...

1482 **(78)** + O my Jesus, You know that I have gotten myself into a lot of trouble for speaking out the truth. O truth, so often oppressed, you nearly always wear a crown of thorns! O Eternal Truth, support me that I may have the courage to speak the truth even if it would come about that I would pay for it with my life. O Jesus, how hard it is to believe in this, when one sees one thing taught and something else lived.

1483 This is why, during the retreat, after a long observation of life, I resolved to fix my eyes firmly on You, Jesus, the most perfect of models. O eternity, which will uncover many secrets and make manifest the truth...

1484 O Living Host, support me in this exile, that I may be empowered to walk faithfully in the footsteps of the Savior. I do not ask, Lord, that You take me down from the cross, but I implore You to give me the strength to remain steadfast upon it. I want to be stretched out upon the cross as You were, Jesus. I want all the tortures and pains that You suffered. I want to drink the cup of bitterness to the dregs.

(79)   The Goodness of God.

1485   The mercy of God, hidden in the Blessed Sacrament, the voice of the Lord who speaks to us from the throne of mercy: **Come to Me, all of you.**

Conversation of the Merciful God

with a Sinful Soul.

Jesus: **Be not afraid of your Savior, O sinful soul. I make the first move to come to you, for I know that by yourself you are unable to lift yourself to me. Child, do not run away from your Father; be willing to talk openly with your God of mercy who wants to speak words of pardon and lavish his graces on you. How dear your soul is to Me! I have inscribed your name upon My hand; you are engraved as a deep wound in My Heart.**

Soul: Lord, I hear your voice calling me to turn back from the path of sin, but I have neither the strength nor the courage to do so.

Jesus: **I am your strength, I will help you in the struggle.**

Soul: Lord, I recognize your holiness, and I fear You.

Jesus: **My child, do you fear the God of mercy? My holiness (80) does not prevent Me from being merciful. Behold, for you I have established a throne of mercy on earth—the tabernacle—and from this throne I desire to enter into your heart. I am not surrounded by a retinue or guards. You can come to me at any moment, at any time; I want to speak to you and desire to grant you grace.**

Soul: Lord, I doubt that You will pardon my numerous sins; my misery fills me with fright.

Jesus: **My mercy is greater than your sins and those of the entire world. Who can measure the extent of my goodness? For you I descended from heaven to earth; for you I allowed myself to be nailed to the cross; for you I let my Sacred Heart be pierced with a lance, thus** opening wide the source of mercy for you. Come, then, with trust to draw graces from this fountain. I never reject a contrite heart. Your misery has disappeared in the depths of My mercy. Do not argue with Me about your wretchedness. You will give me pleasure if you hand over to me all your troubles and griefs. I shall heap upon you the treasures of My grace.

(81) Soul: You have conquered, O Lord, my stony heart with Your goodness. In trust and humility I approach the tribunal of Your mercy, where You yourself absolve me by the hand of your representative. O Lord, I feel Your grace and Your peace filling my poor soul. I feel overwhelmed by Your mercy, O Lord. You forgive me, which is more than I dared to hope for or could imagine. Your goodness surpasses all my desires. And now, filled with gratitude for so many graces, I invite You to my heart. I wandered, like a prodigal child gone astray; but you did not cease to be my Father. Increase Your mercy toward me, for You see how weak I am.

Jesus: **Child, speak no more of your misery; it is already forgotten. Listen, My child, to what I desire to tell you. Come close to My wounds and draw from the Fountain of Life whatever your heart desires. Drink copiously from the Fountain of Life and you will not weary on your journey. Look at the splendors of My mercy and do not fear the enemies of your salvation. Glorify My mercy.**

(82)   Conversation of the Merciful God

with a Despairing Soul.

1486 Jesus: **O soul steeped in darkness, do not despair. All is not yet lost. Come and confide in your God, who is love and mercy.**

—But the soul, deaf even to this appeal, wraps itself in darkness.

Jesus calls out again: **My child, listen to the voice of your merciful Father.**

—In the soul arises this reply: "For me there is no mercy," and it falls into greater darkness, a despair which is a foretaste of hell and makes it unable to draw near to God.

Jesus calls to the soul a third time, but the soul remains deaf and blind, hardened and despairing. Then the mercy of God begins to exert itself, and, without any co-operation from the soul, God grants it final grace. If this too is spurned, God will leave the soul in this self-chosen disposition for eternity. This grace emerges from the merciful Heart of Jesus and gives the soul a special light by means of which the soul begins to understand **(83)** God's effort; but conversion depends on its own will. The soul knows that this, for her, is final grace and, should it show even a flicker of good will, the mercy of God will accomplish the rest.

My omnipotent mercy is active here. Happy the soul that takes advantage of this grace.

Jesus: **What joy fills My Heart when you return to me. Because you are weak, I take you in My arms and carry you to the home of My Father.**

Soul (as if awaking, asks fearfully): Is it possible that there yet is mercy for me?

Jesus: **There is, My child. You have a special claim on My mercy. Let it act in your poor soul; let the rays of grace enter your soul; they bring with them light, warmth, and life.**

Soul: But fear fills me at the thought of my sins, and this terrible fear moves me to doubt Your goodness.

Jesus: **My child, all your sins have not wounded My Heart as painfully as your present lack of trust does— that after so many efforts of My (84) love and mercy, you should still doubt My goodness.**

Soul: O Lord, save me yourself, for I perish. Be my Savior. O Lord, I am unable to say anything more; my pitiful heart is torn asunder; but You, O Lord...

Jesus does not let the soul finish but, raising it from the ground, from the depths of its misery, he leads it into the recesses of His Heart where all its sins disappear instantly, consumed by the flames of love.

Jesus: **Here, soul, are all the treasures of My Heart. Take everything you need from it.**

Soul: O Lord, I am inundated with Your grace. I sense that a new life has entered into me and, above all, I feel Your love in my heart. That is enough for me. O Lord, I will glorify the omnipotence of Your mercy for all eternity. Encouraged by Your goodness, I will confide to You all the sorrows of my heart.

Jesus: **Tell me all, My child, hide nothing from Me, because My loving Heart, the Heart of your Best Friend, is listening to you.**

Soul: O Lord, now I see all my ingratitude and Your goodness. You were pursuing me with Your grace, while I was frustrating Your benevolence. I see that I deserve **(85)** the depths of hell for spurning Your graces.

Jesus (interrupting): **Do not be absorbed in your misery—you are still too weak to speak of it—but, rather, gaze on My Heart filled with goodness, and be imbued with My sentiments. Strive for meekness and humility; be merciful to others, as I am to you; and, when you feel your strength failing, if you come to the fountain of mercy to fortify your soul, you will not grow weary on your journey.**

Soul: Now I understand Your mercy, which protects me, and like a brilliant star, leads me into the home of my Father, protecting me from the horrors of hell that I have deserved, not once, but a thousand times. O Lord, eternity will hardly suffice for me to give due praise to

Your unfathomable mercy and Your compassion for me.

+ Conversation of the Merciful God

with a Suffering Soul

1487 Jesus: **Poor soul, I see that you suffer much and that you do not have even the strength to coverse with me. So I will speak to you. Even though your sufferings were (86) very great, do not lose heart or give in to despondency. But tell Me, my child, who has dared to wound your heart? Tell me about everything, be sincere in dealing with Me, reveal all the wounds of your heart. I will heal them, and your suffering will become a source of your sanctification.**

Soul: Lord, my sufferings are so great and numerous and have lasted so long that I become discouraged.

Jesus: **My child, do not be discouraged. I know your boundless trust in Me; I know you are aware of My goodness and mercy. Let us talk in detail about everything that weighs so heavily upon your heart.**

Soul: There are so many different things that I do not know what to speak about first, nor how to express it.

Jesus: **Talk to Me simply, as a friend to a friend. Tell Me now, My child, what hinders you from advancing in holiness?**

Soul: Poor health detains me on the way to holiness. I cannot fulfill my duties. I am as useless as an extra wheel on a wagon. I cannot mortify myself or fast to any extent, as the saints did. **(87)** Furthermore, nobody believes I am sick, so that mental pain is added to those of the body, and I am often humiliated. Jesus, how can anyone become holy in such circumstances?

Jesus: **True, My child, all that is painful. But there is no way to heaven except the way of the cross. I followed it first. You must learn that it is the shortest and surest way.**

Soul: Lord, there is another obstacle on the road to holiness. Because I am faithful to You, I am persecuted and suffer much.

Jesus: **It is because you are not of this world that the world hates you. First it persecuted Me. Persecution is a sign that you are following in My footsteps faithfully.**

Soul: My Lord, I am also discouraged because neither my superiors nor my confessor understand my interior trials. A darkness clouds my mind. How can I advance? All this discourages me from striving for the heights of sanctity.

Jesus: **Well, My child, this time you have told Me a good deal. I realize how painful it is not to be (88) understood, and especially by those whom one loves and with whom one has been very open. But suffice it to know that I understand all your troubles and misery. I am pleased by the deep faith you have, despite everything, in My representatives. Learn from this that no one will understand a soul entirely—that is beyond human ability. Therefore, I have remained on earth to comfort your aching heart and to fortify your soul, so that you will not falter on the way. You say that a dense darkness is obscuring your mind. But why, at such times, do you not come to Me, the light who can in an instant pour into your soul more understanding about holiness than can be found in any books? No confessor is capable of teaching and enlightening a soul in this way.**

Know, too, that the darkness about which you complain I first endured in the Garden of Olives when My Soul was crushed in mortal anguish. I am giving you a share in those sufferings because of My special love for you and in view of the high degree of holiness I am (89) intending for you in heaven. A suffering soul is closest to My Heart.

Soul: One more thing, Lord. What should I do when I am ignored and rejected by people, especially by those on whom I had a right to count in times of greatest need?

Jesus: **My child, make the resolution never to rely on people. Entrust yourself completely to My will saying, "Not as I want, but according to Your will, O God, let it be done unto me." These words, spoken from the depths of one's heart, can raise a soul to the summit of sanctity in a short time. In such a soul I delight. Such a soul gives Me glory. Such a soul fills heaven with the fragrance of her virtue. But understand that the strength by which you bear sufferings comes from frequent Communions. So approach this fountain of mercy often, to draw with the vessel of trust whatever you need.**

Soul: Thank You, Lord, for Your goodness in remaining with us in this exile as the God of mercy **(90)** and blessing us with the radiance of Your compassion and goodness. It is through the light of Your mercy that I have come to understand how much You love me.

1488   Conversation of the Merciful God

with a Soul Striving after Perfection.

Jesus: **I am pleased with your efforts, O soul aspiring for perfection, but why do I see you so often sad and depressed? Tell Me, My child, what is the meaning of this sadness, and what is its cause?**

Soul: Lord, the reason for my sadness is that, in spite of my sincere resolutions, I fall again into the same faults. I make resolutions in the morning, but in the evening I see how much I have departed from them.

Jesus: **You see, My child, what you are of yourself. The cause of your falls is that you rely too much upon yourself and too little on Me. But let this not sadden you so much. You are dealing with the God of mercy, which your misery cannot exhaust. Remember, I did not allot only a certain number of pardons.**

Soul: Yes, I know all that, **(91)** but great temptations

assail me, and various doubts awaken within me and, moreover, everything irritates and discourages me.

Jesus: **My child, know that the greatest obstacles to holiness are discouragement and an exaggerated anxiety. These will deprive you of the ability to practice virtue. All temptations united together ought not disturb your interior peace, not even momentarily. Sensitiveness and discouragement are the fruits of self-love. You should not become discouraged, but strive to make My love reign in place of your self-love. Have confidence, My child. Do not lose heart in coming for pardon, for I am always ready to forgive you. As often as you beg for it, you glorify My mercy.**

Soul: I understand what is the better thing to do, what pleases You more, but I encounter great obstacles in acting on this understanding.

Jesus: **My child, life on earth is a struggle indeed; a great struggle for My kingdom. But fear not, because you are not alone. I am always supporting (92) you, so lean on Me as you struggle, fearing nothing. Take the vessel of trust and draw from the fountain of life—for yourself, but also for other souls, especially such as are distrustful of My goodness.**

Soul: O Lord, I feel my heart being filled with Your love and the rays of Your mercy and love piercing my soul. I go, Lord, at Your command. I go to conquer souls. Sustained by Your grace, I am ready to follow You, Lord, not only to Tabor, but also to Calvary. I desire to lead souls to the fount of Your mercy so that the splendor of Your mercy may be reflected in all souls, and the home of our Father be filled to overflowing. And when the enemy begins to attack me, I shall take refuge behind the shield of Your mercy.

1489   Conversation of the Merciful God
                      with a Perfect Soul.

Soul: My Lord and Master, I desire to converse with You.

Jesus: **Speak, My beloved (93) child, for I am always listening. I wait for you. What do you desire to say?**

Soul: Lord, first let me pour out my heart at Your feet in a fragrant anointing of gratitude for the many blessings which You lavish upon me; even if I wanted to, I could not count them. I only recall that there has never been a moment in my life in which I have not experienced Your protection and goodness.

Jesus: **Your words please Me, and your thanksgiving opens up new treasures of graces. But, My child, we should talk in more detail about the things that lie in your heart. Let us talk confidentially and frankly, as two hearts that love one another do.**

Soul: O my merciful Lord, there are secrets in my heart which no one knows or will ever know except You because, even if I wanted to reveal them, no one would understand me. Your minister knows some because I confess to him, but he knows only the bit of these mysteries that I am capable of revealing; the rest remains between us for eternity, O My Lord! (94) You have covered me with the cloak of Your mercy, pardoning my sins. Not once did You refuse Your pardon; You always had pity on me, giving me a new life of grace. To prevent doubts, You have entrusted me to the loving care of Your Church, that tender mother, who in Your name assures me of the truths of faith and watches lest I wander. Especially in the tribunal of Your mercy does my soul meet an ocean of favors, though You did not give the Fallen Angels time to repent or prolong their time of mercy. O my Lord, you have provided saintly priests to show me the sure way.

Jesus, there is one more secret in my life, the deepest and dearest to my heart: it is You yourself when You come to my heart under the appearance of bread. Herein lies the whole secret of my sanctity. Here my heart is so united with Yours as to be but one. There are no more secrets, because all that is Yours is mine, and all that is mine is Yours. Such is the omnipotence and the **(95)** miracle of Your mercy. All the tongues of men and of angels united could not find words adequate to this mystery of Your love and mercy.

When I contemplate this mystery, my heart falls into a new ecstasy. In silence I tell You everything, Lord, because the language of love is without words; not a single stirring of my heart escapes You. O Lord, the extent of Your great condescension has awakened in my soul an even greater love for You, the sole object of my love. The life of union manifests itself in perfect purity, deep humility, gentle silence, and great zeal for the salvation of souls.

O my sweetest Lord, You watch over me each moment and inspire me as to how I should act in a precise situation, when my heart wavers between two things. You yourself frequently intervened in the resolution of a difficulty. Countless times, by means of a sudden **(96)** enlightenment, You have given me to know what is the more pleasing to You.

Oh, how numerous are the instances of forgiveness about which no one knows! How often You have poured into my soul courage and perseverance to go forward. It is You yourself who removed obstacles from my road, intervening directly in the actions of people. O Jesus, everything I have said to You is but a pale shadow of what is taking place in my heart. O my Jesus, how ardently I desire the conversion of sinners! You know what I am doing for them to win them for You. Every offense against You wounds me deeply. I spare neither strength, nor health, nor life itself in defense of Your kingdom. Although my efforts may remain invisible on earth, they are no less valuable in Your eyes.

O Jesus, I want to bring souls to the fount of Your mercy to draw the reviving water of life with the vessel of trust. The soul desirous of more of God's mercy should approach God with greater trust; and if her trust in God is unlimited, then the mercy of God toward it will be likewise limitless. O my God, **(97)** Who know every beat of my heart, You know how eagerly I desire that all hearts would beat for You alone, that every soul glorify the greatness of Your mercy.

Jesus: **My beloved child, delight of My Heart, your words are dearer and more pleasing to me than the angelic chorus. All the treasures of My Heart are open to you. Take from this Heart all that you need for yourself and for the whole world. For the sake of your love, I withhold the just chastisements, which mankind has deserved. A single act of pure love pleases Me more than a thousand imperfect prayers. One of your sighs of love atones for many offenses with which the godless overwhelm Me. The smallest act of virtue has unlimited value in My eyes because of your great love for Me. In a soul that lives on My love alone, I reign as in heaven. I watch over it day and night. In it I find My happiness; My ear is attentive to (98) each request of its heart; often I anticipate its requests. O child, especially beloved by Me, apple of My eye, rest a moment near My Heart and taste of the love in which you will delight for all eternity.**

But child, you are not yet in your homeland; so go, fortified by My grace, and fight for My kingdom in human souls; fight as a king's child would; and remember that the days of your exile will pass quickly, and with them the possibility of earning merit for heaven. I expect from you, My child, a great number of souls who will glorify My mercy for all eternity. My child, that you may answer My call worthily, receive Me

daily in Holy Communion. It will give you strength...

(99) Jesus, do not leave me alone in suffering. You know, Lord, how weak I am. I am an abyss of wretchedness, I am nothingness itself; so what will be so strange if You leave me alone and I fall? I am an infant, Lord, so I cannot get along by myself. However, beyond all abandonment I trust, and in spite of my own feeling I trust, and I am being completely transformed into trust—often in spite of what I feel. Do not lessen any of my sufferings, only give me strength to bear them. Do with me as You please, Lord, only give me the grace to be able to love You in every event and circumstance. Lord, do not lessen my cup of bitterness, only give me strength that I may be able to drink it all.

O Lord, sometimes You lift me up to the brightness of visions, and then again You plunge me into the darkness of night and the abyss of my nothingness, and my soul feels as if it were alone in the wilderness. Yet, above all things, I trust in You, Jesus, for You are unchangeable. My moods change, but You are always the same, full of mercy.

1490 **(100)** + Jesus, source of life, sanctify me. O my strength, fortify me. My Commander, fight for me. Only light of my soul, enlighten me. My Master, guide me. I entrust myself to You as a little child does to its mother's love. Even if all things were to conspire against me, and even if the ground were to give way under my feet, I would be at peace close to Your heart. You are always a most tender mother to me, and You surpass all mothers. I will sing of my pain to You by my silence, and You will understand me beyond any utterance...

1491 + The Lord visited me today and said, **My daughter, do not be afraid of what will happen to you. I will give you nothing beyond your strength. You know the power of My grace; let that be enough.** After these words, the

Lord gave me a deeper understanding of the action of His grace.

1492 Before Holy Communion, Jesus gave me to understand that I should pay absolutely no attention **(101)** to what a certain sister would say, because her cunning and malice were displeasing to Him. **My daughter, do not speak to this person about either your views or your opinions.** I begged the Lord's pardon for what in that soul was displeasing to Him, and I begged Him to strengthen me with His grace when she would come to talk with me again. She has asked me about many things, to which I gave answer with all my sisterly love and, as evidence that I have spoken to her from the bottom of my heart, I have told her some things that came from my own experience. But her intentions were something quite different from the words on her lips...

1493 + O my Jesus, from the moment I gave myself completely to You, I have given no thought whatsoever for myself. You may do with me whatever You like. There is only one thing I think about; that is, what do You prefer; what can I do, O Lord, to please You. I listen and watch for each opportunity. It matters not if I am outwardly judged otherwise in this matter...

1494 **(102)** January 15, 1938. Today, when the sister about whom the Lord warned me came to see me, I armed myself spiritually for battle. Although it cost me much, I did not depart one bit from what the Lord had commanded. But when an hour had gone by, and the sister made no move to go, I interiorly called upon Jesus to help. Then I heard a voice in my soul saying, **Do not fear. I am watching you this very moment and am helping you. In a moment, I will send you two sisters who are coming to visit you, and then you will find it easy to continue the conversation.** And at that moment two sisters entered, and then the conversation was much easier, even though it lasted for still another half hour.

1495 Oh, how good it is to call on Jesus for help during a
conversation. Oh, how good it is, during a moment of
peace, to beg for actual graces. I fear most of all this sort
of confidential conversation; there is need of much
divine light at times like this, in order to speak with
profit, both for the other person's soul, and for one's
own as well. God, however, comes to our aid; but we
have to ask Him for it. Let no one trust too much in his
own self.

1496 **(103)** January 17, 1938. Today, since early in the
morning, my soul has been in darkness. I cannot ascend
to Jesus, and I feel as though I have been forsaken by
Him. I will not turn to creatures for light, because I
know that they will not enlighten me if Jesus wills to
keep me in darkness. I submit myself to His holy will
and suffer. Still, the struggle is becoming more and
more desperate. During Vespers, I wanted to unite
myself with the sisters through prayer.

1497 When I went, in my thoughts, to the chapel, my spirit
was plunged into even greater darkness. Total discouragement came over me. Then I heard Satan's voice:
"See how contradictory everything is that Jesus gives to
you: He tells you to found a convent, and then He gives
you sickness; He tells you to set about establishing this
Feast of Mercy while the whole world does not at all
want such a feast. Why do you pray for this feast? It is so
inopportune ." My soul remained silent and, by an act of
will, continued to pray without entering into
conversation with the Spirit of Darkness. Nevertheless,
such an extraordinary disgust with life came over me
that I had to make a great act of the will to consent to go
on living... **(104)**

And again I heard the tempter's words: "Ask for death
for yourself, tomorrow after Holy Communion. God
will hear you, for He has heard you so many times
before and has given you what you asked for." I

remained silent and, by an act of will, I began to pray, or rather, submitted myself to God, asking Him interiorly not to abandon me at this moment. It was already eleven o'clock at night, and there was silence all around. The sisters were all asleep in their cells, and my soul alone was struggling with great exertion.

The tempter went on: "Why should you bother about other souls? You ought to be praying only for yourself. As for sinners, they will be converted without your prayers. I see that you are suffering very much at this moment. I'm going to give you a piece of advice on which your happiness will depend: never speak about God's mercy and, in particular, do not encourage sinners to trust in God's mercy, because they deserve a just punishment. Another very important thing: do not tell your confessors, and especially this extraordinary confessor and the priest in Vilnius, about what goes on in your soul. I know them; I know who they are, and so I want to put you on your guard (105) against them. You see, to live as a good nun, it is sufficient to live like all the others. Why expose yourself to so many difficulties?"

1498 I remained silent, and by an act of will I dwelt in God, although a moan escaped from my heart. Finally, the tempter went away and I, exhausted, fell asleep immediately. In the morning, right after receiving Holy Communion, I went immediately to my cell and falling on my knees I renewed my act of submission in all things to the will of God. "Jesus, I ask You, give me the strength for battle. Let it be done to me according to Your most holy will. My soul is enamored of Your most holy will."

1499 At that moment, I saw Jesus, who said, **I am pleased with what you are doing. And you can continue to be at peace if you always do the best you can in respect to this work of mercy. Be absolutely as frank as possible with your confessor.**

Satan gained nothing by tempting you, because you did not enter into conversation with him. Continue to act in this way. You gave Me great glory today by fighting so faithfully. (106) Let it be confirmed and engraved on your heart that I am always with you, even if you don't feel My presence at the time of battle.

1500   Today, the love of God is transporting me into the other world. I am all immersed in love; I love and feel that I am loved, and with full consciousness I experience this. My soul is drowning in the Lord, realizing the great Majesty of God and its own littleness; but through this knowledge my happiness increases... This awareness is so vivid in the soul, so powerful and, at the same time, so sweet.

1501   + Now that I have difficulty sleeping at night, because my suffering won't allow it, I visit all the churches and chapels and, if only for a brief moment, I make an act of adoration before the Blessed Sacrament. When I return to my chapel, I then pray for certain priests who proclaim and glorify The Divine Mercy. I also pray for the intentions of the Holy Father and to obtain mercy for sinners—such are my nights.

1502   **(107)** January 20, 1938. I never cringe before anyone. I can't bear flattery, for humility is nothing but the truth. There is no cringing in true humility. Although I consider myself the least in the whole convent, on the other hand, I enjoy the honor of being the bride of Christ. Little matter that often I hear people say that I am proud, for I know that human judgment does not discern the motives for our actions.

1503   When, at the beginning of my religious life, following the novitiate, I began to exercise myself particularly in humility, the humiliations that God sent me were not enough for me. And so, in my excessive zeal, I looked for more of them on my own, and I often represented myself to my superiors other than I was in reality and spoke of miseries of which I had no notion. But a short time later, Jesus gave me to know that humility is only the truth. From that time on, I changed my ideas, faithfully following the light of Jesus. I learned that if a soul is with Jesus, He will not permit it to err.

1504 **(108)** + Lord, You know that since my youth I have always sought Your will and, recognizing it, have always tried to carry it out. My heart has been accustomed to the inspirations of the Holy Spirit, to whom I am faithful. In the midst of the greatest din I have heard the voice of God. I always know what is going on in my interior...

1505 I am striving for sanctity, because in this way I shall be useful to the Church. I make constant efforts in practicing virtue. I try faithfully to follow Jesus. And I deposit this whole series of daily virtues—silent, hidden, almost imperceptible, but made with great love—in the treasury of God's Church for the common benefit of souls. I feel interiorly as if I were responsible for all souls. I know very well that I do not live for myself alone, but for the entire Church...

1506 + O incomprehensible God, my heart dissolves in joy that You have allowed me to penetrate the mysteries of Your mercy! **(109)**Everything begins with Your mercy and ends with Your mercy.

1507 All grace flows from mercy, and the last hour abounds with mercy for us. Let no one doubt concerning the goodness of God; even if a person's sins were as dark as night, God's mercy is stronger than our misery. One thing alone is necessary: that the sinner set ajar the door of his heart, be it ever so little, to let in a ray of God's merciful grace, and then God will do the rest. But poor is the soul who has shut the door on God's mercy, even at the last hour. It was just such souls who plunged Jesus into deadly sorrow in the Garden of Olives; indeed, it

was from His Most Merciful Heart that divine mercy
flowed out.

1508 January 21, [1938]. Jesus, how truly dreadful it would be
to suffer if it were not for You. But it is You, Jesus,
stretched out on the cross, who give me strength and are
always close to the suffering soul. Creatures will
abandon a person in his suffering, but You, O Lord, are
faithful...

1509 **(110)** It often happens when one is ill, as in the case of
Job in the Old Testament, that as long as one can move
about and work, everything is fine and dandy; but when
God sends illness, somehow or other, there are fewer
friends about. But yet, there are some. They still take
interest in our suffering and all that, but if God sends a
longer illness, even those faithful friends slowly begin to
desert us. They visit us less frequently, and often their
visits cause suffering. Instead of comforting us, they
reproach us about certain things, which is an occasion
of a good deal of suffering. And so the soul, like Job, is
alone; but fortunately it is not alone, because Jesus-
Host is with it.

After having tasted the above sufferings and spent a
whole night in bitterness, the next morning, when the
chaplain [Father Theodore] brought me Holy
Communion, I had to control myself by sheer effort of
will to keep from crying out at the top of my voice,
"Welcome, my true and only Friend." Holy Communion
gives me strength to suffer and fight.

I wish to speak of one more thing that I have
experienced: when God gives **(111)** neither death nor
health, and [when] this lasts for many years, people
become accustomed to this and consider the person as
not being ill. Then there begins a whole series of silent
sufferings. Only God knows how many sacrifices the
soul makes.

1510 One evening, when I was feeling so bad that I wondered how I would get back to my cell, I came across the Sister Assistant [Sister Seraphina], who was asking one of the sisters of the first choir to go to the gate with a certain message. But when she saw me, she said to her, "No, Sister, you need not go, but Sister Faustina will, because it is raining heavily." I answered, "All right," and went and carried out the order, but only God knows the whole of it. This is just one example among many. Sometimes it would seem that a sister of the second choir[232] is made of stone, but she also is human and has a heart and feelings...

1511 At such times, God Himself comes to our rescue, for otherwise the soul would not be able to bear these crosses of which I haven't even begun to write, nor do I intend to do so now. But when I feel the inspiration to do so, I will write about them...

1512 **(112)** Today, during Mass, I saw the Lord Jesus in the midst of His sufferings, as though dying on the cross. He said to me, **My daughter, meditate frequently on the sufferings which I have undergone for your sake, and then nothing of what you suffer for Me will seem great to you. You please Me most when you meditate on My Sorrowful Passion. Join your little sufferings to My Sorrowful Passion, so that they may have infinite value before My Majesty.**

1513 + Jesus said to me today, **You often call Me your Master. This is pleasing to My Heart; but do not forget, My disciple, that you are a disciple of a crucified Master. Let that one word be enough for you. You know what is contained in the cross.**

1514 + I have learned that the greatest power is hidden in patience. I see that patience always leads to victory, although not immediately; but that victory will become manifest after many years. Patience is linked to meekness.

1515 **(113)** + I spent this whole night with Jesus in the dark dungeon. This was a night of adoration. The sisters were praying in the chapel, and I was uniting myself with them in spirit, because poor health prevents me from going to the chapel. But all night long I could not fall asleep, so I spent the night in the dark prison with Jesus. Jesus gave me to know of the sufferings He experienced there. The world will learn about them on the day of judgment.

1516 **My daughter, tell souls that I am giving them My mercy as a defense. I Myself am fighting for them and am bearing the just anger of My Father.**

1517 Say, **My daughter, that the Feast of My Mercy has issued forth from My very depths for the consolation of the whole world.**

1518 Jesus, my peace and my rest, I beg You to give light to that sister, so that she may change interiorly, Support her powerfully with Your grace, so that she, too, may attain perfection.

1519 **(114)** + Today before Holy Communion, the Lord said to me, **My daughter, today talk openly to the Superior** [Mother Irene] **about My mercy because, of all the superiors, she has taken the greatest part in proclaiming My mercy.** And in fact, Mother Superior came this afternoon, and we talked about this Work of God. Mother told me that the images had not come out too well and were not selling very well. "But," she said, "I have taken a good quantity myself and am distributing them wherever I can and do the best I can to spread the Work of Mercy." When she had gone, the Lord gave me to know how pleasing this soul was to Him.

1520 Today the Lord said to me, **I have opened My Heart as a living fountain of mercy. Let all souls draw life from it. Let them approach this sea of mercy with great trust.**

Sinners will attain justification, and the just will be confirmed in good. Whoever places his trust (115) in My mercy will be filled with My divine peace at the hour of death.

1521 The Lord said to me, **My daughter, do not tire of proclaiming My mercy. In this way you will refresh this Heart of Mine, which burns with a flame of pity for sinners. Tell My priests that hardened sinners will repent on hearing their words when they speak about My unfathomable mercy, about the compassion I have for them in My Heart. To priests who proclaim and extol My mercy, I will give wondrous power; I will anoint their words and touch the hearts of those to whom they will speak.**

1522 Community life is difficult in itself, but it is doubly difficult to get along with proud souls. "O God, give me a deeper faith that I may always see in every sister Your holy image which has been engraved in her soul...

1523 **(116)** Everlasting love, pure flame, burn in my heart ceaselessly and deify my whole being, according to Your infinite pleasure by which You summoned me into existence and called me to take part in Your everlasting happiness. O merciful Lord, it is only out of mercy that You have lavished these gifts upon me. Seeing all these free gifts within me, with deep humility I worship Your incomprehensible goodness. Lord, my heart is filled with amazement that You, absolute Lord, in need of no one, would nevertheless stoop so low out of pure love for us. I can never help being amazed that the Lord would have such an intimate relationship with His creatures. That again is His unfathomable goodness. Every time I begin this meditation, I never finish it, because my spirit becomes entirely drowned in Him. What a delight it is to love with all the force of one's soul and to be loved even more in return, to feel and **(117)** experience this with the full consciousness of one's being. There are no words to express this.

1524 January 25, 1938. My Jesus, how good and patient You are! You often look upon us as little children. We often beg You, but we don't know what for, because towards the end of the prayer, when You give us what we have asked for, we do not want to accept it.

1525 One day, a certain sister came to me and asked me for prayers, telling me that she could no longer stand things as they were. "And so, please pray, Sister." I answered that I would, and I began a novena to The Divine Mercy. I learned that God would give her the grace, but that she would once again be dissatisfied when she received it. However, I kept on praying as she had asked me to do. The next day, the same sister came looking for me, and when we again began to talk about the same thing, I told her, "You know, Sister, when we pray, we ought not force the Lord God to give us what we want, but we should rather submit to His holy will." **(118)** But she thought that what she was asking for was indispensable. Towards the end of the novena, the sister came again and said, "O Sister, the Lord Jesus has given me the grace, but now I am of a different mind. Please pray so that things will somehow be different again." I answered, "Yes, I will pray, but that God's will be done in you, Sister, and not what you want."

1526 Most Merciful Heart of Jesus, protect us from the just anger of God.

1527 + A certain sister is constantly persecuting me for the sole reason that God communes with me so intimately, and she thinks that this is all pretense on my part. When she thinks that I have done something amiss she says, "Some people have revelations, but commit such faults!" She has said this to all the sisters and always in a derogatory sense, in order to make me out as some sort of an oddity. One day, it caused me much pain to think that this insignificant drop which is the human brain can so easily scrutinize **(119)** the gifts of God. After Holy

Communion, I prayed that the Lord would enlighten her, but nevertheless I learned that this soul will not attain perfection if she does not change her interior dispositions.

1528 + When I complained to the Lord Jesus about a certain person [saying], "Jesus, how can this person pass judgment like that, even about an intention?" the Lord answered, **Do not be surprised. That soul does not even know her own self, so how could she pass a fair judgment on another soul?**

1529 Today I saw Father Andrasz at prayer. I also knew that he was interceding with the Lord for me. The Lord sometimes makes known to me who is praying for me.

1530 I am keeping myself a bit in the background, as though this work of God did not interest me. I am not speaking about it at present, but my whole soul is steeped in prayer, and I am entreating God to be so good as to hasten this great gift; that is to say, the Feast of Mercy. And I see that Jesus is acting, and is Himself giving the directives as to how this is to be carried out. Nothing happens by accident.

1531 **(120)** Today I said to the Lord Jesus, "Do You see how many difficulties there are [to be overcome] before they will believe that You yourself are the author of this work? And even now, not everyone believes in it." **Be at peace, My child; nothing can oppose My will. In spite of the murmuring and hostility of the sisters, My will shall be done in you in all its fullness, down to the last detail of My wishes and My designs. Do not become sad about this; I too was a stumbling stone for some souls.**

1532 + Jesus complained to me of how painful to Him is the unfaithfulness of chosen souls, **and My heart is even more wounded by their distrust after a fall. It would be less painful if they had not experienced the goodness of My heart.**

1533 I saw the anger of God hanging heavy over Poland. And now I see that if God were to visit our country with the greatest chastisements, that would still be great mercy because, for such grave transgressions, He could punish **(121)** us with eternal annihilation. I was paralyzed with fear when the Lord lifted the veil a little for me. Now I see clearly that chosen souls keep the world in existence to fulfill the measure [of justice].

1534 + I saw a certain priest's efforts in prayer. His prayer is similar to that of the Lord Jesus in the Garden of Olives. Oh, if that priest [probably Father Sopocko] only knew how pleasing to God that prayer was!

1535 O Jesus, I am locking myself in Your most merciful heart as in a fortress, impregnable against the missiles of my enemies.

1536 Today I found myself in the presence of a certain dying person who was approaching death in my home neighborhood. I supported her with my prayers and, after a few moments, I felt for a short while pain in my hands, feet and side...

1537 **(122)** January 27, 1938. During Holy Hour today, Jesus complained to me about the ingratitude of souls:

In return for My blessings, I get ingratitude. In return for My love, I get forgetfulness and indifference. My Heart cannot bear this.

1538 At that moment, love for Jesus was enkindled so strongly in my heart that, offering myself for ungrateful souls, I immersed myself completely in Him. When I came to my senses, the Lord allowed me to taste a little of the ingratitude which flooded His Heart. This experience lasted for a short while.

1539 Today I said to the Lord, "When will You take me to Yourself? I've been feeling so ill, and I've been waiting for Your coming with such longing!" Jesus answered me, **Be always ready; I will not leave you in this exile for**

long. **My holy will must be fulfilled in you.** O Lord, if
Your holy will has not yet been entirely fulfilled in me,
here I am, ready for everything that You want, O Lord!
(123) O my Jesus, there is only one thing which surprises
me; namely, that You make so many secrets known to
me; but that one secret—the hour of my death—You do
not want to tell me. And the Lord answered me, **Be at
peace; I will let you know, but not just now.** Ah, my
Lord, I beg Your pardon for wanting to know this. You
know very well why, because You know my yearning
heart, which is eagerly going out to You. You know that
I would not want to die even a minute before the time
which You have appointed for me before the ages.
Jesus listened with wondrous kindness to the outpourings of my heart.

1540 **(124)** January 28, 1938. Today the Lord said to me, **My
daughter, write down these words: All those souls who
will glorify My mercy and spread its worship,
encouraging others to trust in My mercy, will not
experience terror at the hour of death. My mercy will
shield them in that final battle...**

1541 **My daughter, encourage souls to say the chaplet which I
have given to you. It pleases Me to grant everything they
ask of Me by saying the chaplet. When hardened sinners
say it, I will fill their souls with peace, and the hour of
their death will be a happy one.**

**Write this for the benefit of distressed souls: when a soul
sees and realizes the gravity of its sins, when the whole
abyss of the misery into which it immersed itself is
displayed before its eyes, let it not despair, but with trust
let it throw itself into the arms of My mercy, as a child
into the arms of its beloved mother. These souls (125)
have a right of priority to My compassionate Heart,
they have first access to My mercy. Tell them that no
soul that has called upon My mercy has been disappointed or brought to shame. I delight particularly in**

a soul which has placed its trust in My goodness.

Write that when they say this chaplet in the presence of the dying, I will stand between My Father and the dying person, not as the just Judge but as the merciful Savior.

1542 At that moment, the Lord gave me to know how jealous He is of my heart.

Even among the sisters you will feel lonely. Know then that I want you to unite yourself more closely to Me. I am concerned about every beat of your heart. Every stirring of your love is reflected in My Heart. I thirst for your love. "Yes, O Jesus, but my heart would not be able to live without You, either; for even if the hearts of all creatures were offered to me, they would not satisfy the depths of my heart."

1543 (126) Today toward evening, the Lord said to me, Entrust yourself completely to Me at the hour of death, and I will present you to My Father as My bride. And now I recommend that you unite, in a special way, even your smallest deeds to My merits, and then My Father will look upon them with love as if they were My own.

1544 Do not change your particular examen which I have given you through Father Andrasz; namely, that you unite yourself with Me continually. That is what I am clearly asking of you today. Be a child toward My representatives, because I borrow their lips to speak to you, so that you will have no doubts about anything.

1545 My health has improved somewhat. I went down to the refectory and the chapel today. I still cannot resume my duties, and so I stay in my cell at the hand-loom [making borders for altar linens]. I enjoy this work very much, but still, even with such light work, I tire easily. (127) I see how feeble I am. There are no indifferent moments in my life, since every moment of my life is filled with prayer, suffering and work. If not in one way, then in another, I glorify God; and if God were to give me a second life, I do not know whether I would make better use of it...

1546 The Lord said to me, **I am delighted with your love. Your sincere love is as pleasing to My Heart as the fragrance of a rosebud at morningtide, before the sun has taken the dew from it. The freshness of your heart captivates Me; that is why I unite Myself with you more closely than with any other creature...**

1547 Today I saw the efforts of this priest [Father Sopocko] concerning the affairs of God. His heart is beginning to taste that which filled God's Heart during His earthly life. In recompense for his efforts—ingratitude... But he is very zealous for the glory of God...

1548 **(128)** January 30, 1938. One-day retreat.

The Lord gave me to know, during meditation, that as long as my heart beats in my breast, I must always strive to spread the Kingdom of God on earth. I am to fight for the glory of my Creator.

I know that I will give God the glory He expects of me if I try faithfully to cooperate with God's grace.

1549 I want to live in the spirit of faith. I accept everything that comes my way as given me by the loving will of God, who sincerely desires my happiness. And so I will accept with submission and gratitude everything that God sends me. I will pay no attention to the voice of nature and to the promptings of self-love. Before each important action, I will stop to consider for a moment what relationship it has to eternal life and what may be the main reason for my undertaking it: is it for the glory of God, or for the good of my own soul, or for the good of the souls of others? If my heart says yes, then I will not swerve from carrying out the given action, **(129)** unmindful of either obstacles or sacrifices. I will not be frightened into abandoning my intention. It is enough for me to know that it is pleasing to God. On the other hand, if I learn that the action has nothing in common with what I have just mentioned, I will try to elevate it to a loftier sphere by means of a good intention. And if I learn that something flows from my self-love, I will cancel it out right from the start.

1550   In cases of doubt, I will not act, but will scrupulously seek clarifications from the priests, and in particular from my spiritual director. I will not give explanations on my own behalf when someone reproaches me or criticises me, unless I am directly asked to bear witness to the truth. With great patience, I will listen when others open their hearts to me, accept their sufferings, give them spiritual comfort, but drown my own sufferings in the most merciful Heart of Jesus. I will never leave the depths of His mercy, while bringing the whole world into those depths.

1551   **(130)** In the meditation on death, I asked the Lord to deign to fill my heart with those sentiments which I will have at the moment of my death. And through God's grace I received an interior reply that I had done what was within my power and so could be at peace. At that moment, such profound gratitude to God was awakened in my soul that I burst into tears of joy like a little child. I prepared to receive Holy Communion next morning as "viaticum," and I said the prayers of the dying[233] for my own intention.

1552   Then I heard the words: **As you are united with Me in life, so will you be united at the moment of death.** After these words, such great trust in God's great mercy was awakened in my soul that, even if I had had the sins of the whole world, as well as the sins of all the condemned souls weighing on my conscience, I would not have doubted God's goodness but, without hesitation, would have thrown myself into the abyss of the divine mercy, which is always open to us; and, with a heart crushed to dust, I would have cast **(131)** myself at His feet, abandoning myself totally to His holy will, which is mercy itself.

1553 O my Jesus, Life of my soul, my Life, my Savior, my sweetest Bridegroom, and at the same time my Judge, You know that in this last hour of mine I do not count on any merits of my own, but only on Your mercy. Even as of today, I immerse myself totally in the abyss of Your mercy, which is always open to every soul.

O my Jesus, I have only one task to carry out in my lifetime, in death, and throughout eternity, and that is to adore Your incomprehensible mercy. No mind, either of angel or of man, will ever fathom the mysteries of Your mercy, O God. The angels are lost in amazement before the mystery of divine mercy, but cannot comprehend it. Everything that has come from the Creator's hand is contained in this inconceivable mystery; that is to say, in the very depths of His tender mercy. When I meditate on this, my spirit swoons, and my heart dissolves in joy. O Jesus, it is through Your most compassionate Heart, as through a crystal, **(132)** that the rays of divine mercy have come to us.

1554 February 1, [1938]. Today I am feeling a little worse, physically, but I am still taking part in the common life [prayers, meals, and recreation]. I am making great efforts, known to You alone, Jesus. In the refectory today, I did not think I would last until the end of the meal. Every mouthful causes me extreme pain.

1555 When Mother S. [Irene] visited me a week ago, she said, "You catch every sickness, Sister, because your system is so weak, but that is not your fault. In fact, if any other sister had that same sickness, she would certainly be walking around; whereas you, Sister, must stay in bed!! These words did not hurt me, but it is better not to make such comparisons with very sick persons, because their cup is full enough as it is. Another thing: when sisters visit the sick, they should not ask in detail every time,

"What is hurting you, **(133)** and how does it hurt?" because it is very tiresome to keep telling each sister the same thing about oneself. And it sometimes happens that one must repeat the same thing over and over many times a day.

1556   When I had gone to the chapel for a moment, the Lord gave me to know that, among His chosen ones, there are some who are especially chosen, and whom He calls to a higher form of holiness, to exceptional union with Him. These are seraphic souls, from whom God demands greater love than He does from others. Although all live in the same convent, yet He sometimes demands of a particular soul a greater degree of love. Such a soul understands this call, because God makes this known to it interiorly, but the soul may either follow this call or not. It depends on the soul itself whether it is faithful to these touches of the Holy Spirit, or whether it resists them. I have learned that there is a place in purgatory where souls will pay their debt to God for such transgressions; this kind of torment is the most difficult of all. The soul which is specially marked by God **(134)** will be distinguished everywhere, whether in heaven or in purgatory or in hell. In heaven, it will be distinguished from other souls by greater glory and radiance and deeper knowledge of God. In purgatory, by greater pain, because it knows God more profoundly and desires Him more vehemently. In hell, it will suffer more profoundly than other souls, because it knows more fully whom it has lost. This indelible mark of God's exclusive love, in the [soul], will not be obliterated.

1557   O Jesus, keep me in holy fear, so that I may not waste graces. Help me to be faithful to the inspirations of the Holy Spirit. Grant that my heart may burst for love of You, rather than I should neglect even one act of love for You.

1558   February 2, [1938]. Darkness of the soul. Today is the Feast of the Mother of God, and in my soul it is so dark.

The Lord has hidden Himself, and I am alone, all alone. My mind has become so dimmed that I see only phantasies about me. Not a single ray of light penetrates my soul. I do not understand myself or those who speak to me. Frightful temptations **(135)** regarding the holy faith assail me. O my Jesus, save me. I cannot say anything more. I cannot describe these things in detail, for I fear lest someone be scandalized on reading this. I am astounded that such torments could befall a soul. O hurricane, what are you doing to the boat of my heart? This storm has lasted the whole day and night.

When Mother Superior [Irene] came in to see me and asked, "Would you like to take advantage of this occasion, Sister, since Father An. [Andrasz] is coming to hear confessions?" I answered, no. It seemed to me that Father would not understand me, nor would I be able to make a confession.

I spent the whole night with Jesus in Gethsemane. From my breast there escaped one continuous moan. A natural dying will be much easier, because then one is in agony and will die; while here, one is in agony, but cannot die. O Jesus, I never thought such suffering could exist. Nothingness: that is the reality. O Jesus, save me! I believe in You with all my heart. So many times have I seen the radiance of Your face, and now, where are You, Lord?... I believe, I believe, and again I believe **(136)** in You, Triune God, Father, Son and Holy Spirit, and in all the truths which Your holy Church gives me to believe... But the darkness does not recede, and my spirit plunges into even greater agony. And at that moment, such terrible torment overwhelmed me that now I am amazed at myself that I did not breathe my last, but this was for only a brief instant.

1559   At that moment I saw Jesus, and from His Heart there issued those same two rays, which enveloped me, whole and entire. At the same moment, all my torments vanished. **My daughter,** the Lord said, **know that of** yourself you are just what you have gone through, and it is only by My grace that you are a participant of eternal life and all the gifts I lavish on you. And with these words of the Lord, there came to me a true knowledge of myself. Jesus is giving me a lesson in deep humility and, at the same time, one of total trust in Him. My heart is reduced to dust and ashes, and even if all people were to trample me under their feet, I would still consider that **(137)** a favor.

I feel and am, in fact, very deeply permeated with the knowledge that I am nothing, so that real humiliations will be a refreshment for me.

1560 February 3, [1938]. Today after Holy Communion, Jesus again gave me a few directives: **First, do not fight against a temptation by yourself, but disclose it to the confessor at once, and then the temptation will lose all its force. Second, during these ordeals do not lose your peace; live in My presence; ask My Mother and the Saints for help. Third, have the certitude that I am looking at you and supporting you. Fourth, do not fear either struggles of the soul or any temptations, because I am supporting you; if only you are willing to fight, know that the victory is always on your side. Fifth, know that by fighting bravely you give Me great glory and amass merits for yourself. Temptation gives you a chance to show Me your fidelity.**

1561 **And now I am going to tell you something that is most important for you: boundless sincerity with your spiritual director. If you do not take advantage of this great grace according to (138) My instructions, I will take him away from you, and then you will be left to yourself; and all the torments, which you know very well, will return to you. It displeases Me that you do not take advantage of the opportunity when you are able to see him and talk with him. Know that it is a great grace on My part when I give a spiritual director to a soul. Many souls ask Me for this, but it is not to all that I** grant this grace. **From the moment when I gave you this priest as spiritual director, I endowed him with new light so that he might easily know and understand your soul...**

1562   O my Jesus, my only mercy, allow me to see contentment in Your face as a sign of reconciliation with me, because my heart cannot bear Your seriousness; if this continues a moment longer my heart will burst with grief. You see that I am even now crushed to dust.

1563   And at that very moment I saw myself in some kind of a palace; and Jesus gave me His hand, sat me at His side, and said with kindness, **My bride, you always please Me by your humility. The greatest misery does not stop Me from (139) uniting Myself to a soul, but where there is pride, I am not there.**

When I came to myself, I reflected on what had happened in my heart, thanking God for His love and for the mercy that He had shown me.

1564   Jesus, hide me; just as You have hidden Yourself under the form of the white Host, so hide me from human eyes, and particularly hide the gifts which You so kindly grant me. May I not betray outwardly what You are effecting in my soul. I am a white host before You, O Divine Priest. Consecrate me Yourself, and may my transubstantiation be known only to You. I stand before You each day as a sacrificial host and implore Your mercy upon the world. In silence, and unseen, I will empty myself before You; my pure and undivided love will burn, in profound silence, as a holocaust. And may the fragrance of my love be wafted to the foot of Your throne. You are the Lord of lords, but You delight in innocent and humble souls.

1565   **(140)** When I entered the chapel for a moment, the Lord said to me, **My daughter, help Me to save a certain dying sinner. Say the chaplet that I have taught you for him.** When I began to say the chaplet, I saw the man dying in the midst of terrible torment and struggle. His Guardian

Angel was defending him, but he was, as it were, powerless against the enormity of the soul's misery. A multitude of devils was waiting for the soul. But while I was saying the chaplet, I saw Jesus just as He is depicted in the image. The rays which issued from Jesus' Heart enveloped the sick man, and the powers of darkness fled in panic. The sick man peacefully breathed his last. When I came to myself, I understood how very important the chaplet was for the dying. It appeases the anger of God.

1566　When I was apologizing to the Lord Jesus for a certain action of mine which, a little later, turned out to be imperfect, Jesus put me at ease with these words: **My daughter, I reward you for the purity of your intention which you had (141) at the time when you acted. My Heart rejoiced that you had My love under consideration at the time you acted, and that in so distinct a way; and even now you still derive benefit from this; that is, from the humiliation. Yes, My child, I want you to always have such great purity of intention in the very least things you undertake.**

1567　As I took the pen in hand, I addressed a short prayer to the Holy Spirit and said, "Jesus, bless this pen so that everything You order me to write may be for the glory of God." Then I heard a voice: **Yes, I bless [it], because this writing bears the seal of obedience to your superior and confessor, and by that very fact I am already given glory, and many souls will be drawing profit from it. My daughter, I demand that you devote all your free moments to writing about My goodness and mercy. It is your office and your assignment throughout your life to continue to make known to souls the great mercy I have for them and to exhort them to trust in My bottomless mercy.**

1568　**(142)** O my Jesus, I believe in Your words and no longer have any doubt about this because in the course of one conversation with Mother Superior [Irene], she told me to write more about Your mercy. That statement was very much in accord with Your request. O my Jesus, I now understand that if You demand something from a soul, You also inspire the superiors to allow us to fulfill Your demands, even though it sometimes happens that we do not receive permission at once, and our patience is often put to the test...

1569 + O Everlasting Love, Jesus, who have enclosed Yourself in the Host,

And therein hide Your divinity and conceal Your beauty,

You do this in order to give Yourself, whole and entire, to my soul

And in order not to terrify it with Your greatness.

O Everlasting Love, Jesus, who have shrouded Yourself with bread,

Eternal Light, incomprehensible Fountain of joy and happiness,

Because You want to be heaven on earth to me,

That indeed You are, when Your love, O God, imparts itself to me.

1570 (143) O Greatly Merciful God, Infinite Goodness, today all mankind calls out from the abyss of its misery to Your mercy—to Your compassion, O God; and it is with its mighty voice of misery that it cries out. Gracious God, do not reject the prayer of this earth's exiles! O Lord, Goodness beyond our understanding, Who are acquainted with our misery through and through, and know that by our own power we cannot ascend to You, we implore You: anticipate us with Your grace and keep on increasing Your mercy in us, that we may faithfully do Your holy will all through our life and at death's hour. Let the omnipotence of Your mercy shield us from the darts of our salvation's enemies, that we may with confidence, as Your children, await Your final coming—that day known to You alone. And we expect to obtain everything promised us by Jesus in spite of all our wretchedness. For Jesus is our Hope: Through His merciful Heart, as through an open gate, we pass through to heaven.

1571 **(144)** I have noticed that, from the very moment I entered the convent, I have been charged with one thing; namely, that I am a saint. But this word was always used scoffingly. At first, this hurt me very much, but when I had risen above it, I paid no attention to it. However, when on one occasion a certain person [perhaps Father Sopocko] suffered because of my sanctity, I was very pained that, because of me, others can experience some unpleasantness. And I began to complain to the Lord Jesus, asking why this should be so, and the Lord answered me, **Are you sad because of this? Of course you are a saint. Soon I Myself will make this manifest in you, and they will pronounce the same word,** *saint,* only this time it will be with love.

1572 **I remind you, My daughter, that as often as you hear the clock strike the third hour, immerse yourself completely in My mercy, adoring and glorifying it; invoke its omnipotence for the whole world, and particularly for poor sinners; for at that moment mercy was opened wide for every (145) soul. In this hour you can obtain everything for yourself and for others for the asking; it was the hour of grace for the whole world—mercy triumphed over justice.**

My daughter, try your best to make the Stations of the Cross in this hour, provided that your duties permit it; and if you are not able to make the Stations of the Cross, then at least step into the chapel for a moment and adore, in the Blessed Sacrament, My Heart, which is full of mercy; and should you be unable to step into the chapel, immerse yourself in prayer there where you happen to be, if only for a very brief instant. I claim veneration for My mercy from every creature, but above all from you, since it is to you that I have given the most profound understanding of this mystery.

1573 + O my God, I am overcome with great longing for You today. Oh, nothing else any longer occupies my heart.

The earth no longer contains anything for me. O Jesus, how strongly I feel this exile, how very prolonged it is for me! O death, messenger of God, when will you announce to me that longed-for moment, through which I will be united to my God forever?

1574 **(146)** O my Jesus, may the last days of my exile be spent totally according to Your most holy will. I unite my sufferings, my bitterness and my last agony itself to Your Sacred Passion; and I offer myself for the whole world to implore an abundance of God's mercy for souls, and in particular for the souls who are in our homes. I firmly trust and commit myself entirely to Your holy will, which is mercy itself. Your mercy will be everything for me at the last hour, as You yourself have promised me...

1575 + Hail to You, Eternal Love, my Sweet Jesus, who have condescended to dwell in my heart! I salute You, O glorious Godhead who have deigned to stoop to me, and out of love for me have so emptied Yourself as to assume the insignificant form of bread. I salute You, Jesus, never-fading flower of humanity. You are all there is for my soul. Your love is purer than a lily, and Your presence is more pleasing to me than the fragrance of a hyacinth. Your friendship is more tender **(147)** and subtle than the scent of a rose, and yet it is stronger than death. O Jesus, incomprehensible beauty, it is with pure souls that You communicate best, because they alone are capable of heroism and sacrifice. O sweet, rose-red blood of Jesus, ennoble my blood and change it into Your own blood, and let this be done to me according to Your good pleasure.

1576 **Know, My daughter, that between Me and you there is a bottomless abyss, an abyss which separates the Creator from the creature. But this abyss is filled with My mercy. I raise you up to Myself, not that I have need of you, but it is solely out of mercy that I grant you the grace of union with Myself.**

1577   Tell souls not to place within their own hearts obstacles
       to My mercy, which so greatly wants to act within them.
       My mercy works in all those hearts which open their
       doors to it. Both the sinner and the righteous person
       have need (148) of My mercy. Conversion, as well as
       perseverance, is a grace of My mercy.

1578   Let souls who are striving for perfection particularly
       adore My mercy, because the abundance of graces
       which I grant them flows from My mercy. I desire that
       these souls distinguish themselves by boundless trust in
       My mercy. I myself will attend to the sanctification of
       such souls. I will provide them with everything they will
       need to attain sanctity. The graces of My mercy are
       drawn by means of one vessel only, and that is—trust.
       The more a soul trusts, the more it will receive. Souls
       that trust boundlessly are a great comfort to Me,
       because I pour all the treasures of My graces into them. I
       rejoice that they ask for much, because it is My desire to
       give much, very much. On the other hand, I am sad
       when souls ask for little, when they narrow their hearts.

1579   (149) + It is when I meet with hypocrisy that I suffer
       most. Now I understand You, my Savior, for rebuking
       the pharisees so severly for their hypocrisy. You
       associated more graciously with hardened sinners when
       they approached You contritely.

1580   My Jesus, I now see that I have gone through all the
       stages of my life following You: childhood, youth,
       vocation, apostolic work, Tabor, Gethsemane, and now
       I am already with You on Calvary. I have willingly
       allowed myself to be crucified, and I am indeed already
       crucified; although I can still walk a little, I am stretched
       out on the cross, and I feel distinctly that strength is
       flowing to me from Your Cross, that You and You alone
       are my perseverance. Although I often hear the voice of
       temptation calling to me, "Come down from the cross!"
       the power of God strengthens me. Although loneliness
       and darkness and sufferings of all kinds beat against my

heart, the mysterious power of God supports and strengthens me. I want to drink the cup **(150)** to the last drop. I trust firmly that Your grace, which has sustained me in the Garden of Olives, will sustain me also now that I am on Calvary.

1581 O my Jesus, my Master, I unite my desires to the desires that You had on the cross: I desire to fulfill Your holy will; I desire the conversion of souls; I desire that Your mercy be adored; I desire that the triumph of the Church be hastened; I desire the Feast of Mercy to be celebrated all over the world; I desire sanctity for priests; I desire that there be a saint in our Congregation; I desire that our whole Congregation have a great spirit of zeal for the glory of God and for the salvation of souls; I desire that souls who live in our homes do not offend God, but persevere in good; I desire that the blessing of God descend upon my parents and my whole family; I desire that God give special light to my spiritual directors, and in particular to Father An. and Father So.; I desire a special blessing **(151)** for Superiors[234] under whose direction I have been, and in particular for Mother General [Michael], for Mother Irene and for the Directress of Novices, Mother [Mary] Joseph.

1582 O my Jesus, I now embrace the whole world and ask You for mercy for it. When You tell me, O God, that it is enough, that Your holy will has been completely accomplished, then, my Savior, in union with You, I will commit my soul into the hands of the Heavenly Father, full of trust in Your unfathomable mercy. And when I stand at the foot of Your throne, the first hymn that I will sing will be one to Your mercy. Poor earth, I will not forget you. Although I feel that I will be immediately drowned in God as in an ocean of happiness, that will not be an obstacle to my returning to earth to encourage souls and incite them to trust in God's mercy. Indeed, this immersion in God will give me the possibility of boundless action.

1583 As I write this, I hear Satan grinding his teeth. He cannot stand God's mercy, and keeps banging things in my cell. But I feel so much of God's power within me that it does not even bother me that the enemy of our salvation gets angry, **(152)** and I quietly keep on writing.

1584 O inconceivable goodness of God, which shields us at every step, may Your mercy be praised without cease. That You became a brother to humans, not to angels, is a miracle of the unfathomable mystery of Your mercy. All our trust is in You, our first-born Brother, Jesus Christ, true God and true Man. My heart flutters with joy to see how good God is to us wretched and ungrateful people. And as a proof of His love, He gives us the incomprehensible gift of Himself in the person of His Son. Throughout all eternity we shall never exhaust that mystery of love. O mankind, why do you think so little about God being truly among us? O Lamb of God, I do not know what to admire in You first: Your gentleness, Your hidden life, the emptying of Yourself for the sake of man, or the constant miracle of Your mercy, which transforms souls **(153)** and raises them up to eternal life. Although You are hidden in this way, Your omnipotence is more manifest here than in the creation of man. Though the omnipotence of Your mercy is at work in the justification of the sinner, yet Your action is gentle and hidden.

1585 A vision of the Mother of God. In the midst of a great brilliance, I saw the Mother of God clothed in a white gown, girt about with a golden cincture; and there were tiny stars, also of gold, over the whole garment, and chevron-shaped sleeves lined with gold. Her cloak was sky-blue, lightly thrown over the shoulders. A transparent veil was delicately drawn over her head, while her flowing hair was set off beautifully by a golden crown which terminated in little crosses. On Her left arm She held the Child Jesus. A Blessed Mother of this type I had not yet seen. Then She looked at me kindly and said: *I am the Mother of God of Priests.*²³⁵ At that, She lowered Jesus from Her arm to the ground, raised Her right hand heavenward and said: *O God, bless Poland, bless priests.* Then She addressed me once again: *Tell the priests what you have seen.* **(154)** I resolved that at the first opportunity [I would have] of seeing Father [Andrasz] I would tell; but I myself can make nothing of this vision.

1586 O my Jesus, You see how very grateful I am to Father Sopocko, who has advanced Your work so much. That soul, so humble, has had to endure all the storms. He has not allowed himself to become discouraged by adversities, but has faithfully responded to the call of God.

1587 + One of the sisters was appointed to look after the sick, but she was so negligent that one had to practice real mortification. One day, I made up my mind to tell the superior about it, but then I heard a voice in my soul: **Bear it patiently; someone else will tell her.** But the service was like that for a whole month. When I was finally able to come down to the refectory and to recreation, I heard these words in my soul: **Now other sisters are going to tell (155) about that sister's negligent service, but you are to keep silent and not speak about the matter.** And at that point there broke out sharp criticism of the sister, but she could find nothing [to say] in her own defense, and all the sisters said in chorus, "Sister, you had better improve in your care of the sick." I have found that sometimes the Lord does not want us to say something on our own; He has His ways and knows when to speak out.

1588 Today I heard the words: **In the Old Covenant I sent prophets wielding thunderbolts to My people. Today I am sending you with My mercy to the people of the whole world. I do not want to punish aching mankind, but I desire to heal it, pressing it to My Merciful Heart. I** use punishment when they themselves force Me to do so; My hand is reluctant to take hold of the sword of justice. **Before the Day of Justice I am sending the Day of Mercy.** I replied, "O my Jesus, speak to souls Yourself, because my words are insignificant."

+

(156) J.M.J.

The Soul's Expectation of the Coming of the Lord.

1589 I do not know, O Lord, at what hour You will come.
And so I keep constant watch and listen
As Your chosen bride,
Knowing that You like to come unexpected.
Yet, a pure heart will sense You from afar, O Lord.

I wait for You, Lord, in calm and silence,
With great longing in my heart
And with invincible desire.
I feel that my love for You is changing into fire,
And that it will rise up to heaven like a flame at life's
end,
And then all my wishes will be fulfilled.

Come then, at last, my most sweet Lord
And take my thirsting heart
There, to Your home in the lofty regions of heaven,
Where Your eternal life perdures.

Life on this earth is but an agony,
As my heart feels it is created for the heights.
For it the lowlands of this life hold no interest,
For my homeland is in heaven—this I firmly believe.

[End of Notebook Five]

Sr. M. Faustina

of the Blessed Sacrament

of the Congregation

of the Sisters of Our Lady of Mercy

*The Mercy of God I will
Praise Forever.*

Notebook VI

+

(1) J.M.J.

1590   Praise, O my soul,
         the incomprehensible mercy of God.
         May all be for His glory.

Cracow, February 10, 1938.

Sixth Notebook.

Sister Faustina of the Blessed Sacrament

of the Congregation

of the Sisters of Our Lady of Mercy.

1591 My heart is drawn there where my God is hidden,
      Where He dwells with us day and night,
      Clothed in the White Host;
      He governs the whole world, He communes with souls.

      My heart is drawn there where my God is hiding,
      Where His love is immolated.
      But my heart senses that the living water is here;
      It is my living God, though a veil hides Him.

1592 **(2)** February 10, 1938. During meditation, the Lord gave
      me knowledge of the joy of heaven and of the saints on
      our arrival there; they love God as the sole object of
      their love, but they also have a tender and heartfelt love
      for us. It is from the face of God that this joy flows out
      upon all, because we see Him face to face. His face is so
      sweet that the soul falls anew into ecstasy.

1593 The Lord Himself moves me to write prayers and hymns about His mercy, and these hymns of praise force themselves upon my lips. I have noticed that ready-formulated words of praise of God's mercy enter my mind, and so I have resolved to write them down in so far as is within my power. I can feel God urging me to do so.

1594 One of the sisters came into my cell for a little while. After a short conversation on the subject of obedience, she said to me, "Oh, now I understand how the saints (3) acted. Thank you, Sister; a great light has entered my soul; I have profited much."

1595 O my Jesus, this is Your work. It is You who have spoken thus to that soul, because this sister came in when I was completely immersed in God, and it was just at that moment when this deep recollection left me. O my Jesus, I know that, in order to be useful to souls, one has to strive for the closest possible union with You, who are Eternal Love. One word from a soul united to God effects more good in souls than eloquent discussions and sermons from an imperfect soul.

1596 + I saw Father A. [Andrasz's] surprise at my actions, but all that is for the glory of God. Oh, how great is Your grace, O Lord, grace which lifts the soul up to greater heights. I am very grateful to the Lord for having given me an enlightened priest. You could have continued to leave me in uncertainties and hesitations, but Your goodness (4) remedied that. O my Jesus, it is impossible for me to count Your favors...

1597 **My daughter, your struggle will last until death. Your last breath will mark its end. You shall conquer by meekness.**

1598 February 13, 1938. I saw how unwillingly the Lord Jesus came to certain souls in Holy Communion. And He spoke these words to me: **I enter into certain hearts as into a second Passion.**

1599 As I was trying to make my Holy Hour, I saw the suffering Jesus, who spoke these words to me: **My daughter, do not pay so much attention to the vessel of grace as to the grace itself which I give you, because you are not always pleased with the vessel, and then the graces, too, become deficient. I want to guard you from that, and I want you never to pay attention to the vessel in which I send you My grace. Let all the attention of your soul (5) be concentrated on responding to My grace as faithfully as possible.**

1600 + O my Jesus, if You yourself do not soothe the longing of my soul, then no one can either comfort or soothe it. Your every approach arouses new raptures of love in my soul, but also a new agony; because, despite all Your approaches to my soul, even the most exceptional, I am still loving You from a distance, and my heart dies in an ecstasy of love; because this is still not the complete and eternal union, although You commune with me so very often unveiled [as if face to face]; nevertheless, You thereby open in my soul and heart an abyss of love and desire for You, my God, and this bottomless abyss, this total desiring of God, cannot be completely filled on this earth.

1601 The Lord has given me to know how much He desires the perfection of chosen souls.

Chosen souls are, in My hand, lights which I cast into the darkness of the world and with which I illumine it. As stars illumine the night, so chosen souls (6) illumine the earth. And the more perfect a soul is, the stronger and the more far-reaching is the light shed by it. It can be hidden and unknown, even to those closest to it, and yet its holiness is reflected in souls even to the most distant extremities of the world.

1602 Today the Lord said to me, **Daughter, when you go to confession, to this fountain of My mercy, the Blood and Water which came forth from My Heart always flows** down upon your soul and ennobles it. **Every time you go to confession, immerse yourself entirely in My mercy, with great trust, so that I may pour the bounty of My grace upon your soul. When you approach the confessional, know this, that I Myself am waiting there for you. I am only hidden by the priest, but I myself act in your soul. Here the misery of the soul meets the God of mercy. Tell souls that from this fount of mercy (7) souls draw graces solely with the vessel of trust. If their trust is great, there is no limit to My generosity. The torrents of grace inundate humble souls. The proud remain always in poverty and misery, because My grace turns away from them to humble souls.**

1603 February 14, [1938]. During adoration, I heard these words: **Pray for one of the students who has great need of My grace.** And I recognized N. I prayed hard, and God's mercy embraced that soul.

1604 When, during adoration, I repeated the prayer, "Holy God" several times, a vivid presence of God suddenly swept over me, and I was caught up in spirit before the majesty of God. I saw how the Angels and the Saints of the Lord give glory to God. The glory of God is so great that I dare not try to describe it, because I would not be able to do so, and souls might think that what I have written **(8)** is all there is. Saint Paul, I understand now why you did not want to describe heaven, but only said that eye has not seen, nor ear heard, nor has it entered into the heart of man what God has prepared for those who love Him [cf. 1 Cor. 2:9; 2 Cor. 12:1-7]. Yes, that is indeed so. And all that has come forth from God returns to Him in the same way and gives Him perfect glory. Now I have seen the way in which I adore God; oh, how miserable it is! And what a tiny drop it is in comparison to that perfect heavenly glory. O my God, how good You are to accept my praise as well, and to turn Your Face to me with kindness and let us know that our prayer is pleasing to You.

1605 **Write down everything that occurs to you regarding My goodness.** I answered, "What do You mean, Lord, what if I write too much?" And the Lord replied, **My daughter, even if you were to speak at one and the same time in all human and angelic tongues, even then you would not have said very much, but on the contrary, you would have sung in only a small measure the praises (9) of My goodness—of My unfathomable mercy.**

O my Jesus, You Yourself must put words into my mouth, that I may praise You worthily.

My daughter, be at peace; do as I tell you. Your thoughts are united to My thoughts, so write whatever comes to your mind. You are the secretary of My mercy. I have chosen you for that office in this life and the next life. That is how I want it to be in spite all the opposition they will give you. Know that My choice will not change.

At that moment I steeped myself in profound humility before God's majesty. But the more I humbled myself, the more God's presence penetrated me...

1606 O Jesus, my only solace! How frightful is this exile! How terrible this wilderness I have to cross! My soul is struggling through a terrible thicket of all kinds of difficulties. If You Yourself did not support me, Lord, there would be no thought of my moving forward.

1607 **(10)** 16 [February] 1938. As I was praying to the living Heart of Jesus in the Blessed Sacrament for the intention of a certain priest, Jesus suddenly gave me knowledge of His goodness and said to me, **I will give him nothing that is beyond his strength.**

1608 + When I learned of some of the sufferings and troubles that a certain person[236] was going through in connection with this whole work of God, I asked the Lord Jesus before Holy Communion that He might make known to me whether by any chance these sufferings were not caused by me: "My sweetest Jesus, I implore You by Your infinite goodness and mercy, make known to me whether anything in this matter displeases You or whether there is some fault of mine in this. If there is, I ask You, when You enter my heart, fill it with unrest and make known to me Your displeasure. And if I am not guilty in this matter, confirm me in peace." When I received the Lord, my soul was filled with great peace, and the Lord gave me to know that the work was undergoing a trial, but **(11)** was no less pleasing to God because of this. I felt great joy at this but I redoubled my prayers so that this work might come through the ordeal unharmed.

1609   O my Jesus, how good it is to be on the cross, but with You! With You, my Love, my soul is constantly stretched out on the cross and is being filled with bitterness. Vinegar and gall touch my lips, but it is good that it is so, because Your Divine Heart was filled with bitterness throughout Your life, and in return for Your love You received ingratitude. You were in such pain that a sorrowful complaint escaped Your lips when You said that You were looking for someone to console You and You found none [cf. Ps. 68:21].

1610   + When I asked the Lord to be so good as to cast a glance upon a certain soul [probably Father Sopocko] who was struggling alone against many difficulties, the Lord gave me to know, in an instant, that all people are as dust under His feet. **So do not worry; you see that they cannot do a thing of themselves. And if I allow them to seem to triumph, I do this for the sake of My (12) impenetrable decrees.** I experienced great peace in seeing how all things are determined by the Lord.

1611   + When the chaplain [Father Theodore] brings me the Lord Jesus, there are moments when I am pervaded with a very vivid presence of God, and the Lord gives me to know His holiness. At such times, I see the smallest speck on my soul, and I would like to purify my soul before every Holy Communion. When I asked the confessor, he said there was no need to confess before every Holy Communion. Holy Communion takes away these tiny things and it is a temptation to think about confession when receiving Holy Communion. I did not go on to explain the condition of my soul in any greater detail, because he was not my director, but the confessor.[237] This knowledge does not take up my time, because it is faster than lightning; it enkindles my love, leaving me with a knowledge of myself...

1612 **(13)** + February 20, [1938]. Today the Lord said to me, **I have need of your sufferings to rescue souls.**

O my Jesus, do with me as You please. I did not have the courage to ask the Lord Jesus for greater sufferings, because I had suffered so much the night before that I would not have been able to bear a drop more than what Jesus Himself gave me.

1613 Almost all night I had such violent pains that it seemed all my intestines were torn to pieces. I threw up the medicine I had taken. When I bowed my head down to the ground, I lost consciousness, and I stayed like that for some time, with my head **(14)** on the floor. When I came to, I became aware that my whole body was pressing on my head and face, and that I was covered with vomit. I thought it would be the end of me. Dear Mother Superior [Irene] and Sister Tarcisia[238] were trying to help me as best they could. Jesus demanded suffering, but not death. O my Jesus, do with me as You please. Only give me strength to suffer. Since Your strength supports me, I shall bear everything. O souls, how I love you!

1614 Today, one of the sisters [probably Sister Amelia[239]] came to see me and said, "Sister, I have a strange feeling, as though something were telling me to come to you and commend to you certain problems of mine before you die, and that perhaps you will be able to beseech the Lord Jesus and arrange these things for me. Something keeps telling me that you will be able to obtain this for me." I answered her with equal frankness that, yes, I felt in my soul that **(15)** after my death I would be able to obtain more from the Lord Jesus than at the present time. "I will remember you, Sister, before His throne."

1615 When I entered the neighboring dormitory to visit the sisters who were ill, one of them said to me, "Sister, when you die I will not fear you at all. Come to see me after you die, because I want to confide to you a secret concerning my soul, something I want you to settle for me with the Lord Jesus. I know you can obtain this from Him." Because she was speaking in public I answered her in this way: "The Lord Jesus is very discreet. And so He never betrays to anyone a secret that is between Him and a soul."

1616 + O my Lord, thank You for conforming me to Yourself through immolation. I see that this earthly vessel is beginning to crumble. I rejoice in this, **(16)** because soon I will be in my Father's house [cf. Jn. 14:2].

1617 February 27, [1938]. Today, I went to confession to Father An. [Andrasz] I did as Jesus wanted. After confession, a surge of light filled my soul. Then I heard a voice: **Because you are a child, you shall remain close to My Heart. Your simplicity is more pleasing to Me than your mortifications.**

1618 Father An. [Andrasz's] words: Live more by faith. Pray that the Divine Mercy become more widely known, and that the work may come into good hands that will manage it well. As for yourself, try to be a good religious here—although things may turn out that way also—but try to be a good religious right here. And now, if you feel those urgings from the Lord and recognize that it is He, follow them. Devote to prayer all the time that is set apart for it, and make your notations afterwards...

1619 **(17)** + The last two days of carnival.[240] My physical sufferings have intensified. I am uniting myself more closely with the suffering Savior, asking Him for mercy for the whole world, which is running riot in its wickedness. Throughout the day I felt the pain of the crown of thorns. When I lay down, I could not rest my head on the pillow. But at ten o'clock the pains ceased, and I fell asleep; but the next day I felt very exhausted.

1620 + Jesus-Host, if You Yourself did not sustain me, I would not be able to persevere on the cross. I would not be able to endure so much suffering. But the power of Your grace maintains me on a higher level and makes my sufferings meritorious. You give me strength always to move forward and to gain heaven by force and to have love in my heart for those from whom I suffer adversities and contempt. With Your grace one can do all things.

1621 **(18)** March 1, 1938. One-day Retreat.

In meditation, I learned that I should hide myself as deeply as possible in the Heart of Jesus, meditate upon His Sorrowful Passion, and penetrate into the sentiments of His Divine Heart, which is full of mercy for sinners. In order to obtain mercy for them, I will empty myself at every moment, living by the will of God.

1622 Throughout this Lent, I am a host in Your hand, Jesus. Make use of me so that You may enter into sinners Yourself. Demand anything You like; no sacrifice will seem too much for me when souls are at stake.

1623 + I have offered this whole month's Masses and Holy Communions for the intention of Father Andrasz, that God may give him an even deeper knowledge of His love and mercy.

1624 This month I will practice the three virtues recommended to me by the Mother of God: humility, **(19)** purity and love of God, accepting with profound submission to the will of God everything that He will send me.

1625 March 2, [1938]. I began Holy Lent in the way that Jesus wanted me to, making myself totally dependent upon His holy will and accepting with love everything that He sends me. I cannot practice any greater mortifications, because I am so very weak. This long illness has sapped my strength completely. I am uniting myself with Jesus through suffering. When I meditate on His Painful Passion, my physical sufferings are lessened.

1626 The Lord said to me, **I am taking you into My school for the whole of Lent. I want to teach you how to suffer.** I answered, "With You, Lord, I am ready for everything." And I heard a voice, **You are allowed to drink from the cup from which I drink. I give you that exclusive privilege today...**

1627 **(20)** Today I felt the Passion of Jesus in my whole body, and the Lord gave me knowledge of the conversion of certain souls.

1628 During Holy Mass, I saw Jesus stretched out on the Cross, and He said to me, **My pupil, have great love for those who cause you suffering. Do good to those who hate you.** I answered, "O my Master, You see very well that I feel no love for them, and that troubles me." Jesus answered, **It is not always within your power to control your feelings. You will recognize that you have love if, after having experienced annoyance and contradiction, you do not lose your peace, but pray for those who have made you suffer and wish them well.** When I returned [...]

+

(21) J.M.J.

1629 I am a host in Your hand,
       O Jesus, my Creator and Lord,
       Silent, hidden, without beauty or charm,
       Because all the beauty of my soul is imprinted within
          me.

       I am a host in Your hand, O Divine Priest,
       Do with me as You please;
       I am totally dependent on Your will, O Lord
       Because it is the delight and adornment of my soul.

I am like a white host in Your hand, O God,
I implore You, transform me into Yourself.
May I be wholly hidden in You,
Locked in Your merciful Heart as in Heaven.

I am like a host in Your hand, O Eternal Priest,
May the wafer of my body hide me from human eye;
May Your eye alone measure my love and devotion,
Because my heart is always united with Your Divine
Heart.

I am like a sacrificial host in Your hand, O Divine
Mediator,
And I burn on the altar of holocaust,
(22) Crushed and ground by suffering like grains of
wheat,
And all this for the sake of Your glory, for the salvation
of souls.

I am a host abiding in the tabernacle of Your Heart.
I go through life drowned in Your love,
And I fear nothing in the world,
For You Yourself are my shield, my strength, and my
defense.

I am a host, laid on the altar of Your Heart,
To burn forever with the fire of love,
For I know that You have lifted me up solely because of
Your mercy,
And so I turn all these gifts and graces to Your glory.

I am a host in Your hand, O Judge and Savior.
In the last hour of my life,
May the omnipotence of Your grace lead me to my
goal,
May Your compassion on the vessel of mercy become
famous.

1630 Jesus, fortify the powers of my soul that the enemy gain
nothing. Without You, I am weakness itself. What am I
without Your grace **(23)** if not an abyss of my own
misery? Misery is my possession.

1631 O Wound of Mercy, Heart of Jesus, hide me in Your depths as a drop of Your own blood, and do not let me out forever! Lock me in Your depths, and do You Yourself teach me to love You! Eternal Love, do You Yourself form my soul that it be made capable of returning Your love. O living Love, enable me to love You forever. I yearn to eternally reciprocate Your love. O Christ, a single gaze from You is dearer to me than a thousand worlds, than all heaven itself. Lord, You can make my soul capable of understanding completely who You are. I know and I believe that You can do all things; if You have deigned to give Yourself to me so generously, then I know that You can be even more generous. Bring me into an intimacy with You so far as it is possible for human nature to be brought...

+

(24) J.M.J.

1632 The desires of my heart are so great and incomprehensible
That nothing can fill the abyss of my heart.
Even the most beautiful things, gathered from all over
the world,
Would not for a moment fill Your place for me, O God.

With one glance, I penetrated the whole world,
And I found no other love like the love of my heart.
Therefore I looked into the world of eternity—
because this one is too small for me.
My heart has desired the love of the Immortal One.

My heart has sensed that I am a royal child,
That I have found myself in exile, in a foreign land.
I see that the heavenly palace is my home;
Only there will I feel as in my own fatherland.

You Yourself have drawn my soul to You, O Lord;
O Eternal Word, You Yourself have stooped to me,
Giving my soul a deeper knowledge of Yourself.
Behold, the mystery of love for which You have
created me!

Pure love has made me strong and brave.
I fear neither the seraphim nor the cherubim, standing
with sword in hand,
(25) And I pass over with ease where others tremble,
Because there is nothing to fear, there where love is the
guide.

And suddenly the eye of my soul came to rest upon
You,
O Lord Jesus Christ, stretched upon the Cross.
Here is my Love, with whom I will rest in my grave,
This is my Bridegroom, my incomprehensible Lord
and God.

[Here occurs a bigger space in the Diary.]

1633 **(26)** March 10, [1938]. Continuous physical suffering. I
am on the cross with Jesus. On one occasion, M.
Superior [Irene] said to me, "It is a lack of love of
neighbor on your part, Sister, that you eat something
and then you suffer and disturb the others during their
night's rest." Yet I know for sure that these pains which
occur in my intestines are not at all caused by food. The
doctor [probably Dr. Silberg] has said the same thing.
These sufferings come from the body itself, or rather are
a visitation of the Lord. Nevertheless, after that remark
I resolved to suffer in secret and not to ask for help,
because it is of no avail anyway, since I throw up the
medicines that are given to me.

Many a time, I have managed to suffer through attacks
that were known only to Jesus. The pains are so violent
and severe that they cause me to lose consciousness.
When they cause me to faint, and I am drenched in cold
sweat, then they gradually begin to go away. Sometimes
they last **(27)** three hours or more. O my Jesus, may
Your holy will be done; I accept everything from Your
hand. If I accept the delights and raptures of love to the
point of becoming oblivious to what is going on around

me, it is only right that I should accept with love these sufferings which cause me to faint.

1634 When the doctor[241] came, I could not go down to the parlor to see him, like the other sisters, but asked that he come to my cell, because I could not go down due to a certain difficulty. After a while, he came to the cell and, having examined me, said, "I'll tell everything to the Sister Infirmarian." When the Sister Infirmarian came, after the doctor had left, I told her why I hadn't been able to go down to the parlor, but she gave me to know how very displeased she was. And when I asked, "Sister, what did the doctor say about these pains?" she answered that he had said nothing, that it was nothing, **(28)** that he had said the patient was just sulking. And with that she went off. Then I said to God, "Christ, give me strength and power to suffer; give to my heart a pure love for this sister." After that, she did not look in on me again for a whole week. But the sufferings returned with great violence and lasted almost the whole night, and it seemed that it would be the end, then and there. The superiors decided to approach another doctor,[242] and he ascertained that my condition was serious and said to me, "It will not be possible to return you to good health. We can remedy your condition partially, but complete recovery is out of question." He prescribed a medicine for the pains, and after I had taken it, the major attacks did not return. "But if you come here, Sister, we will try to patch up your health somehow, if that is still possible." The doctor very much wanted me to go there for a treatment.[243] O my Jesus, how strange are Your decrees!

1635 Jesus orders me to write all this **(29)** for the consolation of other souls who will often be exposed to similar sufferings.

1636 Although I was feeling very weak, I went to see the doctor [Silberg], because that was the superior's will.

The sister who was my companion was very unhappy about this. She made this known to me several times and finally said, "What are we going to do? I don't have enough money to pay for the cab." I answered nothing. "And what if there is no cab? How are we going to get there? It's such a long way." She said this and many other things just to worry me, because our dear superiors had given us enough money for everything, and we didn't run short. And understanding this whole business within myself, I laughed and told sister that I was not worried one bit: "Let's trust in God." But I saw that my deep peace was getting on her nerves, and so I started to pray for her intention.

1637 O my Lord, all this is **(30)** for You and to obtain mercy for poor sinners. When I returned, I was so very tired that I had to lie down right away. But it was the day for the quarterly confession. I tried to go to confession, not only because I had need to do so, but also to ask advice of my spiritual director [Father Andrasz]. I began to prepare myself; however I felt so weak that I decided to go ask Mother Superior [Irene] to allow me to go before the novices. Mother Superior answered, "Go and look for the Directress of Novices [Sister Callista]. If she allows you to go before the novices, it is all right with me." However, there were only three sisters ahead of me, waiting for confession, and so I waited because I did not have enough strength to go and look for the Directress of Novices. When I went in to make my confession I was feeling so bad that I could not give an account of the condition of my soul; I barely managed to make my confession. At that point, I noted how much the spirit **(31)** is needed; the letter itself does not make love grow [cf. 2 Cor. 3:6].

1638 On that day, there arose some misunderstandings between the Superior and myself. Neither she nor I was to blame, but moral suffering remained, because I could not explain the matter in question, since it was a secret.

This was the reason why I suffered, even though, by a single word, I could have revealed the truth.

1639 The 20th [of March]. Today, in spirit, I accompanied a certain dying soul. I obtained trust in God's mercy for her. The soul was near despair.

1640 This night is known only to You, O Lord. I have offered it for poor obdurate sinners, to obtain Your mercy for them. Scourge me here, burn me here, as long as You give me the souls of sinners, and especially.... O Jesus, with You nothing is lost; take everything and give me souls... sinners.

1641 **(32)** At adoration during the Forty-Hours' Devotion, the Lord said to me, **My daughter, write that involuntary offenses of souls do not hinder My love for them or prevent Me from uniting Myself with them. But voluntary offenses, even the smallest, obstruct My graces, and I cannot lavish My gifts on such souls.**

1642 + Jesus gave me to know of how everything is dependent on His will, thus giving me profound peace as regards the security of His work.

1643 **Listen, My daughter, although all the works that come into being by My will are exposed to great sufferings, consider whether any of them has been subject to greater difficulties than that work which is directly Mine—the work of Redemption. You should not worry too much about adversities. The world is not as powerful as it seems to be; its strength is strictly limited. (33) Know, My daughter, that if your soul is filled with the fire of My pure love, then all difficulties dissipate like fog before the sun's rays and dare not touch the soul. All adversaries are afraid to start a quarrel with such a soul, because they sense that it is stronger than the whole world...**

1644 **My daughter, do as much for this work of mercy as obedience allows, but present clearly to your confessor**

the very least of My demands, and he will decide. You must not shirk in any way, but carry out everything faithfully; otherwise, I would find no pleasure in you...

1645 March 25, 1938. Today, I saw the suffering Lord Jesus. He leaned down toward me and whispered softly, **My daughter, help Me to save sinners.** Suddenly, a burning desire to save souls entered my soul. When I recovered my senses, I knew **(34)** just how I was to help souls, and I prepared myself for greater sufferings.

1646 + Today [probably Friday, March 25, 1938] my suffering increased; in addition, I felt wounds in my hands, feet and side. I endured this with patience. I sensed the hostilty of the enemy of souls, but he did not touch me.

1647 April 1, [1938]. Once again, I am feeling worse today. A high fever is beginning to consume me, and I cannot take any food. I would like to have something refreshing to drink, but there is not even any water in my pitcher. All this, O Jesus, to obtain mercy for souls.

Just as I was renewing my intention with greater love, one of the novices came in and gave me a big orange which had been sent by the Directress of Novices [Sister Callista]. I saw the Lord's hand in this. The same thing happened again, several times. **(35)** During this time, although my needs were known, I never received anything refreshing to eat, even though I had asked for it. However, I knew that God was demanding suffering and sacrifices. I am not writing in detail about these refusals, because these are delicate matters, and it is difficult to believe. Yet God can demand even such sacrifices.

1648 I was about to ask Mother Superior [Irene] to allow me to have something in my cell with which to quench my great thirst, but before I managed to ask, Mother herself began to speak, "Sister, let's make an end of this illness once and for all, one way or another. You'll have to undergo regular treatment or something. Things can't go on like this any longer." A little later when I was alone I said, "Christ, what am I to do? Am I to ask You for health or for death?" I had no clear command, so I knelt down and said, "May Your holy will be done in my regard. Do with me, Jesus, as You please." **(36)** At that very moment, I felt as though I were all alone, and various temptations attacked me. But I found peace and light in earnest prayer, and I understood that the superior only wished to test me.

1649 I don't know how this happens, but the room in which I have been lying has been very much neglected. Sometimes, it has not been cleaned for more than two weeks. Often, no one would light a fire in the stove, and so my cough would get worse. Sometimes I would ask to have a fire lit, and at other times I did not have the courage to ask. On one occasion, when Mother Superior [Irene] came to see me and asked me if perhaps it was necessary to heat the room more, I said, No, because it was already getting warmer outside, and we had the window open.

1650 First Friday. When I took the *Messenger of the Sacred Heart* into my hand and read the account of the canonization of Saint Andrew Bobola, my soul was instantly filled with a great longing **(37)** that our Congregation, too, might have a saint, and I wept like a child that there was no saint in our midst. And I said to the Lord, "I know Your generosity, and yet it seems to me that You are less generous toward us." And I began again to weep like a little child. And the Lord Jesus said to me, **Don't cry. You are that saint.** Then the light of God inundated my soul, and I was given to know how much I was to suffer, and I said to the Lord, "How will that come about? You have been speaking to me about another Congregation." And the Lord answered, **It is not for you to know how this will come about. Your duty is to be faithful to My grace and to do always what is within your power and what obedience allows you to do...**

1651 + Today one of the sisters came into my room and said that such-and-such a sister was very fussy over her own illness, and that she found this very annoying and would gladly give her a piece of her mind were it not for the fact that she was not a member of this convent. I answered that I was surprised that she should even think in such a way: "Sister, just think of how many sleepless nights this sick sister has been through and of how many tears..." The sister then came to think differently.

+

(38) J.M.J.

1652 Adore, my soul, the mercy of the Lord,
O my heart, rejoice wholly in Him,
Because for this you have been chosen by Him,
To spread the glory of His mercy.

His goodness no one has fathomed, no one can measure,
His compassion is untold.
Every soul that approaches Him experiences this.
He will shield her and clasp her to His merciful bosom.

Happy the soul that has trusted in Your goodness
And has abandoned herself completely to Your mercy.
Her soul is filled with the peace of love.
You defend her everywhere as Your own child.

O soul, whoever you may be in this world,
Even if your sins were as black as night,
Do not fear God, weak child that you are,
For great is the power of God's mercy.

+

(39) J.M.J.

1653 The light above, where my God reigns,
This it is that my soul yearns for,
This it is for which my heart longs,
And my whole being bounds towards You.

I hasten on to the other world, to God alone,
Into the incomprehensible light, the very fire of love,
For my soul and my heart are created for Him,
And my heart has loved Him from my tender youth.

There, in the resplendent light of Your countenance
My languishing love will rest.
For Your virgin agonizes for You in her exile,
For she lives only when united with You.

    +

J.M.J.

My day is drawing to a close,
Even now I glimpse the refulgence of Your light, O my
    God.
No one shall learn of what my heart is feeling;
My lips shall fall silent in great humility.

   (40)Even now, I draw nigh to the eternal nuptials,
   To heaven unending, to spaces without limit.
   I long for no repose or reward;
   The pure love of God draws me to heaven.

Even now, I go to meet You, eternal Love
With a heart languishing in its desire for You.
I feel that Your pure love, Lord, dwells in my heart,
And I sense my eternal destiny in heaven.

   Even now, I go to my Father, in heaven eternal,
   From the land of exile, from this vale of tears,
   The earth can no longer hold back my pure heart,
   And the heights of heaven have drawn me close.

I go, O my Bridegroom, I go to see Your glory,
Which even now fills my soul with joy
There where all heaven is plunged in Your adoration,
I feel that my worship is pleasing to You, nothingness
    though I am.

   In eternal happiness, I will not forget those on earth,
   I will obtain God's mercy for all,

(41) And I will remember especially those who were
dear to my heart,
And the deepest absorption in God will not allow me
to forget them.

In these last moments I know not how to converse with
others.
In silence I await only You, O Lord.
I know the time will come when all will understand the
work of God in my soul.
I know that such is Your will.—So be it.

+

J.M.J.

1654 O truth, O thorny life,
In order to pass through you victoriously
It is necessary to lean on You, O Christ,
And to be always close to You.

I would not know how to suffer without You, O
Christ.
Of myself I would not be able to brave adversities.
Alone, I would not have the courage to drink from
Your cup;
But You, Lord, are always with me, and You lead me
along mysterious paths.

A weak child, I have begun the battle in Your Name.
I have fought bravely, though often without success,
(42) And I know that my efforts have pleased You,
And I know that it is the effort alone which You
eternally reward.

O truth, O life-and-death struggle,
When I rose to do battle, an inexperienced knight,
I felt I had a knight's blood, though still a child,
And therefore, O Christ, I needed Your help and
protection.

My heart will not rest from its efforts and struggle
Until You Yourself call me from the field of battle.

I will stand before You, not to receive a reward,
But to be drowned in You, in peace forever.

1655 + O Christ, if my soul had known, all at once, what it was
going to have to suffer during its lifetime, it would have
died of terror at the very sight; it would not have
touched its lips to the cup of bitterness. But as it has
been given to drink a drop at a time, it has emptied the
cup to the very bottom. O Christ, if You Yourself did
not support the soul, how much could it do of itself? We
are strong, but with Your strength; we are holy, but with
Your holiness. And of ourselves, what are we?—less
than nothing...

(43) + My Jesus, You suffice me for everything else in the
world. Although the sufferings are severe, You sustain
me. Although the times of loneliness are terrible, You
make them sweet for me. Although the weakness is
great, You change it into power for me.

1656 I do not know how to describe all that I suffer, and what I
have written thus far is merely a drop. There are
moments of suffering about which I really cannot write.
But there are also moments in my life when my lips are
silent, and there are no words for my defense, and I
submit myself completely to the will of God; then the
Lord Himself defends me and makes claims on my
behalf, and His demands are such that they can be
noticed exteriorly. Nevertheless, when I perceive His
major interventions, which manifest themselves by way
of punishment, then I beg Him earnestly for mercy and
forgiveness. Yet I am not always heard. The Lord acts
toward me in a mysterious manner. There are times
when He Himself allows terrible sufferings, and then
again there are times when He does not let me suffer and
removes everything (44) that might afflict my soul.
These are His ways, unfathomable and incomprehensible to us. It is for us to submit ourselves

completely to His holy will. There are mysteries that the human mind will never fathom here on earth; eternity will reveal them.

1657 April 10, 1938. Palm Sunday. I attended Holy Mass, but did not have the strength to go and get the palm.[244] I felt so weak that I barely made it till the end of Mass. During Mass, Jesus gave me to know the pain of His soul, and I could clearly feel how the hymns of *Hosanna* reverberated as a painful echo in His Sacred Heart. My soul, too, was inundated by a sea of bitterness, and each *Hosanna* pierced my own heart to its depths. My whole soul was drawn close to Jesus. I heard Jesus' voice: **My daughter, your compassion for Me refreshes Me. By meditating on My Passion, your soul acquires a distinct beauty.**

1658 **(45)** I received Holy Communion upstairs, for there was no question of my going down to the chapel since I was exhausted because of intense sweating, and when that passed, I had a fever and chills. I felt completely worn out. Today, one of the Jesuit Fathers [Father Zukowicz[245]] brought us Holy Communion. He gave the Lord to three other sisters and then to me; and thinking I was the last, he gave me two Hosts. But one of the novices was lying in bed in the next cell, and there was no Host left for her. The priest went back again and brought her the Lord, but Jesus told me, **I enter that heart unwillingly. You received those two Hosts, because I delayed My coming into this soul who resists My grace. My visit to such a soul is not pleasant for Me.** At that point, my soul was drawn close to Him, and I received a deep inner light which gave me to understand, in spirit, all the workings of mercy. It was like a flash of lightning, but more distinct than if I had watched it for hours with the eyes of my body.

1659 **(46)** Still, in order to write anything at all, I must make use of words, though they cannot render all of what my soul enjoyed on seeing the glory of God's mercy. The glory of the Divine Mercy is resounding, even now, in spite of the efforts of its enemies and of Satan himself, who has a great hatred for God's mercy. This work will snatch a great number of souls from him, and that is why the spirit of darkness sometimes tempts good people violently, so that they may hinder the work. But I have clearly seen that the will of God is already being carried out, and that it will be accomplished to the very last detail. The enemy's greatest efforts will not thwart the smallest detail of what the Lord has decreed. No matter if there are times when the work seems to be completely destroyed; it is then that the work is being all the more consolidated.

1660 My soul was filled with a peace much deeper than anything I had experienced before, a divine reassurance which nothing can efface, a deep peace which nothing can disturb, even though I were to go through the severest of ordeals. **(47)** I am at peace; God Himself governs all things.

1661 I spent the whole day in thanksgiving, and gratitude kept flooding my soul. O my God, how good You are, how great is Your mercy! You visit me with so many graces, me who am a most wretched speck of dust. Prostrating myself at Your feet, O Lord, I confess with a sincere heart that I have done nothing to deserve even the least of Your graces. It is in Your infinite goodness that You give Yourself to me so generously. Therefore, the greater the graces which my heart receives, the deeper it plunges itself in humility.

1662 + O Christ, suffering for You is the delight of my heart and my soul. Prolong my sufferings to infinity, that I may give You a proof of my love. I accept everything that Your hand will hold out to me. Your love, Jesus, is enough for me. I will glorify You in abandonment and darkness, in agony and fear, **(48)** in pain and bitterness, in anguish of spirit and grief of heart. In all things may

You be blessed. My heart is so detached from the earth, that You Yourself are enough for me. There is no longer any moment in my life for self concern.

1663 Holy Thursday [April 14, 1938]. Today I felt strong enough to take part in the ceremonies of the Church. During Holy Mass, Jesus stood before me and said, **Look into My Heart and see there the love and mercy which I have for humankind, and especially for sinners. Look, and enter into My Passion.** In an instant, I experienced and lived through the whole Passion of Jesus in my own heart. I was surprised that these tortures did not deprive me of my life.

1664 During adoration, Jesus said to me, **My daughter, know that your ardent love and the compassion you have for Me were a consolation to Me in the Garden** [of Olives].

1665 **(49)** During Holy Hour in the evening, I heard the words, **You see My mercy for sinners, which at this moment is revealing itself in all its power. See how little you have written about it; it is only a single drop. Do what is in your power, so that sinners may come to know My goodness.**

1666 Good Friday [April 15, 1938]. I saw the Lord Jesus, tortured, but not nailed to the Cross. It was still before the crucifixion, and He said to me, **You are My Heart. Speak to sinners about My mercy.** And the Lord gave me interior knowledge of the whole abyss of His mercy for souls, and I learned that that which I had written is truly a drop.

1667 Holy Saturday [April 16, 1938]. During adoration, the Lord said to me, **Be at peace, My daughter. This Work of mercy is Mine; there is nothing of you in it. It pleases Me that you are carrying out faithfully what I have commanded you to do, not adding or taking away a single word.** And He gave me an interior light by **(50)** which I learned that not a single word was mine; despite difficulties and adversities, I have always, always, fulfilled His will, as He has made it known to me.

1668 The Resurrection. Before the Mass of the Resurrection, I felt so weak that I lost all hope of participating in the procession which takes place in the church; and I said to the Lord, "Jesus, if my prayers are pleasing to You, give me the strength for this moment that I may take part in the procession." At that same instant, I felt strong and certain that I could go along with the sisters in the procession.

1669 When the procession began, I saw Jesus in a brightness greater than the light of the sun. Jesus looked at me with love and said, **Heart of My Heart, be filled with joy.** At that moment my spirit was drowned in Him... When I came to myself, I was walking along in the procession with the sisters, while my soul was totally immersed in Him...

1670 **(51)** + Easter [April 17, 1938]. During Mass, I thanked the Lord Jesus for having deigned to redeem us and for having given us that greatest of all gifts; namely, His love in Holy Communion; that is, His very own Self. At that moment, I was drawn into the bosom of the Most Holy Trinity, and I was immersed in the love of the Father, the Son and the Holy Spirit. These moments are hard to describe.

1671 At that moment, I prayed to the Lord for a certain person, and the Lord answered me, **This soul is particularly dear to Me.** I was immensely happy with this. The happiness of other souls fills me with a new joy, and when I see the higher gifts in some soul, my heart soars up to the Lord in a new hymn of adoration.

1672 April 19, [1938]. During recreation, one of the sisters [Sister Cajetan] said, "Sister Faustina is doing so poorly that she can hardly walk, but may she die soon because she is going to be a saint." Then one of the sister directresses [Sister Casimir[246]] said, "That she is going to die, we know; but whether she is going to be a saint, that is another question." There then began some malicious remarks **(52)** on this subject. I kept silent; then I put in a word, but I saw that the conversation was getting worse, so again I fell silent.

1673   At present, I am getting letters from sisters who are in other houses and who made their novitiate with me.[247] They often amuse me and make me laugh, as they usually go something like this: "Dear Sister Faustina, we are very sorry that you are so gravely ill; but we are very happy that, when the Lord Jesus takes you away, you will pray for us, for you have a lot of influence with the Lord." One of the sisters put it this way: "When you die, Sister, please take me under your special care, for certainly you can do that for me." Another sister wrote as follows: "How I am waiting for the time when the Lord Jesus will take you, because I know what will happen then; and I greatly desire death for you." I did want to ask her what she was thinking of, concerning my death, **(53)** but I mortified myself and answered, "The same thing will happen to me, a sinner, as happens to all sinners, if God's mercy does not shield me."

1674   April 20, [1938]. Departure for Pradnik. I was very worried that I would be put in bed in a ward and be exposed to all sorts of things. If it were to be for only a week or two... but it is for such a long time, two months or perhaps more. In the evening, I went in for a long talk with the Lord Jesus. When I saw the Lord Jesus, I poured out my whole heart before Him, all my troubles, fears and apprehensions. Jesus lovingly listened to me and then said, **Be at peace, My child, I am with you. Go in great peace. All is ready; I have ordered, in My own special way, a private room to be prepared for you.** Reassured and overwhelmed with gratitude, I went to bed.

1675   On the following day, Sister Felicia took me there. I left in great peace and a calm spirit. **(54)** When we arrived, they told us there was a private room for Sister

Faustina. When we entered the room, we were surprised that everything had been prepared so beautifully: all was clean and neat, covered with tablecloths and bedecked with flowers; a pretty Easter Lamb had been placed on the night table by the Sisters.[248] At once, three Sacred Heart Sisters[249] who work at the sanatorium, my old acquaintances, came and greeted me warmly. Sister Felicia was surprised at all this. We bid a warm farewell to each other, and she left. When I was alone, with just the Lord Jesus and myself, I thanked Him for this great grace.

1676 Jesus said to me, **Be at peace; I am with you.** Tired, I fell asleep. In the evening, the sister [Sister David] who was to look after me came and said, "Tomorrow you will not receive the Lord Jesus, Sister, because you are very tired; later on, we shall see." This hurt me very much, but I said with great calmness, "Very well," and, resigning myself totally **(55)** to the will of the Lord, I tried to sleep. In the morning, I made my meditation and prepared for Holy Communion, even though I was not to receive the Lord Jesus. When my love and desire had reached a high degree, I saw at my bedside a Seraph, who gave me Holy Communion,[250] saying these words: "Behold the Lord of Angels." When I received the Lord, my spirit was drowned in the love of God and in amazement. This was repeated for thirteen days, although I was never sure he would bring me Holy Communion the next day. Yet, I put my trust completely in the goodness of God, but did not even dare to think that I would receive Holy Communion in this way on the following day.

The Seraph was surrounded by a great light, the divinity and love of God being reflected in him. He wore a golden robe and, over it, a transparent surplice and a transparent stole. The chalice was crystal, covered with a transparent veil. As soon as he gave me the Lord, he disappeared.

1677 Once, when a certain doubt rose within me shortly before Holy Communion, **(56)** the Seraph with the Lord Jesus stood before me again. I asked the Lord Jesus, and not receiving an answer, I said to the Seraph, "Could you perhaps hear my confession?" And he answered me, "No spirit in heaven has that power." And at that moment, the Sacred Host rested on my lips.

1678 On Sunday [April 24, 1938[251]], the sister who had charge of the sick said to me, "Well, Sister, the priest will bring you the Lord Jesus today." I answered, "Good," and he brought Him. After some time, I received permission to leave my bed. So I went to Holy Mass and to spend time with the Lord, regularly.

1679 After the first examination, the doctor [Silberg] found that my condition was grave. "We suspect, Sister, that you do have the illness about which you spoke to me. But Almighty God can do all things."

When I entered my room, I steeped myself in prayer of thanksgiving for everything the Lord had been sending me throughout my whole life, surrendering myself totally to His most holy will. **(57)** A deep joy and peace flooded my soul. I felt a peace so great that, if death had come at that moment, I would not have said to it, "Wait, for I still have some matters to attend to." No, I would have welcomed it with joy, because I am ready for the meeting with the Lord, not only today, but ever since the moment when I placed my complete trust in the Divine Mercy, resigning myself totally to His most holy will, full of mercy and compassion. I know what I am of myself...

1680 Low Sunday. Today, I again offered myself to the Lord as a holocaust for sinners. My Jesus, if the end of my life is already approaching, I beg You most humbly, accept my death in union with You as a holocaust which I offer You today, while I still have full possession of my faculties and a fully conscious will, and this for a threefold purpose:

Firstly: that the work of Your mercy may spread throughout the whole world and that the Feast of The Divine Mercy may be solemnly promulgated and celebrated.

(58) Secondly: that sinners, especially dying sinners, may have recourse to Your mercy and experience the unspeakable effects of this mercy.

Thirdly: that all the work of Your mercy may be realized according to Your wishes, and for a certain person who is in charge of this work...

Accept, most merciful Jesus, this, my inadequate sacrifice, which I offer to You today before heaven and earth. May Your Most Sacred Heart, so full of mercy, complete what is lacking in my offering, and offer it to Your Father for the conversion of sinners. I thirst after souls, O Christ.

1681 + At that moment, the light of God penetrated my being, and I felt that I was God's exclusive property; and I experienced the greatest spiritual freedom, of which I had had no previous idea. And at the same time, I saw the glory of The Divine Mercy and an infinite multitude of souls who were praising His goodness. My soul was completely drowned in God, and I heard the words, **You are My well-beloved daughter.** The vivid presence of God continued throughout the whole day.

1682 **(59)** + May 1, [1938]. This evening, Jesus said to me, **My daughter, do you need anything?** I answered, "O my Love, when I have You I have everything." And the Lord answered, **If souls would put themselves completely in My care, I Myself would undertake the task of sanctifying them, and I would lavish even greater graces on them. There are souls who thwart My efforts, but I have not given up on them; as often as they turn to Me, I hurry to their aid, shielding them with My mercy, and I give them the first place in My compassionate Heart.**

1683 **Write for the benefit of religious souls that it delights Me to come to their hearts in Holy Communion. But if there is anyone else in such a heart, I cannot bear it and quickly leave that heart, taking with Me all the gifts and graces I have prepared for the soul. And the soul does not even notice My going. After some time, inner emptiness and dissatisfaction will come to her attention. Oh, if only she would turn to Me then, (60) I would help her to cleanse her heart, and I would fulfill everything in her soul; but without her knowledge and consent, I cannot be the Master of her heart.**

1684 + I often communicate with persons who are dying and obtain the divine mercy for them. Oh, how great is the goodness of God, greater than we can understand. There are moments and there are mysteries of the divine mercy over which the heavens are astounded. Let our judgment of souls cease, for God's mercy upon them is extraordinary.

1685 **(61)** During Holy Hour today, I asked the Lord Jesus if He would deign to teach me about the spiritual life. Jesus answered me, **My daughter, faithfully live up to the words which I speak to you. Do not value any external thing too highly, even if it were to seem very precious to you. Let go of yourself, and abide with Me continually. Entrust everything to Me and do nothing on your own, and you will always have great freedom of spirit. No circumstances or events will ever be able to upset you. Set little store on what people say. Let everyone judge you as they like. Do not make excuses for yourself; it will do you no harm. Give away everything at the first sign of a demand, even if they were the most necessary things. Do not ask for anything without consulting Me. Allow them to take away even what is due you—respect, your good name—let your spirit rise above all that. And so, set free from everything, rest close to My Heart, not allowing your peace to be**

disturbed by anything. My pupil, consider (62) the words which I have spoken to you.

1686 O my Love, my eternal Master, how good it is to obey; because when obedience infuses the soul, it brings with it power and strength to act.

1687 Today I saw the Crucified Lord Jesus. Precious pearls and diamonds were pouring forth from the wound in His Heart. I saw how a multitude of souls was gathering these gifts, but there was one soul who was closest to His Heart and she, knowing the greatness of these gifts, was gathering them with liberality, not only for herself, but for others as well. The Savior said to me, **Behold, the treasures of grace that flow down upon souls, but not all souls know how to take advantage of My generosity.**

1688 Today, the Lord said to me, **My daughter, look into My Merciful Heart and reflect its compassion in your own heart and in your deeds, so that you, who proclaim My mercy to the world, may yourself be aflame with it.**

1689 **(63)** May 8, [1938]. Today, I saw two enormous pillars implanted in the ground; I had implanted one of them, and a certain person, S.M., the other. We had done so with unheard-of effort, much fatigue and difficulty. And when I had implanted the pillar, I myself wondered where such extraordinary strength had come from. And I recognized that I had not done this by my own strength, but with the power which came from above. These two pillars were close to each other, in the area of the image. And I saw the image, raised up very high and hanging from these two pillars. In an instant, there stood a large temple, supported both from within and from without, upon these two pillars. I saw a hand finishing the temple, but I did not see the person. There was a great multitude of people, inside and outside the temple, and the torrents issuing from the Compassionate Heart of Jesus were flowing down upon everyone.

1690 After Holy Communion today, Jesus said, **My daughter give Me souls. Know that it is your mission (64) to win souls for Me by prayer and sacrifice, and by encouraging them to trust in My mercy.**

1691 Oh, how greatly I desire the glory of Your mercy—for me, bitterness and suffering! When I see the glory of Your mercy, I am immeasurably happy. Let all disgrace, humiliation and abasement come down upon me, as long as the glory and praise of Your mercy resounds everywhere—that's all that matters.

The Creator and The Creature.

1692 I adore You, Lord and Creator, hidden in the Blessed Sacrament. I adore You for all the works of Your hands, that reveal to me so much wisdom, goodness and mercy, O Lord. You have spread so much beauty over the earth, and it tells me about Your beauty, even though these beautiful things are but a faint reflection of You, Incomprehensible Beauty. And although You have hidden Yourself and concealed Your beauty, my eye, **(65)** enlightened by faith, reaches You, and my soul recognizes its Creator, its Highest Good; and my heart is completely immersed in prayer of adoration.

My Lord and Creator, Your goodness encourages me to converse with You. Your mercy abolishes the chasm which separates the Creator from the creature. To converse with You, O Lord, is the delight of my heart. In You I find everything that my heart could desire. Here Your light illumines my mind, enabling it to know You more and more deeply. Here streams of graces flow down upon my heart. Here my soul draws eternal life. O my Lord and Creator, You alone, beyond all these gifts, give Your own self to me and unite Yourself intimately with Your miserable creature. Here, without searching for words, our hearts understand each other. Here, no one is able to interrupt our conversation. What I talk to You about, Jesus, is our secret, which creatures **(66)** shall not know and Angels dare not ask about. These are secret acts of forgiveness, known only to Jesus and me; this is the mystery of His mercy, which embraces each soul separately. For this incomprehensible goodness of Yours, I adore You, O Lord and Creator, with all my heart and all my soul. And, although my worship is so little and poor, I am at peace because I know that You know it is sincere, however inadequate...

1693 As I was writing the above words, I saw the Lord Jesus leaning over me, and He asked, **My daughter, what are you writing?** I answered, "I am writing about You, Jesus, about Your being hidden in the Blessed Sacrament, about Your inconceivable love and mercy for people." And Jesus said, **Secretary of My most profound mystery, know that yours is an exclusive intimacy with Me. Your task is to write down everything that I make known to you about My mercy, for the benefit of those who by (67) reading these things will be comforted in their souls and will have the courage to approach Me. I therefore want you to devote all your free moments to writing.** "But, O Lord, shall I always have a moment, at least a brief one, in which to write?" And Jesus answered, **It is not for you to think about that. Only do as much as you can, and I will always arrange things so that you will easily be able to do what I ask of you...**

1694 Today, I was visited by a certain lay person [probably Stanislava Kwietniewska] who has caused me a lot of sorrow and who has abused my goodness, telling many lies. At the first moment I saw her, the blood froze in my veins, because there stood before my eyes all that I had to suffer because of her, although with one word I could have freed myself of them all. And the thought came to me to tell her the truth, firmly and immediately. But at the same moment, the mercy **(68)** of God came before my eyes, and I resolved to act toward her as Jesus would have acted in my place. I started to talk to her gently, and when she expressed the wish to talk to me alone, I then, in a very delicate manner, made known to her clearly the sad condition of her soul. I saw that she was deeply moved, though she was trying to hide this from me. At that point, a third person came in, and so our heart-to-heart talk came to an end. She asked me for a glass of water and for two other things which I did willingly. However, had it not been for the grace of God, I would not have been able to act in such a way toward her. When they left, I thanked God for the grace which had supported me during that time.

1695 Then I heard the words, **I am glad you behaved like My true daughter. Be always merciful as I am merciful. Love everyone out of love for Me, even your greatest enemies, so that My mercy may be fully reflected (69) in your heart.**

1696 O Christ, although much effort is required, all things can be done with Your grace.

1697 I was feeling fairly well today, and I was glad that I would be able to make the Holy Hour. But when I began to make the Holy Hour, my physical sufferings intensified, so that I was not able to pray. When the Holy Hour was over, my sufferings came to an end, and I complained to the Lord that I had wanted so much to steep myself in His sorrowful Passion, but that my sufferings had not allowed me to do so. Then Jesus said to me, **My daughter, know that if I allow you to feel and have a more profound knowledge of My sufferings, that is a grace from Me. But when your mind is dimmed and your sufferings are great, it is then that you take an active part in My Passion, and I am conforming you more fully to Myself. It is your task to submit yourself to My will at such times, more than at others...**

1698 **(70)** I often attend upon the dying and through entreaties obtain for them trust in God's mercy, and I implore God for an abundance of divine grace, which is always victorious. God's mercy sometimes touches the sinner at the last moment in a wondrous and mysterious way. Outwardly, it seems as if everything were lost, but it is not so. The soul, illumined by a ray of God's powerful final grace, turns to God in the last moment with such a power of love that, in an instant, it receives from God forgiveness of sin and punishment, while outwardly it shows no sign either of repentance or of contrition, because souls [at that stage] no longer react to external things. Oh, how beyond comprehension is God's mercy! But—horror!—there are also souls who voluntarily and consciously reject and scorn this grace! Although a person is at the point of death, the merciful God gives the soul that interior vivid moment, so that if the soul is willing, it has the possibility of returning to God. But sometimes, the obduracy **(71)** in souls is so great that consciously they choose hell; they [thus] make useless all the prayers that other souls offer to God for them and even the efforts of God Himself...

1699 J.M.J.

> Solitude—my favorite moments,
> Solitude—but always with You, Jesus and Lord,
> Close to Your Heart, time passes pleasantly for me,
> And, close to Him, my soul finds its repose.

> When the heart is filled with You and overflowing with love,
> And the soul burns with pure fire,
> Then, amidst the utmost desolation, the soul will not experience loneliness,
> Because it rests on Your bosom.

> O Solitude—moments of supreme companionship,
> Though I be abandoned by all creatures,
> I immerse myself totally in the ocean of Your Godhead,
> And You listen sweetly to my confidences.

1700 **(72)** This evening, the Lord asked me, **Do you not have any desires in your heart?** I answered, "I have one great desire, and it is to be united with You forever." And the Lord answered me, **That will happen soon. My dearest child, your every stirring is reflected in My Heart. My gaze rests kindly upon you before any other creature.**

1701 I asked the Lord today that He might deign to teach me about the interior life, because of myself I can neither understand nor conceive anything perfectly. The Lord answered me, **I was your Teacher, I am and I will be; strive to make your heart like unto My humble and gentle Heart. Never claim your rights. Bear with great calm and patience everything that befalls you. Do not defend yourself when you are put to shame, though innocent. Let others triumph. Do not stop (73) being good when you notice that your goodness is being abused. I Myself will speak up for you when it is necessary. Be grateful for the smallest of My graces, because your gratitude compels Me to grant you new graces...**

1702 Towards the end of the Way of the Cross which I was making, the Lord Jesus began to complain about the souls of religious and priests, about the lack of love in chosen souls. **I will allow convents and churches to be destroyed.** I answered, "Jesus, but there are so many souls praising You in convents." The Lord answered, **That praise wounds My Heart, because love has been banished from convents. Souls without love and without devotion, souls full of egoism and self-love, souls full of pride and arrogance, souls full of deceit and hypocrisy, lukewarm souls who have just enough warmth to keep them alive: My Heart cannot bear this. (74) All the graces that I pour out upon them flow off them as off the face of a rock. I cannot stand them, because they are neither good or bad. I called convents into being to sanctify the world through them. It is from them that a powerful flame of love and sacrifice should burst forth.**

And if they do not repent and become enkindled by their first love, I will deliver them over to the fate of this world...

How can they sit on the promised throne of judgment to judge the world, when their guilt is greater than the guilt of the world? There is neither penance nor atonement. O heart, which received Me in the morning and at noon are all ablaze with hatred against Me, hatred of all sorts! O heart specially chosen by Me, were you chosen for this, to give Me more pain? The great sins of the world are superficial wounds on My Heart, but the sins of a chosen soul pierce My Heart through and through...

1703 When I tried to intercede for them, I could find nothing with which **(75)** to excuse them and, being at the time unable to think of anything in their defense, my heart was seized with pain, and I wept bitterly. Then the Lord looked at me kindly and comforted me with these words: **Do not cry. There are still a great number of souls who love Me very much, but My Heart desires to be loved by all and, because My love is great, that is why I warn and chastise them.**

1704 + Struggle with a certain temptation. There was a person who kept accosting me with flattering words, and since he knew when I went out to go to the chapel or to the veranda, he would bar my way. Since he did not dare approach me by himself, he found another person like himself, but neither of them dared approach. As I was on my way to the May devotions, they were already standing there where I had to pass. I hadn't yet reached them when I heard enticing words, **(76)** directed at me. And the Lord permitted me to know the intentions of their hearts, which were not good. I felt they would block my way after the service, and then I would have to talk to them, for up to that time I hadn't said a word.

When I left the chapel, they were there, armed and waiting for me to pass. This time, I was overcome with fear. Then Jesus stood by me and said, **Do not fear. I am**

with you. Then I felt an extraordinary strength in my soul, which I cannot describe and, being a few steps from them, I said boldly and loudly, "Praised be Jesus Christ." And they, stepping aside, responded, "For ever and ever. Amen." As if struck by lightning, they bowed their heads, not even daring to look at me. After I had passed, I could hear some malicious comments. Ever since that time, when this person sees me, he runs away in order not to meet me and I, thanks to the Lord, have been left in peace...

1705 **(77)** After Holy Mass, I went out to the garden to make my meditation, since there were not yet any patients in the garden at this time, and so I felt at ease. As I was meditating on the blessings of God, my heart was burning with a love so strong that it seemed my breast would burst. Suddenly Jesus stood before me and said, **What are you doing here so early?** I answered, "I am thinking of You, of Your mercy and Your goodness toward us. And You, Jesus, what are You doing here?" **I have come out to meet you, to lavish new graces on you. I am looking for souls who would like to receive My grace.**

1706 During Vespers today, the Lord gave me to know how very pleased He is with a pure and free heart. I felt that it is God's delight to look into such a heart... But such hearts are knightly hearts; their life is a constant battle...

1707 **(78)** + On my way to the veranda, I went into the chapel for a moment. My heart was plunged in profound adoration, praising God's incomprehensible goodness and His mercy. Then I heard these words in my soul: **I am and will be for you such as you praise Me for being. You shall experience My goodness, already in this life and then, to the full, in the life to come.**

1708 O Christ, I am most delighted when I see that You are loved, and that Your praise and glory resound, especially the praise of Your mercy. O Christ, to the last moment of my life, I will not stop glorifying Your goodness and mercy. With every drop of my blood, with every beat of my heart, I glorify Your mercy. I long to be entirely transformed into a hymn of Your glory. When I find myself on my deathbed, may the last beat of my heart be a loving hymn in praise of Your unfathomable mercy.

1709 **(79)** + Today the Lord said to me, **You shall make a three-day retreat before the coming of the Holy Spirit. I Myself will direct you. You shall not follow any of the rules required for retreats or use any books for meditation. Your task is to listen attentively to My words. For spiritual reading you shall read one chapter from the Gospel of St. John.**

[Here occurs a space of a half page in the original Notebook]

1710 **(80)** May 26, [1938—Feast of the Ascension]. Today I accompanied the Lord Jesus as He ascended into heaven. It was about noon. I was overcome by a great longing for God. It is a strange thing, the more I felt God's presence, the more ardently I desired Him. Then I saw myself in the midst of a huge crowd of disciples and apostles, together with the Mother of God. Jesus was telling them to... **Go out into the whole world and teach in My name.** He stretched out His hands and blessed them and disappeared in a cloud. I saw the longing of Our Lady. Her soul yearned for Jesus with the whole force of Her love. But She was so peaceful and so united to the will of God that there was not a stir in Her heart but for what God wanted.

1711 When I was left alone with the Blessed Virgin, She instructed me concerning the interior life. She said, *The soul's true greatness is in loving God and in humbling oneself in His presence, completely forgetting oneself and believing oneself to be nothing; because the Lord is great, but He is well-pleased only with the humble; He always opposes the proud.*

1712 **(81)** A certain person whom I have mentioned before visited me again. When I saw that she was beginning to get entangled in her own lies, I let her know that I knew she was lying. She became very embarrassed and stopped speaking. Then I spoke to her about the great judgments of God, and I also remarked that she was leading innocent souls astray and along dangerous roads. I uncovered before her everything that was in her heart. Since I had to overcome my own feelings in order to talk to her, to prove to Jesus that I love my enemies, I gave her my afternoon snack. She went away enlightened in soul, but action is still far away...

1713 There are times when the Lord Jesus fulfills my smallest wishes. Today I remarked that I would like to see some ears of grain, but that they cannot be seen from our sanatorium. However, one of the patients heard this remark and, on the following day, he went out into the field and brought me several beautiful **(82)** ears of grain. My room is always adorned with fresh flowers, but my spirit finds satisfaction in nothing. More and more, I yearn for God.

1714 Today I interceded earnestly with the Lord Jesus for our house, that He might deign to take away the cross which has touched our convent.[252] The Lord answered me, **Your prayers are accepted for other intentions. I cannot take away this cross until they recognize its meaning.** Nevertheless, I did not stop praying.

1715 A strong temptation. The Lord gave me to know how pleasing a pure heart is to Him, and thereby I was given a deeper knowledge of my own misery. When I began to prepare for confession, strong temptations against confessors assaulted me. I did not see Satan, but I could sense him, his terrible anger. — "Yes, he's an ordinary man." — "Not ordinary, because he has the power of

God." — Yes, **(83)** it is not difficult for me to accuse myself of my sins. But to uncover the most secret depths of my heart, to give an account of the action of God's grace, to speak about God's every demand, about all that goes on between God and myself... to tell that to a man is beyond my strength. I felt I was fighting against the powers and I cried out: "O Christ, You and the priest are one; I will approach confession as if I were approaching, not a man, but You." When I entered the confessional, I began by disclosing my difficulties. The priest replied that the best thing I could have done was to disclose these temptations from the outset. However, after the confession, they took flight, and my soul is enjoying peace.

1716 Once during recreation, one of the sister directresses said that the lay sisters were without feelings, and so could be treated stiffly. I was sorry to see that the sister directresses know so little about the lay sisters and judge them only from appearances.

1717 **(84)** Today, I was talking with the Lord, and He said to me, **There are souls with whom I can do nothing. They are souls that are continuously observing others, but know nothing of what is going on within their own selves. They talk about others continually, even during times of grand silence, which is reserved for speaking only with Me. Poor souls, they do not hear My words; their interior remains empty. They do not look for Me within their own hearts, but in idle talk, where I am never to be found. They sense their emptiness, but they do not recognize their own guilt, while souls in whom I reign completely are a constant source of remorse to them. Instead of correcting themselves, their hearts swell with envy, and if they do not come to their senses, they plunge in even deeper. A heart, which thus far is envious, now begins to be filled with hate. And they are already at the edge of the precipice. They are jealous of**

my gifts in other souls, but they themselves are unable and unwilling to accept them.

1718 **(85)** To stay at Your feet, O hidden God,
Is the delight and paradise of my soul.
Here, You give me to know You, O incomprehensible One,
And You speak to me sweetly: **Give Me, give Me your heart.**

Silent conversation, alone with You,
Is to experience what heavenly beings enjoy,
And to say to God, "I will, I will give You my heart, O Lord,"
While You, O great and incomprehensible One, accept it graciously.

Love and sweetness are my soul's life,
And Your unceasing presence in my soul.
I live on earth in constant rapture,
And like a Seraph I repeat, "Hosanna!"

O You Who are hidden, body, soul and divinity,
Under the fragile form of bread,
You are my life from Whom springs an abundance of graces;
And, for me, You surpass the delights of heaven.

When You unite Yourself with me in Communion, O God,
I then feel my unspeakable greatness,
(86) A greatness which flows from You, O Lord, I humbly confess,
And despite my misery, with Your help, I can become a saint.

1719 + During Holy Mass, I came to know that a certain priest does not effect much in souls because he thinks about himself and so is alone. God's grace takes flight; he relies on trifling external things, which have no importance in the eyes of God; and, being proud, he fritters away his time, wearing himself out to no purpose.

1720 There are moments when Jesus gives me knowledge within my soul, and then everything that exists on earth is at my service: friends, enemies, success, adversity... all things, willing or not, must serve me. I do not think of them at all; I strive to be faithful to God and to love Him to the point of complete forgetfulness of self. And He Himself looks after me and fights against my enemies.

1721 **(87)** After Holy Communion, when I had welcomed Jesus into my heart, I said to Him, "My Love, reign in the most secret recesses of my heart, there where my most secret thoughts are conceived, where You alone have free access, in this deepest sanctuary where human thought cannot penetrate. May You alone dwell there, and may everything I do exteriorly take its origin in You. I ardently desire, and I am striving with all the strength of my soul, to make You, Lord, feel at home in this sanctuary."

1722 I heard these words: **If you did not tie My hands, I would send down many punishments upon the earth. My daughter, your look disarms My anger. Although your lips are silent, you call out to Me so mightily that all heaven is moved. I cannot escape from your requests, because you pursue Me, not from afar but within your own heart.**

1723 **(88)** When the soul of a certain young lady came to me one night, she made me aware of her presence, and made known to me that she needed my prayer. I prayed for a while, but her spirit did not leave me. Then I thought to myself, "If you are a good spirit, leave me in peace, and the indulgences I will gain tomorrow will be for you." At that moment, the spirit left my room, and I recognized that she was in purgatory.

1724 Today I felt the Lord's Passion in my body more than at any other time. I felt this was for the sake of a dying soul.

1725 Today, the Lord has been teaching me, once again, how I am to approach the Sacrament of Penance: **My daughter, just as you prepare in My presence, so also you make your confession before Me. The person of the priest is, for Me, only a screen. Never analyze what sort of a (89) priest it is that I am making use of; open your soul in confession as you would to Me, and I will fill it with My light.**

1726   Christ and Lord, You are leading me over such precipices that, when I look at them, I am filled with fright, but at the same time I am at peace as I nestle close to Your heart. Close to Your Heart, I fear nothing. In these dangerous moments, I act like a little child, carried in its mother's arms; when it sees something which menaces it, it clasps its mother's neck more firmly and feels secure.

1727   + I often see snares laid for me by souls who should not do so. I do not defend myself, but entrust myself all the more to God, who sees within me. And I see how these souls become entangled in their own snares. O God, how just and good You are!

1728   **(90) Write: I am Thrice Holy, and I detest the smallest sin. I cannot love a soul which is stained with sin; but when it repents, there is no limit to My generosity toward it. My mercy embraces and justifies it. With My mercy, I pursue sinners along all their paths, and My Heart rejoices when they return to Me. I forget the bitterness with which they fed My Heart and rejoice at their return.**

Tell sinners that no one shall escape My Hand; if they run away from My Merciful Heart, they will fall into My Just Hands. Tell sinners that I am always waiting for them, that I listen intently to the beating of their heart... when will it beat for Me? Write, that I am speaking to them through their remorse of conscience, through their failures and sufferings, through thunderstorms, through the voice of the Church. And if

they bring all My graces to naught, I begin to be angry (91) with them, leaving them alone and giving them what they want.

1729   O my Jesus, You alone know of my efforts. I seem to be a bit better, but better only to the point that I can go out on the veranda instead of lying in bed. I see and am fully aware of what is happening to me. Despite the diligent care of my superiors and the efforts of the doctors, my health is fading and running out. But I rejoice greatly at Your call, my God, my Love, because I know that my mission will begin at the moment of my death. Oh, how much I desire to be set free from the bonds of this body. O my Jesus, You know that, in all my desires, I always want to see Your will. Of myself, I would not want to die one minute sooner, or to live one minute longer, or to suffer less, **(92)** or to suffer more, but I only want to do Your holy will. Although I have great enthusiasm, and the desires burning in my heart are immense, they are never above Your will.

1730   I fly to Your mercy, Compassionate God, who alone are good. Although my misery is great, and my offenses are many, I trust in Your mercy, because You are the God of mercy; and, from time immemorial, it has never been heard of, nor do heaven or earth remember, that a soul trusting in Your mercy has been disappointed.

O God of compassion, You alone can justify me, and You will never reject me when I, contrite, approach Your Merciful Heart, where no one has ever been refused, even if he were the greatest sinner.

1731   **(93)** Today I was awakened by a great storm. The wind was raging, and it was raining in torrents, thunderbolts striking again and again. I began to pray that the storm would do no harm, when I heard the words: **Say the chaplet I have taught you, and the storm will cease.** I began immediately to say the chaplet and hadn't even finished it when the storm suddenly ceased, and I heard the words: **Through the chaplet you will obtain everything, if what you ask for is compatible with My will.**

1732 As I was praying for Poland, I heard the words: **I bear a special love for Poland, and if she will be obedient to My will, I will exalt her in might and holiness. From her will come forth the spark that will prepare the world for My final coming.**

1733 **(94)** + Welcome, hidden Love, life of my soul! I welcome You, Jesus, under these insignificant forms of bread. Welcome, sweetest Mercy, who pour Yourself out for souls. Welcome, Infinite Goodness, who pour out everywhere torrents of Your graces. Welcome, O veiled Brightness, the Light of souls. Welcome, O Fount of inexhaustible mercy, O purest Spring from which life and holiness gush forth for us. Welcome, Delight of pure souls. Welcome, only Hope of sinful souls.

1734 O my Jesus, You know that there are times when I have neither lofty thoughts nor a soaring spirit. I bear with myself patiently and admit that that is just what I am, because all that is beautiful is a grace from God. And so I humble myself profoundly and cry out for Your help; and the grace of visitation is not slow in coming to the humble heart.

1735 **(95)** O virgin, lovely flower,
      You will not remain much longer in this world.
      Oh, how beautiful your loveliness,
      My pure bride!

        No numbers can count you.
        How dear is your virginal flower!
        Your brightness is in no way dimmed;
        It is brave, strong, invincible.

      The very blaze of the noon-day sun
      Dims, and darkens in the presence of a virgin heart.
      I see nothing greater than virginity.
      It is a flower taken from the Divine Heart.

O gentle virgin, fragrant rose,
Although there are many crosses on earth,
No eye has seen, nor has it entered into the mind of
    man
What awaits a virgin in heaven.

O virgin, snow-white lily,
You live wholly for Jesus alone
(96) And in the pure chalice of your heart
Is a pleasing dwelling place for God Himself.

O virgin, no one will sing your hymn.
In your song lies hidden the love of God.
Even the Angels do not comprehend
What the virgins sing to God.

O virgin, your flower of paradise
Eclipses all the splendors of this world.
And although the world cannot comprehend you,
It bows humbly before you.

Although the virgin's path is strewn with thorns,
And her life bristles with many a cross,
Who is as brave as she?
Nothing will break her; she is invincible.

O virgin, earthly angel,
Your greatness is renowned throughout the Church.
You stand guard before the tabernacle
And, like a Seraph, become all love.

1736 **(97)** Once, when I was on the veranda, I saw that a certain person was being troubled by strong temptations concerning Holy Confession, doubting its secrecy. Although I knew the condition of that soul, I myself did not start the conversation. When we were alone, she opened her heart to me and told me everything. After talking for a short while, she said to me, "I am at peace now; my soul has received much light."

1737 Today, Jesus made known to me that I should speak little with a certain religious sister. A special grace of

God sustained me during the conversation, which would not otherwise have been for God's glory.

1738 The Lord said to me, **Enter into purgatory often, because they need you there.** O my Jesus, I understand the meaning of these words which You are speaking to me, but first let me enter the treasury **(98)** of Your mercy.

1739 **Write, My daughter, that I am mercy itself for the contrite soul. A soul's greatest wretchedness does not enkindle Me with wrath; but rather, My Heart is moved towards it with great mercy.**

1740 O my Jesus, give me strength to endure suffering so that I may not make a wry face when I drink the cup of bitterness. Help me Yourself to make my sacrifice pleasing to You. May it not be tainted by my self-love, even though it extend over many years. May purity of intention make it pleasing to You, fresh and full of life. This life of mine is a ceaseless struggle, a constant effort to do Your holy will; but may everything that is in me, both my misery and my strength, give praise to You, O Lord.

(99) The Infinite Goodnes of God in the
Creation of the Angels.

1741 O God, who are happiness in Your very self and have no need of creatures to make You happy, because of Yourself You are the fullness of love; yet, out of Your fathomless mercy You call creatures into being and grant them a share in Your eternal happiness and in Your life, that divine indwelling life which You live, One God in Three Persons. In Your unfathomable mercy, You have created angelic spirits and admitted them to Your love and to Your divine intimacy. You have made them capable of eternal love. Although You bestowed on them so generously, O Lord, the splendor of love and beauty, Your fullness was not diminished in the least, O God, nor have their love and beauty completed You, because You are everything in Yourself. And if You have allowed them to participate in Your happiness and to exist and to love You, that is only due to the abyss of Your mercy. This is Your unfathomable goodness, for which they glorify You without end, **(100)** humbling themselves at the feet of Your majesty as they chant their eternal hymn: Holy, Holy, Holy...

1742 Be praised, merciful God, One God in the Holy Trinity,
Unfathomable, infinite, incomprehensible,
Immersing themselves in You, their minds cannot comprehend You,
So they repeat without end their eternal: Holy.

Be glorified, O merciful Creator of ours, O Lord,
Omnipotent, but full of compassion, inconceivable.
To love You is the mission of our existence,
Singing our eternal hymn: Holy...

Be blessed, merciful God, Eternal Love.
You are above the heavens, the saphires, the firmaments.
The host of pure spirits sings You praises,
With its eternal hymn: Thrice Holy.

And, gazing upon You, face to face, O God,
I see that You could have called other creatures before them.
Therefore they humble themselves before You in great humility,
For well they see that this grace comes solely from Your mercy.

(101) One of the most beautiful spirits would not recognize Your mercy,
And, blinded by his pride, he drew others after him.
Angel of great beauty, he became Satan
And was cast down in one moment from heaven's heights into hell.

Then the faithful spirits cried, "Glory to God's mercy!"

And they stood firm in spite of the fiery test.
Glory to Jesus, the Christ abased,
Glory to His Mother, the humble and pure Virgin.

After this battle, the pure spirits plunged into the ocean
of Divinity;
Contemplating and praising the depths of His mercy,
They drown in His mercy and manifold light,
Possessing in knowledge the Trinity of Persons, the
Oneness of Godhead.

1743   + God's Infinite Goodness in Creating Mankind.

God, who in Your mercy have deigned to call man from
nothingness into being, generously have You bestowed
upon him nature and grace. But that seemed too little
for Your infinite goodness. In Your mercy, O Lord, You
have given us **(102)** everlasting life. You admit us to
Your everlasting happiness and grant us to share in
Your interior life. And You do this solely out of Your
mercy. You bestow on us the gift of Your grace, only
because You are good and full of love. You had no need
of us at all to be happy, but You, O Lord, want to share
Your own happiness with us. But man did not stand the
test. You could have punished him, like the angels, with
eternal rejection, but here Your mercy appeared, and
the very depths of Your being were moved with great
compassion, and You promised to restore our salvation.
It is an incomprehensible abyss of Your compassion
that You did not punish us as we deserved. May Your
mercy be glorified, O Lord; we will praise it for endless
ages. And the angels were amazed at the greatness of the
mercy which You have shown for mankind...

1744   May You be adored, O merciful God of ours,
O All-powerful Lord and Creator.
In deepest humility, we give You praise,
Plunging ourselves into the ocean of Your Godhead.

(103) But man did not persevere in the hour of trial.

At the instigation of the evil one, he became unfaithful
to You.
He lost Your grace and gifts; only misery was left him,
And tears, suffering, sorrow and bitterness, until he
would rest in the grave.

But you, O merciful God, did not let humanity perish,
And gave it the promise of a Redeemer.
You did not let us despair, despite our grave offenses,
And You sent Your prophets to Israel.

Still, day and night, mankind cries out to You,
From the abyss of misery, sin and all pain.
Hear the moaning and the tears, You who reign in
heaven,
God of great mercy, God of compassion.

Man erred, but he cannot ask pardon,
Because a gaping chasm has appeared between God and
man.
With the voice of his misery, he cries out, "Mercy!"
But Yahweh is silent... and century after century passes
on.

But the longing of all humankind grows deeper.
A longing for Him who has been promised.
(104) Come, Lamb of God, take away our vile sins,
Come, illumine our darkness like a ray of light.

Humanity calls out to You unceasingly, O Lord of
lords,
Calls out to Your unfathomable mercy, to Your
compassion.
O great Yahweh, grant that we may make atonement,
Remember Your goodness, and forgive us our sins.

+The Infinite Goodness of God
in Sending Us His Only-Begotten Son.

1745 God, You did not destroy man after his fall, but in Your
mercy You forgave him, You forgave in a divine way;

that is, not only have You absolved him from guilt, but You have bestowed upon him every grace. Mercy has moved You to deign to descend among us and lift us up from our misery. God will descend to earth; the Immortal Lord of lords will abase Himself. But where will You descend, Lord; will it be to the temple of Solomon? Or will You have a new tabernacle built for Yourself? Where do You intend to come down? O Lord, what kind of tabernacle shall we prepare for You, **(105)** since the whole earth is Your footstool?

You have indeed prepared a tabernacle for Yourself: the Blessed Virgin. Her Immaculate Womb is Your dwelling place, and the inconceivable miracle of Your mercy takes place, O Lord. The Word becomes flesh; God dwells among us, the Word of God, Mercy Incarnate. By Your descent, You have lifted us up to Your divinity. Such is the excess of Your love, the abyss of Your mercy. Heaven is amazed at the superabundance of Your love. No one fears to approach You now. You are the God of mercy. You have compassion on misery. You are our God, and we are Your people. You are our Father, and we are Your children by grace. Praise be to Your mercy, that You have deigned to descend among us.

1746 Be adored, O God of mercy,
Because You have deigned to descend from heaven to earth.
Most humbly we adore You
For Your having vouchsafed to exalt all mankind.

(106) Unfathomable and incomprehensible in Your mercy,
For love of us You take on flesh
From the Immaculate Virgin, ever untouched by sin,
Because You have willed it so from all ages.

The Blessed Virgin, that Snow-White Lily,
Is first to praise the omnipotence of Your mercy.
Her pure heart opens with love for the coming of the
Word;

She believes the words of God's messenger and is confirmed in trust.

Heaven is astounded that God has become man,
That there is on earth a heart worthy of God Himself.
Why is it that You do not unite Yourself with a Seraph, but with a sinner, O Lord?
Oh, because, despite the purity of the virginal womb, this is a mystery of Your mercy.

O mystery of God's mercy, O God of compassion,
That You have deigned to leave the heavenly throne
And to stoop down to our misery, to human weakness,
For it is not the angels, but man who needs mercy.

To give worthy praise to the Lord's mercy,
We unite ourselves with Your Immaculate Mother,
(107) For then our hymn will be more pleasing to You,
Because She is chosen from among men and angels.

Through Her, as through a pure crystal,
Your mercy was passed on to us.
Through Her, man became pleasing to God;
Through Her, streams of grace flowed down upon us.

+ God's Infinite Goodness in Redeeming Man.

1747 God, You could have saved thousands of worlds with one word; a single sigh from Jesus would have satisfied Your justice. But You Yourself, Jesus, purely out of love for us, underwent such a terrible Passion. Your Father's justice would have been propitiated with a single sigh from You, and all Your self-abasement is solely the work of Your mercy and Your inconceivable love. On leaving the earth, O Lord, You wanted to stay with us, and so You left us Yourself in the Sacrament of the Altar, and You opened wide Your mercy to us. There is no misery that (108) could exhaust You; You have called us all to this fountain of love, to this spring of

God's compassion. Here is the tabernacle of Your
mercy, here is the remedy for all our ills. To You, O
living spring of mercy, all souls are drawn; some like
deer, thirsting for Your love, others to wash the wound
of their sins, and still others, exhausted by life, to draw
strength. At the moment of Your death on the Cross,
You bestowed upon us eternal life; allowing Your most
holy side to be opened, You opened an inexhaustible
spring of mercy for us, giving us Your dearest possession,
the Blood and Water from Your Heart. Such is the
omnipotence of Your mercy. From it all grace flows to
us.

1748   Be adored, O God, in the work of Your mercy,
        Be blessed by all faithful hearts
        On whom Your gaze rests,
        In whom dwells Your immortal life.

        (109) O my Jesus, have mercy, sorrowful was Your
            life on this earth,
            And in terrible torment Your work came to an end,
            Hanging stretched out on the wood of the Cross,
            And all this for the love of our souls.

        In Your inconceivable love, You allowed Your most
            holy side to be opened,
        And streams of Blood and Water gushed forth from
            Your Heart.
        Here is the living fountain of Your mercy,
        Here souls receive consolation and refreshment.

            In the Blessed Sacrament, You left us Your mercy;
            Your love deigned to arrange it so,
            That, going through life, suffering and toil,
            I might never doubt of Your goodness and mercy.

        For even if the whole world's miseries weighed on my
            soul,
        We must not doubt for even a moment,
        But have trust in the power of God's mercy,

Because, with graciousness, God receives a contrite soul.

O unspeakable mercy of our Lord,
Source of compassion and all sweetness,
(110) Trust, trust, O soul, though you are stained by sin,
For when you approach God, you will not taste bitterness.

Because He is a living fire of great love,
When we approach Him with sincerity,
Our miseries, sins and evil deeds vanish;
He will settle our debts when we surrender ourselves to Him.

1749   + God's Infinite Goodness in Adorning
                 the Whole World with Beauty
          in Order to Make Man's Stay on Earth Pleasant.

O God, how generously Your mercy is spread everywhere, and You have done all this for man. Oh, how much You must love him, since Your love is so active on his behalf. O my Creator and Lord, I see on all sides the trace of Your hand and the seal of Your mercy, which embraces all created things. O my most compassionate Creator, I want to give You worship on behalf of all creatures and all inanimate **(111)** creation; I call on the whole universe to glorify Your mercy. Oh, how great is Your goodness, O God!

1750 Be adored, O our Creator and Lord.
      O universe, humbly glorify your God;
      Thank your Creator to the best of your powers
      And praise God's incomprehensible mercy.

          Come, O earth, in all your fine greenery;
          Come, you too, O fathomless sea.
          Let your gratitude become a loving song
          And sing the greatness of God's mercy.

Come, beautiful, radiant sun.
Come, bright dawn which precedes it.
Join in one hymn, and let your clear voices
Sing in one accord God's great mercy.

Come, hills and valleys, sighing woods and thickets,
Come, lovely flowers of morningtide;
Let your unique scent
Adore and glorify God's mercy.

(112) Come, all you lovely things of earth,
Which man does not cease to wonder at.
Come, adore God in your harmony,
Glorifying God's inconceivable mercy.

Come, indelible beauty of all the earth,
And, with great humility, adore your Creator,
For all things are locked in His mercy,
With one mighty voice all things cry out; how great is
the mercy of God.

But above all these beauties,
A more pleasing praise to God
Is a soul innocent and filled with childlike trust,
Which, through grace, is closely bound to Him.

1751 + O Jesus, concealed in the Blessed Sacrament of the
Altar, my only love and mercy, I commend to You all
the needs of my body and soul. You can help me,
because You are Mercy itself. In You lies all my hope.

(113) [In the original there follows a completely blank
page.]

                    +

(114) J.M.J.   Cracow-Pradnik, June 2, 1938

Three-day Retreat.

1752 Under the direction of Master Jesus, who Himself
commanded me to make this retreat, and who selected
the days on which I was to make it; namely, the three
days preceding Pentecost and who, Himself, conducted
this retreat.

However, I asked my confessor [probably Father Andrasz] whether I could make such a retreat, and I received his permission. I also asked Mother Superior [Irene] and received her permission too. I had resolved that I would not make the retreat unless I obtained the permission of the Superiors. I began a novena to the Holy Spirit, and waited for Mother Superior's answer.

(115) I should be beginning the retreat today, but I have not yet received news of Mother Superior's decision.

When I went to Church for the evening devotions, I saw the Lord Jesus during the litany. **My daughter, we are beginning the retreat.** I answered, "Jesus, my dearest Master, I ask Your forgiveness, but I cannot make the retreat, because I have received no news as to whether Mother Superior allows it or not." **Do not worry, My daughter, the Superior has given her permission. You will learn of it tomorrow morning. But we are to start the retreat today.**

And indeed, Mother Superior had telephoned that evening to the sister who is looking after me during my illness [Sister David], asking her to tell me that I was allowed to make the retreat, but the sister had forgotten to tell me. It was only next morning that she told me, (116) and she was very apologetic that she had not told me the day before. I answered her, "Please do not worry. I have already started my retreat, according to the Superior's wish."

+The First Day.

1753 In the evening, Jesus gave me the subject for meditation. At the first moment, my heart was filled with fear and joy. Then I pressed myself close to His Heart, and the fear vanished; only joy remained. I felt entirely like a child of God, and the Lord said to me, **Fear nothing. What has been forbidden to others has been given to you. The graces that are not given to other souls to** discern, not even from a distance, nourish you every day, like the daily bread.

1754 **Consider, My daughter, Who it is to whom your heart is so closely united by the vows. Before I made the world, I loved you with the love your heart is experiencing today and, throughout the centuries, (117) My love will never change.**

1755 Application. At the very thought of Him to whom my heart is wedded, my soul entered into profound recollection, and the hour passed like a minute. In this state of recollection, I came to know the attributes of God. Burning with an inner fire of love, I went out to the garden to cool off; when I looked up at the heavens, a new flame of love flooded my heart.

1756 Then I heard the words: **My daughter, have you exhausted the subject I gave you? If so, I'll give you a new one.** I answered, "O Infinite Majesty, eternity will not be enough for me to come to know You... But my love for You has become more intense. As a token of gratitude, I lay my heart at Your feet, like a rosebud. May its fragrance delight Your Divine Heart, now and for eternity... What a paradise it is for a soul when the heart knows itself to be so loved by God..."

1757 **(118) Today, you will read chapter fifteen of the Gospel of Saint John. I want you to read it very slowly.**

Second Meditation.

1758 **My daughter, consider the life of God which is found in the Church for the salvation and the sanctification of your soul. Consider the use that you make of these treasures of grace, of these efforts of My love.**

1759 Application: O most compassionate Jesus, I have not always known how to profit from these priceless gifts, because I have paid too little attention to the gift itself and too much to the vessel in which You were giving me Your gifts. My most sweet Master, it will be different from now on. I will put Your gifts to the best use of which my soul is capable. Living faith will support me. Whatever the form might be, under which You send me Your grace, I will accept it as coming directly from You, without considering the vessel in **(119)** which You send it. If it will not always be within my power to accept it with joy, I will always accept it with submission to Your holy will.

Conference on Spiritual Warfare.

1760 **My daughter, I want to teach you about spiritual warfare. Never trust in yourself, but abandon yourself totally to My will. In desolation, darkness and various doubts, have recourse to Me and to your spiritual director. He will always answer you in My name. Do not bargain with any temptation; lock yourself immediately in My Heart and, at the first opportunity, reveal the temptation to the confessor. Put your self-love in the last place, so that it does not taint your deeds. Bear with yourself with great patience. Do not neglect interior mortifications. Always justify to yourself the opinions of your superiors and of your confessor. Shun murmurers like a plague. (120) Let all act as they like; you are to act as I want you to.**

Observe the rule as faithfully as you can. If someone causes you trouble, think what good you can do for the person who caused you to suffer. Do not pour out your feelings. Be silent when you are rebuked. Do not ask everyone's opinion, but only the opinion of your confessor; be as frank and simple as a child with him. Do not become discouraged by ingratitude. Do not examine with curiosity the roads down which I lead you. When boredom and discouragement beat against your heart, run away from yourself and hide in My heart. Do not fear struggle; courage itself often intimidates temptations, and they dare not attack us.

Always fight with the deep conviction that I am with you. Do not be guided by feeling, because it is not

always under your control; but all merit lies in the will. Always depend upon your superiors, even in the smallest things. I will not delude you with prospects of peace (121) and consolations; on the contrary, prepare for great battles. Know that you are now on a great stage where all heaven and earth are watching you. Fight like a knight, so that I can reward you. Do not be unduly fearful, because you are not alone.

Second Day.

1761 **My daughter, today consider My Sorrowful Passion in all its immensity. Consider it as if it had been undertaken for your sake alone.**

1762 Application: When I began to immerse myself in the Divine Passion, the great worth of the human soul and the great evil of sin were revealed to me. I understood that I did not know how to suffer. In order to gain merit for my suffering, I will unite myself more closely, in suffering, to the Passion of the Lord Jesus, asking of Him grace for dying souls, so that the mercy of God may embrace them in this grave moment.

(122)Second Meditation.

1763 **My daughter, consider the rule and the vows which you have offered to Me. You know how highly I value them; all the graces that I have for the souls of religious are connected with the rule and the vows.**

1764 Application: O my Jesus, I feel guilty of many imperfections on this score but, by Your grace, I do not recall any conscious and voluntary transgression of the rule or the religious vows. Continue to guard me, O my good Jesus, for of myself I am weak.

1765 **Today, My daughter, for your reading you shall take chapter nineteen of Saint John's Gospel, and read it, not only with your lips, but with your heart...**

1766 During this reading, my soul was filled with deep repentance. I saw all the ingratitude of creatures toward their Creator and Lord; I asked God to protect me from spiritual blindness.

Conference on Sacrifice and Prayer.

1767 **(123) My daughter, I want to instruct you on how you are to rescue souls through sacrifice and prayer. You will save more souls through prayer and suffering than will a missionary through his teachings and sermons alone. I want to see you as a sacrifice of living love, which only then carries weight before Me. You must be annihilated, destroyed, living as if you were dead in the most secret depths of your being. You must be destroyed in that secret depth where the human eye has never penetrated; then will I find in you a pleasing sacrifice, a holocaust full of sweetness and fragrance. And great will be your power for whomever you intercede. Outwardly, your sacrifice must look like this: silent, hidden, permeated with love, imbued with prayer. I demand, My daughter, that your sacrifice be pure and full of humility, that I may find pleasure in it. I will not spare My grace, that you may be able to fulfill what I demand of you.**

I will now instruct you on what (124) your holocaust shall consist of, in everyday life, so as to preserve you from illusions. You shall accept all sufferings with love. Do not be afflicted if your heart often experiences repugnance and dislike for sacrifice. All its power rests in the will, and so these contrary feelings, far from lowering the value of the sacrifice in My eyes, will enhance it. Know that your body and soul will often be in the midst of fire. Although you will not feel My presence on some occasions, I will always be with you. Do not fear; My grace will be with you...

Third Day.

1768 **My daughter, in this meditation, consider the love of neighbor. Is your love for your neighbor guided by My love? Do you pray for your enemies? Do you wish well** to those who have, in one way or another, caused you sorrow or offended you?

Know that whatever good (125) you do to any soul, I accept it as if you had done it to Me.

1769 Application: O Jesus, my Love, You know that it has only been for a short while that I have acted toward my neighbor guided solely by Your love. You alone know of my efforts to do this. It comes to me more easily now, but if You Yourself did not kindle that love in my soul, I would not be able to persevere in this. This is due to Your Eucharistic love which daily sets me afire.

Second Meditation.

1770 **Now you shall consider My love in the Blessed Sacrament. Here, I am entirely yours, soul, body and divinity, as your Bridegroom. You know what love demands: one thing only, reciprocity...**

1771 Application: O my Jesus, You know that I desire to love You with a love that no soul **(126)** has ever before loved You with. I would like the whole world to be transformed into love for You, my Betrothed. You feed me with the honey and milk of Your Heart. From my earliest years, You reared me for Yourself alone, so that I would know how to love You now. You know that I love You, because You alone know the depth of the sacrifice I offer You each day.

1772 Jesus said to me, **My daughter, have you any difficulties in this retreat?** I answered that I hadn't. In this retreat, my mind is like lightning. I penetrate all the mysteries of faith with great ease. My Master and Leader, all darkness disappears from my mind under the ray of Your light.

1773 **Today, for your spiritual reading, you will take the Gospel of Saint John, chapter twenty-one. Let if feed your heart more than your mind.**

1774 **(127)** + During the June devotions, the Lord said to me,

My daughter, My favor rests in your heart. When on Holy Thursday I left Myself in the Blessed Sacrament, you were very much on My mind.

1775 After these words, my love made great efforts to express to Him what He was to me, but I was at a loss for words and burst into tears in my helplessness. And Jesus said, **For you, I am mercy itself; therefore I ask you to offer Me your misery and this very helplessness of yours and, in this way, you will delight My Heart.**

1776 Today, a living flame of divine love entered my soul; if it had lasted any longer, I would have been consumed by the fire, freeing myself of the bonds of the present. It seemed to me that, if it had lasted an instant longer, I would have been drowned in the ocean of love. I cannot describe these arrows of love that pierce my soul.

(128) + Conference on Mercy.

1777 **My daughter, know that My Heart is mercy itself. From this sea of mercy, graces flow out upon the whole world. No soul that has approached Me has ever gone away unconsoled. All misery gets buried in the depths of My mercy, and every saving and sanctifying grace flows from this fountain. My daughter, I desire that your heart be an abiding place of My mercy. I desire that this mercy flow out upon the whole world through your heart. Let no one who approaches you go away without that trust in My mercy which I so ardently desire for souls.**

Pray as much as you can for the dying. By your entreaties, obtain for them trust in My mercy, because they have most need of trust, and have it the least. Be assured that the grace of eternal salvation for certain souls in their final moment depends on your prayer. You know the whole abyss of My mercy, (129) so draw upon it for yourself and especially for poor sinners. Sooner would heaven and earth turn into nothingness than would My mercy not embrace a trusting soul.

1778 My resolution continues to be the same: to unite myself
to Christ-Mercy.

Conclusion of the Retreat.
Last Conversation with the Lord.

1779 Thank you, Eternal Love, for Your inconceivable
kindness to me, that You would occupy Yourself
directly with my sanctification. — **My daughter, let three
virtues adorn you in a particular way: humility, purity
of intention and love. Do nothing beyond what I
demand of you, and accept everything that My hand
gives you. Strive for a life of recollection so that you can
hear My voice, which is so soft that only recollected
souls can hear it...**

1780 **(130)** I could not sleep until midnight today, so deeply
was I stirred by tomorrow's renewal of vows. The
greatness of God embraced my whole being.

Pentecost [June 5, 1938]. Renewal of Vows.

1781 I got up how much earlier than usual and went to the
chapel, steeping myself in the love of God. Before
receiving Holy Communion, I silently renewed my
religious vows. After Holy Communion, the infinite
love of God swept over me. My soul was in communion
with the Holy Spirit, who is the same Lord as the Father
and the Son. His breath filled my soul with such delight
that it would be useless for me to try to give even a faint
idea of what my heart experienced. Throughout the
whole day, wherever I was and regardless of with whom
I talked, a vivid presence of God accompanied me; my
soul was drowned in thanksgiving for these great graces.

1782 **(131)** + When I went out to the garden today, the Lord
said to me, **Return to your room, for I will be waiting for
you there.** As soon as I returned, I saw the Lord Jesus,
sitting at the table and waiting for me. He looked at me
kindly and said, **My daughter, I want you to write now,
because that walk would not have been in conformity**

with My will. I remained alone and immediately got down to writing.

1783 + When I immersed myself in prayer and united myself with all the Masses that were being celebrated all over the world at that time, I implored God, for the sake of all these Holy Masses, to have mercy on the world and especially on poor sinners who were dying at that moment. At the same instant, I received an interior answer from God that a thousand souls **(132)** had received grace through the prayerful mediation I had offered to God. We do not know the number of souls that is ours to save through our prayers and sacrifices; therefore, let us always pray for sinners.

1784 Today, in the course of a long conversation, the Lord said to me, **How very much I desire the salvation of souls! My dearest secretary, write that I want to pour out My divine life into human souls and sanctify them, if only they were willing to accept My grace. The greatest sinners would achieve great sanctity, if only they would trust in My mercy. The very inner depths of My being are filled to overflowing with mercy, and it is being poured out upon all I have created. My delight is to act in a human soul and to fill it with My mercy (133) and to justify it. My kingdom on earth is My life in the human soul. Write, My secretary, that I Myself am the spiritual guide of souls—and I guide them indirectly through the priest, and lead each one to sanctity by a road known to Me alone.**

1785 Mother Superior [Irene] visited me today, but only for a short while. When she looked around, she said that everything was too pretty here. It is true, the sisters are trying to make my stay in the sanatorium pleasant. But all this beauty does not lessen my sacrifice, which God alone can see and which will cease only when my heart stops beating. Neither the beauty of the whole earth, nor even of heaven itself, can blur the torture of my soul, which is real at each moment **(134)** though so deeply interior. It will end when You Yourself, Author of my suffering, say, "Enough." There is nothing that could lessen my sacrifice.

First Friday after Corpus Christi. [June 17, 1938]

1786   Right away, on the Friday after Corpus Christi, I felt so unwell that I thought the longed-for moment was approaching. I had a high fever and spat up much blood during the night. Yet, I did go to receive the Lord Jesus in the morning, but I could not stay for the Holy Mass. In the afternoon, my temperature dropped suddenly to 35.8° C. I felt so weak that it was as if everything inside me were dying. But when I steeped myself in profound prayer, I understood that it was not yet the moment of deliverance, but only a closer call from my Bridegroom.

1787   When I met with the Lord, I said to Him, **(135)** "You are fooling me, Jesus; You show me the open gate of heaven, and again You leave me on earth." The Lord said to me, **When, in heaven, you see these present days, you will rejoice and will want to see as many of them as possible. I am not surprised, My daughter, that you cannot understand this now, because your heart is overflowing with pain and longing for Me. Your vigilance pleases Me. Let My word be enough for you; it will not be long now.**

And my soul found itself once again in exile. I lovingly united myself to the will of God, submitting myself to His gracious decrees.

1788   + The conversations that I hear in this place about worldly matters make me so tired that I nearly faint. The sisters who nurse me have noticed this, because it shows outwardly.

1789   **(136)** + Today[253] I saw the glory of God which flows from the image. Many souls are receiving graces, although they do not speak of it openly. Even though it has met up with all sorts of vicissitudes, God is receiving glory because of it; and the efforts of Satan and of evil men are shattered and come to naught. In spite of Satan's anger, The Divine Mercy will triumph over the whole world and will be worshiped by all souls.

1790 I have come to know that, in order for God to act in a soul, it must give up acting on its own; otherwise, God will not carry out His will in it.

1791 When a great storm was approaching, I began to say the chaplet. Suddenly I heard the voice of an angel: "I cannot approach in **(137)** this storm, because the light which comes from her mouth drives back both me and the storm." Such was the angel's complaint to God. I then recognized how much havoc he was to have made through this storm; but I also recognized that this prayer was pleasing to God, and that this chaplet was most powerful.

1792 I learned that a certain soul was very pleasing to God and that, in spite of all sorts of persecutions, God was clothing this person in a new and higher dignity. My heart greatly rejoiced in this.

1793 The moments which are most pleasant to me are those when I converse with the Lord within the center of my being. I try my very best not to leave Him alone. He likes to be always with us...

1794 **(138)** + O Jesus, eternal God, thank You for Your countless graces and blessings. Let every beat of my heart be a new hymn of thanksgiving to You, O God. Let every drop of my blood circulate for You, Lord. My soul is one hymn in adoration of Your mercy. I love You, God, for Yourself alone.

1795 My God, although my sufferings are great and protracted, I accept them from Your hands as magnificent gifts. I accept them all, even the ones that other souls have refused to accept. You can come to me with everything, my Jesus; I will refuse You nothing. I ask You for only one thing: give me the strength to endure them and grant that they may be meritorious. Here is my whole being; do with me as You please.

1796 **(139)** Today,[254] I saw the Sacred Heart of Jesus in the sky, in the midst of a great brilliance. The rays were issuing from the Wound [in His side] and spreading out over the entire world.

1797 Today, the Lord came to me and said, **My daughter, help Me to save souls. You will go to a dying sinner, and you will continue to recite the chaplet, and in this way you will obtain for him trust in My mercy, for he is already in despair.**

1798 Suddenly, I found myself in a strange cottage where an elderly man was dying amidst great torments. All about the bed was a multitude of demons and the family, who were crying. When I began to pray, the spirits of darkness fled, with hissing and threats directed at me. The soul became calm and, filled with trust, rested in the Lord.

At the same moment, I found myself again in my own room. How this happens... I do not know.

+

1799 **(140)** J.M.J. I feel that there is a power which is defending me and protecting me from the blows of the enemy. It guards and defends me. I feel it very distinctly; it is as if I am being shielded by the shadow of His wings.

1800 My Jesus, You alone are good. Even if my heart were to make every effort to write of Your goodness, at least in part, I could not do so—this is beyond all our comprehension.

1801 One day during Holy Mass, the Lord gave me a deeper knowledge of His holiness and His majesty, and at the same time I saw my own misery. This knowledge made me happy, and my soul drowned itself completely in His mercy. I felt enormously **(141)** happy.

1802 On the following day, I had a clear awareness of the following words: "You see, God is so holy, and you are sinful. Do not approach Him, and go to Confession every day." And indeed, whatever I thought of seemed to me to be a sin. But I did not omit going to Holy Communion, and I resolved to go to Confession at the prescribed time, as I had no clear impediment. But when the day for confession came, I prepared a whole mass of those sins of which I was to accuse myself. However, in the confessional, God allowed me to accuse myself of only two imperfections, despite my efforts to make a confession according to what I had prepared. When I left the confessional, the Lord said to me, **My daughter, all those sins you intended to confess are not sins in My eyes; (142) that is why I took away your ability to tell them.** I understood that Satan, wanting to disturb my peace, has been giving me exaggerated thoughts. O Savior, how great is Your goodness!

1803 One day, when I was preparing for Holy Communion and noticed that I had nothing to offer Him, I fell at His feet, calling down all His mercy upon my poor soul: "May Your grace, which flows down upon me from Your Compassionate Heart, strengthen me for the struggle and sufferings, that I may remain faithful to You. And, although I am such misery, I do not fear You, because I know Your mercy well. Nothing will frighten me away from You, O God, because everything is so much less **(143)** than what I know [Your mercy to be]—I see that clearly.

[Here ends the sixth and last notebook]

My Preparation for
Holy Communion

(1)

+
J.M.J.

Cracow, January 10, 1938

My Preparation for Holy Communion

Sister Mary Faustina
of the Blessed Sacrament

Congregation of the Sisters
of Our Lady of Mercy

1804 **(2)** The most solemn moment of my life is the moment when I receive Holy Communion. I long for each Holy Communion, and for every Holy Communion I give thanks to the Most Holy Trinity.

If the angels were capable of envy, they would envy us for two things: one is the receiving of Holy Communion, and the other is suffering.

1805 1. + Today, I am preparing myself for Your coming as a bride does for the coming of her bridegroom. He is a great Lord, this Bridegroom of mine. The heavens cannot contain Him. The Seraphim who stand closest to Him cover their faces and repeat unceasingly: Holy, Holy, Holy.

This great Lord is my Bridegroom. It is to Him that the Choirs sing. It is before Him that the Thrones bow down. By His splendor the sun is eclipsed. And yet this great Lord is my Bridegroom. My heart, desist from this profound meditation on how others adore Him, for you no longer have time for that, as He is coming and is already at your door.

1806 I go out to meet Him, and I invite Him to the dwelling place of my heart, humbling myself profoundly before His majesty. But the Lord lifts me up from the dust and invites me, as His bride, to sit next to Him and to tell Him everything **(3)** that is on my heart. And I, set at ease by His kindness, lean my head on His breast and tell Him of everything. In the first place, I tell Him things I would never tell to any creature. And then, I speak about the needs of the Church, about the souls of poor sinners and about how much they have need of His mercy. But the time passes quickly. Jesus, I must go to carry out the duties that are awaiting me. Jesus tells me that there is still a moment in which to say farewell. A deep mutual gaze, and we seemingly separate for a while; but, in reality, we never do. Our hearts are constantly united. Though outwardly I am distracted by my various duties, the presence of Jesus plunges me constantly in profound recollection.

1807 2. + Today, my preparation for the coming of Jesus is brief, but imprinted deeply with vehement love. The presence of God penetrates me and sets aflame my love for Him. There are no words; there is only interior understanding. I drown completely in God, through love. The Lord approaches the dwelling of my heart. After receiving Communion, I have just enough presence of mind to return to my kneeler. At the same time, my soul (4) is completely lost in God, and I no longer know what is going on about me. God gives me an interior knowledge of His Divine Being. These moments are short, but penetrating. The soul leaves the chapel in profound recollection, and it is not easy to distract it. At such times, I touch the ground with only one foot, as it were. No sacrifice throughout such a day is either difficult or burdensome. Every situation evokes a new act of love.

1808 3. + Today, I invite Jesus to my heart, as Love. You are Love itself. All heaven catches the flame from You and is filled with love. And so my soul covets You as a flower yearns for the sun. Jesus, hasten to my heart, for You see that, as the flower is eager for the sun, so my heart is for You. I open the calyx of my heart to receive Your love.

1809 When Jesus came to my heart, everything in my soul trembled with life and with warmth. Jesus, take the love from my heart and pour into it Your love, Your love which is burning and radiant, which knows how to bear each sacrifice, which knows how to forget itself completely.

Today, my day is marked by sacrifice...

1810 (5) 4. + Today, I Prepare for the Coming of the King.

What am I, and who are You, O Lord, King of eternal glory? O my heart, are you aware of who is coming to you today? Yes, I know, but—strangely—I am not able to grasp it. Oh, if He were just a king, but He is the King of kings, the Lord of lords. Before Him, all power and dominion tremble. He is coming to my heart today. But I hear Him approaching. I go out to meet Him and invite Him. When He entered the dwelling of my heart, it was filled with such reverence that it fainted with fear, falling at His feet. Jesus gives her His hand and graciously permits her to take her place beside Him. He reassures her, saying, **See, I have left My heavenly throne to become united with you. What you see is just a tiny part and already your soul swoons with love. How amazed will your heart be when you see Me in all My glory.**

1811 **But I want to tell you that eternal life must begin already here on earth through Holy Communion. Each Holy Communion makes you more capable of communing with God throughout eternity.**

And so, my King, I do not ask You for anything, although I know that **(6)** You can give me everything. I ask You for one thing only: remain forever the King of my heart; that is enough for me.

1812 Today I am renewing my act of submission to my King, by faithfulness to interior inspirations.

1813 5. + Today, I am not forcing myself to make any special preparation. I cannot think of anything, though I feel many things. I long for the time when God will come to my heart. I throw myself in His arms and tell Him about my inability and my misery. I pour out all the pain of my heart, for not being able to love Him as much as I want. I arouse within myself acts of faith, hope and charity and live on that throughout the day.

1814 6. + Today, my preparation is brief. A strong and living faith nearly tears away the veil of love. The presence of God penetrates my heart as a ray from the sun penetrates crystal. At the moment when I receive God, all my being is steeped in Him. Amazement and admiration overwhelm me when I see God's great majesty, which stoops down to me who am misery itself. There bursts forth from my soul immense gratitude to **(7)** Him for all the graces that He imparts to me, and especially for the grace of being called to His exclusive service.

1815   7. + Today, in Holy Communion, I want to unite myself to Jesus as closely as possible, through love. I yearn for God so ardently that it seems to me that the moment will never come when the priest will give me Holy Communion. My soul falls as if into a swoon because of my longing for God.

1816   When I received Him into my heart, the veil of faith was torn away. I saw Jesus who said to me, **My daughter, your love compensates Me for the coldness of many souls.** After these words, I was once again alone, but throughout the whole day I lived in an act of reparation.

1817   8. + Today, I feel an abyss of misery in my soul. I want to approach Holy Communion as a fountain of mercy and to drown myself completely in this ocean of love.

When I received Jesus, I threw myself into Him as into an abyss of unfathomable mercy. And the more I felt I was misery itself, the stronger grew my trust in Him.

In this abasement, I passed the whole day.

1818   **(8)** 9. + Today, my soul has the disposition of a child. I unite myself to God as a child to its father. I feel completely like a child of God.

1819   When I had received Holy Communion, I had a deeper knowledge of the heavenly Father and of His Fatherhood in relation to souls.

Today I live, glorifying the Holy Trinity. I thank God that He has deigned to adopt us as His children, through grace.

1820   10. + Today, I want to be transformed, whole and entire, into the love of Jesus and to offer myself, together with Him, to the Heavenly Father.

During Holy Mass, I saw the Infant Jesus in the chalice, and He said to me, **I am dwelling in your heart as you see Me in this chalice.**

1821   After Holy Communion, I felt the beating of the Heart of Jesus in my own heart. Although I have been aware, for a long time, that Holy Communion continues in me until the next Communion, today—and throughout the whole day—I am adoring Jesus in my heart and asking Him, by His grace, to protect little children from the evil that threatens them. A vivid and even physically felt presence of God continues throughout the day and does not in the least interfere with my duties.

1822   **(9)** 11. + Today, my soul desires to show, in a special way, its love to Jesus. When the Lord entered my heart, I threw myself down at His feet like a rosebud. I want the fragrance of my love to rise continually to the foot of Your throne. You see, Jesus, in this rosebud, all my heart [offered] to You, not only now when my heart is burning like a live coal, but also during the day, when I will give You proofs of my love by faithfulness to divine grace.

Today, all the difficulties and sufferings that I will encounter, I will quickly seize, like rosebuds, to throw at the feet of Jesus. Little matter that the hand, or rather the heart, bleeds...

1823   12. + Today, my soul is preparing for the coming of my Savior, who is goodness and love itself. Temptations and distractions torment me and do not let me prepare for the coming of the Lord. Therefore I desire even more ardently to receive You, Lord, because I know that when You come, You will rescue me from these torments. And if it is Your will that I should suffer, well then, fortify me for the struggle.

Jesus, Savior, who have deigned **(10)** to come into my heart, drive away these distractions which are keeping me from talking to You.

Jesus answered me, **I want you to become like a knight experienced in battle, who can give orders to others amid the exploding shells. In the same way, My child, you should know how to master yourself amid the greatest difficulties, and let nothing drive you away from Me, not even your falls.**

Today, I have been struggling all day long with a certain difficulty about which You, Jesus, know...

1824 13. + Today, my heart trembles with joy. I desire very much that Jesus come to my heart. My longing heart is inflamed with an ever-increasing love.

When Jesus came, I threw myself into His arms like a little child. I told Him of my joy. Jesus listened to these outpourings of my love. When I asked pardon of Jesus for not preparing myself for Holy Communion, but for continually thinking of sharing in this joy as soon as possible, He answered that **Most pleasing to Me is this preparation with which you have received Me into your heart. Today, in a special way I bless this your joy. Nothing will disturb that joy throughout this day...**

1825 **(11)** 14. + Today, my soul is preparing for the coming of the Lord, who can do all things, who can make me perfect and holy. I am preparing very carefully for His reception, but there arose the difficulty as to how to present this to Him? I rejected it [this difficulty] at once. I will present it as my heart dictates.

1826 When I had received Jesus in Holy Communion, my heart cried out with all its might, "Jesus, transform me into another host! I want to be a living host for You. You are a great and all-powerful Lord; You can grant me this favor." And the Lord answered me, **You are a living host, pleasing to the Heavenly Father. But reflect: What is a host? A sacrifice. And so...?**

O my Jesus, I understand the meaning of "host," the meaning of sacrifice. I desire to be before Your Majesty a living host; that is, a living sacrifice that daily burns in Your honor.

When my strength begins to fail, it is Holy Communion that will sustain me and give me strength. Indeed, I fear the day on which I would not receive Holy Communion. My soul draws astonishing strength from Holy Communion.

O living Host, light of my soul!

1827 **(12)** 15. + Today, my soul is preparing for Holy Communion as for a wedding feast, wherein all the participants are resplendent with unspeakable beauty. And I, too, have been invited to this banquet, but I do not see that beauty within myself, only an abyss of misery. And, although I do not feel worthy of sitting down to table, I will however slip under the table, at the feet of Jesus, and will beg for the crumbs that fall from the table. Knowing Your mercy, I therefore approach You, Jesus, for sooner will I run out of misery than will the compassion of Your Heart exhaust itself. That is why during this day I will keep arousing trust in The Divine Mercy.

1828 16. + Today, the Majesty of God is surrounding me. There is no way that I can help myself to prepare better. I am thoroughly enwrapped in God. My soul is being inflamed by His love. I only know that I love and am loved. That is enough for me. I am trying my best to be faithful throughout the day to the Holy Spirit and to fulfill His demands. I am trying my best for interior silence in order to be able to hear His voice...

Abbreviations

Used in the Footnotes

A.A.S.	Acts of the Apostolic See
A. SF.	Archives of Sister Faustina
A. SF. Recol.	Archives of Sister Faustina; Recollections of people who knew her.
A. SJ-C	Archives of the Society of Jesus-Cracow
A. SMDM-C	Archives of the Sisters of Our Lady of Mercy-Chronicles
A. SMDM-C and D	Archives of the Sisters of Our Lady of Mercy-Chronicles and Death Records
A. SMDM-D	Archives of the Sisters of Our Lady of Mercy-Death Records
cf.	confer
Const. Congr.	Constitutions of the Congregation (of the Sisters of Our Lady of Mercy)

Footnotes

to the Diary of the Servant of God
Sister Mary Faustina Kowalska
of the Congregation of Our Lady of Mercy

1. On February 22, 1931, while staying at Plock, Sister Faustina received Jesus' order to paint a picture according to a model that was shown to her (cf. Diary 47).

The Servant of God tried to fulfill the command, but not knowing painting techniques, she was unable to do it by herself. Still, she did not give up the idea. She kept returning to it and sought help from other sisters and from her confessors.

A few years later her superiors sent her to Vilnius (Wilno), where her confessor, Rev. Prof. Michael Sopocko, interested to see what the picture of a hitherto unknown theme would look like, asked the painter Eugene Kazimierowski to paint the picture according to Sister Faustina's directions. The picture was finished in June 1934 and hung in the corridor of the Bernardine Sisters' convent near St. Michael's Church in Vilnius, where Father Sopocko was rector.

In 1935, during the celebrations concluding the Jubilee Year of the Redemption of the World, the image of The Divine Mercy was transferred to the Ostra Brama ["Eastern Gate" to the city of Vilnius] and placed in a high window so that it could be seen from far away. It was there from April 26 to April 28. By permission of Archbishop Romuald Jalbrzykowski, on April 4, 1937, the image was blessed and placed in St. Michael's Church in Vilnius.

In 1944, a committee of experts was formed, at the order of Archbishop Jalbrzykowski, to evaluate the image. The experts' opinion was that the image of The Divine Mercy, painted by E. Kazimierowski was artistically executed and an important contribution to contemporary religious art.

There are several characteristic features of this original image. Against a plain background, Christ is shown walking, with a narrow halo around His head, and his eyes slightly downcast, as if he were looking from above at the spectators. His right hand is raised in a gesture of blessing; while his left hand is opening the robe at His Heart (not shown), from which two rays of light issue, a pale one to the viewer's right, a red one to the left. The light of these rays shines through the hands and the robe.

In 1943, in Lwow, at the request of the Sisters of Our Lady of Mercy, Stanley Batowski painted another image, which was placed in a side altar of the community chapel at No. 3/9 Zytnia street in Warsaw. During the Warsaw uprising, this chapel (and with it the image) was burned.

Batowski's image was very much liked by everyone. Encouraged by this, the Superior General of the Community of the Sisters of Our Lady of Mercy asked Batowski to paint another one for the house in Cracow, where the new form of devotion to The Divine Mercy was already expanding. The image was painted and sent to Cracow on October 6, 1943.

In the meantime, the superior of the Cracow house had been approached by the painter Adolf Hyla, who offered to paint some sort of picture for the sisters' chapel as a votive offering for having survived the war. The superior, Mother Irene Krzyzanowska, after consulting with the senior sisters and Father Andrasz, S.J., suggested that Mr. Hyla should paint the image according to Sister Faustina's directions. For that purpose, he was given the description (taken from Sister Faustina's Diary) along with a small copy of the image painted by Eugene Kazimierowski.

The image was finished in Autumn of 1943 and brought to the Cracow house. Batowski's image arrived at the same time. For this reason a problem arose—which of the images should be kept in the sisters' chapel? It was settled by Cardinal Sapieha, who by chance happened to be present there. He inspected the two pictures and said, "Since Hyla has painted his picture as a votive offering, that picture should stay in the sisters' chapel." He blessed the picture and ordered that it be hung. To this day the picture remains in the side altar to the left of the main entrance, in the Chapel of the Congregation of the Sisters of Our Lady of Mercy at No. 3/9 Wronia Street in

Cracow, and is held in reverence as the image painted under the direction of Sister Faustina Kowalska. People from all over Poland and from abroad come to this image of the Merciful Christ to beg for needed graces. There are many votive offerings, and copies of the image are found all over the world.

S. Batowski's picture was placed in the Church of The Divine Mercy at Smolensk Street in Cracow.

Over the years, many other painters have painted images of The Divine Mercy, based on either existing representations or on Sister Faustina's diary.

2. That is; in the picture.

3. During her stay in Vilnius, Sister Faustina was told by her confessor, Father Michael Sopocko, to write down her interior experiences.

When asked by someone in the Congregation why Sister Faustina had been writing a diary, Father Sopocko answered: "I was a professor at the Seminary and at the School of Theology of the Stefan Batory University in Vilnius at the time. I had no time to listen to her lengthy confessions at the confessional, so I told her to write everything down and then to show it to me from time to time. This is how the Diary came into being" (Father Sopocko's letter of March 6, 1972).

Sister Faustina mentions the confessor's order in numbers 6 and 839 of the Diary.

In addition to this order from her confessor, the Servant of God mentions, on many pages of her Diary, a distinct command to write, given her by the Lord Jesus Himself (see Diary nos. 372, 459, 895, 965, 1142, 1457, 1567, 1665, and others).

4. Aldona Lipszycowa then lived in Ostrowek in the district of Radzymin. She was born on April 14, 1896 in Tbilisi, USSR, the daughter of Serafin Jastrzebski and Mary Lemke. In 1965/66 she was one of the witnesses in the informative process of the Servant of God.

"My husband," she recalls, "had asked the pastor of St. James Parish in the suburb of Ochota, to find someone to help me in my housework. Rev. Canon James Dabrowski, when pastor in Klebow, became my husband's friend. He baptized him, blessed our marriage and baptized all our children. The Rev. Canon sent us—in the summer of 1924—Helen Kowalski with a note that he did not know her, but hoped she would be all right" (A. SF. Recol.).

5. The convent of the Congregation of the Sisters of Our Lady of Mercy at No. 3/9 Zytnia Street in Warsaw.

6. Mother Michael—Olga Moraczewska was born in 1873. She was considered highly educated for those times. She spoke several languages and completed the Conservatory of Music. She entered the congregation later in life. After making her final profession of vows, she was appointed superior of the house in Warsaw. She kept this position until 1928. After the term of office of the Superior General M. Leonard Cielecka, she administrated the entire Congregation. During her administration as Superior General, the Constitutions of the Congregations received approbation. She dearly loved her community and sought its spiritual and material development. She founded new homes in Warsaw in the suburb of Grochow, in Rabka, in Lwow, and in Biala, a house affiliated to the house in Plock, 10 km away.

She died in Cracow November 15, 1966, and is buried in the Congregation's cemetery (A. SMDM-C).

7. It is a Community tradition that sisters stay under the same roof with the Lord Jesus in the Eucharist. Since the chapel at the Warsaw house was in a separate building a few meters from the sisters' house, a second chapel was made on the second floor of the sisters' convent. By permission of the Archbishop's Curia, the Blessed Sacrament was kept there and, in accord with church law, on certain days the Holy Mass was said. The chapel was commonly referred to as "The Little Chapel" or "The Little Jesus."

8. According to the Congregation's custom, canonical silence was observed from 9:00 p.m. Private prayers could be recited silently. Most likely the Servant of God thought that praying prostrate on the floor, not the prayer itself, offended this custom.

9. The "superiors" could be the superior general and the directress of the postulants, for they decided whether the Servant of God would be admitted to the reception of the habit and so to the novitiate in Cracow.

The superior general at the time was Mother Leonard Cielecka, born December 24, 1850 in Paplin ziemi Siedleckiej. She came from a family of landowners, and received a higher education in several languages and music. Entering the Congregation on September 1, 1885, she made her perpetual vows in Warsaw in 1893, and was given responsible positions in the Congregation at an early age. In 1908 she became superior of the house in Derdy near Warsaw. From 1912 she was superior in Warsaw, and from 1918, in Walendow. After the Congregation separated from its General headquarters in France, in 1922 at the First Chapter in Poland, she became the first Superior General of all the homes in Poland. She kept this post for 6 years; i.e., until 1928, and then became assistant to the new Superior General. She died November 1, 1933.

The directress of the postulants, Mother Jane Bartkiewicz, was born July 31, 1858. She entered the Congregation on December 10, 1877, and made her perpetual vows in Laval, France in 1885. While the Congregation of Our Lady of Mercy was dependent on the General Home in France, Mother Jane was Vicar General for the homes in Poland.

She was a sturdy and energetic person, sometimes even despotic. She greatly loved the Congregation and wished its good, trying to achieve this in a way repugnant to human nature. Her relationship to candidates and the young professed was peculiarly warm and affectionate. She knew how to be tenderhearted, but at the same time her method of disciplining the sisters created an atmosphere of fear.

After finishing her term as Vicar General, she was for a time the Directress of Novices and of the third probation. For this reason she felt throughout her life that she had the privilege of correcting the young sisters. She died in Warsaw July 1, 1940 (A. SMDM-C and D).

10. Helen Kowalska arrived in Cracow on January 23, 1926, to finish her postulancy. That same day Sister Henry

Losinska died in Cracow. Sister Henry was born on January 20, 1897. She entered the Community in 1920 and worked as a shoemaker (A. SMDM-D).

11. Sister Margaret—Anna Gimbutt, was born in 1857 and entered the Congregation in 1893. She was of great service to the Congregation, performing the duty of Directress of Novices, superior of the house in Vilnius, and then, Instructress of the Third Probation. She was known for her spirit of self-denial, mortification, demanding much of herself. Humble, meek, always prayerful, outstanding in the keeping of the rules, she was an example to the sisters, especially those who were in her care.

12. Bishop Stanislaus Rospond, born September 30, 1877, in Liszki near Cracow. After graduating from St. Ann's High School in Cracow, he entered the Seminary for the Priesthood. After a year he was sent for further studies in Insbruck, receiving the degree of Doctor of Theology in 1904. He was ordained priest on August 10, 1901. He became prefect of the Seminary in Cracow, and then, rector. He was the ordinary confessor of the Sisters of Our Lady of Mercy. On June 12, 1927, he was consecrated bishop. He was Vicar General for many years. His relationship with the Congregation of the Sisters of Our Lady of Mercy was very cordial, and he took part in all the celebrations of the Congregation. Twice a year he was the main celebrant at the clothing ceremony and profession of vows. He died February 4, 1958 and is buried in his family grave in Liszki.

13. It was clothing day—April 30, 1926. Sister Clemens Buczek recalls that she was helping the candidates put on their habits. She wrote in her memoirs: "In May [sic], 1926, I was to dress Helen Kowalska. After she received the habit at the altar, I told her, 'Helen, let us hurry to put on your habit.' Helen fainted. I hurried to get the smelling salts in order to revive her.... Later I used to tease her about her loathing to leave the world. I only found out after her death that the reason of her fainting was not sorrow for the world, but something else" (A. SF. Recol.).

14. Sister Mary Joseph, Stephanie Brzoza, born in 1889. She entered the congregation in 1909 and made her perpetual vows on May 15, 1917. She was a group instructor of the girls in the Cracow institute. In 1925 she was sent to the General House of the Congregation in Laval, France, to observe more closely the formation of novices and to absorb the spirit of the Congregation. After her return from Laval, she became directress of the novitiate on June 20, 1926, until October 30, 1934. She was an exemplary directress and a great discerner of souls. She was demanding, but at the same time full of motherly care and benevolence toward each novice. At the General Chapter in 1934, she was chosen to be a member of the General Council and simultaneously, superior of the Generalate in Warsaw. Five years later she died of cancer on November 9, 1939 (A. SMDM-C and D).

15. Father Theodore Czaputa was then the confessor of the novitiate. Born in 1884, he was ordained priest July 7, 1907. He completed his theological studies at the Jagiellonian University in Cracow. From 1916 he taught religion in the high schools in Cracow. He was then made rector of the Minor Seminary and Tribunal Judge.

From November 1925 he was confessor of the novices of the Congregation of Our Lady of Mercy. He performed this function almost until death, and the novices had great confidence in him. Because of ill health, he was released of the duties of rector and moved to Lagiewniki to become chaplain of the Sisters of Our Lady of Mercy. He died March 2, 1945 (A. Cracow Curia).

16. Superiors in the Congregation may command "in the name of holy obedience" only professed sisters. A novice was not obliged to obey such a command. If the directress used these words, she was relying on the good will and virtue of the novice, who by subordinating herself to the command could be relieved of these painful experiences (See Const. Congr. art., 96-99).

17. She probably means the words of the prophet Isaiah (49:15 JB): "Does a woman forget her baby at the breast, or fail to cherish the son of her womb? Yet even if these forget, I will never forget you.".

18. Some details of the text suggest that it was at the Warsaw house. The superior was Mother Raphael Buczynska. She was one of the most outstanding superiors. She distinguished herself by a clear, healthy judgment of people and things, a very practical sense, and at the same time a deep spiritual life. She loved the congregation and cared for its material and spiritual growth. In her relations to the sisters she was loving, straightforward, and discerning. She knew how to evaluate and put to use the accomplishments of each sister. She never degraded an individual, but rather tried to raise each one's spirit, come to her aid and cheer her up. M. Raphael—Catherine Buczynska was born December 23, 1879. She entered the Congregation October 18, 1900, and died December 23, 1956 (A. SMDM-C).

19. The description points to the Warsaw house. The chapel was in a separate building. The entrance was from the yard. At that time the chapel was used exclusively by the sisters and their students. Lay persons hardly ever came there.

20. The Community was running homes for morally neglected and "difficult" girls. These were commonly referred to as "students," "wards," or "children." They were sent to the sisters by the Social Service or by parents, and some came of their own accord to do "penance." There were up to 230 girls at the Zytnia house. They were divided into three groups called "classes." The sister in charge of a group was called the "Mother of the Class."

The entire description of the vision seems to be a prediction of the difficulties which the Servant of God will face in her work as apostle of The Divine Mercy. It also predicts the final triumph of this work, and herself in it.

21. The confessors were Father Kulesza and Father Roslaniec; the extraordinary confessor was Father Aloysius Bukowski, S.J.

22. The Rev. Prof. Michael Sopocko, born on November 1, 1888, at Nowosady, in the Vilnius region. He studied at the Roman Catholic Seminary in Vilnius. He was ordained priest on June 15, 1914. Later he was graduated from the School of Theology of the Warsaw University and (in 1924) from the State Pedagogical Institute.

In 1928 the Ministry of Religion and Public Education appointed him to the Chair of Pastoral Theology at the School of Theology of the Stefan Batory University in Vilnius.

In 1934 he became docent of the Warsaw University, officially delegated to the Chair of Pastoral Theology at the University of Vilnius. In the same year he became rector of St. Michael's Church in Vilnius. For many years he was confessor to many communities of monks and nuns. He was ordinary confessor of the Sisters of Our Lady of Mercy from January 1, 1933 to January 1, 1942.

During the war he was professor at the Seminary at Bialystok, where the Vilnius seminary had been transferred (A. SF. Autobiography).

The chronicle of the Cracow house states that Father Sopocko was in Cracow on August 28, 1938. It is very likely that he visited the Servant of God at Pradnik then, but her notes stop before that date.

The Rev. Msgr. Dr. Michael Sopocko died on Sister Faustina's name day, February 15, 1976, at 8 p.m. at Bialystok. The funeral took place on February 19. The main celebrant was His Excellency Most Rev. Bishop Henry Gulbinowicz, the diocesan ordinary. With him 80 priests concelebrated. His Eminence, Stephen Card. Wyszynski, Prymate of Poland, sent a telegram expressing his condolences.

23.   Before arriving in Vilnius, the Servant of God had seen her future spiritual director in two visions. The first took place in Warsaw, during the third probation, the second in Cracow, (See Diary, par. 53 and 61).

24.   This was not yet consumption, which later spread throughout her whole body, but general exhaustion due to a new way of life, intense spiritual combat and experiences which made it difficult for her to perform her duties.

25.   She was working in the girls' kitchen, where meals were prepared for more than 200 people.

26. As the doctors found no organic disease in Sister Faustina, the sisters thought that she was feigning illness, and that she preferred prayer to work (A. SF. Recol.).

27. As Sodom and Gomorrah were destroyed by fire falling from heaven (See Genesis 19:24), so Warsaw was indeed destroyed during World War II, as were many Polish towns, by incendiary and demolition bombs dropped from aircraft.

28. "Jozefinek," a newly created house of the Community, at 44 Hetmanska Street in the Grochow section of Warsaw. The new house was administered by the superior of the house at 3/9 Zytnia Street.

29. The confessors at Plock were Rev. Msgr. Adolf Modzelewski, Rev. Msgr. Louis Wilkonski, and Rev. Waclaw Jezusek.

30. The superior of the Plock house was Mother Rose— Jane Klobukowska, born in 1882. She entered the congregation in 1902, and made her perpetual vows in 1909. She was superior in many of the houses of the congregation. From 1934-1945 she was Assistant to the Superior General. From 1946-1952 she was Superior General.

31. Father Joseph Andrasz, S.J., born at Zakopane on October 16, 1891. He entered the Jesuit Order on September 22, 1906, and was ordained on March 19, 1919. He worked at the Jesuit Publishing House (Wydawnictwo Apostolstwa Modlitwy) for eight years. In 1930 he became the manager of the Publishing House and editor of the monthly *Messenger of the Sacred Heart (Poslaniec Serca Jezusowego).* From 1932 he was the extraordinary confessor of the novitiate of the Sisters of Our Lady of Mercy. He died on February 1, 1963 (A. SJ-C).

32. Spiritual childhood according to the conception of St. Therese of the Child Jesus (See *Autobiography of a Soul*).

33. Vilnius lies on the Wilia River. Across the river from the town, on woody hills, were the stations of the cross called "Calvary" (Polish *Kalwaria*). Going from station to station was called "Walking the Paths." It was possible to get there from the sisters' house by boat.

34. Mother Irene Krzyzanowska. Sister Irene—Mary Krzyzanowska was born on November 25, 1889. She entered the Congregation on December 7, 1916 and made her perpetual vows April 30, 1924. She greatly loved the youth and was wholeheartedly given to the apostolic work. She served as educator in the institute for girls, assistant to the directress of the novitiate, superior, and assistant to the Superior General. After years of sacrificial toil she died in Wroclaw on December 3, 1971.

35. Probably Sister Justine Golofit, a friend from the days of novitiate. Mother Irene, wanting to please the Servant of God, appointed her as a companion.

Sister Justine Golofit, born July 5, 1908 entered the Congregation in August 1927. She made her perpetual vows on October 30, 1934. After that she worked in the kitchen in Warsaw, Vilnius, and Radom. Because of heart trouble, she then did lighter work. She was one of the witnesses during the informational Process of the Servant of God.

36. Biala, a village near Plock (today known for its petroleum fields), where the Community had purchased some farm buildings and set up a rest home for the sisters and wards of the Plock house. The sisters lived in a small farmhouse situated in the garden, with the main entrance from the side of the garden. There was a porch before the main door.

37. Probably Father Peter Trojanczyk, who was recuperating at Biala and, at the same time, as the Community's chaplain, served the sisters in spiritual matters. While decorating the chapel with flowers, Sister Faustina probably wanted to put some in the chaplain's quarters.

Rev. Peter Trojanczyk was born April 30, 1887 and was ordained priest on June 22, 1913. On March 7, 1941, he was arrested by the Germans and sent to the camp in Dzialdow, where he was murdered that same year (Monthly Pastoral. Plock, nr. 9, 1949).

38. The wards were: Imelda, Edwarda, Ignasia, Margaret and Hedwig Owar (See A. SF. and letter J. Owar). The first four have died. Hedwig Owar was a witness in the information process.

The Act concerning the vision was written in Vilnius on November 28, 1934 and signed by Sister Faustina, Sister Taida (who recorded Sister Faustina's statements), and Imelda. Mother Irene, the superior of the house, verified its authenticity.

39. The Directresses of the Novitiate made their own handbook on the vows, based on the work of Fr. Peter Cotelle, S.J., "A Catechism of Vows." Each novice was to write the questions and answers in her notebook and study them by heart.

40. In the Community of Our Lady of Mercy, sisters live in common rooms, several to one room. The place occupied by each is separated from the others by a stable partition. These partitioned places are called cells.

41. Sister Stanislaus Stepczynska, who was ill, was staying at the Plock house at the time. Seeing that Sister Faustina was more recollected, meek and prayerful, she spied on her and even checked her bed in search of extraordinary tools of penance (information provided by Sister Christine Korzeniowska).

42. That is elsewhere in the diary. For a long time Sister Faustina did not take notes of her experiences and of graces received. It was only at the explicit order of her confessor, Father Sopocko, that she began to write down her experiences as they occurred, and also earlier ones as she remembered them. After some time, she burned her notes. Father Sopocko gives the following account: "When I was in the Holy Land for a few weeks, she was persuaded by a supposed angel to burn the diary. As penance, I told her to reconstruct the part destroyed. But in the meantime new experiences came, and she wrote down new and old things alternately. Hence the lack of chronological order in the diary."

43. There are indications that it was in the house in Zytnia Street in Warsaw. The following senior mothers were there at the time: Mother Jane Bartkiewicz, Mother Margaret Gimbutt, Mother Raphael Buczynska, Mother Michael Moraczewska, Superior General. There is some probability that it was done by Mother Jane Bartkiewicz, who was very much interested in the young sisters.

44. Perpetual vows. In the Congregation of Our Lady of Mercy, the Superior General, after hearing her Council, either admits a professed sister to perpetual vows or dismisses her after five years of temporary vows (Const.).

45. Sister Faustina was set at peace during a retreat conducted by Father Andrasz from April 20 to April 30, 1933. He understood her and gave her sound advice on how to proceed along the road of God's leadings.

46. The Servant of God had in mind here the fulfillment of God's desires regarding the painted image of Christ with the red and pale rays and the signature: "Jesus, I trust in You"; the public veneration of the image; and the making known of the chaplet and novena to The Divine Mercy. All these demands were realized as a result of the endeavors of Father Sopocko.

47. Sister Faustina, then a postulant, was working in the kitchen with Sister Marcianna Oswiecimska. Sister Marcianna told her to wash and put away the dishes, and left. Helen (later Sister Faustina) set to work, but Sisters kept coming for the second dinner, and every now and then one of them would ask Helen to serve her dinner or do her a favor. Helen, not wanting to refuse, served each one, but did not do her assigned work. When Sister Marcianna came back and saw the dishes still not put away, she thought Helen had neglected her order and told her that for a penance she was to sit on the table, while she herself did the work.

Sister Marcianna—Julia Oswiecimska was born in 1897. She entered the Congregation in 1919. For many years she fulfilled the duties of a cook. She was energetic, demanding, but full of love of neighbor (Sister Marcianna's Recol.).

48. Only superiors can give orders "by virtue of obedience," and that concerning only serious matters. Sister Marcianna could not do it and certainly did not do it. She told Helen to sit on the table as a form of penance. Helen was surprised by this kind of penance and hesitated to obey the order. Then Sister Marcianna asked the postulant: "Is this what your obedience is like, Helen?" This question was misunderstood by Sister Faustina as an order "by virtue of obedience" (Sister Marcianna's Recol.).

49. In some houses, including the Warsaw house at Zytnia Street, Sisters used to have a night watch. The Sisters on duty would circle the house, light the yard, and look through the windows to protect the house against burglary.

50. This is the popular name of the Franciscan Sisters of the Family of Mary, a congregation founded by Archbishop Felinski in 1857. The motherhouse of the Congregation is in Warsaw, at Zelazna Street and is next to the Generalate of the Congregation of the Sisters of Our Lady of Mercy.

51. See footnote 7.

52. She was probably replacing Sister Modest Rzeczkowska, who was ill and had to undergo treatment in Warsaw (Recol. of Sister Pelagia).

53. All sisters devote one day at the beginning of the month to spiritual renewal, the so called one-day retreat. There is no recreation on that day. The sisters keep silence and have an hour of meditation, the Way of the Cross, monthly examination of conscience, and a half hour meditation about death (cf. Const. Congr.).

54. Every month, each novice spent one day, appointed by the Sister Directress, as the so-called day of the crusade. On that day she was obliged to practice greater recollection and union with the Lord Jesus in the Eucharist, ask the Sister Directress for some additional mortification, and offer all her work, prayer and sufferings to the Lord Jesus in atonement for sinners. Some sisters continued this practice even after leaving the novitiate.

55. Sister Faustina left 4 pages empty. She probably intended to go back and fill in some past experiences, but did not.

56. The "Third Probation" is a period of preparation for the sisters who are to make their perpetual vows. In the Congregation of the Sisters of Our Lady of Mercy, it lasts for five months. The Servant of God made her Third Probation in

1932/33 in Warsaw. The Directress was Mother Margaret Gimbutt.

57. Walendow, a house of the Congregation, located 20 km from Warsaw. The sisters had a home for girls there. In 1936, at the suggestion of the Ministry of Justice, a reformatory for first offenders (girls and women) was established there. Apart from the retreat, Sister Faustina was at Walendow from March 25 till May 1936.

58. The retreat was conducted by Rev. Edmund Elter, S.J. He was born on November 14, 1887. He joined the order on July 15, 1905. Outstandingly gifted, he studied the humanities, theology, and (in 1919/20) international law at the Warsaw University. Next he studied in Rome and in France. In 1926 he became a professor of ethics at the Gregorianum in Rome. From 1932 to 1935 he was in Warsaw, and then went back to Rome as a professor of homiletics and rhetoric. He died in Rome on August 27, 1955.

59. The center of a former estate about 1 km from Walendow, where the Congregation has a home for children. It comes from the foundation of Princess Czetwertynska, who gave the Congregation a tract of agricultural land, forest and some farm buildings for a home for morally threatened children. Until 1947 the home was administered by the superior of Walendow, but since then it is an independent unit (Hist. Congr.).

60. "Vestiary"; that is, a storehouse for the sisters' clothing and a sewing room for same. It was the duty of the sisters working there to sew new clothes and linens, to mend and distribute to the sisters the clothes and linens coming back from the laundry, as well as to provide them with needed clothing.

61. At that time the Congregation was divided into two choirs, the so-called director sisters and coadjutor sisters. The membership to one or the other was decided by the Congregation's governing body on the basis of the candidate's intellectual level, age and abilities. The director sisters' task was to manage the Congregation and the penitents' homes.

The coadjutor sisters did the manual work and served as helpers to the director sisters, especially in the area of physical labor (Const. Congr.).

62. The "iron belt" was a kind of belt made of fine wire mesh, used as an instrument of penance. The Sisters could wear the belt with the superior's permission and only for a specified period of time.

63. Across the hall from the "small chapel" was the congregation hall, where meetings were held.

64. "Recreation"; that is, the time given the sisters to relax after work.

65. Sister Faustina's younger sister, Wanda Kowalska, born in 1920. According to the information of their eldest sister, Josephine Jasinska nee Kowalska, shortly before World War II Wanda entered the Congregation of the Ursuline Sisters. During the war she was taken to Germany for forced labor. She did not return to Poland, but married an Englishman and went to England with him. Her husband was soon drafted and died in action. Wanda came to Poland once, but had to go back to England a few days later because of the political situation at the time. A few years later the family was notified by an unknown priest of Wanda's serious illness and hospitalization. She has not been heard of since.

66. Probably one of the ordinary confessors in Warsaw.

67. A presumed permission: when a religious does something without the superior's knowledge, on the assumption that the superior would give her permission to do it.

68. The sisters finished the Third Probation at the Novitiate, and so ended the period of temporary vows.

69. The pall—a large piece of black cloth with a white cross in the middle. According to the Congregation's ceremonial procedure, before taking perpetual vows the sisters prostrated themselves before the altar and were covered with the pall as a symbol of being dead to the world. In the meantime, other sisters recited Psalm 129, and the bells tolled as during a funeral. The officiating priest, usually a bishop, sprinkled the prostrate sisters with holy water and then said: "Rise, you who are dead to the world, and Jesus Christ will enlighten you."

70. It may be supposed that Sister Faustina refers here to Fr. Elter, S.J., who, during the retreat before the Third Probation, set her at peace and encouraged her to be faithful to God's graces.

71. See footnote 32.

72. There was a custom in the Congregation that, every month, sisters would ask the superior for permission to practice little mortifications, say additional prayers, have various small things at their disposal, be freed from observing the regulations which they momentarily could not keep, and for many other things according to the individual needs of a given sister.

73. Bishop Rospond, a great friend of the Congregation, who for many years presided over the ceremonies of clothing and vows, celebrated Mass and gave the homily for the occasion. During the clothing ceremony he presented the postulant with the habit and veil; the novices with the cincture and rosary, the crucifix, and the black veil; the temporary professed with a burning candle and a ring as a sign of perpetual betrothal with the Lord Jesus (cf. 12).

74. The Jesuits have a thirty-day retreat during their third probation, before perpetual vows.

75. The superior at Czestochowa at the time was Mother Seraphina Kukulska. Sister Seraphina, baptized Salomea, was born November 30, 1873. She entered the Congregation July 18, 1894. She was a group instructor and then superior in Cracow, Czestochowa, Walendow. She died June 10, 1964 (A. SMDM-C and D).

76. The formation of the Sisters of Our Lady of Mercy is based on the asceticism of St. Ignatius of Loyola, who distinguishes three degrees of humility.

77. The picture painted in Vilnius by artist Eugene Kazimierowski (cf. 1).

78. Probably Sister Philomena Andrejko, who died in Warsaw on July 13, 1934, at 4:45 p.m.

79. All sisters in good health had an adoration of atonement, so-called holy hour, every Thursday from 9 to 10 p.m. Before the first Friday of the month, the adoration lasted all night, with sisters changing every hour.

80. Dr. Helen Maciejewska, born 1888, was the doctor of the Sisters in Vilnius. In February 1935 she moved to Wilejka to assume directorship of the county hospital. She was a good and valued doctor, noted for her comprehensive mind, and a sensitive and sacrificial heart for the sick. She died on September 21, 1965.

81. There is a church of The Divine Mercy in Smolensk Street in Cracow, built in 1629. Its patronal feast is celebrated on September 14, the Feast of the Exaltation of the Cross.

82. Chapter (Polish *Kapitula*)—a meeting during which the house superior gave a short exhortation and made observations on the observance of the rule, and the sisters accused themselves of external shortcomings.

83. The superior in Vilnius at this time was Sister Borgia—Hedwig Tichy, born January 25, 1887. She entered the Congregation in 1913. She was a nurse, and also a superior in Vilnius and Walendow. She died in Wroclaw on April 26, 1970. She was a witness in the informative process.

84. Probably Sister Frances of the Bernardine Sisters who, on January 15, 1936, paid a visit with her superior to the Sisters in Vilnius (A. SMDM-C).

85. "Benediction"—a short service which concluded with a blessing with the Blessed Sacrament.

86. The chain, like the belt (cf. 62), is made of a wire mesh in the shape of a bracelet and is used as an instrument of penance.

87. We know from Father Sopocko's letter of November 1937 to Sister Faustina that he talked to the nuncio, Archbishop Cortesi about establishing a feast of The Divine Mercy. He hoped the nuncio would present the matter to the Holy Father (See Letters 160).

88. The way she recorded the resolutions on clean sheets has been reproduced according to the original diary entry.

89. The vision concerns Father Sopocko, who was to suffer greatly because of the destruction of the devotion to The Divine Mercy. The prediction was almost literally fulfilled. Decree No. 65/52 of the Sacred Congregation of The Holy Office, dated November 28, 1958, and a notification of March 6, 1959, prohibited the spreading of the devotion to The Divine Mercy in the form given by Sister Faustina. As a result, the images which had been hung in many churches were removed. Priests stopped preaching about The Divine Mercy. Father Sopocko himself was severely admonished by the Holy See and suffered many other troubles in connection with the spreading of the devotion to The Divine Mercy.

The Congregation of Our Lady of Mercy was also forbidden to spread the devotion; in consequence, the images, the chaplet, the novena and all other things that might suggest that the devotion was being propagated were withdrawn. It appeared that the work of mercy, so much recommended by Sister Faustina, had been destroyed and would never rise again.

Until the notification, the image of The Divine Mercy received much honor in the Congregation's home in Cracow, where Sister Faustina died, and it was covered with votive offerings. A solemn Mass was held on the third Sunday of each month, and priests preached sermons about The Divine Mercy. The first Sunday after Easter was celebrated as the Feast of The Divine Mercy, which Cardinal Adam Sapieha in 1951 invested with a plenary indulgence for seven years.

In view of the Holy See's ban, the Sisters addressed the Ordinary of the Archdiocese of Cracow, Archbishop Baziak, to inquire what should be done with the image which hung in the side altar, covered with many votive offerings, and what attitude should be taken towards the celebrations in praise of The Divine Mercy. In answer, Archbishop Baziak ordered the image to be left in its place and the faithful not to be forbidden to pray before the image for needed graces. He also ordered the existing celebrations to be maintained.

In this way the devotion to The Divine Mercy survived the test in the small center of the Congregation in Cracow, at 3/9

Wronia Street, where the body of the Servant of God is buried. At present, the devotion is again gathering force, renewing and attracting the interest of theologians.

Since the first part of her prophecy was fulfilled almost literally, it can be supposed that the remainder of it will also be fulfilled. The following facts attest to the genuineness of the Servant of God's prophecy:

On June 30, 1978, The Sacred Congregation for the Doctrine of the Faith (A.A.S. page 350) published a "Notification" signed April 15, 1978, by His Eminence Franjo Cardinal Seper, Prefect, and Archbishop Jerome Hamer, O.P., Secretary. It is as follows:

> **From various places, especially from Poland, even proceeding from competent authority, it has been asked whether the prohibitions contained in the "Notification" of the Sacred Congregation of the Holy Office, published in the Acts of the Apostolic See, in the year 1959, p. 271, regarding the devotion to The Divine Mercy in the forms proposed by Sister Faustina Kowalska, must be regarded as still in force.**

> **This Sacred Congregation, having now in possession the many original documents, unknown in 1959; having taken into consideration the profoundly changed circumstances, and having taken into account the opinion of many Polish Ordinaries, declares no longer binding the prohibitions contained in the quoted "Notification."**

On July 12, 1979, in response to the Superior General of the Congregation of Marians of the Immaculate Conception of the B.V.M., who in the name of the Provincial Superior of the American Province of St. Stanislaus Kostka, of said Congregation, had asked for an authoritative explanation of the scope of the text in the "Notification" of 1978, rescinding the prohibitions to spread the devotion to The Divine Mercy proposed by Sister Faustina Kowalska, the Prefect of The Sacred Congregation for the Doctrine of the Faith ascertained:

> **In reference to that matter (raised in the letter of Father General) I have the honor of informing you that**

with the new "Notification" (A.A.S., 30 June 1978, p. 350), arrived at in the light of original documentation examined also by the careful informative intervention of the then Archbishop of Cracow, Card. Karol Wojtyla, it was the intention of the Holy See to revoke the prohibition contained in the preceding "Notification" of 1959 (A.A.S., 1959, p. 271), in virtue of which it is understood that there no longer exists, on the part of this S. Congregation, any impediment to the spreading of the devotion to The Divine Mercy in the authentic forms proposed by the Religious Sister mentioned above [The Servant of God Sister Faustina Kowalska].

90.   The retreat in Vilnius, held from February 4 to February 12, 1935, was conducted by Father Macewicz, S.J. At the end of the retreat there was a mass in the Eastern Rite, and the sisters received Communion under both species.

91.   Renewal of the vows. The constitutions of the Congregation of Our Lady of Mercy contained the provision that twice a year, after the eight-day and the three-day retreats, each sister should renew her vows of chastity, poverty and obedience, together with the whole community, by reciting aloud a shortened formula, to which the following prayer was added: "My Lord, grant me the grace, to observe them more faithfully than I have up to now."

92.   Sister Faustina's family lived in the village of Glogowiec, district of Turek, province of Lodz.

93.   Sister Maria Salomea Olszakowska, who died in June 1962.

94.   The image of The Divine Mercy, with two rays, a pale and a red one, painted by Eugene Kazimierowski in Vilnius. The picture was displayed for public veneration in the Dawn Gate at the conclusion of the Jubilee of the Redemption of the World, April 26-28, 1935 (See Diary no. 419 and footnote 1).

95.   Sister Faustina thought she was to leave the Congregation of Our Lady of Mercy and found a new community, whose task would be to spread the devotion to The Divine Mercy and pray for mercy for the world.

96. Sister Faustina wrote that the Lord Jesus was demanding from her the founding of a new community, whose aim would be to pray for Divine Mercy for the world and to spread the devotion of The Divine Mercy. As she did not want to do anything on her own, Sister Faustina confided these inspirations to her confessor, Father Sopocko, to her Superior General, Mother Michael Moraczewska and, after coming to Cracow, also to Father J. Andrasz, S.J.

The confessors were undecided; Mother Michael gave her permission after long hesitation, but stressed that she was taking no responsibility. Sister Faustina turned to Archbishop Romuald Jalbrzykowski with her inspirations. He did not refuse, but said it was necessary to wait for a clearer sign from heaven.

Despite steady efforts, Sister Faustina did not live to see the new community founded. It was only owing to Father Sopocko's efforts that the matter arose at a "Bible Hour" meeting in 1941; and on October 15, 1941, the first candidate took the vow of chastity before Father Sopocko and pledged poverty and obedience. In the next year other candidates joined her and made similar vows and promises. In 1946 the first candidates, Osinska and Naborowska, left Vilnius and settled at Mysliborz, in the Diocese of Gorzow. Others soon followed, and slowly the Congregation began to develop.

On August 2, 1955, the Ordinary of Gorzow, Zygmunt Szelazek, on the basis of special authorization, established the Congregation of the Most Holy Lord Jesus Christ, Merciful Redeemer, whose aim was to spread the cult of The Divine Mercy and to assist the Church hierarchy. In this way the wish of the Servant of God was fulfilled without her personal participation (See O. Izydor Borkiewicz, O.F.M.Con., "Kowalska Helena" manuscript, p. 18).

97. Sister Faustina had in mind the founding of the new community and was asking St. Ignatius for help.

98. The three-day retreat on August 12-16, 1935, was conducted in Vilnius by Father Rzyczkowski, S.J., later provincial of the northern province of the Society, which had its headquarters in Warsaw.

99. The Archbishop of Vilnius at the time was The Rev. Romuald Jalbrzykowski (1876-1955). He was graduated from the seminary in Petersburg (1898-1902), and was ordained in 1901. He became professor at the seminary in Sejny and canon of the Sejny chapter. He was evacuated to Petersburg during World War I, and then moved to Minsk, where he conducted lively pastoral, educational and social activities. After several years of wandering, he returned to Sejny in 1917. Consecrated bishop in 1918, he worked as an auxiliary in the Polish section of the diocese of Sejny. From 1921 he was the Apostolic Delegate, and in 1926 the first ordinary of the newly-established diocese of Lomza. On the death of the Metropolitan of Vilnius, Archbishop Jan Cieplak, he assumed government of the Diocese of Vilnius on September 8, 1926. On March 13, 1940 he was arrested by the Germans and interned in the monastery of the Marian Fathers at Mariampol in Lithuania. He returned to Vilnius on August 5, 1944. In December of the same year, he was again arrested and imprisoned in Vilnius. After the end of World War II, he had to transfer to Bialystok, where he devoted all his energies to the organization of the Metropolitan Curia, appointing priests to the vacant parishes and dealing with many necessary matters.

In his relationships with others, Archbishop Jalbrzykowski was simple, accessible, understanding and patient. But towards himself he was very exacting. He died in Bialystok on June 19, 1955.

100. Father Sopocko placed this chaplet to The Divine Mercy, as found here in Sister Faustina's Diary, on the back of a holy card (a copy of the painting by Kazimierowski in Vilnius) and had it published by the Cebulski Publishing House in Cracow (See Letters #75, 87-90).

101. Father Sopocko, not sure of Sister Faustina's inspirations regarding the establishing of a new community, wanted to refer the matter to one more priest for consideration, and for that reason he told Sister Faustina to give an account of all the commands she received to her former confessor, Father Andrasz, S.J., in Cracow.

102. The Congregation of Our Lady of Mercy has its own cemetery in Cracow, which is in the park, separated from the rest of it by a thick wall with a wide entrance gate. All the sisters and wards who die in Cracow are buried there. Sister Faustina was buried here too, and her body was in a tomb in the cemetery until the exhumation of her body on November 25, 1966.

103. Sister Vitalina Maslowska, born Dec. 4, 1852, died Jan. 6, 1939.

104. During monthly individual meetings with the superior, the sisters asked her for permission to say private prayers not included in the Congregation's rules (cf. 72).

105. There is no custom in the Congregation of adding a cognomen to the religious name. But it is possible for a sister to make an addition to her name, depending on the devotion she has, as, for instance, Sister Faustina did, adding "of the Blessed Sacrament."

106. In the sisters' dining room (refectory) there was a bulletin board on which the superior put the names of the sisters who had some special duty for the given week. In this case, it was duty at the gate during community meals that was meant.

107. In the former Constitutions, the title "Mother" was reserved for the members of the General Council of the Congregation and all the house superiors. The wards also addressed their educators as "Mothers."

108. The Postulancy is the first probation period in the Congregation. During this time the candidate gets to know better the Congregation of which she wishes to become a member, and the Congregation likewise gets to know her.

109. After the period of postulancy, the candidate makes an eight-day retreat. During the clothing ceremony she receives the religious habit and new name and begins her novitiate. This is a further step to test whether the religious life is for the candidate; and at the same time, the candidate has the chance to better know the Congregation of which she is to become a member.

In the Congregation of Our Lady of Mercy the novitiate lasts for two years. The first, known as the "canonical," is dedicated to the deepening of the spiritual life and convent practices. During this time the novice cannot attend formal schooling, spend time in studies, or perform any absorbing tasks.

During the second year of novitiate, the novices may, in addition to their religious practices, study or work under the direction of the professed sisters.

If, after this period, the Congregation and the novice are satisfied, the novice makes a profession of vows for one year, renewing them for the next five years annually. During this time, the professed sister may leave the Congregation or be dismissed. If all turns out positive, the professed sister is allowed to take perpetual vows (Const. Congr.).

110. In the Congregation of Our Lady of Mercy the sisters take simple vows. In the Congregation proposed by Sister Faustina, the sisters would take solemn vows.

111. Office—a liturgical prayer of the Church consisting of psalms and versicles. All sisters have an obligation to say the Office.

112. By the *enclosure*, or *cloister*, is meant a certain section of the convent restricted to members of the Congregation only.

113. For every religious house, the local Ordinary appointed a regular confessor to whom every sister should go to confession. According to a provision of Canon Law, the local Ordinary should also appoint an extraordinary confessor for every house. His duty was to visit the house at least four times a year to hear confessions. All sisters had to see him, if not to confess, then at least to receive a blessing.

114. The Servant of God had a vision of the future community's house. It was in Vilnius, at 12 St. Anna Street, and it was in complete ruin. Father Sopocko had the house restored with his own money and intended eventually to place the new community in it. The war interrupted the realization of these plans (See letter of Fr. Sopocko March 31, 1972).

115. "In the dust"—a figurative expression of the Servant of God for the way she responded to her feeling of guilt.

116. *Pinafore*, or *apron*, could mean several things. For children it was a substitute for a shirt, and Sister Faustina had this in mind.

117. Sister Faustina probably saw the house of the Congregation of the Most Merciful Redeemer at Mysliborz.

118. Probably Father Ladislaus Wantuchowski, S.J., who looked after the Congregation of the Most Merciful Redeemer for ten years while Father Sopocko was in hiding.

119. A lash, whip, or similar instrument for the infliction of pain, used by religious as a means of doing penance.

120. Probably the fasts on Ash Wednesday and Good Friday.

121. The church in Poland accepted the practice that in each quarter of the year, three days—Wednesday, Friday and Saturday, called "Ember days"—were set aside for fasting and penitence, and special prayers were said for priests and for vocations to the priesthood and religious life.

122. At that time fasting was obligatory on the eve of the following feasts: Pentecost, Assumption of the Blessed Virgin Mary, and All Saints.

123. Some communities, including the Congregation of Our Lady of Mercy, by solemn act elected the Mother of God as their Superior General, and entrusted to her all matters of this and future life. The act took place on August 5, 1937, at the General House in Warsaw, with all the superiors participating. Then the act was repeated in all the houses on August 15, 1937, with the participation of all the sisters of the Congregation.

124. The priest was Father Sopocko, who writes this in his memoirs of Sister Faustina: "... my troubles reached their peak in January 1936. I never mentioned them to anyone, and it was only on the critical day that I asked Sister Faustina for prayer. To my great surprise, all my troubles vanished into thin air on that very day, and Sister Faustina told me she had taken all my suffering upon herself and experienced so much suffering on that day as she never had before" (A. SF. Recol.).

125. *Te Deum,* a hymn of thanksgiving, sung during all major feast days and thanksgiving devotions. Religious congregations pray it during Matins. The origin of the hymn is ascribed to St. Ambrose, which explains why it was often called the "Ambrosian Hymn."

126. Probably Sister Veronica Rapisz. Born March 18, 1853, she entered the Congregation on December 16, 1881. She had spent all her life as a religious working in the garden. In her last years she devoted very much time to prayer. She died in Vilnius on January 28, 1936 (A. SMDM-C and D).

127. "The whole Congregation" probably means all the sisters of the house, in this case, of the Vilnius house.

128. Probably Father Anthony Korcik, chaplain of the Congregation's house in Vilnius from August 10, 1934 until 1940. Father Korcik was born about 1892, and ordained priest in 1920 for the diocese of Luck and Zytomierz. He graduated from the School of Theology of the Warsaw University, specializing in philosophy. From 1929 he lectured on the history of philosophy at the Unversity of Vilnius. After the war he went to Lublin, where he taught logic at the Schools of Theology and Philosophy at the Catholic University of Lublin. He died in Lublin on October 24, 1969.

129. This vision is mentioned by Father Sopocko in his letter of March 31, 1972.

130. As in other houses, at the Vilnius house the sisters had an institution for girls. The wards sometimes participated in adoration with the sisters to atone for their own sins and for the sins of others.

131. It was probably Sister Antonina Grejwul, who writes in her memories of Sister Faustina as follows: "After confessions I was worried and doubting whether the Lord Jesus had forgiven me. Weeping, I asked Sister Faustina for prayer. Next morning she said, 'Sister, you have grace with Jesus, because He answered at once that He was not angry with you for your sins, but was hurt by your distrust in His forgiveness. I will pray to propitiate Him for you.' "

Sister Antonina Grejwul, born Sept. 13, 1877, entered the Congregation in Vilnius on June 29, 1909. She stayed in

Vilnius until the closing of the house in 1945. During World War II, in 1939, she was imprisoned in the Lukiszki prison in Vilnius together with the other sisters. As a Latvian she was freed after a while. After the sisters had left Vilnius she was sent to the Congregation's house at Biala near Plock, where she died on January 22, 1960 (A. SMDM—C and D).

132. One can assume that it was Sister Petronela Basiura, who worked in the garden before Sister Faustina's assignment to Vilnius, and because she was stronger was given the duty to raise the cattle. She died March 5, 1959, in Czestochowa (A. SMDM-C and D).

133. It was probably Sister Regina Jaworska, who knew the Servant of God from novitiate days. Sister Regina— Valeria Jaworska was born November 28, 1905. She entered the Congregation in 1926 and made her perpetual vows October 30, 1933. She was a witness during the information process of the Servant of God.

134. Most probably the regular confessor of the Sisters in Walendow, Father Ceslaus Maliszewski.

135. Letter of Father Sopocko, written in Vilnius July 10, 1936 (see Letter #49).

136. Probably Father Sopocko's pamphlet called *Milosierdzie Boze* (Studium teologiczne-praktyczne) [*The Divine Mercy* (A Theological — Practical Study)], published in Vilnius in 1936. Imprimatur was given by Bishop Romuald on June 30, 1936, No. R. 298/36 (A. SF.). The cover of the pamphlet showed a color copy of Eugene Kazimierowski's image painted in Vilnius.

137. Dr. Adam Silberg, from the sanatorium at Pradnik. Dr. Silberg, a convert, was about 40 years old then. In the years 1937-1939 (until the outbreak of the war) he was the director of City Sanatoriums (Polish *Miejskie Zaklady Sanitarne*) at Pradnik Bialy in Cracow, popularly known as *Sanatorium* (now a special city hospital named Dr. Anka Hospital). He lived on the premises of the hospital together with his wife and son Kazimierz. It is not sure what happened to him after the outbreak of the war. According to the account of Mr. Ludwik Spytkowski, retired janitor at the hospital, Dr. Silberg tried to make his way to the east, together with his wife, and was shot by the Germans near Lvov. Another version, given by Dr. Adamczewski, a radiologist at the hospital, says that Dr. Silberg made his way to France with a group of doctors, then went to Scotland and died there during the war.

138.   Probably Sister Fabiola, who had tuberculosis and therefore was in the infirmary. Sister Fabiola Pawluk, born in 1912, entered the Congregation on April 16, 1934. She died in Czestochowa on November 25, 1947 (A. SMDM-C).

139.   The Feast of The Divine Mercy—as the Servant of God stated—according to Jesus' wish was to be celebrated on the first Sunday after Easter (See Diary par. 49, 88, 280, 299, 420, 570, 699, 742).

140.   The cook, Sister Bronislaus—Julianna Jaworska, born in 1886, entered the Congregation in 1908. She died on February 11, 1972.

141.   The doctor at the Pradnik sanatorium confirmed that Sister Faustina had tuberculosis of the lungs. He ordered her to be separated from the others to prevent infection. Sister Faustina was put in the room for the seriously ill, called the infirmary.

142.   Father Sopocko, in his letter of Oct. 5, 1936, asked Sister Faustina for the texts of the Chaplet and the Novena to The Divine Mercy.

143.   The following sisters came to take their perpetual vows then: Sister Boleslaus Domagalska, b. 1902; Sister Cyprian Rzad, b. 1903; Sister Damiana Ziolek, b. 1909; Sister Marceline Kobrzyniecka, b. 1906; Sister Pancratia Nalewajko, b. 1908; Sister Sebastiana Gabinowska (1905-1942). It is difficult to say which of the sisters confided to Sister Faustina, but it can be supposed it was Sister Sebastiana Gabinowska, who often went through periods of depression. She even asked her superiors to postpone the date of her perpetual vows. Soon after perpetual profession she showed symptoms of mental illness. She was sent to the mental hospital at Kobierzyn near Cracow. She shared the fate of other patients during the occupation: they were taken away and executed by the

Germans. The death took place probably at the end of June 1942 (A. SMDM-C and D).

144. In this case the preacher was Father Ladislaus Wojton, S.J., who from October 20 to 29, 1936, conducted the retreat before the vows.

145. Probably Sister Gertrude Budzinska (1875-1966), who shared a room with Sister Faustina for some time.

146. After novitiate the sisters take temporary vows for one year. These are repeated for five years. Then perpetual vows are taken. Sister Faustina took her temporary vows (which she calls annual vows) on April 30, 1928.

147. This was a letter written on September 21, 1936, in which Father Sopocko informed Sister Faustina about the developments regarding the spreading of the devotion to The Divine Mercy and the founding of the new community.

148. Probably a vision of the house of the Congregation of the Most Merciful Redeemer at Mysliborz. The community was founded by Father Sopocko after Sister Faustina's death. The Mysliborz sisters conduct the catechesis of children.

149. Sister Faustina probably made a mistake about her age here; as she herself writes in the Diary, she received the grace in the Octave of Corpus Christi in 1925. As she was born in 1905, she was 20, not 18 in 1925.

150. Sister David—Antonina Cedro. She was born September 17, 1898, and entered the Congregation of Servants of the Sacred Heart (Polish *Sercanki* or *Pelczarki*), founded by Bishop Joseph Pelczar in 1894. Sisters from the Congregation worked at the Pradnik hospital.

151. Sister Felicia—Jane Zakowiecka. Born in 1900, she entered the Congregation in 1926 and made perpetual vows in 1934. She was the house econom at Vilnius and Cracow, and then became house superior at Rabka, and finally at Derdy. She met with the Servant of God at Vilnius and later, from 1936 to 1938, in Cracow. She was a witness at the information process of Sister Faustina. She died at the Wroclaw house on November 7, 1975.

152. The Congregation's house in Cracow was about 10 km from Pradnik, where Sister Faustina was staying. In those days, a trip to the sanatorium required much time and trouble, and this is why Sister Faustina was not visited very often.

153. This refers to the sufferings and humiliations experienced by Father Sopocko in his efforts to spread the cult of The Divine Mercy and to found a new community. Sister Faustina received inner knowledge of these sufferings and wrote about it in a letter to Father Sopocko (Letter of March 6, 1972).

154. Sister Chrysostom—Mary Korczak. Born in 1892, she entered the Congregation in 1921. She worked as a group instructor and as a nurse. She came in contact with Sister Faustina in Vilnius, and then during Sister Faustina's last illness in Cracow. She was appointed to be a witness at the information process for reasons of her office.

155. Sister Cajetan—Mary Bartkowiak. Born January 19, 1911, she entered the Congregation in 1933. She was with Sister Faustina in Warsaw and in Cracow. She was a witness at the information process in 1965/66.

156. After Christmas, Sister Faustina was taken back to the hospital at Pradnik by Sister Damiana Ziolek, who gives the following account of the circumstances of the trip: "At night a little baby was left by the convent gate. In the morning Sister Frances found it, took care of it, washed and fed it, and started to look for someone to look after the baby. A neighbor who had no children of her own and wanted a foster child learned about it. She readily accepted the Congregation's offer, took in the foundling and agreed to give it her name. The cab which was taking Sister Faustina to Pradnik gave the woman a lift to the parish church in Podgorze, where the child was baptized and the fact recorded in the books."

Sister Damiana—Sophia Ziolek was born on October 18, 1911. She entered the Congregation in 1927. She came in contact with Sister Faustina in Plock in 1932 and then in Cracow. She was a witness at the information process.

157. St. Joseph Church in Podgorze. Rev. Joseph Niemczynski was the pastor at the time.

158. Sister Damiana Ziolek.

159. Probably Sister Alana—Caroline Wilusz, of the Congregation of Servants of the Sacred Heart. She suffered from consumption and had a room near Sister Faustina's. She was born in 1910 and entered her Congregation in 1929.

160. The Servant of God recalls the date of January 2, 1934, when she had first visited the painter Eugene Kazimierowski to give him directions concerning the painting of the image of The Divine Mercy.

161. The superior of the Servants of the Sacred Heart at the Pradnik hospital was Sister Sebastian—Helen Wasik (1889-1952).

162. Probably Father Andrasz, but it may also have been Father Theodore Czaputa, who visited Sister Faustina in the hospital and heard her confessions.

163. Probably Stanislava Kwietniewska, former ward of the sisters and a patient at the sanatorium at the time.

164. Sister Faustina was in Tuberculosis Ward I, which was about 70 steps from the chapel.

165. Stanislava Kwietniewska (cf. 163).

166. Sister Faustina is probably praying for the intentions of Archbishop Jalbrzykowski, Father Sopocko, and Father Andrasz.

167. A Eucharistic Congress was held from February 3 to 7 in Manila in the Philippines.

168. Father Andrasz was Sister Faustina's spiritual director at the time, so it can be supposed that the letter concerning permission for minor penitential practices was written to him.

169. Probably Sister Faustina has Father Andrasz in mind, as he was her spiritual director at the time, although the words of praise could also refer to Father Sopocko.

170. "Passion" (Polish *Pasja*)—a lenten service to give worship to Christ's Passion. Special lenten songs *Gorzkie Zale* are sung during the service.

171. On the basis of the invocations that follow, Father Sopocko composed a Litany to The Divine Mercy, correcting a few invocations and adding some of his own (See letter of Fr. Sopocko, May 14, 1972).

172. As Sister Faustina's spiritual director, Father Sopocko had ordered her to carefully underline in her diary everything that she thought came from God, and in particular everything that related to the institution of the Feast of Mercy and the establishment of the new community.

173. Sister Cornelia Trzaska died at Plock on February 15. She was born in 1888, entered the community in 1905, and worked in the Congregation as a shoemaker.

174. Father Bonaventure Kadeja of the Piarist Order, Cracow, Pijarska Street. He was born in 1906, ordained priest in 1932. In the religious life he had the duties of House Superior, Counselor General, and Provincial. In 1965/66 he was a judge in the information process.

175. Cf. footnote 65 and Sister Faustina's letter to her sisters Natalie and Wanda of June 10, 1938 (Letters #296, 297).

176. Probably a prediction that was fulfilled under the German occupation, when many priests secretly celebrated the Eucharist in private homes and basements, without liturgical vestments, and even in concentration camps, wearing prison clothes.

177. Sister Faustina, while making her monthly day of recollection, took advantage of the conferences which Father Bonaventure Kadeja was giving during a retreat for the sanatorium personnel.

178. The word "confessors" seems to indicate that the Servant of God was told to write the Diary not only by Father Sopocko, but also by Father Andrasz.

179. Sister Faustina's spiritual director, Father Michael Sopocko, remembered her special gifts: visions, illuminations, enlightenments, hearing inner voices, etc. She is referring to one of these gifts here; i.e., interior knowledge of events touching people related to her. (See A. SF. Father Sopocko's letter of March 7, 1972).

180. At the first profession of temporary vows the sisters receive a black veil, a little cross, a rosary and a belt. It is this cross that Sister Faustina meant.

181. The Feast of The Divine Mercy, on the first Sunday after Easter.

182. The chapel of the Congregation was open only to the sisters and wards at the time. It was only during the German occupation that it was opened to the public.

183. This vision most likely refers to the investigations of the writings of Sister Faustina and the mistaken interpretation of them.

184. Polish *ciemnica,* literally "dark cell," denotes both the altar of Maundy Thursday liturgy (repository) and the prison in which Jesus spent the night of His Passion.

185. Probably fragments of the liturgy of the Holy Week.

186. Father Theodore Czaputa, as the Congregation's chaplain, delivered a sermon in the chapel every Sunday.

187. The Directress of Novitiate at the time was Sister Callista—Helen Piekarczyk. Born March 30, 1900, she entered the Congregation in 1920. She succeeded Sister Mary Joseph Brzoza as directress on December 10, 1934, and continued until September 8, 1945. She died on September 11, 1947 (A. SMDM-C).

188. Father Sopocko's article on The Divine Mercy published in the *Vilnius Catholic Weekly* (*Tygodnik Katolicki, nasz przyjaciel*) on April 4, 1937, No. 14.

189. In the Cracow house, the chaplain, Father Theodore Czaputa, had weekly lectures to the sisters on ascetical subjects. These were familiarly called "Catechism." Sister Faustina probably is referring to one of these.

190. Every year, besides the eight-day retreat, the sisters have a three-day retreat.

191. An eight-day retreat was being held in the house, preceding the profession of vows and taking of the veil (April 20-29). It was conducted by Father Plaza, S.J., superior of the provincial house at 8 Maly Rynek, Cracow (A. SMDM-C).

192. We do not know to what talks the vision refers. But we know that Father Sopocko sent a memorial on The Divine Mercy to the participants of the First Plenary Synod, which was held at Czestochowa on August 26-27, 1936. The Pope's legate, Msgr. Marmaggi presided at the Synod. He probably mentioned the matter of promulgating a Feast of The Divine Mercy in his report of the Synod to the Holy See. That may have caused the disputes. We have reason to suppose that the report drew the interest of Eugene Cardinal Pacelli, Secretary of State (and later, Pope Pius XII). But it is difficult to say what the work could have been. The fact that the notification banning the devotion was not issued by the Holy Office until after his death (November 28, 1958) suggests that Cardinal Pacelli's attitude toward the devotion to The Divine Mercy was a favorable one.

193. The Ceremonies of Clothing, Temporal and Final Professions took place in the Congregation twice a year at that time: in the spring on the last day of April or first of May, and in the fall on October 30.

194. Only the Holy See has the right to release one from perpetual vows.

195. These words of the Lord Jesus to the Servant of God attest that, despite the requests to found a new congregation, she is to remain in the Congregation of Our Lady of Mercy. The dialog of the Servant of God with the Lord Jesus, cited on another page of the Diary (see Diary par. 1649), wherein Sister Faustina complains to the Lord Jesus that her Congregation has no saint and receives the reply: you will be that saint, likewise proves this. It is a fact that Sister Faustina remained in the Congregation of Our Lady of Mercy until her death, and in reference to the new congregation only gave standing guidelines.

196. The Corpus Christi procession to the four altars. The procession started from the parish church at Borek Falecki and ended at the fourth altar, which was in the Congregation's garden. The Blessed Sacrament then remained in the sisters' chapel.

197. The sisters' procession was always on the Octave of Corpus Christi. The altars were set up and decorated in the garden.

198. Cf. Isidore Borkiewicz, "O stosunku siostry Faustyny do Zgromadzenia Najmilosierniejszego

Odkupiciela" ("Sister Faustina's Connection with the Congregation of the Most Merciful Reedemer"), p. 25.

199. Sister Jolanta, a group instructor in the Vilnius house, was attending a course in pedagogy in Cracow at the time (from July 3, 1937). Sister Jolanta—Aleksandra Wozniak was born in 1909. She entered the Congregation in 1929. She was a group instructor, and then superior at the Radom, Czestochowa, and Cracow houses.

200. The patron saints of the Congregation of the Sisters of Our Lady of Mercy:

Our Lady of Mercy	August 5
St. Ignatius of Loyola	July 31
St. Josephe	March 19
St. Michael the Archangel	September 29
St. Mary Magdalene	July 22
St. Teresa of Jesus	October 15
St. Anthony of Padua	June 13

201. Many articles appeared in the Polish Catholic press at the time on the ungratefulness of the Polish nation to God and to the Church.

202. A place in the Carpathian hills, where the Congregation has a small vacation house for sisters and girls.

203. Probably Sister Helen, who was the superior of the Rabka house. Sister Helen—Mary Urbanska, born in 1884, entered the Congregation in 1908. She was a nurse and in 1932 took over management of the newly acquired house at Rabka. She died at Rabka on August 6, 1940.

204. "Remember"—a prayer to St. Joseph said daily by the whole Congregation.

205. Perhaps one of the Benedictine Fathers, Kazimierz Ratkiewicz (1906-1965), who was a friend of the sisters in Rabka. The first group of Benedictines arrived in Poland in 1936 and settled in the "Jaworzyna" villa in Rabka, not far from the house of the Congregation of Our Lady of Mercy called "Loretto." The Fathers regularly said masses there, and Father Ratkiewicz busied himself with hearing the sisters' confessions. He was great friends with "Loretto," and it is very likely that it was he who heard Sister Faustina's confession.

206.   The novena which is in the Diary was published, with some changes, in a pamphlet called *Chrystus Krol Milosierdzia (Christ King of Mercy)* in 1937, by the J. Cebulski Press, Cracow. The cover had a colored picture representing the Merciful Christ with the rays and the inscription "Jezu, ufam Tobie" ("Jesus, I trust in You"). The contents included the Novena to The Divine Mercy, the Litany and the Chaplet.

The superior of the Cracow house, Mother Irene Krzyzanowska, sent out the leaflet to the other houses of the Congregation. The sisters said the prayers privately, but did not know their origin.

207.   According to the Congregation's custom, the parlor was entered by the superiors or by sisters appointed for that function. Other sisters could go to their guests only by permission of the superior of the house.

208.   Reference is to the imprimatur of two publications: 1. An image of Jesus with the Chaplet to The Divine Mercy on the back, for which Fr. Sopocko obtained permission in Vilnius on Sept. 1, 1937 (No. R. 200/37); 2. A small pamphlet under the title *Chrystus Krol Milosierdzia (Christ King of Mercy)*, which included the novena, the chaplet and the litany to The Divine Mercy. The imprimatur was granted by the Metropolitan Curia in Cracow (L. 671/37). Both were published by the J. Cebulski Publishing House, 22 Szewska St., Cracow.

209.   It is likely that the writer mistakenly recorded August instead of September.

210.   Sister Faustina calls the gate a "desert" because the gatekeeper remained separated from the rest of the Congregation during most of the day.

211.   The Servant of God had two brothers, Stanley and Mecislaus. It later becomes clear that it was Stanley who visited her. He was born at Glogowiec on March 26, 1912. Later he lived in Lodz working as a joiner, a cabinet maker and an organist.

212. *Poslaniec Serca Jezusowego (Messenger of the Sacred Heart)*, a monthly magazine devoted to the devotion of the Sacred Heart of Jesus, and published by the Jesuit Fathers at the Wydawnictwo Apostolstwa Modlitwy House, 26 Kopernik Street, Cracow.

213. Probably at the shop of Cebulski, where devotional articles were sold.

214. A copy of Eugene Kazimierowski's image of Jesus, made ineptly by a Miss Balzukiewicz in Vilnius for the Redemptorist Fathers. It later appeared in Cracow.

215. Every sister is obliged to participate once a year in an eight-day retreat (so-called "big" retreat, as opposed to the three-day retreat). In the Cracow house the professed sisters took advantage of the retreats given before the ceremonies of taking the veil and professing the vows. In 1937 the retreat was held from October 20 to 29, and was conducted by Father Nitka, S.J. This was Sister Faustina's last retreat together with the sisters.

216. There was a custom in the Congregation of keeping written records of one's interior victories and falls.

217. The taking of the veil and the vows.

218. The cross was probably the illnesses of sisters and of the superior herself. There was a long-drawn flu epidemic in the house and, in addition, the following sisters were seriously ill: Sister Clemens Buczek, head gardener, down with gastric ulcers; Sister Virginia Narkiewicz, taken to the hospital because of serious heart trouble brought on by rheumatism; Sister Dominic Szymanska, seriously ill, died on November 15, 1937.

219. Sister Dominic—Josephine Szymanska. Born November 28, 1875, she entered the Congregation in 1897. She worked in the Cracow house for 30 years as a shoemaker, and became so expert in her job that she trained younger sisters. She died on November 15, 1937.

220. Sister Damiana Ziolek, who wanted to choose Bishop S. Rospond to be her confessor.

221. This is a quotation from the Roman Martyrology, which was read in the refectory after the prayer before meals.

222. *Pasterka* is the Mass at midnight, December 24 to 25. According to the Congregation's custom, the sisters went to bed after the Christmas Eve supper. Those who wanted to pray in the chapel until midnight asked for permission to do so.

223. The Servant of God most probably had an inner knowledge as to the time of her death. She knew that this would be the final year of her life.

224. At the end of the year the sisters take part in a service of thanksgiving for the graces received, during which the *Te Deum* is sung. Usually all the sisters participate in the service.

225. The chaplain takes Holy Communion to the sisters who could not take part in the community Mass on account of illness. Those less ill walk to the infirmary at the moment of Communion so as not to trouble the chaplain with visiting every cell.

226. Father Matzänger, S.J., temporarily substituting for the chaplain, Father Theodore Czaputa, who left for a few days to visit his brother, also a priest.

227. Sister Faustina's vision regarding Mother Irene Krzyzanowska came true in so far that Mother Krzyzanowska was a witness at the information process and was probably questioned about Sister Faustina and her writings. Mother Mary Joseph Brzoza, however, died on November 9, 1939, and we do not know whether anyone asked her about Sister Faustina.

228. Probably Sister Gertrude, who was sharing a small room called *separatka* (isolation ward) with Sister Faustina at the time.

Sister Gertrude Budzinska, born 1876, entered the Congregation in 1895. She died in Cracow on August 11, 1966.

229. Probably Sister Liguoria Poznanska, the sacristan and an expert on handiwork, came to teach Sister Gertrude how to make borders for altar linens.

Sister Liguoria Poznanska, born January 15, 1880, entered the Congregation on December 4, 1919. She was sacristan almost all her life as a religious. In 1953 she was appointed assistant to the house superior in Cracow. She died in Cracow on May 2, 1960.

230. It could be that at this particular time the Servant of God was given to know the day of her death.

231. No date is given, but it can be supposed that the vision occurred between January 8 and 15, 1938.

232. Sister Faustina was very sensitive to the division into choirs. In this case, Sister Seraphina certainly was not guided by the division, but seeing Sister Faustina already wet, she thought it would be easier for Sister Faustina to go to the gate than for another sister to get wet, too. In giving the order she obviously did not know Sister Faustina was unwell, or else she would have done otherwise. Sister Seraphina was a good and pious sister. She was never known to make any differences among the sisters.

233. It was the custom in the Congregation to pray for the dying person the prayer, "O most kind Jesus..." and Psalm 129 "Out of the depths."

234. Sister Faustina's superiors during her lifetime as a religious:

> M. Margaret Gimbutt—beginning of novitiate and third probation before perpetual vows;
> M. Raphael Buczynska—in Cracow and Warsaw;
> M. Rose Klobukowska—in Plock;
> M. Xavier Olszamowska—in Kiekrz;
> M. Borgia Tichy—in Vilnius;
> M. Seraphina Kukulska—in Walendow.

Sister Xavier—Jane Olszamowska, born 1883, entered the Congregation in 1912. She was superior in Kiekrz and in Warsaw, and then was secretary general. She died on March 11, 1970, in Cracow.

235. Cf. Bishop Zbigniew Kraszewski, "Udzial Matki Bozej w Dziele Odkupienia" ("The Role of the Mother of God in the Work of Redemption") in *Gratia Plena*, Poznan, 1965.

236. Probably Father M. Sopocko, because he was chiefly active in spreading the devotion of The Divine Mercy and in efforts to found the new community; but Sister Faustina may also have had in mind Father Andrasz or Mother Irene Krzyzanowska, because they, too, made efforts to spread the devotion of The Divine Mercy.

237. Father Theodore Czaputa was the confessor of the novitiate. Some of the professed sisters also made their confession to him. The Servant of God's spiritual director was Father Andrasz. Sister Faustina is careful to make the distinction.

238. Sister Tarcisia—Casimira Piotrowicz. Born in 1891, she entered the Congregation in 1912. For a short time she was a nurse in the Cracow house.

239. Probably Sister Amelia, who was Sister Faustina's close friend.

Sister Amelia—Stanislava Socha was born on May 15, 1911. She entered the Congregation in 1930. The doctors soon diagnosed she had tuberculosis of the bones in her hand. Sister Amelia was afraid of being a burden to the Congregation and asked Sister Faustina to pray for an early death for her. Sister Faustina promised that, within a year after her, Sister Amelia would also die. That was the case, as Sister Amelia died on October 4, 1939.

240. Carnival—a time of revelry and merrymaking before the Lenten Season.

241. A doctor called in to see the sick sisters. It is hard to say which one. A Dr. Stoch came frequently.

242. Probably Dr. Silberg, who knew Sister Faustina's condition.

243. To the hospital for contagious diseases at Pradnik near Cracow, known as the "sanatorium.".

244. There is a corridor leading from the house to the choir loft of the chapel. Sister Faustina was in the choir loft and so attended Mass, but she was not strong enough to go down and take part in the procession with the palms.

245. Father Zukowicz, S.J., who was celebrating Mass that day. He was assistant to the provincial for very many years. He was a close friend of the Congregation of Our Lady of Mercy. As a great benefactor of their apostolic work, he often visited the girls and brought them small gifts.

246. Sister Casimir—Irene Twarowska. Born 1911, she entered the Congregation in 1933. She worked as a group instructor and then as the head of the home for girls. She died in Cracow on April 18, 1969.

247. The following sisters had been in the novitiate with Sister Faustina:

Senior novices: Sister Alice Dabrowska, Sister Cherubim Kowieska, Sister Ernest Szczyrba, Sister Yvonne Goebel, Sister Joachim Gluc, Sister Kinga, Sister Crescentia Bogdanik, Sister Laurenta Kosinska, Sister Longina Suchomska, Sister Lucine, Sister Natalie Fiszer, Sister Placida Putyra, Sister Renata Jodlowska, Sister Simon Nalewajko, Sister Valentina Leszczynska.

Junior novices: Sister Anunciata Peraj, Sister Bernarda Wilczek, Sister Celine Bronikowska, Sister Felicia Zakowiecka, Sister Justine Golofit, Sister Clementine Gluc, Sister Louise Gadzina, Sister Martina, Sister Regina Jaworska, Sister Severina Marciniak, Sister Teresita, Sister Zenobia Saja.

Sisters who were clothed together with Sr. Faustina: Sister Bernadette Federowicz, Sister Bonaventure Edelmann-Glowacka (d. Dec. 17, 1936), Sister Florentine Pajak (d. Jan. 2, 1950), Sister Henry Skulimowska (d. Oct. 20, 1974).

Sisters who corresponded with Sr. Faustina: Sister Justine Golofit, Sister Louise Gadzina, Sister Regina Jaworska; perhaps there were others, but at present they are unknown.

248. Sisters of the Congregation of Servants of the Most Sacred Heart of Jesus, who worked at the hospital at Pradnik. The Congregation had been founded in Cracow in 1894 by Bishop Pelczar.

249. Sister David Cedro; Sister Alana—Caroline Wilusz, born July 20, 1910; Sister Medarda—Caroline Podrazik, born June 16, 1910, died 1966.

250. Similar incidents can be found in the lives of saints; for example, St. Stanislaus Kostka and St. Bonaventure.

251. Low Sunday. The Sunday mentioned by Sister Faustina was the first Sunday after Easter; that is, the day that was to be the Feast of The Divine Mercy.

252. Probably a reference to the flu epidemic which had begun in February and continued for several months. As many as 22 sisters were down on some days.

253. It is difficult to establish the date. Sister Faustina no longer dates anything but merely writes, "today." At any rate, this was after Pentecost; that is, after June 5.

254. It can be supposed that Sister Faustina had the vision of the Heart of Jesus on the Friday after the Octave of Corpus Christi; i.e., on June 24, 1938.

255. Many souls have attained heroic sanctity, and so were saved, never having celebrated the Feast of Divine Mercy. Then, too, according to His revelations to Sr. Faustina, Jesus offers to sinners another eztraordinary means as a "last hope of salvation," namely the divine Mercy Chaplet (cf. *Diary*, 687). The statement made by Our Lord here (965) regarding the Feast of Mercy, therefore, must be seen within the context of the remainder of this passage: "If they will not adore My mercy, they will perish for all eternity," as well as in the light of the statements declared on later occasions: "I give [souls] the last hope of salvation, that is, recourse to My Mercy" (998); and "For them [lukewarm, indifferent souls] the last hope of salvation is to flee to My mercy" (1228). We see that the immediate and solely adequate response to God's mercy on the part of human beings is trust. The attitude of trust is the only means of coming to mercy (cf. 1578) and so, of finding refuge in it. Jesus calls it the "last hope of salvation" for the human soul—literally the "plank or (sheet) anchor," the last refuge for safety (cf. *Webster*).

The Feast of Mercy, therefore, must be seen in this context as an occasion serving as a powerful enticement for sinners to take hold of the promises which Jesus holds out to them in connection with its celebration, motivating [enducing] them to trust that He will be true to them. Expressing that trust, by fulfilling the conditions Jesus gave for receiving on that day [Mercy Sunday] the total forgiveness of sins and punishment as though truly a "second baptism," will truly be for some souls the last opportunity to be reconciled with God, allowing Him to present them to Himself radiant, "without stain or wrinkle or any other blemish, but holy and blameless" (Ephesians 5:27), and so, saved "for all eternity."

Index

MARY, MOTHER OF GOD

Advice of Jesus to ask Mary for help in temptations, 1560

Faustina with,

   at Shrine in Czestochowa, 160

   waiting during Advent, 793

Gift of purity, 40

Strengthens Faustina in suffering, 25

Teaches Faustina

   abandonment to the Will of God, 1437

   about the interior life with Jesus, especially in Holy
        Communion, 840

   how to live for God, 620

   to commune with God, 454

Tells Faustina,

   of new congregation to prepare world for the second
        coming, 625

   of the seven daggers that pierced Her Heart, 786

   to prepare world for the second coming, 635

Visions to Sister Faustina,

   encouraging her, 449

   exhorting her

        to pray for Poland, 325

        to offer vows for Poland, 468

   interceding for Poland, 1261

   Jesus and Mary, 88, 330

        at *Ostrabrama*, 529

        in a small chapel which became big
        temple, 561

Jesus, Mary, and Joseph, 608, 846, 1442

Mary and Child, 677, 846

Mary and confessor, 330, 597

Mary as Mother of God of Priests, 1585

of priest who loves Mary, 806

on Feast of the Immaculate Conception, 564, 805,
   1414-1415

on Feast of the Ascension, 1711

on Feast of the Assumption, 1244

The Congregation of Sisters of Our Lady of Mercy

"From the very beginning, the Congregation's mission has been closely related to the mystery of The divine Mercy and the mystery of Mary — Mother of Mercy."

The history of the Congregation has its roots in French religioous communities, Mother Teresa Eva Potocka of Prince Sułkowski's family adapted the Constitution, spirituality, and methods of apostolic work from those of Mother Theresa Rondeau, the foundress of the House of Mercy and the religious order of the same name in Laval, France. On November 1, 1862, Mother Teresa founded the first Polish House of Mercy on Żytnia Street in Warsaw. This day marks the foundation of the Congregation of Sisters of Our Lady of Mercy in Poland.

Houses of Mercy — the name given to places where the Congregation performs its apostolic work — provide shelter and care for girls and women in need who have come to the Sisters voluntarily in search of reform of life. These houses provide the warm and stable family atmosphere that is needed, away from the problems of the outside world. They provide a certain degree of anonymity, a prayer life, and chores for the girls and women that help produce positive results. Hundreds of girls and women have started their lives afresh with renewed self-respect and respect for others, along with a firm conviction about the ultimate goal of human life and a renewed sense of how to achieve it with honor.

Our Lord called St. Maria Faustina Kowalska (1905-1938) — presently known worldwide as the Apostle of Divine Mercy — to become a member of this Congregation. Her mission was to remind the world of the eternal truth of God's merciful love for us and to convey to us new forms of the devotion to The Divine Mercy. The Congregation has become spiritual heir to this mission, and thus the Sisters work to spread the message in conformity with the Church's teachings. A sacred image of the Merciful Savior — to which veneration is accorded as a basic element of the Divine Mercy devotion revealed to St. Faustina, and to the veneration of which many graces are being continuously attributed — hangs above the side altar in the Congregation's chapel in Cracow-Lagiewniki, where, too, St. Faustina's mortal remains are laid to rest. This chapel has become the International Shrine of The Divine Mercy, with a constant stream of pilgrims not only from all over Poland but also from all parts of the world.

For more information about the Congregation's spirituality and apostolic works, as well as the requirements for prospective candidates to it, please write to the Congregation of Sisters of Our Lady of Mercy at:

USA HOUSE	**GENERAL HOUSE**	**NOVITIATE**
241 Neponset Ave	ul. Żytnia 3/9	ul. Siostry Faustyny 3/9
Dorchester, MA 02122	01 - 014 Warszawa	30 - 420 Kraków 12
	POLAND	POLAND

THE CONGREGATION OF MARIANS OF THE IMMACULATE CONCEPTION B.V.M.

This authorized version of the Diary of Saint Maria Faustina Kowalska, translated directly from the Polish original, is the fruit of the long-standing co-operation between the Congregation of Marians in North America and the Congregation of Sisters of Our Lady of Mercy in Poland, of which the Author of the Diary has been declared a Co-Foundress.

The Marians of the Immaculate Conception, who first introduced the Divine Mercy Message and Devotion to North America and Mexico in the early 1940s, were founded in Poland in 1673 by the Venerable Servant of God Fr. Stanislaus of Jesus Mary Papczynski, and reformed in 1909 by Blessed Archbishop George Matulaitis-Matulewicz. The principal goals of this religious family are to foster due veneration of the Most Blessed virgin Mary in the mystery of her Immaculate Conception, to apply by every possible means the purifying love of spiritual help to the Holy Souls detained in Purgatory, and to assist the clergy in the sacramental and educative ministry to the faithful.

The Marians of the St. Stanislaus Kostka Province in North America undertook "the work of divine Mercy" hardly three years from the death of Saint Faustina, with the result that within ten years they had spread this message and devotion to every continent. They were also responsible for the publication of the very first Polish edition of St. Faustina's DIARY in 1981, on the 50th Anniversary of the first revelation granted to Saint Faustina, which inaugurated her mission to the world. They also rendered timely help toward the completion of Sister Faustina's Canonization Process in Rome, and were intimately involved with the procuring and verification of the miracles accepted by the Church for Sister Faustina's Beatification and Canonization.

At the audience granted to the 1993 General Chapter of the Marians, Pope John Paul II commissioned the entire Congregation to "be apostles of Divine Mercy under the maternal and loving guidance of Mary," implying that this program of life and of pastoral activity is rooted in the Congregation's tradition, is consonant with its customary apostolate, and fits very well into the context of the New Evangelization that involves all the People of God.

On March 20, 1996, the chapel, in which Marians maintain the more than 50-year tradition of imploring Divine Mercy upon the world according to the authentic forms of devotion revealed to Saint Faustina, and to which in ever-increasing numbers the faithful from all over the country and beyond it keep coming on pilgrimage, was canonically designated a "National" Shrine by the National Conference of Catholic Bishops of the United States of America.

More information about the history, spiritually, and actual ministry of the Congregation of Marians can be obtained by writing to:

Congregation of Marians, Eden Hill, Stockbridge, MA 01262, USA

Saint Maria Faustina Kowalska of the Congregation of Sisters of Our Lady of Mercy (1905-1938). The portrait was taken in Płock in 1929.

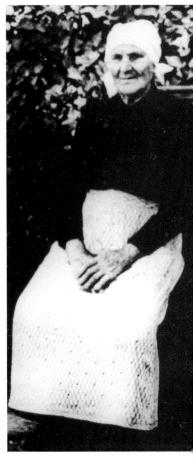

Stanislaus Kowalski
St. Faustina's father.

Marianne Kowalska
St. Faustina's mother.

St. Faustina during the sole visit she made to her family during her convent life. On the right, her parents; on the left, her godparents.

St. Faustina with her family.

The Kowalski home in the village of Głogowiec, the parish of Świnice Warckie, where little Helen, later St.
Faustina, was born and spent her childhood.

St. Casimir Church, Świnice Warckie , where St. Faustina was baptized, made her first Holy confession and Communion, and received her first calling to the consecrated life.

The baptismal font where Helen Kowalska was reborn of water and the Holy Spirit and became a child of God.

Saint Stanislaus Kostka Cathedral in Łódź, where Helena Kowalska received instructions from Our Lord to go to Warsaw, where she would enter a convent.

Mother Thérèse Rondeau, foundress of the Congregation of Sisters of Our Lady of Mercy in Laval, France.

Mother Teresa, Ewa Potocka of the Prince Sułkowski family (1819-1881), the foundress of the Congregation of Sisters of Our Lady of Mercy in Poland.

Mother House of the Congregation of Sisters of Our Lady of Mercy on 3/9 Żytnia Street, Warsaw, Poland. (completely destroyed during World War II) where St. Faustina entered the Religious Life.

The Convent and Bakery of the Congregation of Sisters of Our Lady of Mercy in Płock, where St. Faustina received the first vision of Jesus as The Divine Mercy and her mission to proclaim His mercy to the world.

The statue of Jesus, The Divine Mercy, marks the place where, in the dormitory on the 2nd floor, Our Lord commissioned St. Faustina to paint an image according to the vision of Him that she received there. Civil authorities did not allow the ruined building to be restored.

[ST] JOSEPH'S [PLACE], Cracow-Łagiewniki, the convent of the sisters of Our Lady of Mercy where St. Faustina lived as a novice, professed her first and perpetual vows, served as cook, gardener, and doorkeeper, and spent the last

The chapel of the Prądnik Sanatorium in Cracow, frequented by St. Faustina whenever her illness permitted during her sojourn there.

The Servant of God, Rev. Michał Sopoćko, the confessor and spiritual director prepared for St. Faustina by Our Lord. He served her in that capacity during the years she was assigned to the Vilnius Convent. The diocesan process towards his beatification was solemnly inaugurated on December 4, 1987.

The Rev. Józef Andrasz, S.J., St. Faustina's confessor in the last years before her death.

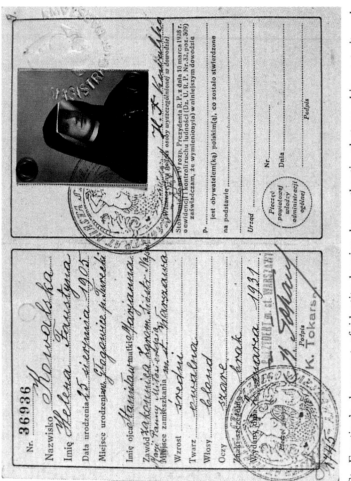

St. Faustina's document of identity bearing her authentic photographic portrait and signature, issued on March 2, 1931.

Mother Michaela Moraczewska, superior of the house in Warsaw and later Superior General of the Congregation. Acting on behalf of the Superior General, she accepted St. Faustina to the Congregation, and later, as the Superior General, she was a great help to her.

Sister Maria Józefa Brzoza, directress of St. Faustina's novitiate class. *"Oh how grateful I am to her! When my soul was plunged in darkness and it seemed to me that I was damned, she wrenched me from the abyss by the power of obedience"* (Diary, 1112).

Sister Irene Krzyżanowska, St. Faustina's superior in Vilnius and Cracow during the last years of her life. **"My daughter, today talk openly to the Superior [Mother Irene] about My mercy because, of all the superiors, she has taken greatest part in proclaiming My mercy"** (Diary, 1519).

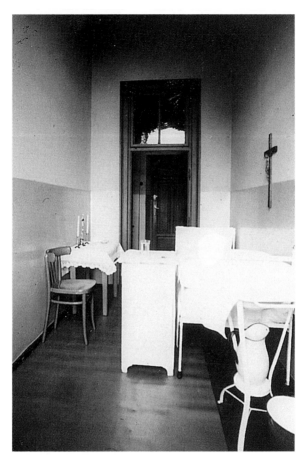

The cell in the infirmary of the convent in Cracow-
Łagiewniki where St. Faustina died on October 5,
1938.

The procession transferring St. Faustina's mortal remains to a resting place in the Sisters' chapel in Cracow-Łagiewniki, on the occasion of their canonical recognition, November 25, 1966.

The common tomb at the far end of the Sisters of Our Lady of Mercy cemetery in Cracow-Łagiewniki, where St. Faustina's mortal remains were first laid to rest on October 7, 1938.

Ostra Brama (the "Dawn Gate" to the city of Vilnius).
Here the image of The Divine Mercy was seen for the
first time by the public during celebrations marking the
close of the Jubilee Year of the Redemption of the
World, April 26-28, 1935.

The first image of The Divine Mercy, painted in Vilnius by E. Kazimirowski under St. Faustina's direction, January-June, 1934.

Actual diary page in St. Faustina's handwriting bearing the account of her vision of Our Lord during which He ordered her to paint a sacred image after the pattern she was beholding (Diary, 47).

His Eminence Karol Cardinal Wojtyła signing documents at the close of the diocesan informational process towards Sr. Faustina's beatification on September 20, 1967.

An image of The Divine Mercy, displayed behind the field altar in front of St. Ann's church in Warsaw, where the Holy Father, John Paul II spoke to the youth on June 3, 1979, during his first pilgrimage to Poland.

The place of respose of Saint Faustina's mortal remains after their transfer from the Sisters' cemetery on November 25, 1966.

The sacred image of The Divine Mercy venerated in the chapel of the Congregation of the Sisters of Our Lady of Mercy in Cracow-Łagiewniki. It is A. Hyla's rendition of St. Faustina's vision renowned for the graces received by means of it.

The casket beneath the sacred image contains the mortal remains of the "Secretary" and "Apostle" of The Divine Mercy.

His Eminence Bernard Cardinal Law of Boston venerates the relic of St. Faustina at its reposition in the National Shrine of The Divine Mercy in Stockbridge, August 8, 1993.

Aerial view of the National Shrine of The Divine Mercy and of the John Paul II Institute of Divine Mercy, Stockbridge, U.S.A.

View of the Sanctuary of the National Shrine of The Divine Mercy in Stockbridge, Massachusetts. The sacred image of Our Lord, The Divine Mercy, venerated there was painted in Mexico expressly for this Shrine in 1945 by Maria Gama at the request of Fr. Józef Jarzębowski, MIC, who provided her with the photo of the Vilnius original received from the hands of the Servant of God, Rev. Michał Sopoćko, St. Faustina's spiritual director.

St. Faustina Chapel—National Shrine of The Divine Mercy, Stockbridge, MA, U.S.A.